MW00529714

"O mother, they are all asleep."

— August Bussee to his mother

DAKOTA

DAWN

Gregory F. Michno

Background: "The siege of New Ulm, Minnesota," by Henry A. Schwabe. *Library of Congress*

The Decisive First Week
of the Sioux Uprising, August 17-24, 1862

SB

Savas Beatie
New York and California

Cataloging-in-Publication Data is available from the Library of Congress.

ISBN 978-1-932714-99-9

05 04 03 02 01   5 4 3 2 1
First edition, first printing

SB

Published by
Savas Beatie LLC
521 Fifth Avenue, Suite 1700
New York, NY 10175

Editorial Offices:

Savas Beatie LLC
P.O. Box 4527
El Dorado Hills, CA 95762
Phone: 916-941-6896
(E-mail) sales@savasbeatie.com

Savas Beatie titles are available at special discounts for bulk purchases in the United States by corporations, institutions, and other organizations. For more details, please contact Special Sales, P.O. Box 4527, El Dorado Hills, CA 95762, or you may e-mail us at sales@savasbeatie.com, or visit our website at www.savasbeatie.com for additional information.

Frontis photos: Big Eagle (*author*), and Merton Eastlick and his mother Lavina Eastlick, holding baby Johnny (*Minnesota Historical Society*).

To the innocent victims . . . on both sides.

"People Escaping from the Indian Massacre of 1862," by Adrian J. Ebell. The four girls closest to the camera from left to right are: Sophia Robertson, Martha Williamson, Anna J. Riggs, and Nancy Williamson. The woman on the right kneading dough is Martha T. Riggs. *Author*

Contents

Contents (continued)

Photos

A gallery of photographs is centrally located following page 256

Maps

A gallery of maps is located following page xii

Preface

Almost every book requires a Preface. Turabian's Manual for Writers suggests a Preface should include motivation for the study, scope of research, and its purpose. I wrote this book for a selfish reason—I wrote it for me. I had read quite a bit about the Sioux uprising, or Dakota conflict, or whatever term is acceptable today. The episode encompassed one of the greatest massacres in American history, and the survivors passed down a dramatic and tragic story. The dimension of pathos in their experience is nearly overwhelming. The volume of individual stories is vast and previous attempts to explain what happened are, in my humble estimation, insufficient. As readers will soon discover, trying to sort out the large number of people and families with similar names and convoluted genealogies is a challenge. For much of the genealogical work, I thank my wife, Susan, because deciphering family trees makes me pull my hair out.

Because I am a visual person, I decided early on that my study would include numerous detailed maps of the various areas involved in the first week of the uprising. Unfortunately, other published accounts on this topic lack maps with sufficient detail to show where these events occurred. It is not enough to write that Dakota warriors attacked Jones, who farmed about a mile from Smith, who lived across the creek from Johnson. I want and need to see the spatial relationships on a map, which allows me to understand the sequence of events more easily.

In order to prepare maps, I had to figure out the location of individual houses. It was not easy to plot these cabins and farms. Some I found on old maps, and others I deduced from participant narratives. My wife spent many long hours in the Bureau of Land Management records locating the townships, ranges, and sections, at least for those settlers who were kind enough to record their plots. Sometimes we could not get an exact location for a house or two, and in some instances had to make our best estimate for others. For example, if we knew "Tom Smith" lived on the SW ¼ of the NE ¼ of Section 22, and Smith wrote that "Michael Jones" lived half a mile east of him, we could plot Jones with a reasonable assurance of accuracy. If one cabin was said to be "about two miles downriver," the placement would be a bit more tentative, but still accurate enough to show the general spatial relationships in the neighborhood.

The potential for name misunderstandings, especially with some of the German and Scandinavian names, is significant. Because recorders often phonetically wrote down what they thought they heard, multiple spellings appear. Many immigrants anglicized their names when they arrived in America. For example, a German with the last name Huber might become Hoover, a Finn named Seppa might be anglicized to Smith, a Swede named Soderlund to Sutherland, and a Norwegian Jonsson to Johnson. This was also true with first names. John could be spelled Jon, Johan, Johann, or Johannes. Many Scandinavians complicated matters further by adding a birthplace or region to their last name. Anders might have a son, name him Jon, and the boy would become Jon Anderssen; a daughter might be called Anne Andersdatter. If Jon Anderssen came to America, he might add the name of the farm he left and become Jon Anderssen Bakken. This has led to some confusion in the past when recording casualties; when a "Schwartz," "Swartz," and "Schwarz" are listed as killed, each name may well be a variation of only one person.

I relied on a number of secondary and primary sources for this study, including books, magazines, journals, newspapers, microfilm, archival records, and the Internet, all of which are listed in both the footnotes and bibliography. The number of eyewitness accounts is voluminous. Even if one could collect them all, it would be impossible to incorporate them one volume. A seldom used but absolutely invaluable resource is the Indian Depredation Claims. After the Dakota uprising, settlers filed nearly 3,000 claims for damages caused by the Indians. These are of interest to researchers because the settlers itemized their losses and told of their experiences, painting firsthand slices of their life on the frontier and information about their cabins, tools, clothes, crops, animals, and other possessions, from hay wagons to musical instruments. Unfortunately, the majority of these claims are missing from the National Archives, but I have utilized about 100 of them, which I do not believe have ever been incorporated into a book. They illuminate many episodes and correct some previous misconceptions.

I have not used any taxpayers' money to research this book. I received no fellowships, grants, or stipends. No one gave me time off and paid for my research expenses. No one waived my photocopying fees, which amounted to nearly 2,000 pages from microfilm and original documents. As I noted earlier, I wrote this book for me, simply to make the story more comprehensible for my own satisfaction. It was not written to prove or disprove any particular point or with any ax to grind. There is enough innocence and guilt to spread around on both sides, human nature being human nature. No animals were harmed in the making of this book. In fact, my dog rather enjoyed romping through the Minnesota cornfields as I walked the terrain and pondered the fates of the many people you will read about in the pages to come.

I would also like to thank Mike Kirchmeier in Jackson County, Minnesota, and Darla Gebhard in Brown County, Minnesota, for providing me with valuable information that helped me prepare this book.

Gregory F. Michno
Longmont, Colorado

Dakota Dawn Map Gallery

The following 19 maps have been placed in a central location for the convenience of readers. A solid understanding of the location of the various cabins, towns, forts, rivers, creeks, ferries, and other important landmarks is critical to understanding the first week of the Dakota Uprising of 1862.

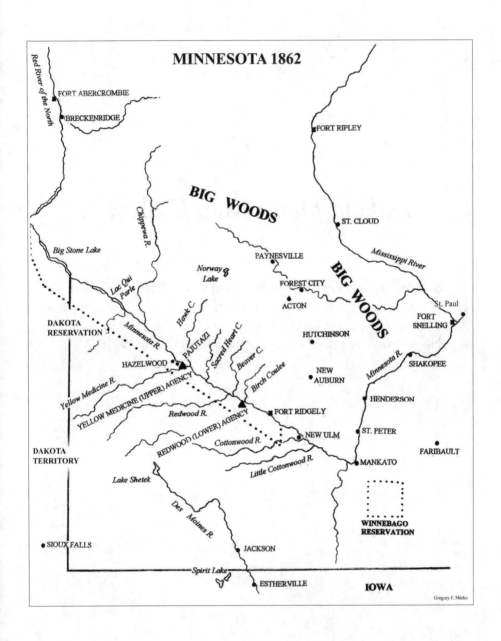

MINNESOTA 1862

Red River of the North

FORT ABERCROMBIE
BRECKENRIDGE

FORT RIPLEY

BIG WOODS

Chippewa R.

Big Stone Lake

ST. CLOUD

Mississippi River

PAYNESVILLE

Norway Lake

BIG WOODS

FOREST CITY

Lac Qui Parle

ACTON

St. Paul

DAKOTA RESERVATION

Minnesota R.

Hawk C.

PAJUTAZI

Sacred Heart C.

Beaver C.

HUTCHINSON

FORT SNELLING

HAZELWOOD

Birch Coulee

NEW AUBURN

Minnesota R.

SHAKOPEE

Yellow Medicine R.

YELLOW MEDICINE (UPPER) AGENCY

Redwood R.

REDWOOD (LOWER) AGENCY

FORT RIDGELY

HENDERSON

Cottonwood R.

NEW ULM

ST. PETER

DAKOTA TERRITORY

Little Cottonwood R.

MANKATO

FARIBAULT

Lake Shetek

Des Moines R.

WINNEBAGO RESERVATION

SIOUX FALLS

JACKSON

Spirit Lake

ESTHERVILLE

IOWA

Gregory F. Michno

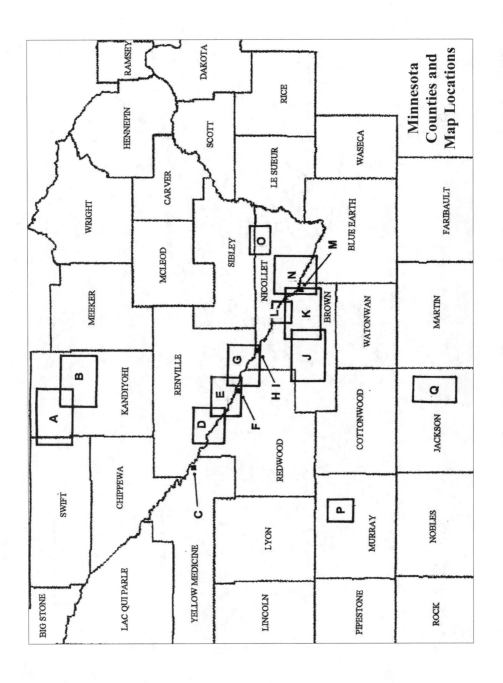

Minnesota
Counties and
Map Locations

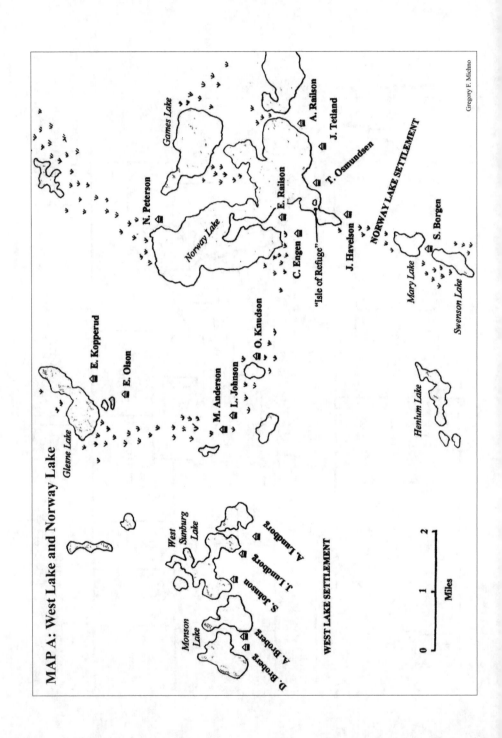

MAP A: West Lake and Norway Lake

Glesne Lake

Games Lake

Norway Lake

West Sunburg Lake

Monson Lake

Henlum Lake

Mary Lake

Swenson Lake

E. Kopperud

E. Olson

N. Peterson

M. Anderson

L. Johnson

O. Knudson

C. Engen

E. Railson

"Isle of Refuge"

T. Osmundsen

A. Railson

J. Tetland

J. Havelson

NORWAY LAKE SETTLEMENT

S. Borgen

A. Lundborg

J. Lundborg

S. Johnson

A. Broberg

D. Broberg

WEST LAKE SETTLEMENT

0   1   2

Miles

Gregory F. Michno

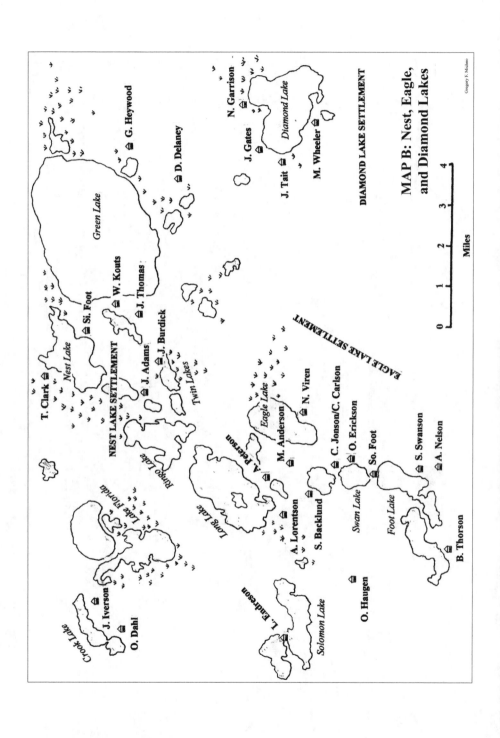

MAP B: Nest, Eagle, and Diamond Lakes

Miles

DIAMOND LAKE SETTLEMENT

Gregory F. Mediro

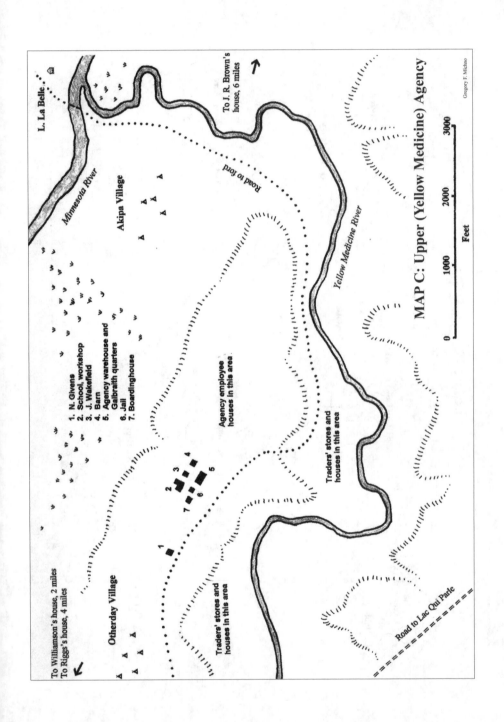

MAP C: Upper (Yellow Medicine) Agency

L. La Belle

Minnesota River

Akipa Village

To J. R. Brown's house, 6 miles

Road to ford

Yellow Medicine River

Feet

0   1000   2000   3000

1. N. Givens
2. School, workshop
3. J. Wakefield
4. Barn
5. Agency warehouse and Galbraith quarters
6. Jail
7. Boardinghouse

Agency employee houses in this area

Traders' stores and houses in this area

To Williamson's house, 2 miles
To Riggs's house, 4 miles

Otherday Village

Traders' stores and houses in this area

Road to Lac Qui Parle

Gregory F. Michno

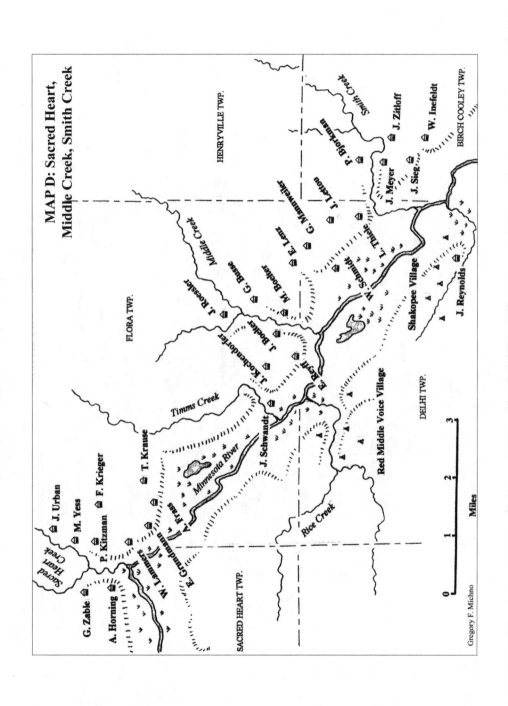

MAP D: Sacred Heart, Middle Creek, Smith Creek

Gregory F. Michno

Miles

0   1   2   3

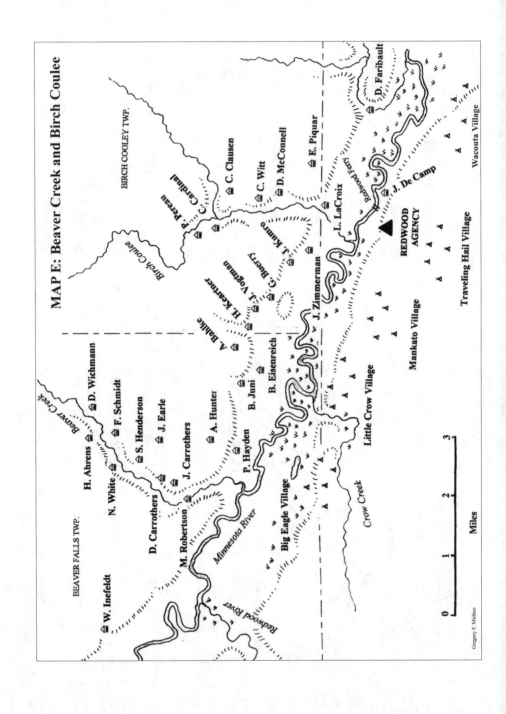

MAP E: Beaver Creek and Birch Coulee

Gregory F. Michno

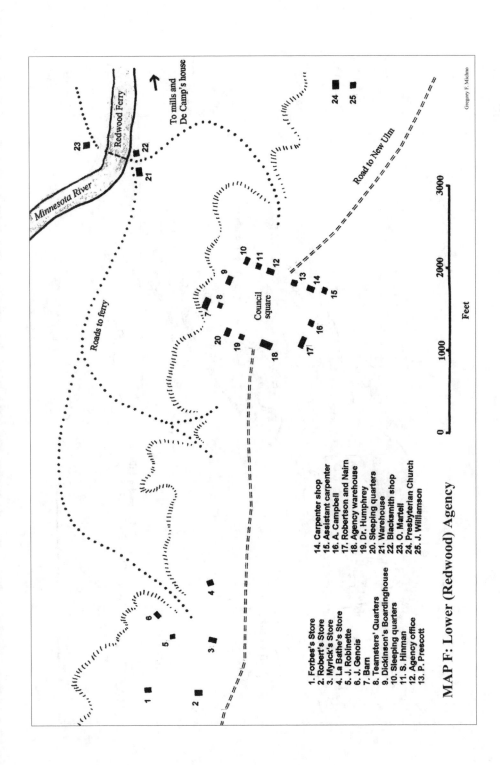

MAP F: Lower (Redwood) Agency

1. Forbes's Store
2. Robert's Store
3. Myrick's Store
4. La Bathe's Store
5. J. Robinette
6. J. Genois
7. Barn
8. Teamsters' Quarters
9. Dickinson's Boardinghouse
10. Sleeping quarters
11. S. Hinman
12. Agency office
13. P. Prescott
14. Carpenter shop
15. Assistant carpenter
16. A. Campbell
17. Robertson and Nairn
18. Agency warehouse
19. Dr. Humphrey
20. Sleeping quarters
21. Warehouse
22. Blacksmith shop
23. O. Martell
24. Presbyterian Church
25. J. Williamson

Minnesota River

Redwood Ferry

To mills and De Camp's house

Roads to ferry

Road to New Ulm

Council square

Feet

0   1000   2000   3000

Gregory F. Michno

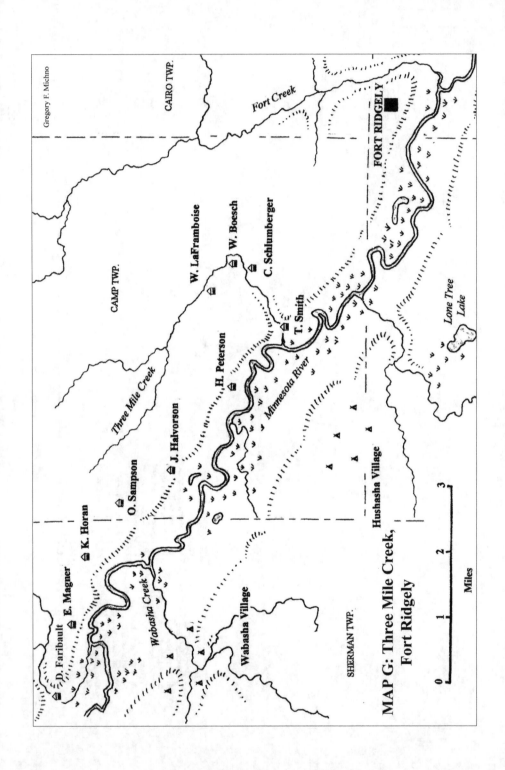

Gregory F. Michno

CAIRO TWP.

Fort Creek

FORT RIDGELY

W. LaFramboise

W. Boesch

C. Schlumberger

CAMP TWP.

T. Smith

Three Mile Creek

H. Peterson

Minnesota River

Lone Tree Lake

J. Halvorson

O. Sampson

K. Horan

D. Faribault

E. Magner

Wabasha Creek

Wabasha Village

Hushasha Village

SHERMAN TWP.

MAP G: Three Mile Creek,
Fort Ridgely

0   1   2   3

Miles

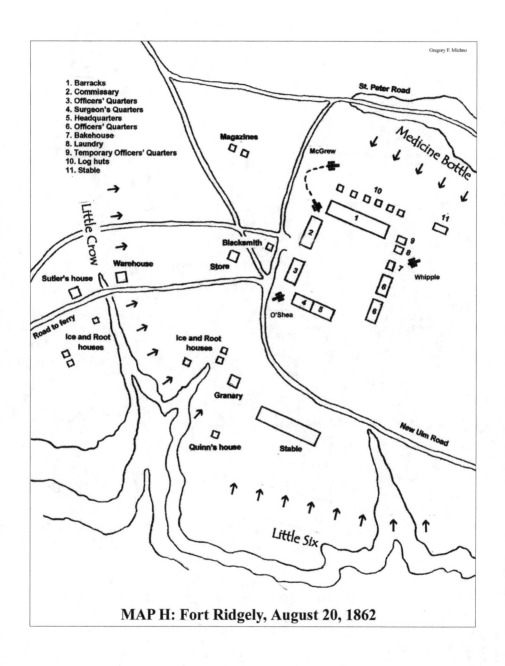

MAP H: Fort Ridgely, August 20, 1862

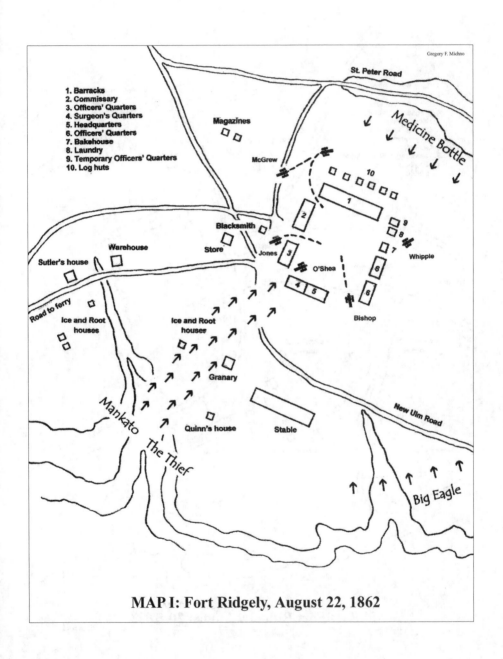

Gregory F. Michno

1. Barracks
2. Commissary
3. Officers' Quarters
4. Surgeon's Quarters
5. Headquarters
6. Officers' Quarters
7. Bakehouse
8. Laundry
9. Temporary Officers' Quarters
10. Log huts

St. Peter Road

Medicine Bottle

Magazines

McGrew

Blacksmith

Store

Warehouse

Sutler's house

Jones

O'Shea

Whipple

Bishop

Road to ferry

Ice and Root houses

Ice and Root houses

Granary

New Ulm Road

Mankato

The Thief

Quinn's house

Stable

Big Eagle

MAP I: Fort Ridgely, August 22, 1862

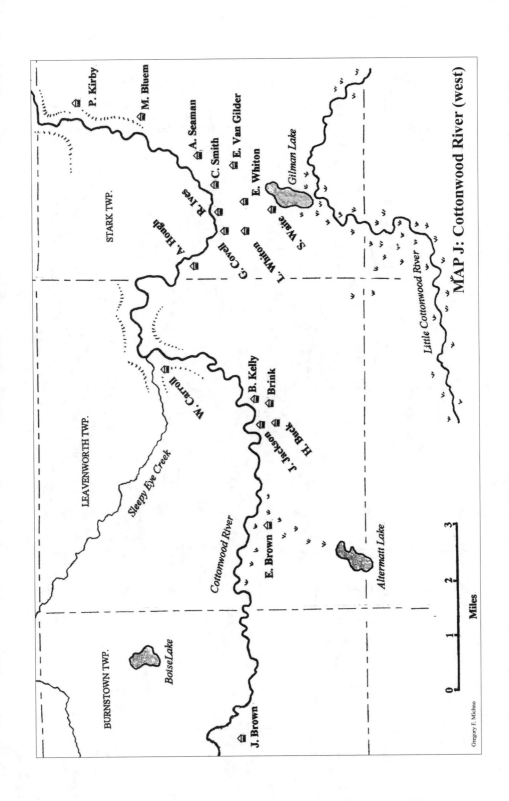

MAP J: Cottonwood River (west)

Gregory F. Michno

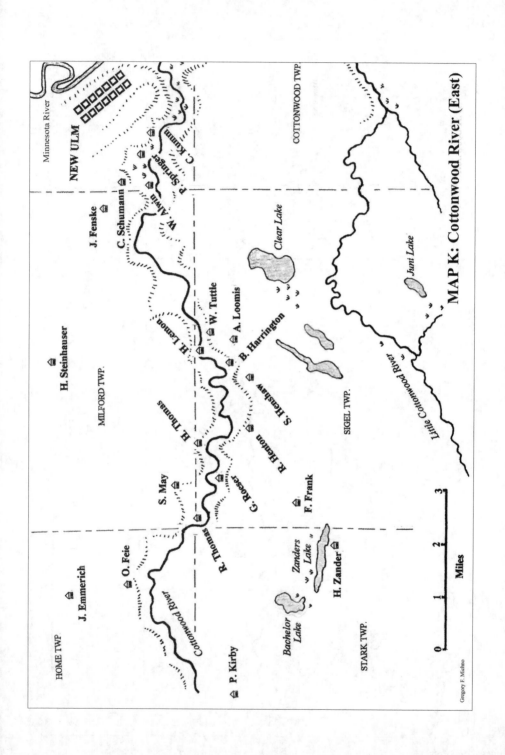

MAP K: Cottonwood River (East)

Gregory F. Michno

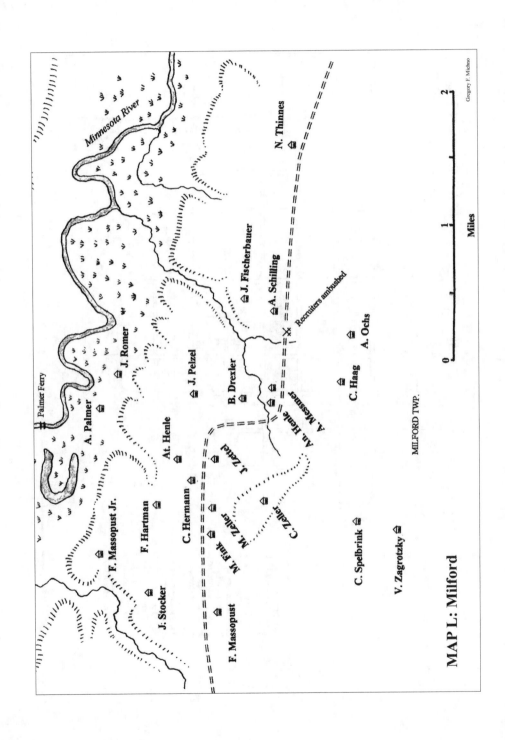

MAP L: Milford

Palmer Ferry

Minnesota River

A. Palmer

J. Romer

F. Massopust Jr.

F. Hartman

J. Stocker

C. Hermann

At. Henle

J. Pelzel

M. Fink

M. Zettel

J. Zettel

B. Drexler

J. Fischerbauer

A. Schilling

F. Massopust

C. Zeller

An. Henle

A. Messmer

N. Thinnes

Recruiters ambushed

C. Spelbrink

C. Haag

A. Ochs

V. Zagrotzky

MILFORD TWP.

0   ½   1   2

Miles

Gregory F. Michno

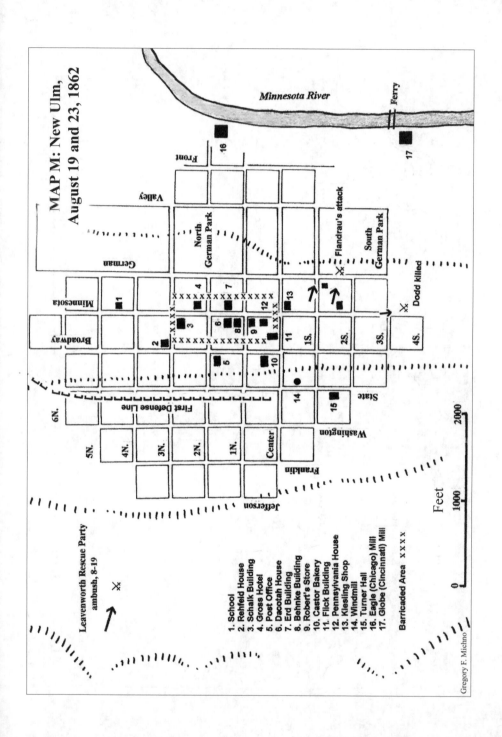

MAP M: New Ulm,
August 19 and 23, 1862

Minnesota River

Ferry

Front

16

17

Valley

German

North German Park

Flandrau's attack

South German Park

Minnesota

Broadway

1

2

3

4

5

6

7

8

9

10

11

12

13

14

15

1S.

2S.

3S.

4S.

Dodd killed

State

First Defense Line

Washington

9N.

5N.

4N.

3N.

2N.

1N.

Center

Franklin

Jefferson

Feet

0   1000   2000

Leavenworth Rescue Party
ambush, 8-19

1. School
2. Rehfeld House
3. Schalk Building
4. Gross Hotel
5. Post Office
6. Dacotah House
7. Erd Building
8. Behnke Building
9. Robert's Store
10. Castor Bakery
11. Flick Building
12. Kiesling House
13. Kiesling Shop
14. Windmill
15. Turner Hall
16. Eagle (Chicago) Mill
17. Globe (Cincinnati) Mill

Barricaded Area   x x x x

Gregory F. Michno

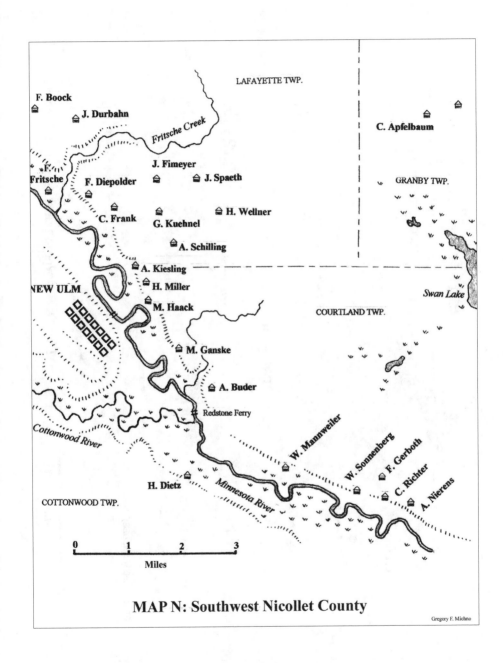

LAFAYETTE TWP.

F. Boock

J. Durbahn

Fritsche Creek

C. Apfelbaum

J. Fimeyer

F.
Fritsche

F. Diepolder   J. Spaeth

GRANBY TWP.

C. Frank   H. Wellner

G. Kuehnel

A. Schilling

A. Kiesling

H. Miller

M. Haack

NEW ULM

Swan Lake

COURTLAND TWP.

M. Ganske

A. Buder

Redstone Ferry

W. Mannweiler

Cottonwood River

W. Sonnenberg   F. Gerboth

C. Richter

A. Nierens

H. Dietz

Minnesota River

COTTONWOOD TWP.

0   1   2   3

Miles

MAP N: Southwest Nicollet County

Gregory F. Michno

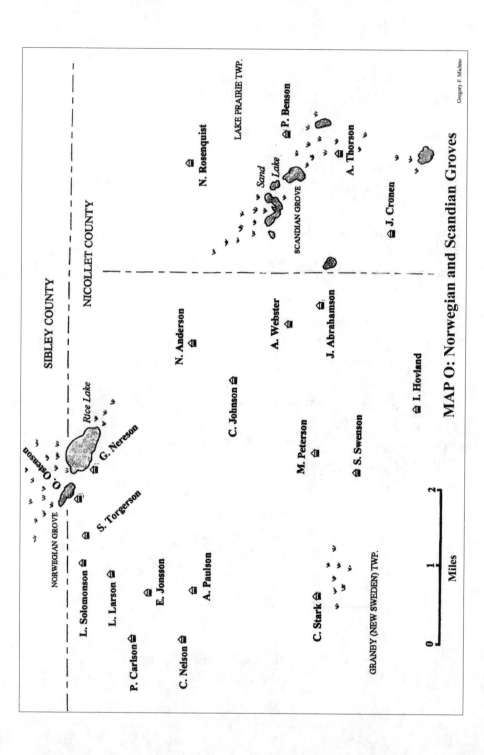

SIBLEY COUNTY

NICOLLET COUNTY

LAKE PRAIRIE TWP.

NORWEGIAN GROVE

Rice Lake

O. Ostenson

G. Nereson

S. Torgerson

L. Solomonson

L. Larson

E. Jonsson

A. Paulson

P. Carlson

C. Nelson

C. Johnson

N. Anderson

A. Webster

J. Abrahamson

M. Peterson

S. Swenson

C. Stark

I. Hovland

GRANBY (NEW SWEDEN) TWP.

Sand
Lake

SCANDIAN GROVE

P. Benson

A. Thorson

J. Cromen

N. Rosenquist

0   1   2

Miles

MAP O: Norwegian and Scandian Groves

Gregory F. Michno

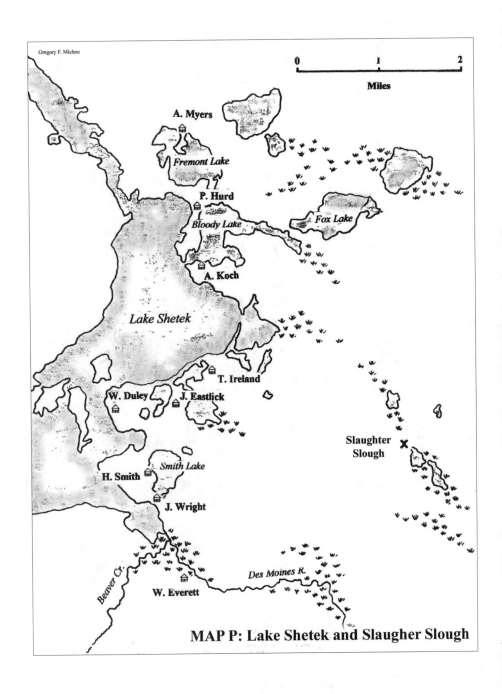

Gregory F. Michno

0   1   2

Miles

A. Myers

Fremont Lake

P. Hurd

Bloody Lake

Fox Lake

A. Koch

Lake Shetek

T. Ireland

W. Duley   J. Eastlick

Slaughter
Slough   ✕

Smith Lake

H. Smith

J. Wright

Beaver Cr.

Des Moines R.

W. Everett

MAP P: Lake Shetek and Slaugher Slough

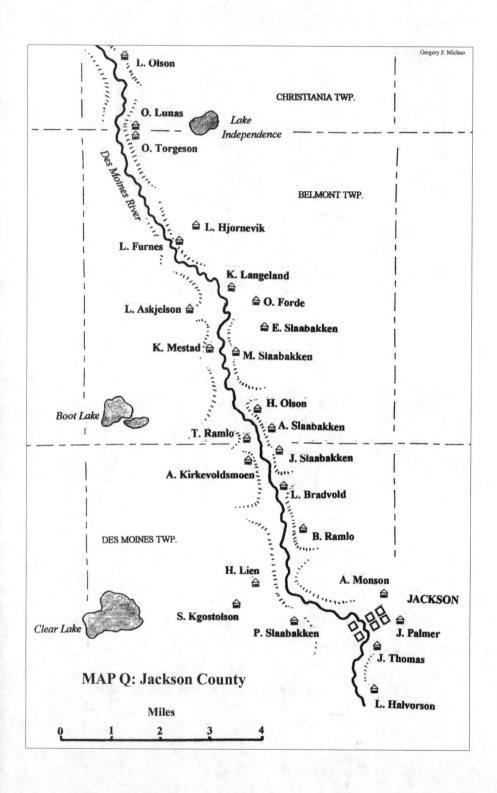

L. Olson

CHRISTIANIA TWP.

O. Lunas

Lake
Independence

O. Torgeson

Des Moines River

BELMONT TWP.

L. Hjornevik

L. Furnes

K. Langeland

O. Forde

L. Askjelson

E. Slaabakken

K. Mestad

M. Slaabakken

H. Olson

Boot Lake

A. Slaabakken

T. Ramlo

J. Slaabakken

A. Kirkevoldsmoen

L. Bradvold

B. Ramlo

DES MOINES TWP.

H. Lien

A. Monson

JACKSON

S. Kgostolson

J. Palmer

Clear Lake

P. Slaabakken

J. Thomas

MAP Q: Jackson County

L. Halvorson

Gregory F. Michno

Miles

0   1   2   3   4

C hapter 1

"Some men will rob you with a fountain pen."

Causes of the Uprising

Gold ~ Causes of the uprising ~ Treaty of 1851 ~ Little Crow ~ Treaty of 1858 ~ Inkpaduta ~ Farmer and blanket Indians ~ Thomas Galbraith ~ Clark Thompson ~ Russell, Majors & Waddell ~ Crooked traders ~ Land hunger ~ Bread Raid ~ Let them eat grass ~ Conspiracy

T he $71,000 in gold coins weighed about 220 pounds. The large keg the coins rested in and the five gun-toting men escorting it required a sturdy wagon. This was a rush job. After all the procrastination and delays it had come down to this: if the payment wasn't made immediately, all the warnings of dire consequences would come to pass. Except for those intimately involved in the negotiations, few believed it. The Civil War was being fought and money was in short supply, especially hard coin. The Sioux could have waited, or they could have been paid in greenbacks, but they didn't want greenbacks—nobody wanted greenbacks. Secretary of Treasury Salmon P. Chase finally authorized the transaction. The shipment left New York on August 11, 1862, by express rail and wagon to St. Paul, Minnesota. "Every effort was made that could be thought of to get the gold," wrote Acting Commissioner Charles E. Mix to Commissioner William P. Dole two days later, ". . . and the efforts in the end appear, from present appearances, to have been successful."

The shipment arrived in St. Paul on Saturday the 16th. Superintendent Clark W. Thompson, about to leave on a peace mission to the Chippewas (Ojibways) with Commissioner Dole, President Lincoln's Secretary John G. Nicolay, and others, could not personally escort the money to the Sioux. "Knowing their unsettled condition," however, Thompson said he "took immediate steps towards forwarding the money to the agent, and succeeded in starting it by safe hands on the 17th."

Riding shotgun in the money wagon were Thompson's clerk, Cyrus G. Wykoff, J. C. Ramsey, A. J. Van Vorhees, C. M. Dailey, and Edward A. C. Hatch, a former agent for the Blackfeet Lakotas. They traveled throughout the night, making the 125 miles between St. Paul and Fort Ridgely and arriving exhausted at the fort at noon on Monday, August 18. They were only 13 miles from the Lower Sioux Agency. The Indians began the massacre earlier that same morning.

The gold shipment was six hours late.[1]

*   *   *

At daybreak on August 18, 1862, the Dakota Indians of Minnesota commenced a massacre on a scale never before experienced by Americans. How did it happen?

Almost everyone had an opinion about the causes, but there were two main reasons: greed and land hunger—from both white and Indian. There is no question that Indian tribes coveted land and the stronger tribes took it from the weaker tribes whenever it suited their needs. If they had no concept of legal ownership as did the white man, they certainly understood ownership by conquest. The white man coveted land also, and although he may have used more subtle "legal" measures, if they failed, physical conquest was a tried and true option. To paraphrase an American folk song, some men will rob you with a six-gun, while others will rob you with a fountain pen. White Americans were practiced at both.

As Indian tribes were forced west, even the idea of a permanent Indian Country beyond the Mississippi was eventually scrapped; there was just too much good land out there needed by an expanding America in the throes of a fever that many called Manifest Destiny. Indian tribes could be put on reservations, colonized, and eventually they might integrate into white society. The Preemption Act of 1841 allowed Americans to settle on public land prior to purchase, without being considered trespassers. They moved to lands they considered "public," even while tribes already occupied them, becoming de

1   *Commissioner of Indian Affairs 1862*, 199, 205, 212; Anderson, *Little Crow*, 222n1. Hatch said the keg contained $84,000 in gold.

facto owners. The government needed treaties with the tribes to make them de jure owners. The fountain pen was a great conscience-soother.

The Dakotas had been slowly forced west from their lands around the upper Great Lakes by the Chippewas in the process of conquest that the tribes were all familiar with. In 1849 when Minnesota Territory was organized, the whites who began moving in created more problems for the Dakotas than the Chippewas ever did. By 1851, it was evident that something had to be done to move the Indians out of the way again. Of the four Dakota bands, agents and traders believed the Upper Sioux Sissetons and Wahpetons were less sophisticated and cautious than the Mdewakantons and Wahpekutes and that they would sign any treaty if simply for all the good presents they would receive.[2]

On July 23, 1851, at Traverse des Sioux on the Minnesota River, Commissioner Luke Lea and Minnesota Territorial Governor Alexander Ramsey presided over the meeting in which the Sissetons and Wahpetons sold their lands in the state of Iowa and in western Minnesota for $1,665,000 in cash and annuities and agreed to move to a 20-mile wide reservation stretching along both banks of the western Minnesota River. Out of the money, $275,000 was to be paid to the chiefs to relocate their people and $30,000 was earmarked for the building of mills, schools, blacksmith shops, and farms. Of the remaining $1,360,000, they were to be paid five percent interest, or $68,000, annually. From that, $28,000 was also subtracted to pay for agricultural improvement, education, and purchase of goods and provisions. Thirty five Indians signed the agreement, including Running Walker, Sleepy Eyes, Metal Horn, Grey Thunder, Cloud Man, and He Who Shoots as He Walks (Mazakutemani). Missionary Stephen R. Riggs interpreted, read, and explained each article to the chiefs several times. The bottom line was that the two bands would get only $40,000 a year.[3]

With the sale, the Wahpekutes and Mdewakantons were faced with a *fait accompli*, and likely realized it would do no good to hold out. At Mendota on August 5, the bands signed a treaty that sold their lands in southeast Minnesota for $1,410,000. It was not a smooth process, however. There was discord, especially among some of the older chiefs who had sold their lands east of the Mississippi back in 1837. They claimed they had not yet been paid all the money

---

2   Anderson, *Little Crow*, 58-59.

3   Kappler, *Indian Treaties*, 588-90.

due to them from that transaction. Red Leaf (Wabasha) was in opposition, but Little Crow (Taoyateduta), a man whom the Mdewakantons increasingly looked to as their spokesman, realized that the treaty might be the solution to their economic problems.

Born about 1810 near the Mississippi River about ten miles below the mouth of the Minnesota River, Taoyateduta had become more politically astute than many of his people. Although the first of Big Thunder's many sons, Taoyateduta was not at first seen as one who would lead his people, for he was wandering the west much of his life, and when he was home, he was considered a troublemaker, a womanizer, and a debauchee in morals and habits. He had married and discarded two wives when he lived among the Wahpekutes, and acquired four more wives among the Wahpetons.

Taoyateduta would likely have continued his wayward existence if his father had not died and given the trappings of his chiefdom to his younger half-brothers. Faced with the threat to his succession, Taoyateduta came home to confront his half-brothers, who threatened his life.

"Shoot then, where all can see," Taoyateduta challenged. One of them fired, the ball going through and shattering both of his forearms. The brothers fled. Taoyateduta's brave stance convinced the elders that if he lived, the Great Spirit must have destined him to be chief. He did live, but his hands evermore hung awkwardly from his deformed wrists and he never had full use of his fingers.

The experience appeared to transform Taoyateduta. His supporters killed his half-brothers, paving the way for his assumption of control. He adopted the name Little Crow and suddenly he was a changed person. "I was only a brave then; I am a chief now," he said.[4]

Little Crow's biographer claimed that his understanding of the nature of Indian and white relationships was superior to his contemporaries, and that he developed a rational policy for dealing with the whites based on negotiation and accommodation rather than war. Seeing the destructive results of drunkenness, Little Crow encouraged temperance and invited Presbyterian Dr. Thomas Williamson to establish a mission at his village—yet he would not call himself a Christian. He supported farming efforts and wore white man's clothing—but he still preserved his Indian identity by not personally tilling the soil. Little Crow

4 Kappler, *Indian Treaties*, 591; Oehler, *Great Sioux Uprising*, 17, 19; Anderson, *Little Crow*, 9-10, 44-46, 59.

became a power broker who sought to get the best deal for his people while trying "to satisfy an insatiable personal hunger for power." He "was a politician who happened to be an Indian. . . ."[5]

The chief showed what he was made of during the negotiations at Mendota. Wabasha again broached the subject of unpaid money from the 1837 treaty when the Dakotas sold their lands east of the Mississippi. Lea and Ramsey promised that the money would be included in the new treaty, but the Indians were not convinced. As the talks progressed, Little Crow supported the Indians' interests, but was willing to compromise. Another point of contention was the boundary of the new reservation. The government wanted the southeastern boundary to be where the Redwood River enters the Minnesota River; the Mdewakantons and Wahpekutes wanted it as far east as Traverse des Sioux— these Dakotas were essentially woodland Indians and did not want to live out on the open prairies as did the Nakotas and Lakotas.

Little Crow gained the support of a few other chiefs, and it appeared that they would sign, if only the boundary could be settled. Lea and Ramsey suggested a compromise line about halfway between the two points, at the mouth of the Little Rock River. The Indians appeared willing, but Wabasha turned to the crowd and asked if anyone intended to kill the first chief who signed. Red Middle Voice said it would not happen and indicated his willingness for a treaty. Ramsay took the quill and asked Medicine Bottle who should be the first. He pointed to Little Crow.

Sensing the appropriate time for theatrics, Little Crow stood and addressed the crowd: "I am willing to be the first, but I am not afraid that you will kill me. If you do, it will be all right." Taking a page from Shakespeare's Julius Caesar, he commented that a man must die sometime, and a brave one could be killed but once. He held up the document and said, "I believe this treaty will be best for the Dakotas, and I will sign it, even if a dog kills me before I lay down the goose quill." Little Crow did not have to scratch an "X." Instead, he spelled out "Taoyateduta."[6]

The politician had taken office. It is difficult to argue that Little Crow and the other chiefs and headmen did not know what they were signing. They had discussed the terms for two years, while the council's explanations,

---

5   Anderson, *Little Crow*, 3-4. Anderson presents a thorough and balanced treatment of the causes of the Sioux uprising.

6   Anderson, *Little Crow*, 62-63.

interpretations, and arguments had taken eight days, and 65 men made their marks on the agreement. When $30,000 from the old 1837 treaty was handed over there was an orgy of spending, much of it on horses and liquor, and the merchants in and around St. Paul experienced a minor windfall.[7]

The temporary euphoria notwithstanding, after the subtractions for education, relocation, and infrastructure—much as with the treaty with the Sissetons and Wahpetons—the Mdewakontans and Wahpekutes would get only $30,000 a year. In total the four tribes would get $70,000 divided up among 7,000 people, making about $10 per person. That was not all, for the U.S. Senate was not finished with it. Former Secretary of the Interior Alexander H. H. Stuart had warned Ramsey and Lea that a reservation should not be established within the confines of the land purchase, but rather off to the west in Dakota Territory. He knew many senators were not in favor of the concept and he knew it might affect votes, but he may not have realized it might also affect life and death.

Ramsey and Lea were hamstrung; they could not get Indian signatures without the reservation closer to their old homelands. They included it, and the Senate promptly scratched it out. The Dakotas felt betrayed and would not accept the amended version. Governor Ramsey scrambled for a solution, coming up with a temporary expedient that allowed the Dakotas to occupy the reservation lands for 25 years, after which the president could decide if they were to stay or move. Perhaps reluctant to face the chiefs again, Ramsey got trader Henry M. Rice to persuade them. The proceedings were not recorded; Rice got signatures on the amended treaty, but many Dakotas came away with the idea that they could stay on the reservation forever.[8]

After all the legalities and paper chasing, the issue was still unresolved. There was more. A lot of money was floating around, and the traders wanted a hand in it. Moments after the Indians had signed the treaties, the traders handed them a second document to sign, called the "traders' paper." This pact said the Indians agreed to hand over $210,000 of their treaty money to pay the traders for past debts. Most of the Dakotas agreed that the debts should be paid, but they wanted control over the distribution to cover only legitimate debts. Only the Mdewakantons refused to sign. Henry H. Sibley, who had once hunted with Little Crow and was a territorial delegate, merchant, and trader, was destined to

---

7   Kappler, *Indian Treaties*, 591-93; Anderson, *Little Crow*, 64.

8   Anderson, *Little Crow*, 61, 66.

play a large role in the upcoming story. The Wahpekutes had signed the paper, setting aside $90,000 for their debts, but Sibley could not get the Mdewakantons to do likewise. He tried cutting off credit to them at his store, but they went elsewhere.

In November 1852, Governor Ramsey picked up the treaty money. After much discussion, all the Dakotas now wanted him to give them the money directly so they could pay their debts. Ramsey refused. Instead, he told them they must sign a receipt for the money and let him distribute it. Wabasha and Wakute adamantly disagreed, along with many of the mixed-bloods, who also wanted to get their fingers into the large pot. On the other hand, chiefs such as Good Road and Bad Hail supported Ramsey. All had their reasons; Bad Hail had a son in prison and Ramsey offered to free him for his support.

Greed and self-interest took over, as it usually did. The whites sought Little Crow's help. Mixed-blood Alexander Faribault, Little Crow's trader and a Sibley protégé, made a deal with Little Crow to pay him $3,000 in exchange for signing Ramsey's receipt. Probably rationalizing that the solution would be best for all, Little Crow agreed, as did Wabasha, Wakute, and others. With $20,000 added into the Mdewakanton and Wahpekute chiefs' pockets, Ramsey went to the Sissetons and Wahpetons. This time, Red Iron resisted so vehemently that Ramsey threw him in jail. With him out of the way, the others signed, got paid, and Ramsey was free to distribute the money as he saw fit. By the end of the year $495,000 was gone into the traders' coffers, and Governor Ramsey had deducted a 10% handling fee for all his hard work. Charges were brought against the governor for misappropriation of funds, but although it was found that he "was not warranted under the circumstances in paying over the money," he was exonerated by a senate resolution. Ramsey, as ex officio superintendent, was supposed to have the Indians' interest at heart—instead he looked to protect the traders at the Indians' expense.

The money designated for removal and subsistence was gone, whites were moving into the Dakotas' lands west of the Mississippi, and there was no money to relocate them or set up the new reservation.[9]

The Dakotas tried to exist under the rules that seemed ambiguous at best. Several years later, however, they were forced back to the treaty table. Minnesota had been admitted to the Union as a state in May 1858. More whites were moving in, encroaching on the reservation, and clamoring for the lands

---

9   Anderson, *Little Crow*, 64-69; Robinson, *History of the Dakota*, 260-61.

that the Indians weren't utilizing in ways they thought they should be used. In the summer of 1854, about 30 men, most of them recent German immigrants, left Chicago and searched for new farmland near the junction of the Cottonwood and Minnesota Rivers. Due mainly to the persistence of men such as Athanasius Henle, Ludwig Meyer, Alois Palmer, and Franz Massopust, the first place for a potential town site they found having just the right amount of fertile land, timber, and water was in a temporarily abandoned Dakota village! They moved in, and when the Indians returned, naturally there was a confrontation. Bloodshed was avoided, however, mainly through the intercession of the trader, Joseph La Framboise, who lived several miles up the Minnesota.

The settlers survived by living in the Indians' bark huts through the winter. The impasse was settled by territorial Governor Willis A. Gorman, who ruled that the Indians were technically off their reservation, which began about nine miles upriver at the mouth of Little Rock Creek. The Dakotas reluctantly moved away and more Germans moved in, their town site eventually becoming the village of New Ulm. Within three years, every quarter-section open for settlement had been pre-empted and hundreds of newcomers were in the area. Although most settlers had no serious confrontations with the Indians in the 1850s, the boundary between the "Dutchmen" and the Dakotas would remain a sore point, and the settlers would pay the price in 1862.[10]

Although the Dakotas cleared out of the area, it may not have mattered where they went. Back in 1852 the Senate had removed that part of the treaty that guaranteed the Dakotas a reservation in Minnesota. To prevent future confrontations with the settlers and to finally secure legal title, government officials convinced the Indians that it would be better to sell a portion of the reservation that they didn't really own than to have the state take it by force.

In the spring of 1858 a delegation of 27 Dakotas, including Little Crow, Wabasha, Shakopee, Mankato, Big Eagle, Red Iron, Mazakutemani, and Otherday, traveled to Washington D.C. Escorted by Agent Joseph R. Brown and Superintendent William J. Cullen, they went to the negotiating table again. Accompanying the party were a number of people, including Rev. Thomas S. Williamson and traders Andrew J. Myrick, William H. Forbes, and a few others, all with various motives, from saving souls to making money. This time the commissioner, Charles E. Mix, was not so conciliatory and was not averse to

10 Berghold, *Indians' Revenge*, 33-39; Tolzmann, ed., *Brown County*, 65-66.

bullying. In a series of meetings stretching from March through June, the Dakotas met with President James Buchanan once and with Mix a number of times. Little was resolved.

Little Crow complained of German settlers moving on to his lands, but Mix showed him a map where the boundary was made at Little Rock Creek, and besides, the Senate had removed not only the boundary, but the reservation. The Dakotas occupied the land only "by the courtesy of their Great Father." If they wanted to stay there they should sell the northern half above the Minnesota River and become farmers on the southern half, which would be divided into 80-acre individual allotments.

Disgusted with the bickering, Reverend Williamson went back to Minnesota. He believed that the Dakotas' supposed benefactors only pretended to "take considerable interest in the welfare of the Indians. . . but they are destitute of religious principle and so not fully reliable especially as they are here constantly in contact with men at least as wise and shrewd as themselves who think their pecuniary interests may be much advanced by measures detrimental to the Indians."[11]

By June the weather grew extremely hot, humid, and stifling. Tempers were on edge and the Indians were being worn down. They wanted to go home. At times Little Crow and Mix exchanged heated words. Little Crow complained about Brown, but would not give particulars. Brown replied, "I am not afraid to have him say what he knows of my conduct." Mix said that Little Crow was being unjust, and added, "If he has anything to say against his Agent, he must say it to his face, or hereafter hold his tongue." Mix asked the Dakotas who their chief was, "and if he is a man why does he not speak out." Little Crow was ashamed of what they were being forced to sign, but he rationalized once again that the deal would at least give them more money to pay off those ever-present trade debts. The chiefs signed the agreement on June 19, without even knowing what they would be paid for the land, and granted the secretary of the interior discretionary power in the amounts and use of future annuities. Two years passed before the Senate resolved to pay them, but only at 30 cents per acre for lands said to be worth five dollars an acre. The Lower Sioux (Mdewakantons and Wahpekutes) got $96,000 and the Upper Sioux (Sissetons and Wahpetons) got $170,880. Of course, the traders' claims were subtracted from that, leaving

---

11 Newcombe, "The Sioux Sign a Treaty," 83-88.

the Upper Sioux with about half of the amount, and the Lower Sioux with virtually nothing.[12]

Although 27 chiefs had signed the treaty, most of the Indians back in Minnesota were outraged, especially at the loss of half the reservation. The money issue was another sore spot. The Indians never seemed to get what they thought was their due. When Abraham Lincoln was elected president, a whole new set of Republican administrators came to office in the spring of 1861, including the Minnesota Superintendent Clark W. Thompson, and Agent Thomas J. Galbraith. The Mdewakanton Big Eagle succinctly summed up the regime change: the Indians "did not like the new men."

Usually, presidential changes meant good news for the tribes. John Nairn, a carpenter at the Lower Agency, recorded a conversation that may have been apocryphal, but nevertheless illustrated the Dakotas' mindset. Two Indians sat smoking. One said, "Have you heard the news? We are getting a new great father." The other man was pleased. "That is news indeed," he replied with a laugh, "I wonder if his pockets are deep? Our great father always sends us a new father with deep pockets and the Dakotas have to fill them."[13]

Galbraith quickly learned that the Lower Sioux believed they would be paid "one hundred boxes of money" per year (a box meaning to them $1,000), and the Upper Sioux a similar amount. Instead, the Lower Sioux fund was used to pay off debts and two-thirds of the Upper Sioux money disappeared the same way. If the plan was to have debts subtracted every year, Galbraith said, "I shall not pretend to relate in detail." All he knew for a fact was that "from the first day of my arrival upon the reservation, up to the outbreak, this matter was a perpetual source of wrangling, dissatisfaction, and bitter, ever-threatening complaints on the part of both the upper and lower bands."[14]

If the Dakotas hadn't realized it earlier, they certainly now knew what it meant to be robbed with a fountain pen.

*   *   *

---

12 Kappler, *Indian Treaties*, 781-88; Anderson, *Little Crow*, 102-03; Newcombe, "The Sioux Sign a Treaty," 95-96.

13 Anderson and Woolworth, *Through Dakota Eyes*, 25; John Nairn recollection, Microfilm Reel 3, Dakota Conflict, Minnesota Historical Society.

14 *Commissioner of Indian Affairs 1863*, 286.

There were other causes of the outbreak not directly related to land issues, but related to annuity payments. In March 1857, Dakotas, generally considered to be Wahpekute renegades led by Inkpaduta (Scarlet Point), massacred 39 settlers around Spirit Lake, Iowa, and Springfield (now Jackson), Minnesota. They evaded soldiers and civilians and fled west with four female captives. Dakota Agent Charles Flandrau requested immediate help to track down Inkpaduta and rescue the captives. Infantry from Fort Ridgely went out, but returned without finding their quarry. Flandrau stressed the importance of bringing the perpetrators to justice, but subsequent expeditions also came up empty-handed. In the meantime, there was panic on the northwestern frontier, as rumors of widespread Indian massacres swept across the land and settlers fled their homes.[15]

It was an accepted tenet in the American jurisprudence system that those guilty of crimes should be punished, and the case was especially true as it concerned Indians on the frontier, who were considered child-like by many whites, and would persist in bad behavior without correction. "Spare the rod and spoil the child" was an aphorism taken to heart by many. Harriet E. Bishop was an early settler who taught Indian children at Little Crow's village at Kaposia in 1847, moved to a district school in St. Paul in 1850, and later opened a female seminary for would-be teachers. Bishop, who married John McConkey in 1858, was sympathetic to the Indians' plight, nevertheless, she entertained the accepted belief. "Inkapaduta," she wrote, "was the vilest wretch un-hung. It had been feared that his going unpunished would embolden the evil inclined—that the leniency would be a precedent on which they might base future deeds."[16]

Agent Thomas Galbraith was of a similar mind. According to him, punishment was not a matter of revenge or hate, but was simply "stern justice." Because Inkpaduta was not killed, caught, or tried after the massacre, the Indians interpreted the government's non-action in a logical, if simple way: "The whites either have not the ability or the inclination to punish us." The United States government, whether from "false philanthropy or morbid

15 Beck, *Inkpaduta*, 5-6, 74, 87; Gardner Sharp, *Spirit Lake Massacre, passim*; Michno, *Fate Worse Than Death*, 190-98; Folwell, *History of Minnesota*, II, 223-24.

16 McConkey, *Dakota War Whoop*, xviii-xxi, 8.

sentiment" acted improperly. Galbraith went on to assert that if the Indians had been punished in 1857, the 1862 "outbreak would never have occurred."[17]

Those opinions were expressed after the fact, but other contemporary warnings were clear. On May 6, 1857, less than two months after the massacre, an editorial in the *St. Peter Courier* stated, "It is highly important that these rascals should be promptly punished, unless we would give encouragement to other Indians that the most flagrant outrages may be committed against the frontier settlers with impunity." The next day, the *Henderson Democrat* declared, "If you don't punish them, within two years will be a general uprising by all the Indians." The prophetic editor's time-frame was off only by a few years.[18]

The government did try to apprehend the culprits, but the methods and ramifications may not have been well thought out. In June 1857, Agent Flandrau got word that some of Inkpaduta's followers and one of his sons, Roaring Cloud, were camping at the Upper Agency. Flandrau, with Lt. Alexander Murray, 15 10th Infantrymen, 12 white volunteers, and John Otherday as guide, went to apprehend them. The Indians saw the soldiers approaching and fled. There was a short fight, Roaring Cloud was killed, and Flandrau took his wife and child prisoner, despite Lieutenant Murray's objections. As they marched away, the woman called for help, exciting the inhabitants of the other villages they passed through. They were soon surrounded by an angry mob and had to release the prisoners, plus hand over two cows.

At the Upper Agency, Murray sent to Fort Ridgely for assistance, and Maj. Thomas Sherman arrived with 25 more soldiers. Dakota Missionary Stephen Riggs urged them to go after the rest of Inkpaduta's band. While contemplating a course of action, Superintendent William J. Cullen arrived with instructions from Commissioner James W. Denver, and on July 19, he told the Dakotas that there would not be any annuity payment until the Dakotas themselves caught or killed Inkpaduta.[19]

The chiefs were incensed by what they considered an unjust demand. They may have believed that the whites were acting like petulant children, but the behavior was not unknown to them either. Vengeance and retaliation were

---

17 *Commissioner of Indian Affairs*, 1863, 298.

18 *St. Peter* (Minnesota) *Courier*, May 6, 1857 and *Henderson* (Minnesota) *Democrat*, May 7, 1857, in Beck, *Inkpaduta*, 93.

19 Beck, *Inkpaduta*, 103-04.

primary motivators in Sioux society. Not only in warfare involving entire tribes, but in day to day affairs, their responses often appeared to be that of a spoiled child. For a perceived insult, or the denial of a request, or to assuage grief for example, the Sioux response was often to vent anger or frustration through destruction. Social rebuffs could lead to horse or cattle killings, and if the person who committed the alleged offense was not available, an innocent victim would suffice. "Dakota men and women," explained one historian, "typically sought to ease their grief by causing either themselves or others to suffer."[20]

White men were perhaps a bit different in one aspect: they seldom wanted themselves to suffer; others would suffice just fine.

Thus, Superintendent Cullen ordered the Dakotas to do what the soldiers could not do. "Our Great Father has asked us to do a very hard thing," said Standing Buffalo, ". . . to go and kill men and women who do not belong to our bands." The Indians resisted. Cullen, who was inexperienced and, according to Agent Joseph Brown, didn't know the difference between "a Sioux Indian and a snapping turtle," telegraphed Commissioner Denver for advice. "Adhere to your instructions," Denver answered, "there will be no yielding." Cullen told the Dakotas they must catch Inkpaduta or fight the U.S. Army.[21]

There was a tense stand-off, and when a Sisseton warrior stabbed one of Major Sherman's soldiers, it looked like there would be a war. At that juncture, however, Little Crow arrived and defused the situation by agreeing to go after Inkpaduta. He gathered 100 men and headed out onto the Dakota prairie. At Lake Herman in late July they found Inkpaduta's camp, although he was absent. Little Crow's men attacked, and in a short fight, killed three warriors, wounded one, and captured two women and one child. A few others rushed into the lake to escape and drowned. John Otherday killed Inkpaduta's son, Fire Cloud. The three dead warriors were participants in the Spirit Lake Massacre. Feeling that they had complied with the government's wishes, Little Crow led his party back to the Upper Agency, returning on August 4.

The army seemed pleased with the effort, as was Cullen, and he telegraphed Commissioner Denver on August 18 that he believed the Sioux had "done all in their power to punish or surrender Inkpaduta and his band" and wanted to pay their annuities. Agent Flandrau and Democratic Governor Samuel Medary

20 Hassrick, *The Sioux*, 76, 80, 91; Anderson, *Little Crow*, 31, 42-43.

21 Beck, *Inkpaduta*, 105.

concurred. Other Bureau of Indian Affairs officials were not satisfied and still wanted Inkpaduta. They asked for a military expedition, and Commissioner Denver still refused to allow distribution of annuities. The commissioner's temper may have stemmed from his aversion to the whole idea of passing out money in the first place. He believed that annuities converted the Indians into paupers, made them less civilized, and more "naturally disinclined to labor." He was a fatalist. "There seems to be no likelihood of a termination of this pauper system," he wrote, "but with the extinction of the whole race."

Once again the Dakotas were irate at what they saw as another broken promise. Agency officials pleaded the Indians' cause, but nothing changed until Denver temporarily left office to take care of personal business. Acting Commissioner Charles Mix realized that the Indians had done all they could and authorized Cullen to distribute the annuities in late August 1857, but the affair only increased hard feelings.[22]

The whole idea of the Trade and Intercourse Act of 1834 and its various amendments was to provide a mechanism to allow whites and Indians a means to peacefully settle their disputes. Both parties could legally seek compensation for damages, but many claims were denied. When whites won their cases, the money they received was deducted from tribal annuities. Punishment was thus visited upon innocents; in effect, white justice was not so different from Indian justice.

Both sides were being petty and vindictive and there was no statesman with wisdom enough to interrupt the destructive spiral. In the spring of 1857, J. Brandt, one of the first Germans who came to settle in the New Ulm area in 1854, was murdered. His body was found in the brush near some abandoned tipis on the banks of the Little Cottonwood six miles south of New Ulm. It was not known if his death was related to the other killings done by Inkpaduta's band about the same time.[23]

Brandt was not on reservation land, but before the Treaty of 1858 had even been ratified by the Senate, hundreds of additional whites began moving to the lands north of the Minnesota River, cutting timber, starting farms, and blocking pathways the Dakotas traditionally used to travel north and east to the Big Woods to hunt or to raid the Chippewas. The Big Woods was a region of elm,

---

22 Anderson, *Little Crow*, 84-87; Beck, *Inkpaduta*, 105-06; Bryant and Murch, *Great Massacre*, 44-45; Kvasnicka and Viola, *Commissioners of Indian Affairs*, 70.

23 Berghold, *Indians' Revenge*, 28, 71.

oak, and sugar maple covering a land of hills and lakes stretching from about Faribault and Mankato in the south to St. Cloud in the north, and northwest from there halfway to Fort Abercrombie. Dakotas and Chippewas hunted in the northern half and it was a rough dividing line between the tribes.

By 1859, there were several thousand white families obstructing the Dakotas' routes to the Big Woods, and with only the Minnesota River separating the whites and Indians, depredations were bound to increase. In addition, when Chippewas bested Dakota war parties, the latter took vengeance on innocents by killing stock or people. John B. Schmitz was imprudent enough to go just beyond the reservation boundary about ten miles west of New Ulm where he dug a cellar for his new house. On April 27, 1860, a Dakota shot and killed him. The murderer was caught and imprisoned in New Ulm. During his trial he was shackled and well-guarded, but at one point he had to attend a call of nature. As he was being escorted to an outbuilding, the Dakota broke away from three surprised deputies and ran off, never to be caught again.[24]

Because of depredations whites filed damage claims. Whenever there was a successful petition, the government deducted money from the annuities, punishing guilty and innocent alike. Agent Joseph Brown saw the harm in the system and tried to deduct the money only from guilty individuals, but they either denied guilt or went into hiding.[25] Besides, a pro-rated deduction from an individual might only net several dollars. The innocent would have to suffer too. Those who were punished simply vented their anger by destroying more white property, initiating another round of damage claims. It was a never-ending and self-defeating cycle.

In contrast with events on the Central or Southern Plains where Comanches and Kiowas ran rampant, stealing stock, destroying property, and taking lives, the Dakotas in Minnesota in 1860 still generally managed to restrain their anger. The whites were not their only problem. While settlers built farms north of the Minnesota River, the Dakotas on the south side were having an internal struggle over farming. As early as 1854, Rev. Stephen R. Riggs and Dr. Thomas S. Williamson set up Presbyterian missions and farming communities at the Upper Agency. Williamson's, about three miles north of the Upper Agency was known as Yellow Medicine, or Pajutazi, with followers centered around the Wahpeton, Inyangmani, Little Crow's father-in-law. About

---

24 Berghold, *Indians' Revenge*, 71.

25 Anderson, *Little Crow*, 110-11.

three miles beyond, just above Hazel Creek, Riggs set up Hazelwood, which consisted mostly of Mdewakantons, among them Paul Mazakutemani, Lorenzo Lawrence, and members of the Renville clan.

Although the Dakotas made some of their earliest farming attempts at the Lower Agency (Redwood), they had no mission. In 1860, the Episcopal Bishop of Minnesota, Henry B. Whipple, visited the Lower Agency and Wabasha, Good Thunder, and Taopi approached him with, as usual, complaints about non-payment of annuity money. In addition, Wabasha said they had been promised $8,000 for schools, but nothing had been done. When they asked Whipple for a school and a missionary he was pleased, and he knew just the man for the job. He ordained as deacon a young man named Samuel D. Hinman, and by September 1860, Hinman began services at the St. John Mission at Redwood.[26]

Now, there were missionaries enough. On the other hand, according to the government officials there weren't enough farmers, while most of the Dakotas would have said that there were already too many. In October 1857, Charles Flandrau was elected a state supreme court judge and his position as agent was taken by Joseph R. Brown. Brown, a one-time trader and land speculator, was considered immoral by the missionaries, but he had married a mixed-blood Sisseton woman, had lived with the Indians for three decades, and knew their ways. He realized that the Dakotas would not work the soil if white farmers were doing it for them, and they would never break their dependency on traders unless they had an alternative. By getting the money designated for schools, houses, and agricultural equipment, and by paying and rewarding Indians who would build houses and work the farms, Brown made great progress. In his 1859 report, Brown wrote that more than 200 men, most of them heads of families, had moved to their allotted farms, worked the soil, cut their hair, discarded their blankets, and wore white men's clothing. Superintendent Cullen stated that Brown's experiment was "an assured success." Commissioner Alfred B. Greenwood believed that, counting the family members, there were more than 700 "Farmer Indians," and he prophesied that within three years the farmers would outnumber the "blanket Indians."[27]

---

26 Anderson, *Little Crow*, 79; Folwell, *History of Minnesota*, II, 118; Whipple, *Lights and Shadows*, 60-61.

27 Anderson, *Little Crow*, 107; Folwell, *History of Minnesota*, II, 219-20.

As more Indians farmed the opposition became more unyielding. Brown and Cullen wanted to give two pairs of pants, two coats, two shirts, a yoke of oxen, and a cow to every male who would cut his hair and join the farmers, which was more than ten times the annual annuity of $10 to $20 each Indian would normally receive. The "blanket Indians" saw this as unfair and actually allied with the traders, who naturally opposed civilization efforts that ruined their lucrative business. Little Crow, who tried to be progressive, witnessed a change in his peoples' lifestyles and did not like what he saw. Indians were ignoring the sacred feasts and ceremonies. Some of them, instead of sharing their crops with their people, were selling them to the government. They were becoming little white entrepreneurs and he believed it was destroying their cultural and social fabric. He did not believe a man could dress and work like a white man and still be a Dakota.

The "blanket Indians" struck back. "Bad men," said Agent Brown, tried to get some of the free gifts, and when they could not, resorted to traditional behavior. They teased and tormented the farmers, condemned them for being white "toadies," and tried to sabotage all their efforts. For the traditional Indians the farmers were nothing more than "Dutchmen," no better than the meek Germans who were crowding them off their lands. They stole the farmers' pigs, drove off their cattle, and raided their cornfields. Dakota medicine men were particularly bitter in their denunciation. At Hazelwood, where Dr. Williamson had begun a program similar to Brown's, the farmers could not stand the pressure, and the experiment failed.[28]

Joe Brown might have overcome the resistance, but party politics meant that he didn't have a chance. When the Republicans took over in 1861, he was gone. The spoils system dictated that only party members got the jobs. Thomas J. Galbraith, who had been involved in Minnesota's constitutional convention, took over Redwood Agency. Harriet Bishop McConkey said that Galbraith "had no frontier experience to equip him for his job. No amount of character could make up the difference." Even his character, however, was in question. Judge Martin Severance described the new agent as a red-haired, hard-drinker, whose overindulgence of liquor impaired his mental faculties. "Half the time he was out of his head," Severance said. "He had no diplomacy and treated the

28 Anderson, *Little Crow*, 108-09; Folwell, *History of Minnesota*, II, 221-23.

18

Indians arrogantly," and was "wholly unfit to manage a turbulent lot of savages."[29]

Coming in at the same time as a replacement for Superintendent Cullen was Clark W. Thompson. He toured the Upper and Lower Agencies in June and July 1861 to see his charges and distribute annuities, but there was trouble, particularly at Yellow Medicine Agency. Depredations committed the previous year resulted in $5,500 being deducted from the money, once again punishing the innocent and fomenting more resentment. As if there weren't enough problems, now the Yanktonais—Nakotas who lived to the west of the Dakotas—had come to Yellow Medicine seeking a portion of the Dakota annuities. Ever since they learned that the Dakotas sold part of their homeland back in 1851, the Yanktonais had been insisting that some of the land was theirs, and they deserved some of the money. Thompson distributed the annuities to the Mdewakantons and Wahpekutes at the Lower Agency on June 26, 1861, and to the Sissetons and Wahpetons at the Upper Agency on July 16. He thought the Yanktonais would cause trouble, but he promised to make their grievances known to the Great Father and gave them presents of beef cattle. With the timely arrival of two companies of soldiers from Fort Ridgely, they went away "apparently satisfied." The Yanktonais wanted their share. Had they known what the Dakotas were getting they might have realized that nothing from nothing leaves nothing.

In his annual report, Thompson believed that the effort to convert the Indians into farmers was proceeding satisfactorily. "I was much surprised to find so many of the Sioux Indians wearing the garb of civilization," he wrote. Thompson, however, was as untutored as Galbraith. A white shirt and top hat did not make an Indian into a white man, and the farming efforts had actually tapered off since Joe Brown left. Thompson did learn that the Sioux were inveterate horse thieves, there was too much liquor available on the reservations, and he believed that nearly all the depredations committed "are the immediate effects of intoxication."

Thompson was engaged in on-the-job training. Visiting the tribes was eye-opening and he learned that theories didn't support reality. There was "a very different state of facts from what we were induced to believe by reading reports," he stated. "One week's actual residence with the Indians is usually enough to eradicate nearly all preconceived notions and theories from a

29 McConkey, *Dakota War Whoop*, 7; Folwell, *History of Minnesota*, II, 222.

thinking mind." Thompson's solution was to "change the disposition of the Indian to one more mercenary and ambitious to obtain riches."[30] Apparently, once the Indian became more avaricious and materialistic he would value possessions, become more productive, appreciate law, and respect property. Thompson would bring about peace and harmony by having the Indian become as mercenary as the white man. Today the concept appears ludicrous; in 1862 it illustrated how bankrupt U.S. Indian policy had become.

Unbeknownst to Thompson, he sowed the seeds of more discontent. Feeling overwhelmed and threatened, and with the exuberance of inexperience, he promised more than he could deliver. The new Republican administration, he said, would treat them better than the Democrats did. Thompson told the tribes that in the autumn they would have a great bounty. He could not divulge where it would come from, but it would be very large and "the Great Father was going to make them all very glad."[31]

The Sissetons and Wahpetons were thus led to believe that they could expect great things in the fall, and instead of attending to their crops or going on their fall hunt, they waited in expectation. When Thompson showed up with the "windfall," which turned out to be $20,000 worth of goods amounting to only about $2.50 per capita, it was hardly enough to make a dent in what the people needed for the upcoming winter. Galbraith was faced with trying to feed more than 1,000 people who might have been able to supply their own needs if they had hunted and reaped. There were not enough supplies and the Indians had to go deeper in debt to the traders.

The Mdewakantons and Wahpekutes were leery of Thompson's promise and they went about their usual business. They would not accept the "bonus" until they learned where it came from. Thompson was compelled to admit that it had been deducted from the annuity money due to them the next summer! This was no windfall and Thompson's deception was seen as another in a long line of lies fed to them by the whites.

Thompson's trickery was, of course, a rich tidbit for the recently displaced Democrats such as Flandrau, Brown, and all the other traders and agency employees who had been replaced by the spoils system. Democrats in the background filled the Indians' heads with discontent, spreading stories that the

---

30 *Commissioner of Indian Affairs*, 1861, 69-73.

31 Riggs, *Mary and I*, 147-48.

Republicans planned to take away cash annuities and substitute payments in goods—an idea that had actually been discussed by several administrations.[32]

The Indians were not nearly as naïve and susceptible to subterfuge as some later historians would paint them. Agency employee John Nairn said that the councils followed a familiar pattern. The agent, usually "some pot-house politician," spoke in high terms about the white and red man living in peace and harmony, but an Indian orator usually disabused him of his pretensions. He would launch into a litany of the wrongs they suffered and condemn the course of previous agents and the government, "almost knocking the breath out of his white father by his knowledge of treaty and agency affairs, abolishing and annihilating the preconceived notions of the white father, clipping his soaring wings and landing him on the earth among pork and flour."[33]

The Dakotas were not easily hoodwinked, and they were keen observers. They also knew very well that the Civil War was not going well for the North. There were rumors that cash was short and since the money had to be used elsewhere, the payments would stop completely. The Great Father had been calling for more of his people to leave their farms and go away to fight the Southern white men. Soon there would be no one left except women and children. Perhaps the Indians could seek revenge when so few men were around.

Even with a great civil rebellion in progress, however, the Dakotas may not have felt the need for revenge if only the whites would have given them their promised money. Unfortunately, businessmen and politicians could not keep their hands out of the Indians' pie. More turmoil stemmed from the Mormon War of 1857-58. Trouble with Brigham Young in Utah drew soldiers out of Minnesota Territory who might have been used for going after Inkpaduta, but the main problem, besides a manpower shortage, was a money shortage. The freighting firm of Russell, Majors & Waddell had its fingers in a number of freight, passenger, and mail enterprises in the 1850s. By 1857 the partners had a near monopoly on business across the Central Plains and they contracted with the U.S. Army to supply the Army of Utah on its trek west to suppress the Mormons. Unfortunately, Mormons and Indians attacked their trains and stole or destroyed much of their stock, property, and provisions and the expedition

---

32 Robinson, *History of the Dakota*, 262-63; Folwell, *History of Minnesota*, II, 237; Riggs, *Mary and I*, 148-49.

33 John Nairn recollection, Microfilm Reel 3, Dakota Conflict, Minnesota Historical Society.

stalled. The war department was out of money. The campaign continued in 1858, but Russell, Majors & Waddell presented the army with a bill for transportation and losses for more than $642,000.

The public believed claims for such losses were a swindle and the Buchanan administration was accused of promoting the Mormon War simply to fill the firm's coffers. With Secretary of War John B. Floyd's influence, a deficiency bill was passed in May 1858, granting the company 2.4 million dollars; even so, it still had to go into debt to outfit itself. In January 1859, the partners wanted out of their contract. They were still losing money and they saw that perhaps by supplying the gold rushers for the new strikes in Colorado they could work their way out of debt.

In the summer of 1859, *New York Tribune* editor Horace Greeley went west on a Leavenworth and Pike's Peak Express stage, another of William H. Russell's subsidiary operations. Instead of glowing reports, however, Greeley complained of fraud. The Army of Utah was in the West only to "enrich the contractors favored by the War Department and the saintly speculators of Mormondom."[34]

There may have been some truth to it, but Russell, Majors & Waddell's losses were real. In January 1860, 2,500 of their oxen died in a blizzard in Nevada, and Russell hit on the idea of a Pony Express carrying mail across the country to make money and save the company. Unfortunately, the scheme didn't work and they lost even more. Russell went to Washington in the summer of 1860 looking for help. He told his troubles to Luke Lea, a former commissioner of Indian affairs and now a partner in a bank. Lea couldn't help, but he knew a man named Godard Bailey, a relative of Secretary Floyd's wife, and a lawyer and clerk in the Department of the Interior who might.

Secretary Floyd had been endorsing drafts, often called acceptances, written by William Russell, on the War Department, and against the future earnings of the company. Floyd believed he either had to help Russell raise money or else abandon sending supplies to the Army of Utah. His predicament was not unlike that faced by Colorado's Gov. William Gilpin, who issued similar drafts and lost his job because of it. Floyd wrote to various banks and urged them to accept the drafts. They were cashed, but Russell could never make enough money to repay them. The whole scheme teetered near collapse, and when it was explained to Bailey, he believed it was his duty, not to help

---

34 Settle, *War Drums and Wagon Wheels*, 49, 52, 56-57, 66, 82, 85, 86, 92, 94, 105.

Russell, but to prevent discomfiture to Floyd. Bailey "loaned" Russell $537,000 in bonds from the Indian Trust Fund, representing unpaid Indian annuities being held by the Interior Department. Russell accepted that money, and more. Later, when he learned where the money came from, he said, "The disclosure completely overwhelmed me."[35]

On December 1, 1860, concerned that he was guilty of embezzlement and realizing that Russell could not repay the bonds, Bailey wrote out a full confession. On January 29, 1861, a grand jury indicted William Russell, John Floyd, and Godard Bailey for conspiracy to "combine, confederate and agree together by wrongful means to cheat, defraud, and impoverish the United States" by removing $870,000 worth of bonds from the Department of the Interior. In the midst of a Civil War, with enough problems already, President Lincoln had to ask Congress for more money to reimburse the Indian Trust Fund. The appropriation was reluctantly passed in July 1861. Seen in this context, Superintendent Clark Thompson's promising the Dakotas windfall money in the fall of 1861 appears to be the height of folly. The Indian Trust Fund had been robbed, the Union was struggling for existence and in dire need of money, and prompt payment of Indian annuities was not a priority.[36]

There were a myriad of causes for the Sioux uprising, including unfulfilled treaties, broken promises, land issues, non-punishment of transgressions, cultural and societal breakdowns, non-payment of annuities, bad credit, swindles, inexperienced officials, and the spoils system. Bishop Henry Whipple had a slightly different take. Because we treated Indian tribes as independent nations and then ruined their weak government by inserting our own rules, we destroyed the chiefs' independence, power, and control. We dismantled tribal government and put power in the hands of chiefs who became tools for traders and agents, "powerful for mischief, but powerless for good."

Whipple said that our policies did not encourage Indians to live by honest labor, but fostered idleness instead. By unabashedly giving liquor to the Indians for trading advantages he said we have "made devils" of them. Our trade system was ruinous to honest traders and pernicious to the Indians. Whipple declared

---

35 Settle, *War Drums and Wagon Wheels*, 106, 109, 131-35.

36 *Ibid.*, 143, 150-52. Russell was freed on a technicality regarding the question as to whether a bond was a "paper or document." Floyd was freed when attorneys entered a *nolle prosequi*, because they could find no proof to sustain the indictment. Bailey skipped bond and disappeared from Washington.

that the entire nation knew that the Indian Department was the most corrupt in the government, and making unqualified people agents simply as political rewards was almost to guarantee inefficiency and fraud. The nation knew this, Whipple said, but nevertheless "has winked at it." Americans lacked the moral courage to stand up and demand reforms. Because we failed, the bishop rhetorically asked, "At whose door is the blood of these innocent victims? I believe that God will hold the nation guilty."[37]

White men have speculated much about why the Sioux rose up to murder them. Many of their explanations are valid, but what did the Dakotas have to say? Big Eagle (Wamditanka) was a Mdewakanton born in 1827 on the south bank of the Minnesota near where Mendota would take root. He succeeded his father as chief in 1857 and tried his best to work with the whites, joining the farmer Indians at the Redwood Agency, and suffering verbal abuse and threats because of his progressive stance. The Dakotas might have struggled and survived on the 20-mile wide reservation as established in the 1851 treaties, but when the northern ten-mile strip was taken away in the 1858 treaty, the restriction was too great. On the south side there was less game and the whites were breaking the land into small farm plots. Little Crow was blamed for signing the treaty and his status took a downturn. The Dakotas, said Big Eagle, "were induced to give up the old life and go to work like white men, which was very distasteful to many." He believed that if the Indians had forced the whites to give up their way of life and live like Indians they would have resisted just the same.

Big Eagle listed other causes. The whites would not let the Dakotas go to war against their enemies like the Chippewas; they wanted to fight their old foes, hunt where they pleased, and trade furs to anyone. The traders were a major problem. Indians bought on credit, and when the time came for payment, "the traders were on hand with their books," showing the Indians owed money. The Indians had no books and could not disprove the claims, "and sometimes the traders got all of their money." Big Eagle later learned that white men often disputed their bills, and when they did they refused to pay and could "go to law" to fix the problem. "The Indians could not go to law," Big Eagle said.

Another problem was that "many of the white men often abused the Indians and treated them unkindly." They were condescending. Big Eagle:

---

37 Whipple, *Lights and Shadows*, 125-27.

"Many of the whites always seemed to say by their manner when they saw an Indian, 'I am much better than you,' and the Indians did not like this."[38]

Isaac V. D. Heard lived in Minnesota for a dozen years, knew many of the people involved, and studied the events leading up to the outbreak. He took a cultural view of events and saw the conflict as nearly inevitable. "The Indians were predisposed to hostility toward the whites," he wrote. They regarded whites with "that repugnance which God has implanted as an instinct in different races for the preservation of their national integrity." Their "inborn feeling," Heard wrote, was increased because of cheating traders, the debauchery of their women, and the sale of liquor. Another important factor was when the U.S. Government ordered the Dakotas to stop fighting the Chippewas. They viewed the prohibition as tyrannical and hypocritical, especially as the white men were currently fighting one another. Their rhetorical inquiry was, as Heard phrased it, "Our Great Father, we know, has always told us it was wrong to make war, yet now he himself is making war and killing a great many. Will you explain this to us? We don't understand it."[39]

Heard's view that the Indians' ethnocentrism had a great deal to do with the war would be looked at with disfavor in the 21st Century, when historians appear more comfortable ascribing racist arrogance as solely an Anglo provenance. Heard, however, was not far off the mark. The whites' attitude of superiority was hard for the Indians to stomach, because they owned a similar mind-set. Philander Prescott, who married into the tribe and lived with the Dakotas for four decades, said that the Dakotas thought they were "wiser and better than the others." In council with the whites they acted humble, but "by themselves they would say the whites were the greatest fools they ever saw." Big Eagle affirmed the sentiment: "The Dakotas did not believe there were better men in the world than they."[40]

When two ethnocentric peoples try to co-exist there is little chance for compromise. Some, like Wabasha, to his credit, did try to defuse the situation and make the best of the circumstances. Born about 1800 near present-day Winona, Minnesota, Wabasha did not at first walk the middle road. He was opposed to the treaties of 1851 and was a rival to Little Crow. He reluctantly

---

38 Anderson and Woolworth, *Through Dakota Eyes*, 21, 23-24.

39 Heard, *History of the Sioux War*, 31.

40 "Recollections of Philander Prescott," 491, *MHSC*, Vol. 6; Anderson and Woolworth, *Through Dakota Eyes*, 24.

participated in the treaty talks of 1858 and did not want the lands north of the Minnesota River taken. Nevertheless, he went along with the decision, learned to farm, wore white man's clothes, and had his hair cut.

Wabasha knew what the main problem was all about: land. The Dakotas did not disdain land or shun the products that came from it. They wished to own and use it much as did the whites. Wabasha came to believe that white ways were good because they "obtain land and hold it," and plant corn and raise animals. "I wish you to give my people land where we may do the same," Wabasha dictated in a letter to the president. "If we are left without a country, we will be obliged to go out on the plains." Illustrating the Dakotas' penchant for the woodlands, Wabasha declared that on the plains his people would perish of cold and starvation and other tribes would kill them. When Wabasha got to see President Buchanan in 1858, he personally reiterated to the Great Father "about what was my chief desire, which was to have land."[41]

Land ownership, by treaty or conquest, was the sine qua non of Dakota and American existence.

In addition to the underlying issues, more immediate events brought the situation to the boiling point. Effects of a terrible drought in 1860 carried over into 1861, making a poor corn crop. Then cutworms arrived, destroying much of the remaining corn. Many Dakotas, believing Superintendent Thompson's "bonus" promise, had not made adequate food plans for the winter. Galbraith had to request an additional $5,000 out of a special fund so he could help feed the Indians. He asked Reverend Riggs for a list of the neediest, and they fed about 1,500 Dakotas from mid-December until April 1862. Galbraith used up his stores, and had to buy flour and pork from the traders on credit. A great snowstorm hit in late February 1862, delaying the spring hunt and exacerbating the Indians' desperate situation. Some of the elderly and the children starved to death. When the weather permitted, the Dakota farmers planted their crops, but it would be months before the annuities were due, and even longer before harvest.[42]

Although most of the blanket Indians were in dire straits, Agent Galbraith helped the farmers, often giving them what little he had in his own warehouse to get them through the hard times. The farmers had the houses and the food, and,

41 Anderson and Woolworth, *Through Dakota Eyes*, 27-29.

42 Berghold, *Indian's Revenge*, 69; Folwell, *History of Minnesota*, II, 228; Heard, *History of the Sioux War*, 42; *Commissioner of Indian Affairs*, 1863, 267.

said Big Eagle, "The other Indians did not like this. They were envious of them and jealous, and disliked them because they were favored."[43]

Backlash came from the soldiers' lodge. The old quasi-military society was organized primarily for hunters, but by the 1860s it was becoming a militant institution where the young men could gather to discuss tribal matters, protest conditions, and seek options—options which often included violent solutions. Galbraith viewed the soldiers' lodge at Yellow Medicine as particularly dangerous. Farmer Indians privately informed him that the soldiers' lodge had the power to kill anyone who failed to follow their wishes, and many farmers were becoming targets.

About the same time the soldiers' lodge received news that would raise tensions even higher. Most of the Indians had assumed that all old debts were finally paid off with the annuity distribution of 1861. Now, however, government farmer Philander Prescott and trader William S. Forbes were said to have told the Dakotas that the debts were not paid, and more would be deducted from the 1862 money. Big Eagle heard that half of the money would be taken and said that the young men "felt very angry." If that wasn't bad enough, other rumors indicated that there wouldn't even be any annuities this year because the Great Father was out of money, using it all to fight the other white men in the south.

Henry Whipple was visiting the agencies in June. At Yellow Medicine, an old Indian named Pay-Pay stopped the bishop and asked him how much money they would receive. Whipple told him he believed it would be $20 per head, about the same they always received. Pay-Pay went away, but returned again with Wakute and asked Whipple to tell him what he had said. Whipple repeated his statement, but Wakute did not believe it. Whipple was nervous. At Redwood he talked to one of the trader's clerks and told him that Major Galbraith was coming soon "to enroll the Indians for payment."

"Galbraith is a fool," the clerk replied. "Why does he lie to them? I have heard from Washington that most of the appropriation has been used to pay claims against the Indians. The payment will not be made. I have told the Indians this, and have refused to trust them." Whipple was astounded and wondered how the clerk seemed to know more than the agent. "I had never seen the Indians so restless," he said. They were constantly doing "some heathen dance" and sometimes refused to shake hands with him. Whipple knew

---

43 Anderson and Woolworth, *Through Dakota Eyes*, 26.

that those men would later boast that they had not taken the hand of a white man, "which was always a danger signal."[44]

Factions within the Dakota ranks were forming into hard divisions. Little Crow was seen as an appeaser. Old Shakopee died in 1860, and his son, Young Shakopee (Little Six), called "a tall scowling ruffian," was a belligerent.[45] He and Red Middle Voice became hard-liners and sympathized with the soldiers' lodge. In June the time came for the selection of a new tribal speaker. Little Crow was in disfavor, likely because of his waffling; blanket Indians thought he favored the farmers and vice versa, plus he was not trusted since he had agreed to sell half of the reservation in 1858. Big Eagle was a candidate, but he was relatively new on the scene and a moderate. Traveling Hail was a farmer and had the backing of Galbraith. Big Eagle explained that many whites believed that Little Crow was always the main chief, but he was not—he had only been principal chief once since his blunder in 1858. Before the June 1862 election, Wabasha was the principal chief. It was "an exciting contest" according to Big Eagle. "We had politics among us," he said, "and there was much feeling." Traveling Hail won and Little Crow "felt sore" at being spurned. He came to believe that the way to regain control would be to get with the program. He began attending the Episcopal Church, dug a cellar for his new house, began to work the soil, and decided that if the future meant he must become a "white man," so be it.[46]

Tribal factions would not heal so easily, and the heat turned up a notch as rumors grew that the annuities would not be paid. The rumors had a basis in fact. When the Dakotas heard that the $20,000 "windfall" of goods they received in the fall of 1861 would be subtracted out of their 1862 annuities, and that future payments might all be made in goods and not money, they were incensed. The Indian department, realizing the blunder it had made, did not dare to come to the table with a partial payment. It pleaded for help, but money to replace the $20,000 had to come from the appropriations for 1863. The House passed the bill in February 1862 and the Senate, with many amendments, passed it in May. The House did not agree and the bill went to conference, with its final version not being approved until July 5, 1862. The Dakotas had said long before then that they were starving.

---

44 Anderson, *Little Crow*, 81-82, 118; Anderson and Woolworth, *Through Dakota Eyes*, 30; Whipple, *Lights and Shadows*, 106-07.

45 John Nairn recollection, Microfilm Reel 3, Dakota Conflict, Minnesota Historical Society.

46 Anderson, *Little Crow*, 119, 121; Anderson and Woolworth, *Through Dakota Eyes*, 24-25.

Further delays came because the money-strapped Federal Government figured it could save a few bucks by paying the Indians with treasury notes called "greenbacks." The paper money was cheaper. The government could have obtained greenbacks quicker, but the traders told the Indians that paper money was no good, and worth only half the value of coin. This was true, but the Indians would never see it in either form, for the traders knew they would get it all when they presented the bills of debt. When the traders lobbied for gold through the Indians it only delayed the payment longer. It was not until August 8, 1862, that Treasury Secretary Chase authorized the payment in gold.[47]

By then it was too late. Greed and parsimony had triumphed. The old English adage about being penny-wise and pound-foolish was borne out. Hundreds of people lost their lives and millions of dollars of damages resulted, but, the cynic might look back and say, at least the U.S. didn't have to worry about paying the Dakotas for a few years.

Given all the resentment and anger literally boiling at the Upper and Lower Agencies, it is remarkable that Agent Galbraith seemed to have little inkling of the powder keg he presided over. He spent the spring and summer purchasing agricultural equipment, cutting timber, making bricks, and obtaining construction materials for buildings. He boasted that his farmer Indians on both reservations had made 30,000 fence rails and posts during the winter and spring. The farmers were industriously planting and all the agency employees were busy making improvements. Nelson Givens, the assistant agent, was at Big Stone Lake directing agricultural operations; August H. Wagner, superintendent for farms at Redwood, reported that all the Indians were following instructions; John Nairn, carpenter at Redwood, was busily cutting lumber and making plans for building Little Crow's new house; contractor Joseph W. De Camp had the mills running at full capacity; H. G. Billings was engaged in cutting 550 tons of hay; Amos W. Huggins and Julia La Framboise ran a new school to teach the Indian children at Lac Qui Parle; George Lott was building a new blacksmith shop at Big Stone Lake; Galbraith supervised the construction of 18 bridges over the creeks and sloughs running along the roads between the Upper and Lower Agencies, facilitating transportation and cutting freighting costs by one-quarter; and Galbraith proudly counted the land in cultivation by early summer of 1862: 2,135 acres of corn, 560 of potatoes, 150

47 Robinson, *History of the Dakota*, 264; Folwell, *History of Minnesota*, II, 237-38.

of turnips and rutabagas, 24 of wheat, and numerous quantities of beans, squash, beets, peas, and pumpkins.

Galbraith was proud and optimistic. "Thus, to all appearance, the spring season opened propitiously," he wrote. It appeared that the Indians would not starve or have reason for discontent the upcoming winter, but it was not to be. "I need hardly say that our hopes were high at the prospects before us, nor need I relate my chagrin and mortification when, in a moment, I found those high hopes blasted forever." Never underestimate the power of little men to do harm.[48]

Galbraith was taken aback when, about June 25, a number of Sisseton and Wahpeton chiefs and headmen came to him at Yellow Medicine Agency and asked him if they were going to get any money, when, and how much. Galbraith did not know himself, but he answered that of course they would be paid, "very nearly, if not quite, a full payment," but probably not before the 20th of July. He issued a token amount of provisions, tobacco, powder and shot, and told them not to come back until he called for them. Galbraith then went to Redwood, issued a small amount of similar items, and spent a week supervising the building and planting.

Earlier in June, Dr. Williamson at Yellow Medicine learned from Cloud Man and Scarlet Plume that some of Inkpaduta's band and a large number of Yanktonais were coming to the Upper Agency to demand what they considered was their share of the annuity money. If they did not get the money, they would kill all the Indians who dressed like white men. Galbraith was apprised of the threats and wrote to Superintendent Thompson requesting that soldiers be present at the distribution.

On June 30, Lts. Timothy J. Sheehan and Thomas P. Gere took 100 men of Companies B and C, 5th Minnesota, with one 12 pounder mountain howitzer, on a march to the Upper Agency, arriving there on July 2 while Galbraith was away. Nothing seemed to be happening and Gere wrote in his diary that the mosquitoes "are likely to prove our most formidable enemy." On the 8th, warriors sent word through interpreter Peter Quinn that they wished to talk. They told Lieutenants Sheehan and Gere that when their money arrived, "We wish you to keep the traders away from the pay table," plus they wanted "a present of a beef." The officers responded that money distribution and beef issuance were in the hands of their agent, and that they didn't have enough

48 *Commissioner of Indian Affairs*, 1863, 269-73.

rations to give out any extra. Gere, still taking the Dakotas lightly and imitating the contemporary humorist, Artemus Ward, described them as "a emfatic noosens," but the Dakotas were deadly serious. More arrived every day, including 78 lodges of Yanktonais, just as had been forewarned. Galbraith returned on July 14 and discovered "to my surprise," soldiers and thousands of Indians camped around the agency.[49] The agent conferred with the Indians. They said they feared something was wrong and they would not get their money "because white men had been telling them so." Galbraith talked to Sheehan and Gere who thought it best to give the Indians some provisions. On July 17, Reverend Williamson, who had a son, A. W. Williamson, serving in Gere's company, gave Gere's men permission to go to his garden and pick all the peas they wanted. On the 18th, Gere said, they had "one grand pea dinner," but a garden full of peas would not feed the multitudes. More Indian delegates arrived and said they were starving. The officers talked again to Galbraith, but he said that there was no cause for alarm because the Indians were still peaceful and making no overt threats. In his report, the agent said, "I supplied them as best I could, parsimoniously, indeed, from necessity it was; still I did all in my power." Lieutenant Sheehan was under the agent's orders and could do little, but he did send a messenger to Fort Ridgely to ask for another mountain howitzer, which arrived on the 21st.[50]

While awaiting a resolution, warriors had confrontations with the traders. The soldiers' lodge apparently planned to get as much goods as they could on credit before the annuity money arrived, and then, believing they could keep the traders away, renege on their debts and refuse to pay them back. Word of the plan was relayed to the traders and warriors of the soldiers' lodge went after the three who they believed were the squealers. They killed one in the woods and caught the other two in the street at the agency and sliced the clothing from their bodies in front of all the people. Now, when hunters came in to ask for credit, the traders told them, "Go to the Soldiers' Lodge and get credit." Some

49 *Commissioner of Indian Affairs*, 1863, 273-274; Robinson, *History of the Dakota*, 265; Gere, "Uncle Sam's Army," Brown County Historical Society; *Minnesota in the Civil and Indian Wars*, I, 245.

50 *Minnesota in the Civil and Indian Wars*, I, 245-46; Gere, "Uncle Sam's Army," Brown County Historical Society; *Commissioner of Indian Affairs*, 1863, 274.

of them apparently replied: "If we could, like our women, give ourselves up to you, we could get all the credit we ask for; but, since we are men, we cannot."[51]

With the soldiers' lodge warriors denied credit and having no money for food, they were essentially told to starve, or, as in the phrases commonly heard around the agencies in times of hunger, were told to go eat wild potatoes or grass. A party of irate hunters went to Andrew J. Myrick's store and they shouted at each other. "You have said you have closed your stores . . . and that we should eat grass. We warn you not to cut another stick of wood nor to cut our grass," the warriors threatened.

"Ho! all right!" Myrick replied. "When you are cold this winter, and want to warm yourselves by my stove, I will put you out of doors."[52]

About July 22, a party of Chippewas raided the area and killed two Dakotas 18 miles from the agency. A war party of more than 1,000 Dakotas responded, sweeping past Yellow Medicine on the 24th, leaving Sheehan and Gere wide-eyed and no doubt glad that the angry Indians were not after them.

On July 26, in order to make it look like something was being done, Major Galbraith agreed to count all the Indians who would later receive annuities, thus having one less task to do when the money arrived. The count took more than 12 hours, and the soldiers distributed some of their hard cracker rations to the appreciation of the hungry Indians. In the meantime, Galbraith received word that Inkpaduta and his band were camped up the Yellow Medicine River. On the 27th he instructed Lieutenant Sheehan to take a small detachment upriver and catch him—something that the army had been unable to do since the Spirit Lake Massacre in 1857. As if it was a foregone conclusion, Galbraith said, "You will take said Inkpaduta and all the Indian soldiers with him, prisoners, alive if possible, and deliver them to me at the Agency. If they resist, I advise that they be shot."

Sheehan left Gere in charge at the agency and took 14 soldiers, four citizens, and Good Voiced Hail, a Christian Indian guide who had helped rescue some of the Spirit Lake captives, and went after the renegades. Notwithstanding their caution and secrecy, Indian spies warned Inkpaduta and

51 Heard, *History of the Sioux War*, 48-49; Berghold, *Indians' Revenge*, 70.

52 Anderson, *Little Crow*, 122, 219; Heard, *History of the Sioux War*, 49; Berghold, *Indians' Revenge*, 74. This exchange has been reported in various versions, with the statements being to eat grass, potatoes, hay, or even ordure. Andrew Myrick wrote of the confrontation to his brother Nathan, on July 20.

Sheehan found only an empty camp. He chased Inkpaduta to Lake Benton in Dakota Territory before giving up, and returned to Yellow Medicine on August 3.[53]

On the morning of August 4, about 800 Indians flooded the agency, aiming at the warehouse. With the Minnesota infantrymen rubbing the sleep from their eyes and too startled to act, the Indians broke down the door and began unloading the supplies. They had taken about 100 sacks of flour outside before Lieutenant Sheehan lined up his outnumbered men to cover the building. A warrior grabbed Pvt. James W. Foster's gun, which discharged, and the warrior seized Foster's hair as if he was going to scalp him. Sheehan ordered his men to stand back and the warrior let Foster go. With cocked weapons the soldiers stood there, not knowing what would happen. One thing is certain, if a soldier had shot an Indian at that moment, there would have been a massacre with about 100 dead soldiers the probable result. Sheehan tried to stay cool, realizing that the Indians were only taking food, and that if they had meant to kill, they would have already done so.

When Lieutenant Gere had the men of Company B train one of the howitzers on the warehouse door, the Indians stopped looting and rapidly pulled back to either side of the howitzer's line of fire. Lieutenant Sheehan, Sgt. Solon A. Trescott, and 15 men marched to the door and bluffed the Indians back. With Trescott holding a tentative perimeter, Sheehan went to Galbraith, who had not yet come out of the dubious protection of his brick house, and told him he must do something now. Galbraith still believed that a concession to threats would be destructive to future negotiations, but he talked to the Indians and agreed to issue two days worth of pork and flour on the condition that they all leave and only the chiefs return the next day, unarmed, for a council. They agreed, and another crisis had been defused.[54]

The exact sequence of events over the next few days is difficult to determine, since witnesses' reports differed. Galbraith sent for Stephen Riggs and when the Reverend arrived, Galbraith said, "If there is anything between the lids of the Bible that will meet this case, I wish you would use it." Riggs went to see Standing Buffalo of the Sissetons, who was usually a voice for restraint,

53 *Minnesota in the Civil and Indian Wars*, I, 246; Robinson, *History of the Dakota*, 266; McConkey, *Dakota War Whoop*, 10-11; Beck, *Inkpaduta*, 112.

54 *Commissioner of Indian Affairs*, 1863, 274; McConkey, *Dakota War Whoop*, 12; Gere, "Uncle Sam's Army," Brown County Historical Society; *Minnesota in the Civil and Indian Wars*, I, 246-47.

and asked him to attend the council.[55] On August 5 the chiefs returned, but this time Little Crow was among them. Having heard of the troubles at Redwood he hurried to Yellow Medicine, and even though Traveling Hail was elected chief spokesman, it was Little Crow whose talk was remembered. Riggs was present, as was John P. Williamson, a son of missionary Dr. Williamson. Galbraith was present, as were a number of the clerks and traders, including Andrew J. Myrick.

The Indians began the talk by stating the obvious: they had no money and their families were starving. Galbraith could only offer the same answer: the money was coming soon and he had little left in the government warehouse. Little Crow said that the government supplies might be gone, but suggested that there were four traders' stores full of supplies that could be used. Why couldn't Galbraith "make some arrangement" with the traders? Little Crow had his own account at Myrick's store at Redwood and had been conciliatory in the past, often siding with the traders' claims in arguments over debts. It seemed like a reasonable solution, but then Little Crow added, "When men are hungry they help themselves."

Whether the comment was a justification of the Bread Raid made on the warehouse or a threat for the future is unclear. Interpreter Peter Quinn caught his breath, hesitated, and refused to translate the statement into English. The impasse was remedied when Galbraith turned to John P. Williamson, who was fluent in the Dakota language. Williamson explained what was said. Galbraith and the traders sat in silence for a moment, when Galbraith turned to them and said, "Well, it's up to you now. What will you do?"

Most of the stores at Yellow Medicine were operated by clerks, and they turned to Myrick, who was the only owner there. After a brief consultation, one of the clerks said, "Whatever Myrick does, we will do." Disgusted with the affair, Myrick got up to leave the room, but an angry Galbraith demanded an answer. Myrick no doubt recalled his recent confrontations with men of the soldiers' lodge who warned him not to use their timber or grass, and his response to boot them out of his store and stop their credit. He was fed up with these lily-livered, pusillanimous conciliations. Only a tough stance would keep the Indians in their place.

Myrick turned and said, "So far as I am concerned, if they are hungry, let them eat grass." Again, Quinn refused to translate, and Galbraith turned to

---

55 Riggs, *Mary and I*, 151.

Williamson. When he spoke the words in Dakota the chiefs reportedly jumped up and trilled their war whoops in anger.[56]

Myrick's phrase has been passed down by historians for generations, almost always used as an illustration of the white man's insensitivity, outright meanness, and stupidity. But did he say it? Did he say it at that time and place, or was the phrase one that was mentioned in many variations, by many people, many times, and telescoped into that one snapshot moment of time? Abel B. Murch, who later co-authored a thorough study of the outbreak, was at Yellow Medicine Agency at the time and joined Agent Galbraith when he recruited about 50 men known as the "Renville Rangers" to fight in the Civil War. Murch was acquainted with the players in the drama, but he never mentioned that Myrick was in any council or that he made any such statement.[57]

Reverend Riggs was there and wrote a book about his experiences, yet, he did not mention Myrick being at the council. Thomas Galbraith and Lts. Sheehan and Gere made no mention of it in their reports, which one would think would have been important enough to record in light of subsequent events. Galbraith in particular, looking to shift blame away from himself as a cause of the outbreak, would certainly have referred to Myrick's egregious gaffe. In his 32-page report to the superintendent, Galbraith made no mention of Myrick in connection with these events. Sarah Wakefield, who lived at Yellow Medicine, wrote a narrative in 1863, stating, "The traders said to them [the Indians] they would get no more money; that the Agent was going away to fight, and they would have to eat grass like cattle, etc."[58] In a number of histories or remembrances written after the uprising, there are no references to Myrick making that statement.[59]

In 1904, Doane Robinson, secretary of the South Dakota Historical Society, was collecting material for his *History of the Dakota or Sioux Indians*. One of his friends and informants was the Rev. John P. Williamson, the same person

56 Anderson, *Little Crow*, 127-28; Folwell, *History of Minnesota*, II, 233; Barton, *Brother to the Sioux*, 50. This statement has been rendered several ways, such as "If they are hungry, let them eat grass," or "If they are hungry, let them eat grass or their own dung." Examples are in Carley, *Dakota War of 1862*, 6; Schultz, *Over the Earth I Come*, 28; Koblas, *Let Them Eat Grass*, I, 187.

57 Bryant and Murch, *Great Massacre*, 78.

58 Wakefield, *Six Week in the Sioux Teepees*, 65.

59 Examples are McConkey, *Dakota War Whoop* (1863); Heard, *History of the Sioux War* (1863); Bryant and Murch, *Great Massacre* (1864); Riggs, *Mary and I* (1880); Berghold, *Indians' Revenge* (1891); Whipple, *Lights and Shadows* (1899).

who translated during that 1862 conference. Williamson said nothing to Robinson about Myrick's supposedly infamous words to the Indians, or if he did, Robinson chose not to mention it. In fact, Myrick is not mentioned once in Robinson's history. The chances are slim that Robinson would have omitted such dramatic words of historical irony if he had known about them.

In their 1908 book *Minnesota in Three Centuries*, authors Lucius Hubbard and Return Holcombe reconstructed the events based on an interview with Big Eagle, which was translated and given to Holcombe in 1894. Holcombe first published the story in the *St. Paul Pioneer Press*, July 1, 1894, and later the same year it appeared in a Collections of the Minnesota Historical Society publication. Big Eagle spoke of many incidents, but as to this episode he only said, "Mr. Andrew Myrick, a trader, with an Indian wife, had refused some hungry Indians credit a short time before when they asked him for some provisions. He said to them, 'Go and eat grass.'"[60]

From that, Hubbard and Holcombe expanded the story. It was in June 1862 that men of the soldiers' lodge went to Captain Marsh at Fort Ridgely. Through interpreter Quinn they asked if he planned to send soldiers to help the traders collect debts when the annuity money arrived. Marsh said his soldiers were not debt collectors and the Indians were satisfied. At the Lower Agency they boasted of what had transpired, the traders heard, and Andrew Myrick supposedly vowed not to give them any more credit.

"You will be sorry for what you have done," Holcombe has Myrick saying. "After a while you will come to me and beg for meat and flour to keep you and your wives and children from starving and I will not let you have a thing. You and your wives and children may starve, or eat grass, or your own filth."[61]

Hubbard and Holcombe gave no documentation for this quote, but presumably it was from Big Eagle's much sparser rendition. A little poetic license from a newspaper reporter, therefore, is apparently at the root of the Myrick insult story. The authors were aware of the impact of irony, and this is just what Myrick's utterance may be—apocryphal irony that may not be totally accurate, but it is such a historical gem that few subsequent authors would want to qualify it, let alone deny it.

The first time Myrick's phrase is connected to a white eyewitness and printed in its popular context is in Winifred W. Barton's 1919 book about her

60 Anderson and Woolworth, *Through Dakota Eyes*, 32n1, 56.

61 Hubbard and Holcombe, *Minnesota in Three Centuries*, III, 285-86.

father, John P. Williamson, entitled *A Brother to the Sioux*. From that time on, Myrick had evermore been depicted as telling the Indians to eat grass or dung.[62]

The depiction is fitting: an obstreperous man telling starving Indians to eat grass, and then getting his just deserts by being killed and having grass stuffed in his mouth is such great historical irony that it will probably never be excised from the files of urban legend. This is not to say that historians have not questioned the event. William Folwell, writing his *History of Minnesota* in 1924, referenced *Minnesota in Three Centuries* and *A Brother to the Sioux*. When he corresponded with Barton about the "grass" story, she replied that her father mentioned it later in life when his thoughts returned to the early years. Folwell concluded that Williamson "doubtless repeated it many times" to his daughter. Why only to his daughter and not to his friends who were writing books? The fact that Little Crow later dictated a letter to Colonel Sibley mentioning that Myrick "told the Indians they would eat grass or dirt," said Folwell, "also adds a degree of credibility" to the incident. Folwell, however, was still a bit puzzled why it was "difficult to assign a date" to that particular council. He concluded that August 14 or 15 was a good estimate, and he was certain it took place at Redwood Agency.[63]

Marion P. Satterlee moved to southern Minnesota as a young boy in 1863, knew many of the survivors of the uprising, and spent much of his life studying the events. He correctly states that John P. Williamson was the Lower Agency missionary, says that the event occurred at the Lower Agency, and Philander Prescott, an old government farm instructor who lived with the Dakotas for 40

---

62 No white contemporaries witnessed and wrote of Myrick's "eat grass" statement. Yet, after it was first mentioned in a secondary source 57 years after the fact, it has proliferated as truth in virtually every subsequent history. Repetition, unfortunately, is equated with accuracy. The phenomenon has been described in remarkably similar context by historian John H. Monnett in his 2008 book, *Where a Hundred Soldiers Were Killed*. Monnett was confronted with an analogous phrase that he could not show was in existence until 38 years after it was supposedly uttered. The statement, "Give me eighty men and I'll ride through the whole Sioux Nation," attributed to a boastful, arrogant Capt. William J. Fetterman before his demise near Fort Phil Kearny on December 21, 1866, is a perfect illustration. Having supposedly said those words, Fetterman promptly went out with 80 men and was massacred. His commanding officer at the time, Col. Henry B. Carrington, and his two wives, were instrumental in starting the story, and author Cyrus Townsend Brady gave literary form to the suggestion in his 1904 book, *Indian Fights and Fighters*. The point is, Fetterman never said it, but as Monnett argues, "irony often outlasts historical fact."

63 Folwell, *History of Minnesota*, II, 233-34n24. Priscilla Russo, in "The Time to Speak is Over," 101, gives essentially the same story as Folwell, but says it occurred on August 13.

years, was the interpreter.[64] If Prescott was the interpreter, there probably wouldn't have been the fuss made over "firing" interpreter Peter Quinn. Then again, perhaps both of them were present, or the Quinn firing occurred at the Upper Agency and had nothing to do with the council at the Lower Agency which may have taken place a week or more later.

Historian Gary Anderson studied the affair and said it occurred at Yellow Medicine Agency, even though Reverend Riggs and Lieutenant Sheehan were present on August 5, and neither of them mentioned Myrick or the council. Because Captain John Marsh arrived in the afternoon of August 6 and took an active part in the negotiations, Anderson concluded that the council took place at Yellow Medicine Agency on the morning of August 6. There is something to be said for the argument, but we also have to consider the letter written by Agent Galbraith to Lieutenant Sheehan dated August 5, stating that interpreter Quinn "is a man whom I cannot trust to communicate or correspond with my Indians," and requesting that Quinn be removed to the custody of Captain Marsh. Sheehan thus ordered Lieutenant Gere to escort Quinn back to Fort Ridgely. They left at four p.m. on the fifth, passed the Lower Agency at midnight, and arrived at the fort at three a.m. on August 6. Marsh promptly left, and with an exhausted Gere, rode back to Yellow Medicine, arriving at one-thirty in the afternoon of August 6. The council could not have taken place on the morning of the sixth, when Galbraith wrote the letter to remove Quinn on the fifth.

Anderson argues that John Williamson's daughter did not specify the location of the council and it does not fit Redwood Agency, yet it appears clear enough while following the story line. The 26-year-old Williamson had graduated from Lane Seminary in Ohio in 1860, and was a missionary at the Redwood Agency. He had lived in and done his preaching based out of the tipi of his friend, Napesni. They had just finished constructing the mission building that spring. Barton gave no date for the council, but her description places the event at Redwood. She also said her father left the next morning for a business trip to Ohio. Per Anderson, Williamson left on August 11. If Barton's recollections are correct, the council therefore was on August 10. On that day, however, Galbraith was still at Yellow Medicine. Williamson went by horse to St. Paul, steamship down the Mississippi to Galena, Illinois, and railroad to Ohio. There, he picked up a Cincinnati paper and read about the "Great Indian

64 Tolzmann, ed., *Outbreak and Massacre*, 8.

Massacre in Minnesota." The uprising began on August 18 and word had reached St. Paul by late that evening. The next morning telegraph news spread across the country. It would have only taken a few days before papers all across the Midwest were screaming the headlines.[65]

Unfortunately, none of the scenarios fit well together. Instead the details serve to confuse, rather than resolve, the matter.

In his *History of the Santee Sioux*, Roy W. Meyer writes that Little Crow was present at Yellow Medicine when Galbraith distributed supplies on August 8 and 9, and obtained a promise from him that the agent would also issue provisions at Redwood. About August 16 Little Crow, Galbraith, and the traders held another council at Redwood, and it was there that Myrick made his "grass" statement.[66]

In an article in *Minnesota History*, Patricia Russo added more ingredients into the mix. She logically argued that during the early August Bread Raid at Yellow Medicine, Little Crow was the chief speaker, as he was on August 13 at Redwood. It is there, Russo said, that Myrick made his "grass" insult, and Little Crow was still clearly the chief speaker. It was this slap in the face by the whites that caused the Mdewakantons to seek another representative. The Dakotas, Russo stated, exercised political initiatives through majority election, not heredity. The village was the main socio-political unit, but tribes took precedence in crisis periods. This was a crisis. Thus, Myrick's insult came on August 13, and it triggered the election for a new speaker. Little Crow couldn't seem to alleviate the Dakotas' frustration—perhaps Traveling Hail could.[67] Russo's argument has merit, but if the Dakotas were so angry with Little Crow's seemingly conciliatory manner, it appears that they would have chosen the more militant Red Middle Voice perhaps, instead of the moderate Traveling Hail who did not want war with the whites.

As mentioned above, Big Eagle could not ascribe any more particulars to the incident other than at some time and place some Indians went to Myrick and asked him for credit. "He said to them: 'Go and eat grass.'" A Mdewakanton, Good Fifth Son (Robert Hakewaste), participated in the events but did not mention Myrick. He said that men of the soldiers' lodge tried to get

---

65 Anderson, *Little Crow*, 127, 220n22; Anderson, "Myrick's Insult: A Fresh Look," 198-206; *Minnesota in the Civil and Indian Wars*, I, 247-48; Barton, *Brother to the Sioux*, 46-50.

66 Meyer, *History of the Santee*, 114.

67 Russo, "Time to Speak is Over," 101-04.

credit from the traders at Redwood, but the traders "were not going to give us any credit and we were going to eat grass." Another version was told by the Mdewakanton Good Star Woman (Wicahpewastewin). She recalled that two traders had one day called the Indians to a council to tell them that they must sign a paper so the traders could collect money from the government. The Indians demurred, and an unnamed trader threatened that if they didn't sign they would get nothing from his store. "If you have to eat grass," he said, "go ahead and eat grass but don't come around here asking for food." Good Star Woman said that from that time on the Indians and the trader were unfriendly, "but the trouble did not begin right away."[68]

Why all this confusion in time, place, personnel, and phraseology? The reason may stem from the simple fact that the incident never happened in the manner it has been popularly depicted. Perhaps Williamson's daughter erred in remembering what her father told her—which is a major drawback in relying on oral history, especially four decades or more later. It appears that the statement was likely made in various forms by several clerks and/or traders, at various times, and in different places. Myrick, as one of the more obnoxious white men at the agencies, was the man branded with the statement and given the primary onus of guilt for starting a war. If Myrick was to blame, or if he shared the responsibility with several others, one thing becomes clear: a culture clash did not start a war; a few petty, mean, and greedy individuals orchestrated life and death for thousands.

There is another factor that needs assessment in the causation equation: was the uprising an impromptu paroxysm set-off by accident, or was it pre-planned? Many people have a penchant for conspiracy theories, but most can be dismissed by examining the evidence thoroughly. Although unlikely, the possibility of premeditation in the Sioux uprising deserves a look.

Charles S. Bryant and Abel Murch, eyewitnesses to some of the incidents and involved in settling many of the depredation claims, contend that the outbreak was part of a "deep-laid conspiracy." Their witness was a Frenchman who attended an Indian council held on Sunday, August 3. At that meeting the chiefs decided they would strike to avenge all the injustices the whites had done to them over the years. They were starving, the annuities had not come, and there were few soldiers around. Little Crow was said to be the main voice in agitating the chiefs to take that final step to drive the whites from their land.

68 Anderson and Woolworth, *Through Dakota Eyes*, 32, 36, 38, 56.

The next day was the Bread Raid at Yellow Medicine, discussed above. Warriors broke into the warehouse and would have begun the massacre, except for some unexpected circumstances. Early on the morning of the 4th, two Dakota messengers came to the agency with the news that their tribesmen were coming to the agency grounds, said Lieutenant Gere, "to fire a salute and make one of their demonstrations," and they wanted "to inform us beforehand so we would understand that it was all right." As the Indians frequently came to the agency, the soldiers likely assumed it was another visit to air their grievances. Yet, sending two messengers to give notice may have seemed odd. The Dakotas soon arrived, but it was apparent that this was something out of the ordinary. The messengers were probably spies, but they had something disconcerting to report: more soldiers were there—Sheehan had returned late the previous night with his squad after searching for Inkpaduta. With more long knives and a manned howitzer, perhaps this was not the time to fight. The tense stand-off was barely resolved with the distribution of food.[69]

That same day, 96 warriors approached Fort Ridgely and notified Captain Marsh that they wished to hold a "green corn dance" on the fort's parade ground. There were only 30 soldiers, five civilians, and a number of women and children in the fort at the time. Captain Marsh consented, but Sgt. John Jones protested. Young Howard Clarke was friends with the sergeant, who sometimes let him pull the lanyard when he fired his artillery in salute. Clarke was standing nearby and heard Jones say to Marsh "with all due respect," he refused "to allow those red devils to come in here." He said he was in charge of government property and protecting the grounds, and the Indians "must stay outside the fort." The two men argued for a time and Marsh finally told the Indians they could not enter, but must hold their dance out by the horse pond.

Young Clarke went out to watch. The warriors deposited their guns, tomahawks, and ammunition pouches in the brush, and when they stripped off their blankets or shirts, all of them, said Clarke, "was in the red and yellow war paint of the Sioux." The Indians danced for about an hour and got permission to camp on rising ground about a quarter of a mile west of the fort. That evening, Jones was uneasy. He told his wife he had business to attend to and told her not to wait up. Jones got a few men and trained his howitzers on the

---

69 Bryant and Murch, *Great Massacre*, 54-55; Gere, "Uncle Sam's Army," Brown County Historical Society; *Minnesota in the Civil and Indian Wars*, I, 246.

Indian camp. They manned the guns all night. In the morning the Indians were gone.

Two weeks later the fort was attacked, and about tens days following that, Colonel Sibley arrived to break the siege. Coming in at that time was the Frenchman who was privy to the Indian council of August 3, and Bryant and Murch's informant. The Frenchman talked to Sergeant Jones, but begged that he must never disclose his name or his secret. Jones asked why, and the Frenchman replied, "They will kill me, sir; they will kill my wife and children."

Jones promised secrecy and the man asked him if he recalled when the Indians came to the fort to hold their dance. He said they were all Little Crow's warriors and were there the same day that others of the tribe planned to attack the Upper Agency. The plan was to gain access to the fort, hold a dance, "and, when all suspicion should be completely lulled, in the midst of the dance, to seize their weapons, [and] kill every person in the fort." They then planned to get all the arms, ammunition, and howitzers, join with the rest of the Indians and sweep down the Minnesota River, driving every white man beyond the Mississippi.

Jones asked why the Indians didn't carry out their plan. "Because," the Frenchman answered, "they saw, during their dance, and their stay at the fort, that big gun constantly pointed at them."[70]

Mrs. Margaret Hern, wife of David W. Hern, 4th Minnesota, was at the fort at that time. She remembered the event as happening about three weeks before the outbreak. She said the Sioux indicated they wanted to hold a war dance before going against the Chippewas. A mixed-blood she knew as "Indian Charlie" came to talk to her, and said "Too bad! Too bad!" Mrs. Elizabeth Dunn, another soldier's wife, asked her to find out what he meant, and Margaret did so. "Injins kill white folks," he said. It was too bad because he liked the whites and did not want to have to fight them. Elizabeth told Margaret to report what she heard to Sergeant Jones, but he seemed to dismiss the warning. Yet, Jones kept his guns trained on the dancers that night.[71]

The spark at Acton that eventually set off the conflagration was not planned, but it was difficult to convince many early settlers that there was no conspiracy involved. One of them, Adam Rieke, was at the fort on August 14 and saw 200 Dakotas. When they had arrived on the bluff and wanted to enter

70 Bryant and Murch, *Great Massacre*, 56-59; Koblas, *Let Them Eat Grass*, II, 157-59.

71 Morris, *Old Rail Fence Corners*, 144-45.

the grounds, interpreter Peter Quinn halted them and told them they must leave their guns outside. They agreed, entered, and were loaded with provisions. Rieke always believed that if they were allowed to enter the fort with their guns "the story of Fort Ridgely would have been much different."[72]

A few alert men, and the Indians' fear of the big guns that shoot twice, may have prevented a massacre—at least temporarily. They may never have pre-planned any attacks before August 18, but there was enough smoldering anger amongst the Dakotas that any number of propitious opportunities may have served the purpose just as well.

72 Curtiss-Wedge, *History of Renville County*, I, 635.

C hapter 2

"Ta-o-ya-te-du-ta is not a coward."

Acton

Dakota and settler interactions ~ Renville Rangers ~ A propitious time to strike ~ Acton ~
Midnight meeting ~ Little Crow's speech

The Bread Raid on the Upper Agency and the dance at Fort Ridgely on
August 4, 1862, were close calls. It will probably never be known with
certainty whether they were part of a conspiracy to begin a war. Howitzers and
food were enough to defuse the situations for the time being. Captain Marsh
arrived on August 6, and discussions continued for two more days. Agent
Galbraith and the traders distributed 130 barrels of flour and 30 barrels of pork.
Lieutenant Sheehan later testified that he heard Galbraith tell Little Crow they
would also "immediately issue rations to the Lower Indians." The issuances and
the promises were enough to convince the Sissetons and Wahpetons to vacate
the agency, and they were gone by August 10. Many of them headed west to Big
Stone Lake to begin a buffalo hunt.

"Thus this threatening and disagreeable event passed off," Galbraith later
reported, "but, as usual, without the punishment of a single Indian who had
been engaged in the attack on the warehouse." The agent was unable to drop his
hardline stance. The Indians weren't punished because the Army didn't have
the power, and thus, Galbraith complained, they had to adopt what he called the
same "sugar plum" policy that had not worked since the Spirit Lake Massacre in
1857.[1]

---

1 Folwell, *History of Minnesota*, II, 232 (note 23); *Commissioner of Indian Affairs, 1863*, 274.

At least things seemed to have quieted down. Around New Ulm, Indians continued to visit and beg for food from the civilians. Rudolf Leonhart, a German schoolteacher who had moved with his family from Pennsylvania to Minnesota, witnessed little change in the Indians he met from the summer of 1861, through the subsequent severe winter, and into the following summer. "Don't think that the settlers never saw any Indians before the uprising," Leonhart wrote in his reminiscences. "On the contrary, almost every day they were on our backs, as they surpass even the slickest Caucasian tramps as beggars. They practice the business with dignity, as if it were the most honorable profession on earth."

One Indian with his "half-grown" son visited the Leonhart home during the winter. When they indicated they were hungry and the boy was sick, Mrs. Leonhart prepared a meal. The pair consumed six pounds of beef and took with them the bones, two loaves of bread, and three gallons of coffee. "We hoped to see if the stomachs of these gourmet lovers might be filled," wrote Leonhart. "Vain expectations!" When they asked for a third serving, Rudolf declared supper over and it was time for them to leave.

Leonhart saw the same Indian on many occasions. One time he arrived at the schoolhouse with a note for Rudolf to copy for him. The message indicated his name was Tomahah, that he was a good Indian, a friend to the whites, and all aid and sustenance should be given to him. Leonhart copied the note and Tomahah thanked him and went on his way. Leonhart saw him and many other Dakotas around New Ulm up until the massacre began. As for the note, Leonhart reported that it was later found amid the refuse on the floor of a neighboring farmhouse next to the bodies of several murdered settlers.[2]

Jacob Nix moved with his family to New Ulm in 1858, ran a general store, and made similar observations. The townsfolk and farmers recognized that the Indians had been given a bad deal and were often tricked by traders and government officials, and the civilians did their best to mitigate their misery. "The begging Indians were given every possible help," Nix explained. They had been "on the friendliest of terms," the settlers "even sharing with them their last provisions." Since the whites had shown the Dakotas every kindness, they did not believe the Indians would consider them enemies. They had no way of knowing about the Sioux predilection for taking out their anger against

---

2 Leonhart, *Memories of New Ulm*, 34-36.

innocent parties. It was the settlers' "blind confidence," Nix concluded, that led to their ruin.[3]

It may have been business as usual around New Ulm, but closer to the agencies some whites noticed a marked change in the Indians. Were the Dakotas getting surlier? In the spring of 1862, settlers along Middle Creek (Map D) on the north side of the Minnesota River about midway between the two agencies experienced increased harassment. Wilhelmina Busse lived with her five brothers and sisters and her parents, Gottfried and Wilhelmina. "It was about this time that the conduct of our Indian neighbors changed toward us," she remembered. "They became disagreeable and ill-natured." Indians who once visited them often now rarely came by, and when they met, "they passed by coldly and sullenly and often without speaking."

On one occasion Dakotas entered the woods on Gottfried Busse's plot and began cutting down the young timber. Gottfried confronted them and said they could use what they wanted for tipi poles, but they could not cut his trees for no good reason. An old woman picked up a big knife and chased Gottfried home. When he told his wife she chuckled at him "for allowing an old squaw to drive him from his own woods." Only one week before the uprising, Ernest Lenz, one of Busse's neighbors, caught a string of fish in the Minnesota River and took them home. Indians followed him and demanded some. "Go and catch your own fish," Lenz told them. One Indian shouted angrily in reply, "You talk most now but wait awhile and we will shoot you with your own gun." According to Wilhelmina Busse, Lenz was the only man in the area who owned a gun and the Indians knew it. These incidents cast a pall on the community, but most of the residents shrugged it off and went about their business.[4]

When the Dakotas dispersed from the Upper Agency, Lieutenants Sheehan and Gere figured the crisis was over and marched out on August 11, arriving at Fort Ridgely on the evening of the 12th. "All prospect of trouble in this region seemed now to have disappeared," wrote Gere. The Upper Indians were gone hunting and the Lower Indians had not participated in the confrontation at the agency. "All had apparently decided to wait patiently for the arrival of the annuity money." With no need for extra troops, Captain Marsh released Sheehan and Company C, 5th Minnesota, and sent them back to Fort Ripley. The soldiers marched out at 7:00 a.m. on August 17. That same day, Marsh

3 Nix, *Sioux Uprising*, 81.

4 Tolzmann, ed., *German Pioneer Accounts*, 31-32.

detached Lt. Norman K. Culver and six men of Company B with transportation to escort about 50 recruits to St. Peter.[5]

The recruits had expressed a desire to join the U.S. Army. Papers replete with woodcuts depicting scenes and news from the Civil War circulated among the traders. They were of interest to white civilians as well as the Indians, who took note that many whites were being killed and the war was not going well. After the disastrous showing of Gen. George B. McClellan and the Army of the Potomac during the recent Peninsula Campaign, President Abraham Lincoln had issued a desperate call for 600,000 more men to fight the Confederacy. When the call for more troops arrived at the agencies that July, many young men, mixed-bloods, unemployed whites, and employees who were about to be discharged told Galbraith of their wish to join the Northern army. There were several would-be leaders who could not agree on anything, and they asked Galbraith if he would take charge. The agent told them he "would go with them to Fort Snelling, and even to Richmond," as long as he could safely leave his duties as agent "without injury to the public service."[6]

With encouragement from Captain Marsh, Galbraith began recruiting. On August 12, 30 men joined at Yellow Medicine and about 20 more joined at Redwood two days later. The next day, August 15, the self-styled "Renville Rangers" marched to Fort Ridgely, where Marsh gave them transportation and wished them Godspeed. With Sheehan and Culver's detachments gone and Galbraith and his Rangers on the road, only two officers and 76 men remained at Fort Ridgely.

The Dakotas were very interested in this development. The war must be going badly if the Great Father had to ask for help from the Frenchmen and mixed-bloods. According to Reverend Riggs, their thought was, "Now we can avenge our wrongs and get back our country." Riggs's assessment was correct. Big Eagle voiced the same sentiment: "The Indians now thought the whites must be pretty hard up for men to fight the South, or they would not come so far out on the frontier and take half-breeds or anything to help them." Big Eagle continued, "It began to be whispered about that now would be a good time to go to war with the whites and get back the lands. It was believed that the men who had enlisted last had all left the state, and that before help could be sent the Indians could clean out the country." Big Eagle believed that even the

---

5   *Minnesota in the Civil and Indian Wars*, I, 248.

6   *Commissioner of Indian Affairs*, 1863, 275.

Chippewas and Winnebagoes would join them and they would once more be masters of their old realm. A war would also permit the Dakotas "to forget the troubles among themselves and enable many of them to pay off some old scores."[7]

Galbraith's leaving with his "Renville Rangers" at that moment was either very good or very bad timing, depending on the point of view. For the Dakotas it might have been the final weight tipping the scale to convince them to go to war. If the 50 men had remained, perhaps no outbreak would have occurred. Then again, they may have stayed and added more casualties to the list of dead and wounded on both sides. It was probably just good luck for Galbraith and the recruits that they happened to leave when they did. Although their absence made it easier for the Indians to massacre many helpless civilians, Galbraith didn't leave because he and his recruits knew or even suspected a murderous attack was imminent. Yet, some speculated that was in fact exactly the reason the soldiers left.

In New Ulm, for example, Jacob Nix wondered why the agent would pick that specific moment to take leave of his job and march away toward Fort Snelling. "Didn't this man know that during the past days the starving Indians had assumed a more than threatening attitude, or did he not wish to know? This has been an unsolved riddle up to the present time." According to Nix, several others insisted "that the gentleman wished to escape the threatening thunderclouds in order to save his hide before lightning struck."[8]

*   *   *

A large number of people from Hazelwood and Pajutazi gathered on a Sunday morning at the Upper Agency on August 17, 1862. As Reverend Riggs oddly expressed it, "As our custom was, both churches came together to celebrate the Lord's death." None of them that August day knew it would be the last time they would meet in the mission chapel. "A great trial of our faith and patience was coming upon us, and we knew it not. But the dear Christ," Riggs continued, "knew that both we and the native Christians needed just such a quiet rest with Him, before the trials came." Riggs's rationalization may read

---

7   Riggs, *Mary and I*, 108; Anderson and Woolworth, *Through Dakota Eyes*, 25-26.

8   Nix, *Sioux Uprising*, 83.

rather bizarrely today—his deity was apparently giving them a timeout before the slaughter.[9]

At the Lower Agency, John Williamson had recently constructed his Presbyterian mission but was now on the road to Ohio. Episcopal Missionary Samuel Hinman still had the largest congregation, and Little Crow and the Christian Indians attended services there that morning. When it was over, Little Crow shook hands with everyone. Good will and peace appeared to be the order of the day. Although unknown to any of them at that time, the wagon containing $71,000 of the Dakotas' gold had left St. Paul that morning. Tomorrow, it would be at the agency and distribution of the money could begin.[10]

A number of Dakotas did not attend church services that day. About 20 men from Shakopee's village had gone north to the Big Woods, either looking for Chippewas or simply to hunt. They would provide the accidental spark that triggered the lightning.

The party divided. Island Cloud (Mak-pe-yah-we-tah) and a few warriors moved to George C. Whitcomb's home on Lake Minnie Belle, about 12 miles south-southwest of Forest City, Minnesota. Apparently, they had left a wagon there the previous fall as security for the purchase of a sleigh and they wanted the wagon back. Unfortunately, they did not have the rest of the money agreed upon to finish the purchase of the sleigh. When Whitcomb refused to give them back the wagon, Island Cloud and his men brandished their axes and threatened to chop it to pieces. Although no one was hurt and nothing was damaged, they left after they "hinted that an outbreak would occur." Eight-year-old Elizabeth Whitcomb asked her father if the whites and Indians really were going to fight. "They wouldn't dare," Whitcomb replied.[11]

Four other warriors, Brown Wing (Sungigidan), Breaking Up (Ka-om-de-i-ye-ye-dan), Killing Ghost (Nagi-wi-cak-te), and Runs Against Something when Crawling (Pa-zo-i-yo-pa) wandered near a settler's house. They later said they were not out to kill anyone, but simply hunting game. Near a fence they found a hen's nest with eggs in it. When one of them took the eggs,

9 Riggs, *Mary and I*, 152.

10 Folwell, *History of Minnesota*, II, 239.

11 Hubbard and Holcombe, *Minnesota in Three Centuries*, III, 303; Heard, *History of the Sioux War*, 52, 57; Elizabeth Whitcomb interview, Microfilm Reel 3, Dakota Conflict, Minnesota Historical Society.

another cautioned, "Don't take them, for they belong to a white man and we may get in trouble."

The first warrior was hungry, but anger overcame him and he smashed the eggs on the ground. "You are a coward," he said. "You are afraid of the white man. You are afraid to take even an egg from him, though you are half-starved. Yes, you are a coward, and I will tell everybody so."

"I am not a coward," the other replied. "I am not afraid of the white man, and to show you that I am not I will go to the house and shoot him. Are you brave enough to go with me?"

"Yes, I will go with you," said the first warrior, "and we will see who is the braver of us two." The other two companions agreed to come along and also prove their manhood.[12]

The house belonged to an older man named Robinson Jones. He and Howard Baker took up preemption claims there in 1857 in what would become the little community of Acton, west of Long Lake near the western border of Meeker County. They both farmed, but Jones also opened a small general store, gave lodging to travelers, and became the postmaster. In 1861, Jones married Ann, Howard Baker's mother. They adopted two children of a deceased relative, 15-year-old Clara D. Wilson and her 18-month-old half-brother. Staying at Baker's house about one-half mile from Jones were Viranus and Rosa Ann Webster, immigrants from Michigan who had parked their covered wagon at Baker's for the past three weeks while searching for a place to settle.

The Indians approached Jones's place. According to Big Eagle, who heard their story, Jones grew alarmed at their approach and went to Baker's. The Indians followed and killed five people. The white survivors had a different take. Two of the four Indians had on white men's coats. One wore two feathers in his cap and one wore three. One was tall, one was small, and one was "thick and chubby." All were middle-aged. It was not the Indians' first visit. The previous winter Jones loaned one of them a gun but he failed to return it. Jones, who spoke some Dakota, argued with the same Indian, refused to give any of them liquor, and threw them out of the house. The Indians headed toward Baker's place, where Jones's wife was visiting. Robinson Jones may have believed they were up to mischief and followed.

According to Howard Baker's wife, the Indians reached the house about 11:00 a.m. They asked for water and received it, and asked for tobacco and Mr.

12 Anderson and Woolworth, *Through Dakota Eyes*, 35.

Webster gave them some. They smoked for 15 minutes. It was about then that Jones arrived, and they picked up their ongoing discussion about the gun he had loaned them. Apparently they reached an agreement when Jones traded one of Baker's guns to an Indian for one of his, plus some cash. The Dakotas proposed testing the weapons against a target. Jones and Baker fired at the target, as did the Indians. On the porch, Mrs. Baker noticed two Indians reloading in the yard as the men walked back toward the house. She turned to go inside when she heard a shot and saw Mr. Webster fall at the doorstop. At the same time, an Indian ran up and shot Howard Baker with one barrel of his shotgun. Baker staggered backward and the warrior shot him with the second barrel. Robinson Jones tried to run, but bullets brought him down in the yard.

"My mother [in-law] (Mrs. Jones) walked to the door and another Indian shot her," Mrs. Baker recalled, "she turned to run and fell in the buttery; they shot at her twice as she fell. I tried to get out of the window, but fell down [the] cellar; [I] saw Mrs. Webster pulling her husband into the house; don't know where she was prior to this; Indians immediately left the house; while I was in the cellar I heard firing out of doors."[13]

Within a few short minutes Mr. Jones, Mrs. Jones, Mr. Webster, and Mr. Baker were dead or dying. The Indians didn't go after Mrs. Baker or her two children, or Mrs. Webster, who was said to have been in the covered wagon and thus escaped the Indians' attention. The four murderers hurried away to the southwest. Mrs. Webster and Mrs. Baker emerged and went to help Robinson Jones and Viranus Webster. When Rosa Ann asked Viranus why they shot him, he replied, "I do not know. I never saw a Sioux Indian before, and never had anything to do with one." In a short time, both he and Jones were dead.

The women gathered up the two children and fled north to the home of Nels Olsen a few miles away. Although they could not speak each other's language, the women did their best to communicate what had happened. Ole Ingemann understood and mounted his horse for a 14-mile gallop to Forest City to spread the word. A number of civilians rode for Acton that evening.

In the Acton area, half a dozen neighbors gathered to discuss what to do. John Blackwell rode to Olsen's house and heard the story. He was worried about the two children who were left at Jones's. With Ole Ness, Henry

---

13 Folwell, *History of Minnesota*, II, 415; Anderson and Woolworth, *Through Dakota Eyes*, 35-36; McConkey, *Dakota War Whoop*, 16-18; Heard, *History of the Sioux War*, 52-56; Smith, *Sketch of Meeker County*, 42-43. According to Mrs. Baker there were six Indians; two arrived about an hour after the first four.

Hulverson, A. N. Fosen, and a few others made for Baker's and, stumbling about in the darkness, finally found the four bodies. They next went to Jones's place, where their lamp revealed Clara Wilson shot dead and lying on the floor. In the bed was the toddler, who mumbled to his rescuers that Clara was "hurt" and he wanted his supper. Blackwell took him away. The boy was later adopted by Charles Ellis in Wright County.[14]

Clara was killed after the massacre at Baker's when Brown Wing, Killing Ghost, Breaking Up, and Runs Against Something when Crawling passed by Jones's place a second time. Perhaps one of them had not yet proven his bravery by killing a white. When they spotted Clara in the window they burst in through the door and killed the girl, but left the little boy alone. Oddly enough, they did not touch any of Jones's whiskey, take any of his goods, or damage his property, which reinforces the contention that they were not there to rob or destroy, but only to prove to each other that they were not cowards.

The four Indians continued traveling southwest toward Lake Elizabeth in eastern Kandiyohi County. They approached Peter Wicklund's place on the lake's north shore where P. M. Johnson, Jonas Peterson, and Andrew M. Ecklund were eating dinner. Depending on the version of the story, a couple of Dakotas distracted the whites by threatening them with weapons from outside the window while the others stole two horses from Ecklund, who was Wicklund's son-in-law and had come with his wife to visit her father that Sunday. Another version has the Dakotas luring the men to come outside where they indicated that the Chippewas had just killed the Jones and Baker families. The settlers, however, did not believe them and went back inside. It was later that evening when the Indians stole Ecklund's horses. In any case, the Dakotas made off with the horses and headed south, stealing two more on the way as they rode hard for the agency about 40 miles distant.[15]

The next morning, August 18, about 60 people gathered in Acton. Judge A. C. Smith of Meeker County presided over an impromptu inquest. Mrs. Baker and Mrs. Webster appeared and gave testimony. Coffins were made for the five bodies. At this time, 11 mounted Indians under Island Cloud made an appearance. Two of them had been near the Baker house the day before, but left

14 Hubbard and Holcombe, *Minnesota in Three Centuries*, III, 306-08; Smith, *Sketch of Meeker County*, 39-41.

15 Hubbard and Holcombe, *Minnesota in Three Centuries*, III, 308, 310-11; Jonas Peterson Depredation Claim #261; Satterlee, "Narratives of the Sioux War," 353.

before the killings. They heard shots and reported to Island Cloud. Since Brown Wing and his accomplices had not been seen since then, Island Cloud assumed they might have gotten into a fight with the whites and been killed. As his band approached the Baker cabin during the inquest a number of mounted settlers rode after them. What appeared to them as an unprovoked attack confirmed their fears, and the Indians fled. Neither the whites nor the Indians around Acton knew that morning of the great uprising just beginning in the Minnesota Valley.[16]

*   *   *

The four Dakotas who killed five whites knew there would be big trouble as they rode their stolen horses toward the Agency. They could not have galloped all the way, but averaging even seven or eight miles an hour, it would have taken them about five hours to cover the distance. It was late at night when they arrived at Red Middle Voice's village at Rice Creek. Noisily tripping into camp on horses near dead from exhaustion they created quite a stir.

"Get your guns!" they reportedly said. "There is a war with the whites and we have begun it." Red Middle Voice arrived as did men from the soldiers' lodge. They moved down to Shakopee's village on the Redwood where the excitement spread like a prairie fire. What should they do? From past experience they realized that the whites would seek punishment—depredations meant they would all lose money, and murders meant the guilty would likely be tried and either imprisoned or executed. The entire tribe would suffer for the folly of a few, just as had occurred after the Inkapaduta affair. They would not submit to such a fate. Now was the time to drive all the whites from the Minnesota Valley and reunite the Dakotas in a common purpose. The whites were easy to kill at Acton, and almost all of the men were gone fighting in the South. The hot-heads believed this was the course to take, but they needed approval from other bands.

"Let us go down and see Little Crow and the others at the Agency," Shakopee said. It was nearly dawn before the crowd arrived. Little Crow, recalled Big Eagle, "sat up in his bed and listened to their story." Disturbed by

---

16 Hubbard and Holcombe, *Minnesota in Three Centuries*, III, 309. Mrs. Baker and Mrs. Howard were taken to Forest City and the five dead were buried in a common grave at the Ness Lutheran Cemetery at Lake Harold about four miles east of the Baker's.

the news, but still stung from his loss to Traveling Hail in the recent speaker election, Little Crow snapped, "Why do you come for me for advice? Go to the man you elected speaker and let him tell you what to do." The firebrands knew Traveling Hail was a moderate, and if he and other farmer Indians were brought into the discussion, their rebellion would fail.

They insisted that Little Crow must decide. They argued that blood was already spilled, "the payment would be stopped, and the whites would take a dreadful vengeance because women had been killed." Big Eagle, Wabasha, and Wacouta argued for restraint, but their voices were drowned out in the fever. "Kill the whites and kill all these cut-hairs who will not join us," they cried out.[17]

Little Crow painted his face black and lowered his head in contemplation. He understood the implications of what would happen if they went to war. The action was foolish, but he felt vindicated. Little Crow's biographer suggests that Little Crow was flattered by the attention and appeal from Dakota warriors outside his own band who did not think they could go to war without his support and approval. Being a political opportunist he saw this as a way to regain leadership and influence. Still, Little Crow hesitated and may not have taken the final plunge—until one warrior openly accused him of cowardice.

Little Crow jumped up, grabbed and threw the man's headdress to the ground. "Ta-o-ya-te-du-ta is not a coward, and he is not a fool!" he roared. "When did he run away from his enemies? When did he leave his braves behind him on the war-path and turn back to his teepees?" Little Crow continued, explaining that when the Chippewas defeated them it was he who was last from the battle and covered their backs "as a she-bear covers her cubs!" He challenged them to look at his war feathers and count his scalps and dead enemies. "Do they call him a coward? Ta-o-ya-te-du-ta is not a coward, and he is not a fool. Braves, you are like little children; you know not what you are doing."

Little Crow accused them of being drunk on "the white man's devil-water. You are like dogs in the Hot Moon when they run mad and snap at their own shadows." The whites, he continued, were "like the locusts when they fly so thick that the whole sky is a snowstorm. You may kill one—two—ten; yes, as many as the leaves in the forest yonder, and their brothers will not miss them . . . ten times ten will come to kill you."

17 Anderson, *Little Crow*, 131-32; Anderson and Woolworth, *Through Dakota Eyes*, 36; Hubbard and Holcombe, *Minnesota in Three Centuries*, III, 311-12.

It was true, Little Crow admitted, that the whites were then fighting among themselves, "but if you strike at them they will all turn on you and devour you and your women and little children. . . . You are fools. You cannot see the face of your chief; your eyes are full of smoke. You cannot hear his voice; your ears are full of roaring waters. Braves, you are little children—you are fools. You will die like the rabbits when the hungry wolves hunt them in the Hard Moon."

Little Crow had driven home his point: They were crazy to go to war and they would all be killed. Nevertheless, logic and fine speeches could not overcome the overriding insult to his manhood. "Ta-o-ya-te-du-ta is not a coward," he reiterated. "He will die with you."[18]

People usually act in their own self-interest, but actions are often driven by emotion rather than reason. Little Crow simply could not abide being called a coward. From Myrick's grass, Brown Wing's eggs, and Little Crow's "chicken," fools rather than philosopher-kings have dictated life and death for entire nations.

18 Anderson and Woolworth, *Through Dakota Eyes*, 39-42. Little Crow's speech is offered with a caution. Chiefs who were present did not ascribe to him any such lofty phrases. The speech in its popular form was passed down orally from Little Crow's 15-year-old son, Wowinape, who was in the room and supposedly memorized the words. He did not record the talk until he gave the story to attorney and author Hanford L. Gordon, who reproduced it in two books of poetry published in 1891 and 1910. The white reiteration of Little Crow's words may more accurately characterize our fondness for historical irony than actual fact.

C hapter 3

"Run away, run away quick!"

Redwood Agency

Coursolle warned ~ Campbell at Forbes ~ Spencer captured ~ Robinettes attacked ~ Hinman escapes ~ Nairn flees ~ Prescott flees ~ Humphrey leaves late ~ De Camp captured ~ Martell spreads warning ~ Killings at Birch Coulee

As the Dakotas argued their options throughout the night, most of the white and mixed-blood families around the Lower Agency slept securely with not an inkling of what the morning would bring. One exception was Joseph Coursolle and his family. Coursolle, about 31 years old, was the son of Pierre Coursolle and a Sisseton woman. When his parents died he was partly raised and educated through the efforts of trader, merchant, and later congressional delegate Henry H. Sibley. Coursolle married Jane Murray Kilcool in 1850 and they began raising what would become a large family. Coursolle worked as a blacksmith, trader, and teamster, but in August 1862 he lived in the mixed-blood community at the Lower Agency and clerked in the agency stores.

The night was hot and humid and Joe had trouble sleeping. He could hear drums beating two miles upriver in the direction of Little Crow's village. It was a familiar sound, but he recalled an "anxious feeling in my stomach." Late that night one of his female Dakota kinsmen slipped into his house so quietly it barely alerted Coursolle's red setter named Duta. "Shhh," the woman cautioned as she whispered Coursolle's Indian name and spoke in Dakota, "Hinhankaga (The Owl), be still. I am a friend. Big trouble coming. Tomorrow warriors kill all whites. Go, now, before too late. Tell no one I warned you or I, too, will die." And then she was gone.

The warnings sent a shiver up Joe's back. Should he heed the warning? After all, he was half Dakota and so reasonably believed no one would kill him. Still, he was worried for his family. When the sun rose enough to see, he gathered his wife, daughters Elizabeth (6) and Minnie (4), and nine-day-old baby Cistina (Little) Joe to leave. He left Duta behind so he would not give them away by barking.

The family walked down the path to the river where Joe had a small dugout canoe. It was too small for everyone, so he told Elizabeth and Minnie to wait while he paddled Jane and the baby across to the north bank. When he was about to go back he heard someone coming, waved at the children and softly called to them to hide. Four Indians slipped down the path, passed the girls, and continued down the river trail. Coursolle waited in a plum thicket to make sure no one else was coming. He was about to cross when he heard shots and war whoops from the direction of the agency. The warning was real! He waited until it seemed safe to cross and then paddled to rescue the balance of his family. "Elizabeth and Minnie were gone!" he later remembered. "My heart turned to stone."[1]

There was no red sky at morning on Monday, August 18, 1862. When the sun broke above the horizon at 5:24 a.m., the bottomlands remained fog enshrouded and even along the bluffs it took time for the hazy mists to burn off. It would be another clear and hot day, but during the early morning hours it was difficult to see the Indians as they moved quietly down from Rice Creek to Redwood River and beyond, gathering warriors from Big Eagle's, Little Crow's, Mankato's, and Traveling Hail's villages. (Map E) They approached the Lower Agency from the northwest, a small village of two dozen or more buildings centered around a council ground on the top of the bluffs on the south (or west) side of the Minnesota River. (Map F)

The Lower Agency was about a dozen miles upstream from Fort Ridgely though on the opposite bank. The road from New Ulm to the Upper agency ran along the bluffs and through the center of the council grounds. There were a few trails that snaked down the wooded 200-foot bluffs to the Redwood Ferry where another road went along the north (or east) bank of the river to the fort. Several other buildings were located at the ferry and on both sides of the river.

---

1 Joseph Coursolle story, Microfilm Reel 1, Dakota Conflict, Minnesota Historical Society.

There were nearly 200 brick, frame, and log houses spread along the bluffs from ten miles above the agency to nearly as far below.[2]

Being a Monday, many people were up before dawn to get ready for work. On the south side of the council ground lived the extended mixed-blood Campbell family: Antoine Joseph Campbell, wife Mary Ann Dalton Campbell, and children Emily (15), Cecelia (13), Mary (9), Joseph (7), Martha (5), Willie (2), and Stella (two months); Antoine's mother, Margaret Scott Campbell; Antoine's brothers, Hypolite, Baptiste, and Scott; Hypolite's wife, Yuratwin (a cousin of Standing Buffalo), and their two children, John and Theresa.

Antoine worked as a clerk in Myrick's store. He and Baptiste intended to take a wagon to New Ulm that day to get a load of goods and they wanted to get an early start. Andrew Myrick was not an early riser, however, and Antoine had to wake him to ask for the bill of lading he needed to complete the task. Clerk George Washington Divoll wasn't quite ready to go to work either, and he asked Baptiste to prepare some Kinnikinnick (a tobacco, sumac, and willow mixture) in a pipe so they could smoke. James W. Lynd, a former newspaper editor and state senator, was in charge at Myrick's. Antoine talked to him briefly but he seemed detached, "laboring under some presentiment that morning." He left his paperwork to stand outside near the east door. Impatient with the delay, Antoine also went outside, sat on a box for awhile, and then got up to crack his whip at some high weeds nearby. He was so engaged when several Dakotas approached and said something about going to war with the Chippewas. Soon after, shots were fired.

Antoine headed inside while Baptiste emerged. "Brother," he said, "Divoll and Lynd are killed." Lynd may have been the first person murdered. Much Hail (Ta-wa-su-ota) ran up to him as he stood near the door and called out as he shot: "Now I will kill the dog who would not give me credit." As Lynd fell, other Indians entered and killed Divoll and the inoffensive old German cook named "Fritz."[3]

"Let's go back in," Antoine yelled to Baptiste, hoping to shut the doors, seize the guns and ammunition, and make a defense. The Indians grabbed him.

2   John Nairn recollection, Microfilm Reel 3, Dakota Conflict, Minnesota Historical Society.

3   Anderson and Woolworth, *Through Dakota Eyes*, 44, 47, 51-52, 54-55; Heard, *History of the Sioux War*, 62; Hubbard and Holcombe, *Minnesota in Three Centuries*, III, 312-13. Red Face was convicted of killing Divoll. Much Hail's words raise the possibility that it may have been Lynd who made the "grass" statement.

Baptiste, more sympathetic to the Dakotas, was not so inclined to resist. As the Indians struggled to hold Antoine, he looked to the upstairs windows in the hope that Myrick might be watching and would shoot the Indians. He had a 16-shot Henry Rifle and was said to be a marksman. A warrior leveled his gun at Antoine's breast when several others, including Iron Elk (Hahakamaza), Chattan, and Grey Eagle arrived to intercede. They were all blood relatives of Antoine's father, Scott Campbell, and made it known that if the Campbell brothers were harmed they would have to fight them also. Symbolically shielding them with blankets, the Dakotas escorted the two brothers back to their house.

Upstairs above the store Myrick did indeed hear the firing. When he spotted the events transpiring below he slammed the door. The Indians were reluctant to come up after him. As they discussed burning the building down, Myrick crept out through a trapdoor in the roof, climbed down a lean-to, and ran toward the spring at the bluffs. The Indians spotted him, however, and their arrows brought him down. Someone shoved a scythe blade through his body. Years later a story spread that grass had been stuffed into his mouth.[4]

Antoine Campbell's daughter Cecelia was up and helping with breakfast after her father and uncle left for Myrick's store. When she looked out the door in the morning gloom, she saw "something dark moving along the ground as far as I could see." She likened it to a boa constrictor snaking along the road. It took her some time before she realized it was a long line of Indians moving in column. Her grandmother joined her and wondered why there were so many. She concluded they were probably on their way to a supply distribution. When she asked an Indian servant girl to find out, she returned quickly with two stories: there was going to be a distribution, and they were going to fight Chippewas. One warrior left the column and walked to the house to inquire on Antoine's whereabouts. When he learned that Antoine had left for Myrick's, the

---

4   Anderson and Woolworth, *Through Dakota Eyes*, 48-49. The first accounts of the massacre at Redwood by Heard, McConkey, and Bryant and Murch written in 1863 and 1864 do not mention Myrick with grass in his mouth. Myrick's brother, Nathan, who went to recover the body, stated that he had an arrow in his arm and "an old burned scythe thrust through him." Anderson, *Little Crow*, 222 n3. Not until Big Eagle gave the story to Return Holcombe 32 years later, does an eyewitness mention the grass. Big Eagle said he found Myrick dead "with his mouth stuffed full of grass," while an Indian mocked him: "Myrick is eating grass himself." Anderson and Woolworth, *Through Dakota Eyes*, 56. Like Myrick's supposed "Let them eat grass" statement, his being found dead with his mouth stuffed with grass may be apocryphal, but it is such classic historical irony that it will forever be repeated.

warrior wanted to know if he had a team and horses available "to take us off." The reply meant one thing: trouble. Only Uncle Hypolite was at the house, and he grabbed his Henry Rifle and shotgun and waited. In a few minutes, Iron Elk and the others brought Antoine and Baptiste home. They were safe, at least for the time being, but it appeared that others would not be so lucky.[5]

*   *   *

While the killings were taking place at Myrick's, Dakotas hit the other traders' stores as well, all located west of the main agency grounds. Louis Robert was absent that day, but Indians broke into his store and killed Patrick McClellan. Mixed-blood Moses Mireau was a widower with two children who were not with him that day. He had been working for the past year as a storekeeper for Robert while residing at Dickinson's boardinghouse. When the Indians broke in he escaped out the back while they killed four men and one woman in the kitchen. A shocked Mireau crossed the river and watched from the woods for a few hours as Robert's and Dickinson's burned, and with them all the property he had in the world, which he later reported was worth $169. Joseph Fortier was also a clerk for Robert, but he had just joined the "Renville Rangers" and so avoided the bloodshed that morning. Fortier lost $177 worth of property.[6]

Mixed-blood trader Francois La Bathe was home and the Indians murdered him. William H. Forbes was away, but many people were at his store that morning. When the Indians first rushed it, Francis Giard, a 23-year-old French-Canadian who had worked off and on for the Campbell's since 1857, but at this time was working at De Camp's sawmill, was outside. When the Indians arrived and began shooting, Giard began to flee when more Indians appeared. He decided instead to hide inside Forbes's, but fell over Joe Belland's body while bounding through the doorway. When he realized Indians were still inside looking for loot, Giard remained on the floor feigning death.

George Spencer shouldn't have been there at all. Spencer was born in Kentucky in 1831 and by the time he was 20 years old had become a fur trader in St. Paul, Minnesota. He was a member of the First Baptist Church of St. Paul and had many friends there, although he was currently employed as a clerk at

5   Anderson and Woolworth, *Through Dakota Eyes*, 45-46.

6   Moses Mireau Depredation Claim #159; Joseph Fortier Depredation Claim #272.

William H. Forbes's trading post on Big Stone Lake about 90 miles upriver. Spencer was en route to visit friends in St. Paul when he stopped to spend Saturday night at the Lower Agency. He attended church the next day, and made the mistake of spending one more night.

Early on Monday morning, Spencer and six other people were at Forbes's Redwood store when the sound of Indian war whoops drew them outside. Myrick's store was being attacked a short distance away. When the Indians spotted the men at the trading post they fired and killed four of them: Joe Belland, Antoine Young, George Thomas, and William Taylor. Bullets hit Spencer in his right arm, in his right breast, and in the stomach. Somehow he managed to run with his two uninjured companions for the stairs leading to the second floor.

A warrior took point-blank aim at the stumbling Spencer and pulled the trigger, but his double-barreled shotgun misfired. Spencer struggled up the stairs and collapsed on a bed. William Bourat and the mixed-blood Paulite Osier were with him. Osier looked through a trap door to the scene below and saw 25 or 30 Indians ransacking the store. An Indian looked up and called for him to come down, assuring him he would not be hurt. Probably believing they had no other choice, the two uninjured men climbed down. Once at ground level, however, William Bourat bolted out of the store and ran for his life. An Indian blasted him in the side and hip with duck-shot about 200 yards from the store. Bourat played dead while the Indians stripped his clothes and shoes and piled logs on him. Convinced he was dead, the Indians left to plunder the store. Bourat crawled away and escaped. He fled to Glencoe, then to Carver, and finally hitched a ride to St. Paul on the ship *Antelope*.[7]

Osier saved his skin by joining with the Indians in ransacking the store. The looters left George Spencer alone for the time being, but they had not forgotten him. They knew that guns were stored above the store and they were sure he would shoot anyone who came up. Spencer had become fluent in the Dakota language during his business ventures. When he heard them discussing burning the building, he tied a bed cord to a bedpost and tossed the cord out the window intending to slide down if they started a fire.

---

7   Anderson and Woolworth, *Through Dakota Eyes*, 66 n11; Oehler, *Great Sioux Uprising*, 39; McConkey, *Dakota War Whoop*, 36, 38-41. According to Samuel Hinman, Heard, *History of the Sioux War*, 67, Taylor, a black man, escaped from the agency but was shot on the north side of the Minnesota River.

From below George heard the familiar voice of His Thunder (Wakinyantawa), his friend for the past ten years and at one time one of Little Crow's head warriors, asking about his whereabouts. George shouted to announce his location and the Dakota climbed upstairs. When His Thunder asked Spencer if he was mortally wounded, George responded that he was badly hurt and unsure whether he was going to die. His comrade helped him downstairs while other Indians in the store yelled "Kill him!" "Spare no Americans!" "Show mercy to none!" His Thunder brandished a hatchet and threatened anyone who harmed Spencer. About this time Big Eagle arrived and also assisted in protecting Spencer. Together they lifted him into a wagon and His Thunder told two Indian women to take him to his lodge in Little Crow's camp. His Thunder treated George's bullet wounds with an Indian remedy of roots and herbs. From this time on, His Thunder chose not to take part in the hostilities against the whites. Little Crow realized that Spencer's presence was keeping one of his head warriors out of the fighting, and the two exchanged heated words about what to do with the white man.[8]

Francis Giard was still playing dead on the floor at Forbes's. When the Indians began discussing burning the building he jumped up to get out, startling some of them. One large warrior blocked his path and raised his hatchet. "How, Cola!" Giard said while standing still and pointing to his forehead. "Strike me here." The warrior lowered his weapon and said to Giard that he was too brave to kill, but he did order him to prepare a yoke of oxen and a wagon to help haul away his plunder. Giard did so, but the shooting and chaos made the oxen difficult to control. As they rode past Campbell's place, Giard jumped off and ran inside.

He might have thought he was safe there, but Giard's presence endangered everyone else inside. If the Indians came for him, the Campbell brothers would defend him but, explained Cecelia Campbell, "it would be war between our defenders and the hostiles." Iron Elk, who had just delivered Antoine and Baptiste, told Mrs. Campbell that she should have Giard hide upstairs. When the Indians came looking for him, Iron Elk told them that "he must have gone on because there was no Frenchman there." An Indian opened the door but Iron Elk told him to leave because he was frightening the women and children. When it looked clear, Iron Elk put his blanket around Giard, escorted him to

---

8   McConkey, *Dakota War Whoop*, 35, 41-44; Anderson and Woolworth, *Through Dakota Eyes*, 56.

the cornfield out back, and told him to circle around to the river and hide. Giard hit the bluffs near Jean Genois' boardinghouse north of Myrick's store. There he met Genois and a boy named Lefevre. They laughed when he told them what was happening, unwilling to believe the Indians were killing anyone. Giard eventually convinced them to flee with him.[9]

Near Forbes's store was a cabin at that time occupied by the Robinettes. Joseph Robinette was born in Montreal, Canada, about 1804 and moved to Minnesota in 1831. He married Cecile Turpin about 1837 and they had four children living with them at the time: Harriet, Mary, Emma, and Louis. Cecile had a daughter by a former marriage, Jane Kilcool, who was married to Joe Coursolle and lived a short distance from them. With Joe Robinette's extended family were his adult son, Vanesse (Vanosse, Vanoise) Robinette, Vanesse's wife, Matilda, and their four children ranging in age from six years to three months. Matilda was the daughter of Francois La Bathe, who had just been murdered. They had moved in only three months ago. Joseph Robinette worked as a blacksmith and had gone early down to the ferry. Vanesse worked for Joseph W. De Camp who had the contract to run the government sawmill. Both men were down at the river when the Dakotas arrived.

The family had a short warning when two Indian women rushed in to tell Cecile, a mixed-blood Dakota, that the Indians were killing all the whites. They urged her to go to her daughter, Jane Coursolle, who just had a baby and probably needed help, and they would take care of her four children. Cecile left and was gone only a few minutes when Little Crow came in. "Harriet and I were glad to see him," 14-year-old Mary recalled, "for he was father's friend and we were sure he wouldn't let any harm come to us." Little Crow had often eaten with them and Mary asked if he wanted breakfast. He shook his head no, but asked for the tomahawk that Joe Robinette was making for him. Mary gave it to him. Little Crow put his hand over his breast, bowed slightly, and said in English, "My heart is sad." Then he spoke rapidly in Dakota to the other Indians. Harriet understood some and told Mary that it appeared that they were to be taken care of and sent to the village. Mary turned back to ask Little Crow if he had seen her father, but "like a phantom he had vanished. We never saw him again."

The Dakotas cleared the Robinettes out of the cabin, took what they wanted, and set the building ablaze. Vanesse and Matilda later claimed they had

9 Anderson and Woolworth, *Through Dakota Eyes*, 49-50.

lost $454 worth of property in the conflagration. Little Crow's instructions to care for the women and children were followed. No harm came to them, however, old Joe Robinette was not so lucky; warriors not knowing or caring of his friendship with Little Crow killed him near the blacksmith shop. Vanesse got away and later joined the Minnesota 1st Regiment of Mounted Rangers.[10]

*   *   *

Several early risers saw the Indians slipping among the agency buildings. Philander Prescott, the 61-year-old interpreter and government farmer who had lived with the Indians for four decades and was married to a full-blood Dakota, spotted Little Crow walking past. When he asked what was happening, Little Crow told him to get back in his house and stay there. Prescott obeyed and listened as the gunfire outside intensified. Soon thereafter Big Eagle arrived and told him about the widespread killing and that he wanted to prove he was not involved. He urged Prescott to "write me a letter to the fort, for that I would have no part in the matter." Prescott was shaking so hard he could barely write, but Big Eagle eventually got his letter and left. Unable to wait any longer, Prescott discussed his options with his wife Mary. Since she was a full-blood Dakota and the daughter of Cloud Man, he figured she and their daughter, Julia, would be safe. Prescott fled alone.[11]

Reverend Samuel D. Hinman, who lived a few houses north of Prescott, was preparing to travel to Faribault that morning when the killing began. He finished breakfast and went outside to smoke, where he talked with John C. Whipple (38), an ex-artillerist who had served in the Mexican War and was now a stonemason working on Hinman's new St. John's Church. "Presently I saw a number of Indians passing down, nearly naked and armed with guns," recalled Hinman. Whipple thought they were going to hold a dance. Instead, the Indians, continued Hinman, "commenced sitting down on the steps of various buildings." The sound of gunfire from the upper town soon reached them. Another man standing nearby suggested that the Chippewas must have come and that a battle was being fought. The men watched as Indians left Prescott's

10 St. Paul *Pioneer Press*, June 7, 1917; Rose and Borden Family Papers, P1957, MHS; Vanesse Robinette Depredation Claim #1136.

11 Curtiss-Wedge, *History of Redwood County*, I, 135; Anderson and Woolworth, *Through Dakota Eyes*, 30.

house with Frank Robertson, a young government clerk. Hinman asked Robertson what was going on. The clerk answered that he didn't know, but the Indians had told them to stay in the house. Robertson figured there was trouble and decided to go to his mother's house across the river at Beaver Creek.

When an obviously agitated White Dog ran past the puzzled Hinman stopped him and asked for news. The answer must have shocked the Reverend: There was "awful work" going on, explained White Dog. "The Indians have bad hearts and are killing the whites. I am going to Wabasha to stop it." Little Crow was the next to pass by Hinman's gate. The Reverend, who had just shaken hands with the chief after church the day before, inquired about what was taking place. "He was usually very polite," Hinman remembered, "but now he made no answer, and, regarding me with a savage look, went on toward the stable, the next building below."

The next person to pass by Hinman's gate was August H. Wagner, the superintendent of farms at the agency. Hinman collared him and again demanded to know what was happening. According to Wagner, the Indians were on their way to the stables to steal horses and he was going to stop them. Hinman warned him that there was serious trouble afoot and that Wagner should not interfere, but the superintendent ignored the wise advice and continued on. Unable to remain behind, Hinman made his way to the stables and saw Wagner and hostler John Lamb confronting the Indians. Little Crow approached and asked the warriors, "What are you doing? Why don't you shoot these men? What are you waiting for?"

Another hostler, Lathrop Dickinson, was standing nearby. When either Dickinson or Lamb tried to stab one of the warriors with a pitchfork, both men and Wagner were gunned down. When John Fenske (19) ran into the barn a warrior shot him in the back with an arrow from a distance of only 12 feet. The wounded Fenske hid in the hayloft and tried to extract the arrow, but was unable to do so and instead broke it off. He threw a blanket over himself and, mustering all his calmness and courage, slowly walked away from the plundering Indians and down to the river. James Powell, who lived at St. Peter, was at the agency herding cattle. He had just saddled his mule when Wagner was killed and he heard Lamb scream for help. Bullets whistling past his head, however, convinced Powell to put spurs to the mule and head for the ferry.[12]

---

12 Heard, *History of the Sioux War*, 65-66; Curtiss-Wedge, *History of Redwood County*, I, 136.

John P. Kratke worked for contractor Henry G. Billings, who was hired by Agent Galbraith to cut hay for the agency. Kratke would have been at the stable that morning had he not just left on business with his horses and Billings's wagon for Henderson, Minnesota. He escaped but the Indians got his wagon, blankets, and other property.[13]

Carpenter John Nairn shared a double cabin with the Robertson family on the south side of the council ground next to Campbell's house. He was up early and on his way east to his shop when he saw several people moving among the buildings, particularly at the stables on the north side. When he asked some Dakotas what the trouble was all about, none of them could give him a straight answer. "Suddenly, there was a great discharge of guns and instantly there was a break for the stables, in which were many fine horses," recalled Nairn. More rounds were fired, and "then scattering shots as individuals were killed." It was 6:45 a.m.—the minute when "the storm broke over the agency." The Dakotas may have harbored an intense hatred for the people they believed had cheated them, but for many it was not murder, but booty that was the first object. The Dakotas near Nairn ran to get as many horses as they could as the carpenter broke for his house to get his family. "A few persons only escaped because of the eagerness of the Indians for their share of the plunder," he said.[14]

John Nairn was determined to be counted among the few. Born in Scotland in 1828, Nairn married Magdalene Nisbet in 1852, moved to Minnesota the same year, and had served as the head carpenter at the Lower Agency for the past three years. He gathered his wife and children, Cecelia (10), James (6), Margaret (3), and John (six weeks) and together they made for the ferry. When they discovered Indians blocking the route Nairn decided to take everyone back up on the bluffs. His assistant carpenter, Edward Bibeau, would probably have been with him had he not just joined the "Renville Rangers," who were now marching away. Bibeau lost carpenter's tools worth $72, but got away with his life. Somewhere in the timber Nairn and his family met Alexander Hunter and his wife, Marion Robertson Hunter, whose father was a Scotsman, Andrew Robertson, and whose mother was Jane Anderson, a mixed-blood Dakota. Hunter and Nairn had worked together for several years and were friends.

The families were discussing their options when White Spider (Unktomiska) approached them. The Dakota, Little Crow's half-brother who

13 John Kratke Depredation Claim #259.

14 John Nairn recollection, Microfilm Reel 3, Dakota Conflict, Minnesota Historical Society.

often went by the white name of John Wakeman, was one of the progressive "farmer" Indians. The dichotomous actions of so many Dakotas, torn between kin, friends, and enemies, were simply impossible to understand. Conscience, whim, and rational thought dictated different actions even by the same person at a moment's notice. Little Crow, for example, had warned Prescott, refused to speak with Hinman, ordered warriors to kill Wagner, Lamb, and Lathrop, and directed White Spider to save the women. "Go and gather up what white women and children you can," Little Crow told White Spider. "This state of things won't last very long, The Indians will have to go pretty soon, and the captives will perish; so, go quick."

White Spider obeyed, taking his staff and a few young warriors in search of anyone he could help. When he found Nairn and Hunter, he pointed out a ravine that followed the bluffs downriver and instructed them to hide and travel only by night to New Ulm. Mrs. Nairn offered him her wedding ring in thanks, but he refused the gift. "No, no! I don't want your ring," he said. "Just look at my face and if anything happens, remember it." With that, the families made their way down the south bluffs. "Our escape from the agency was very Providential," Nairn concluded. Providence aside, a little human help sometimes made the difference.[15]

After seeing the men at the stable gunned down Reverend Hinman finally decided it was time to get out. He stopped at Philander Prescott's to warn him, but the interpreter already knew and was preparing to flee. Hinman's wife, Mary Ellen, was absent from the mission, but he paused long enough to get Emily J. West (52), a teacher at the Episcopal school, and together they ran for the ferry. Somewhere along the way, recalled Hinman, West "ran into a house and I lost sight of her." After leaving Hinman's side Emily West met another white woman with a child and they crossed at the ferry and walked together until a band of warriors approached them. One of them laughed and said in English, "You belong to the missionary. Washte! (Good!) Where are you going?" West pointed to a house in the distance. "No," the Indian replied, "we are going to kill them." He motioned for the women and children to take the road up the far bluffs leading to Fort Ripley. The Indian was White Spider. "I took Miss West, he said, "and another woman and two children and they were saved."

15 John Nairn recollection, Microfilm Reel 3, Dakota Conflict, Minnesota Historical Society; Edward Bibeau Depredation Claim #160: Curtiss-Wedge, *History of Redwood County*, I, 138; Anderson and Woolworth, *Through Dakota Eyes*, 55, 61.

Hinman didn't wait around after he lost Emily. Near Dickinson's government boardinghouse on the north side of the council grounds, he found a wounded German and helped him down the hill and onto a skiff. They crossed to the north side and got away. Many people were congregating at the ferry, each trying to be the first to get across.[16]

Boardinghouse manager Joseph C. Dickinson, his wife Emily, and a son and daughter quickly weighed their options. At the barn, which was only 40 yards from the boardinghouse, they watched as Indians killed some of the teamsters who lodged with them and took their horses. Dickinson knew they had no choice but to run to the ferry and to find some form of transportation. Two employees, Dora Pelzel and Katherine Glock, went with them. Left behind were all their worldly possessions, which for Glock included two good woolen dresses, summer shawls, a new silk bonnet, and other items worth $139. They were among the first to reach the ferry, obtained a team and wagon, and were probably the first to reach Fort Ridgely.[17]

Those who responded quickly to the outbreak of hostilities had a better chance of escaping. Others generally paid with their lives. Philander P. Humphrey was one of the procrastinators. Born in Connecticut in 1823, he studied medicine at Oberlin College, married Susan Ames, and moved to Minnesota. In 1861, Humphrey took the position of government physician at Redwood Agency for the salary of $1,000 per year. The opinionated abolitionist was well-read and loved to discuss politics, religion, or philosophy. He and Mary had three children: John Ames (12), Jay Phelps (4), and Gertrude (1).

Twelve-year-old John A. Humphrey remembered his father as a disciplinarian with a temper. John sometimes accompanied his father when he visited the Indians to give them medicines and cure their ailments. He "visited their villages fearlessly," learned their language, and they called him "little medicine man." Although John had an opportunity to mingle with the Dakotas, his father was often overly protective. For instance, Philander never learned to swim and threatened his son with severe punishment if he ever discovered that

16 Heard, *History of the Sioux War*, 67; Whipple, *Lights and Shadows*, 109; Curtiss-Wedge, *History of Redwood County*, I, 158; Anderson and Woolworth, *Through Dakota Eyes*, 61, 65n2.

17 Katherine Glock Depredation Claim #258. According to some histories, the Dickinsons escaped with horses and wagon from the agency, but Glock is clear that the Indians took the horses. She says they walked to Faribault's, where they got his team and rode on to Ridgely. Nancy Faribault, however, is also clear that they had horses, but no wagon. The Dickinsons, Pelzel, and Glock must have obtained the wagon at the ferry.

he had "been in swimming." John, of course, found the time to sneak down to the Minnesota River and swim (and nearly drowned on one occasion) despite his father's threats.

As the hours dragged past midnight into early Monday, John Humphrey could not sleep. "Like a nightmare," he later wrote, "apprehension of impending doom settled down." It was barely gray in the east when the youngster awoke, dressed, and decided to take the water buckets to the spring, "expecting every instant to see or hear something horrible." Nothing happened, however, and John made the several trips needed to fill the tubs to the brim. He was hauling the heavy buckets on the last trip when he saw Indians moving around the buildings. Some of them approached a teamster with a wagon and demanded his horses. When the man refused a warrior shot him in the stomach. The unnamed teamster rolled on the ground in agony, where another assailant clubbed him in the head with the butt of his rifle. The shocked youngster ran to his house where he found his father dressed and in his office.

"Father, something awful is going to happen," John announced.

"Nonsense," Philander replied, turning back to his work.

John begged him to go outside and look, but he wouldn't move. When the son explained what he had witnessed, the elder Humphrey finally displayed enough interest to walk reluctantly outside. What he saw convinced Philander to leave, but he took some time to reach that conclusion. He finally collected his wife and ordered John to prepare the two younger children to travel. Within minutes the family was heading out the back door toward the ferry. "But father had been too slow," John lamented.[18]

Nearly everyone was taken by surprise that morning, including most of the Indians. Good Star Woman was about eight years old at the time of the uprising. She and her mother, Archargowe, were outside gathering wood when the first shots were fired. "Hurry, the Chippewa must be here," exclaimed Archargowe, and they ran to the camp. It was early and almost everyone was still in bed. A man galloped in and they asked him what the trouble was all about. "The Sioux are killing the whites," he informed them. The agency was more than four miles away but they could hear the firing. "The children wakened and began to cry," Good Star said. Everyone was shocked at the news.

Blue Sky Woman (17), also known as Esther Wakeman, was the wife of White Spider. Although he was Little Crow's half-brother, White Spider was not part of the impromptu war council. Blue Sky Woman was outside early that morning chasing crows away from the corn. She saw warriors traveling from Redwood River toward the agency and heard part of a conversation when someone stated, "If we do this, we will not have to worry for at least two years." When Blue Sky Woman heard shooting, she ran to her house and saw Little Crow there. She assumed he had been hunting and told him about the gunfire. Little Crow said nothing in reply.

Concerned, she ran to the agency when she saw two men supporting her brother. He had been at Forbes's helping the traders when Much Hail burst in and shot down James Lynd. "My brother," Blue Sky Woman said, "who had been sitting next to the storekeeper became covered with blood and fainted. The place had been ransacked," she remembered after walking through the rooms. "It was horrible." She continued searching until she found White Spider, who had helped the Nairns, West, and others escape. "Everything was confusion," Blue Sky Woman continued. "It was difficult to know who was friend and who was foe."[19]

Taopi, one of the leading farmer Indians, was preparing to visit Reverend Hinman that morning to discuss laying out a cemetery plot near the new church. Before he reached the reverend an old man came to his house and told him that the upper bands were armed and coming to the agency. Taopi hurried on, and another man ran toward him shouting, "They are killing the traders." Taopi turned back and climbed to his rooftop, where he could see Indians plundering the agency. More farmers gathered to discuss the deteriorating situation. Taopi tried to send a messenger to Wabasha, but a hostile band blocked his passage. At the village the Indians demanded that the farmers remove their white man's clothes and put on blankets and leggings. They threatened to kill all of the "bad talkers" if they didn't join them. Taopi and others wanted to escape to the fort, but were outnumbered and surrounded.[20]

The Dakotas hit the traders' stores and agency buildings first, but soon enveloped Redwood Ferry. Downriver one-quarter mile from the crossing was Joseph W. De Camp's house. De Camp was born in Ohio in 1826 and Jannette E. Sykes was born in New York in 1833. The pair married in Ohio in 1852 and three years later moved to Shakopee, Minnesota. In 1861 they moved again, this time to Redwood Agency when Agent Thomas Galbraith appointed De Camp

19 Anderson and Woolworth, *Through Dakota Eyes*, 52-55.

20 Whipple, *Lights and Shadows*, 111.

to run the saw mill. De Camp also built a mill for grinding corn for the Indians. The Dakotas were there almost daily with their bags, waiting for the corn to be ground and asking questions about the mill operation. Mainly, Jannette recalled, they were interested in the fighting between the North and South and believed the government was "in the last throes of dissolution."[21]

Joseph De Camp left his wife and three sons on Sunday, August 17, to go to St. Paul on business. He expected to return in less than a week. The next day Jannette was gardening when she saw an Indian harness her horses from the stable, hitch them to the wagon, and drive toward her. When she demanded to know where he thought he was taking her horses, he replied that all her property was his, the whites at the agency had been killed, and she should flee for her life. "I did not believe a word of it," she later admitted. She and her husband had often helped the Indians when they were hungry, opening their cellar and distributing bushels of vegetables on many occasions. The Indians called Joseph "the friendly man," and because Dr. Philander Humphrey "was not a favorite with them," the Dakotas often went to see Jannette, who prepared medicines for their sick children.

Jannette believed the tale was nothing but a ruse to steal horses, but the two girls who helped her with the housework, a German and a mixed-blood named Lucy, were convinced he was telling the truth. The unnamed German girl ran away. Lucy screamed and wanted to flee, but she helped Jannette gather her three children and together they climbed the hill. Below them spread a scene of chaos. The agency and trader stores were ablaze as hundreds of painted warriors shouted and brandished their weapons. Not a sound had carried to their house below the bluffs, so the revelation was a shock. Lucy ran away.

An elderly Indian woman, Chief Wacouta's mother, scurried past Jannette and yelled in Dakota, "Fly! Fly! They will kill you, white squaw!" The woman picked up De Camp's son (4), Jannette grabbed her infant, and along with Willie De Camp (9) followed the woman to Chief Wabasha's village.[22]

Several men worked for Joe De Camp. One was James L. Bennett, who escaped the conflagration when he headed for St. Peter on Friday, August 15. Bennett was on his way back when he was warned about the killings and turned around. Some of De Camp's employees stayed at his small boardinghouse, including Francis Giard, who shared a room with Narcisse Guerin. While Giard

21 "De Camp Sweet's Narrative," 354-56, *MHSC* Vol. 6.

22 "De Camp Sweet's Narrative," 357-58, *MHSC*, Vol. 6.

was having his own problems up at Forbes's store and at Campbell's, Indians surrounded De Camp's house at the river. Guerin heard the warnings and saw Mrs. De Camp and some of the girls run off. When he stepped out to investigate, a Dakota shot him down. Somehow Guerin staggered into the thick brush along the riverbank and hid there. Indians stole his shotgun and other property worth $100. Guerin managed to cross the river but did not take the popular route to the fort. Instead, he stumbled his way east across the prairie all the way to Henderson.[23]

By the time Philander Humphreys' family reached the river, no one was to be seen and the ferry and all the boats were on the north bank. Their neighbors and the last wagons were already across and moving toward Fort Ridgely. The doctor's face was ashen with hopelessness, and he may have wondered what happened to the ferryman.

Ferry owner Oliver Martell was born in Quebec, Canada, in 1818. He moved to Wisconsin at age 17, worked as a lumberjack and trader, married Louise Johnston in 1843, and had three children. They moved to Minnesota in 1855. With his partner, St. Germain, they built a sawmill at Waterville. When they lost it in the Panic of 1857, they moved to the Lower Agency and began operating the ferry in 1859. From the doorway of his house about 7:30 on the morning of the outbreak, Martell watched as Wacouta and his son signaled and shouted to each other from opposite banks. Martell's partner, St. Germain, ferried Wacouta across the rver. Minutes later, Martell heard scattered shots and then volleys of gunfire rumbling down to the valley.[24]

A short time later Reverend Hinman, John Whipple, and a dozen others arrived in a hurry and signaled frantically to be ferried across the river. Hinman later told Martell that he saw John Lamb killed and that Indians were killing many others, but they let his party pass through. When Hinman asked if he had any horses, Martell replied that he had a team and a single horse. "Give me the team to take my family and these people to the fort," suggested Hinman, "and you saddle the single horse and go to Fort Ridgely and notify the commandant of the outbreak."

Martell agreed, climbed on his horse, and began his Paul Revere-like ride. Just north of the ferry he warned Louis La Croix and his family. Nearby was the empty house of Antoine Young, who was already dead at Forbes's store. Martell

23 James Bennett Depredation Claim #171; Narcisse Guerin Depredation Claim #278.

24 Oliver Martell story, Microfilm Reel 2, Dakota Conflict, Minnesota Historical Society.

spread the word at David Faribault's place about two miles east of the ferry. Nancy McClure Faribault was in the doorway when Martell galloped by. "Oh, Mrs. Faribault," he called out, "the Indians are killing all the white people at the agency! Run away, run away quick!" Martell also warned Magner, Peterson, LaFramboise, and Schlumberger, giving them a chance to escape.[25]

When Martell, Hinman and his party, and other stragglers left the river, only the ferryman remained. The Indians eventually killed him. According to some accounts, he was disemboweled and his head, hands, and feet cut off. Most people who mentioned the ferryman praised him. Sam Hinman's words to contemporary and later historian Isaac Heard led him to conclude, "Obscure Frenchman though he was, the blood of no nobler hero dyed the battle-fields of Thermopylae or Marathon." Joseph Schneider, however, was not at all pleased when he reached the ferry and found no one there to take him across. Perhaps the ferryman was already dead by the time he arrived. Schneider dragged himself across the river by holding on to the ferry rope.[26]

The ferryman's identity is open to dispute because different men ran the ferry at different times. Almost every history names Oliver and a brother, Peter Martell, as the owners of the ferry. Several accounts claim the ferryman that fateful day was Hubert Miller, Hubert Millier, Jacob Mauley, Jacob Mayley, Charlie Martell, or a number of other variations. According to Oliver Martell, his brother was named Augustus, but he was not there and did not co-own the ferry. Martell's partner was a man named "St. Germain," who apparently operated the ferry on occasion, just as Oliver did. The 1860 census listed Louis Fleury as ferryman and Henry La Pine as an assistant. Theodore Morin, who was employed by Nathan Myrick but joined the "Renville Rangers" a few days before the uprising, left all of his property "in the charge of Hubert Milier," who he claimed "kept the ferry at the Lower Agency." Morin lost his property when Milier was killed and the Indians burned his cabin.[27]

25 Oliver Martell story, Microfilm Reel 2, Dakota Conflict, Minnesota Historical Society; Anderson and Woolworth, *Through Dakota Eyes*, 82; Curtiss-Wedge, *History of Renville County*, I, 99, 100, 103.

26 Heard, *History of the Sioux War*, 67; Curtiss-Wedge, *History of Redwood County*, I, 139.

27 Oliver Martell story, Microfilm Reel 2, Dakota Conflict, Minnesota Historical Society; Connors, "Elusive Hero of Redwood Ferry," 233, 235; Theodore Morin Depredation Claim #163. Examples of name variations are in Curtiss-Wedge, *History of Redwood County*, I, 139; Koblas, *Let Them Eat Grass*, I, 197; Hubbard and Holcombe, *Minnesota in Three Centuries*, III, 313. Jacob Mauerle, whose story follows, is another possibility.

What this confusion makes clear is that there were several "ferrymen," and all of them assisted in saving lives. Sadly, they were all killed or were gone by the time the Humphrey family arrived. The ferry and a few smaller boats were all on the north bank and their neighbors and the last of the wagons were gone. Young John looked into his father's face and saw utter hopelessness. Many times in the past John had been in the river learning to swim and had gone home hoping his hair was dry when his father cast suspicious glances in his direction. It was time to show his father that he had disobeyed his warning. "I now boldly plunged into the river," John later recalled, "swam to the other side, secured a small boat and rowed back to them, and we all crossed in silence." The family plodded east along the road as the sun rose in the sky and the day grew hot. Looking back, John believed at the time that this exhibition of his swimming skill should have allowed them to escape. "[H]ad we been only those few minutes earlier," he lamented, everyone would have gotten away safely.[28]

The Humphreys were not alone in the area. When Joe Coursolle got his wife and infant daughter across the river he went back to discover his daughters Elizabeth and Minnie had vanished. He scurried up and down the bank looking in bushes and gullies but could not find them. When his setter Duta, who had escaped the house, caught his scent and came running to him he climbed the bluffs to quiet him. His barking would alert the Indians! Joe grabbed the dog and pulled him into the trees. "I was forced to do the cruelest task of my life," he related. "I slipped off my belt and pulled it tight around Duta's neck." Joe cried as the dog struggled for breath and then, finally, struggled no more. "Forgive me Duta," he said, as he laid his head in his lap for a moment.

Coursolle continued searching for his girls. Several agency buildings were burning, his cabin among them. "I saw many dead men, scalped and tomahawked with brains oozing out of their skulls." The grounds were empty of life and after a few hours he gave up and returned to his wife.

"Are they dead?" she asked.

"I don't know," Joe replied. "I couldn't find them. But I saw no bodies of women or girls so I think they are alive."

He wanted to keep looking, but first he had to get his wife and daughter to the fort.[29]

---

28 Humphrey, "Boyhood Remembrances," 343-44, *MHSC*, Vol. 15.

29 Joseph Coursolle story, Microfilm Reel 1, Dakota Conflict, Minnesota Historical Society.

C hapter 4

"Pa, let me go with you."

Beaver Creek

Thomas Robertson ~ David Carrothers ~ Helen Carrothers ~ Stephen Henderson ~ Jonathan Earle ~ Urania White ~ Diedrich Wichmann ~ Ezmon Earle chases horses ~ Attempted escape ~ Hayden, Juni, and Eisenreich ~ Nancy and David Faribault ~ Kearn Horan ~ Ole Sampson ~ Benidict Juni caught ~ Humphrey family caught

T he Dakotas' first major strike was at the Lower Agency, but attacks began nearly simultaneously in surrounding areas. Confusion reigned at the Lower Agency. Most of the Indians were as surprised as the whites when the violence erupted. The mixed-bloods increased the chaos because there were no clear battle lines. Kinship ties resulted in diverse loyalties. Generally, the mixed-bloods were spared but not all were so fortunate. Sometimes life or death depended on how kind the potential victim had been to the assailant. According to Big Eagle, almost every Indian had a relative or friend he wanted to save. On the north side of the Minnesota River, the racial divide was more apparent, and there was little reluctance to kill at the white homesteads.

The Dakotas made short work of the agency and continued the destruction at the ferry. The crossing was just downstream from the mouth of Birch Coulee, originally called La Croix Creek for Louis La Croix, the first settler in the area in 1845. On his ride Martell warned some of the settlers near the mouth of the creek, including Louis La Croix. He and his extended family escaped. Others lived farther up the creek and on the surrounding bluffs, including George Buerry, John Kumro, Peter Pereau, Joseph and David McConnell, John Vogtman, Clement Cardinal, Carl Witt, and Charles Clausen. (Map E) Some got away, and others did not.

Mrs. Carl Witt was stacking hay when an Indian shot her dead. Her son, William (14), who was pitching the hay, jumped down and ran to his father. When the Indians abruptly left, Carl Witt (45) and William buried the body and fled with the four younger children to Fort Ridgely. Indians killed Eusebius Piquar and captured his young daughter, Elizabeth, while his wife, Elizabeth (22), and son, Eusebius (6), escaped. On their way to the fort, Carl and William Witt found Piquar's body and also buried it.

The rampaging Dakotas moved north. Charles Clausen with his wife and son John, his married son Frederick, Frederick's wife Martha, and their two children, plus Thomas Brook, were preparing for a trip when the Dakotas appeared. Had they left the day before all of them would have survived. The Indians killed Charles and Frederick Clausen and Thomas Brook and captured Martha Clausen and her two children. Mrs. Charles Clausen and John Clausen made it to the fort.[1]

About two and one-half miles from the mouth of Birch Coulee lived the Pereaus and Cardinals. Peter Pereau was born in Canada and had several children. When his wife died they moved to Minnesota and Peter remarried. Clement Cardinal (25), also from Canada, moved to Minnesota when he was 13, worked at farming and fur trading, found a piece of land at Birch Coulee, and settled down near the Pereaus. He and Margaret Pereau married in 1858. On the morning of the uprising, Margaret Cardinal was at the Clausens while they were packing their wagon. When the Dakotas attacked, a man named Te-he-hdo-ne-cha captured Margaret and others took Mrs. Clausen and her two children. Warriors fanned out to the nearby homes and killed Peter Pereau, but his wife and six children escaped. Clement Cardinal got away and joined the 5th Minnesota Infantry and served for one year "in the campaign against the spoilers of his home."[2]

Brothers David McConnell (40) and Joseph McConnell (25) were from Massachusetts and had a place about two miles north of the mouth of Birch

[1] Curtiss-Wedge, *History of Renville County*, II, 928, 1290-91, 1347; Tolzmann, ed., *Outbreak and Massacre*, 37-38, 106. Today, the creek Birch Coulee is spelled differently from Birch Cooley Township.

[2] Holcombe, *Monuments and Tablets*, 29; Neill, *History of the Upper Mississippi Valley*, 268. Te-he-hdo-ne-cha later confessed that he raped Margaret Cardinal: "I slept with this woman once—I did bad towards her once—I tell you the truth. Another Indian may have slept with her." Te-he-hdo-ne-cha was one of the 38 Indians hanged at Mankato in December 1862. Heard, "Dakota Conflict Trials," www.law.umkc.edu/faculty/projects/ftrials/dakota/trialrec1.

Coulee. The Indians arrived and wounded their nephew, Mark Brook (16), probably Thomas Brook's brother, as he gathered eggs for his Uncle David's breakfast. The Indians moved on. David sent his family to the fort while he remained behind to tend to the livestock. He slipped away that evening and made it to the fort. Joseph, who left his wife behind in Massachusetts, arrived in May 1862 and worked as a plasterer for John Nairn. He lived most of the week at Dickenson's boarding house at the agency, but stayed at his brother's place each weekend. On Monday morning, Joseph went to work and so was able to flee with Nairn until he got separated and made his own way to the fort.[3]

Thomas A. Robertson (22) was the oldest of nine children of Andrew Robertson and mixed-blood Jane Anderson. His father was superintendent of the agency schools until his death in 1859, so Thomas was adequately educated. He taught in one of the schools for six months, was in charge at Alexander Bailley's store at Redwood for a year, and worked as an interpreter for Reverend Hinman. In 1860, Thomas, his mother, and a few other brothers and sisters, moved to the same quarter section of land near the mouth of Beaver Creek where his sister Marion had a house with her husband, Alexander Hunter. The two were not home (they were attempting their own escape from the Lower Agency). Thomas's sister, Martha C. Robinson, also had a claim farther downstream on Beaver Creek.

Jane Anderson shook Thomas awake at sunrise to tell him "there was something strange going on in the flat below our house." Thomas saw Indians running and driving cattle but did not know why or what else was happening. An old Indian who lived just across the river named Ka-kpan- kpan-u stopped by and concluded it was probably a war party of Chippewas and asked Thomas for his gun, which he had borrowed many times before. Robertson handed him the weapon and he left, only to return a short time later with a different explanation: the Sissetons were stealing horses. Once again, he was not positive. When he returned a second time he was shaking, and this time he was sure: the Lower Sioux were stealing stock and they intended to kill all the whites. Ka-kpan-kpan-u's wife, who was Jane Anderson's aunt, was with him. She instructed her niece to take the family across the river to their house for safety. Ka-kpan-kpan-u told Thomas that a party of warriors was on the hill surrounding the white settlers, waiting only for a signal to attack them. He asked

---

3 Joseph McConnell Depredation Claim #200. A number of histories, including Marion Satterlee's account, list David McConnell as being killed. He survived.

that Thomas go with him "and tell these Whites to get out of the country as fast as they could."[4]

North of Hunter and Robertson and on both sides of Beaver Creek lived a number of families who had settled the area soon after the 1858 Treaty, including Carrothers, Ahrens, Henderson, Schmidt, Earle, White, Wichmann, and Wedge. (Map E) Robertson and Ka-kpan-kpan-u went to David Carrothers nearby house. There were already several Indians and a few whites talking there. One Indian, a Winnebago, spoke English. Robertson realized it would not be safe for him to warn Carrothers within earshot of him. Ka-kpan-kpan-u distracted the Winnebago as Robertson edged closer to Carrothers and whispered the news. When he asked if he had any horses, David replied that he already had three teams hitched at Henderson's barn. Robertson told him to get away while Ka-kpan-kpan-u led the Indians off in another direction. When Robertson returned to his sister's, his family was already across the river and the stock was missing. When Ka-kpan-kpan-u arrived the Indian announced, "There is nothing for us to stay here for. We will go to my place and see what is best to do."[5]

David Carrothers, who household consisted of his wife Elizabeth, an infant, and two sons William (7) and John (6), was already aware something was terribly wrong. He had earlier witnessed Indians trying to round up loose horses and had sought out neighbors to help. His brother, James Carrothers, lived close by, but James was absent. His wife, Helen Mar Paddock, was only 14 years old when she married James, who had worked as a carpenter at the Lower Agency since the brothers moved to Beaver Creek in 1858. James and Helen had two children, Althea (4) and Tommy (2). The Dakotas were always friendly with them and visited Helen daily. She learned their language and their traditions. The tribal medicine man taught her about various herbs, roots, and barks and how to use them to cure a variety of ills.

That morning Helen Carrothers was at Stephen R. Henderson's house helping care for Mrs. Clarissa Henderson, who was seriously ill with what was thought to be appendicitis. When Agency physician Dr. Humphrey announced that she would not recover, the Hendersons appealed to a Dakota medicine

4   Thomas Robertson reminiscence, Microfilm Reel 3, Dakota Conflict, Minnesota Historical Society.

5   Thomas Robertson reminiscence, Microfilm Reel 3, Dakota Conflict, Minnesota Historical Society.

man as a last resort. The medicine man agreed to assist only if Helen would help him. When the Indian doctor had no better luck, Dr. Humphrey was called again. He was scheduled to visit them that day. Helen Carrothers and the Hendersons were eating breakfast about half past six that morning when they spotted four Indians peeking in the window. A short time later they left without incident in the direction of Jonathan Earle's house.[6]

Jonathan W. Earle, a Vermont native, graduated from the University of Vermont in 1841 and taught school for nine years. In 1842 he married Amanda M. Macomber of Westford, Vermont. Eight years later they moved to Pardeeville, Wisconsin, where Jonathan practiced law. They had six children: Chalon (19), Ezmon (17), Radnor (15), Julia (13), Herman (9), and Elmira (7). The Earle family moved to Beaver Creek in late June 1862, taking with them their entire library of 1,200 books, plus medical stores, a melodeon, and several violins. The three oldest boys played the violin; Julia played the melodeon. Ezmon didn't consider he and his brothers to be violinists, "but we certainly were fiddlers." On Sundays, missionary John P. Williamson held services in the Henderson's front yard, and afterward John, Jonathan, and Mrs. Henderson would sing while the children played their instruments.

Indians were always in the area talking, borrowing, or digging wild turnips. Only three days earlier, Little Crow showed up to make the case that the Indians were in dire need of their annuity money. Accompanied by several tribesmen and Thomas Robertson, Little Crow negotiated the deal. Ezmon Earle, who knew some Dakota, was also there. He described Little Crow as "tall, spare, with a nose like a hawk's bill, and sharp piercing black eyes. He was by no means good looking." Ezmon took special note of his "very much deformed" wrists. The chief and his men gave Jonathan Earle two double-barreled shotguns as security for one cow, but Earle demanded Little Crow's own gun, a double-barreled shotgun with a yellow stock, as additional collateral for a second cow. Little Crow agreed reluctantly to leave the gun, but only after Earle wrote out a receipt that he would return it when he was paid for the cow. A man would not likely pawn his favorite gun if he planned to go to war three days later.

On Sunday night, Radnor Earle stood at the door and commented on how plainly he could hear the Indian drums. Ezmon and Chalon listened also. "This

6   Bryant and Murch, *Great Massacre*, 283-84.

was something unusual, yet it did not disturb us," Ezmon recalled. "And so we went to bed and to sleep."[7]

Jonathan Earle rose early the next morning, August 18, to finish shingling the house. From the roof he noticed four Indians in the corner of his fenced yard, but he paid them little attention. When he climbed down for breakfast, Jonathan walked over to ask them what they were doing. As Earle later explained it, they were "pretending to be in pursuit of Chippewas." The Indians walked to the house and asked if they could look at his rifles. When one of them tried to climb on the bed to reach the gun rack, Jonathan objected and interposed himself. The Indians grew angry and left. Suspecting that something wasn't quite right, Jonathan dispatched his sons to round up his horses.

Chalon and Radnor moved east to see if any had wandered onto the prairie, while Ezmon went to Beaver Creek. He walked down to Robertson's, but the family was gone and Indians were driving horses into their fenced yard. A Dakota asked Ezmon to help them catch the horses. When the boy refused because the animals did not belong to him, the warrior insisted. The horses were being brought in when several broke toward Ezmon, who made a half-hearted and unsuccessful attempt to turn them back. The Indians tried again, forcing Ezmon to participate, when an old woman (likely Ka-kpan-kpan-u's wife) who had just helped the Robertsons across the river, walked up to Ezmon and told him to "puckachee tehan"—go far away.

Ezmon was thinking the woman knew that his attempt to round up the horses was insincere when the same Indian who had tried to take his father's gun approached him. The Indian put his arm around his neck, squeezed, and told him he would like to scalp him and guessed he might do so before nightfall. A hard punch in the ribs forced the Indian to let go and walk away. An old Indian he had seen many times called Old Beaver Creek (likely Ka-kpan-kpan-u) was very agitated when Ezmon approached him and he refused to speak. Something was very wrong. Ezmon left and headed back up the creek, using the bushes as cover. Back at his house he told his father what had transpired and they decided to gather their seven horses and take them to the agency until the trouble, or whatever it was, blew over.

Chalon and Ezmon mounted two steeds and went after the rest. Ezmon was on the prairie when another neighbor, Diedrich Wichmann, ran past and

---

7   Bryant and Murch, *Great Massacre*, 275-76; Ezmon Earle reminiscences, Microfilm Reel 1, Dakota Conflict, Minnesota Historical Society.

yelled that the Indians were killing all the whites at the agency. Ezmon galloped to find Chalon, and the two rode off to warn their neighbors.[8]

Jonathan Earle and his daughter Julia ran to the Hendersons. While Jonathan helped them gather some belongings, Julia Earle and Julia White (14) hurried to warn White's mother. Julia White had been at the Hendersons helping Mr. Henderson take care of his ill wife and her two small children, as was Helen Carrothers. The two girls ran down into the Beaver Creek bottom to White's house. Julia White's mother, Urania S. Frazer White, was born in 1825, in Alexander, New York. She married Nathan Dexter White in New York in 1845, and two years later they moved to Pardeeville in south-central Wisconsin, where they spent 15 years. It was there that they met the Jonathan Earle family, and in May 1862 joined the Earles in moving to Renville County, Minnesota. Nathan built his cabin at the base of the bluff in the valley of Beaver Creek, about two miles from its junction with the Minnesota River.

Nathan White and James Carrothers were delegates on their way to a political meeting in Owatonna in Steele County, and Nathan was going to pick up Mrs. Henderson's parents in Blue Earth County on his return. Urania, on this day of her 20th wedding anniversary, was doing the laundry when her excited daughter Julia Earle entered the house to tell her the Indians were on the warpath. The news frightened Urania. "In fact," she remembered, "it seemed to strike me dumb." Forgoing the chance to collect extra clothing and food, she instead grabbed a large purse containing money and important papers, a gun, and her five-month-old son Frank. Together with her daughter Julia and Julia Earle, they ran to the centrally located Earle home. Urania's sons Millard (12) and Eugene (16) were already there helping the Earles warn people and readying the horses and wagons. Eugene had also heard Mr. Wichmann's warning when he ran by.[9]

Diedrich Wichmann lived a little farther north on Beaver Creek, as did the Ahrens, Schmidt, and Shepherd families. Wichmann moved into the area in the fall of 1860 with his wife, sons Cosmos Fred, Diedrich H., Henry J., and William, and daughters Dorothy and Fredericke. The next year a prairie fire

---

8 Bryant and Murch, *Great Massacre*, 276; Ezmon Earle reminiscences, Microfilm Reel 1, Dakota Conflict, Minnesota Historical Society.

9 White, "Captivity Among the Sioux," 395-98, *MHSC*, Vol. 9; Bryant and Murch, *Great Massacre*, 105; Ezmon Earle reminiscences, Microfilm Reel 1, Dakota Conflict, Minnesota Historical Society. Urania White believed the gun she took was one that Little Crow had pawned to her husband.

threatened to consume their barn, but when an old Indian living nearby saw it begin, he soaked his blanket in water and helped Mrs. Wichmann put it out. Friendly Dakotas were always in the area, and the Wichmanns often fed them during the winter. The Wichmann's added another son (John C.) on August 14, 1862 who, according to the family, was the first white child born in Renville County. The days were unremarkable. Cosmos was working at Fort Ridgely as a butcher, Diedrich Wichmann and his other boys had cut and shocked the rye, and with that done, Wichmann got a job at the agency putting up hay.

That morning Diedrich had reached the ferry and was waiting to be taken across when he heard shooting and learned Indians were on a killing spree. He pulled off his heavy work boots, and with them in hand, ran barefoot back home. After calling the warning to Ezmon Earle he found Mr. and Mrs. F. W. Schmidt hauling hay and gave them the same alarm. Diedrich gathered his family and prepared the horses and wagon for an escape. Henry ran to notify Judge Henry Ahrens while Diedrich Jr. ran to alert the Shepherds, the area's most recent arrivals. All of them congregated at the Wichmann place. The boys, who had just loaded a wagon with hay, worked frantically to dump it out to make room for others. The procession of four families, with ox teams and wagons, set out toward Fort Ridgely but avoided the more heavily traveled road along the Minnesota River. The bumpy ride somehow jostled three-year-old William Wichmann through a hole in the bottom of the hay wagon. Miraculously, he missed being crushed by the wheels. No one knew he had fallen until Judge Ahrens in the following wagon spotted him in the road and picked him up. The families continued on. Farther south, fires burned along the river and bluffs.[10]

They were a little too slow getting ready at the Earle house, where the Hendersons, Carrothers, and Whites gathered to plan their escape. Only three wagons were available for their exodus. The ill Clarissa Henderson lay on a feather mattress in their family buggy. Two single men who lived nearby, Jehiel Wedge and John Doyle, joined the group which totaled 27 people: five adult males, four teenage boys, and 18 women and children. Ezmon Earle prepared two rifles and three of the Dakotas' double-barreled shotguns, all muzzle-loaders, for action. One of the rifles had a small bore so Ezmon put in two bullets for good measure. He loaded two of the shotguns, "but for the third I had no shot," he explained, "so I put in a few small stones. Our shot and

10 Curtiss-Wedge, *History of Renville County*, II, 917-18.

bullets were all gone and only one flask of powder partly filled remained. This shows how utterly defenseless we were."[11]

The small procession had barely traveled one-half mile when 16 Indians blocked their path. Others who had been hanging around the house closed in from behind. Stephen Henderson, who could speak Dakota fluently, together with David Carrothers, approached them to determine their intent.

"We are going to kill you," one Indian replied. Henderson gave the talk of his life, negotiating with them for ten minutes. He returned to the others and explained that the Indians would not kill everyone if they gave up their horses, wagons, and guns. Henderson agreed to some of the demands but refused to surrender the guns and insisted on keeping the buggy and one team for his wife and children. The Indians agreed. As the Indians claimed their property and unhitched the teams, the women and children walked ahead to put some distance between themselves and the warriors. At that point the Indians changed their minds and demanded Henderson's horses. He protested to no avail: The men would have to pull the buggy by hand.

When the unusual exchange ended, the Dakotas shook hands with the whites recalled Helen Carrothers, "and seemed well pleased." At the time she believed that with "this sacrifice [the surrendering of the animals and wagons] all were safe." Given what was to take place, Ezmon Earle was perplexed by the course of events. "Why they did not kill us then and there," he said, "I cannot understand."

The Dakotas allowed the party to walk a short distance before experiencing yet another change of heart or, perhaps, they had planned to kill or capture everyone from the start. Helen Carrothers was about 50 yards in front of the buggy when she heard the Dakotas singing, followed by shots fired. "The Indians were actually killing us." Elizabeth Carrothers was in the buggy shielding Mrs. Henderson from the sun with an umbrella when the mayhem began. She jumped out and ran toward her sister-in-law as two bullets cut through her dress without hitting her. When the bullets started flying, David Carrothers yelled, "Look out!" but no one else said a word. When the Indians drew closer and the firing increased, the men hauling the buggy realized they could not haul the buggy out of harm's way and save themselves. Jonathan Earle, Ezmon Earle, and David Carrothers dropped the buggy and ran. Stephen

---

[11] Ezmon Earle reminiscences, Microfilm Reel 1, Dakota Conflict, Minnesota Historical Society.

Henderson told them he could not leave, and Jehiel Wedge announced that Mrs. Henderson had once nursed him when he was sick, so he would stay as well.

Clarissa Henderson insisted they surrender and gave her husband a white pillowcase to wave. He was attempting to do so when bullets knocked off his hat, riddled his clothing, and clipped off the forefinger on his right hand that held the pillowcase. The warriors closed in quickly, killing Wedge and surrounding the buggy. Henderson broke and ran, overtaking the overweight and slower Jonathan Earle. By the time Ezmon caught up to the women, Elizabeth Carrothers was too tired to keep running and carry her baby. Ezmon took the infant from her and they continued on. The survivors covered perhaps one mile before Urania White dropped out from exhaustion. White, "a very fleshy woman" according to Ezmon, explained she could run no farther and simply slumped to the prairie with her baby. "The bullets were continually whizzing by my head," Urania later recalled as she awaited her fate. The Dakotas could come back and get her later, so they ignored her and continued after the others.[12]

The few guns carried by the fleeing whites did them little good except as a deterrent that kept their pursuers from charging in too close. The Indians had no way of knowing they contained only one shot apiece (and that one shotgun was loaded with pebbles). When the Indians left Urania behind, it appeared to some as though the women might be spared or simply captured instead of killed. When Elizabeth Carrothers stopped Ezmon handed back her baby and continued running. Seven-year-old John Carrothers was doing his best to keep up with his father and called out for him to wait. David stopped, turned to face his son, and instructed him to go back to his mother on the assumption the Indians would not kill a young boy. Unsure what to do John stood and cried—until an Indian reached him and killed him.

Seven-year-old Elmira Earle caught up to her plodding father. "Pa, let me go with you," she pleaded. Jonathan stopped long enough to notice the Indians had caught his wife but had not killed her. Rationalizing as David Carrothers had just done that the children would be safe, Jonathan told her to go back to her mother, turned around, and ran.

---

12 Bryant and Murch, *Great Massacre*, 278-79, 285-86; Ezmon Earle reminiscences, Microfilm Reel 1, Dakota Conflict, Minnesota Historical Society; White, "Captivity Among the Sioux," 399, *MHSC*, Vol. 9.

Some warriors stopped for the women as the others moved on to pick off the fleeing men and boys. William Carrothers was the next to die. Chalon and Ezmon Earle and Eugene White were running close together. The Earle boys looked back as a warrior stopped and leveled his gun. They both dropped to the ground and the bullet hit Eugene White in the back of the right knee. When Ezmon asked if he was hit, Eugene replied that he thought his leg was broken. He got up, but limped badly. After a short distance Eugene hopped into some tall grass and hid. Ezmon watched as an Indian ran to the spot, aimed into the grass, and emptied a double-barreled shotgun into him.

By this time the Indians were gaining rapidly on the overweight Jonathan Earle, who stopped, aimed his rifle, and fired. The Indians stopped and may have fallen back a bit, but then Jonathan did a foolish thing: he threw away his weapon. He knew he had only one shot, but the Indians did not. With his weapon gone they closed in for the kill. Jonathan yelled for help but only his son Radnor was close enough to hear him. Armed with a shotgun loaded with pebbles, he stopped to defend his father. Jonathan trotted past him and shouted, "Shoot at the Indians, drop your gun, and run!" Radnor stooped in the grass and let his father get a few yards past him before leveling his weapon and pulling the trigger. Jonathan saw the puff of smoke and watched as a pair of warriors ran up to the boy and fired. When he turned back to look again, Jonathan recalled, the Indians "were busy, apparently, scalping him. Noble boy! He saved my life by the sacrifice of his own." Jonathan overtook Chalon Earle and Millard White, while Ezmon ducked into some tall grass and took a roundabout path out of the area. Stephen Henderson and David Carrothers went off in separate directions.[13]

The Indians who had dropped out of the chase gathered up their captives. Oddly enough, the Dakotas put on a friendly face, shook hands with the women and, as Helen Carrothers recalled, "said we were going now to live with them." They sat on the prairie for 15 minutes until the other warriors returned. During the walk back toward the Earle house the Indians refused to allow them to go near Henderson's buggy, but they could see what was going on.

"Woe and despair now seized all of us who were made captives," wrote Urania White. Clarissa Henderson was too ill to be of any use to anyone, and if she was to be killed, so must her two-year-old daughter and nine-month-old

13 Bryant and Murch, Great Massacre, 280-81; Ezmon Earle reminiscences, Microfilm Reel 1, Dakota Conflict, Minnesota Historical Society.

baby. The captives watched in horror as the warriors threw the children out of the buggy and beat their heads with violins. They dumped Clarissa on the ground with her dead or dying children, threw the feather mattress over them, and set it on fire. "The bravest among us lost courage, being so helpless, defenseless, and unprepared for this act of savage warfare," admitted Urania. "With blanched faces we beheld the horrible scene and clasped our helpless little children closer to us."

There were now 11 captives: Elizabeth Carrothers and her baby; Amanda Earle and her daughters Julia and Elmira; Urania White and children Frank and Julia; and Helen Carrothers with Althea and Tommy. The Indians returned them to Jonathan Earle's home, where the Indians loaded a wagon full of useable items and destroyed everything else. Thereafter they continued down the bluffs to the Hunter and Robertson houses. When a warrior drove his hatchet into Robertson's door, another scolded him saying, "This is an Indian's house." The captives were divided on two wagons and they continued to the Hayden house. A warrior Helen Carrothers called Indian John told her that he had cut off Mrs. Hayden's head—a false story meant to frighten her. When they passed the Juni and Eisenreich houses, the Indians shot some hogs and chickens and told the captives they had also slaughtered those families. The women learned they were going to cross the river and head for Little Crow's village.[14]

*   *   *

August Gluth (13) was herding horses somewhere in the area between Birch Coulee and Beaver Creek when the war reached him. The Gluths emigrated from Germany in 1856 and settled in Milford Township a few miles west of New Ulm.[15] There were several children, including Fred (who was killed while serving in the Union army), John (22), August (13), and Henry (6). The family had little money. In the summer of 1862 an opportunity arrived for young August to work herding stock near Beaver Falls. He had been on the job a few weeks and was daydreaming on the back of his horse when a band of

---

14 Bryant and Murch, *Great Massacre*, 286-87; White, "Captivity Among the Sioux," 399-400, 403, *MHSC*, Vol. 9.

15 Although the nation wasn't unified until 1871, chroniclers made many references to Germany as the country of origin.

Dakotas rode up and captured the stock and herding boys in one sweep, August among them. The Dakotas had a hard time handling the oxen, and Gluth and the other boys were probably spared so they could take care of the livestock.[16]

East of the mouth of Beaver Creek lived Patrick Hayden and his wife Mary (19), their one-year-old child Catherine, and Patrick's brother John. That morning Pat Hayden was traveling to Redwood River to see Joseph B. Reynolds when he met Thomas Robinson, who told him to get his family out because the Indians were coming to kill the whites.[17] The Haydens packed quickly, hitched a wagon, and headed downriver. The next house belonged to Benedict Juni (Eune) and his wife, son Benedict Jr. (11), and four other children. That morning the Junis heard what they thought were drums beating at the agency; in reality it was gunfire. Benedict Jr. had taken the family's only horse to round up the oxen when the Haydens arrived and raised the alarm. Mr. Juni refused to believe the shocking news, but the women pleaded so insistently that he took the hayrack off the wagon, tossed in some clothing, bedding, and provisions, placed his wife and other children in it, and sent them off with Mary Hayden. John Zimmerman, who lived two miles down the valley, was there with his eldest son John Jr., and they took charge of the wagon. According to Benedict Jr., "They had two guns and a sword with which Mr. Zimmerman declared he would defend the occupants." The group headed downriver to get the rest of Zimmerman's family, which consisted of his blind wife Mary, another son named Gottfried, and two daughters. Patrick and John Hayden were as skeptical as Mr. Juni about the news and they returned to their house. According to Mary Hayden, her husband was "still thinking the Indians would not kill anyone, and intended to give them some provisions if they wanted them. I never saw him again."[18]

16 West, "A Lad's Version of Chief Little Crow," Microfilm Reel 1, Dakota Conflict, Minnesota Historical Society. Frederick Gluth served in the 6th Wisconsin Infantry (Company B, the Prescott Guards), part of the legendary Iron Brigade, Army of the Potomac. He enlisted May 10, 1861, and was killed in action on September 17, 1862 at Antietam. *Roster of Wisconsin Volunteers, War of the Rebellion, 1861-1865*, Vol. 1 (Madison, Wisconsin, Democrat Printing Company, 1886), 502.

17 Bryant and Murch, *Great Massacre*, 109. Mary Hayden recalled the name of the man who warned her husband as the mixed-blood Thomas Robinson. It is quite possible the man was Thomas Robertson, who lived near Hayden and had warned David Carrothers. Robinson, on the other hand, did not give a danger warning to other whites (Inefeldt, Zitloff) who were fleeing.

18 Bryant and Murch, *Great Massacre*, 110; Brown, *Cottonwood and Watonwan Counties*, 337.

When they started off, Mr. Juni told his son to run the cows to a penned area they kept where the village of Morton now stands. Then, his father told him to ride down the valley and warn the neighbors while Mr. Juni and a younger son guarded the stock. When the Indians showed up, Mr. Juni and his son reassessed the situation and their inability to guard their property and took off running for Fort Ridgely. Benedict Jr. penned the cows as instructed and rode to the homes of George Buerry and John Kumro. (Map E) Buerry was born in Germany in 1826 and arrived in America at age 20. He worked as a cooper in Canada and New York before moving near Birch Coulee in 1859. He had already heard the alarm when Benedict appeared, so the boy continued down the road to Kumro's place. Another German immigrant, Kumro was born in 1826, served three years in the military, and moved to America in 1850. He married Mary Coffman six years later and they began raising a family of ten children. They relocated to the Birch Coulee area in 1859 to try their hands at farming.

Kumro had also gotten the word and he and Buerry were preparing to flee. They asked Benedict to come with them, but he declined because his father told him to warn the neighbors. Benedict left the river road to cut through the brush but ran into three Dakotas who leveled their guns and grabbed the reins of his horse. One of them, speaking in broken English, asked if he wanted to resist. Benedict only smiled and slipped off the horse, figuring the warriors wanted the horse more than they wanted him. The Indian mounted the animal and left with the other two following on foot. Benedict decided to give the road a wide berth and cut through the brush along the bluffs. He reached the road again near the ferry where he saw "the body of a Frenchman" he believed was one of two brothers who operated the ferry. A dog was sitting next to the corpse. "I can never forget the appealing look the murdered man's little dog gave me as he sat beside his master licking the clotted blood from his face." The bloody scene convinced Benedict to remain hidden. He crouched in the brush a few yards away and remained there even as his own family and neighbors rolled by in wagons. He thought Indians were behind every bend and decided it was smarter to stay out of sight, darting occasionally from cover only to continue his dangerous journey.[19]

*   *   *

19 Brown, *Cottonwood and Watonwon Counties*, 338; Neill, *History of the Minnesota Valley*, 806, 808.

The hit and miss nature of the outbreak is illustrated by the fates of the various families, where a handful of yards or a few minutes meant the difference between life and death. Indians killed Henry Kaertner (28), who lived near the road just west of Buerry. Kaertner's wife escaped to Fort Ridgely. On the bluff above and west of Kaertner's lived the widow Maria Bahlke Frohrip (65) and her brother Andrew Bahlke. Both were born in Germany, as were some of Maria's children, which made them special targets as hated "Dutchmen." When Dakotas entered the yard and shot the family's barking dog, Andrew ran out to scold them and they shot and killed him. The rest of the family bolted. Maria had five adult daughters, four of whom were there that day. Dorothea (28) and Frederica (21) were killed. Mary (31) was captured and later killed, as was son John Frohrip (22). Maria escaped with her youngest daughter Louisa (18) who worked at the Lower Agency, but not before the old woman caught a few loads of buckshot in the back and legs. Mother and daughter made it to Fort Ridgely.[20]

Traveling the road below the Frohrip place were the Hayden-Juni-Zimmerman wagons. They made it to the ferry area where Mary Hayden commented on the same touching sight Benedict Juni had seen: "We had gone about four miles, when we saw a man lying dead in the road, and his faithful dog watching by his side."[21]

The party drove on until they approached David Faribault's place. (Map E) The log house stood at the foot of the bluff known as Faribault Hill about two miles east of the ferry on the north bank where the road from Fort Ridgely ran off the prairie down to the bottomlands. David, born in 1815, was the son of Jean Baptiste Faribault and mixed-blood Pelagie Ainse. A brother of trader Alexander Faribault, he joined with Henry Sibley in 1844 to open a general merchandise outlet in St. Paul. The store's later manager was William Forbes, whose store at Redwood had just been sacked. David married a Dakota named Suzanne Weston and they had three children: David Jr., William, and Louis. Thereafter the couple separated. In 1851 David married Nancy McClure, the daughter of Lt. James McClure of the 1st U.S. Infantry and a Dakota woman named Winona. Nancy, born at Mendota in 1836, did not know her father, who

20 Curtiss-Wedge, *History of Renville County*, II, 1347-48; Tolzmann, ed., *Outbreak and Massacre*, 104. Maria did not survive long. She went to her daughter Wilhelmina's home in Blue Earth County and succumbed to her wounds in September.

21 Bryant and Murch, *Great Massacre*, 110.

was soon transferred to Florida and died there in 1838. Nancy lived with her mother and stepfather, Antoine Renville, at Lac qui Parle for about ten years, attending schools run by Dr. Thomas Williamson and Jonas Pettijohn. When her mother died in 1850 she moved with her grandmother to Traverse des Sioux. David Faribault Sr. met her there in 1851 and was smitten. "I was only about sixteen, and too young to marry," Nancy explained, but after getting the approval of Henry Sibley who testified that David was a good man and "a fine money-maker," she consented. David continued in the trading business, moving to Le Sueur, Faribault, and to Redwood Agency, but the money was never very good. "He trusted the Indians to a large amount," she admitted, "and they never paid him."[22]

David's largesse in dealing with the Dakotas was about to be tested. That morning he and his wife heard shooting from the direction of the agency. The gunfire that could not be heard at De Camp's house only a quarter mile away but directly below the bluffs was heard clearly at Faribault's. Nancy was at the door when Oliver Martell rode by with the warning. What she believed to be blood on his shirt may have convinced her of the truth of the alarm. The couple contemplated their limited options. They had a few horses in the stable but no wagons, so they were about to saddle the animals and ride away when an ox-drawn wagon lumbered down the road loaded with six men, three or four women, and several children "all in a great fright." The arrivals suggested hitching the horses to the oxen so the four beasts could pull faster. While the men hitched the teams Nancy ran inside where, "woman-like," she said, "I tried first to save my jewelry." The strong drawer was swollen tight, and as she struggled with it David urged her to go. Nancy grabbed her daughter (8) and ran outside where everyone else was in the wagon. She looked up the road and saw Indians approaching. "I was afraid they would overtake the wagon so I declined to get in." Nancy, David, and the child ran for the woods.

At the edge of the timber they met the mixed-bloods Louis P. Brisbois (47), wife Elizabeth (37), and children Antoine (10), Louis (8), and Margaret (6). Together they hid in the woods but the Dakotas found them. One of Indians called out loudly: "Oh, Faribault, if you are here, come out; we won't hurt you." Although David was armed, he decided it would be best to surrender. When they stepped out the warriors rushed toward Brisbois and his family. David demanded to know what was happening. "We have killed all the white people at the agency;" one of the Indians replied. "[W]e are not going to hurt you, for you have trusted us with goods, but we are going to kill these Brisbois." One of them struck Mrs. Brisbois in the face, saying that she had treated them badly. Nancy intervened and begged for their lives, to no avail. When she explained that she did not want to witness any killing and asked that they wait until she left, her request seemed to work; the Dakotas moved them all back to the house. At that moment two more wagons loaded with white refugees approached along the road. Excited, the warriors left their recent captives and ran toward the new prey.[23]

Once the Indians left Nancy herded the Brisbois family into her house and "put them out a back window." They ran through a cornfield and got away. The whites on the road were not so fortunate. The warriors stopped the wagons and shot down Mr. Zimmerman and his two boys in spite of the two guns and sword they carried to defend the women and children. According to Mary Hayden, she "sprang out of the wagon, and with my child, one year old, in my arms, ran into the bushes." She eventually found Nancy, who explained that "an Irish woman named Hayden came running up to the house crying out for me to save her." A young Dakota who had once worked for the Faribaults was chasing her. Nancy called out for him to spare the woman, and Mary made her escape through the brush and timber.

After killing several people, including the Juni's eldest daughter Anna Maria, the warriors took the remaining Junis and Zimmermans to Faribault's house and held them inside, taunting them with threats that they would be locked in and the house set afire. Three Dakotas ordered Nancy and David into one of the wagons to drive it with them back to the agency. They were heading west when Indians jumped another wagon of settlers heading in the opposite direction. Pat and John Hayden had left the Junis and Zimmermans because they did not believe the situation was that serious. Soon thereafter, however, something transpired that changed their minds. They joined the Eisenreichs who lived just down the road from Juni and continued together toward the fort with Pat Hayden no doubt hoping to catch up with his wife. Indians jumped them near the ferry and killed John Hayden. Closer to Faribault's they killed Pat Hayden, and then Balthasar Eisenreich. Mrs. Eisenreich and her children Peter,

23 "Story of Nancy McClure," 449-50, *MHSC*, Vol. 6; Nancy McClure Huggan letter, Microfilm Reel 2, Dakota Conflict, Minnesota Historical Society.

Sophie, Mary, and Joseph, were taken to Faribault's, where they joined the surviving Junis and Zimmermans.

Nancy Faribault saw dead bodies near the road as they drew near the ferry. One of them, a boy, appeared to be alive and a Dakota walked over to shoot him. "Just then," Nancy said, "a Dutchman rode up. One of the Indians said to the other to shoot him and take the horse." Once again Nancy pleaded with them to spare the man the Indians called "Big Nose." When she asked her husband to plead with them as well, "he seemed to be unable to speak a word." Nancy called to the German to get off his horse and run. When he did the warrior seemed to be satisfied with the horse and let the German escape. The Faribaults crossed at the ferry and moved up to the agency grounds where Nancy saw more bodies, specifically recalling one of La Bathe's clerks and Andrew Myrick.[24]

Edward Magner lived east of Faribault and just west of Kearn Horan (37), both on the Ridgely road where the village of Franklin would later grow. (Map G) Magner got the warning from Martell and sent his family to the fort. Like many others, however, Magner did not take the warning seriously and remained at his house to guard his cattle. The Indians killed him along with Patrick Kelly and David O'Conner. Patrick Horan was near the agency early that morning. When he heard shooting and shouting he rode back to his brother's house to warn him. Kearn Horan sent his wife Bridget (24), daughter Millie (3), and infant to the fort while he discussed with his brother Patrick, Thomas Smith, and Smith's son William what to do. Smith lived about five miles east near the mouth of Three Mile Creek, but was moving to a new claim at Birch Coulee. Smith left his wife Ellen (38), and children Millard (12), John (10), and Mary (5) back with the cattle near Christian Schlumberger's place on Three Mile Creek. When the men spotted people at Magner's, explained Kearn, "Thomas Smith went to them thinking they were white men, and I saw them kill him."

The reports were all too real, and the males turned to flee. Others with ox-drawn wagons came by and they joined them in the exodus. The Indians were gaining on them when one of the men dropped his gun in the excitement. When the pursuers ran to claim the dropped weapon, the whites took the opportunity to whip the oxen into a run and escape.

---

24 Bryant and Murch, *Great Massacre*, 110; Paulson, Franz Massopust, 21; "Story of Nancy McClure," 450-51, *MHSC*, Vol. 6; Nancy McClure Huggan letter, Microfilm Reel 2, Dakota Conflict, Minnesota Historical Society. Nancy did not mention seeing grass in Myrick's mouth.

The next house they passed belonged to Ole Sampson, who immigrated from Kvam, Norway. He was cutting hay about a quarter-mile from the house. His wife Anna (34) was standing in the doorway with her three children crying out for help. "We told her to go into the brush and hide, for we could not help her," said Kearn Horan. As the wagons pulled away the Horans ducked into a ravine. When Kearn spotted Sampson's dog he grew concerned it might bark and give away their location. Fortunately, the animal remained quiet because the Dakotas suddenly appeared along the opposite side of the ravine.

"Come out boys;" one of them, likely a mixed-blood, called out to them in plain English. "What are you afraid of? We don't want to hurt you." The warriors remained on the far side of the ravine for a few minutes before going back to the Sampson farm, where they found and killed Ole. The Sampsons had recently arrived from Waseca County and their big "prairie schooner" wagon was parked nearby. The Dakotas entered the house, took all they wanted, and, explained Ole's wife Anna, "went out and piled grain and hay sheaves around the house, set it on fire and left. I got out with the three children, but all were badly burned."

Anna hid with her injured kids in the covered wagon where they were discovered. "They took her babe from her, and, throwing it down upon the grass, put hay under the wagon, set fire to it, and went away," recalled Kearn, leaving the two older children inside the wagon. "My two little girls were burnt to death," said Anna. Somehow she managed to rescue the infant and they hid in the grass until dark before making their way to the fort.[25]

Young Benedict Juni had been dodging Indians from the ferry up to Faribault's house, which he reached about noon. There, he saw Indians on the premises who, he learned later, were "deciding the fate of my people." Benedict circled around the house, climbed the hill, and walked up the road leading to the Magner farm. He ran into two warriors who aimed their weapons at him.

"Where go?" one of them asked.

"Teepee tauke," Benedict answered, which meant "Big house," as the Indians called Fort Ridgely.

The Indian shook his head, grabbed Benedict, and turned him around. He was a prisoner.

25 Bryant and Murch, *Great Massacre*, 111-12; Curtiss-Wedge, *History of Renville County*, II, 1360-61, 1364; Tolzmann, ed., *Outbreak and Massacre*, 37-38, 104, 106; Dunn, "Sioux Massacre of '62," *Jackson Republic*, July 20, 1888. Ole Sampson is sometimes called Ole Sampson Quam, possibly a corrupted version of his hometown of Kvam.

Back down the hill the boy spotted young John Zimmerman laying in the grass. He looked like he was sleeping and Ben tried to rouse him only to discover he was dead. Gottfried's body was at the edge of the creek flowing down from the bluff near Faribault's. Mr. Zimmerman's body was on the west side. A warrior approached the corpse and smashed the skull with his rifle, just to make sure he was dead.

As they moved toward the ferry one of Benedict's captors used a whip on his bare legs to make him walk faster. The crossing was jammed with several ox wagons full of plunder waiting to get across. The Indians weren't having much luck because the oxen seemed afraid of them. Benedict stepped up and led the lead team off the landing and onto the boat. "Hocksheta washte" (Good boy) the Indians said, and they clapped for him. Benedict was going to be a useful captive.[26]

*   *   *

Somehow Dr. Philander Humphrey and his family avoided the Dakotas on their journey to the ferry. When John swam across and got them a boat it looked as if they might get away. Having had nothing to eat or drink, as the sun climbed higher in the sky the heat took a toll on Mrs. Humphrey and the children had trouble walking. Up Faribault Hill they climbed until they reached the Magner farm. When Susan Humphrey began to faint they went to the cabin. "Until then we had neither seen nor heard Indians," explained John, "and prospects for escaping seemed to brighten."

Philander found a pail, gave it to John, and told him to follow a footpath that likely led to a spring. The boy did as he was told and was halfway back with a full pail of water when he heard shots from the direction of the house. Deciding he could do nothing to help his family, John dropped the pail and ran into the ravine to hide. He waited there for more than an hour before deciding to move through the brush paralleling the road in an attempt to reach the fort. While doing so he stumbled across John Magner (Edward's brother) and Pvt. John L. Magill. Magill served in Company B, 5th Minnesota and was on furlough visiting the Magners when the uprising erupted. The three men crept away.

26 Brown, *Cottonwood and Watonwon Counties*, 338-40.

Unbeknownst to them, Mary Hayden and her baby were also hiding nearby. She had run from Faribault's and made it to Magner's. When she saw Indians throwing furniture out the door she carried her child into the thickets south of the road and hid there until sundown.[27]

27 Humphrey, "Boyhood Remembrances," 344-45, *MHSC*, Vol. 15; Hughes, et. al., *Welsh in Minnesota*, 69; Bryant and Murch, *Great Massacre*, 110.

C hapter 5

"O mother, they are all asleep."

Middle Creek

Middle Creek massacre ~ Wilhelmina Inefeldt ~ Michael Zitloff ~ Siegs, Hauffs, Thieles, and Meyers ~ Peter Bjorkman ~ Smith Creek massacre ~ Middle Creek ~ Emanuel Reyff ~ Justina Boelter ~ Minnie Busse ~ John Kochendorfer ~ Mannweiler and Lenz

T raveling up the Minnesota River from the Lower Agency required passing several streams flowing into the river from the north side. The first was Birch Coulee (La Croix Creek), followed by Beaver Creek, Smith Creek, Middle Creek, Timms Creek, and Sacred Heart Creek, although Smith Creek and Timms Creek had not yet received their current names. (Maps D, E) Homesteads were scattered along the river as well as on the prairie above. A significant number of families clustered around the streams, which gave rise to their common designations, such as the Beaver Creek, Middle Creek, and Sacred Heart Creek communities. The Dakotas rushed out of their villages closest to the Lower Agency and spread like ripples on a pond, breaking and eddying around settlement clusters before moving on. Generally, settlements farther from the epicenter were hit later, although small parties of warriors congregated around individual homes before the main killing began.

South of Middle Creek (near the stream now known as Smith Creek) lived the Meyer, Sieg, Inefeldt, Nelson, Mannweiler, Thiele, Schmidt, Hauff, Bjorkman, Zitloff, and Lettou families. (Map D) A few miles north of Smith Creek were the Middle Creek settlers, including Busse, Boelter, Roessler, Reyff, Lenz, Kochendorfer, and Schwandt. Many of them belonged to the German Evangelical Association and had moved there in 1859-60. Because there was no local church, preachers rode the circuit and met in one family's house to conduct services every several weeks. The Rev. Christian L. Seder was scheduled to arrive on Sunday, August 17, to hold services for some 100 men and women and 30 children between the two creeks at John Lettou's house. Sunday school superintendent Gottlieb Mannweiler organized the prayer meetings and classes. He closed the school just before Rev. Seder began services and handed the children blue cards with scriptures printed on them. He told the children that if they memorized the verse for the following Sunday they would all get new red cards. "We were all greatly pleased at this," recalled seven-year-old Wilhelmina (Minnie) Busse. Not everyone could fit inside the Lettou home, so the children and most of the men and boys remained outside. Louis Thiele and Mike Zitloff sat on a wagon tongue watching the children play. "None realized," another preacher commented, "that this would be the last service that some of them would ever attend on this earth."[1]

Wilhelmina Inefeldt and her husband William had moved south of Smith Creek from New Ulm in 1858, and Wilhelmina gave birth to a daughter named Bertha in early 1862. The Inefeldts lived south of Wilhelmina's father, John Zitloff, a widower, and his son Michael Zitloff, who married Mary Juni less than a year earlier. John had two daughters. One of them, Caroline, was married to John Meyer and had three children. The other daughter, born to his first wife, was also named Caroline and was married with three children to John Sieg.

On Monday morning, Wilhelmina, her brother Michael Zitloff, and Michael's wife's sister Lena Juni were taking an ox-wagon to the agency to trade butter and eggs for other groceries. They were near Beaver Creek when they spotted fire and smoke at the agency. Mixed-blood Thomas Robinson lived across the Minnesota River near the mouth of Redwood River, and they asked him whether the Indians had broken out.

"He replied 'no,'" Wilhelmina said, "the Indians were hungry," and that if the Dakotas "took our cattle to let them have them; they would not harm us." Robinson appeared nervous and they suspected that he was lying.[2] The group thanked him, but hesitated going forward. When they saw Indians riding some of Stephen Henderson's distinctive white horses, Michael concluded that the

---

1   Tolzmann, ed., *German Pioneer Accounts*, 32; Curtiss-Wedge, *History of Renville County*, II, 1276.

2   Tolzmann, ed., *German Pioneer Accounts*, 70; Thomas Robinson Depredation Claim #1217. The assurances given by Robinson differ from the warning given by Robertson. Robinson may have first sided with the Dakotas and passed incorrect information to the settlers, but when he was taken prisoner by them and his property, worth $133, was stolen, he later assisted the soldiers.

Indians must have broken out or they would not have Henderson's horses. Lena Juni climbed down off the wagon and proceeded to her folks downriver while Michael and Wilhelmina hurried back upstream. Somehow they would have to convince their families and closest neighbors that big trouble was brewing and they should all flee.

Back at the Zitloff's, Michael acted to warn the neighbors while the others loaded wagons. Wilhelmina left her baby with her sister, Mrs. Sieg, and ran home to tell her husband. They were discussing options when the first Indians appeared. William Inefeldt instructed his wife to run back to Sieg's, but to use a more concealed path through the woods while he remained behind to see what the Indians would do. She complied, but when William failed to show up later Wilhelmina ran back to find her husband. "I found him dead on the floor," she remembered, with a butcher knife in his heart, and "my furniture all thrown out of doors, my feather beds all ripped open and the feathers all scattered to the winds." Wilhelmina ran again, this time using the shorter prairie road.

She was back at her sister's home when a breathless Ernest Hauff arrived to spread the word that the Indians had just killed his wife. His two daughters were visiting with the Sieg's three children. Many people congregated there, but there was only one wagon with a hayrack attached. Twenty-one people climbed aboard: John Meyer with his wife Caroline and their three children; John Sieg and his wife Caroline and their three children; Ernest Hauff and his two daughters; Louis Thiele with his wife and child; Michael Zitloff and his wife Mary; John Zitloff; and Wilhelmina Inefeldt and her child.

Unfortunately, the settlements at Smith and Middle Creeks were right across the Minnesota River from the villages of Red Middle Voice and Little Six, two of the most bellicose chiefs. The settlers were gathering when Little Six and about 50 warriors swept in. Peter Bjorkman's place was close by. The 41-year-old was heading toward Meyer's when Little Six recognized him.

"There is Bjorkman;" he shouted. "Kill him!"

Bjorkman ran behind his house in an effort to keep out of the line of sight of the Dakotas, plunged into a slough, and eluded his pursuers. He remained there—wet, muddy, burned by the sun and engulfed by mosquitoes—until nightfall. From his vantage point Bjorkman could see the Meyer and Sieg cabins and an overcrowded wagon pulling away. He also witnessed the massacre of nearly an entire neighborhood.

The wagon only made it a short distance before Little Six and his warriors emerged from a cornfield and surrounded it. There were no negotiations. The Dakotas stepped out and began firing. John Sieg stood and called out,

"Everybody jump from the wagon and scatter and save your lives as well as you can!" Most were cut down quickly. Mr. Hauff grabbed his two daughters under his arms and made his way toward the bluffs. An Indian shot him in the back and several others kicked and stomped the girls to death.

Wilhelmina Inefeldt was running with Mary Zitloff. She couldn't stand leaving the others alone. "O, Mary," she cried, "let us go back and die where the rest are dying." They turned back. Almost immediately a warrior appeared in front of Wilhelmina and placed his gun to her breast. "The cap snapped and the gun did not go off," Wilhelmina said. "He tried three different caps. Each one snapped." The perplexed warrior put the gun down. Perhaps he concluded the white woman was spiritually protected. Instead of killing her he took her hand and said, "Washte" (good). The warrior had three Indian women guard her while he went back to Mary.

Wilhelmina called out, "What is he doing with you, Mary?"

She answered, "Nothing; he told me to sit down." It was the last Wilhelmina saw or heard from her. They killed Mary the next day.

The settlement was almost wiped out. Of the 21 people in the wagon, only Louis Thiele and John Meyer escaped, while Wilhelmina Inefeldt and her baby were taken prisoner.[3]

Brothers John and Michael Boelter and their families moved to Middle Creek from Germany in June 1862. They first settled in Wisconsin, and with the passage of the Homestead Act took land in Minnesota. On May 20, 1862, President Abraham Lincoln signed the act that was an extension of the Preemption Act of 1841. A person could now settle on up to 160 acres of public land and own the land by continuous residence of five years with only a payment of $34 on the Pacific Coast or $26 in other states. If he didn't want to wait five years for title he could buy it at $1.25 an acre, or simply "improve" at least one acre, which would commute all other fees. The Boelters were some of the first settlers to claim lands north of the Minnesota River under the Homestead Act.[4]

Another family new to the area hailed from Switzerland. The Reyffs first moved to Wisconsin before shifting to Forest City, Minnesota, for two years and finally arrived at Middle Creek in the spring of 1862. Eusebius Reyff Sr. and

3 Tolzmann, ed., *German Pioneer Accounts*, 70-72; Curtiss-Wedge, *History of Renville County*, II, 924-25; Tolzmann, ed., *Outbreak and Massacre*, 26-27.

4 Robbins, *Our Landed Heritage*, 206-07.

his wife Anna had 12 children before sailing to America in 1845, a trip Anna did not survive. The surviving Reyff children, all adults in 1862 and with 21 years separating the oldest from the youngest, lived in various parts of Wisconsin and Minnesota. Eusebius Jr. (42) built a cabin just west of the Boelters. He lived there with wife Margreth, and two children Benjamin (10) and Annie (8). The oldest son (18), also named Eusebius, was working on a farm near New Ulm, and two other girls, Mary and Emma, were working away from home.

Emanuel Reyff (21), Eusebius Sr's youngest son, lived with his eldest brother, Eusebius Jr., and worked rafting logs down the Minnesota River to the sawmill at New Ulm. On Monday, his boss told him the river was too low to float logs so he paid off his employees and they went home. Emanuel was walking into the pasture when he saw Indians running toward his house. Ten seconds earlier he would have been caught. The quick-thinking young man ducked into some nearby timber and climbed a tree covered in grape vines. His brother and young Benjamin were stacking hay when an Indian ran up and shot Eusebius Jr. in the jaw with an arrow. After he fell, wrote Emanuel, "the Indians grabbed him, cut off both his hands and scalped him before he was dead."

Ten-year-old Benjamin tried to run, "but there were about forty Indians and poor little Ben had no show." The Dakotas caught and carried him to the wagon, turned it over, raised the tongue, "and tied Ben's feet together with a rope and hung him to the wagon tongue by his heels. They then cut off his pants with a butcher knife and slashed up his body . . . then they poured powder over his body and set it on fire." Watching from his perch, Emanuel thanked God he had died quickly, although whether he suffered a quick death is open to some debate. "He was such a fat little fellow and they seemed to like the job."

Margreth came out of the house and begged for her and her daughter's lives. They staked her to the ground and mutilated her with knives and when she was dead, they scalped her. Annie screamed in terror when a pair of warriors grabbed her and "cut her to pieces with butcher knives on the doorstep."

From his tree, Emanuel aimed his revolver at the Indians twice but lowered the pistol each time without pulling the trigger. Even if he killed one or two of them they would inevitably catch and torture him as well. Once the massacre ended the Dakotas passed directly beneath Emmanuel's tree. If they kept to their direction they would reach the Kochendorfer place, so when Emanuel climbed down he headed instead for the Schmidt house.

William Schmidt (33), his wife Louisa (30), and their three children lived about one and one-half miles downriver. By the time Emmanuel got there the Indians had already done their work. He stepped over a dead dog on the doorstep and crept into the house only to find "one of the most horrible sights I ever witnessed in my life. Mrs. Schmidt's head was lying on the table with a knife and fork stuck in it," he recalled. "They had cut off one of her breasts and laid it on the table beside the head and put her baby nursing the other breast. The child was still alive."

A thoroughly sickened Emmanuel Reyff picked up the baby and ran from the house toward the brush along the Minnesota River. When he discovered more Indians walking along the bluffs he decided to swim the river and head toward New Ulm. Emmanuel left the Schmidt baby behind and he soon died. He failed to realize that five-year-old Minnie Schmidt although badly wounded, was still alive. Minnie recovered consciousness, wandered for some time in the woods, and finally sought refuge at the Busse's house.[5]

While Emanuel was in the tree watching the massacre at his brother's house, the Boelters just to the east also took note of the commotion. Justina Wendland (28) left Prussia and arrived in Wisconsin in 1856, where she married another Prussian named John Boelter (39). They arrived at Middle Creek in June 1862. They had three children: Emilia (5), Ottilie (3), and baby Julius. John's parents, Gottlieb Boelter and his wife, lived with them. John's brother, Michael Boelter (31), lived on the east side of Middle Creek with his wife, Justine Koberstein Boelter, and their three children.

That morning while at breakfast a Dakota woman appeared at Justina's kitchen for no apparent reason. She seemed very happy about something, but left just as abruptly as she had appeared. The Indian woman joined a few other Dakota women and a short time later Justina saw her carrying an ax. A curious Justina followed them some distance until she heard gunfire from the direction of the Reyff house. Justina ran back and told John, who left to round up his cattle in case there was trouble. John was gone when seven male and female Indians walked up to the house and asked Justina for water. While she was helping them, two Indians took John's gun down from the wall, checked to see if it was loaded, and replaced it. They left without incident and walked back toward Reyff's.

The Indians had just left when Michael Boelter ran up and reported, "the Indians are killing the whites." Earlier that morning Michael had joined Emil Grundmann and August Frass, who lived more than four miles upstream near

---

5   Bryant and Murch, *Great Massacre*, 324; Tolzmann, ed., *German Pioneer Accounts*, 62-63; Tolzmann, ed., *Outbreak and Massacre*, 31.

Sacred Heart Creek, in a trip to the Lower Agency for supplies. About 11:00 a.m. they discovered the bodies of a woman and two children on the river road near the Smith Creek settlements. The shocked trio hurried to the nearest house only to find more bodies. Unsure what was happening, they rushed back upriver. Michael Boelter left Frass and Grundmann, who continued on to Sacred Heart Creek. After he told his sister-in-law, he ran for the bottomland where his father was making hay. Not knowing what else to do, Justina walked home and put a loaf of bread in the stove, but she was too nervous to wait any longer and took her three children toward the Reyff farm. When a running Michael reappeared after his terrible discoveries, she recalled that he didn't speak a word. "I knew that something dreadful had taken place there." Michael took baby Julius from her as Justina told him to find her husband John. She looked toward the Reyff's and froze: "I saw the Indians killing Mrs. Reyff and the children. We heard Mrs. Reyff halloo; the cry was heard but a moment, when all was hushed!" By now there was no doubt what was taking place. Michael ran off with Julius. He probably concluded that Justina would follow with the other two children, but unable to keep up with him she changed course toward the timber on the river. Her brother-in-law was gone with her baby and, she later explained, "I never saw nor heard of my husband after he left."

Indians followed after Justina, but for reasons unknown they turned around and she safely reached the timber and concealed herself and the children all that day and through the night. While the children slept that night she heard Indians conversing as they often walked past her hiding place.[6]

Just north of Michael Boelter's house was the Gottfried Busse farm. (Map D) Gottfried and Wilhelmina Busse emigrated from Germany in 1858. After living in Wisconsin for two years they moved to Middle Creek in the spring of 1862. The family consisted of Gottfried (33), Wilhelmina (30), a son August (14), and five daughters named Wilhelmina (Minnie) (7), Augusta (5), Amelia (4), Caroline (3), and Bertha (3 months).

On August 18, Gottfried was working in his hay field about one mile from his home. Dinner was late and Gottfried arrived back home somewhat testy that it was not ready because he wanted to go to Yellow Medicine to put up hay for the government. August climbed on his roof to locate the family cattle that were often stampeded by Indians trying to steal them. From his high perch the teenager heard gunshots and screams from the nearby Roessler house. When he

6   Bryant and Murch, *Great Massacre*, 324-27; Tolzmann, ed., *Outbreak and Massacre*, 28.

reported this to his mother, she dismissed it as the Indians having target practice, but she did send August to the Roessler place to borrow some sewing needles. The notorious Mdewakanton, Cut Nose, had already been there.

Cut Nose and his followers had walked up in a friendly manner and offered his hand to John Roessler, who had stopped mowing to grind his scythe. When John reached out to shake his hand, Cut Nose plunged his knife into the man's breast. Roessler grabbed him and they fell to the ground. The men wrestled there, and Roessler nearly bit off Cut Nose's thumb before the Dakota worked his knife into a vital spot and finished the job. Now, in addition to having one of his nostrils missing, Cut Nose had lost nearly half a thumb. His face was painted black. When he smeared blood from his chewed thumb all over his body, he presented a truly frightening spectacle. Cut Nose's warriors also killed Frederick Roessler, who was likely John's brother, and dispatched the rest of the family. Roessler's body was later found with the scythe sticking in it.

August Busse arrived seeking his sewing needles, found part of the slaughtered family, and ran home crying out, "O mother, they are all asleep. Mrs. Roessler and the little boy," he said, "were lying on the floor and the boy's ear was bleeding. The big boy was lying in the clay pit and was all covered with clay." August didn't see John and Frederick Roessler's bodies.[7]

Mrs. Busse sized up the situation immediaely and set off to warn her husband. She instructed her children to meet with them on the south side of the cornfield. The children spotted the Indians heading for their house from Michael Boelter's, but the warriors did not notice them. The family successfully rendezvoused in the cornfield. Gottfried Busse began to act irrationally by grabbing baby Bertha and running across the open prairie. His wife tried to stop him, but was too late. Twenty Indians saw him and encircled the family. Gottfried pled with the Indians to take their possessions but let them live. One warrior replied that the Sioux were "cheche" (bad), and blasted Gottfried and Bertha with his double-barreled shotgun, killing them both. They murdered Mrs. Busse and her daughter Caroline next, and then daughter Augusta. Another warrior tried twice to shoot August but missed both times. Minnie later recalled that if an Indian shot twice at an enemy and failed to kill him, he

---

7 Tolzmann, ed., *German Pioneer Accounts*, 33; Anderson and Woolworth, *Through Dakota Eyes*, 77; Tolzmann, ed., *Outbreak and Massacre*, 28. Some histories say that John Boelter bit Cut Nose's thumb. This is a possibility, but John Boelter was looking for cattle that morning, not mowing.

allowed the person to live, for it was the will of the Great Spirit. Directive of the Great Spirit or not, the warriors took August, Amelia, and Minnie prisoner.

The marauding warriors took their captives to Michael Boelter's house. Minnie looked for the children she used to play with and saw their bodies outside between the house and the well. The oldest girl's face was shot away and a second girl was covered up with clothes. When August tried to remove them and look at her the Indians stopped him. Minnie saw the youngest daughter's body and believed someone had taken her by the feet and beaten her against a log, "for her dress was unfastened and her back was bare and was all black and blue." Minnie noticed Justine Boelter's flower garden. She had always envied it and wished she could pick the many pretty flowers. Now, everyone was dead and she could have all the flowers she wanted, but did not want them. By the doorstep Minnie discovered "Grandma Boelter on the floor with every joint of her body chopped to pieces." Of all the things she saw, that one haunted her dreams all winter, and said she "would cry in my sleep over it." Minnie was struck by the incongruity of the situation. "The birds were singing in the trees above them and the sun shown just as bright as ever. There was not a cloud in the sky. I have often wondered how there could be so much suffering on earth on such a perfect August day."[8]

The killing was not finished in the settlement. The Indians who Emanuel Reyff watched slaughter his brother's family made for the Kochendorfer farm. John Kochendorfer Sr. was in the field haying when he was called to the cabin for lunch. He had just gone inside when an Indian appeared and called for him. John Jr. (11) saw the Indian, who had a gun, take an ax off the porch and toss it into the brush. "I noticed that was something wrong," John Jr. later explained, and he called his father's attention to it. By this time other Indians were approaching. The elder Kochendorfer took a stand in front of the cabin, but none of them realized what was to happen, for "they had always shown the greatest kindness" to the Indians. A shot rang out and Kochendorfer fell backward. Still alive, he yelled for everyone to run. His wife Catherine was washing clothes. She didn't get far. The youngest child, Sarah, hid under the bed, but was soon found there and killed. John Jr. rushed his sisters, Rose (9), Katie (7), and Maggie (5), outside and into the woods. They covered about seven miles before stumbling across Michael Boelter, who was still carrying

8   Tolzmann, ed., *German Pioneer Accounts*, 34-36.

Justina's baby. A wagon overtook them and together the lucky few rode to Fort Ridgely.[9]

Southeast of the Busses and Boelters were the Mannweiler and Lenz homes. Only one week earlier, when refused some of the fish Ernest Lenz had caught, an Indian vowed to shoot Lenz with his own gun. It was one of the few wishes the angry Dakotas were unable to fulfill. As Minnie Busse and the other captives were being led away, she watched as another band of warriors headed toward Lenz and Mannweiler. Mrs. Caroline Mannweiler, a daughter of Ernest Lenz, had already recognized the seriousness of the situation and insisted they all leave as quickly as possible. She was at her father's house, and when she saw he was packed and ready, she and her sister Augusta Lenz hurried back to Augusta's house to make sure her husband, Gottlieb, was also ready to leave. They were just emerging from the woods when Indians shot Gottlieb out of the wagon. The women turned and ran back to the Lenz home. Augusta was captured, but Caroline made it in time to jump in the wagon as it pulled away. Mrs. Mannweiler and the Lenz family made it to Fort Ridgely. Minnie Busse later wondered if Mr. Mannweiler "would hold Sunday school in heaven and distribute the pretty red cards?"[10]

As Caroline Mannweiler and the Lenzs hurried east, they passed near the Lettou house. John Lettou had provided overnight accommodations to Reverend Seder, who had preached the day before and would be on his way back to New Ulm in the morning. When they heard word of the uprising they left with haste. Indians killed John Lettou and one child. Seder hopped into his buggy and tried to escape, but only got a quarter mile from the house before the warriors caught him. Dashing by in their wagon, Caroline Mannweiler saw Indians stop the buggy and shoot Seder out of it. She said she watched for five minutes until she was out of range, but Seder never moved from where he fell. The Indians destroyed his hymnals, stole his silver watch, horse, buggy, and other property totalling $235.[11]

9   Curtiss-Wedge, *History of Renville County*, II, 930-31.

10 Tolzmann, ed., *German Pioneer Accounts*, 36, 41; Tolzmann, ed., *Outbreak and Massacre*, 30-31, 105.

11 Curtiss-Wedge, *History of Renville County*, II, 1276; Louis Seder Depredation Claim #1085. John Lettou's last name is also spelled Lateau, Lettau, and Lettow.

Mrs. Ann Lettou (42) and four children ran off. The two oldest boys, 10 and 12 years of age, separated from their mother, who continued on with Augusta (5) and an infant.

Peter Bjorkman emerged from his hiding place in the mosquito-ridden slough that night and approached a house to gather scraps of food and clothing before heading toward the fort. Somewhere in the darkness he ran into Ann Lettou, who was nearly naked and without shoes or stockings. Bjorkman ripped up his his shirt and wrapped pieces around her feet so she could continue walking. He carried five-year-old Augusta and they moved on together.

When they reached Ridgely, Ann finally had something to smile about: her sons had arrived before her.[12]

12 Tolzmann, ed., *Outbreak and Massacre*, 30, 105; Stevens, *Minnesota and Its People*, 367.

C hapter 6

"Come across; everything is right over here."

Redwood Ferry

The garrison at Fort Ridgely on the morning of August 18 consisted of but two officers and 76 men. Two days earlier, Agent Galbraith and about 50 "Renville Rangers" left for Fort Snelling to enlist in the army, and Lieutenant Culver and six others went along as an escort. At 7:00 a.m. that Sunday, Lieutenant Sheehan headed back to his post at Fort Ripley with about 50 men of Company C, 5th Minnesota. Sheehan marched 22 miles due east on the old Government Road, camping at the junction of the road running north to New Auburn and Glencoe. On Monday he and his men turned north, putting more miles between themselves and the Dakotas just then enveloping Fort Ridgely.

Under normal circumstances Fort Ridgely's small garrison was more than adequate for the needs at hand. It was the fort itself that was the problem. Said to be "more fit for a county fair than for a fort," Ridgley sat on the north bank of the Minnesota River about one mile from the waterway. The loose square of buildings with a large gap to the south did not have an outer protective wall and so was wide open to assault from every side. Except from the west, wooded ravines offered an attacker a covered approach nearly all the way to the buildings. This arrangement was adequate during peace time, and it had been decades since Indians had assaulted any forts east of the Mississippi River. Most people assumed an enlightened Indian policy precluded warfare on such a drastic scale.[1]

* * *

The opening day of the uprising began as every other one had until just before 10:00 a.m., when frightened refugees began streaming into Ridgely. Sutler Benjamin H. Randall, whose store was across a ravine west of the fort, was in his buggy about two miles to the west when a wagon pulled by two jaded horses lumbered up with Joseph Dickinson and his family and a few of his boardinghouse employees aboard. When Dickinson sputtered out the alarming news of what was transpiring, Randall cracked his buggy whip and returned as fast as possible to the fort. Oliver Martell beat him there by a few minutes, but both men reported to Capt. John S. Marsh. Once he digested the startling news, the captain scribbled out an order and dispatched Cpl. James C. McLean of Company B to find and recall Lieutenant Sheehan and his 50 men from Company C, 5th Minnesota: "It is absolutely necessary that you should return with your command immediately to this post. The Indians are raising hell at the Lower Agency."

Marsh had the long roll sounded and the garrison mustered on the parade ground. About that time, Louis La Croix and his family arrived. Martell and La Croix mounted a pair of horses and rode back along the road to try and find out more about what was happening. Four miles from the Lower Agency they began discovering the corpses. Ed Magner, Thomas Smith, and one other man, possibly Kelly or O'Conner, had just been killed, recalled Martell, "for fresh blood was oozing from the wound in Magner's neck. So La Croix and I put back to the fort."[2]

Within thirty minutes of the warning, Captain Marsh selected 46 infantrymen and interpreter Peter Quinn to march to the agency. "I am sure we are going into great danger," Quinn confided to Sutler Randall. "I do not expect

1   Orlando McFall narrative, Microfilm Reel 2, Dakota Conflict, Minnesota Historical Society; Tolzmann, ed., *Outbreak and Massacre,* 62.

2   Morris, *Old Rail Fence Corners,* 231; *Minnesota in the Civil and Indian Wars,* II, 167, 178; Carley, *Dakota War of 1862,* 15; Oliver Martell story, Microfilm Reel 2, Dakota Conflict, Minnesota Historical Society. Gere reported the first refugees arrived about 10:00 a.m., but Cpl. John F. Bishop claimed they arrived about 8:30 a.m. The earlier time is doubtful because it was about a three-hour trip from the agency to the fort.

to return alive. Good bye; give my love to all." Marsh and Quinn mounted mules, while mule teams with extra ammunition and one day's rations followed behind. According to Lieutenant Gere, Marsh marched out with a cadence "as regular and exact as if it were a parade. I was left in command of the Fort with less than 25 effective men." About three miles out the wagons caught up to the infantry and they climbed aboard for a ride. More fleeing settlers appeared with tales of destruction and murder. Five miles from the fort Captain Marsh met Martell and La Croix on their return journey.

"How do things look up there?" Marsh asked.

"We went as far as Magner's place," Martell replied, "and found Ed Magner, Smith and another man dead and we could see fire at the agency." Martell admitted that he wasn't the one to give advice, but he warned, "I wouldn't go up there at all . . . you haven't enough men to do any good." Martell went on to describe the ferry: "On one side is willow brush as thick as they can grow and on the other side is an old field grown up to artichokes as high as a man's head. This is a splendid place for Indians to ambush, and whatever you do, don't try to cross the river there."

Marsh listened, but in the end discounted the advice and continued. He was later censured for pushing on. One of his men, 19-year-old Sgt. John F. Bishop, took a soldier's view of the decision and claimed that "no brave officer could have turned back and left those defenseless women and children between that band of Indians and ourselves." Bishop estimated more than 200 refugees passed them on the road. "An officer who would order his men back in the face of these facts would deserve to be shot without a trial, and dishonor would certainly have followed him," he concluded. Bishop claimed many of those who escaped would have been murdered because the Indians were forced to concentrate on the soldiers instead of the citizens. Had they retreated, the Indians would have followed them all to the fort and captured the place that night.[3]

Marsh and his command forged ahead past the Horan cabin and approached Magner's place, which by now was enveloped in flames. (Map G) John Magner, John Magill, and John Humphrey emerged from the brush, and told Marsh what they knew. Although he was on furlough, Magill joined his

---

3   Hubbard and Holcombe, *Minnesota in Three Centuries*, III, 316; Gere, "Uncle Sam's Army," Brown County Historical Society; Oliver Martell story, Microfilm Reel 2, Dakota Conflict, Minnesota Historical Society; *Minnesota in the Civil and Indian Wars*, II, 170.

company. Magner also came along, as did young Humphrey, figuring it was his chance to learn what happened to his family. It was also safer with the soldiers than on their own. In a few minutes they reached Magner's home. The younger Humphrey moved along the footpath with several soldiers and found his father's body. "A bullet had pierced the center of his forehead, and the fiends had cut his throat," he later wrote. His only weapon, an ax, lay a few feet away, which proved "that he went outside the cabin and met them like a brave man."

According to Sgt. Bishop, Dr. Humphrey was tomahawked on the doorstep and Mrs. Humphrey lay dead in the center of the room with an infant on her breast. John Humphrey had a different recollection. He claimed the burning cabin had collapsed into the cellar, taking "the mortal remains of my mother and brother and sister" with it. "How long I stood there, I do not know; the shock was so great that I became momentarily insensible to material surroundings and saw only in spirit the scene of death—truly I was alone with my dead."

By the time John snapped out of his reverie he was indeed alone. He ran back up the path to the road and caught up with the wagons, climbed aboard one of them, and sat on a provision barrel contemplating all that had transpired. His family was Christian and God-fearing, especially his saintly mother. "The atheist, the agnostic, or the nominal Christian, can give no reasonable explanation for the fate that befell this Christian woman, and indeed the entire family, excepting one," John later wrote, "and it would be equally impossible for such persons to give any sufficient reason why the eldest boy escaped with his life." For John, the explanation had to be that there was no God.[4]

Captain Marsh moved on to the top of Faribault Hill where the road descended from the bluffs to the bottomlands. Four dead civilians littered the slope. In and around the small creek at the bottom were four more bodies. To the surprise of many, two dozen women and children, many from the Juni, Eisenreich, and Zimmerman clans, poured out of the Faribault house. The Indians had rounded them up there, tormented them with threats of burning them alive, but left them for other prey. The women and children were afraid to move until they saw the soldiers, at which time they fled to the fort.

Marsh and his small column were approaching the ferry when the wagon containing the Dakotas' $71,000 in gold reached Fort Ridgely. Had it arrived

4 Humphrey, "Boyhood Remembrances," 339, 345-46, *MHSC*, Vol. 15; *Minnesota in the Civil and Indian Wars*, II, 167.

one day earlier, the captain and his men would, in all likelihood, not be marching to the agency under such dire circumstances.

What Marsh did not know was that the Indians were aware of his approach. The warriors chasing refugees toward the fort spotted Marsh and his men and prudently fell back. Word spread through the various bands about the approach of the soldiers and hundreds congregated at the ferry to set up an ambush. When the Campbells learned of the arrival of the soldiers, some family members made their way to the bluffs to watch. "We ran to the hill and saw a handful of glistening bayonets just passing David Faribault's house across the river," recalled Cecelia Campbell. Her mother was afraid that their arrival could upset the tentative respite. "What foolish soldiers," she exclaimed. "They'll all be killed. Come we must get away out of earshot; I don't want to hear a shot that kills them." Cecelia thought it was about two in the afternoon when they found a cart that had been left behind, packed it, and left on foot for Traveling Hail's village. They had covered perhaps two miles when the sound of small arms fire reached them. "Mother dropped as tho she was dead," Cecelia said, "with her baby Stella on her back, she had fainted."[5]

Marsh and his men moved beyond the Faribault place and the soldiers climbed out of the wagons and continued in single file toward the ferry. Two more bodies were discovered along the way. The troops advanced to Martell's house on the north bank of the landing. (Map F) The boat was on their side, apparently in readiness for them to cross. The soldiers offered various recollections of the time they reached the ferry. Some believed it was as early as noon and others as late as 1:30 p.m., but the latter time was more likely given the time it would have taken to reach the river after the first warning reached the fort.

Captain Marsh and Peter Quinn walked to the river's edge and saw White Dog on the far side. The presence of White Dog in this context is problematical. A man by that name warned Reverend Hinman that morning that he was going to Wabasha to try to stop the uprising. White Dog was also said to have been a peaceful farmer who had taught the Indians how to till the soil until he was replaced by Taopi when the Republicans came into office. Nevertheless, witnesses place White Dog at the river ferry and Marsh used an interpreter to speak with him.

5 *Minnesota in the Civil and Indian Wars*, II, 167; Anderson and Woolworth, *Through Dakota Eyes*, 51.

"Come across," White Dog beckoned. "Everything is right over here. We do not want to fight and there will be no trouble. Come over to the agency and we will hold a council."

"I don't know this Indian," Quinn told the captain. "He don't belong here." Sergeant Bishop told Marsh that he had seen the same Indian at Yellow Medicine and thought he was one of Standing Buffalo's people.

When Marsh asked White Dog what he was doing at Redwood, the Indian replied that he was "on a visit for a few days," and once again urged Marsh to cross the river and hold a council. He went on to say that there was some trouble with the traders, but the captain could fix it.[6]

Sergeant Bishop moved to the river to dip his cup in for a drink only to discover muddy water swirling with twigs and leaves drifting downstream. Bishop looked upstream to find out what was causing the disturbance, thought about it for a moment, and then turned to quietly inform Marsh, "I believe we are being surrounded by Indians crossing the river above us." In an effort to get a better handle on what was transpiring, Bishop climbed a small sand hill and looked across the river. In a shallow ravine he "saw a lot of ponies switching their tails in the bush." When he passed the information to Marsh, the captain directed Quinn to ask White Dog what the ponies were doing there. White Dog's reply was to raise his gun and fire.

"Look out!" Quinn shouted. They were his last words.

A volley blasted them from across the river and from the brush and high grass behind them on the same side. Quinn went down as about a dozen balls riddled his body, but Marsh and Bishop escaped the flying lead. Most of the men were facing the river as scores of warriors rushed them from behind, many firing double-barreled shotguns. "Steady men," Marsh called out as the soldiers moved up the bank to fire a return volley. Within a short time the Indians were upon them and a hand-to-hand fight broke out with every man, recalled Bishop, "fighting the best he knew how to cut his way out of the terrible looking mob around us. They were all painted and naked, except breech-clouts."

Sergeants Bishop and Trescott—the latter had bluffed the Indians at the warehouse during the Bread Raid—along with two other men, ran toward the ferry house. Trescott fell about 200 feet from the building and the other two

---

6 *Minnesota in the Civil and Indian Wars*, II, 167, 179; Anderson and Woolworth, *Through Dakota Eyes*, 93. Big Eagle conceded, "I do not know what the truth is about this." Big Eagle later heard that White Dog did not tell the soldiers to cross, but to go back.

were shot farther on. The place was full of Indians. Bishop cut between the house and a barn and headed into the brush. A musket ball splintered his rifle stock and cut his thigh, but he kept running. He would later participate in the Civil War battle at Nashville in late 1864, calling it "a quiet promenade for me in comparison to this dash."

A discharge from a warrior's shotgun right in front of Bishop tore up the sand at the soldier's feet. The two men stood facing each other, both trying to be the first to reload and fire. It was at this moment that Pvt. James Dunn arrived behind Bishop and killed the warrior. The two men ran down the road, but when more warriors blocked their path they cut south into the thicket. A dense tangle of willow and choking brush some 50 yards wide ran along the river south of the road and stretched east nearly to Faribault's. It turned out to be the soldiers' salvation. John Humphrey, who had been sitting in a wagon, jumped out and joined the fleeing men, trying "to keep in about the middle of them." Only a knot of about 15 soldiers succeeded in gaining the thicket and the Indians moved quickly to surround them, blasting the foliage with buckshot and ball. Marsh ordered his men to return fire, but the rate of gunfire slowed considerably as both sides sought to preserve their dwindling supply of ammunition. The soldiers moved slowly downstream with the Indians doing their best to match their movements.[7]

*   *   *

Joe Coursolle had crossed the river northwest of the ferry after the fruitless search for his daughters. Jane and their infant remained hidden in the woods. When he found them, she told Joe no one had come by while he was gone, "but there were many gun shots and much yelling down the river. I think there was a battle and the Indians won." Joe also heard the shooting and shouting. "If there was a battle and the Indians won," he concluded, "now is the time to go—while they are scalping the dead and celebrating their victory."[8]

*   *   *

7 *Minnesota in the Civil and Indian Wars*, II, 168-69, 179-80; Humphrey, "Boyhood Remembrances," 346, *MHSC*, Vol. 15.

8 Joseph Coursolle story, Microfilm Reel 1, Dakota Conflict, Minnesota Historical Society.

The fighting heard by the Coursolles continued in fitful fashion until about 4:00 p.m., when the soldiers reached the downstream edge of the thicket. Indians were already beyond them and the soldiers would have to cross open ground before reaching the wooded bluffs by Faribault's. Captain Marsh decided the only way to escape was to cross the Minnesota River, which was about 50 yards wide at that point.[9] Marsh held his sword and revolver above his head and waded into the water until about two-thirds of the way across, when he stepped into a hole and vanished. When he popped up and called for help, Pvts. John Brennan, James Dunn, and Stephen Van Buren swam after him. Brennan reached the struggling officer first. Marsh grabbed his shoulder for a moment, lost his grip, and sank beneath the water.

Once Marsh was gone, command devolved to Sergeant Bishop. In addition to Bishop there were three corporals and 11 privates, John Magner, and John Humphrey. Bishop was wounded and Pvt. Ole Svendson was shot severely enough that he had to be carried. They spent some time crouched under the riverbank figuring what to do and decided to make their way down the same side of the river rather than cross it. It was a lucky choice. When the Indians saw Marsh and the others in the water, they assumed all the men were crossing. Warriors congregated on the south side farther downstream and set up an ambush, but the soldiers never made an appearance. At dusk, Bishop and the surviving men were still some five miles from the fort. Bishop sent Pvts. Dunn and William B. Hutchinson in advance to get help. The men made it through and told Lieutenant Gere about the ambush and disaster that had befallen them. Gere sent out a rider with dispatches for the governor and to warn everyone he could find. He was anxious to locate Galbraith, Culver, and the recruits and get them back as soon as possible.

In the darkness Bishop and his soldiers stumbled across two women and an infant. Bishop never identified them, but recalled that one of them exclaimed, "Have I found help at last? Am I saved?" Somewhere along the march two soldiers dropped their rifles. John Humphrey found them and believed the men were either demoralized or had relaxed their vigilance. He picked up the weapons, figuring they would certainly be needed again. When the unarmed men saw him carrying their weapons, they took them back. Bishop and his

---

9   Almost all of the accounts at this time measure distances in rods (one rod = 5.5 yards, or 16.5 feet) and miles. Most of the distances have been converted into yards, a more familiar unit of measurement.

survivors reached the fort about ten that night. Mary Hayden, still holding her baby, was hiding in the woods near Magner's when she heard the fighting at the ferry and in the thicket. She waited until after dark and made her way to the fort, where she arrived about three hours later.[10]

Several others straggled in after Mary. Pvt. Thomas Parsley was in the thicket with three others who were all killed before dark. He escaped and reached the fort alone. Pvts. Ezekiel Rose and Ole Svendson were wounded. When Svendson could be carried no longer, he and Rose helped each other through the woods and made it back. Pvts. William H. Blodgett and William A. Sutherland were both shot but remained hidden until after dark. Sutherland, who took a ball through his right lung, crawled to the river in the darkness, climbed into a half-sunken skiff, and floated downriver. Caught in currents and eddies, he made only a dozen or so miles by Wednesday morning. Stuck on land, Sutherland crawled out but when he realized he was on the wrong bank he had to "swim" back across to the north side. He finally stumbled into the garrison about 9:00 a.m., just before Little Crow's forces surrounded the fort to make their first assault.

Private Blodgett was shot through the abdomen. He lay near the riverbank for a time while bullets splattered all around him, throwing sand into his face. When he found an opportunity, he crawled into the thicket and later to the ferryman's house, which was now vacant. When he left, he made his way through the brush and ran into Pvt. Edwin F. Cole. They traveled together until Cole took a left path and Blodgett turned right. When Indians appeared, Blodgett dropped under some morning glory vines to hide. He heard Cole cry out, and Indians laugh and call him a squaw. Then, recalled Blodgett, he "heard the most sickening sound imaginable. It was a blow with a tomahawk, and poor Cole was no more." Blodgett remained hidden in the brush until nightfall, when he began walking and crawling along the bank until he was too exhausted to go any farther. Even after he was somewhat refreshed in the morning he figured he could never get to the fort by crawling through the tangle of brush and traversing the rough ravines that cut across his path. He would have to go up by way of the trail, even if it increased the chances of his discovery.

It was night again by the time Blodgett reached Three Mile House (Map G), so named for its location on a creek of the same name and that distance from

10 *Minnesota in the Civil and Indian Wars*, II, 169-70, 180-81; Humphrey, "Boyhood Remembrances," 346-47, *MHSC*, Vol. 15; Bryant and Murch, *Great Massacre*, 110.

the fort. Blodgett snuck inside and found an old ham bone. He was gnawing on it when someone knocked on the door. Blodgett froze until a German-sounding voice asked if anyone was inside. A silhouette at the window appeared and the voice said, "We had better hurry to the Fort, as the Indians are coming."

The man at the window was John Fenske, a citizen of New Ulm who was at the stables at the Lower Agency when he was shot in the back with an arrow. Fenske threw a blanket over himself and got away. The arrowhead worked its way into his lung, and he began spitting up blood. Fenske spent the next couple days much as Blodgett did, crawling and dodging through the woods in an attempt to stay alive, all while seriously injured. Now the two joined together and assisted each other the last three miles to the fort, which they reached about 2:00 a.m. on Wednesday.[11]

The "battle" at Redwood Ferry is better described as a near-massacre. Marsh's expedition cost him about one-half of his command—24 men killed and five wounded—but his efforts very likely saved Fort Ridgely.

---

11 Tolzmann, ed., *Brown County*, 148-50; Wall, *Recollections of the Sioux Massacre*, 63-74. Blodgett and Fenske survived. Fenske's injury was written about in the *American Anthropologist* (1901). The three-inch barbed arrowhead penetrated between the third and fourth ribs to the left of his backbone. The doctor had to make a large incision to extract the head because its barbs wedged between the ribs and bent over each side. The head had penetrated the lung. Fenske left the hospital on September 30, 1862, 42 days after being wounded.

C hapter 7

"After we kill, then we will have dinner."

Milford Massacre

Milford massacre ~ Recruiting party

About the time the first white refugees reached Fort Ridgely, a party of recruiters seeking to enlist men in the U.S. Army left New Ulm and moved eight miles west for Milford, a settlement of about 100 mostly German residents. The recruiters intended to hold a rally at Anton Henle's inn, sometimes called the "Travelers Home." A small band marched along playing martial music and five teams and wagons rolled along. Henle's was the first stop. If similar efforts drummed up enough men to enlist in scores of little towns across Minnesota, maybe the hated draft would not be reinstated.

As the recruiters marched out of New Ulm, parties of Dakotas arrived on the western edge of Milford. They had slipped down the south bank of the Minnesota River paralleling the refugees on the north bank, but moved about twice as fast. Before 10:00 a.m. they were already at Milford, a dozen miles below Ridgely. The Massopust homes dotted the western edge of the settlement, almost on the border of the reservation. (Map L) Franz Massopust Jr. was one of the original "pathfinders" who selected the area for settlement. He was born in German Bohemia in 1828, one of ten children, six of whom eventually came to America. Franz married Ernestine Klingbeil in Traverse de Sioux in 1855, and by 1860 almost all of their relatives had joined them.[1]

---

1 Nix, *Sioux Uprising*, 87; Paulson, *Franz Massopust*, 2, 4, 7, 11.

On the morning of August 18, Franz Jr. (34), his wife Ernestine (26), sons Franz (6) and Rudolph (4), and daughter Augusta (2) lived on the north side of the road between New Ulm and Redwood Agency. One mile southwest of them lived Franz Massopust Sr. (60) and his children Mary Ann (28), Julia (18), and John (15). Two other sons, Joseph (25) and Wenzel (23), were employed but not living at home. Their mother Katherina had died the year before.

Indians arrived at Franz the elder's house between 9:30 and 10:00 a.m. It was time to pay back the hated Dutchmen who had taken their lands. Mary Ann and Julia were doing the dishes while Franz sat in his chair. One of the "Indians" in the party was Joseph Godfrey (Otakle or Many Kills). His story illustrates the complexities of the unfolding tragedy. Godfrey (27) was the son of a French-Canadian voyageur and a black woman, raised for a time by mixed-blood fur trader Alexis Bailley. In 1857 he married the daughter of Wakpaduta and lived with Wabasha's band. That same morning he had been making hay in the far southeast end of the reservation when a war-painted Indian told him that "all the white people had been killed at the agency," and he must choose a side.

It wasn't much of a choice. "I was afraid," Godfrey admitted, "because he held his gun as if he would kill me." The warrior said he must go home, take off his clothes, and put on a breech-clout. Godfrey obeyed, and while at home discussed with his wife and family what to do. They urged him to flee, and his father-in-law agreed. His wife's uncle, however, said that if they went toward the whites they would be killed. Others convinced Godfrey he must join the Indians. As they walked toward New Ulm, other warriors joined them and scolded Godfrey for not being painted and having no weapon. "They painted me," he explained. "I was afraid to refuse." They also gave him a hatchet and told him that "I must fight with the Indians, and do the same they did, or I would be killed."[2]

As the party of about 20 Dakotas approached Franz Sr.'s house, a pair of wagons rolled toward them along the road. Half the Indians went to the house while the other half waited for the wagons. Godfrey stood in the road until a warrior ordered him to go to the house. He ordered Godfrey to tell the whites that Chippewas were in the area and the Dakotas were hunting for them. He did as he was told. When the war party asked for water, one of the Massopust girls left to get some. The Dakotas followed her and entered the house. One of the

---

2 Paulson, *Franz Massopust*, 11-14; Heard, *Sioux War*, 191-93.

warriors pointed to a firearm on the wall and said to Godfrey, "Here is a gun for you." The Massopusts had no idea what was about to happen. When an Indian spotted food on the table, he joked, "After we kill, then we will have dinner."

Just seconds later several Indians opened fire without warning and Franz, Mary Ann, and Julia were mortally wounded. John, who was standing nearby, received a glancing blow from a tomahawk and ran upstairs. Among those who did the killing were Comes for Me (Mahoowayma) and Little Thunder (Wakinyanna), who were later convicted and hanged on Godfrey's testimony. The warriors were preparing to finish off John Massopust, but just then the two wagons hauling goods from New Ulm to the agencies rolled up near the house. The Indians ran outside to kill the teamsters and called Godfrey to help in the attack. John saw his chance and fled out the back door. On the way he passed his older sister Julia, who had crawled out on the porch. She begged him to take her along, but he could not. Half-crazed with fear, he ran off to the south. The house was on a slight hill, and because the Indians had moved north, they could not see John running away on the opposite slope.

Out on the road, meanwhile, the Indians set about killing the white teamsters. According to Godfrey, Great Spirit (Wakantanka) attacked one white man with his knife. "He cut his side open, and then cut him all to pieces," he later testified, which guaranteed a death sentence for the murderer as well. Godfrey's brother-in-law told him to get on and drive one of the captured wagons, and they turned them around and headed toward New Ulm. A few warriors went back in Massopust's house to look for John, who had run a short distance and tried to hide in a slough. When the Dakotas spotted him, John—his clothes soaked and heavy with water—ripped off his pants and ran for his life on a beeline toward Victor Zagrotzky's place more than one mile to the southeast. One of the warriors, perhaps angered because he could not find or catch John, cut off the head of one of the Massopust girls, snagged it on a fishhook, and hung it on a nail.

Now fully immersed in their killing routine, the Indians and wagons headed leisurely down the road in search of victims. "When we got near to a house," Godfrey recalled, "the Indians all got out and ran ahead of the wagons, and two or three went to each house, and in that way they killed all the people along the road." They weren't the only war parties in the neighborhood. Godfrey "could see them and hear them all around. I was standing in the wagon, and could see three, or four or five Indians at every house."[3]

Joseph and Caroline Stocker lived one-half mile north of Franz Massopust Sr. From his window, Joe watched as the Indians attacked the wagons. Joseph felt helpless because Caroline was bedridden. He could not carry her, and he couldn't leave her. His problem was compounded because he was also unarmed. There was little he could do other than lock the door and hope for the best. When the Indians found the door locked they smashed a window and climbed inside. When one of them pointed his gun at Caroline, Joe grabbed the barrel and tried to wrench it away. While they wrestled, Scarlet Leaf (Wapaduta), Godfrey's father-in-law, shot and killed her. Caroline had always been kind and fed the Indians whenever they came to her house. She may have believed they would spare her, but it was not to be.

Joe pushed away his adversary and ran to the trap door cellar in another room, where a frightened ten-year-old Cecelia Ochs had been helping them with the housekeeping. He pulled her by the arm down the steps and bolted the trap door above them as the Indians rummaged above them, plundering, and breaking items. They had no way of knowing whether Stocker had a gun, and so were reluctant to climb down after him. Instead, they set fire to the house. Once the structure was ablaze the warriors watched the south end where the only door and windows were located. Joe would have to come out or burn to death.

As the flames engulfed the upper floor, Stocker and Cecelia found some shingles and, using them as shovels, began digging on the north side of the dirt wall where the ground met the floor of the house. By this time smoke was beginning to seep into the cellar. The pair worked frantically until they poked a hole wide enough to allow air in. Before too long they enlarged it enough for them to squeeze through. Joe peered out and, when he determined no one was watching that side of the house, crawled out and pulled Cecelia through after him. Together, they ran for the wooded bluffs a short distance to the north.[4]

The next house along the bluffs and about one-half mile northeast of Joe Stocker's belonged to Franz Massopust Jr. The day before, Franz had borrowed a buggy to take his family to visit the Christian Kumm family south of New Ulm

---

3 Heard, *Sioux War*, 193-94; Bryant and Murch, *Great Massacre*, 141; Anderson and Woolworth, *Through Dakota Eyes*, 96n14; Paulson, *Franz Massopust*, 14-16.

4 Berghold, *Indians' Revenge*, 93; Tolzmann, ed., *Outbreak and Massacre*, 41; Tolzmann, ed., *Brown County*, 72-73.

(Map K), where Maria Klingbeil, Ernestine's mother, was living after her husband had died. When they returned home it was late Sunday evening. The Indians arrived on Monday morning, while Franz was returning the buggy. Ernestine was in the woods fetching the cow to milk, and had left the children in the yard with instructions to get the cow in the pen if it came home before she got back. When she heard gunfire, she figured it was someone shooting at blackbirds. Indians appeared and she engaged them in conversation. They were acting strangely, she remembered, and some had horses pulling travois. When Ernestine pressed them about what was wrong, they told her that Chippewas were after them.

Ernestine hurried home only to find six-year-old Franz dead in the yard. The Indians had already swept through the area. One of them slashed Augusta across the cheek with a knife and another clubbed four-year-old Rudolph in the head. "I knelt down but the Indian saw me and I can still hear the ting tingle as he tommyhawked me," he remembered. Rudolph concluded the Indians were afraid of his father. While constable of New Ulm, Franz had shot one of them for stealing and butchering a neighbor's cow. When a depredation claim was filed, the Indians had to pay for the animal out of their annuity money. Another time, Massopust fought with two inebriated Indians and was severely injured. One of them, Rudolph recalled, used to come to their house to visit.

The Indians may have thought Massopust was around, but did not stay long enough to find out. A stunned Ernestine went inside and found the bleeding and crying Rudolph and Augusta huddled together in a wooden cradle. After making sure they were safe, she carried Franz's body into the root cellar. While outside she heard more shooting and saw houses farther south on fire. Gathering Augusta in her arms and Rudolph by the hand, she walked quickly to Alois Palmer's house and ferry below the bluffs on the Minnesota River. (Map L) Ernestine removed her shoe and dipped it in the river so her children could drink. Rudolph recalled the sip "was the best drink of water he ever had." She waved to Palmer and Joseph Romer, who were working at the sawmill, and told them what happened. They had already heard rumors about an Indian outbreak, but Ernestine's story convinced them it was time to flee. Palmer and Romer left to warn settlers across the river in Nicollet County while Ernestine and the children made it to New Ulm.[5]

5   Paulson, *Franz Massopust*, 16-19.

The next houses along the road to the east belonged to Fink and Zeller. John Martin Fink's house was just south of the road. He and his family—Martin (67), his wife Monika (60), son Max (23), and grandson Carl Maerkle (2)—were wiped out. Max Zeller lived a quarter mile farther east. Max (39) was married to Lucretia (37), who was John Fink's daughter. Indians killed both plus their daughters Monica (10) and Cecelia (6), and sons Conrad (3) and Martin. Only their son John (16) escaped.[6]

Florian Hartman's place was a half mile north of the road opposite Zeller. Florian was working in the field binding wheat with a hired man, Swiss emigrant John Rohner (Rehner). Florian's wife Maria, sister of Anton Henle who ran the "Traveler's Home," was preparing dinner when she heard a commotion outside. She stepped outdoors only to find several houses on fire and people around them acting as if they were trying to save the buildings. A few seconds later, however, she heard the cry "Nippo!" (kill), and rifles firing. An Indian appeared close by, locked eyes with her, and ran off. Maria ran out into the field about 200 yards south near the road to alert her husband. Just across the road she saw Rohner on the ground and her first thought was that he was asleep. It was then that she saw the blood. She found her husband lying on the ground just 30 steps away from the Swiss helper's corpse.

"He motioned me to keep quiet and to drag him into the cornfield, because he was shot. Stricken with fear," Maria recalled. "I was powerless to do it." She sat down next to him, not knowing what to do. Two Indians approached Rohner's body and fired two more balls into him. Florian whispered to his wife that she could not help him and she should hide in the cornfield. Maria crawled into the corn, dug a hole with her hands, and hid there until evening. Warriors passed within yards of her, but did not see her.

About 8:00 p.m. Maria thought she heard someone crying, but was afraid to move from her hiding place. When it was fully dark she crept to her husband's side and "found him cold and stiff in death." She took some of his hair as a remembrance and ran into the woods below the bluffs, where she hid until the first gray light the next morning. Maria wanted to cross the river at Palmer's Ferry, but the boat was on the north shore and no one was around to operate it.

6 Berghold, *Indians' Revenge*, 93; Tolzmann, ed., *Brown County*, 75, 125. Marion Satterlee, in Tolzmann, ed., *Outbreak and Massacre*, 42, gives the Zellers the names Max, Lucretia, Pauline, Theresa, Max, and an infant.

She tried and failed to pull herself across with the rope. Maria Hartman's 17-day ordeal for survival was just beginning.[7]

East of Zeller's house and also on the south side of the road was where John Baptist Zettel lived. Indians killed the entire family: John (36), daughters Elizabeth (8) and Johanna (2), and sons Stephen (5) and Anton (4). John's wife Barbara Zettel (36), who was Lucretia Zeller's sister and the daughter of Martin Fink, was badly wounded and recovered by a rescue party later that same day. She lingered for two weeks before dying. Across the road to the north, the families of Casimer Hermann and Athanasius Henle saw the Indians performing their bloody work at the Zettels and burning buildings farther west. The families fled north to the river, the Henles on horseback warning Palmer and Romer just before Ernestine Massopust arrived with a similar alarm.

About one-half a mile east of the Henle home, just beyond where the road made a 90-degree turn from east-west to north-south, sat Johann Pelzel's cabin. (Map L) Johann lived there with his wife Brigitta. Indians killed them both. Their daughter Dora worked at Redwood Agency and escaped with Joseph Dickinson. When Christian Haag, who lived farther southeast, saw Fink's house burning he jumped on his horse to hurry over and help them extinguish the flames. The Dakotas met him in the road and shot him.[8]

One-half mile south of Max Zeller lived his brother Conrad. Nearly one mile to the south were the Spelbrinks, and farther south yet were the Zagrotzkys. The first notice that something was amiss was about 10:00 a.m., when Mrs. Spelbrink saw "a man with nothing but a shirt on" running as fast as he could west of the house toward the Zagrotzky cabin with Indians chasing after him. The "man" was John Massopust escaping from his house. Mrs. Spelbrink also saw a mounted Indian who "held like a statue all morning" watching from a nearby hill. Four more Indians hanging around Zagrotzky's house all morning "set up a terrible howl" when they left.

Mrs. Spelbrink was observing this strange behavior when Christopher Spelbrink and his son Christopher Jr. (13) were working the wheat in a rented ten-acre plot north of their house. Just south of them, Anton Messmer (61), his grandson Martin Henle (12), and an unidentified young girl worked another ten

---

7   Tolzmann, ed., *Brown County*, 83-84. Sometime during this episode, Rohner's wife Regina was also killed. See Dahlin, *Dakota Uprising Victims*, 132-33.

8   Dahlin, *Dakota Uprising Victims*, 48, 130, 132; Berghold, *Indians' Revenge*, 93-94; Tolzmann, ed., *Brown County*, 75.

acres. Before noon, the Spelbrinks were taking a load of wheat home and crossed paths with Messmer and Henle, who were hauling a load of barley home in the opposite direction.

"I guess this will be the last load," old man Messmer said. Chris Spelbrink later related that "he meant the last load before noon, but it was the last load of his life." Messmer headed for his home on the main road a little more than one mile northeast of Spelbrink's cabin. They crossed over a low ridge running northwest to southeast between the houses and the parties lost sight of each other. The Indians attacked Messmer, Henle, and the girl on the north side of the hill. The Spelbrinks had barely moved 50 yards south when young Chris heard two or three shots. He told his father, who was hard of hearing, but the old man said there were only "some drunken Indians about, wasting their powder." Father and son continued home and ate dinner. When Mrs. Spelbrink told them what she had seen during the morning, neither seemed unduly alarmed.[9]

About 2:00 p.m. that afternoon, the Spelbrinks left for another load of wheat. They had not gone far when Conrad Zeller, who lived on the low ridge north of them, ran up to tell them the Indians were killing everyone. He had just found Martin Henle lying on the ground. The boy showed signs of life, so Zeller picked him up and took him to his house. Still certain it was the work of a few drunken Indians, old man Spelbrink told his son Chris to "take your fork and come along!" They rode to Zeller's place and went inside only to find the family hiding in the cellar. Mr. Spelbrink saw a house burning and wanted to investigate, despite Zeller's warning that it was a bad idea.

Spelbrink and his son were moving northeast toward Zettel's house when a dozen mounted Indians left the road and galloped toward them. Young Chris saw them first and shouted to his father to get his attention. When Mr. Spelbrink realized the seriousness of the situation, he designed a plan to make it harder for the Indians to get them both. He instructed his son to stay put and watch, but if the Indians went after him to run into the slough or back to Zeller's cellar. He, meanwhile, was going to drive the wagon home to get his wife and the other children. Before they could execute the plan, however, Conrad Zeller and his family came up, climbed into Mr. Spelbrink's wagon, and they all drove away "as fast as an ox-team will go." Chris found Martin Henle at Zeller's. The boy moved his hand but did not respond when Chris spoke to

---

9   Tolzmann, ed., *Brown County*, 77.

him. Where the New Ulm-Redwood Agency road made a sharp north-south to east-west bend, Chris spotted several groups of Indians who looked as if they were discussing their options. While they talked, Chris "made for home in a three-mile-a-minute gait and reached home a little later than the ox-team."

While the Spelbrinks and Zellers hurried to pack a few things and make their escape, Victor Zagrotzky arrived. He had been to town, heard of the outbreak, and hurried home to secure his family. He arrived to find his windows smashed, his belongings strewn across the yard, and no one around to explain what had transpired. He was afraid to go inside, believing he would find his family butchered. What the frantic Zagrotzky did not know was that the trouserless John Massopust had already reached his home earlier, warned his family, and together they had all escaped to the south.

Zagrotzky joined the Spelbrinks and Zellers heading to New Ulm and met the Albrecht and Ochs families along the way. Halfway to New Ulm but overcome with anxiety about the fate of his family, Zagrotzky begged someone to go back with him to discover their whereabouts. Spelbrink and Conrad Zeller agreed to accompany him and, despite the protests of their families, the three men walked back to see what they could do.[10]

Anton Messmer, Martin Henle, and the unidentified girl, meanwhile, were taking their barley home, crossing the low ridge and turning east. Messmer's house was on the main road just east of the east-west to north-south bend and less than one mile east of Conrad Zeller's cabin. The Indians attacked them before they reached the road. Messmer was killed outright. A mounted warrior chased Henle, striking him numerous times with a tomahawk until he dropped unconscious. The warrior assumed he was dead and rode on. Zeller later found the boy and carried him to his house.

Maria Messmer (61) had no way of knowing what had just happened to her husband and grandson. One of her sons, Anton (24), was not at home but Joseph (26) was working in a nearby field. Maria's daughter Theresa Henle and her husband Anton lived about 100 yards to the west where, in addition to running a traveler's rest stop, they cultivated acreage. They had three children: Maria (4), Anton (8), and Martin, the latter already lying critically wounded less than one mile away. Anton was returning from New Ulm to continue the Union army enlistment drive. That morning about nine Theresa bid goodbye to an overnight guest she called "a Frenchman." He was on his way to the Redwood

10 Tolzmann, ed., *Brown County*, 78-79.

Agency with a load of freight. An hour later the man came speeding by in his wagon in the opposite direction without so much as a word. Theresa found his behavior most unusual because he never passed without offering a greeting. And what was his hurry?

About noon, Theresa walked over to her mother's to get some lettuce. She was walking back home when she noticed "three naked Indians." The sight startled her, and she turned around to warn her mother. She approached Maria, who was working in the garden, when an Indian appeared and shot Mrs. Messmer. "O Theresa!" she cried as she fell to the ground.

Terrified, Theresa fled toward her house in fear for her children's lives. The party of 20 warriors, with Joseph Godfrey still driving the wagon, had arrived near the eastern end of the Milford settlement. The Indians ordered Godfrey to stop while they ran toward the Henle and Messmer homes. According to Godfrey's testimony, Blows on Iron (Mazabomdu) knocked Maria and Anton down and stomped and kicked them. Godfrey averted his eyes and did not see what happened next, but he heard shots and believed Blows on Iron also killed Mrs. Messmer in her garden.

Theresa reached her home only to find Indians inside. She turned and fled into a creek behind the house that ran north into the Minnesota River, where she hid for a short while. Now she knew why the Frenchman had gone by in such haste. Mustering her courage, Theresa crept back toward the house to find her children. When she found too many Indians walking about, she crossed the creek bed to Benedict Drexler's home about 150 yards to the north. She crawled in through an open window only to discover that no one was there to help her. The Indians had just killed Benedict and cut off his head and carried it away. His wife Margaretha and their children Mary (9), Ursula (7), Matilda (6), and Crescentia (4) were hiding in the cornfield. The Indians shot at them but they escaped. A frantic Theresa Henle heard the shooting in the cornfield and ran back to see if she could reach her mother.[11]

Once the killing ended at Henle's and Messmer's, Blows on Iron and the Dakotas ordered Godfrey to drive east, where they caught Joseph Messmer in the field near the roadside. The warriors struck him down with a tomahawk and cut off one of his arms and one of his ears. They left him alive in terrible agony bleeding to death. The Dakotas, explained Godfrey, had discovered a jug of

---

11 Berghold, *Indians' Revenge*, 91-92; Tolzmann, ed., *Brown County*, 81; Dahlin, *Dakota Uprising Victims*, 45; Anderson and Woolworth, *Through Dakota Eyes*, 88.

whiskey in the wagon and had been drinking it for some time "and were now almost drunk." The next house they came to belonged to Adolph Schilling. Blows on Iron ordered Godfrey to get out of the wagon. When he did so, he was handed a hatchet and told to accompany Blows on Iron to the house. An old man lived there, and Blows on Iron had traded three guns to him for some flour. It was up to Godfrey to kill the people and get the guns back.

Schilling (59) and his family were from Mecklenberg, Germany. He and his wife, Christine, daughter Louise (21), son Joseph, and another unnamed man were eating dinner when the warriors arrived. The Indians shoved Godfrey in first. He struck "the old man on the shoulder with the flat of the hatchet, and then the Indians rushed in and commenced to shoot them." The occupants tried unsuccessfully to save themselves. Louise Schilling was killed and her brother Joseph stabbed by a small Indian with a face scarred by smallpox. Somehow he and his mother slipped out of the house and escaped into a cornfield. The unnamed man Godfrey struck also got outside but was shot and killed. Adolph Schilling made it as far as the road before he fell mortally wounded.[12]

The Dakotas were finishing their murderous work at the Schilling home when they caught sight of men and wagons coming up the road from New Ulm. One of the wagons had a flag flying above it. Thinking they might be soldiers, the Dakotas turned back. Less than one-half mile east of Henle's Inn a steep-banked ravine cut across the road from the south toward the Minnesota River to the north. (Map L) A small wooden bridge spanned the creek. The country to the south was open prairie, but the timber near the Minnesota River extended close to the road at this point, with numerous trees and shrubs growing along the creek and obscuring the bridge. The Dakotas told Godfrey to drive the wagon beyond the bridge while they got out and hid along the ravine in ambush.

*   *   *

The recruiting party, consisting of 25 men in five wagons with flag flying and music playing, had taken about two hours to amble along the road from New Ulm to Milford. The party was a mile from Henle's when someone in one

---

12 Anderson and Woolworth, *Through Dakota Eyes*, 88-89; Dahlin, *Dakota Uprising Victims*, 44-45.

of the rear wagons spotted something in the grass along the side of the road. Anton Henle, who had left home early that morning to go with the recruiting party, walked over and discovered it was his brother-in-law, Joe Messmer. According to John W. Young, Messmer was "lying on his face and groaning, apparently in great agony." The three rear wagons stopped to help and their occupants noticed several Indians far ahead. Some of the men loaded the wounded Messmer into a wagon while the last two wagons turned back to New Ulm. Ten men raced to the two lead wagons and climbed on. The first wagon was owned by Julius Fenske (28), whose younger brother John was already gravely wounded with an arrow in his back and hiding in the brush below Redwood Agency trying to reach Fort Ridgely. Julius was married to Ernestine and lived with her and their two children near New Ulm. The second team and wagon was owned by John Schneider. After a quick discussion the men decided to rush the Indians even though they were unarmed. "We drove with a dash and a shout," recalled John Young, "hoping to intimidate them, and drive them back."

Theresa Henle was watching the episode unfold from her hiding place in the woods. She had fled from Drexler's house in the hope of getting back to her mother, but that plan didn't work because there were still Indians milling around the Messmer house. Theresa hid again in the dry creek bed. To the east she "could hear the rattling of the wagons coming from New Ulm" as she watched "hardly five hundred steps from the place where the Indians were lying in ambush." She was in agony about her children and worried about her husband, who was with the approaching wagons. As she waited, the two family dogs found and sat next to her.

The recruiters' horse teams and wagons made a quarter-mile dash toward the Indians in the road, who dropped out of sight. When the wagons approached the bridge, the Dakotas popped up and fired. Fenske and Schneider reined in their horses and tried to turn the wagons while many of the riders hopped out, all in an effort to place the wagons between themselves and the Indians. "As we struck the ground," reported Young, "we heard Fenske scream, and he fell dead, pierced through with a ball." Ernst Dietrich (33), a cabinetmaker living in New Ulm with his wife Paulina and their four children, was sitting up front near Fenske when the warriors attacked. Dietrich was also shot and killed. In the second wagon, a bullet found and killed John Schneider, knocking him out of the wagon and onto the ground.[13]

The survivors ran as fast as they could back to the single remaining wagon, in which Anton Henle had finally placed his brother-in-law. A volley of shots rang out from the timber to their left. A load of buckshot hit John Haupt and tore out his left eye and punctured his left side and leg. Haupt staggered but kept running. Adolph Steimle was also badly wounded but made it to the last wagon. Once the men clambered aboard they whipped the horses to get away. Somewhere along the road they met up with a family fleeing on foot and took them aboard the overloaded wagon.

Just outside town the wagon load of people came upon one male and two female Dakotas who had been to New Ulm trading and buying goods. The Indians were oblivious to what had been occurring just a few miles away. Some of the settlers wanted vengeance and called out "Shoot him!" "Kill him!" "Take his gun!" John Young was acquainted with the male Dakota and approached him asking for his weapon. He refused to give it up. When Young spoke to all three in Dakota and explained what was happening, the Indians were as shocked as the whites had been. Without another word, all three turned and ran into the timber along the Minnesota River.[14]

Joe Godfrey, who witnessed the ambush of the wagons near the bridge, reported that at the first volley the men in the lead wagon flying the flag were either killed or jumped out and the horses continued across the bridge. The second wagon was abandoned and the Indians got it, too. Now they had four teams and wagons. The Dakotas, continued Godfrey, discussed what to do next and decided that it was getting late and they needed to look after their families they had sent walking to Redwood. One of the captured teams was frightened and difficult to control, so the Indians forced Godfrey to ride in that wagon. They turned around and drove back up the road past burning houses and scattered bodies, part of the destruction they and others had wrought.

When the Indians approached the Massopust property, where the carnage had first begun, Godfrey was told to guide the wagon close to the house. A few warriors walked around as if inspecting the damage. "I saw one [Massopust] girl

13 Anderson and Woolworth, *Through Dakota Eyes*, 89; Dahlin, *Dakota Uprising Victims*, 42-43; Tolzmann, ed., *Brown County*, 40, 81-82; Roos, "The Battles of New Ulm," Brown County Historical Society; Nix, *Sioux Uprising*, 87; Bryant and Murch, *Great Massacre*, 176-77.

14 Bryant and Murch, *Great Massacre*, 177-78.

with her head cut off; the head was gone," recalled Godfrey. Wazakoota, who Godfrey described as "a good old man," inquired as to who cut off the head and remarked that it was too bad it was done.

No one answered. "The girls' clothes were turned up," Godfrey continued, and Wazakoota got off the wagon to decently put the dresses back down. As they continued up the road, more parties of Dakota warriors joined them, no doubt satisfied with a good day's work and eager to head home for the night. They traveled about seven miles, close to where the road branched to the ferry near Fort Ridgely.

Perhaps their day was not yet over after all: coming toward them out of the west was another wagon.[15]

15 Anderson and Woolworth, *Through Dakota Eyes*, 89-90.

Chapter 8

"They will not kill me; they will shoot you and take me prisoner."

Murders on the New Ulm Road
and Cottonwood River

Mary Schwandt ~ Martha Williams ~ Joseph and Valencia Reynolds ~ John Nairn ~ Philander
Prescott ~ Alexander Hunter ~ Francois Patoile ~ Joseph Godfrey ~ Sarah Wakefield ~ Chaska
and Hapa ~ Attacks along the Cottonwood River ~ Roos rescue party

In the Minnesota River valley, about one-quarter mile west of
Kochendorfer's near the mouth of what would later be called Timm's
Creek, sat the home of Johann Schwandt. (Map D) Given its location between
the Middle Creek and Sacred Heart settlements, it was a little more isolated than
some of the other cabins. Schwandt, his wife Christina, and their five children
Karolina (19), Mary (14), August (10), Frederick (6), and Christian (4) moved
from Germany to Wisconsin in 1858, and to Minnesota in the spring of 1862.
Karolina recently married John Walz and the couple lived with the Schwandts,
as did hired man John Frass. John was the son of August Frass, who that
morning had ridden down the road to the Lower Agency with Grundmann and
Boelter.

Mary Schwandt recalled that there were few white neighbors and she often
felt lonely. Indians from Shakopee's village across the river visited the
homestead more often than did other settlers. "Their ways were so strange they
were disagreeable to me," she admitted. "They were always begging, but
otherwise well behaved. We treated them kindly, and tried the best we knew to
keep their good will." Karolina, however, "was much frightened" by them and

cried in terror and hid whenever they appeared. Mary thought it was a premonition.

A few weeks earlier LeGrand Davies was seeking a girl to work for Joseph B. Reynolds, who ran the government agricultural school at Shakopee's village as well as a traveler's rest. The school was south of the Minnesota River above the mouth of the Redwood River on the main road between the two agencies. Mary was so lonesome that she begged her mother to let her take the job. She had two companions at Reynolds's named Martha M. "Mattie" Williams (Reynolds's niece) and a hired girl named Mary Anderson (Maja Stina Andersdotter). Reynolds had two children. A hired man named William Landmeier and Davies also lived with them. Taking the job saved Mary Schwandt's life.

On the afternoon of August 18, Little Six's and Red Middle Voice's warriors approached the Schwandt cabin. After all the killings at Smith and Middle Creek, one might believe their rage had been sated, but such was not the case. Johann was on the roof making repairs when they shot him dead. The Indians tomahawked and slashed Christina to death. Her body was discovered in a nearby field but her head was never found. John Walz was shot three times and died on the doorstep. John Frass was also killed. Warriors tomahawked and beat 10-year-old August severely and left him for dead, but he watched as the Indians killed his two younger brothers. What they did to Karolina was nearly unspeakable: the warriors cut her open, took out her unborn child, and nailed it to a tree. Sickened and bloody, August crawled away and somehow reached the Busse home, where he found another charnel house of corpses and one person alive—little five-year-old Minnie Schmidt. August walked with, prodded, and carried the dazed girl three or four miles until he could take her no farther. He finally put her in an abandoned house and told her to wait there for help. August eventually reached the fort but Minnie was captured.[1]

Mary Schwandt escaped the fate of most of her family, but faced haunting trials of her own. She later remembered that the day began as a "red morning," for after the fog burned away in the bottoms scarlet shafts of light illuminated the valley and bluffs. An old German soldier's song came to mind: "O, morning red! O, morning red! You shine upon my early death!"

---

1 Schwandt, *Captivity of Mary Schwandt*, 5-8; Berghold, *Indians' Revenge*, 131, Bryant and Murch, *Great Massacre*, 300-01. Minnie was recovered, but died at Fort Ridgely.

Mary Schwandt and Mary Anderson were doing the laundry that morning at Reynolds'. Francois Patoile (usually pronounced "Patwell" by the English speakers), a licensed trader at Yellow Medicine Agency, stopped by for breakfast. It was mixed-blood Antoine La Blaugh (sent by another mixed-blood named John Moore who lived at Shakopee's village) who delivered the horrifying news that the Indians were on the warpath and intended to kill all the whites. La Blaugh told them the Lower Agency and Beaver Creek settlement had already been attacked and that everyone must flee.

Joseph Reynolds, described by Lieutenant Gere as "a fine old fellow, with a tremendous belly," took the warning seriously and he and his wife Valencia and their two children prepared to leave. To Valencia's surprise, several Indian women were already ransacking her kitchen. One of them told her, "Your face is so white you had better put some water on it." Valencia grabbed a few things and climbed into a buggy. Hired man William Landmeier decided to go off on his own rather than ride in the buggy, and eventually reached the fort. The Reynolds crossed Redwood River and headed southeast, avoiding the road and bypassing south of the agency. East of the agency, as they angled back toward the main road, they ran into an old Indian who asked Joseph to write him a paper saying he was a good Indian and wanted nothing to do with the killings.[2]

The Reynolds family continued along the road to New Ulm. They began spotting refugees about eight miles east of the agency: John Nairn, his wife Magdalene, and their four children, and Alexander Hunter and his wife. Valencia Reynolds saw a girl she later identified as Maria Frohrip.[3] Nairn flagged them down and asked if Joe Reynolds would take their oldest children, Cecilia and James, in his buggy. They could not walk any farther, but John and Magdalene could carry the three-year-old and the baby. Reynolds agreed.

*   *   *

The Nairns and Hunters continued walking along the road until John and his wife decided to head for the fort about five miles away. And so they parted with the Hunters and went off on their own. When they reached the river Nairn

2 Schwandt, *Captivity of Mary Schwandt*, 10-11; Josephine Patoile Depredation Claim #836; Gere, "Uncle Sam's Army," Brown County Historical Society; Bryant and Murch, *Great Massacre*, 404-06.

3 Bryant and Murch, *Great Massacre*, 407. This may have been Louisa Frohrip, who worked at the Lower Agency, but she is also said to have escaped her house with her mother Maria.

spotted a boat on the opposite shore, swam across, brought it back, and rowed his family across. They were nearly at the fort when they had second thoughts about sending off their two children in the buggy. John swam across and scaled the bluffs, but when he discovered Indians between him and the road he backtracked and together with his wife finished their journey to Fort Ridgely. With nothing to do but wait, the Nairns did just that, wondering all the while whether they had made the right decision.[4]

Old Philander Prescott ran into the same Indians Nairn had spotted. Philander had left his mixed-blood wife and child at the agency, where they were captured but not harmed. He was trying to reach Fort Ridgely when a handful of warriors found him. They knew he was the interpreter with a Dakota family, but to them it made no difference.

"I am an old man;" Philander pleaded. "I have lived with you now forty-five years, almost half a century. My wife and children are among you, of your own blood; I have never done you any harm, and have been your true friend in all your troubles; why should you wish to kill me?"

They replied that they would save him if they could, but their orders were "to kill all white men; we cannot spare you." With that, two Dakotas shot and killed him.[5]

In the same area, Alexander Hunter and his wife Marion were making their way to the river. It was a long and slow journey. Years earlier, Alexander had frozen his feet and lost some toes, so he was somewhat lame. An Indian discovered the couple and urged them to come with him, promising to aid them in their escape. The Hunters were not far from Hushasha's village, where the Indians were much friendlier than some of the other bands. (Map G) Once at the village, however, their unnamed savior would not or could not help them, and the couple had not choice but to slip away on their own and hide in the woods that night. With the Tuesday sun Alexander and Marion started for Fort Ridgely. Another warrior, Walks Clothed with an Owl's Tail, discovered them

---

4   John Nairn recollection, Microfilm Reel 3, Dakota Conflict, Minnesota Historical Society.

5   Curtiss-Wedge, *History of Redwood County*, I, 138-39; Folwell, *History of Minnesota*, II, 446. During the subsequent military tribunals held after the uprising had been extinguished, a witness claimed to have heard Medicine Bottle admit that "he and one other Indian shot at him." That allegation, along with other charges of killing whites, was enough to hang Medicine Bottle.

and, without speaking a word, walked up to Alexander and shot him dead. He took Marion Robertson Hunter captive.[6]

After leaving Joe Nairn, Joe Reynolds drove his buggy to a point opposite Fort Ridgely, wavered in his decision as to where to go, and then continued on toward New Ulm. Although they passed a number of Indians, none of the Dakotas molested the family. When they drew near Milford, however, which was undergoing a brutal attack, they ran into about 60 Indians plus some cattle and wagons. As was often the case, determining who was a friend and who was a foe was difficult. One warrior approached the buggy, aimed his double-barreled shotgun at Joseph, "and snapped both caps, but they failed to ignite the powder." The warrior was trying to fix his weapon when another Indian rode up on a white horse and called out, "Puckachee!" (go far away) and urged Joseph to turn the buggy around and make for the agency as fast as possible. Joseph wasted little time and within a few seconds the buggy was racing away with their protector riding alongside them, placing his body between the buggy and other Indians raising their weapons to try and kill them. Cecelia Nairn was riding in the back of the buggy when a mounted warrior closed in and pointed his gun at her. "Let me get in front," she screamed. "He'll shoot me first!" A terrified little James sat almost motionless repeating "Oh dear!" over and over.

The buggy pulled slightly ahead, but after nearly a three-mile run the horse was exhausted. Joseph and Valencia climbed out and urged the animal to continue at a walk off the trail and through head-high grass. In that manner they moved down the bluff to the river, where Joseph unharnessed the horse, climbed on his back, and swam toward the far shore. Horse and rider went under water for a moment, but popped back up and reached the far bank safely. Valencia and the children hid in the willows and listened as Indians searched for them.

At the fort, meanwhile, John Nairn still questioned whether sending his children with the Reynolds' family was the right decision. He was about to leave a second time to search for them when Reynolds arrived on horseback about 3:00 p.m. The men found a wagon and a party of soldiers and hurried back to

---

6 Curtiss-Wedge, *History of Redwood County*, I, 138; John Nairn recollection, Microfilm Reel 3, Dakota Conflict, Minnesota Historical Society. Walks Clothed with an Owl's Tail was convicted of murdering Hunter. Missionary Stephen Riggs (Riggs, *Mary and I*, 124) says it was Andrew Hunter who was badly frozen and maimed in December 1852.

the river where, with the help of a small boat they ferried Valencia and the children across. "I drove into the fort a happy man," admitted Nairn.[7]

* * *

Francois Patoile left Redwood River that morning slightly behind the Reynolds family. The trader had agreed to take Reynolds' employees in his wagon. Mary Schwandt, Mary Anderson, and Mattie Williams climbed in, but only Mattie brought along many belongings, including a feather bed and a trunk full of possessions. LeGrand Davies also climbed aboard, while Antoine La Blaugh rode alongside. The party headed east following Reynolds and was swinging south around the agency when a mounted Indian rode up and ordered Patoile to turn around. He refused and continued on. Smoke coming from the agency added another sense of urgency to the journey but the horses were getting winded and Patoile had no choice but to slow down.

In mid-afternoon, mounted Indians approached and shot several arrows from long distance. A few hit the wagon and the girls collected them as souvenirs. When they reached the Minnesota River opposite Fort Ridgely, Patoile concluded they could not get across safely and continued on toward New Ulm. The occupants occasionally climbed out of the wagon and walked to lighten the load for the horses. Seven or eight miles from Milford some 50 warriors approached, some of them mounted, some on foot, and some in wagons loaded with plunder—including the wagon driven by Joseph Godfrey. Reynolds turned the wagon in an attempt to escape, but the refugees were surrounded almost immediately.

"We are lost," LeGrand Davies informed Patoile just before several rifle balls crashed into the driver and knocked him backward over the seat. Davies and the girls jumped from the wagon and ran toward high grass near a slough. Davies didn't get far and was the next to die. La Blaugh took off in another direction about the same time, but the Indians caught and killed him. Indians threw Patoile out of his wagon and a young warrior stuck a knife in his ribs while another smashed his head with a rifle. Joseph Godfrey and a few Indians, meanwhile, jumped out of their wagon and ran after the women. Lead balls

---

7 Bryant and Murch, *Great Massacre*, 408-10; John Nairn recollection, Microfilm Reel 3, Dakota Conflict, Minnesota Historical Society. James Nairn's health deteriorated with an undiagnosed malady and he died in Iowa in October 1862. Before he died, he told his mother that he heard constant "Indian drumming" in his head.

snapped through the folds of Mary Schwandt's dress, but Mary Anderson was not as fortunate. One of the Dakota rounds struck her in the back and lodged in her abdomen. Blows on Iron caught Mary Schwandt and Old Buffalo (Tazoo) seized Mattie Williams. The wounded Mary Anderson was thrown roughly into the back of a wagon with Mattie and her trunk, which held items worth about $225.

Mary Schwandt, who was forced into Godfrey's plunder-filled wagon, had a very different view of his participation in the uprising than the one Godfrey portrayed at his trial. Instead of being an unwilling participant, Mary believed he enthusiastically took part in the robbing and killing spree. She later testified that she heard him boast of killing seven whites. His Indian name was Otakle, or Many Kills. The "old villain," as Mary called him, was wearing a number of stolen watches around his wrist. When she asked him what they were going to do with her, Godfrey replied that he didn't know, but they were going to look for their women, whom they had left behind while destroying the settlement at Milford. When the Indian women were located, they ran joyfully to the wagons to get their shares of the plunder.

"What time is it?" Mary asked Godfrey.

He looked at one of the watches and answered, "It is 4 o'clock."

The war party and captives headed back to the Lower Agency.[8]

*   *   *

There were also a few other refugees on the road coming down from the Upper Agency. Those farther removed from the outbreak's epicenter at the Lower Agency did not feel the murderous shockwaves for some time. By noon, rumors circulated at Yellow Medicine that something was going on at Redwood. (Map C) Around dinner time, agency physician John L. Wakefield was concerned enough to arrange to send his wife Sarah to Fort Ridgely.

Sarah Brown and her husband John Lumen Wakefield were born on the east coast, Sarah in 1829 in Kingstown, Rhode Island, and John six years earlier in Winsted, Connecticut. John graduated from Yale medical school in 1847 and in April of 1854 established a medical practice in Shakopee, Minnesota. They

---

8   Martha Williams Depredation Claim #165; Schwandt, *Captivity of Mary Schwandt*, 12-15; Anderson and Woolworth, *Through Dakota Eyes*, 90; Tolzmann, ed., *German Pioneer Accounts*, 84n6. Antoine La Blaugh's wife and two children were captured at the Lower Agency. Tazoo was later convicted of raping Mattie Williams and was hanged at Mankato.

married two years later. In June of 1858, Dr. Wakefield treated many Dakotas for wounds suffered while fighting Chippewas. Sarah's first child, James Orin, was born that same year and their second child, Lucy Elizabeth (Nellie), arrived in 1860. The following summer, June 1861, Dr. Wakefield was appointed the physician for the Upper Agency.[9]

Dr. Wakefield sent his family away once before to the Lower Agency to stay with Reverend Hinman during the Bread Raid troubles just two weeks earlier. This time he suggested that Sarah and the children visit his mother-in-law back east. Sensing the urgency of the situation, he decided not to wait for the stagecoach, but how then would he get them out of harm's way? His dilemma was solved by a storekeeper at the Lower Agency warehouse named George Gleason. The merchant had been visiting the area but had no return transportation, so he agreed to take Sarah, James, and Lucy to Fort Ridgley if the doctor would lend him his horses and wagon to do so.[10]

Gleason and the Wakefield family left about 3:00 p.m. Stewart Garvie, manager of Nathan Myrick's store, flagged them down to report that he had heard Indians had killed some settlers up in the Big Woods and were now discussing what to do next. Sarah asked Gleason to return her and the kids to their home but Gleason refused; her husband wanted her and the children at Fort Ridgely and he intended to deliver them there. When she inquired whether he carried a pistol, he confirmed that he did. Halfway to the Lower Agency they saw smoke rising in the distance. Sarah became frantic, began to cry, and tried to jump from the wagon. Gleason scolded her, adding that she was being very unpleasant.

"Very well," Sarah shot back, "go on; they will not kill me; they will shoot you and take me prisoner."

"Why, who are you talking about?" asked Gleason. "The lower Indians are just like white men; you must not act so hysterical."

They drove on until they approached Joseph Reynolds' house. "It is now a quarter past six," Gleason announced. "We will eat supper at Old Joe's, and at eight o'clock we will be at Fort Ridgely." He was barely done speaking when

---

9   Wakefield, *Six Weeks in the Sioux Tepees*, 25-26, 43-44.

10 John F. Meagher indicates Gleason was one of Agent Galbraith's clerks and worked at both agencies. He indicates that Gleason left the Upper Agency in the company of George Spencer, although Spencer was already at Redwood early that morning. John F. Meagher letter, Microfilm Reel 1, Dakota Conflict, Minnesota Historical Society.

two Indians named Hapa and Chaska approached the wagon. Worried, Sarah begged Gleason to draw his gun, but he refused and instructed her to remain quiet. After exchanging a few words Gleason tried to drive off, but Hapa lifted his gun and fired, hitting Gleason in the shoulder and knocking him into Sarah's lap in the back seat. The warrior fired a second time and Gleason fell from the wagon to the road.

Chaska, who had not fired a shot, recognized Sarah and asked her whether she was the doctor's wife. When she confirmed that she was, the Dakota warned her to say nothing because Hapa was a bad man and "has too much whiskey." Sarah spoke out despite Chaska's warning, begging to be spared and offering to sew, wash, and cook for them. Before either Indian could reply the wounded Gleason moaned, "Oh, my God, Mrs. Wakefield!" Hapa shot him a third time and finally killed him. When Hapa lifted the barrel and waved his gun in Sarah's face, Chaska knocked it away and the two men began to argue.

According to Sarah, Hapa said, "She must die; all whites are bad, better be dead." Hapa believed Sarah was really Henrietta, Agent Galbraith's wife, and that if he could do so, "he would . . . cut her in pieces on her husband's account." Doctor Wakefield, however, had treated the Dakotas and Chaska felt a deep obligation to save his wife. After some discussion Hapa finally agreed to spare Sarah, but declared the children must die for they would be trouble. "No!" Chaska said, "I am going to take care of them; you must kill me before you can any of them." With that, Hapa finally relented.

The two warriors and the Wakefields traveled a few miles to an Indian camp numbering some 200 people. Many of them, Sarah realized, were the same ones who had camped during the winter around Shakopee. Some had visited her home, where she had always fed them. They recognized her, too. "They promised me life," she recalled, "but I dared not hope, and felt as if death was staring me in the face."[11]

* * *

While Schwandt, Williams, Anderson, and Wakefield were being captured along the road to New Ulm, other Dakota war parties were fanning out in the Milford area and south along the Cottonwood River. When word of the outbreak spread to settlers living along the Cottonwood, from New Ulm to the

11 Wakefield, *Six Weeks In The Sioux Tepees*, 63, 66-69.

Leavenworth settlement twelve miles southwest of Milford, they reacted in much the same way: some fled immediately, some took a wait-and-see approach, and others dismissed the warnings as alarmist nonsense.

Joseph Emmerich and Henry Heyers (Heuyers) left their families behind to drive to New Ulm to learn what was happening. During Heyers' absence Dakotas attacked his house and killed his wife Dorothea and their sons Carl, John, and Joachim. Heyers never knew his family's fate. He and Emmerich stopped at Sebastian May's house about the same time a Dakota war party swept in (Map K), killed them both, and stole their ox-team. Sebastian May (30), his wife, Barbara (28), son, Henry (4), and infant Bertha were also slaughtered. Somehow their other children, Anne Mary (7) and three-year-old twins Magdalena and Friederich, were wounded but survived.

The house farthest west in Brown County probably belonged to Joseph L. Brown. A Massachusetts native, Brown (73), with his son Jonathan (37) and daughter Oratia (36), worked a farm and ran a rest stop much like Anton Henle. Their place was on the road not quite halfway from New Ulm to Lake Shetek, about three miles east of present-day Springfield. (Map J) The Browns left for New Ulm sometime after hearing word of the Dakota uprising. They made it five miles before the Dakotas caught and killed them all within a space of 100 yards. Their corpses were found on August 21 when fleeing refugees "Dutch Charlie" Zierke and his wife, who also kept a traveler's rest about 25 miles beyond Brown's place, found them along with one other unidentified man. Oratia, one of the witnesses reported, "had been killed with exceptional brutality."[12]

Eli C. Brown moved to Leavenworth Township in 1860 and lived about five miles down the Cottonwood from Joe Brown. Eli got away.

Hiram A. Buck and his wife Louesa lived two miles farther downriver. The Bucks had been renting a house on John Jackson's property since 1861, sharecropping and splitting the profits equally with the landowner. The Bucks fled on Monday night and camped on the prairie only two miles away. By Tuesday morning they convinced themselves their exit had been too hasty and went back to retrieve their cattle. As it turned out, their timing had been perfect: Indians were already milling about their property shooting guns. The couple

---

12 Dahlin, *Dakota Uprising Victims*, 51, 63, 145-46n158; Tolzmann, ed., *Outbreak and Massacre*, 41-42, 44; Tolzmann, ed., *Brown County*, 125; Hughes, et. al., *Welsh in Minnesota*, 102. Brown's house was in section 22, Burnstown Township.

changed their plans again and headed east past Bernard Kelly's empty house and made it to New Ulm.[13]

The Martin Bluem family left Bavaria for America in the mid-1850s and had a home near the Cottonwood River in Stark Township, about four miles southeast of present-day Sleepy Eye. (Map J) The family consisted of Martin and wife Elizabeth, daughters Margaret and Lizie, and sons John, Adam, and Charles. The children ranged in age from six to 18. Margaret, the oldest daughter, was visiting a neighbor's house when a Dakota woman told her about the uprising. She conveyed the news to her father who decided to move everyone to New Ulm. They were too late. The Dakotas raided their house, destroyed $400 worth of property, and caught the fleeing family about three miles east of Iberia, about six miles southeast of present Sleepy Eye. Only John Bluem (12) escaped.

George Roeser lived along the Cottonwood River in western Sigel Township about eight miles southwest of New Ulm. (Map K) He and his wife Barbara were killed at their home. Their 18-month-old child was left untouched and was rescued the following day.[14]

On the north side of the Cottonwood about nine miles west of New Ulm, Ole Anderson Feie heard rumors of an uprising and watched as a group of distant Indians moved south in his direction. A schoolteacher from Norway, Feie had farmed in Northfield, Minnesota, for a time before moving to Brown County only three months earlier. Without taking much besides what they were wearing, Ole got his wife and three children into his ox wagon and rode hard for town. Mounted Indians chased him for a few miles before giving up. By this time Ole's oxen were played out, but his luck held when he ran into a neighbor with a horse and wagon team. Ole abandoned his oxen and wagon and climbed into the neighbor's wagon to continue the flight to New Ulm. His property losses were $390, but he and his family were still alive.[15]

On Monday afternoon, one of the Jacksons (either Philetus or John) who lived along the Cottonwood River in the Leavenworth area heard the murderous rumors. Jackson stopped at the houses of Luther Whiton and his brother, Elijah Whiton, to share the grim news: a family had been murdered on

---

13 Hiram A. Buck Depredation Claim #1153. Hiram would be wounded in three places during the upcoming battle for New Ulm.

14 Dahlin, *Dakota Uprising Victims*, 64, 146n164; Tolzmann, ed., *Outbreak and Massacre*, 44.

15 Ole Feie Depredation Claim #1019.

the Minnesota River. Elijah was not unduly concerned, but Luther thought there was something to it. George W. Covell, who lived one-half mile west of Elijah and another half-mile north of Luther, was stacking grain for Luther (Map J) when Jackson arrived with the news. Covell left for home about 4:00 p.m. and told his wife Mary Jane (33) and their son James (11). Like Luther, they thought there was truth behind the report and decided to leave. Covell shared the news with Thomas Riant (Ryant), a recent resident from faraway Maine. Riant agreed to flee and made ready his team and wagon and two large trunks—one said to have held $2,000 in gold. The Covells climbed aboard Riant's wagon, as did an unnamed family recently arrived from Tennessee consisting of a man, his wife, a four-year-old child, and a toddler about two years old. The youngest, remembered Mary Jane, was "a corpse whose eyes they were just closing when the alarm came," but the mother refused to leave the body behind. The solemn little caravan avoided the road and headed south across the prairie. The party camped Monday night in high grass only three miles from Covell's house. The original bearer of the news, Philetus Jackson, also fled with his family. The Dakotas caught and killed him while his family escaped into the brush.[16]

Several families lived between Leavenworth and Iberia along a southern bend of the Cottonwood River in today's Stark Township. In addition to the Whitons and Covells, these families included the Ives's, Waite's, Van Gilder's, and Seaman's. Russel Ives (45) was born in Connecticut. He and his wife Lucretia (44), who was from New York, had at least three living children: Luther C. (22), Electra (16), and Clarice (8). They moved to Minnesota in 1860 and for the past two years were sharecropping on land owned by Luther Whiton and Sidney L. Waite. Russel and Luther worked three acres of wheat, two acres of corn, and one-half acre of turnips and potatoes for Waite, and kept one-third of what they produced. When they heard of the outbreak, Russel fled with his family to New Ulm late Monday evening together with neighbor Bernard Kelly. Luther intended to return with a rescue party the next day.[17]

---

16 Bryant and Murch, *Great Massacre*, 132; George W. Covell Depredation Claim #127; Tolzmann, ed., *Outbreak and Massacre*, 44. Philetus Jackson was killed, but the record is unclear whether the news bearer was Philetus or John.

17 Bryant and Murch, *Great Massacre*, 133; Russel Ives Depredation Claim #2034. Waite claims Ives also had two younger children who died of exposure during the family's flight, but Ives doesn't mention them.

On the eastern edge of Stark Township about nine miles southwest of New Ulm lived Hubert Zander. (Map K) His house was on the south shore of what is today Zanders Lake. Hubert was three miles from home when he heard the warning. He took it seriously and rushed home to gather his wife Gertrude and their children Agnes (8), Mary (6), Catherine (3), and Clara (1) and a few possessions. Hubert had just hitched up his ox-team when six mounted Indians appeared from the west. They chased the Zanders as Hubert whipped his oxen as fast as they could run. When the family reached the far side of a slough on the eastern end of Zanders Lake, the Indians quit the pursuit and turned back to raid the cabin. By the time Hubert returned in October, his crops were destroyed and his hogs and cattle were gone. He estimated his losses at $456.[18]

Frederick Frank lived one mile northeast of the Zander home in today's Sigel Township with his family, his father Christian Frank (70) and his mother Elizabeth (65). They fled late on August 18 and reached New Ulm.[19]

Farther down the Cottonwood, Mrs. Benjamin Harrington (Philetus Jackson's daughter) and Mrs. Hill, whose husbands were both absent, got together and decided to flee. Seth Henshaw, a single man living on a plot adjoining the Harrington land, allowed Benjamin to farm an acre of his land to grow sugar beets. Mrs. Harrington convinced Seth to harness his team to his wagon and take the two women to New Ulm. Mrs. Harrington had two children with her. The small party had gone but a short distance when the Indians found them. The speeding wagon overturned trying to negotiate a curve and the passengers were thrown out. While the Indians were killing Henshaw, Mrs. Harrington scooped up her one-year-old boy and began to run, as did Mrs. Hill. A bullet pierced the boy's small hand and slammed into his mother's shoulder, but she managed to stay on her feet and eventually find a hiding place in a slough. The youngster seemed to know they were in great danger, she recalled, "and kept as still as a mouse."

The Indians eventually left the area, but Mrs. Harrington was too dizzy from the loss of blood to walk any substantial distance. Mrs. Hill left the wounded infant with her but took the other child and left. On the way she met John Jackson and William Carroll, who lived in Leavenworth and were traveling

18 Hubert Zander Depredation Claim #202.

19 Christian Frank Depredation Claim #2019. Christian Frank was too old to fight in the subsequent battles for the town. Nevertheless, he received a severe wound in the head from a stray bullet and, explained his son Frederick, "his mind has been greatly impaired ever since."

to New Ulm to learn the latest news. The men took Mrs. Hill and the child into town with them. Mrs. Harrington and her young boy, meanwhile, spent the next eight days wandering through sloughs, prairies, and timber eating roots, berries, and raw vegetables. Wounded, exhausted, cold, and nearly starving, they finally stumbled into Crisp's Store midway between New Ulm and Mankato, where men from Lt. J. B. Swan's Le Sueur Company were guarding New Ulm evacuees. A private on guard duty that cold and rainy night heard something or someone approaching through tall grass. He called out the challenge but no one answered. Doing as he was ordered, he lifted his rifle and pulled the trigger, but the cap was wet and the gun misfired. Moments later Mrs. Harrington and her boy appeared.[20]

*   *   *

A peaceful dawn on Tuesday greeted the Covell party, which included George Covell and his wife Mary Jane, Thomas Riant, and an unnamed Tennessee family consisting of a husband and wife (still carrying her dead child) and their four-year-old. They had fled the day before and camped the previous evening in tall grass barely three miles from George's house. The morning was lovely and quiet. There were no Indians in sight and no burning buildings. Had they overreacted?

After some discussion they retraced their path a short way north to Eli Van Gilder's home. The Van Gilder family consisted of Eli, his mother, his wife, and two children. (Map J) The Covell party also found there Edward Allen and his wife, Charles Smith and his family, and Mrs. Mercie Carroll, whose husband William had helped Mrs. Hill make it to New Ulm the previous night but had not yet returned. The Van Gilders were still preparing their team of oxen, so Riant, Covell, and the unnamed family decided to leave them behind to catch up later. About two and one-half miles across the prairie they met a party of Indians driving a wagon. When the Indians gave chase, Thomas Riant turned his team around and sped back toward the Van Gilder cabin. The others brought up the rear. George Covell had a double-barrel shotgun—the only gun in the entire party—but the ammunition was wet and useless. Nevertheless, he was smart enough to keep it pointed at the Indians to keep them as far away as

---

20 Tolzmann, ed., *Outbreak and Massacre*, 43-44; Bryant and Murch, *Great Massacre*, 135-36, 179; Hughes, et. al., *Welsh in Minnesota*, 93; Benjamin Harrington Depredation Claim #215.

possible. The ruse likely worked because the Indians fired four times, but no one was hit.

Van Gilder had just gotten his oxen moving when Riant's and then Covell's wagon rolled into view. Within a few moments everyone was running for the house. A Dakota bullet tore through Riant's coat, and another crashed through a window and hit Van Gilder's mother Ruth, (who Mary Covell called Mrs. Howard), breaking her left arm. The warriors fired at the cabin for thirty minutes before stealing Riant's horses, waving and whooping at the huddled settlers, and riding away. Left with only Van Gilder's oxen and wagon, the refugees headed southeast in an effort to reach Mankato some 30 miles away. Riant was not among them. He decided to strike out on his own on foot for New Ulm. The mother from Tennessee was finally convinced to leave her dead child behind.

More refugees joined them, including Sidney L. Waite and Luther Whiton, who had been hiding in the grass waiting for the Indians to leave. Alva B. Hough had a house about two miles northwest of Waite's cabin. Alva was on business in St. Peter and his wife Mary and children John (13), Josephine (2), and Abraham (one month) made their way downriver to join the little caravan heading east. There were now at least 15 people in the party, and most of them had to walk. They traveled across the prairie all day and crossed the Little Cottonwood River southwest of New Ulm on Tuesday night. "[B]eing weakly," recalled Mary Jane Covell, "[I] frequently fell down on this journey but borrowed strength from despair" and stumbled to the campground "just before the descent of a heavy rain which fell on us that night." The wet, destitute, and hungry refugees remained hidden there until Friday.[21]

* * *

The fortunate survivors of the murderous attacks on Milford spent the afternoon and evening of August 18 hiding or trying to make their way to New Ulm. After they burrowed their way out of the cellar of the burning cabin, Joe Stocker and 10-year-old Cecelia Ochs hid in the woods before walking about one mile east to the Zettel house. (Map L) They found John Zettel lying on the

---

21 Bryant and Murch, *Great Massacre*, 133-35; George Covell Depredation Claim #127; Alva B. Hough Depredation Claim #2029. Hough claimed property damages of $457, but they were not caused by Indians. A prairie fire destroyed 25 rods of three-rail fence and rain leaked into the roof he was repairing, ruining much of their clothing and book collection.

floor clutching a loaf of bread soaked with blood. Three children were dead in the next room and a fourth was on the ground outside. Someone called out from under a shock of wheat, where they found Mrs. Zettel bleeding from several hatchet wounds to the head. The Indians attacked them just as the family was sitting down for the noon meal. Her husband was trying to give the Dakotas a loaf of bread when they killed him.

Stocker and Ochs helped Mrs. Zettel to bed and continued on, taking to the woods along the river and heading toward New Ulm before angling back to the road near John Fischerbauer's place. Fischerbauer was about to shoot them when he recognized Cecelia and welcomed them inside, where the wounded Mrs. Schilling and her son Joseph were also hiding. The Fischerbauers were probably next in line to be attacked after the Schilling place when the recruiting party arrived and diverted the Indians' attention.

Cecelia Ochs left the Fischerbauer house for her nearby father's home, but Anton Ochs had already fled. Christian Haag, another neighbor, ran up to her and broke the sad news that his own father had been killed, but that his mother and the rest of the family were still at home. Cecelia accompanied Christian to his house, and she and the Haag survivors left for New Ulm.

East of Fischerbauer's was the house of Nicholus Thinnes. Nicholus was at Fort Ridgely at this time, but a cousin who lived with him named Michael Arnold somehow managed to move much of their property to a warehouse in New Ulm.[22]

The Ochs family (minus Cecelia) was already on the road to New Ulm when they met up with the Zellers, Spelbrinks, and Zagrotzky. It was at that point when Victor Zagrotzky convinced Conrad Zeller and Christopher Spelbrink to return with him to look for his family. "The chances, of course," explained young Chris Spelbrink, "were that they might meet the Indians and be killed, but they went." The men approached Zagrotzky's with caution, but when they got up enough courage to go inside they found the place plundered but there were no bodies to be found. Zagrotzky began hoping his family might have escaped. Zeller wanted to go back to his house to get 12-year-old Martin Henle's body. To everyone's surprise the boy was still alive. He even lifted himself while trying to smile. They gave him water but found it impossible to

---

22 Koblas, *Let Them Eat Grass*, I, 284-85; Nicholus Thinnes Depredation Claim #1210. The Indians later burned down the warehouse the following Saturday, destroying the property inside. Joe Stocker vanishes from the record at this point.

move him since there were no horses or wagons. They were wondering what to do when a group of whites approached on the road: Brown County Sheriff Charles Roos and his party of rescuers had arrived.[23]

When the Union recruiting party was ambushed at the bridge near Henle's about noon, Indians captured two of the wagons and the other three had turned around—the last one barely getting away after loading aboard the badly wounded Joe Messmer. The wagons picked up other refugees along the way, but one of the party, Henry Behnke, could not wait. Behnke (29) and his family had emigrated from Mecklenburg (later Germany) in 1853 and moved to New Ulm two years later. Henry was selected as the first probate judge when Brown County was organized in 1856. The next year he married Esther Tuttle, whose father Albert was Brown County's first state representative. When the Indians struck, Henry took off on foot for the nearest cabin, grabbed a fast horse, and rode south to the Cottonwood River to warn his father-in-law and his neighbors. After that Behnke turned east and, like Paul Revere, galloped past numerous farms calling out the warning.

Charles Roos may have been wondering how the recruiting was going when, sometime after noon on Monday, a man galloped into town shouting "The Indians are coming. . . . They have already killed the recruiting party!" Roos never identified the man. It may have been Behnke, but his detour to the Cottonwood River implies that he may have gotten back to New Ulm after the surviving members of the recruiting party. Regardless of who shouted the alarm, Roos acted quickly although he mistakenly believed that "only some drunken Indians needed to be arrested and called out a posse."

While the men comprising the posse gathered, Roos walked to the school and informed teacher Rudolph Leonhart that "an uprising has broken out at the Agency. Indeed, they are only stories at present, yet foresight is better than hindsight, and I ask you, therefore, to send the children home." Leonhart sent the children home with instructions that they inform their parents of the news and then set out to get his own family into town.

Roos appointed Jacob Nix as Commandant of New Ulm. Liberty-loving Nix (40) had participated as a captain in Franz Zitz's Free Corps in the 1848 Revolution in Germany. He was captured there and sentenced to death for treason, but escaped to Antwerp and made his way to America. He married Margaret Schneider and moved to Minnesota in 1858, where he ran a general

23 Tolzmann, ed., *Brown County*, 79.

store. After tapping the best man for the job of commanding the town, Roos gathered 30 men armed with a variety of rifles, shotguns, and assorted weapons, commandeered several teams and wagons, and headed for Milford. Nix, meanwhile, set about recruiting men to build barricades at the edge of town.[24]

Sheriff Roos's skepticism about an uprising dissipated the farther west his company traveled as refugees, including the wounded Haupt and Steimle, streamed past the advancing posse. Steimle was unable to speak because of his throat wound (he would die a few weeks later), but wrote on a piece of paper that Schneider, Fenske, and Dietrich were dead. After reading those words from a witness and finding bodies along the road and in the fields, Roos realized fully the seriousness of the situation. Warriors still lurked in the area, and a few took long distance shots at them, but no one was hit. The rescuers filled wagons with wounded and dead and sent them back to New Ulm. The cargo convinced any doubting townsfolk that they were in the middle of a war and must prepare a proper defense. Henry Behnke, meanwhile, continued his Paul Revere-like ride, galloping to St. Peter to spread the warning and find help.

*   *   *

Others were also spreading the warning. Athanasius Henle and Alois Palmer left the ferry with a wagon carrying wounded Milford people. They remained on the north bank of the Minnesota River and told Frederick Fritsche that evening. Fritsche, who lived about two miles north of New Ulm, put his wife Louise and their baby Louis Albert into the wagon that safely carried them into town. (Map N) Frederick, meanwhile, gathered some clothing, bedding, and supplies and followed in his own wagon after dark. They stayed with Frederick's father, John Karl Fritsche, who lived in the southeast part of New Ulm.[25]

Roos's posse found Fenske's corpse just east of the bridge, and the bodies of Schneider and Dietrich about 100 yards beyond. Schneider was stripped of everything but his shirt. The group continued, passing Messmer's and heading

---

24 Dietz, "New Ulm's Paul Revere," 111-13; Leonhart, *Memories of New Ulm,* 42-43; Folwell, *History of Minnesota,* II, 361; Nix, *Sioux Uprising,* ix, 89-90.

25 Berghold, *Indians' Revenge,* 96; Roos, "The Battles of New Ulm," Brown County Historical Society; Frederick Fritsche Depredation Claim #142. The baby, Louis Albert, would later practice medicine in New Ulm and write a history of Brown County.

for Henle's. Anton Henle was riding with Sheriff Roos. Anton was within one-half mile of his house when the Indians jumped the recruiting party that afternoon. Now he had a chance to go back but his anxiety was overwhelming: would he find even a single member of his family alive? The men stopped at Anton's and found two of his children and his mother-in-law dead. The grieving father walked behind the house and called out—he was sure in vain—for his wife. Unsure what to do or where to go, Theresa had been hiding in the creek bed with her dogs since the ambush. "Toward evening I heard the voice of my husband in the direction of the house calling me," she recalled, "and I came forth from my hiding place." Sorrow and joy accompanied their reunion. Now they had to find Martin. What they didn't know was that the 12-year-old had already been found and was lying wounded at Zeller's waiting for rescue.

Roos's men were moving west picking up bodies when they spotted a man driving a wagon. When the stranger stood to wave a cloth and shout a war whoop, John Hauenstein leveled his rifle and fired. The Indian fell out of the wagon, but got up and ran. The posse chased him for a while, but since they were approaching woods and it was getting dark, they thought better of it and turned back toward the Henle cabin. It was at this time that Zeller, Spelbrink, and Zagrotzky spotted the Brown County sheriff and his party of rescuers. There was little time for pleasantries. The trio of refugees acquired a wagon and continued on to Zeller's to help the badly injured Henle son. Anton would get back his boy, if only for a short while.

Roos also found Mrs. Barbara Zettel, wounded and in her bed where Stocker and Ochs had placed her. By then it was too dark to safely continue on, so Roos called off the operation and returned to town, which they reached about 10:00 p.m. Ten-year-old Cecelia Ochs reunited with her happy parents, who were convinced their little girl had been killed. Schoolteacher Rudolph Leonhart, one of those detailed to remain behind to defend the town, watched as the solemn procession of wagons returned filled with the dead and the wounded. When the schoolteacher asked Roos what had happened, the exhausted sheriff merely pointed inside one of the wagons, where "three corpses lay under the blankets and that the same had been scalped and horribly mutilated by the Indians."

No formal announcement was made about the return of the bodies, but before long many of the hundreds of refugees and townsfolk flooded to the wagons to see if they could locate any missing kin. "Heart-rending cries of the women and children soon arose who had been made widows and orphans as a result of this atrocity committed by the Redskins," recalled Leonhart. "That same night coffins were completed and the next morning the mutilated corpses committed to the earth."

Few families were as devastated as the Henles and their relatives. Barbara Zettel and young Martin Henle would both die of their wounds within two weeks, adding to the list of the dead that now included Martin Fink and his wife, Max Fink and a nephew, Max Zeller, his wife and four children, the Zettels and their four children, the Messmers, Florian Hartman, and Henle's children. All told, the Henles lost 21 relatives.[26]

26 Tolzmann, ed., *Brown County*, 79, 82; Roos, "The Battles of New Ulm," Brown County Historical Society; Leonhart, *Memories of New Ulm*, 44, 46.

Chapter 9

"You are a good man; it is too bad you should be killed!"

Sacred Heart Creek

Settlers flee from Sacred Heart Creek ~ Dakotas escort settlers back home ~ Kitzman-Krieger massacre ~ Survivors trek to Fort Ridgely

By Monday afternoon the Dakotas fanning out from the Lower Agency had swept 18 miles southeast to Milford and hit settlements at Beaver Creek, Smith Creek, and Middle Creek from six to 14 miles to the northwest. Sacred Heart Creek, another substantial settlement about 18 miles above Redwood and 12 miles below Yellow Medicine, was about to feel the murderous wrath.

Like those at the lower settlements, the first white pioneers in the area selected a spot where a substantial stream flowed down to the Minnesota River. Settlers described the area as "an expanse of rich land, covered with waving violet blue-joint grass, and with many sightly groves along creeks running merrily into the river." Mosquitoes, however, invaded the idyllic setting. "They were thick enough to obscure sunlight on warm days and came near killing the settlers' cattle," recalled a resident. One could easily locate the dwellings by the thick smoke of smudge-pots that smoldered constantly in vain attempts to drive the pests away. Until August 18, 1862, mosquitoes were a worse foe than Indians.[1]

---

1 Curtiss-Wedge, *History of Renville County*, II, 1, 329.

A number of families lived along Sacred Heart Creek and above Patterson's Rapids, including those with the last name of Kitzman, Krieger, Lammers, Laramie, Yess, Grundmann, Frass, Krause, Zabel, Heining, Neuman, and Urban. (Map D) That Monday morning, Emil Grundmann and August Frass left for the Lower Agency and picked up Michael Boelter on Middle Creek. On the river road near Smith Creek about 11:00 a.m. they discovered the bodies of a woman, two children, and their scattered belongings. The shocked men hurried to the Mannweiler house, and then to the Busse and Roessler homes, only to find dead bodies at each of them. Boelter, who lived in the same neighborhood, had remained with the wagon each time. When Frass and Grundmann reported what they found, he made for home while his companions returned to Sacred Heart Creek.

Frass and Grundmann reached their homes early that evening, warned their own families, and then rode straight to the Krieger's and Kitzman's to warn them about what they had found. One of 14 children, Justina Kitzman Lehn Krieger (27) was a native of Prussia and there married Daniel Lehn. The couple had three children: John, Gottlieb, and Lizzie. When Dan died five years later Justina and her parents and siblings immigrated to Wisconsin, where Justina married Frederick Krieger in 1857. Frederick already had three daughters from a previous marriage: Caroline (11), Tillie (10), and Minnie (6). Justina and Frederick had one daughter, Henrietta (5), and another baby daughter born early in 1862. The Krieger family moved to Sacred Heart Creek just 11 weeks before the uprising. Justina's brother, Paul Kitzman, together with his wife and their five children Louis (Ludwig), Wilhelmina, Pauline, Gustav, and baby Paul lived about one-half mile to the west.[2]

Fred Krieger and Paul Kitzman were both fishing in the Minnesota River when Frass and Grundmann arrived, so Louis Kitzman (14) ran to tell them. Just the previous evening, Louis and John and Gottlieb Krieger were out looking for stray cows on a journey that carried them nearly three miles away down by the river. While there, the three boys heard faint shooting and shouting. "We thought it was Indians," remembered Gottlieb, but Louis was convinced "it was only Indians hunting."[3]

While Louis ran to tell his father, the older Krieger and Kitzman children were sent running to the other families in the neighborhood with a call to

---

2 Justina's three children from Dan Lehn later went by the anglicized name of Lane.

3 Bryant and Murch, *Great Massacre*, 298-300; Tolzmann, ed., *German Pioneer Accounts*, 64-65.

assemble at the Kitzman house. Within an hour, 13 families were gathered there. Paul Kitzman was selected as the nominal leader of the gathering, but "My uncle had so much faith in the Indians he could not believe that they had done the killing," explained Gottlieb.

Nearly everyone was there except the Schwandt family. When their absence was noticed, Kitzman sent two men to find Johann to make sure he knew what was happening. The Schwandt cabin, roughly between the Middle Creek and Sacred Heart settlements, was somewhat isolated. When the messengers arrived they found everyone dead. As related earlier, 10-year-old August Schwandt had been tomahawked and left for dead, but managed to slip away and was now on his way to the fort. The sight of an unborn child nailed to a tree especially sickened the visitors, who grabbed John Frass' bloody coat as evidence of the murders and hurried back to report what they had found. "This convinced my uncle," explained Gottlieb. A mad rush got underway to gather up household goods and provisions.

It was after 8:00 p.m. when the 13 families packed themselves into 11 wagons and headed for Fort Ridgely. They decided to avoid the river road and head instead across the prairie. Initially the wagon train of refugees rolled northwest toward the Chippewa River, but about 2:00 a.m. on Tuesday morning they circled back east, crossed the headwaters of Beaver Creek, and angled southeast to upper Birch Coulee. By 8:00 a.m. they were about 14 miles from Sacred Heart when eight mounted Indians approached. The men circled the wagons in a rough box formation for defense, but had only two firearms between them. The eight warriors made hostile moves, but the prepared settlers gave them pause. Instead of attacking, the Dakotas changed their demeanor, put away their weapons, and made signs not to fire.

One of the warriors who spoke English knew Paul Kitzman, and had often visited him. The Indian approached, shook his hand, and embraced him. The friendly gestures did nothing to convince Justina Krieger. "The Indian kissed my brother and showed great friendship," she wrote. "Judas-like, he betrayed us with a kiss!" When the warrior asked them where they were going, Paul explained that Indians were killing people and they were fleeing to the fort.

"The Sioux did not kill anybody," Justina recalled the warrior replying. "The people had been murdered by the Chippewas; they were now on their way after the Chippewas to kill them." Paul's Indian acquaintance went on to warn them that Chippewas were blocking the road and that if they continued to the fort they would be killed. "You are a good man," he continued. "It is too bad you should be killed!"

With that, the Indians went around to everyone, shaking their hands and saying that they would protect them on their return journey. Their apparent sincerity lulled most of the party into a false sense of security. The Indians made a poor attempt to hide their weapons behind them as they approached, sat in a circle, and asked if the travelers would share some of their food. The whites passed out bread and milk, with some of the settlers even offering money to seal the deal. "All of us were now fully assured that they were really friendly," remembered Justina.

Gottlieb Krieger wasn't one of them. "I have often wondered why no one in the crowd noticed the Indians' guns," he said. "My uncle could have taken all of them as he passed the bread around and the other men could have run out to meet him and each one have a gun and we would have had the brutes at our mercy." When Gottlieb told his mother about the weapons, she told him to keep still.[4]

After they ate, the reassured settlers turned their wagons around and started for home with the Indians riding along as an escort. Sometimes the Dakotas rode ahead and sometimes they dropped back. After five miles the settlers decided it was time to unyoke the oxen and let them feed. The Indians once again dined with them on a dinner of bread, butter, and watermelon. Once they re-harnessed the oxen and continued on, however, the Dakotas took up positions on either side of the wagons. Several of the whites thought the unusual arrangement threatening and they talked together in German about what to do. Some wanted to shoot at the Indians; their guns were in the wagons, however, while the Indians carried theirs with them. Paul Kitzman persuaded them not to take any rash action.

When the wagons rolled through the area of Middle Creek where Grundmann and Frass had discovered bodies the day before, the Dakotas became agitated and moved closer to the wagons. This time their shotguns were out. "They came up and demanded our money," remembered Justina Krieger. When one of the warriors approached her, Justina handed him five dollars but hid the rest. Frederick Krieger whispered to her that "he was going to be killed" before slipping her his pocket knife as a remembrance. Instead of opening fire, however, the Dakotas rode off toward the houses at Middle Creek.

---

4   Bryant and Murch, *Great Massacre*, 301-03; Berghold, *Indians' Revenge*, 132; Tolzmann, ed., *German Pioneer Accounts*, 65.

Bewildered but relieved, the anxious settlers decided to continue on to their homes. They were on the prairie about one and one-half miles from the Krieger house when a pair of unidentified dead white men and a dead dog were found lying along the roadside. Mr. Krause, who owned the only horses in the settlement and who was riding a mare, decided enough was enough. The Indians were nowhere in sight and he saw his chance. "He suddenly bolted the track and rode over the hills east toward Fort Ridgely," young Gottlieb wrote. "I can see him yet as he passed us. His wife was screaming and everything was in confusion."[5]

Indians appeared out of the west just minutes after Krause bolted. The settlers made a quick decision to pull out the few guns they had and fight. If they could reach the nearest house just a quarter-mile distant, perhaps they could put up a good defense. The Indians—who now numbered about 14—rode up and inquired where the man on horseback had gone. When no one answered, they rode off a short distance, dismounted, spread out, and walked back, surrounding the stalled wagons. It was four in the afternoon on Tuesday.

"The firing commenced. Confusion reigned supreme," related Gottlieb. "Everybody was screaming and flying for their lives." Each Dakota selected an adult male to kill first. "All the men but three fell at the first fire," reported Justina. "It was done so quickly that I could not see whether our men fired at all." Among the first to die was a bachelor named Uris Andermack (or Untermach) and another named Wagner, who was said to be Mrs. Kitzman's epileptic brother. After the first devastating volley only August Frass, Gottlieb Zabel, and Frederick Krieger remained standing. Although some members of the party had run, most remained frozen in their wagons. The Dakotas issued the women an ultimatum: come with them now or die. Some agreed, but others refused. Justina defiantly replied that she would stay and die with her husband and children, but Frederick urged her to go, telling his wife that the Indians would not kill her and she could escape later. She refused.

One of the women who agreed to go with the Indians began walking away with a warrior. When she stopped to wave at Justina and urge her to come along the warrior shot her dead. As if granting permission to slaughter, the other warriors began killing the rest of the women and men. Justina watched in horror as the Dakotas bashed the children with the stocks of their shotguns so as not to waste ammunition on the young. Frederick Krieger was the last adult male alive.

5   Bryant and Murch, *Great Massacre*, 304-05; Tolzmann, ed., *German Pioneer Accounts*, 65-66.

He was standing outside the wagon begging Justina to go when a pair of warriors leveled their guns and shot him almost simultaneously. One of the balls passed through him and cut Justina's dress. Frederick fell between the oxen where his assailants shot him again, this time in the shoulder and the head. Justina tried to jump from the wagon but a load of buckshot slammed into her back, knocking her into the wagon bed, where she landed in the middle of eight screaming children. Most of them scrambled out and tried to run. Some got away and some were cut down. The scene was duplicated up and down the wagon train. When an Indian found Justina he threw her onto the ground and someone drove the wagon over her body. She fainted from the pain.[6]

The quick-thinking Lizzie Lehn (13) told the girls in her wagon to jump down, face the ground, and play dead. Her half-sisters Caroline, Tillie, and Minnie did as she ordered. Shouting, shooting, and crying engulfed the prone children. Eventually the Indians left. "We arose among the dead and wounded," six-year-old Minnie Krieger remembered. "An awful thunderstorm came up; the rain was terrible. The wounded children were all crying."

The girls tried to carry the wounded children and headed to the nearby Krieger house. "The little ones were all partly helpless," said Minnie, "and we could do nothing more for them. There were eighteen of them." After getting some of the wounded to the house, Caroline and Tillie carried water back to the dying women and men. Justina Krieger was unconscious and the children thought she was dead. The only adult they found "alive" was Mrs. Anna Zabel. They helped her to the house. Lizzie used some of her own clothing to wash and dress Anna's hip and shoulder wounds.

Justina, meanwhile, faded in and out of consciousness. She saw a boy perhaps four years old sitting and holding his father's hand, saying over and over, "Papa, papa, don't sleep so long!" The Indians found him and took him away. Later, she was aware of Caroline taking her baby from her, but she could not move or speak. When her step-children returned they secured August Heining's two sons, a son and daughter of Emil Grundmann, two sons of a Mr. Tille (Thiel?) and another boy they thought was Gustav Kitzman, and helped them back to the house. All of them were wounded. The hand of Grundmann's four-year-old daughter had been shot off. August Urban (13), a member of the

6 Bryant and Murch, *Great Massacre*, 305-07; Tolzmann, ed., *German Pioneer Accounts*, 66; Tolzmann, ed., *Outbreak and Massacre*, 35; Curtiss-Wedge, *History of Renville County*, II, 1276, 1,347.

party who had disappeared, showed up and helped the girls with the wounded children.[7]

When the Indians opened fire, several of the older children did not wait around to see what would happen. August jumped from a wagon and hid in the tall grass, but his mother, Ernestine, Rose, Louise, and Albert (6) were all captured. Mrs. Urban carried one daughter on her back and another in her arms as the Dakotas led them away. According to Albert, the Indians did not mistreat his mother. After some days he was stripped naked and allowed to play with the other Indian boys. Once, however, they forced him to stand still, placed pieces of bark on his head, and shot them off with arrows. "I was terribly frightened," he admitted, and his "knees nearly wilted" as he tried to keep still. Albert didn't know if he moved or if one of the archers shot low, but "it was then that I received the 'stamp of Minnesota,' which I will bear to my grave. The point of the arrow struck me on the forehead and knocked me out, and I stayed that way for three days."[8]

Michael Yess was absent on business that day or he would have been with his family on the doomed wagon train. When the Dakotas attacked, Mrs. Yess (48) tried to get off her wagon but became entangled in the oxen's trace chains and was dragged into the tall grass. She freed herself and crawled away. Her daughter Henrietta (3), however, was captured. August Yess (14) hopped out and ran south toward the timber near the Krause house. John and Gottlieb Krieger followed him. As he did so, Gottlieb noticed a group of 50 or so Indians watching the fight from a nearby hill. He didn't know whether they moved down to participate in the slaughter, but he "could hear shooting and screaming" as he ran. The boys made it to the woods and scrambled for a place to hide. Not a single Indian followed them. By the time they caught their breath and discussed what to do next, the sun was setting. Gottlieb walked cautiously up on the bluff for a look around and spotted the Indians gathered together. To his horror, they began approaching the timber but suddenly changed course and

---

7 Tolzmann, ed., *German Pioneer Accounts*, 72-73; Bryant and Murch, *Great Massacre*, 307, 309-10. The child holding his papa's hand could have been one of the Lammers, Frass, or Kitzman boys. Justina believed Paul Kitzman was one of those recovered by her stepdaughters, but Wilhelmina Inefeldt stated that young Paul was a captive with her for a time, until the Indians took knives and left him "all cut to pieces" because of his crying and obstinacy. Heining is sometimes spelled Horning.

8 *Mankato Free Press*, January 28, 1931.

headed toward the Kitzman cabin. The relieved boys remained hidden in the woods all night.

Lizzie Lehn and her half-sisters Caroline, Tillie, and Minnie did a remarkable job finding and caring for as many survivors as they could find. Caroline and Tillie mustered all the courage they possessed and ventured out during the night to see if they could find other survivors, followed by Lizzie and Mrs. Anna Zabel, while Minnie remained in the Krieger house with the baby and the other wounded children. They were not the only ones hunting that night.

The scene of the massacre was too tempting to avoid for long, and several Dakotas returned to scavenge through the debris to gather up anything of use they may have missed earlier. Two warriors approached the wounded and barely conscious Justina, who had collected enough of her wits to get up and try to slip away. When she discovered Indians approaching she dropped to the ground and pretended to be dead. One Indian kicked her and knelt to feel whether she had a pulse. She held her breath and tried to remain still as the warrior pulled out his knife and, with one stroke, cut through her dress from her throat to her abdomen. The Dakota might have believed she was dead and wanted nothing more than to remove the dress, but his blade cut deep, laying open her intestines. "My arms were then taken separately out of the clothing," Justina remembered. "I was seized rudely by the hair, and hurled headlong to the ground, entirely naked."

Justina fainted again. When she regained her senses a short time later, she saw a light glimmering in the north and believed it to be the aurora borealis. Silhouetted against its shimmering curtain was a warrior in the process of discovering Wilhelmina Kitzman, Justina's wounded niece. The Dakota picked up the little girl by her foot and dangled her upside down. With his knife, he cut through the leg below the hip, and "by twisting and wrenching, broke the ligaments and bone, until the limb was entirely severed from the body." All the while little Wilhelmina screamed, "O God! O God!" The Indian took her clothing and left her to die.

Numb with horror and pain, Justina lay still for some time before deciding she had to escape the murderous scene. Somehow she managed to crawl toward her house, hoping to find a body and use its clothing to cloak her naked bleeding body. Ironically, she crawled across her own dress an Indian had carved off her and then discarded. Justina bound the torn garment around her body and continued, but was overcome with the fear that Indians might be waiting at the house. She turned around and resolved that she would make it all the way to Fort Ridgely, more than 30 miles away.[9]

The surviving children and Anna Zabel played an exceedingly lucky game of hide and seek with the Indians. They carried wounded children between the houses or down to a branch of Sacred Heart Creek to wash and drink as the Indians visited the cabins, plundered, and moved on. They were back at the Krieger cabin later that night when Justina decided it was not safe to go there. Dawn was breaking on Wednesday, August 20, when Anna Zabel convinced the oldest unwounded children that they must leave the house. The Indians, she told them, were certain to return. The Grundmann child, her small hand severed, had spent the night crying, moaning that "Mother always took care of [me] when [I] was hurt, but now she [will] not come to [me]." There was little the older survivors could do to help her. The only adult, Anna, was wounded in the hip and shoulder, and the nominal leader of the group the 13-year-old Lizzie. They had to make a tough decision: remain and be found, or leave and seek help. They decided to leave the dead and the wounded behind and strike out for assistance. Minnie Krieger carried Justina's baby much of the time during the trek to Mr. Tille's house, which was somewhere nearby.[10] There, they found some flour and butter, mixed it with water, and ate it. Worried about remaining in one place any length of time, they went outside to see who else they might find at the massacre site. As they did so, a man rode by on horseback.

Antoine Frenier reined in his horse in front of the Kreiger house, stunned by what he discovered. The mixed-blood interpreter had been dispatched the previous day by Agent Galbraith to scout the agencies, learn what he could, and report back; no doubt Galbraith also hoped he could also learn the fate of the agent's family. Frenier cut a rapid circuit of both agencies and was on his way back when he passed Sacred Heart. His decision to stop at the Krieger's, which was near the road, left him face-to-face with the seven Tillie, Grundmann, and Heining children who had been left behind. The youngsters were so traumatized, hungry, and exhausted that they "appeared to be stupid and unconscious of their condition." Frenier promised them he would get help, set

9 Tolzmann, ed., *Outbreak and Massacre*, 34; Tolzmann, ed., *German Pioneer Accounts*, 66, 73; Bryant and Murch, *Great Massacre*, 314-16.

10 Bryant and Murch, *Great Massacre*, 310. I have been unable to place the location of Tille's (or Thiele's) cabin. Louis Thiele lived about eight miles downstream near Smith Creek. Perhaps this was another branch of the Thiele family Justina spelled phonetically as Tille. In any event, this Tille cabin was near the Krieger cabin.

his spurs, and galloped off. The Krieger children, Lizzie Lehn, Anna Zabel, and August Urban, saw him coming, believed he was an Indian, and hid in the grass. One of them thought she heard the rider exclaim, "O, my soul, bless God!" or something to that effect, as he rode by the strewn bodies in the road. By the time they realized he was a white man he had galloped away.[11]

The refugees—Caroline, Tillie, Minnie Krieger, Lizzie Lehn, August Urban, Anna Zabel, and Justina Krieger's baby—struck out for Fort Ridgely. They wandered around part of the day but, unsure of the route, decided to return to the Krieger house thinking the rider they had seen might return with help. They were approaching Sacred Heart Creek once again when they found the Krieger house smoldering and in ruins. The Indians had returned, just as Anna Zabel predicted, and burned the cabin to the ground with the wounded children still inside. The horrendous act killed Tille's one- and two-year-old sons, Grundmann's one-year-old son and four-year-old daughter, Heining's one- and three-year-old sons, and one other child (possibly Pauline Kitzman). The group walked to Tille's place and scrounged for the last morsels of food. When they saw Indians plundering the Frass cabin in the distance, they knew they had no choice but to leave the area. "We left the baby [Justina's] to die," admitted Minnie Krieger, "and although it broke Lizzie's heart, it could not be otherwise."

The refugees initially traveled by day, but when they spotted Indians decided to hide and travel mainly at night. They chewed grass, drank water, and once, when Lizzie found some red onions in an abandoned garden, they enjoyed a big feast.[12]

* * *

August Yess and John and Gottlieb Krieger were moving faster and had already passed through the area days earlier. The boys hid near the Krause house on Tuesday night. The next morning they saw Indians all around them; they had Krause's mare and colt with them. Krause had abandoned the wagon train and his wife the previous day on horseback, and to the boys it appeared he did not get very far when in fact he had made it safely to Fort Ridgely. His mare

11 *Minnesota Pioneer & Democrat*, August 23, 1862, cited in Koblas, *Let Them Eat Grass*, I, 246-47; Bryant and Murch, *Great Massacre*, 311; Heard, *History of the Sioux War*, 97.

12 Tolzmann, ed., *German Pioneer Accounts*, 73; Bryant and Murch, *Great Massacre*, 311-12.

had a colt that could not keep up and the mare would not speed up and leave it behind. Krause abandoned the animals and went off on foot. When Indians approached the house again the boys scurried back down the bluff into the timber and waited there until dark. That night they moved on to Kitzman's, found a cow and milked it, drank, and hung the pail back so it looked like no one had been there.

On Thursday morning the boys returned to the Krause place, but there was little left because the Indians had picked it clean. They did, however, find half a loaf of bread. "We divided it into three equal parts and ate it," Gottlieb recalled. "Bread never tasted so good to me before." While back in hiding several cows wandered by. The boys "caught one of them by the horns and held her while the other would milk directly into his mouth. So we took turns until we all satisfied our hunger."

That night the boys started out for Fort Ridgely, walking slowly along the road in the dark and hiding by day. After what seemed an exhausting and harrowing eternity the boys awoke one morning to see the fort ahead. They walked past three abandoned houses and stopped to look for something to eat, almost stepping on a body lying in the grass. The grisly discovery frightened them so much they left the road and circled around on the prairie. A soldier in the distance appeared waving his cap and calling, "Hurry up, boys; you are so close to the fort, but you may be killed yet before you reach it." The boys heeded the warning and ran to him as fast as they could. They had been alone on their journey for six days.[13]

It took even longer for Caroline, Tillie, and Minnie Krieger, Lizzie Lehn, August Urban, and Anna Zabel to reach the fort. After their "feast" of red onions Lizzie was overcome with despair. "She threw herself onto the ground, hid her face and cried as if her heart would break," related Minnie. There was little else they could do but push on. One night they stumbled across 15 bodies. Another night they nearly walked right into a band of Dakotas traveling the road in the opposite direction. After that close call they decided to travel during the daylight hours.

Finally, in the distance they made out buildings and tents, but could not determine whether it was Fort Ridgely or a large Indian camp. Minnie Krieger collapsed while they determined what to do. "I played out completely and could

13 Tolzmann, ed., *German Pioneer Accounts*, 67-68; Satterlee, "Massacre at Sacred Heart," Microfilm Reel 2, Dakota Conflict, Minnesota Historical Society.

go no farther," she admitted. "Mrs. Zabel told Lizzie to leave me to die, but she dragged me to the brook and bathed my face and said she would stay with me." The other children protested and would not leave without Minnie. Someone found a melon rind in the road and they fed it to her. When she revived they continued on, but by this time Anna Zabel was convinced they were approaching an Indian camp and refused to go any farther. Soldiers found them and rushed a wagon out to pick them up. Anna, certain the approaching men were Indians, stumbled off in the opposite direction. The soldiers soon caught up with Anna and convinced her otherwise. Together, they brought in the ragged, bruised, and starving party. Their ordeal had lasted twelve days.

"I never forgave Mrs. Zabel," Minnie said, referring to her suggestion that they leave the girl behind to die. Rewards and punishments are rarely allotted fairly. The company's true leader and inspiration was Lizzie Lehn. "Poor Lizzie was never strong after that awful trip," Minnie continued. "She was never rewarded for her kindness on earth. May she reap her reward in heaven."[14]

Lizzie's mother, Justina Lehn Krieger, wandered the woods and prairies from August 19 until soldiers found her on September 1. She was lying in a wagon when the Battle of Birch Coulee broke out on September 2. Some 200 bullets pierced the vehicle and the robes she was wrapped in, but she miraculously escaped further injury.

14 Tolzmann, ed., *German Pioneer Accounts*, 73-74.

C hapter 10

"Shoot me, but I shall first kiss my wife."

Yellow Medicine Agency

Ebell's description of Yellow Medicine ~ John Otherday in council ~ Mixed-bloods give warning ~ Whites gather at the agency ~ Peter Patoile ~ Joseph La Framboise Jr. ~ Duncan Kennedy's escape ~ Joseph Brown family captured ~ Susan Frenier Brown saves lives ~ Charles Crawford searches for his sister ~ Flight of the refugees with Otherday ~ Dr. Williamson hesitates ~ Stephen Riggs and Jonas Pettijohn flee Hazelwood ~ Richard Orr wounded ~ Williamson joins Riggs ~ Andrew Hunter visits Ridgely ~ Divine providence credited

L ocated about 30 miles northwest of Redwood Agency, Yellow Medicine Agency was situated in roughly the same configuration on the bluffs on the south bank of the Minnesota River and on the road running between New Ulm and Lac Qui Parle and Big Stone Lake farther upriver. (Map C) Contemporary pictures and descriptions of the area were made by journalist-photographer Adrian J. Ebell, who arrived at the agency to photograph Dakota Indians only three days before the uprising. Traveling with assistant Edwin R. Lawton, Ebell described the approach to the agency across a wide and beautiful Yellow Medicine River running with clear rippling water. Storehouses for four traders stood at the bottom of a slight hill, which climbed to the brickyard, a boarding house for employees, corn and potato fields, and finally the government stores and residences. Beyond that stretched a three-mile farming district and Dr. Thomas Williamson's mission house at Pajutazi, with Rev. Stephen Riggs's house another two miles beyond.[1]

---

1 Woolworth and Bakeman, eds., *Camera and Sketchbook*, 11, 33-34.

On Sunday, August 17, Ebell thought "the Indians acted strangely." An Indian woman approached Stephen Riggs to demand a calf as payment for damage his hogs had caused to her potato patch. Riggs refused, and the Indian left saying, "he might as well give it to her then, as she would have it any how pretty soon." Dakotas went to Williamson's barn and took two horses. When he confronted them, they told him someone would soon take the horses and "they might have them as well as any one else." In Ebell's estimation, the Dakotas knew something was brewing.[2]

Monday morning began as any other weekday, but by mid-morning rumors of trouble at Redwood Agency were spreading. As usual, the Dakotas were aware first. John Otherday (Ampatutokacha) said he heard word by eight in the morning, which if true was remarkable considering it was 30 miles between agencies. Otherday, son of Wahpeton leader Red Bird (Zitkaduta), was said to have been a brawling, intemperate, wild youth, much as Little Crow had been. In a rough fight with One Who Stands on a Cloud, Otherday bit off part of his opponent's nose, causing the man to be known ever after as Cut Nose. Cut Nose never outgrew his pugnacity and was one of the most murderous of the warring Dakotas. Otherday, however, walked a different path. In 1856 he joined the Hazelwood community, became a farmer, and adopted some white customs. In 1857 he assisted in rescuing Abbie Gardner, one of Inkpaduta's Spirit Lake captives, and killed Inkpaduta's son Fire Cloud in battle. Otherday was one of the delegates who traveled to Washington in 1858 to negotiate the treaty. There, he became infatuated with a white woman who worked as a waitress (and who was also said to be a prostitute) at the hotel in which the Indians stayed. She moved back to Minnesota with him to become his wife. Otherday was a prime example of a progressive who realized that cooperation and assimilation were necessary for the Dakotas to survive in a rapidly changing world. He also illustrated the sharp divide between his party and the Dakotas who embraced their traditional lifestyle.[3]

Otherday was cutting hay when he stopped for water and heard drums at Inyangmani's camp on the prairie. About 100 Wahpeton and Sisseton leaders had assembled to discuss the unfolding situation, joined by about 30 visiting Yanktons. Otherday joined them, and the talks lasted much of the day. Otherday argued that they should keep out of the trouble the Mdewakantons

---

2   Woolworth and Bakeman, eds., *Camera and Sketchbook*, 46.

3   Holcombe, *Monuments and Tablets*, 50-51; Newcombe, "The Sioux Sign a Treaty," 95.

began. "We are a different tribe," he admonished those around him. "Their actions are nothing to us. I do not want to see a white man killed." An Indian named Mazamani, however, replied that the Mdewakantons were relatives and lived next to them, and that it would be impossible to stay out of the affair. "The whites will not discriminate," Mazamani predicted, adding that the Mdewakantons "have involved us in their ruin."

Meanwhile, messengers arrived to report on what else was happening downriver, including the attack on Captain Marsh's men at Redwood Ferry. According to Otherday, the council "was greatly divided in sentiment." The general position of the Sisseton members was that they should kill the whites and take their property because the whites would see them all as enemies. The Wahpetons wanted to take the whites' property, but did not want to kill anyone. Otherday told them that they might kill five, ten, or even 100 whites, but soldiers would come and engulf their entire country and kill them all or drive them away. That mattered not, was the majority position; that result would occur whether they killed whites or only stole their property. White Lodge and his people arrived and added their voices to the argument for killing the whites and plundering the stores. Otherday described them as "the most unruly Indians at the Upper Agency." Some of the chiefs arguing for killing the whites were Lean Bear, White Lodge, and Blue Face, while those who argued for restraint included Mazamani, Akipa, Simon Anawangmani, and Inyangmani, Little Crow's father-in-law. When some Indians began to leave, Otherday realized the killing and plundering was about to begin, and that he must save as many people as he could.[4]

The mixed-bloods got the news a little later. Gabriel Renville was the son of mixed-bloods Victor Renville and Winona Crawford and was raised by the full-blood Wahpeton, Akipa. Ex-agent Joseph R. Brown was his brother-in-law. Gabriel lived about six miles below the Upper Agency on the north side of the Minnesota River. His son Victor (13) attended school at Williamson's mission. He was returning home when two Indians stopped him and took his saddle blanket. He wondered what the strangers were doing there and rode to the house of Solomon Two Stars (Wicanrpinonpa) to tell him what happened. Two Stars already heard the stories and told the boy to hurry home: Indians were killing whites and mixed-bloods. "This is a rumor," he added, "but your father

4 Whipple, *Lights and Shadows*, 119-20; Anderson and Woolworth, *Through Dakota Eyes*, 120-121, 123.

had better look out." Two Stars and his wife visited Gabriel's house about eight that evening and remained there overnight.

Twenty-five-year-old Charles R. Crawford (Wakanhinape), the son of Akipa and mixed-blood Winona Crawford and half-brother of Gabriel Renville, got word of the uprising about noon. While the mixed-bloods were usually second to hear the news, the whites scattered from Dr. Williamson's house in the west to the traders' stores in the east were last in the chain. Crawford, a government warehouse clerk and part-time interpreter at Yellow Medicine, told Noah Sinks, an Ohio native who supervised the government warehouses at both agencies and was in charge while Galbraith was gone. Sinks voiced skepticism and even Crawford didn't believe the rumors.[5]

The agency blacksmiths wondered what was going on when Dakotas began bringing in their weapons to have them repaired. Head blacksmith Nehemiah A. Miller and his assistant, Edward Cramsie, had never done such a brisk business. When they asked about it, the Indians replied that they were going on a buffalo hunt or an expedition against the Chippewas. Cramsie (62), a native of Ireland, came to America in 1826, married, raised a family, and moved them to St. Paul in 1857, where he built the city's first blacksmith shop. When two of his sons enlisted to fight in the Civil War, Cramsie left the rest of his family in St. Paul to work as blacksmith at Yellow Medicine Agency. He roomed at John Fadden's boarding house.[6]

By Monday evening both Cramsie and Miller realized they were being duped, abandoned the shop, and made for home. Frederick Patoile stopped by Miller's and told him what he had heard about the outbreak. Miller was still somewhat skeptical and replied that "we had heard many such stories before." Patoile advised him that John Otherday had moved his wife to the warehouse and that others were in the process of doing the same, himself included. Mazamani had warned him of the outbreak and Frederick was moving his sickly wife, child, and sister Josephine. They worked in their Uncle Francois Patoile's store and Josephine also kept house in his dwelling next door. What they did not yet know was that their uncle had been killed late that afternoon. Frederick's brother, Peter Patoile, decided to stay at the store and finish up some business.

---

5   Anderson and Woolworth, *Through Dakota Eyes*, 100, 105-06, 112-13.

6   Woolworth and Bakeman, eds., *Camera and Sketchbook*, 84; Newson, *Pen Pictures of St. Paul*, 645; Edward Cramsie Depredation Claim #232.

The clerks at Louis Robert's store escaped, but Louis Constans, a Frenchman who worked at Forbes's store, remained there. William L. Quinn (33) was in charge of the store but was in St. Paul on business, unaware that his father Peter Quinn lay dead at Redwood Ferry. When Constans finally decided to run the Indians chased him down and killed him. William Quinn returned as a scout for Colonel Sibley weeks later and found Constans's body in the bottoms by the Minnesota River.

Two men who received no warning at all were James W. Lindsay and Charles Lauer, a pair of bachelors who worked a plot of land about a dozen miles up the Yellow Medicine from the agency. Warriors killed them both.[7]

By the time Peter Patoile realized he had made a mistake by staying at the store, he tried to get away but was shot down outside. The bullet went into his back, through one lung, and exited his chest. A warrior turned him over, said "He is dead," and left. While the Dakotas plundered the stores Peter crawled into the bushes by the Yellow Medicine and hid all day Tuesday. After dark he made his way up the bluff to the agency, but found it plundered and abandoned. By then his uncle's store and house were burned, and all of Peter's belongings, worth about $143, were destroyed. After making his way to the Minnesota River near the mouth of the Yellow Medicine, Peter crossed over and found the deserted house of a settler, named Louis LaBelle. Badly wounded and completely exhausted, Patoile fell into bed and slept until Wednesday morning. He made a breakfast of some crackers, tripe, and onions before heading northeast, avoiding the roads leading to Fort Ridgely. Peter wandered several days, sleeping in deserted houses while scrounging any food wherever he could find it. Twelve days later he was far to the north in Stearns County at the Sauk River, where settlers found him and carried him in a wagon to St. Cloud. It was only then that his terrible wound was finally dressed.[8]

Mixed-blood Joseph La Framboise Jr., son of the trader who assisted the first German immigrants at New Ulm, also spent much of Monday trying to

---

7   Bryant and Murch, *Great Massacre*, 129, 396; Josephine Patoile Depredation Claim #836; Peter Patoile Depredation Claim #1097; Holcombe, *Monuments and Tablets*, 32; Renville, "A Sioux Narrative," 605, MHSC, Vol. 10.

8   Peter Patoile Depredation Claim #1097; Bryant and Murch, *Great Massacre*, 118-20; Stevens, *Minnesota and its People*, 371-72. According to the latter two sources, Joseph La Framboise Jr. and Narcisse Frenier found Patoile at LaBelle's and assisted him with food and blankets. La Framboise makes no mention of this in his narrative (Anderson and Woolworth, *Through Dakota Eyes*, 140), saying instead he went to a house to get his brother, Alexis La Framboise.

warn the whites. His first visit was to 31-year-old Stewart B. Garvie. The Scotsman ran Myrick's store at Yellow Medicine and was reading a newspaper with his feet propped up against the door when La Framboise broke the news. Garvie didn't appear overly concerned and remained at Myrick's. La Framboise took his warning next to Robert's, Forbes's, and Patoile's stores. Dr. Wakefield responded to the news by telling La Framboise that it was foolish to believe rumors of that kind. Noah Sinks, however, wasn't so sure. "I believe there is something in this," he said, "because we have not received any mail for two days." When Dr. Wakefield was finally convinced something serious was afoot, he made arrangements with George Gleason to take his wife Sarah out of harm's way. When Sinks asked La Framboise what they should do, the mixed-blood messenger suggested they get all the whites together in one of the agency brick buildings and defend themselves.[9]

La Framboise gathered his wife and children and took them to Francis Frenier's, his mother-in-law's home. His next stop was the Daily, Pratt & Company store, where he had begun working just three days earlier. There, La Framboise told Duncan R. Kennedy and J. D. Boardman to get away as fast as possible. The men left for the agency to see what was happening. La Framboise and his brother-in-law, Narcisse Frenier, heard some of the heated discussions among the Indians that evening. When arguments turned toward killing the mixed-bloods (who some argued were no more deserving of life than the whites), Joe and Narcisse left for the Frenier home, but stopped back at the Daily, Pratt & Company store when they saw the lights burning inside. Kennedy and Boardman had returned from their visit to the agency and, convinced the rumors of murders and proper destruction were exaggerated, busied themselves stocking the shelves. La Framboise blew the light out, stressed the seriousness of the latest developments, put blankets over them, and rushed them out the back door.

The men were making their way through the darkness when two Dakotas stumbled into La Framboise and asked whether the white men were still in the store. When the mixed-blood answered yes, the Indians continued on. A few moments later La Framboise and his brother-in-law pulled the blanket off the shopkeepers, pointed the way to the river, shook their hands, and hastened Kennedy and Boardman on their way. Then they ran as fast as possible for the Frenier house.

9   Anderson and Woolworth, *Through Dakota Eyes*, 108-09.

They had barely taken ten steps when shots rang out. La Framboise and Narcisse ducked behind some bushes as a man in a white shirt ran past followed by two Indians. When the Dakotas returned a short time later Joe and Narcisse—who could speak Dakota fluently—listened as one of them admitted, "I shot him in the back and I think I hit his heart." The other replied that if such was the case, the wounded man could not have gotten far, adding, "He must be hiding in the bushes somewhere." La Framboise and Narcisse crawled away as fast as they could for home. The man shot in the back was probably Peter Patoile.

Another casualty that night was Stewart Garvie. The Scotsman had remained at the store until Indians arrived and opened fire. Garvie ran upstairs, jumped out a back window, and was crawling through a potato patch when his pursuers spotted him and opened fire again. Bullets struck him in the wrist and side. Garvie crawled uphill toward the agency, probably hoping there was still someone there to help him and wishing all the while he had taken La Framboise's advice hours ago.[10]

Duncan Kennedy had a slightly different recollection of these events. According to Kennedy, he and Boardman were asleep at the store when La Framboise arrived to awaken them about 2:00 a.m. Tuesday morning. The mixed-blood, he continued, told them that traders had been killed at Redwood, threw buffalo robes over them, and ushered them outside. Boardman was ill will "consumption" (possibly tuberculosis) and Kennedy assisted him almost every step of the way. Kennedy locked the door and threw the key in the river. The men had only covered about 50 yards when three Dakotas approached along the same path. The whites jumped down the bank of Yellow Medicine River to hide as they passed by. According to Kennedy, they listened to them conversing in Dakota and heard his name mentioned. Boardman wanted to leave but Kennedy was curious and followed the warriors as they approached his store, pounded at the door, called out his name, and finally returned down the same path.

Kennedy wanted to flee, but returned instead to help Boardman join the other whites gathering in the stone buildings. Once Boardman was safe Kennedy left on what would turn out to be a remarkable journey. Moving speedily in the dark, he crossed the Minnesota River and walked about ten miles

10 Anderson and Woolworth, *Through Dakota Eyes*, 111-12, 123; Joseph La Framboise Jr. Depredation Claim #1108. Woolworth and Bakeman, eds., *Camera and Sketchbook*, 85.

northeast, detouring around the roads closely paralleling the river. He avoided a couple of Indians during the daylight and reached the headwaters of Beaver Creek by four in the afternoon. When Kennedy spotted more Indians he hid for a while and used the cover provided by a rolling thunderstorm to keep moving. He was still about ten miles from Fort Ridgely when he heard a rider approaching in the darkness. Kennedy raised his shotgun and was about to fire when he decided to call out a challenge.

"Who comes there?"

"For God's sake don't shoot!" the man responded, "I am a white man!" It was Antoine Frenier, who had just left Ridgely on his scouting mission. The two men exchanged a few words and were on their way. Kennedy reached the fort during the early hours of Wednesday morning after traversing 52 miles from the Upper Agency, plus several more miles of detours—all in about 24 hours. Kennedy's journey confirmed his wife's claim that he was quite a physical specimen. He could trot all day long, she said, and once "walked" the 75 miles from Traverse des Sioux to St. Paul in a single day.

Kennedy remained at Ridgely until the following Monday, when a call was made for a volunteer to carry a message to St. Peter. Kennedy promptly stepped forward. Sutler Randall offered him a horse, but Kennedy declined, replying, "If the Indians hear the horse they will know the difference between a shod horse and an Indian pony. I will go alone." And so Kennedy took off again. He had a brush in the darkness with some Dakotas near Nicollet, but answered their challenge in their own tongue and they let him pass. He reached St. Peter safely.[11]

* * *

The atmosphere at Yellow Medicine was charged with tension on Monday afternoon when stories of the outbreak spread and individuals were forced to decide what course of action to take. Sixteen-year-old Samuel J. Brown arrived at the agency about noon. He was the son of Joseph R. Brown and Susan Frenier, a mixed-blood Dakota and the step-daughter of Akipa. Ex-agent Joe Brown built a three-story brick "mansion" on the north bank of the Minnesota about six miles below Yellow Medicine Agency, where he housed his large family along with other relatives. That morning young Sam and his older sister

11 Bryant and Murch, *Great Massacre*, 376-78; Morris, *Old Rail Fence Corners*, 120-21.

Ellen arrived in their carriage with a load of clothes to wash. While on the road to the agency an Indian farmer named Little Dog, who attributed his prosperity to the programs initiated by Sam's father, stopped them. After he told Sam and Ellen about the outbreak and advised them to get their mother and family away, Sam thanked him and they rode on. Little Dog was known in the area as an inveterate liar.

At the agency, the pair passed George Gleason making ready to leave with Sarah Wakefield. To Sam, it looked and sounded more like George was taking her on the first leg of a pleasure journey to visit relatives back east rather than hurrying her away in an effort to save her life. Gleason promised Sam that when he returned he would bring James Lynd with him and they would all enjoy some hunting and fishing. No one had the slightest idea that Lynd had been lying dead on the floor at Myrick's Redwood store for the past six hours—the first victim of the uprising. Sam and Ellen rode another three miles to Williamson's, where they dropped the clothes off for the washerwoman. They were returning when an old Dakota woman approached and urged them to get away. Sam and Ellen dismissed the warning and rode to John Fadden's boarding house near the agency, where they stopped to talk and have dinner. Fadden was Angus Brown's (Sam's brother's) father-in-law. They asked an Indian woman who worked there if the rumors of trouble were true. She denied them.

Sam and Ellen left the agency at 3:30 p.m. shortly after Gleason and Wakefield. At home that evening they told everyone all they had heard and seen, but Angus Brown and Charles Blair, Ellen's husband, "pooh-poohed the idea of trouble with the Indians." Ex-agent Joseph Brown was away on business and Susan Frenier Brown was in charge of the household. She thought differently. Once everyone was in bed she locked and bolted the doors. The silence was shattered about 4:00 a.m. on Tuesday morning when an old Canadian Frenchman named Peter Rouillard appeared outside yelling "Brown! Brown!" Peter had lived with the Indians for many years and had taken a Dakota wife. Ellen's husband Charles opened a window and asked what on earth he was shouting about. "For God's sake hurry!" Peter exclaimed. "Indians are burning everybody at the agency," and he had barely escaped with his life.[12]

Susan Brown ordered Sam to wake up Mr. Lonsman, the hired hand, and have him get the horses and wagons ready. The horses were running loose,

---

12 Brown, "In Captivity," *Mankato Weekly Review,* as cited in Anderson and Woolworth, *Through Dakota Eyes,* 70-73.

however, so Lonsman hitched up six pair of oxen to three wagons. By the time they were ready several other families had arrived, including at least one survivor from the Ingalls family. Late the previous evening, while John Otherday and other chiefs argued the fate of the whites, warriors who had already made up their own minds set out to rob and kill. Either late Monday or early Tuesday at the small Hawk Creek settlement a few miles downriver of Yellow Medicine they attacked Scotsman Jedidiah H. Ingalls and his family. They killed Jed and possibly his wife. They captured George Washington Ingalls (10) but spared the boy (as the story goes) because of his bright red hair. Sisters Amanda (12) and Lavinia (8) escaped to Brown's house.[13]

The large group of people gathered at the Brown's included several families and individuals. Joseph and Susan Brown's extended family consisted of Lydia Ann Brown Blair (26), her husband Charles Blair (27), and their children Minnesota (Minnie) (4) and Stuart (2); Angus M. A. Brown (24), his wife Elizabeth Fadden Brown (21), and their son Edmund (infant); Ellen Brown (21); Samuel J. Brown (16); twins Amanda and Emily Mary Ann Brown (15); Maria (12); Joseph R. Brown Jr. (10); Sibley H. Brown (6); and Susan Jane Brown (2). Charles Holmes, a single man who lived on a claim west of Brown, joined them. Leopold Woehler and his wife Frances arrived. Leopold and his brother Charles (30) burned lime at the government kiln three miles east of the agency, but Charles had joined Galbraith and his Renville Rangers a few days before the uprising and was gone. Leopold and Frances took the outbreak warning seriously and fled to the Brown's late Monday. Stewart Garvie's cook arrived, as did a few other refugees from the agency. Frenchman Peter Rouillard also joined them. At least 26 people climbed aboard the three wagons and urged the oxen toward Fort Ridgely.[14]

The wagons had traveled about six miles and were beyond Sacred Heart Creek when a sizeable band of warriors appeared. Among them were Cut Nose, Little Six, and Dowanniye. They had just finished butchering the Busse, Boelter,

---

13 Brown, "In Captivity," *Mankato Weekly Review*, as cited in Anderson and Woolworth, *Through Dakota Eyes*, 73; Bryant and Murch, *Indian Massacre in Minnesota*, 131; "The Ingalls Inquirer," http://home.comcast.net/~ingallspages/Inquirer/4-2.html and 9-1.html. Ingalls is said to have been either a widower, married twice, or married with his wife living in Wisconsin, with two daughters and a son, three daughters and a son, or two daughters and two sons. Sources also conflict as to his wife's fate: she was either killed with him or absent.

14 Bryant and Murch, *Great Massacre*, 130-31; Charles E. Woehler Depredation Claim #237. James Fadden also was employed by and lived with the Browns. On August 10, he took a wagon to Henderson to buy a load of flour for Major Brown and thus avoided capture.

and Roessler families on Middle Creek. Susan Brown realized that the only way to save lives was to talk fast and forcefully. Mustering incredible bravery, she stood in the wagon, waved her shawl, and cried out that she was a Sisseton, a relative of Scarlet Plume, Sweet Corn, and Akipa. All of the people with her were seeking protection, she continued. Most of the Indians seemed inclined to murder them anyway, but one of them rode closer, pointed to Susan, and announced, "This woman saved my life last winter, and I shall save her's now." The warrior launched into an impassioned speech and the other Indians withdrew to talk it over. A few minutes later they returned to declare that they would spare everyone—except the white men. Susan refused to back down. "Remember what I say," she threatened. "If you harm any of these friends of mine, you will have to answer to Scarlet Plume, Ah-kee-pah, Standing Buffalo and the whole Sisseton and Wahpeton tribe." After several more councils and arguments the Dakotas agreed reluctantly to spare the women and children and let the white men go—all that is except hired man Lonsman, who they ordered to drive the wagons, and Charles Blair, who they planned to kill later.

Cut Nose was leading Frances Woehler off when her husband Leopold ran toward her. Cut Nose cocked his gun and threatened to shoot him if he did not leave immediately. Leopold left, but returned a short time later. The Dakotas moved to kill him, but Susan Brown's scream brought them to a halt. Leopold backed away again but returned a third time. On this occasion he approached Cut Nose, tore open his shirt, and declared, "Shoot me, but I shall first kiss my wife." Leopold Woehler's audacity astonished the Indians, who stood and watched as he showered Francis with kisses and then ran away.

Once Leopold departed the white women were parceled out among the Indians. On the way toward their camp on Rice Creek they passed several mutilated white bodies. One of them was a woman with a pitchfork sticking in her, and another a man with a scythe in him. According to Sam Brown, Cut Nose "gleefully told that he had killed this man" by first shaking his hand and then stabbing him in the chest. They fought, the warrior continued, and the white man almost bit off Cut Nose's thumb before he killed him and stuck the scythe into his body. The Dakota proudly displayed his bloody thumb to the horrified onlookers. The hushed and frightened captives were taken to mixed-blood John Moore's house near Redwood River. There, some of the warriors took the Ingalls girls and Frances Woehler while the rest continued to Little Crow's, where the chief gave them water, robes, and blankets and assured them he would treat them as his family. Little Crow was a "wily old fellow!" declared Sam Brown. "He was working for the aid and support of the Upper

Sioux. He knew of [Sam's] mother's influence over Standing Buffalo, Waanatan, Scarlet Plume, Sweet Corn, Red Iron, A-kee-pah, and other influential Sisseton and Wahpeton chiefs."[15]

As the Browns and other refugees were preparing to flee in the pre-dawn of August 19, matters were coming to a head at Yellow Medicine Agency. About sundown on Monday, Haponduta, who had seen the beginnings of the outbreak at Redwood, arrived at Yellow Medicine and confirmed the news. Haponduta, Charles Crawford, Mazamani (Iron Walker), and Supihiye (His Guts Came Out) visited Noah Sinks at the government warehouse and told him he had better get away. Sinks thought it might be better if they all remained in the warehouse until they knew more, as La Framboise suggested. A few others streamed in, the result of additional efforts by John Otherday and his wife to convince them to go to the brick "Agency house."

As the whites gathered so did the Dakotas. The Indians arrived in groups of five to ten and soon formed a loose circle around the buildings. Otherday concluded they intended to kill him and his four companions and then attack the whites. Thinking they might be in for a long siege, during the night Crawford obtained a key to the supply room and he and others rolled out a barrel of pork and sugar while boarding house owner John Fadden eyed them suspiciously.

Crawford and company may have been hoarding the food about the time shots were fired down the hill in the direction of the traders' stores. Soon the orange glow of a fire was visible beyond the crest of the hill. The Dakotas encircling the agency buildings broke away and hurried down to the stores "to participate in the booty," explained Otherday, who together with some 60 whites gathered there decided it was their best chance to flee.

Before they left the mixed-blood Crawford slipped over to see his mother Winona, who lived nearby. She was very worried about what was happening and asked her son to look after his sister, Susan Frenier Brown. He promised her he would do so. Back at the agency, the party was readying to flee before sunrise. When Crawford told them about his promise to his mother, Fadden— whose daughter was married to Angus Brown—told him that when the party got as far as Brown's place, he and Otherday would go down and check on Crawford and the Browns.

15 Brown, "In Captivity," *Mankato Weekly Review*, as cited in Anderson and Woolworth, *Through Dakota Eyes*, 73-78, 131.

Despite his promise, Crawford was afraid to travel there alone. When a Mdewakanton Indian named Bogaga arrived from Redwood, Winona inquired whether her daughter was alive. He didn't know about the fate of the Browns, but he informed her that whites living as far up as Sacred Heart had been killed. At Winona's request, Bogaga agreed to accompany her son to find out. To arouse less suspicion Crawford stripped down his clothes, applied paint, and the "farmer" Indians left. John Fadden had been paying close attention to what was transpiring. "Our party then left under guidance of Otherday," Fadden later testified in a depredation claim, "but before we left I noticed claimant (Crawford) was naked and had daubed on the war paint. He acknowledges he was in one or two battles and it is my opinion he joined voluntarily. He could have escaped with us if he had been disposed."[16]

Crawford and Bogaga reached the Minnesota River on the opposite shore from Brown's about sunup. The ferryboat was north of the river, but when Crawford shouted for Angus Brown no one returned the call. Crawford took off his remaining clothes, wrapped only his shirt around his head, and swam across. Back on dry land, he wrapped his shirt around his waist as a breech clout and made his way to the Brown house. It was empty. Crawford walked to the hilltop and there met up with Otherday and Fadden. Seeing Crawford clad only in breech clout and adorned with paint only served to further confirm the boardinghouse keeper's suspicions that the mixed blood was a renegade. Neither Otherday nor Fadden wanted to stay and investigate the fate of the Brown family, so Crawford walked back to the house, gathered some clothes, put on one of Joe Brown's military coats, and left. Bogaga, who had been waiting on the far bank of the river, waved to hurry Crawford across because two Dakotas were approaching. Crawford crossed over and hid in the background while Bogaga asked the warriors if they knew the whereabouts of the Brown family. They didn't have any information, but told him that most of the whites in the area had been killed. They were on their way to the Brown house to get powder and shot. When they left, Bogaga told Crawford to go home as quickly as possible.

Crawford was making his way home when two Frenchmen approached in a buggy heading toward Brown's. He warned them about the Indians at the ferry

<hr>

16 Anderson and Woolworth, *Through Dakota Eyes*, 113, 115-16, 122; Charles Crawford Depredation Claim #152. Testimony from Fadden and others made trouble for Crawford, who was brought before the military commission twice for participation in the war, but was acquitted both times.

and they promptly pulled off the road. Farther on Crawford passed an old woman, mixed-blood Elizabeth Jeffrey (Winonagina), her daughter Angeline Jeffrey Quinn, the wife of William L. Quinn, and their children Ellen, William, and Thomas. Crawford shared the same news with them and made sure they understood that if they went to the ferry they would be killed. They turned their buggy around and headed back toward Yellow Medicine, but they were not quick enough and were soon all captured.

Back at the agency Crawford found his mother a nervous wreck. She was certain her children and family had been killed. He was reassuring her otherwise when his half-brother, Gabe Renville, arrived with news that the Riggs and Williamson families hadn't left yet, but that other Indians were guarding them.[17]

While Crawford was at Brown's house, the whites at the agency warehouse had finally fled. More than 60 of them had gathered there during the past 24 hours, straggling in all day. John Otherday brought in his wife and child. Mrs. Galbraith, the agent's wife, was there with her three children. She realized her life was in danger because of the bad feelings the Dakotas had toward her husband. Sub-agent Nelson Givens, his wife, his wife's mother, and three children also arrived, as did Noah Sinks with his wife and two children and Frederick Patoile, his wife and child, and his sister Josephine Patoile. John Fadden brought in his wife and three children. Mr. and Mrs. John German arrived, as did Henry Eschle with his wife and five children, Mrs. Links with her children, Mr. Rotwell and his family, and boardinghouse owner Ebenezer Goodell with his wife and children.

There were many others, including Jane K. Murch, Edward Cramsie, Nehemiah Miller, Mary Charles, Lizzie Sawyer, Oscar Canfil, J. D. Boardman, Parker Pierce, Z. Hawkins, E. Rider, Dr. John Wakefield, Mr. Parker, Mr. Ashley, Matthew E. Hurd, and Carter H. Drew. Hurd had worked as an engineer at the government mill for three years and boarded at Fadden's. He left behind $112 worth of clothes and equipment. Drew was a surveyor who worked for Renville County. For the past year he had made his office in Fadden's boarding house while plotting a road from Fort Ridgely to Yellow Medicine along the north side of the river. Drew had to leave behind his equipment, including surveying compass, stakes, and chains, valued at $148.

17 Anderson and Woolworth, *Through Dakota Eyes*, 116-19. Crawford also explained that Otherday and the whites at the warehouse had fled. Crawford knew this because he spoke with Otherday and Fadden near the Brown house.

Mary Hayes came to work for Goodell in May of that year and fled with him. Elizabeth Zeiher worked for Noah Sinks and stayed with his family. For the past one-and-a-half years, Mary J. Dailey kept house for Agent Galbraith and lived with his family. Widow Ellen Hanrahan arrived in the spring and worked in Nelson Givens's house, just one-quarter mile from Galbraith's. None of the latter four women owned much in the way of property, but all they left with that day was what they were wearing.[18]

There would have been more people available to join Otherday's escape party or to share the fate of the others had not Galbraith recruited so many men to join the Renville Rangers. Abel B. Murch left his wife behind when he went to enlist. David Carpenter, a cook at Robert's store, joined with his friend Medard Lucier. Rocque Berthiaume worked for Stewart Garvie but joined the rangers with his friend Theophilus Richer, who became a sergeant in the company. Cyprian Le Clair worked at Yellow Medicine for six years farming, haying, and storekeeping. He spent the past year learning the business from Stewart Garvie, but decided to join the Union army with several of his friends. James F. Dickinson worked for Galbraith and Givens for one year before leaving with the other recruits. John McCole joined because his friend James Gorman, who worked with Garvie the past four years, caught war fever and decided to enlist. The men voted him lieutenant of the company. Henry Resca, on the other hand, did not join the rangers but was fortuitously absent during the uprising. Resca, who worked as assistant carpenter to head carpenter Henry Eschle, was given a leave of absence to visit friends in St. Paul. As a result of patriotism, serendipity, or for other motives these men and more were absent from the Upper Agency and so escaped the conflagration. Most of them, however, did not escape the subsequent fighting in the larger war sweeping the country.[19]

The 60-plus people in the warehouse spent an anxious night wondering whether they would escape, whether everything would blow over, or whether

18 Bryant and Murch, *Great Massacre*, 121; *New York Times*, August 26, 1862; Matthew E. Hurd Deprtedation Claim #255; Carter H. Drew Depredation Claim # 618; Mary Hayes Depredation Claim #274; Elizabeth Zeiher Depredation Claim #238; Mary Jane Dailey Depredation Claim #501; Ellen Hanrahan Depredation Claim #245. The four women filed claims for items such as dresses, bonnets, shawls, cloaks, bedding, draperies, and shoes, losses ranging from $40 to $80 apiece.

19 David Carpenter Depredation Claim #315; Rocque Berthiaume Depredation Claim #748; Cyprian Le Clair Depredation Claim #161; James F. Dickinson Depredation Claim #757; James Gorman Depredation Claim #343; Henry Resca Depredation Claim #166.

they would all be killed or taken captive. According to Nehemiah Miller, at some time before 11:00 p.m. several gunshots rang out below the hill from the direction of the traders' stores. Many of the Dakotas guarding them, plus the Dakotas who had surrounded the place trying to harm them, disappeared over the hill. Somehow in the confusion and darkness the injured Stewart Garvie made it to the warehouse, where Dr. Wakefield dressed his wounds. "The most dreadful noise continued outside, at the stores, all night," continued Miller. "We placed men on guard, and prepared for the worst. The night was passed in the most dreadful suspense!"[20]

John Otherday slipped away several times during the night to discern what was going on. He left again with Fadden about 5:00 a.m. on Tuesday to plan an escape. The Dakotas were nearly done plundering the stores, and when they finished they would almost certainly return to deal with the trapped whites. All the men could find, however, were two buggies and three wagons. The dozens of whites piled on, packing the wheeled vehicles to overflowing. When Miller inquired why Garvie was not among them, he was told there was no room, he was going to die, and would be left behind. Miller replied that if the Scotsman was going to be left behind, he would stay with him. Fadden intervened and gave up his spot for Garvie. The caravan left just before sunrise with 62 people crammed aboard.

The five vehicles crossed the Minnesota River near the mouth of the Yellow Medicine. Some wanted to take the direct route along the River Road to Fort Ridgely, but Otherday insisted they move instead onto the prairie. They paralleled the river on the road for a time until they drew near Joseph Brown's house, where Otherday and Fadden left the wagons to check on the family. On the way they met mixed-blood Charles Crawford, explained what they were doing, and returned to the caravan, angling northeast to give the river a wide detour. Most of the refugees were suspicious of Otherday, and only Noah Sinks appeared to have full confidence in him. This distrust, admitted Otherday, made him "very sad." His wife interpreted as he tried to give them hopeful reassurances, and this seemed to cheer up many of the refugees.

That night the caravan rolled into Kandiyohi County and stopped near the shore of Little Kandiyohi Lake at the home of Charles Peterson, about six miles southeast of present Willmar, Minnesota. The critically wounded Garvie was

20 Woolworth and Bakeman, eds., *Camera and Sketchbook*, 85; Bryant and Murch, *Great Massacre*, 397.

still alive and carried into the house, where the women did their best to make him as comfortable as possible. The next morning, Wednesday, Peterson fled alone and Otherday's party headed southeast toward Hutchinson. When the refugees reached the village of Cedar City, in the extreme northeast corner of McLeod County, they found it deserted. The settlers had fled to an island in Cedar Lake. Otherday's party joined them, and everyone spent a miserable night in the rain. By this time it was obvious to everyone that Garvie was failing. Thursday morning, the 21st, the refugees traveled several miles south before stopping at a house owned by a man named Peck. They left Garvie there in his care and continued to Hutchinson. Beyond Hutchinson the party split up, with some heading to Glencoe and the balance to Henderson.[21]

Ebenezer Goodell and his family reached Glencoe on Saturday the 23rd, where he spoke with a newspaperman. Three days later the harrowing story of what was transpiring in distant southern Minnesota appeared in the *New York Times*. According to Goodell's account, Otherday's party consisted of 20 men and 42 women, all of whom were saved. He went on to speculate that about 40 families, including all those between Lac Qui Parle and Yellow Medicine Agency, had been killed. Some farmer Indians gathered at Reverend Riggs's house to defend him, Goodell continued, but they had been overpowered. It was through this newspaper article that word spread that all the missionaries and the people with them had been slaughtered. It wasn't the case. [22]

* * *

The whites living above Yellow Medicine Agency endured the same dilemma as all the others: should they remain with their homes and property or flee? Adrian Ebell was staying at Dr. Williamson's house at Pajutazi. He was out taking photographs of the area on Monday and returned to find the family "in great alarm" because of rumors of war. Many farmer Indians had come by to pass on the news of the uprising and three of them—Robert Chaska, Paul Mazakutemani, and Enos Good Voiced Hail—remained overnight. By

---

21 Woolworth and Bakeman, eds., *Camera and Sketchbook*, 85; Bryant and Murch, *Great Massacre*, 398-99; Anderson and Woolworth, *Through Dakota Eyes*, 125. Garvie died a day later. Nehemiah Miller arranged for his body to be moved to Hutchinson, where a sermon was read and he was properly buried.

22 *New York Times*, August 26, 1862.

Tuesday morning, Ebell recalled, "Some were for instant flight, others thought it was only a 'scare,' and had no doubt that it would blow over shortly. Not one of us, even the most timid, had the least conception of its magnitude."

Indian women boldly walked into Dr. Williamson's home and took whatever they wanted, carrying off the sugar barrel and even dumping out the feathers from the mattresses to wear the ticking as coats. Ebell, in a classic understatement, explained that it was at this time "We began to think it was time to leave."[23]

Gabriel Renville and his son Victor left their house Tuesday morning and rode to Yellow Medicine Agency. There was no one at the west door of the warehouse. Puzzled, they moved around to the east side only to find Dakotas carrying off supplies. Otherday and the whites had fled just hours earlier. The startled pair rode to Winona Crawford's (Gabriel's mother) and she told what she knew, including that she had sent Gabriel's half-brother, Charles Crawford, to Brown's house. Gabriel ordered his mother to remain indoors and promised he would come back for her later.

Father and son next rode to Williamson's home and found the doctor standing in the road. Gabriel broke the news that all the people at Redwood and the settlers across the river had been killed, but those at Yellow Medicine had all fled in wagons and buggies under the guidance of John Otherday. The doctor may have expressed disbelief, for the mixed-blood added, "These things are true. Therefore, my friend, flee."

"I have been a long time with the Dakotas," Dr. Williamson replied, "and I don't think they will kill me." He was an old man, continued the doctor, and he was not afraid and would rather die than run away.

Gabriel next walked into the house and shook hands with several people. He remembered how frightened everyone looked—pale and wild-eyed. The whites climbed into a hay wagon and Chaska led them to a little-used ford on the Minnesota River. Dr. Williamson, his wife Margaret, and his sister, Jane Williamson, remained behind.

Gabriel and Victor rode toward Riggs's Hazelwood mission two miles farther up the road. On the way they met He Who Brings What He Wants (Ecetukiya), a brother of Solomon Two Stars, and Enos Good Voiced Hail (Wasuhowaste). The Indians explained that they had just hidden Riggs and his family in a thicket along the Minnesota River and were on their way to make

---

23 Woolworth and Bakeman, eds., *Camera and Sketchbook*, 47.

sure Dr. Williamson was safe. "It was a good thing they were doing," concluded Gabriel.[24]

* * *

According to Stephen Riggs, the sun was setting Monday when they heard the news from Antoine Renville (52), one of the elders of his church. Renville was a mixed-blood trader and the step-father of Nancy McClure Faribault. Like so many others, Riggs refused to believe what to him was the unbelievable. Surely it must be "only a drinking quarrel." But when some of the mixed-blood and Dakota parents arrived to take their children home from the boarding school, Riggs knew it was serious. Definitive confirmation arrived from the mouth of Jonas Pettijohn.

Pettijohn was born in Virginia in 1813, married Fannie Huggins of Ohio in 1845, and moved to Lac Qui Parle as Presbyterian missionaries to the Dakotas. Jonas and Fannie taught at Indian schools and assisted Riggs in translating the Bible into Dakota. They had five children between 1846 and 1854. In November 1859, Agent Joe Brown asked the Pettijohns to move to Red Iron's village a dozen miles above Hazelwood to teach in the government school. The Pettijohns worked there until August 1862, when James W. Holtsclaw enlisted in the Union army and offered Jonas the opportunity to run his farm near St. Peter during his absence. Exhausted after so many years of teaching the Dakotas, Jonas "didn't feel that I was doing much where I was," and accepted the offer.

On Monday, August 18, Jonas and his family were in the process of hauling their possessions down to Hazelwood in shifts. He hired a few Indians to help and sent his sons Albert (13) and William (10) down with their cow and calf. Jonas, Fannie, and daughters Laura (14) and Alice (6) hauled a load later in the day. On the way they met Thomas Riggs (15) driving back one of the empty wagons. Jonas traded places with Thomas and the boy rode back to Hazelwood with the Pettijohn children. Jonas was returning to his house for the last load when he caught word of an uprising. Skeptical about its merit, he collected the remainder of his goods and started for Hazelwood about sundown. Along the way a pair of Dakotas joined him on his wagon with the explanation that they were on their way to the mission for tobacco. Coming on the heels of news of

24 Anderson and Woolworth, *Through Dakota Eyes*, 102-03, 107.

an uprising, the rationale seemed a rather strange one. A short time later two more Indians Jonas had hired arrived with his other wagon, stopped him, and demanded he get out. They told him that whites were being killed and they wanted his property—but they were not going to harm him. Perhaps because of his kindnesses the warriors left him with one horse and admonished him to ride quickly but that he might well be killed before he could reach his family.[25]

This was the terrifying news Jonas related to Stephen Riggs. Soon thereafter they received a note from Nelson Givens at Yellow Medicine, delivered by a Dakota messenger, urging that they all move to the agency as soon as possible to join them. It was after midnight when they concluded to heed the advice. When Paul Mazakutemani stopped by to ask for some blue cloth so he could "dress like an Indian to be safe," any doubts that may have lingered vanished. If Paul was worried, they were in mortal danger. Riggs was tremendously concerned for his three oldest daughters, Isabella (22), Martha (20), and Anna (17), as well as for Mrs. Moore, the wife of D. Wilson Moore. The Moores were newlyweds from New Jersey and in Minnesota for their honeymoon. They met Riggs in early July in St. Paul when Riggs officiated the wedding of Alexander Hunter and Marion Robertson. To Riggs's surprise, the New Jersey couple arrived at his house after hearing that an annuity payment was going to be made soon and they wanted to see live Indians. There were no accommodations for them at the agency, so they sought out Riggs. Their curiosity had landed them in a heap of trouble. Even a friend of the Dakotas such as Riggs still reflected the prevailing frontier sentiment. The Indians, he reflected, would "kill us to get possession of" his daughters and Mrs. Moore.[26]

The party left Hazelwood about one o'clock on Tuesday morning with a two-horse wagon and a light buggy. Joining them were H. D. Cunningham, who was in charge of the Hazlewood boarding school, his wife, his sister, and his child. All together the caravan included Stephen Riggs, his wife Mary Ann, and their children Isabella, Martha, Anna, Thomas, Henry (13), Robert (7), and Mary Cornelia (3); Jonas Pettijohn, his wife Fannie, and their children Laura, Albert, William, and Alice; four Cunninghams, and two Moores. Martha Riggs counted 21 persons in their company. The lack of weapons among settlers living on the frontier is notable: Wilson Moore had the only good revolver, and Thomas and Henry Riggs each had a double-barrel shotgun. He Who Brings

25 Riggs, *Mary and I*, 154; Pettijohn, *Reminiscences of Jonas Pettijohn*, 6, 62, 67-71.

26 Riggs, *Mary and I*, 149-50, 155.

What He Wants and Enos Good Voiced Hail led the party to an island in the Minnesota River where they could hide.

It was not until about dawn that someone realized they had left behind much of the bread the women had baked for the trip. A short time later the voice of a Dakota woman called out to them. Stephen Riggs remembered her name as "Zoe," while Jonas Pettijohn referred to her as "Rainbow." She had risked her life to bring them their bread as well as some meat. "We received it as a God-send," acknowledged Martha Riggs. The refugees sat on their little island, miserable under a drenching rain, waiting to see what was to be done.

New York native Andrew Hunter (32) arrived in Minnesota in 1852, worked at Williamson's mission, and married Williamson's daughter Elizabeth. He was hiding along the Minnesota River with others from Pajutazi when he and Paul Mazakutemani discovered the Hazlewood group huddled on the island about noon and suggested they join forces. Hunter recommended that everyone move from the island to the north bank of the river, and volunteered to drive one of his wagons over to help carry people across. While Hunter was preparing a wagon, Cunningham and Pettijohn rode to the south bank to round up more horses. After securing one additional mount they returned to find the island had already been evacuated. Cunningham took the horse and a buggy and rode downriver to a ford while Pettijohn crossed back in a canoe. The heavy rain made for slow going, but quickly masked them and their tracks. Their numbers swelled when several employees from the government sawmill also found them. According to Pettijohn the party now numbered 36. Martha Riggs, however, counted 38, while Adrian Ebell put the number at 40. Once all was set the party headed downriver toward Hawk Creek. A short time later someone turned around and spotted a white man hobbling in their direction. Like so many, he too had a horrendous story to share.[27]

Richard Orr (21) worked at the Daily, Pratt & Company store below the mouth of the Chippewa River near the government school where the Pettijohns had also been employed. At daybreak on Tuesday, Dakotas from Red Iron's village knocked at the door and Orr's partner, Peter Guilbault, let them inside. Chippewa war parties were roaming nearby, explained the warriors, and they wanted to make sure the whites had loaded their guns. The Chippewas, explained Guilbault, never entered white men's houses. One of the Dakotas

---

27 Riggs, *Mary and I*, 155-57, 171-72; Pettijohn, *Reminiscences of Jonas Pettijohn*, 72; Woolworth and Bakeman, eds., *Camera and Sketchbook*, 47.

leaned over and sharpened a large knife on the grindstone and another asked for a pipe to smoke. Guilbault handed the Dakota a pipe and was building a fire when Orr finished dressing and walked outside.

Seconds later a shot came from inside the store. Orr ran back to the porch just as the warriors exited. The Dakota with the newly sharpened knife pulled it from behind his back and plunged it in his arm and shoulder. Twisting free, the young wounded storekeeper bulled his way inside and slammed the door. Guilbault was lying on the floor moaning, "My God! My God!" When Orr turned back toward the door and demanded to know what was going on, one of the Dakotas shot him in the groin. Orr stumbled backward and pulled out his own weapon, but it was unloaded. When he couldn't quickly find his ammunition, Orr sent his two dogs outside to attack the Indians and buy him time to escape. While the dogs attacked the Dakotas, Orr slipped out the back of the store and staggered into the woods. Exhausted and bleeding, the young man sought refuge in some willows, where one of his dogs later found him. When the Indians appeared Orr sent his dog after them again and moved downriver two miles before crossing to the north side. Although he "vomited blood," Orr told his rescuers, he staggered on until the wagons stopped to pick him up. "Our wagons were more than full," Stephen Riggs recalled, "but we could make room for a wounded white man."[28]

*   *   *

One white man who wouldn't be joining the escaping wagons was Amos W. Huggins, the eldest son of Alexander D. Huggins. Amos, born in Ohio in 1833, was given the middle name of Williamson in honor of his father's friend, Dr. Thomas Williamson. Both families moved to Dakota country as Presbyterian missionaries in 1835 and Amos spent his formative years there, making friends and learning the Dakota language. Amos left for school at 16 and worked in other fields. When he returned to the Lac Qui Parle region he did so with his bride Sophia Josephine Marsh Huggins, and together the young couple worked as government agents and teachers. They had two children, Eletta (4) and Charles (1). Julia La Framboise lived with them and also worked as a teacher at the school.

---

28 Bryant and Murch, *Great Massacre*, 270-71; Tolzmann, ed., *Outbreak and Massacre*, 49-50; Riggs, *Mary and I*, 157.

After Red Iron's warriors attacked Orr and Guilbault early Tuesday morning near the mouth of the Chippewa, they moved on and reached Lac Qui Parle, about ten miles farther north, later that afternoon. According to Sophia Josephine Huggins, August 19 "dawned on me full of hope and happiness. It was the twenty-fourth anniversary of my birth. But before its close it proved to be the saddest day of my life." Rumors of an outbreak reached Huggins about the same time three armed Dakotas appeared. Talkative and friendly, they asked to come inside and once there, demonstrated a deep interest in the sewing machine Julia was using. When they heard Amos arrive home in his wagon about 4:00 p.m., the warriors went outside to greet him. Within minutes, Amos was shot dead. According to later testimony, the murderer was Leather Blanket (Tainna). He Brought the News (Hosihdi) was also there, as was Makes the Wind (Tatekage), a grandson of Spirit Walker (Wakanmani) who was said to be mentally defective.

When Julia heard the gunfire and the Indians rushed back in "looking so wild and frightened," she thought the Chippewas were attacking them. The Dakotas yelled at her, "Go out, go out; you shall live—but go out. Take nothing with you." In the yard, Sophia Josephine Huggins saw her husband Amos's body and Julia kneeling over it. The woman looked and cried, "Oh Josephine, Josephine!" "An ocean of grief rolled over me," recalled Sophia Josephine.

Heeding the Dakota warning, Julia, the new widow, and her two young children left and took nothing with them. After staying a short time with a mixed-blood Chippewa trader who had a Dakota wife, they returned to secure Amos's corpse but found a gathering of angry Dakotas plundering the house. Spirit Walker found them and vowed to protect them. He denounced the killing and told Sopia Josephine that if he had been there, he would have protected Amos with his life. A few friendly Wahpetons buried Amos later that day and the women and children sought shelter in Spirit Walker's tipi, where he kept them from harm.[29]

*   *   *

29 Heard, *History of the Sioux War*, 209-10; McConkey, *Dakota War Whoop*, 100-02; Riggs, *Mary and I*, 169-70; Anderson and Woolworth, *Through Dakota Eyes*, 266n14. Hosihdi was later tried and sentenced to be hanged for Huggins's murder, but was given a reprieve. In a miscarriage of justice, Tatekage was tried and hanged.

Once the wounded Richard Orr was safely aboard a wagon the Riggs-Pettijohn party moved to put more miles between them and those who would do them harm. By nightfall the caravan was beyond Hawk Creek. Mr. Cunningham in his horse and buggy finally rejoined them, which enabled a few more people to ride instead of walk. Wednesday morning the party decided to head toward Glencoe and Hutchinson. Andrew Hunter had three milk cows with him, but during the day the calves drank all their milk. In the evening, however, Hunter tied up the calves to allow each person a turn to get "quite a good drink of fresh milk." Pettijohn was amused by the Moores, "educated and cultured people" from New Jersey who had "never before tasted warm cow's milk." Participants recalled that it seemed to rain incessantly throughout the perilous journey. Women and children crawled under the wagon beds at night, but the water dripped through the cracks and drenched them anyway. When Riggs spotted Mrs. Moore looking particularly wretched and inquired as to how she was, she replied "that one might as well die as live under such circumstances."

Four unnamed men—three Germans and a Scot according to Pettijohn—joined up with party on Wednesday. The men were from New Ulm and wanted the company to head in that direction. The caravan's eventual destination was still unclear. "We arose" Thursday morning after another night of rain, recalled Adrian Ebell, "and performing our toilets, like a Newfoundland dog just out of a mill-pond, with a hearty shake to dry ourselves," waddled toward a thicket ten miles distant in hope of finding some firewood. When a wide marsh blocked their course, some of the men sloshed through and brought back some firewood. Although they were only about 20 miles from the Upper Agency, the party stopped in the middle of the prairie at three in the afternoon to kill a heifer and eat. "[We] had our breakfast of partly roasted or smoked veal."

Martha Riggs saw a divine hand guiding their exodus: "The God who had led us during these long days, would neither suffer us to perish in this prairie wilderness, nor be taken by savages." Reasons why that same God allowed hundreds of others to perish apparently did not weigh on Martha's mind as she and the others "luxuriated on meat roasted on sticks." Ebell used the opportunity to set up his photographic equipment. "Here our party was immortalized by a young artist," Martha recalled.[30]

---

30 Riggs, *Mary and I*, 158, 173-74; Pettijohn, *Reminiscences of Jonas Pettijohn*, 73; Woolworth and Bakeman, eds., *Camera and Sketchbook*, 48-49.

On Friday, August 22, the company decided to head southeast toward Fort Ridgely. They had no way of knowing that on that same day, the Dakotas made their second and most serious attempt to overrun the outpost. The day started clear and bright, and by noon the caravan was between Beaver Creek and Birch Coulee. (Map E) Andrew Hunter drove his buggy to a claim he owned along lower Beaver Creek (not to be confused with Alexander Hunter and Marion Robertson, who also lived in the area) and there met up with an old Indian acquaintance. The unnamed Indian told Hunter that all the whites had either been killed or had fled to the fort. Hunter returned to the rest of the party with the news about the same time a wagon was seen approaching from the west carrying Dr. Williamson and his wife and sister. They had remained at Pajutazi when friendly Dakotas took them to the agency, where they stayed Tuesday night with Mazamani, His Guts Came Out, Solomon Two Stars, Gabe Renville, Akipa, and others. Early Wednesday, Simon Anawangmani and Chaska helped the three whites get across the river and sent them on their way. Williamson followed the wagon tracks Riggs and company carved into the muddy earth whenever he could see them, and guessed along the way when he could not. Although a full day behind, he was able to move faster and caught up with them on Friday.

Any doubts about the mortal threat still facing them were erased by the graphic carnage they discovered traveling along the east side of Beaver Creek. Two sons tried to get away from their home with their sick mother. They "carried her out on a straw mattress, and in a wagon had tried to escape," recalled Ebell. "The Indians overtook them, killed the sons, and piling some brush around the mattress, burned the sick woman alive." Ebell was probably describing the death site of Clarissa Henderson and her children.[31]

Even with the addition of the four men seeking to get to New Ulm the caravan still counted only four weapons. Ill-equipped but undaunted, the party formed "in military order" and continued along the road to the fort, finding bodies, burned dwellings, and discarded plunder along the way. When darkness fell they were still about seven miles from Fort Ridgely. They stopped when they saw silhouettes of Indians along a hilltop and a red glow from what appeared to be rockets fired from the direction of the fort. Andrew Hunter

---

31 Riggs, *Mary and I*, 159, 174; Pettijohn, *Reminiscences of Jonas Pettijohn*, 74-75, 78; Anderson and Woolworth, *Through Dakota Eyes*, 119; Woolworth and Bakeman, eds., *Camera and Sketchbook*, 48-49.

volunteered to take the buggy and ride ahead to examine the situation. After riding as far as he deemed prudent he hid the buggy as best he could and crept into the fort, where he found Lieutenant Sheehan. The Indians had attacked the fort throughout the day and the defenders had held on only by the slightest margin. They were nearly out of ammunition, continued the lieutenant, and there were already far too many women and children in the fort to guard or feed. Riggs's unarmed company would only make the situation worse. The officer suggested they drive on to Henderson.

Anxious to find out something, the impatient Dr. Williamson followed Hunter and met up with him when he was returning to get his buggy. The pair drove back and joined the balance of the refugees. The discussion that followed left the company divided as to the best course of action. Williamson, who owned two of the teams, made up his mind and announced, "As for me, my family and teams, we are not going into the Fort. Drive on." Pettijohn followed. The three Germans and one Scot who had joined the party on Wednesday remained determined to reach New Ulm and declared they would seek refuge in the fort. Perhaps worried that they would be caught and reveal their presence to the Indians, Wilson Moore cocked his pistol and threatened to shoot anyone who tried to leave. That settled the debate, and the caravan headed back out onto the prairie.

Although they traveled through much of the night, they were never out of sight of the glow of burning dwellings. Nerves were shot and everyone was exhausted. Any sound or shadow was thought to be a lurking Indian ready to pounce and kill them. "Ah! If a night of fear and dread was ever spent, that was one," admitted Martha Riggs. They finally stopped when they reached a creek across their path and were unable to find a fording place for the exhausted animals to haul them across. Few were able to get any sleep. Martha Riggs, as she was wont, turned her thoughts to God and her possible fate. Life was sweet and dear. Heaven would be glorious, but going to it "by the tomahawk and scalping knife" was "a hard way to go." She asked God, "must it be?" She shrank from being taken captive, "from the dishonor which is worse than death," but she wondered if it would be a greater sin to take her own life or suffer such a fate. For Martha and everyone else, "the night wore on . . ."[32]

---

32 Riggs, *Mary and I*, 159-60, 175-76; Pettijohn, *Reminiscences of Jonas Pettijohn*, 76-77; Woolworth and Bakeman, eds., *Camera and Sketchbook*, 50-51.

At first light on Saturday the caravan of refugees found themselves at what Stephen Riggs called the Lac Qui Parle crossing of Mud River, probably in the vicinity of present Mud Lake on upper Little Rock Creek, several miles northeast of Fort Ridgely. It was there that the four unarmed men bent on reaching New Ulm finally left the company. About 7:00 a.m., after having walked only a couple of miles, they were jumped by a band of warriors. After failing to capture the fort on Friday, the Dakotas had moved downriver for a second attempt to destroy New Ulm—and the Germans and Scotsman had walked right into them. Ebell, Riggs, and Pettijohn remembered hearing the gunfire that killed all four. Once more the survivors looked for an otherworldly answer to explain their survival. "The Lord of hosts was there with us," explained Jonas Pettijohn, "The God of Jacob was our refuge." Martha Riggs agreed: "Surely God led us and watched over us."

Divine protection or not the company continued east. They passed near Norwegian Grove, which the Dakotas would also attack later in the day. After traveling all day Sunday, they decided they were close enough to safety on Monday to separate and go their own ways. Williamson and his group rode on to St. Peter and Riggs's group, with the Moores and Ebell, went on to Shakopee. Like everyone, Riggs was overwhelmed by the events of the past week but could not get a thought out of his mind: "What will become of our quarter-century's work among the Dakotas? It seemed to be lost."

Riggs was still unaware of the scale of the disaster that had befallen both the whites and the Dakotas.[33]

33 Riggs, *Mary and I*, 161-62, 176; Pettijohn, *Reminiscences of Jonas Pettijohn*, 77; Woolworth and Bakeman, eds., *Camera and Sketchbook*, 51, 121. Many of the missionaries and teachers professed a sincere concern for the Dakotas' well-being, but it did not prevent them from filing damage claims against the tribe. Several of the Riggs and Pettijohn clans received compensation from the Dakotas' annuities. Stephen Riggs received $2,875. Ebell's claim was denied because he had gone on the reservation without permission.

Chapter 11

"Nature itself turned to their favor."

First Battle of New Ulm

Description of New Ulm ~ Defense preparations ~ Leavenworth rescue party ~ Dakotas attack
the town ~ Leavenworth rescue party ambushed ~ Relief attempts ~ Thunderstorm

O n August 19, as the uprising of murder and mayhem spread as far
northwest as the Chippewa River, Dakota warriors re-visited the New
Ulm area 70 miles to the south. They had moved around the outskirts of the
town on Monday when they devastated Milford and swept along the
Cottonwood River, but on Tuesday decided to strike the town directly. It was a
close decision whether Fort Ridgely or New Ulm would be the first to feel the
wrath of a full Dakota attack. Scattered raids by comparatively small war parties
were one thing; what was sweeping toward New Ulm was something altogether
different.

Fort Ridgely was spared (for the time being) because an Indian force strong
enough to launch an attack could not be gathered in time to make a Monday
effort. As a result, many refugees had time to flee there. By mid-morning on
Tuesday, Little Crow, Mankato, Big Eagle, and other chiefs, assembled west of
the fort to argue for an assault. Younger warriors overruled their advice and
urged instead an attack against New Ulm, where there would be no soldiers, no
cannons, and plenty of easy plunder. Little Crow had more than 300 warriors,
but after the division he was left with only about 125. Now too weak to attack
the fort, Little Crow decided to wait until the next day. While the Dakotas
argued about where to attack first, the townsfolk of New Ulm prepared to
defend themselves.

Laid out generally southeast to northwest between a tight "V" formed by the junction of the Cottonwood River with the Minnesota River, the town was not built with defense in mind. The land rose about 200 feet from the Minnesota in two terraces, dropped off slightly in a marshy depression, and then rose again to the third terrace or bluff above the Cottonwood. The terraces, recalled one witness, provided the Dakotas "with sloping springboards for invasion." Timber close to the town covered approaches, and the dispersed dwellings designed to give everyone "elbow room" made a concentrated defense much more difficult. Most of the buildings were on the lower terrace, but others were scattered elsewhere, too dispersed for mutual protection but ideal as cover for an attacker. The main street, Broadway, ran between the "V" a little closer to the Minnesota River side. Center Street bisected Broadway in the middle of town. (Map M)[1]

According to the 1860 census New Ulm's population was 635, but by 1862 had grown by perhaps another 200 people. The ratio of men to women and children in this town full of industrious growing families was about one in five, meaning all told about 170 adult New Ulm males in various stages of preparedness would be available to fight. However, the real number from this pool was smaller because some men gathered their families and fled. On the other hand, large numbers of refugees were swarming into the town, which should have increased the potential number of armed men—if they had weapons. Given the numbers of men gathered for defense, it appears many or most of those swarming into New Ulm did so without a viable means of defense. Sheriff Roos gathered about 30 men with firearms to accompany him when he left Monday night to recover the killed and wounded from the Milford attack. Jacob Nix, the German ex-captain appointed the town's commandant, rounded up 14 men with rifles led by Louis Theobald; 18 men with double-barrel shotguns, commanded by E. F. Brunk; and another dozen led by J. Chaikowitz and armed with what one witness described as "poor shotguns." Some 18 additional men with firearms of varying quality arrived but did not join any particular company. Using these numbers, perhaps 92 men with firearms were available to defend the town.[2]

---

1   Carley, *Dakota War of 1862*, 32-33; Wall, *Recollections of the Sioux Massacre*, 76-77; "New Ulm 2009 Visitor's Guide," 30-31.

2   Nix, *Sioux Uprising*, 89-90.

Knowing that they would need help, Roos and Nix sent messengers to Mankato and to Governor Alexander Ramsey in St. Paul. The capital was far away, however, and Henry Behnke, who had ridden to town with the news of the attack on the recruiting party volunteered to ride to Traverse des Sioux to find Judge Charles E. Flandrau, the ex-agent, who was one of the best-known and influential men in the state. Behnke left at near midnight and reached St. Peter about four a.m. on Tuesday. He aroused William B. Dodd, one of the town's founders, and then rode a mile north to tell the judge. Flandrau knew immediate action was needed. He told Behnke to wake the people of St. Peter and by 6:00 a.m. Flandrau was there to find that Dodd had already gathered a relief force of about 100 men. It would be hours before any help would arrive; until then the people of New Ulm were on their own.[3]

Many families abandoned the outer dwellings and came to the town center, which was generally along the parallel Broadway and Minnesota Streets. There were only three brick buildings near the center, the Forster (post office), Flick, and Erd buildings, and that is where many people went. Schoolteacher Rudolph Leonhart took his family to Frank Erd's Variety Store at 108 N. Minnesota, along with scores of families. The place was jammed from the basement to the second floor. Rudolph spent the night outside making barricades and taking turns at a sentinel post—armed only with a club. At dawn he went to visit his family, finding the building "overfilled to the point of suffocation" and "the air so foul that only the need to see my family could have forced me to go any further." His wife hadn't slept all night because of crying, moaning, sick people, and the stench. To top it off one pregnant woman delivered a baby during the night. "I absolutely cannot stand it here another night," Mrs. Leonhart said, and Rudolph led them up on the flat roof where at least they had some room and fresh air. Surveyor H. Brockmann joined them there, placing his telescope in a spot where he could spy the countryside and hopefully give warning of an Indian approach.[4]

Jacob Nix said that Tuesday dawned as "a beautiful morning," but the townsfolk were full of gloom when they considered their predicament. Nix saw the irony in a situation where so many of his fellow countrymen had fled Europe because they refused to fight for a "petty prince in the old Fatherland," who chose not to fight for the Union to suppress the Confederacy, and who

---

3   Dietz, "New Ulm's Paul Revere," 114-15; Carley, *Dakota War of 1862*, 34.

4   Leonhart, *Memories of New Ulm*, 46; Berghold, *Indians' Revenge*, 98.

now had to assume the mantle of heroic defenders of their families and farms and fight a people with whom they had no quarrel.[5]

Most of the people in town organized into companies. Many of the Nicollet County farmers formed the Lafayette Company. Fidel Diepolder was elected lieutenant; Mathias Lump, orderly sergeant; Frederick Fritsche, second sergeant; and Charles Frank, corporal, along with 33 privates. As people came into town, others were leaving. Upon hearing warnings of an Indian uprising on Monday afternoon, a dozen or more settlers along the Cottonwood came to town for news. Learning that the stories were true, they banded together with several others who had gone to town on business, but were dissuaded from returning that night because of the danger. By Tuesday morning they were very concerned for their families and organized a company to go to the rescue, nine men in three wagons and eight men on horseback. Most townsfolk wanted them to stay, but Sheriff Roos approved their expedition and appointed William B. Carroll as captain.

Only a mile or so out of town they found a man walking alone who said he had seen Indians skinning a heifer at Ralph Thomas's house—one of the men in the party. Farther on they met John Thomas and Almon Parker. Indians had chased them, but they got away and managed to hide in a grove a mile or more from Thomas's place. Thomas and Parker reported seeing Indians everywhere, moving generally south from the Minnesota River toward the Cottonwood River. The rescue party stopped at Thomas's to feed the horses while Ralph and several others went with him to check on his neighbor, Sebastian May. (Map K) There, they found Sebastian's body, along with his wife's, both children, and those of Joseph Emmerich and Henry Heyers. Incredibly, seven-year-old Anne Mary "rose up from the ground, and commenced crying piteously." Ralph Thomas took her in his arms. They also discovered that the three-year-old twins were wounded, but still alive.

The group stopped next at George Roeser's house and found him and his wife dead, but their toddler still alive trying to get water out of a bucket to quench his thirst. They gave the boy water and food and returned to Thomas's, from there sending the four children on to New Ulm in one of the wagons driven by John Thomas and Almon Parker. Somewhere along the road the rescuers found the bodies of the Martin Bluem family. Luther C. Ives said that

5 Nix, *Sioux Uprising*, 91.

Margaret, the oldest girl, "was treated in a most shameful manner before killing."[6]

The rescue party continued on toward the Leavenworth settlement. They found Thomas Riant hiding in tall grass near Abner Seaman's home. (Map J) Riant told them that he had been with the Covells, Whitons, Van Gilders, and others, but Indians chased them and scattered everyone across the prairie. The rescuers searched for them for two hours before giving up. Riant joined them and the party headed back for New Ulm. The people they searched for were already miles southeast of them heading for the Little Cottonwood.

Near Thomas's house, the rescue party split up; eleven went down the south side of the Cottonwood to William Tuttle's place, and seven crossed to the north bank. (Map K) They planned to meet again at Tuttle's and go into town together, but the larger party reached Tuttle's first and decided not to wait. This group consisted of William B. Carroll, Almond D. Loomis, George Lamb, Jan Thomson, Samuel McAuliffe, Charles Koehne, Robert A. Henton, Luther C. Ives, Philip Kirby, Thomas Riant, and one other. Crossing to the north bank they approached New Ulm from the west and noticed fires burning in several buildings on the outskirts of town. It is likely they now fully realized why they were begged not to leave that morning: the town was under attack.[7]

As the Leavenworth Rescue Party, as it came to be called, was moving up the Cottonwood River, other settlers were moving downriver toward town. Rudolph Leonhart reported that about noon he saw dark smoke clouds to the southwest from burning granaries. About the same time another party of refugees entered town with confusing stories about families being cut off and needing help. Not knowing where these settlers were or when the Indians might attack, town commandant Nix refused to allow anyone else to leave. Unable to stem the desperate pleas, however, Nix finally relented and allowed Louis Theobald to take his company out but advised not to be gone long. After half an hour with no word, and worried that Theobald might be in trouble, E. F. Brunk and his company went out at double-time to lend a hand.

At three o'clock, from the roof of Erd's store, Brockmann signaled that the Indians were coming. They approached from the northwest, most of them on horseback, and as they neared the town cemetery they split in two groups and

6 Tolzmann, ed., *Brown County*, 11; Bryant and Murch, *Great Massacre*, 178-79; Dahlin, *Dakota Uprising Victims*, 146n, 164.

7 Bryant and Murch, *Great Massacre*, 179-80; Berghold, *Indians' Revenge*, 100.

rode in wide semicircles around the town. There were still several families on the outskirts of town that had not vacated their homes; they came running now. Said Leonhart, "It was a frightening moment."[8]

The Holls were one of the tardy families. They had chosen a homestead about three miles from town in Milford Township and for several years expanded their one-room shanty with a grass roof into a more respectable dwelling. Their diet consisted mostly of potatoes, bread, a little salted meat, and plums and strawberries that they gathered in the summer. Frank Holl befriended an old Dakota and fed him when he was hungry. Because of this, the old man always visited whenever he was in the area, and brought Mrs. Holl wild duck or goose eggs, which was a great addition to their diet.

On August 18, Dakotas had attacked Milford, but did not go as far east as Holl's. Frank was in a quandary. He was preparing to thrash, and needed to get supplies to feed the men who were going to assist him. It was past noon on Tuesday, no one had reported Indians around, and Frank Holl decided to go to town, taking his wife and youngest child, Henry, with him. Six children remained at the farm: Margareta (15), John, Francis, Anna, Maria, and Josephine. An hour or so after their departure the old Dakota showed up at Holl's door, pounding and gesticulating to the children. Margareta could not understand what he wanted, and her brothers and sisters didn't pay him much attention. Finally, the old man got them to come outside just as another farmer with his family rode by in their wagon. The Dakota stopped the farmer and "practically forced the Holl children into the wagon." Margareta said his act no doubt saved their lives. Then the Indian disappeared and it was the last time they ever saw him.

When the crowded wagon got to New Ulm there was a trench dug across the main road and men were standing guard at the barricades. The farmer dropped the Holl children off at Koehne's grocery store. The place was already packed with women and children Margareta described as "more dazed than excited." Luckily, they found their mother and brother. Frank Holl had already been commandeered to man the barricades.[9]

---

8   Nix, *Sioux Uprising*, 92-93; Berghold, *Indians' Revenge*, 98; Leonhart, *Memories of New Ulm*, 47. According to Berghold, the report of settlers in trouble arrived at 11:00 a.m; Nix put the time at 2:00 p.m.

9   Margareta Holl Hahn interview, Microfilm Reel 2, Dakota Conflict, Minnesota Historical Society.

The old Dakota had saved the childrens' lives while risking his own. Minutes later, scores of warriors appeared, heading straight for New Ulm. However imposing the Dakotas appeared to the town defenders, they did not constitute an overwhelming force. Little Crow's "army" shrunk that morning after leaving Fort Ridgely. Many sought easier targets in Nicollet County and along the Cottonwood in Brown County. Perhaps 100 warriors remained. That was probably not sufficient strength to capture or destroy a well defended New Ulm.[10]

The Dakotas burned several houses outside town, including Gropper's, Bellm's, and Steinhauser's. Nix said only three houses were burned, but others were reported going up in flames. Christian Scheible, a carpenter who had built his own substantial two-floor dwelling with a stone cellar, was working at Fort Ridgely on August 19. He rented a room in his home to Nicholas Wentz, who escaped before the Indians torched it. Neighbor Otto Scheuffler testified to its destruction. The brewery was also burned.[11]

The houses were burning when the first half of the Leavenworth Party approached the embattled town. Robert Henton was riding in advance when he spied Indians working their way toward New Ulm. When he suggested to his fellow refugees that they cross the Cottonwood River and take the road to Mankato, some accused him of cowardice. William Carroll suggested that they fight their way into town. A good road ran down the upper bluff, across a slough at its base, and into town. If they moved quickly, the journey would take perhaps five minutes. (Map M) It was about three o'clock.

The party reached the edge of the slough before spotting two more Indians. Luther Ives proposed moving around to the other side of town, and if they failed to get in from that direction they could make a run for St. Peter. Others disagreed, arguing that it was hopeless to try to avoid a fight and their predicament would be no better anywhere else. Henton, who had just minutes earlier urged his comrades to make for Mankato, drew his revolver and charged. No doubt surprised by a mounted white man with a revolver making for them, the two Indians fell back. While Henton was clearing the way the rest of the

10 Heard, *History of the Sioux War*, 79-80, wrote that Little Crow started the day with 320 warriors, but only 100 remained to make the attack on New Ulm. Estimates of Indian numbers vary considerably from 25, 30-40, 50, 100, and 200-300. See Folwell, *History of Minnesota II*, 361-73.

11 Hughes, et. al., *Welsh in Minnesota*, 76-77; Koblas, *Let Them Eat Grass*, II, 106, 108; Christian Scheible Depredation Claim #56.

party attempted to punch their way through in the wagons. The party was strung out along the road when additional Dakota warriors appeared out of the tall grass on both sides and opened fire. According to Samuel McAuliffe, the Indians had been waiting to spring the trap all at the same time. George Lamb jumped out, dropped to a knee, and returned fire. Ives, McAuliffe, and a few others did the same thing. When Lamb fell wounded a warrior ran behind him and finished him off. Another bullet struck Almond Loomis in the heart and knocked him out of the wagon. Terrified by the noise and shouting, the horses bolted straight through the few Indians blocking the road. Ives vaulted back into a wagon and shouted for everyone to follow behind the runaways.

When William Carroll rolled past in a wagon McAuliffe decided it was time to hitch a ride out and tried to jump aboard. As he did so his gun got entangled in the rear wheel and was torn from his hands. Moments later Carroll was shot and the wagon careened from side to side as Phil Kirby, who was nearly thrown out when the wagon hit a log, grabbed for the reins and got the vehicle back under control. He hung on as the horses careened first left and then right. "Three times the Indians turned the team away from town," explained McAuliffe, "but each time the horses veered back with almost human intelligence and finally they succeeded in running the gauntlet." Just when the horses reached the Dakotah House the reins twisted in the wheels tight enough to lock them up and skid the wagon to a halt. "Had that happened in the open prairie," McAuliffe continued, "it would have meant the death of the entire party." Still, the Indian ambush inflicted serious losses: William Carroll, Almond Loomis, George Lamb, Jan Thomson, and Thomas Riant were killed running the gauntlet; the rest of the party made it into New Ulm.

The smaller party of seven men who had crossed to the north bank of the Cottonwood was about half an hour behind "Captain" Carroll's group. Unaware of the danger ahead, they moved down the same hill and across the slough. As they did so, an estimated 150 Indians "sprang up out of the grass and fired upon us," reported Ralph Thomas, "killing five horses and six men." The dead included William H. Tuttle, DeWitt Lemon, Ole Olson, Nels Olson, Tore Olson, and Uriah Loomis, 17-year-old brother of Almond Loomis, who had just been killed the same way and in nearly the same spot. Only Ralph Thomas escaped. "My own horse was shot through the body . . . killing him instantly," Thomas reported. "My feet were out of the stirrups in a moment, and I sprang to the ground. . . . I dropped my gun, jumped up, and ran." A warrior fired a shotgun from nearby and the charge tore up the ground at Thomas's feet, but he sped past and "into town on foot as fast as I could go." The Leavenworth "Rescue Party" lost 11 out of 18 men.[12]

*   *   *

When the Indians were first spotted approaching New Ulm, former German officer Jacob Nix shouted, "To your posts! Get ready to fight!" Men dashed to man the barricades and the Indians fired a few wild volleys. Since they were firing downhill, most of the bullets flew over the barricades and into the buildings beyond. Despite orders that no one was to go outside, 13-year-old Emilie Pauli (or Pauly) stepped out of one building so she could see the action. One of the first shots struck her in the head and killed her. One of the first rounds also struck Nix, severing the ring finger of his left hand.

There were only some 40 armed men in the town. Most sported short-range shotguns; only a couple were armed with rifles. Nix surely regretted his decision to allow Theobald and Brunk to leave with their companies and immediately dispatched runners to recall them. Thankfully they had not marched far and ran back to town at double-time, filling in the gaps along the barricades on State, Minnesota, Broadway, and German streets. Their added firepower was enough to force the Dakotas to probe left and right in search of easier avenues of approach. "Wilder and wilder now raged the combat on all sides of the attacked town," Nix reported with some exaggeration. He believed the Indians were better armed than the town's defenders. Ammunition was also a concern; his men had sufficient gunpowder but were short of bullets. In an effort to remedy that deficiency, bags of buckshot were melted down and cast into larger caliber bullets.

"The fiercest fighting took place over the possession of the barricades which had been built at the southern part of town," explained Nix. The Indians tried several times to take them, "but each time the defenders forced them back with bloody heads." According to Nix, the German defenders deserved the credit for the repulse. They pushed the Indians back in the south and then repelled an attack from the northwest. The Indians also tried an approach

---

12 Berghold, *Indians' Revenge*, 100-01; "The Ill-Fated Leavenworth Expedition and Marker," Brown County Historical Society; Bryant and Murch, *Great Massacre*, 180-81; Dahlin, *Dakota Uprising Victims*, 52-55.

against the northeast side of town by slipping through the high grass and cornfield in North German Park, but defenders also drove them back from that sector. Thrown back at all points, the Dakotas grudgingly broke off the attack. "The German town of New Ulm was defended and saved by Germans on the 19th of August," Nix proclaimed with pride. Nix's proclamation notwithstanding, other non-German defenders were on hand to defend New Ulm.[13]

Henry Behnke's horseback arrival in St. Peter early that Tuesday morning created enough of a stir to awaken Lieutenant Governor Henry A. Swift and many of the townspeople. With Judge Flandrau's approval Swift climbed into his buggy with Nicollet County auditor William G. Hayden and rolled out as advance scouts to learn what was happening and to report if the reinforcements should head first to New Ulm or Fort Ridgely. Nicollet County Sheriff L. M. Boardman, meanwhile, organized a mounted party of 16 men and rode out of St. Peter for New Ulm at 11:00 a.m.

Swift and Hayden took the shortest route, crossing the Minnesota River and heading west through the Nicollet and Swan Lake settlements. The settlers called a meeting, elected Aaron M. Bean as captain and Samuel Coffin as lieutenant, and formed a small company of 16 or 18 men who followed Swift and Hayden on the ride to New Ulm. Along the way the pair fell in with a German minister and the three entered New Ulm about 3:00 p.m.—just before the Indians appeared.[14]

Although they found it difficult to communicate because most of the townspeople spoke only German, Swift and Hayden determined quickly the danger was very real. Evan Bowen, who lived between New Ulm and Mankato, volunteered to carry a message to Judge Flandrau to tell him to make New Ulm his destination. Bowen slipped out of town just before the Dakotas closed in. Swift and Hayden walked from the Dacotah House to the next terrace in time to

---

13 Nix, *Sioux Uprising*, 94-95, 97-98, 102; Roos, "The Battles of New Ulm," Brown County Historical Society; Berghold, *Indians' Revenge*, 98; Leonhart, *Memories of New Ulm*, 48.

14 *Minnesota in the Civil and Indian Wars*, I, 731-32; Hughes, et. al., *Welsh in Minnesota*, 76. Boardman's company included: J. B. Trogdon, J. K. Moore, James Horner, William Wilkinson, Lewis Patch, Henry Synder, Salmon A. Buell, Jacob and Phillip Seltzer, and Horace Austin. Included in Bean's company were James Hughes, T. B. Thompson, Charles Wetherell, Merrick Dickinson, Frank Kennedy, James Parker, E. G. Corey, Andrew Friend, A. H. Thurston, Hiram Caywood, C. A. Stein, Henry and Frederick Otto, and Griffith and Thomas Williams. See Bryant and Murch, *Great Massacre*, 165. Henry A. Swift became Minnesota's governor eleven months later.

see Indian warriors approaching. The sight sent them hurrying back to the barricades. The Indians occupied the ground Swift and Hayden had just evacuated and opened fire, "not at us, fortunately," reported Hayden, "but into the crowded street and over our heads, killing a woman [Pauli] who was standing in the doorway of a store on the main street."[15]

The St. Peter company of 16 to 18 men under Bean and Coffin arrived to find the townsfolk huddled in confusion around two squares on the main street.[16] According to one of Bean's men, Andrew Friend, who was from Judson about a dozen miles below New Ulm, the reinforcements arrived before the fighting "and took dinner at the Dakota House" while a man named Brockmann kept watch on a rooftop using a surveyor's theodolyte. The reinforcements had sufficient time, he continued, to help finish building barricades and then man the lines. Friend was there when young Emilie Pauli was killed (during the first round of fighting) and recalled he manned the barricade on the southwest side of town and opened fire. "I had a good double barrel Hyatt rifle and in those days I could shoot as well as anybody," Friend claimed. "I took good aim and fired at one of the Indians and he fell. A German standing close by rushed up and hugged Friend saying, 'Oh you kill Indian, you kill him I see him fall.'"

Friend left the barricade to climb upstairs above a butcher's shop to continue firing. He claimed he hit another Indian "square," after which a pair of other warriors pulled down part of a picket fence and hauled off his corpse. "My gun was empty else I could have killed these two who carried him off." According to Friend, the butcher was killed right outside his own store.[17]

About 20 men, some from Bean's command and some townsmen, moved to clear the Indians out of Frederick Rehfeld's house at the corner of Broadway and Third North Street. The men used other buildings as cover until they got

15 Hayden, "Account of the relief expedition," Microfilm Reel 2, Dakota Conflict, Minnesota Historical Society.

16 As with most accounts of any historical event, time estimates vary considerably. Hayden and Swift reached New Ulm a little ahead of Bean's company. Hayden claimed he and Swift arrived at 3:00 p.m., while others claim Bean's men arrived at 1:00 p.m. Roos wrote that the Nicollet County men arrived between 4:00 and 5:00 p.m.

17 Andrew Friend, in Thomas J. Hughes, "Collected statements," Microfilm Reel 2, Dakota Conflict, Minnesota Historical Society; Minnesota Statesman (St. Peter), August 22, 1862; Hayden, "Account of the relief expedition," Microfilm Reel 2, Dakota Conflict, Minnesota Historical Society.

close enough to attack. "Come on, boys!" someone cried, but only eight men joined in the charge through Rehfeld's front door: John Hauenstein, Charles Wagner, August Hellman, Julius Guetling, John Peller, August Riemann, August Westphal, and Frederick Fritsche. The Dakota warriors opened fire, killing August Riemann and wounding Guetling, Peller, and Westphal, before fleeing out the back door.

Once the gallant deed was done, however, it became apparent the small party was not strong enough to hold Rehfeld's house. A deadly chaos ensued as the Dakotas, recalled Fritsche, "opened a murderous fire on our few men" from State Street, which was at a slightly higher elevation; Peter Gropper's nearby house was burning. Men from John Bellm's company opened fire from the Schalk Building just behind Rehfeld's recaptured house. The covering fire allowed Fritsche and his comrades to pull back. Some of Bean's men tried to take another house held by several warriors but also found they could not hold it. Armed with six good rifles, however, his men contributed much to the town's firepower.[18]

Rain began to fall about 4:30 p.m. The thunderstorm rolling in from the southeast brought "unexpected help" to the embattled town's defenders. "Nature itself turned to their favor," recorded Nix. Fritsche also commented on the weather, recalling that during the fighting "a thunder shower broke loose, which sounded just as though artillery from heaven had mixed in with our firing." Water poured down in streams, he continued, soaking buildings and haystacks alike. Everything was so wet "the Indians ceased setting fires." Schoolteacher Rudolph Leonhart also remembered nature's spectacular display, and how "lightning bolts flashed down brilliantly from the sky as thunder rolled with full force throughout the valley as only a storm can do on the western prairie." The rain came down so hard that Leonhart recalled disregarding the bullets slamming into the buildings as he ran from porch to porch in search of a place to keep dry.[19]

Some of the early chroniclers of the New Ulm battle—including Heard, McConkey, Malmros, and Flandrau—wrote that Nicollet County Sheriff L. M. Boardman's mounted company arrived in New Ulm just in time to save the

---

18 Folwell, *History of Minnesota*, II, 362; August Riemann Depredation Claim #325; Tolzmann, ed., *Brown County*, 12-13.

19 Nix, *Sioux Uprising*, 98; Tolzmann, ed., *Brown County*, 13; Leonhart, *Memories of New Ulm*, 47-48.

day.[20] Sheriff Boardman and his 16 riders, however, were still on the road well behind the buggy carrying Swift and Hayden and Bean's marching company. In fact, they were still about ten miles from New Ulm when "a most terrific rain storm" drove them to seek shelter in an unoccupied farmhouse. According to Salmon A. Buell, he and his comrades approached the town from the lower Redstone Ferry a few miles downriver. From the high bluff on the Nicollet County side they spotted "a dense black cloud, against which, as a background, could be plainly seen the flash of guns, fired in either attack or defense, and burning stacks or buildings." They would have to hurry. The ferry boat was on the other bank, however, and a man swam over to retrieve it. The approach to New Ulm on that side, however, was on low ground and everyone was justifiably apprehensive about a Dakota ambush. No Indians were waiting for them, and they reached the town without further incident. Members of the party had different recollections about what they saw and did next.[21]

Salmon Buell, a member of Boardman's mounted company, recalled that after arriving in town Boardman decided to attack the Indians. He led his men to the barricade and Buell jumped his horse over it. Some of the townsfolk, however, caught wind of the proposed charge and begged the men not to expose themselves needlessly. According to Buell, Boardman canceled the attack and rode his men back to the town center.

Horace Austin offered an entirely different account. Austin, who would take the oath as Minnesota's sixth governor eight years later, recalled seeing the Swan Lake men constructing barricades while Nix did his best to replace confusion and chaos with order and calm. Sheriff Boardman, continued Austin, rode his cavalry into open country where the Indians were deploying for an attack, but suddenly decided he was not competent to command and resigned. According to Austin, he assumed command and ordered the charge "regardless of consequences," but the Dakotas refused to stand and receive it. The warriors fired a few times for good effect and disappeared.

20 Heard, *History of the Sioux War*, 80; McConkey, *Dakota War Whoop*, 65; Malmros, *Perspectives on the Sioux War*, 17; *Minnesota in the Civil and Indian Wars*, I, 732; Hubbard and Holcombe, *Minnesota in Three Centuries*, III, 324.

21 Buell, "Defense of New Ulm," 786-87, MHSC, Vol. 10, pt. 2. Their arrival time is also in question. Horace Austin said they waited out the strongest part of the storm about ten miles outside town and did not arrive there until 4:00 p.m. Nix, however, reported that the storm did not start until 4:30 p.m.

After the "charge" episode, town resident D. G. Shillock informed Boardman that a wounded refugee was trapped in a house at the lower end of town, the same area Boardman had just passed through to enter New Ulm. A few of Boardman's men and a squad of town volunteers led by Shillock hurried out to get him, successfully avoiding the Dakotas' fire along the way and back again.

The rescuers were returning to the lower barricade, remembered one witness, when a man was seen "coming at full speed over the prairie ridge just back of the town, the Indians firing at him from behind it." The embattled rider was Ralph Thomas, the last survivor of the doomed Leavenworth Rescue Party. The only reinforcements known to be on the way were from St. Peter. Nix, Roos, and others consulted with Boardman and Henry Swift about what to do next. The men agreed that the sheriff had the best horse and should ride back to find Judge Flandrau and the reinforcing column and hurry them along. Since the Dakotas had blocked the road to the lower ferry, Boardman dashed out to the upper ferry abreast of the town and crossed safely.[22]

Jacob Nix was technically correct: Boardman's men did not save New Ulm; the Germans did. Bean's company certainly lent a hand. Excluding the 11 killed in the Leavenworth expedition, the New Ulm defender's escaped with relatively light losses. The dead included Emilie Pauli, possibly an unnamed butcher, and August Riemann. In addition to the wounding of Westphal, Guetling, and Peller, Frederic Peuser received a non-lethal neck injury and another man, said to be "in a state of drunken courage," went out too far and was shot through the side.

Nix later claimed that the thunderstorm saved the town, and he may well be right. Whether the Indians were superstitious, their bowstrings went slack in the rain, or their powder was too wet to continue, they pulled back shortly after the storm reached its fury. By 5:00 p.m. they were gone.[23]

New Ulm had survived the first test.

---

22 Folwell, *History of Minnesota*, II, 367-69; Buell, "Defense of New Ulm," 786-87, MHSC, Vol. 10, pt. 2. J. K. Moore, another member of Boardman's mounted party, recalled entering the town and hitching their horses while deciding what to do. According to him, nothing much of consequence happened. Bullets flew for a time, but the firing ended quickly and he did not see any Indians.

23 Nix, *Sioux Uprising*, 101.

C hapter 12

"I kill him one. I kill him one."

First Battle of Fort Ridgely

Fort Ridgely ~ Rieke Brothers ~ Defense dispositions ~ Messengers ride for help ~ Corporal
McLean returns with Lieutenant Sheehan ~ Ezmon Earle joins Sheehan ~ Private Sturgis's ride ~
Return of the Renville Rangers ~ 5th Minnesota ~ Disposition of the defenders on August 20 ~
Little Crow attacks ~ Artillery saves the day ~ The killed and wounded

F ort Ridgely, declared Charles Flandrau, "was in no sense a fort. It was
simply a collection of frame buildings forming a square and facing
inwards." (Map H)

Established in 1853 near the mouth of Rock Creek (later called Fort Creek)
at the head of navigation on the Minnesota River, the "collection of frame
buildings" was named Ridgely after three Maryland officers of the same name
killed in the Mexican War. The purpose of the fort was to protect the frontier
from the Sioux, but as Flandrau made clear it offered little in the way of
protection. The only defensible structures consisted of two stone buildings, one
a barrack and the other a commissary. There was no outer protective wall and
the complex didn't even have its own well for water. The structures were
erected in a loose square around an open parade ground about 90 yards wide.
The terrain surrounding the fort further complicated matters for its occupants.
Ravines well within musket range—perfect for shielding attackers—scarred the
earth north, east, and southwest of the fort. To the south about 300 yards
distant was an abrupt bluff overlooking the Minnesota River. Indians
determined to attack the fort could approach very close without being seen.

The site of construction was optional, but the weather in that part of
Minnesota was not. Thomas Gere, who was a sergeant when he arrived there

with Company B in March 1862, was unimpressed with his new post. It was "away out in the wilderness," he explained, and the snow and ice seemed to stick around forever. The first steamboat of the season did not arrive until April 25, and even in May Gere was still complaining about the weather: "Fort Ridgely beats any place we have seen, for wind; the average number of windy days in each week being eight-and-a-half."

On Monday afternoon, August 18, 1862, only a handful of men were available to defend a post that was largely indefensible even if held with double their number. The defenders were being sent away. Once Agent Galbraith passed through with his rangers and Lieutenant Culver and six men left with them as an escort. After the "Bread Raid" trouble ended, Lieutenant Sheehan headed back to Fort Ripley with 50 men of the 5th Minnesota, leaving just two officers and 76 men at the fort. After Captain Marsh marched out to meet disaster at Redwood Ferry, Lieutenant Gere, who was only 19 years old, was left at the post with less than 30 men—and of those, seven were ill, leaving 22 soldiers available for duty.

Reinforcements of a sort arrived when the wagon hauling $71,000 in gold coins pulled in with five men aboard. Cyrus G. Wykoff, J. C. Ramsey, A. J. Van Vorhees, C. M. Dailey, and Edward A. C. Hatch were briefed by Gere of the dangerous situation, hid the money keg in one of the buildings, and added their guns to the defense. Scores of refugees also swarmed in, but most of them were women, children, and unarmed farmers.[1]

Some of those farmers could fight, however. Brothers George (28) and Victor Rieke (26) arrived in America from Germany and settled in Ohio in 1855 before moving to Cairo Township about four miles east of Fort Ridgely in 1859. The next year more of the family arrived including their parents, Johann (66) and Gertrude (58), brothers Adam (22), Henry (19), Ernst August (16), and Herman (9), and sisters Anna Maria (15) and Lisetta (12). The large Rieke family homesteaded near Mud Lake not far from Johann Buhrer (33), who had finished a five-year hitch in the army before settling with his wife Agathe (32) and their son Henry (2).

The Rieke brothers contracted with the Army earlier that summer to furnish Fort Ridgely with 150 tons of hay, and made a hay camp less than one mile from the post. George and Adam were hauling in two loads of hay that

---

1   *Minnesota in the Civil and Indian Wars*, I, 733-34; Frazer, *Forts of the West*, 64, 66; Gere, "Uncle Sam's Army," Brown County Historical Society; Carley, *Dakota War of 1862*, 26.

Monday morning when a horseman sped by shouting words neither brother understood. The Riekes were at the hay scales before 10:00 a.m. when an ashen-faced soldier ran past. Something was seriously amiss. The brothers unloaded their hay as fast as possible and were returning when they met a man they knew who had been wounded in the arm. The Indians, he told them, were killing everyone. With the terrible news ringing in their ears, the brothers rode to the hay camp, picked up their father and brothers, August and Victor, and drove them to the fort.

Adam, George, and August returned to Mud Lake with a wagon to get the rest of the family. While Adam and George piled everyone aboard, together with whatever goods they could carry, August rode to Buhrer's cabin to tell Agathe what was happening and to pick up Henry. The three of them trotted to Rieke's and joined them for the flight to Ridgely. On the way they passed Johann Buhrer and Patrick Heffron, who were haying near the Nicollet County line and informed them of the uprising. Both men dismissed the warning and poked fun at the Rieke boys for taking it seriously. "Take my wife and Henry if you want to," said Buhrer. "But don't be afraid. Heffron and I are old soldiers, no Indians can hurt us. You go on. Maybe we will come into the fort tomorrow, or maybe some other day."[2]

Three miles from the fort the road branched in two directions, one trail leading toward Henderson and the other to St. Peter. The junction boasted two inns. One was owned by James Ryan but rented to Jacob Schmahl, who had already fled with his wife to the fort. The other inn was run by William Mills and his family. Mills and his brother-in-law, Thomas Graham, also worked as mail carriers between Fort Ridgely and St. Peter. As the Riekes rode past, Mills and Graham promised they would follow along as soon as possible, but then changed their minds.

Instead, Mills took his family to a wooded and secluded slough about three miles away and hid them there while he rode to the fort to find out more information. When he discovered the uprising was indeed serious and deadly Mills made for his house, packed up supplies, and carried them to his hidden family. When he was sure they were well taken care of, he rode once again back to the fort. It was not until early the next morning that he finally returned a second time and shepherded his family to Henderson.

2   Curtiss-Wedge, *History of Renville County*, I, 634-37; Johann Buhrer Depredation Claim #338.

The Riekes were approaching Fort Creek ravine when a trader warned them that Indians were lurking there. George lifted his gun as a precaution and Adam drove the wagon safely through as quickly as possible. Victor Rieke, meanwhile, had joined sutler Benjamin H. Randall to help haul water from the spring under the bluff until all the fort's tanks were full.[3]

"All the available arms in the Fort were placed in the hands of the refugees," reported Lieutenant Gere, "although we could hardly think that the Indians intended to attack us." The young officer assigned the men he guessed were the most capable to defend positions where they would do the most good. Because they were from Germany, Gere assumed (wrongly) the Riekes had had some sort of military training. He placed George, Victor, and Adam with the squads in charge of the field guns.[4]

*   *   *

After failing to find his daughters at the river, Joe Coursolle took his wife Jane and their young son Joe and hitched a ride to the fort on what he described as "an army ambulance." Once Jane and the boy (who was hot, flushed, and seriously ill) were in the barracks, Joe was put to work. "I grabbed a shovel," he recalled, "and began digging dirt for barricades with the others."

Many soldiers were engaged in the same activity. Orlando McFall spent much of his time "throwing up rude breastworks and piling up cordwood at the entrances between the buildings." Ezmon Earle, however, arrived later with Lieutenant Sheehan and recalled "there was no sign of a breast work about the fort." When Ezmon asked Lieutenant Gere for a gun and was told there were none left to distribute, he sought out a sergeant on a work detail and asked him for his weapon. According to Ezmon's rather implausible recollection, the sergeant loaned it to him. So armed, he joined a company of citizens under Joseph De Camp, who had been selected to serve as captain. De Camp had left his family at Redwood Agency on Sunday to go to St. Paul, but only got as far as the fort when the sudden uprising changed everyone's plans. Ezmon was assigned to one of the windows on the first floor of the north side of the stone

---

3   Bryant and Murch, *Great Massacre*, 143-44; Curtiss-Wedge, *History of Renville County*, I, 621, 637-38.

4   Gere, "Uncle Sam's Army," Brown County Historical Society.

barracks. Other civilians who were only armed with axes or crowbars were stationed at the other doors and windows.[5]

One of those arriving at the fort was Joseph Jack Frazer, the nearly 60-year-old son of a British fur trader and a mixed-blood half-sister of Wacouta. Frazer had lived as an Indian for 35 years before adopting the ways of the white man, learning his language, working in the fur trade, and becoming a hunting partner and a scout with Henry Sibley. On the morning of the outbreak Frazer left his family, slipped out of Wacouta's village, made his way to Ridgely, and was placed on picket duty.[6]

Sunset that Monday was about 7:20 p.m. Lieutenant Gere prepared to survive the night by arranging most of his soldiers on picket duty. All told, remembered Pvt. Oscar G. Wall, they formed "a thin and slender line." The refugees realized the defenders were few in number, continued the private, a realization that kept them "in a constant state of nervous tension." If Gere was hoping for good news from the outside world, the "fearful tidings" he received shortly before 8:00 p.m. that night must have been crushing. Two exhausted and wounded privates, James Dunn and William Hutchinson, staggered into Ridgely to announce that Captain Marsh and about one-half of his command had been wiped out. Dunn found his wife Elizabeth quartered in a log hut on the north side of the post with a neighbor named Margaret Hern. The private, "caked with blood and sweat," stumbled in about dusk. "For God's sake, what is the news, Jim?" asked Mrs. Hern. "Give me something to eat quick," Dunn responded. After swallowing a few mouthfuls of food he told them about the disaster at the ferry and his efforts to get back to the fort. The women prepared to move closer to the center of the post.

While Dunn was eating and sharing his harrowing tale, Gere was busy penning a letter inside the headquarters building logged with the time of 8:00 p.m. It was addressed to the commanding officer at Fort Snelling and included a request that it be forwarded to Governor Ramsey. In the letter Gere explained that Marsh had been defeated, only 13 of his men had survived, the Indians were plundering and murdering, and Ridgely needed immediate help. Company

---

5   Joseph Coursolle story, Microfilm Reel 1, Dakota Conflict, Minnesota Historical Society; Orlando McFall narrative, Microfilm Reel 2, Dakota Conflict, Minnesota Historical Society; Ezmon Earle reminiscences, Microfilm Reel 1, Dakota Conflict, Minnesota Historical Society.

6   Gilman, *Henry Hastings Sibley*, 69, 174; Anderson and Woolworth, *Through Dakota Eyes*, 98n28; Curtiss-Wedge, *History of Renville County*, I, 622.

B's Pvt. William J. Sturgis, part of the 5th Minnesota, took the dispatch and set off in the darkness on one of the horses that had hauled in the gold. Fort Snelling was a 125-mile ride. Sturgis was ordered to go to St. Peter first and see if he could find Lieutenant Culver and Agent Galbraith. Before he had set out for the Redwood Agency, Captain Marsh had sent Corporal McLean in search of Lieutenant Sheehan. One of those couriers (Sturgis or McLean) would have to find help for the fort's defenders to have a decent chance of survival. After midnight Gere penned another message, this time to Lieutenant Sheehan, informing him of Marsh's crushing defeat and asking him to return as quickly as possible.

Second-guessing his dispositions, Gere decided it would be better to move the more than 200 women and children scattered amongst the wooden houses forming three sides of the fort into the stone barracks on the north side. He was setting about to get this done when one of the outer pickets leveled his weapon, fired into the darkness, yelled, "Indians!" and ran back toward the buildings.

"The scene that followed beggars description," said Private Wall. The shot and shouting "set the affrighted mass into a pell-mell scramble for such security as the stone building might afford." Many of the men also "lost their heads in the mad rush for the barracks, the windows of which they crushed to facilitate ingress." Some of the men beat the women to safety "in the scurrying bedlam that made the night hideous." The pell-mell stampede frustrated Lieutenant Gere, who reported that "Regardless of all orders to stay outside, they seemed only anxious to get out of danger." It took some minutes to realize that the soldier had discharged his gun at a shadow. The lieutenant figured the false alarm scare got everyone out of the way. "How I did wish I had a soldier in the place of every citizen!" lamented the young post commander.[7]

Several of the soldiers' families lived in log huts erected along the north side of the post. Margaret Hern moved there from Hutchinson when her husband enlisted in the fall of 1861. The recruiting officer, she recalled, told them that families would be welcome at the fort, but "the officer had lied. We were not expected or wanted at the fort." She and others in the same position were able to remain only because they made arrangements to board with blacksmith John Resoft. During the winter, when the 4th Minnesota was occupying Ridgely, the only women there were: the doctor's wife, Mrs. Eliza Muller; Capt. James C.

---

7   Morris, *Old Rail Fence Corners*, 146; Carley, *Dakota War of 1862*, 26; Wall, *Recollections of the Sioux Massacre*, 70-71, 110; Gere, "Uncle Sam's Army," Brown County Historical Society.

Edson's wife; Elizabeth Dunn and her three children; Julia Sweet, the chaplain's wife, and her three children; Sgt. Cyrus L. Snyder's wife and their three children; Mrs. C. G. Mickel and her three children; Mrs. John Jones and her three children; and Mrs. Randall, the sutler's wife.

On Monday evening most of the families headed for the stone barracks. Margaret Hern carried her baby while her children Walter and Minnie followed her upstairs. And there they sat, huddled with hundreds of other people. When "lights out" was ordered, the room became "dark as pitch." Margaret listened as several people conversed in the Dakota tongue. Frightened, she wondered how she came to be in such a dreadful situation. At least she had a butcher knife wrapped in a piece of rubber stuck in her belt, and Mrs. Dunn, the wounded private's wife, was armed with a pair of scissors. Margaret suggested they could at least "put out their eyes with them" if attacked, for they "expected death every minute after hearing those Indian voices." When Jim Dunn arrived with a lamp, Margaret turned up the flame just enough to see who was around her. "This was the crucial moment of my life," she admitted. When the soft light fanned out around her she breathed a slight sigh of relief: the voices were from only a few Indian women with some mixed-blood children.

Still, the darkness served to compound the fear pounding within her. How could Margaret trust these Indian women? The more she thought about it, the more certain she became that they were spies who would try to slip out and tell the Dakotas how weakly the fort was defended.

When the picket fired at imaginary Indians, bedlam broke out around Margaret in the barracks. Cpl. Charles H. Hawley, who had just returned from the battle at the ferry, had been checked out by Doctor Muller and posted in the barracks. When he left his post to assist someone, one of the Dakota women Margaret had been watching broke for the door. Margaret sprang up and beat her there, grabbed Hawley's bayonet-fixed musket, and leveled it in her direction. When the woman tried to shove past her, Margaret announced, "Go back or I'll ram this through you!" The woman retreated, cursing Margaret in English and Dakota. Perhaps stunned at what she had done, Margaret relinquished her musket to another soldier and returned to her spot, where she clutched tightly her butcher knife until dawn.[8]

Palpable fear notwithstanding, no attack came that night. In fact, there were only a handful of Indians in the immediate vicinity. One of them was

8   Morris, *Old Rail Fence Corners*, 144, 147-48.

19-year-old George Quinn (Wakandayamani or The Spirit that Rattles as It Walks), who may have been the mixed-blood son of interpreter Peter Quinn. He lived near St. Paul, where Protestant missionaries Samuel and Gideon Pond taught him to read and write Dakota, and was visiting Redwood when the uprising began. Quinn took part in the fight against Marsh and his men at the ferry and later explained that he was anxious to distinguish himself in war, but "had no wish to murder anyone in cold blood." He fought soldiers, he insisted, "but not the unarmed white settlers."

After the fight and ensuing celebration, several scouting parties were sent out. One group composed of Quinn and four other young warriors moved downriver to keep an eye on what was happening at Fort Ridgely. They reached the fort late that night, hitched their horses, and crawled up a ravine on the southwest side of the post. When they didn't spot anything unusual they fell asleep, unaware of the chaos transpiring inside the fort.[9]

The Dakotas had no intention of attacking Ridgely on Monday. Although we will never know why, it is possible that Captain Marsh's gallant stand and sacrifice at the ferry dissuaded Little Crow and his chiefs from assaulting more soldiers defending their own ground. If they had known that the fort was so weakly defended, the course of events might have unfolded differently. If the Dakotas could have attacked in force at any time from the afternoon on Monday to early Tuesday morning, they would probably have taken the fort and killed or captured all of the soldiers and settlers in the vicinity. With their rear secured they might have united for a coordinated attack against New Ulm and captured that as well.

While the Dakota scouts slept and the refugees in Ridgely struggled with their nerves, Corporal McLean reached Lieutenant Sheehan. McLean had followed Sheehan's track east on "the old Government Road" twenty-two miles to where Sheehan had camped Sunday night. There, the trail turned north to New Auburn and Glencoe. Sheehan had marched twenty miles from the junction near Norwegian Grove and camped one-half mile north of New Auburn after the men voted they had tramped far enough for one day. The men were making coffee and frying bacon and potatoes when "the boys happened to look to the southward and saw a cloud of dust in the air," remembered Pvt. Orlando McFall. "There emerged from that cloud of dust a jaded and almost lifeless horse. His rider was James Mc[Lean]."

9   Anderson and Woolworth, *Through Dakota Eyes*, 93-94.

The exhausted McLean sought out Sheehan, handed him the dispatch from Lieutenant Gere, and added that he was requested to return to the fort "as quickly as a merciful God would permit him to do." Sheehan ordered his men to fall in. "Every man was alive now," McFall said, "no one tired, no one hungry, we threw our supper out on the ground." The soldiers secured their guns, which were packed in boxes in the wagons, and within twelve minutes of McLean's arrival were back on the road retracing their steps. Sheehan confiscated two teams and a pair of wagons in New Auburn. One farmer did it the easy way and accompanied the soldiers. The other refused to let him take his wagon because it was full of wheat waiting to be stacked. Sheehan offered to stack it for him. A dozen of "the boys," explained McFall, "took hold of the rack on one side and dumped it in the road." The irate farmer refused to ride with them, so Sheehan took his wagon and left without him.[10]

Lieutenant Sheehan realized that haste was required and kept his men moving. They stopped at Norwegian Grove at 11:00 p.m. for a light "lunch" and continued on their way, the horses trotting half the distance while the men moved at double-time. The first refugees fleeing in the night spilled across their path about ten miles from the fort. Sheehan stopped his column for thirty minutes to give his men a break and interrogate the terrified civilians, who told him all the settlers behind them had been killed, the fort had been taken, and Sheehan should not go any farther. The lieutenant ignored their advice, pointed them in a safe direction, and ordered his exhausted men to fall in. Several climbed into the wagons, but the jolting ride was worse than walking. The column was about seven miles from the fort when the eastern sky began to lighten. Sheehan wisely threw out flankers to avoid an ambush and continued on.

The sun was above the horizon when a solitary figure approached from the north. It was Ezmon Earle. He had been on the run since the previous afternoon when he escaped the massacre suffered by his family and that of the Hendersons, Carrothers, and Whites at Beaver Creek. He figured the fort was about fifteen miles away and he struck off across the prairie roughly paralleling the road about one-half mile north of it. When night fell he tried to use the north star as a guide, but about midnight clouds made that impossible. When he found a swale with tall grass he crawled in and rested there until dawn. He didn't

---

10 Wall, *Recollections of the Sioux Massacre*, 110, 117; Orlando McFall narrative, Microfilm Reel 2, Dakota Conflict, Minnesota Historical Society.

sleep well. Ezmon heard what he later described as two night hawks calling to each other, followed by something that sounded like the taps of a knife against a powder horn, followed by a response. The Indians were searching for him! In what could only have been a terrifying ordeal, he lay still as someone walked through the tall grass close by. When Ezmon eventually talked to his father, he learned that Jonathan Earle had also tried to get to the fort several times, but that Indians in the area forced him back north. The person he heard moving through the grass that night may well have been his own father.

Once there was enough light to see that morning Ezmon started east. The coarse grass had cut up his pants and his legs were bare and bleeding. By this time he had lost the road so he decided to turn south closer to the Minnesota River. After a few miles he spotted a man on horseback and knew the road must be close by. When he reached it and identified that the horse was shod he breathed a sigh of relief; almost certainly the rider was a white man. Ezmon continued along the road, topped a rise, and spotted three wagons in front of him "one of the pleasantest sights of my life, a body of troops. I could see their uniforms and the glistening of their guns and bayonets in the sunshine."[11]

Lieutenant Sheehan questioned Ezmon about the uprising but the teenager could not tell him anything other than what had happened to him and the people at Beaver Creek. The lieutenant sent him to the commissary wagon to get something to eat, and Ezmon "did not wait for the order to be repeated." The famished boy didn't care that there was nothing available but raw pork. "I found the pork barrel and went into the brine up to my elbow and fished out a chunk of pork from which I cut off a few slices with my knife," Ezmon recalled. "I think I never ate a more delicious morsel."

Sheehan and his men continued moving toward Ridgely. About one mile from the fort they met William Mills, who had left his family in hiding and was returning for them. Sheehan, perhaps irritated that he was rushing men to the fort while a man with a good weapon was leaving it, demanded to know where Mills was going. When his explanation failed to satisfy the officer, Sheehan

---

11 Orlando McFall narrative, Microfilm Reel 2, Dakota Conflict, Minnesota Historical Society; Ezmon Earle reminiscences, Microfilm Reel 1, Dakota Conflict, Minnesota Historical Society. As in so many recollections there is a discrepancy as to when particular events occurred. According to McFall, the sky began to lighten while they were six or seven miles from the fort; Earle, however, claimed he met the soldiers ten miles east of the fort about 10:00 a.m. on Wednesday morning.

wrested his gun from him and left him unarmed. Undeterred by the lack of a firearm, Mills hurried off to get his family and flee to Henderson.

The relief column drew near Fort Creek when Sheehan asked Ezmon Earle if he could drive a four-mule team. When he answered in the affirmative, Sheehan ordered the soldiers in the wagon to get out and form in a column. Sheehan tied on a bright red scarf, a move Ezmon thought brave but indiscreet. How the men reached the fort is a matter of some debate.

According to Ezmon's recollection, Sheehan sent the three wagons running along the road across the creek bed while he took his men "on a wide detour to the right where the bluffs were lower and the woods less thick." At the time the teenager thought this a cowardly move, but he later realized it was probably the best way to get his soldiers into the fort and simultaneously avoid an ambush on the road—small comfort for the three wagon drivers. Private McFall remembered the approach differently. The ravine along Fort Creek was half a mile wide, claimed the private, and so thick "with alder brush and willows the eye could not penetrate into these jungles four feet." To his recollection, Sheehan placed twenty-five men in single column in front, followed by the three wagons and another twenty-five men in line in the rear. When the order to move was given, the men ran at double-quick "and the last grand dash to the rescue began."

It took the column about six minutes to push down the banks, slip across the creek, and move up the other side, where they were met by an escort and ushered to the fort's parade ground. There, McFall said, "we saluted the remnant of Company B who were drawn up in line in front of us." It was a joyful and sorrowful reunion; one-half of the boys they had spent the summer with were now dead. McFall was proud of their forced march to Ridgely and claimed they covered the last forty-five miles in less than ten hours.[12]

*   *   *

Dawn on Tuesday brought to a close the night Oscar Wall forever remembered as one the uneasy occupants of Fort Ridgely filled with

---

12 Ezmon Earle reminiscences, Microfilm Reel 1, Dakota Conflict, Minnesota Historical Society; Bryant and Murch, *Great Massacre*, 144; Orlando McFall narrative, Microfilm Reel 2, Dakota Conflict, Minnesota Historical Society.

"supplication, moaning and ceaseless wailing in the barracks." If nothing else, the morning sun dispelled the gloom and "had a mollifying effect."

The Dakotas watching the fort were also stirring. Peter Quinn rose at daybreak and realized with a start that Jack Frazer, one of the few men who had maintained his composure and remained on picket duty throughout the night, was right in front of him. When Frazer saw the Dakotas he "called out to us to get right away from there or he would shoot us, and he said that if he did not know our fathers and mothers so well he would shoot us anyhow." Quinn and his fellow warriors slipped down the bluff and escaped.

Another Dakota scouting party discovered Sheehan and his relief column approaching Fort Ridgely and rode to Redwood to notify Little Crow. This initial report of reinforcements frightened the Dakotas, who began breaking camp to flee to Yellow Medicine. When another warrior rode in and reported the reinforcements appeared to be only about fifty men, the order to break camp was canceled.[13]

*   *   *

Private Sturgis had a longer ride than Corporal McLean and left the fort nine hours later. Like his counterpart he did not spare the horseflesh, and after a twelve-mile run the animal was too exhausted to continue. When Sturgis overtook a peddler with a team and wagon heading east he dismounted and walked alongside for a while to rest his horse. He rode again until he came to a settler's cabin, pounded on the door, told the sleepy man who answered what had transpired, and demanded a fresh horse. The unnamed settler complied and Sturgis continued. He reached St. Peter just after three o'clock in the morning, beating Henry Behnke from New Ulm by about one hour. It was there, not long before dawn, that Sturgis found Lieutenant Culver, Thomas Galbraith, and the Renville Ranger recruits.

After leaving Fort Ridgely on August 16, Galbraith marched his recruits to New Ulm. According to Sheriff Charles Roos, a cheering crowd gathered the next day when he spoke at the Gross Hotel to assure everyone "there was absolutely no danger to be feared from the Indians because he had complied

---

13 Wall, *Recollections of the Sioux Massacre*, 72; Anderson and Woolworth, *Through Dakota Eyes*, 94-95. The Dakotas would make a move toward Fort Ridgely, but as described in Chapter 11, the younger warriors opted instead to attack New Ulm. The decision provided enough time for the Renville Rangers to arrive and bolster the fort's defenses.

with their every wish." Ever the recruiter, Galbraith urged the young men to join his company. Those who could not join, including Schneider, Fenske, and Dietrich, agreed to do all they could to recruit others.[14]

Galbraith's company marched out on the morning of the 18th and reached St. Peter in the afternoon. When Private Sturgis found Galbraith there, the agent already knew about the uprising. One man beat all the messengers. Joe Dickinson had escaped from Redwood Agency, ridden to Fort Ridgely, reported to Captain Marsh, and continued almost nonstop with Martell's team and wagon all the way to St. Peter, which he reached about sundown on Monday. Dickinson, Galbraith recalled, arrived "in a state of excitement, bordering on insanity." The reason for his terrified state of mind became clear as he spoke of a murderous outbreak and Captain Marsh's decision to head to the Lower Agency, but the tale was so "confused, conflicting, and disconnected" the men had trouble believing it. They gathered the rangers and had Dickinson tell the story a second time, but the men still "doubted him, and most of them refused to return to the fort."

Galbraith, however, thought there was something to the story and dispatched a man to carry a request for 200 men to Governor Ramsey; Culver sent his own request for 500 men. The state of Minnesota had 50 old Harpers Ferry muskets on hand, but it took until midnight, "after great trouble, by giving bonds," to secure them. Louis Robert, who ran some of the trading houses on the reservations, paid the $1,000 bond to secure the arms. By this time fugitives from New Ulm were streaming into town, which "satisfied us of the reality of the outbreak," confirmed Galbraith. It took more time to locate sufficient ammunition. By the time the powder, lead, and buckshot were apportioned there was enough for about ten rounds apiece. Private Sturgis found the men about 4:00 a.m. and shared the unwelcome news that Marsh and half his command were dead.

By daybreak St. Peter was in pandemonium and it was difficult to find Sturgis another horse. Sheriff R. W. Tomlinson took him in his buggy 12 miles north to Le Sueur, where he obtained a livery horse and continued on to Shakopee. There, he obtained a fresher mount and reached a ferry farther downriver. Sturgis found two men taking a team to St. Paul and asked if he could climb aboard. When they refused, Sturgis fingered his revolver and

14 Wall, *Recollections of the Sioux Massacre*, 111; Roos, "The Battles of New Ulm," Brown County Historical Society.

threatened to take the team by force, if necessary. Recognizing the soundness of his argument, the men took him the rest of the way and Sturgis reached Fort Snelling at 3:00 p.m. on Tuesday after an 18-hour journey. Luckily, Governor Ramsey and Adjutant General Oscar Malmros were there and within three hours part of the 6th Minnesota Infantry was on a steamboat heading up the Minnesota River.[15]

At "dawn of day," said Galbraith, they started for Fort Ridgely "but with very slender hopes indeed." Within a few miles the men began running into fugitives armed with dire tales of woe. "Still we went on," Galbraith continued, "and, about five o'clock p.m., in a drenching rain [the same rain that ended the Indians' attack on New Ulm] arrived at the fort, and found the little garrison yet safe." That discovery, the agent pronounced, "was well, yea, providential."

*   *   *

Providence, in fact, had nothing to do with it. Dissension within the ranks of the Dakota and an inability of the chiefs to force a warrior into a fight he didn't want saved Fort Ridgely. Unsure how many soldiers were at the fort, the Indians bypassed it on Tuesday in favor of the "easier" target of New Ulm. Even those who moved on New Ulm were leaderless. "I do not think there was a chief present at the first fight," recalled Big Eagle. "I think that the attack was made by marauding Indians from several bands, every man for himself."[16] The lack of command control that Tuesday may have both precluded an attack against Fort Ridgely and saved New Ulm. By Wednesday, however, the Dakotas' command control improved measurably.

After the failed New Ulm assault the disgruntled Dakotas congregated back at Little Crow's village above Redwood Agency. It is fair to speculate that recriminations were expressed and that Little Crow lamented the fact that they could not come together for a unified attack against either place. Scouts reported the countryside empty, and that all whites who had not been killed or captured were holed up in Fort Ridgely or New Ulm. Little Crow, Big Eagle, Little Six, and Medicine Bottle agreed that one or the other must be attacked with the combined might of the Dakotas, and they hoped to include the

---

15 Wall, *Recollections of the Sioux Massacre*, 112-13; *Commissioner of Indian Affairs, 1863*, 275-76.

16 *Commissioner of Indian Affairs, 1863*, 276; Anderson and Woolworth, *Through Dakota Eyes*, 147.

Winnebagoes in the uprising. As usual there was discord; Wabasha and Wacouta refused to fight. According to Lightning Blanket (Hachinwakanda, later David Wells), a 32-year-old Mdewakanton, Wabasha refused to follow any of Little Crow's plans because he was jealous of him. The Dakotas spent all night Tuesday arguing and managed about as much sleep as the whites at the fort.

Despite their exhaustion, by sunup there were more than enough warriors ready to fight. According to Lightning Blanket, they put on their war paint, breech clouts, and leggings and tied a large sash around their bodies to hold their food and ammunition. The warriors crossed the river at Redwood ferry and traveled to Faribault Hill, where they stopped to rest. After Little Crow passed out his final instructions they followed the bluff road to Three Mile Creek about noon, stopped to eat, and then split up. One group on foot under Medicine Bottle and possibly Big Eagle (he later claimed he did not participate in the first fight at Fort Ridgely) moved east to Fort Creek two miles above the fort and turned downstream to cover the fort on the north and east side. The mounted warriors under Little Crow and Little Six rode down to the river road and approached from the south and west. (Map H) The plan called for Medicine Bottle's men to fire three volleys in the north to draw the soldiers' attention so Big Eagle in the east, Little Six in the south, and Little Crow in the west "could rush in and take the fort."[17]

*   *   *

By this time (Wednesday afternoon) the odds of a successful attack against Fort Ridgely were much lower than they would have been on Tuesday. As described earlier, Lieutenant Sheehan arrived Tuesday morning with 50 men of Company C, 5th Minnesota. Because he ranked Lieutenant Gere, Sheehan assumed overall command of the fort. That afternoon Lieutenant Culver's squad arrived with Galbraith and Lieutenant James Gorman and 50 Renville Rangers. Company B was now reunited and had 56 men, although many were too sick or incapacitated to aid in the defense.

Those waiting in Ridgely had high expectations for the two companies of the 5th Minnesota and looked upon these Union soldiers as their saviors. The men may have looked sharp in their uniforms and marched reasonably well, but

17 Anderson and Woolworth, *Through Dakota Eyes*, 153-54.

they were not well-trained veterans. Only a handful had ever been in battle, and the summer trouble at the agencies was the first real "action" or baptism of fire for the companies. The simple fact was that these young men were but one step removed from the civilian refugees seeking their assistance.

The 5th Minnesota was the last of the volunteer regiments to complete the state's quota under President Lincoln's first call for 500,000 men. The various pieces of the regiment came together at Fort Snelling in late 1861 and was not finished organizing until March 1862. Its first colonel, Rudolph von Borgersrode, resigned that August and was replaced by Lt. Col. Lucius F. Hubbard. At the same time, Maj. William B. Gere—Lieutenant Thomas Gere's brother—took over as lieutenant colonel. Captain Marsh did not join Company B until mid-April, when 2nd Lieutenant Culver became 1st lieutenant and Sergeant Gere was elevated to 2nd lieutenant. In the same process, John F. Bishop, who mustered in as a private in February 1862, was promoted to sergeant when Gere moved up.

Company B was recruited mainly from Fillmore County and Company C from Freeborn and Faribault counties, all located along Minnesota's border with Iowa. Before the regiment was organized, Company B was assigned to Fort Ridgely while Company C was dispatched to Fort Ripley in Crow Wing County, near the confluence of the Mississippi and Nokasippi rivers. Company B drilled in manual of arms and infantry evolutions and when a minimum proficiency was obtained, Ordnance Sergeant John Jones—the only Regular Army soldier in the bunch—exercised some of the men in artillery drill. The training was done "more to promote the general efficiency of the company than in anticipation of its necessity or actual use at the fort." It remained to be seen how they would stand up in a tough fight. In many ways Lieutenant Gere was a microcosm of the whole: he was still in his teens, had been in the army only eight months, an officer for just four months, had never fought in a battle, and was said to have been ill with the mumps when the Dakotas launched their attack.[18]

Gorman's 50 Rangers added additional welcome firepower. Although armed with old muskets and only ten rounds each, many of them were mixed-bloods with frontier experience who knew how to fight. When they marched in, Ranger Abel Murch shook hands and exchanged words with Joe De Camp, an acquaintance who also worked at the agency. Neither man knew

---

18 *Minnesota in the Civil and Indian Wars*, I, 243-44; Carley, *Dakota War of 1862*, 26.

what had become of their loved ones. (By this time Mrs. De Camp and the children were captives, and Mrs. Murch was making her escape with John Otherday.)

Choking with emotion, De Camp uttered, "Well, the red devils have got our families."

"We will make them pay the forfeit with their lives," Murch replied.

"Yes," De Camp agreed, the tears were running down his cheeks as he added, "but, curse them, they have not lives enough in the whole Sioux nation to pay it."

Joseph De Camp, "whose Sharp's carbine became familiar music," boasted Private Wall, would prove to be a steadfast fighter throughout the upcoming battles. This was not the case for the majority of the 300 civilians, who were more of a hindrance than a help. Private Wall estimated there were only "some twenty-five men of sterling worth" who made significant contributions to the defense of Ridgely, including the Riekes, who the private described as "brave and brawny fellows."[19]

Other arrivals that Tuesday afternoon included Johann Buhrer and Patrick Heffron and his family, who finally took seriously the warning they received the day before. Heffron had gunsmithing experience and used that valuable trade to repair 20 old dragoon carbines at the fort that would not otherwise have been useable. On Wednesday morning Agathe Buhrer raised concerns about property they had left behind in their hurried flight, in particular a fine green silk dress and some good furniture left by her first husband. She convinced Johann to return to the house and retrieve it. Still making light of the danger, Johann hitched a yoke of oxen with his friend Felix Schmidt, a former soldier from Nicollet County, and left. Concluding that they could also retrieve more of their property, Frederick Rieke and his wife climbed aboard. Only the last minute pleading of their friend Patrick Glassner persuaded the Riekes to climb back out of the wagon. Buhrer and Schmidt rode out of Ridgely alone.

Henry Diepolder showed up at the fort on Wednesday morning. Diepolder lived near the Minnesota River in West Newton Township in Nicollet County, about halfway between the fort and New Ulm. His farm was close to Alexander Harkin's store, one of the first settlers in the area in 1856. Diepolder was the first postmaster in 1860, but Harkin took over the duties shortly after. The two men weren't the best of friends. Diepolder sent his wife to the fort on Tuesday

---

19 Bryant and Murch, *Great Massacre*, 198; Wall, *Recollections of the Sioux Massacre*, 82-87.

and was one of the last men to arrive before the Indians surrounded the post. Because of his two years of service in the Prussian Army, his presence was welcome.

Diepolder was getting settled in the fort not long after Buhrer and Schmidt reached Buhrer's house, loaded the wagon with goods, and headed back to the fort. The wagon was rolling down into the narrow valley to cross Fort Creek when the men ran into Dakota warriors who had just invested the eastern ravine. When Buhrer was shot and killed, Schmidt jumped out of the wagon and ran for his life, stopping a few times to shoot his revolver at the approaching Indians. Somehow he managed to cover nearly a mile of ground before being cut down. He was found with a dead warrior lying next to him. The Dakotas left the oxen in their yoke but scattered most of the goods on the prairie. Agathe Buhrer's claim for $466 in lost property was a trifling remuneration for the cost of three lives.[20]

Xavier Zollner was probably the last person to slip into Ridgely before the Indians encircled the place. He arrived about noon on Wednesday after a hard ride from New Ulm with a message for Lieutenant Sheehan. Zollner described the attack on his town the day before and asked for soldiers and cannon to be sent to them. While waiting for his answer he spotted the Riekes family, who lived close to him. Zollner warned them that his horse's actions told him there were Indians in the neighborhood, and that to calm the nervous animal he left the road and rode around by way of the open prairie. Before Zollner could ride back the Indians had surrounded the fort and he was stuck. Sheehan, meanwhile, discussed the matter with Sergeant Jones and they agreed they could spare one gun for New Ulm, but the townsmen would have to come and get it themselves because they could not spare any men.[21]

After Zollner pitched his case to Lieutenant Sheehan for reinforcing New Ulm, the lieutenant gathered a squad of 20 soldiers to reconnoiter the grounds. According to Private McFall, the squad moved down the wagon road leading to St. Peter and into the ravines on the north and east. From there, Sheehan guided his men down Fort Creek to the Minnesota River, upstream below the bluff, and then north on the prairie to the west side of the fort. Sheehan either

20 Curtiss-Wedge, *History of Renville County*, I, 624, 639-40; Henry Diepolder Depredation Claim #2013; Reddemann, Henderson to Fort Ridgely Trail, 35; Dahlin, *Dakota Uprising Victims*, 84; Johann Buhrer Depredation Claim #338.

21 Curtiss-Wedge, *History of Renville County*, I, 640; Tolzmann, ed., *Brown County*, 14.

completed his scout just minutes before the Dakotas arrived, or they remained hidden and let the soldiers pass in order to not expose themselves and perhaps their battle plan. McFall remembered that he and his comrades were making for the high ground west of the fort "to see what there was beyond when bang, bang, bang, the ball had opened from the east side of the fort." The reconnoitering party "about faced and ran with race horse speed for the fort . . . Sheehan was mounted on a mule," remembered McFall, but he was no match for the soldiers. "We beat him into the fort," boasted the private.[22]

About half past one in the afternoon Little Crow, riding a black pony, appeared on the open high ground west of the fort. He stopped there just out of musket range. From that safe position the Dakota leader tried to distract the soldiers by signaling for a parley. Sergeant Bishop moved out to the picket line in an effort to induce him to ride closer. Neither side was willing to make the first move. This stalemate of sorts was unfolding when Medicine Bottle's men on the north fired the three-volley signal.[23]

When the volleys were fired, Medicine Bottle's warriors charged up to the north and northeast side of the fort. According to Lightning Blanket, the warriors on the other three sides "were slow in coming up." The warriors in the north ran toward the log quarters running parallel with and north of the stone barracks. Warning shots were fired to alert the fort's defenders when pickets there spotted the approach of the Dakotas. Credit for firing the first shot is generally attributed to Joseph Osier of the Rangers.[24]

All the corners of Ridgely were vulnerable to attack, with the gap at the northeast end particularly so. Lieutenants Sheehan and Gere realized this and had placed an artillery piece at the northeast, northwest, and southwest corners. No gun was placed to defend the approach leading toward the southeast corner because that route was comparatively open and free of the encroaching ravines. There were barely enough soldiers with artillery experience to handle three of the six pieces available, and the crews still had to be fleshed out with civilians.

22 Orlando McFall narrative, Microfilm Reel 2, Dakota Conflict, Minnesota Historical Society.

23 The feigned conference and invitation of Bishop seems implausible if Lieutenant Sheehan and his squad were west of the fort at that time. Lightning Blanket's recollection of the plan of attack did not include Little Crow distracting the soldiers from the west side of the fort. The plan was for Medicine Bottle to make the signal and begin the contest.

24 Wall, *Recollections of the Sioux Massacre*, 89, 95; Anderson and Woolworth, *Through Dakota Eyes*, 154-56.

John C. Whipple, who had recently escaped from Redwood Agency, was in charge of a 12-pounder mountain howitzer unlimbered between the bake house and the laundry on the northeast corner. Whipple made good use of his artillery experience and was assisted by Werner Boesch (33), an ex-Swiss artilleryman who lived along Three Mile Creek with his wife Anna. Several other soldiers helped them, and Lieutenant Gere placed a squad of Company B nearby to support the gunners. In the northwest corner was another 12-pounder howitzer under the command of Sgt. James McGrew, with Pvt. James Dunn and a few other soldiers assisting. A squad of Company C men, put in place by Lieutenant Sheehan, remained in reserve to support McGrew and his artillerists. A 6-pounder field gun bolstered the southwest corner commanded by Dennis O'Shea, also an ex-artilleryman. With him were four soldiers and George, Victor, and Adam Rieke. Ordnance Sgt. John Jones, the only Regular Army soldier in the fort, was loosely in charge of all the guns but spent most of his time with O'Shea's crew. Most of the Renville Rangers supported that quarter of the post.[25]

According to several sources someone had tampered with Whipple's gun. The claims vary: a few of the mixed-blood Renville Rangers stuffed either rags or cotton into the vent; one of the rangers who deserted Wednesday night was to have plugged it with rags before he left; Whipple discovered the gun would not fire and Sgt. Jones found a rag inside that indicated carelessness in inspecting and maintaining the weapons, or; the Indians who visited the fort on August 14 had done it. Whatever the reason, the obstruction was easily removed and the gun ready for action.[26]

Lightning Blanket claimed 400 Indians participated in the attack; if the four chiefs each fielded approximately equal numbers, it would be reasonable to conclude that perhaps Medicine Bottle's attack consisted of some 100 warriors

---

25 Wall, *Recollections of the Sioux Massacre*, 90-93; Curtiss-Wedge, *History of Renville County*, I, 624-26; Belanger, "The Fort Ridgely Medal," 235-36; *Minnesota in the Civil and Indian Wars*, II, 182. The 6-pounder field gun (the number equaled the weight of the shot/shell) was obsolete by 1861, supplanted by the 12-pounder Napoleon; many of the smaller caliber pieces were still in use by necessity. Its tube weighed 884 pounds and its range was 1,500 yards. Although it fired a larger and heavier shot, the 12-pounder mountain howitzer only weighed 220 pounds with a range of 900 yards. It was more maneuverable and could be broken down and carried on pack animals. It was very common in the Indian fighting army. See Thomas, *Cannons*, 27, 32.

26 Curtiss-Wedge, *History of Renville County*, I, 625-26, 640-41; Wall, *Recollections of the Sioux Massacre*, 151; Heard, *History of the Sioux War*, 83. Folwell, *History of Minnesota*, II, 131n27, calls these tales "farcical."

charging along the north and northeast sides of the fort. The picket fire offered Whipple a timely alert to prepare for combat. "As we were running in we saw the man with the big guns," recalled Lightning Blanket, "and as we were the only ones in sight he shot into us." If Little Crow had attacked when the signal volley was given, complained Lightning Blanket, "the soldiers who shot at us would have been killed."

Shrapnel from Whipple's howitzer and small arms fire from soldiers of Company B killed a pair of Dakotas outright and wounded three more, two of them mortally. The Dakotas fired through the gaps between the buildings and their charge carried them to the log structures in the northeast quarter. Seeing an opportunity for a flanking fire, some Company C men moved north out from the northwest corner of the fort, turned east, and fired into the attacking Dakotas who returned fire. Company C's Pvt. Mark M. Greer was killed in the first exchange of fire and Pvt. William Good of Company B was badly wounded when a bullet struck him in the center of his forehead. His comrades thought he had been instantly killed, but somehow Good hung on, passing in and out of consciousness throughout the siege. Surgeries were unable to extract the bullet. Good lingered for several more years, "a greater mental than physical sufferer," wrote Oscar Wall. According to Orlando McFall, however, the unfortunate private dropped dead on a Minneapolis street in 1893.

If Private McFall remembered correctly, it must have been about this time that Little Crow began his attack from the west side, chasing Sheehan's squad into the Ridgely. Little Crow's warriors "were in hot pursuit of us when we entered the fort," recalled McFall. "The reception they received when they got in range sent them flying down over the bank onto the Minnesota bottom." O'Shea and Sgt. Jones sent their shells into the oncoming Indians, aided by some Company B men under Lieutenant Culver and many of the Rangers under Lieutenant Gorman. Once the soldiers reached the fort they ran for shelter "as the bullets from the Indian forces on the east were sweeping the parade ground like a hail storm." The men made a dash for the stone barracks, ran up to the second floor, and took position on the north side. "We did not stop to shove the windows up but beat them out with the butts of our muskets. Pandemonium and hell now reigned."[27]

27 Anderson and Woolworth, *Through Dakota Eyes*, 154-55; Curtiss-Wedge, *History of Renville County*, I, 625-26, 640-41; Wall, *Recollections of the Sioux Massacre*, 90, 150-51; Orlando McFall narrative, Microfilm Reel 2, Dakota Conflict, Minnesota Historical Society.

Medicine Bottle's warriors gained a footing at the northeastern corner, where they took over an old stable at the outer edge. Sergeant Jones's pregnant wife was trapped inside a hut just to the west. Maria had taken their three children into the barracks, but returned to the hut to get some items when the Dakotas burst out of the ravines. Depending on which story you believe, she hid in a small closet and wedged her body between the door and back wall so warriors could not push the door open, or a warrior thrust his musket through a window and fired but she ducked behind the iron stove and the bullet missed. When the Indians fell back Maria made a successful break to the barracks. The terrifying ordeal exhausted her, and the next morning she gave birth to a stillborn child. According to refugee Mrs. Catherine Meade, "twelve of the women were prematurely confined during the first twenty-four hours," i.e., they were pregnant and went into labor. Catherine helped Dr. Muller deliver babies and care for the wounded for 48 hours before falling asleep on the floor.

Elizabeth Bell, the wife of Pvt. Charles R. Bell was hiding a few huts west of where Maria Jones was trapped. Pvt. Bell had left with Captain Marsh on Monday and would never return. The Indian attack Wednesday had driven off two of the Bell's cows, said to be a Devon and a Durham of superior stock. Without a husband and with her livestock gone, Elizabeth gathered her seven children, ages ranging two to 15, and ran from the hut to the barracks.[28]

Lightning Blanket later voiced disappointment that Little Crow and Little Six did not charge from their sides when the signal was given. If they had not been tardy, argued Lightning Blanket, "we could have shot at the same time and killed all, as the soldiers were out in a big opening between the buildings." In reality, Lightning Blanket was likely so focused on his own attack that he did not realize Little Crow had attacked, as Private McFall explained.

When Sergeant McGrew saw Company C men move out of the northwest corner to fire to the east, he used the opportunity to move his howitzer forward just beyond the corner of the westernmost log buildings and do the same. The tactic offered him and his gun a perfect enfilade along the northern facings of the buildings into the right flank of the warriors charging Whipple and the Company B men holding the northeast corner. McGrew trained his howitzer on the ravine in an effort to diminish or end the heavy gunfire pouring out of it. The fuse was cut to explode the shell one-quarter mile distant, but the round

---

28 Bryant and Murch, *Great Massacre*, 199-200; Morris, *Old Rail Fence Corners*, 300; Elizabeth Bell Depredation Claim #1201.

skimmed the grass and traveled beyond the ravine before exploding. McGrew ran the piece back behind the building, re-loaded, and cut the fuse as short as possible. Once everything was ready he had the howitzer run forward amidst a storm of bullets, aimed, and fired. This time the shell burst directly over the mass of warriors using the northern ravine as cover. McGrew's artillery fire from the northwest, coupled with Whipple's fire from the northeast, along with the musketry support, produced a converging fire too hot for the Dakotas to stand.

Not knowing whether the warriors in the other quarters would support them, and taking a hot fire from two sides, Medicine Bottle's men withdrew or, as Lightning Blanket succinctly put it, "We ran back into the creek."

When Little Crow and Little Six finally launched a full assault some time after chasing Sheehan's 20-man reconnoitering squad back into the fort, Medicine Bottle and Big Eagle were no longer in a position to support them. Lightning Blanket and his warriors "didn't know whether the other men would come up close or not, but they did and the big guns drove them back from that direction." Jones's and O'Shea's 6-pounder gun and the Renville Rangers turned back the initial charge from the west. "We did not fight like white men, with one officer; we all shot as we pleased," confessed Lightning Blanket. "The plan of rushing into the buildings was given up, and we shot at the windows, mostly at the big stone building, as we thought many of the whites were in there."[29]

Lightning Blanket was correct on that point. By the time Pvt. McFall and the other Company C men joined the others at the second floor windows, the scene unfolding inside the barracks was simply chaotic. According to McFall there were about 300 civilians in the fort, with 200 women and children huddled inside the barracks. After claiming he did not have the words to describe the scene, he did his best to try, adding, "There was singing and praying and crying and screaming and about 50 children came in with their cows." The room he was in had 14 windows, explained McFall, with three men working each one. Two men in each team would load while the third lay on the floor. When he was handed a loaded musket, he "would peak over the window sill and let fly, sometimes at random and sometimes at a redskin."

29 Curtiss-Wedge, *History of Renville County*, I, 626; *Minnesota in the Civil and Indian Wars*, II, 183-84; Wall, *Recollections of the Sioux Massacre*, 90-91; Anderson and Woolworth, *Through Dakota Eyes*, 155.

Robert Baker, a civilian who had escaped from the Lower Agency on Monday, was standing by a window when a bullet hit him in the head and killed him instantly. Women and children were ordered to get flat on the floor, but some were hit by pieces of flying glass, wood, and stone. "They were awful hard to manage," McFall recalled, though he conceded, "who could blame them." Almost everyone had lost one or more family members or had been wounded in their flight to Ridgely.

Ezmon Earle was stationed at a window on the first floor of the barracks, where there were few if any women and children. A row of small log houses in front of him built for families of the non-commissioned officers limited his field of vision. Some soldiers were fighting in and around the structures. It was "About two o'clock the music began and it seemed for a while as though pandemonium itself had broken loose," Ezmon wrote. He guessed the Indians numbered between 400 and 500, and "each time they fired they uttered the war whoop." Ezmon said the noise of the firing and bullets crashing through doors and windows was bad enough, but "the war whoop was worse yet." He described it as "blood-curdling" and admitted he dodged more for the whoops than for the bullets. For a time, he confessed, "my hair stood on end."

Ezmon calmed down, though he found it difficult to participate in the fight because he risked hitting one of the soldiers in and around the huts in front of him. The bluish cloud of gun smoke from their rifles, which only increased with each passing minute, further complicated Ezmon's dilemma. As a result, "I simply remained guard at the window." The post's surgeon, Dr. Alfred Muller, set up a temporary hospital in the same room, and as the day wore on Ezmon admitted that "the sight of those poor fellows taxed my nerves severely."

One of the wounded was Robert J. Spornitz of Company B. Early in the fight, explained Wall, a bullet hit Spornitz in the cheek, tore out the roof of his mouth, and passed out the other side. McFall, however, recalled that his wound was in the leg. Either way, he lived for several years.[30]

When their initial assault failed, the Dakotas hiding in the north and east ravines focused their fire at the windows of the buildings along the northern face of the fort, particularly the stone barracks. They could not see the whites inside, explained Lightning Blanket, "so were not sure we were killing any."

30 Bryant and Murch, *Great Massacre*, 188; Orlando McFall narrative, Microfilm Reel 2, Dakota Conflict, Minnesota Historical Society; Ezmon Earle reminiscences, Microfilm Reel 1, Dakota Conflict, Minnesota Historical Society; Wall, *Recollections of the Sioux Massacre*, 150.

They also tried to shoot fire arrows into the structures, "but the buildings would not burn, so we had to get more powder and bullets."

At least one of the fire arrows did its job. Joe Coursolle recalled that when the attack came it hit from every side with nearly naked warriors "rushing at us with screaming yells" and bullets and arrows whizzing above their heads. "A flaming arrow stuck in the shingles of the officers' quarters and a blaze started to spread."

An officer called out to Joe to "climb up on that roof and chop out the fire!" Joe hesitated, believing "Every Indian bow and gun will be shooting just at me." Nevertheless, he found a ladder and, although his legs felt wobbly, scaled it two rungs at a time as bullets whizzed by his head. "Never did an axe swing faster than mine as I whacked out the fire," Joe declared. When he finished he determined it was too slow and risky going back down the ladder, so he moved to the edge of the roof and rolled off, landing with a grunt on an earth wall. "I thought there would be more holes in me than a sieve," he explained, "but I didn't have a scratch. They were bum shots."[31]

Unable to break through in the north and east, the Dakotas settled for a long-range fire in that quarter while Little Crow and Little Six tried to arrange a coordinated attack from their respective sides. Sergeant Jones and O'Shea worked their 6-pounder in the southwest, but converging fire from the Indians forced them to pull back onto the open parade ground. Jones took position on the porch of the barracks, roughly midway between the three guns, and tried to direct them all. It was quickly becoming apparent that the battle might last until nightfall or even longer, and that a potentially fatal mistake had been made in not hauling all the artillery ammunition from the magazine to a central location in the fort proper.

Sergeant Jones sought out volunteers to remedy the situation. The first to step forward were Pvts. Charles E. Chapel and Charles A. Rose of Company C. The pair agreed to run to the magazine which, for safety's sake, had been built about 200 yards northwest of the fort. He still needed more men and even

---

31 Anderson and Woolworth, *Through Dakota Eyes*, 155; Joseph Coursolle story, Microfilm Reel 1, Dakota Conflict, Minnesota Historical Society. Joe Coursolle is said to have later claimed that the officer who told him to put out the fire was Capt. Joseph Anderson. Anderson, however, didn't get to Fort Ridgely with the mounted Cullen Guards until August 27, and Coursolle joined them at that time. Joe's story was passed down to his son and grandson, who related it to interviewer Floyd J. Patten in 1962. As is usually the case with oral history, the story becomes garbled over time.

called on the civilians for help. Adam Rieke claimed that Jones issued a challenge to the superintendent's clerk, Cyrus Wykoff, claiming that one of the principal reasons for the uprising was the failure to bring the Dakotas' money in time. Now, the least Wykoff could do was help carry in ammunition. The accusation was unfair, at least on a personal level, but Wykoff accepted the challenge and he and the other four members of the money guard dashed out to the magazine.

The ground to the northwest was more open and thus harder for the Indians to approach unexposed. McGrew ran out his howitzer with some soldiers as back-up and covered the men running to and fro carrying the heavy shells. They placed the ammunition in the stone barracks, only to discover yet another problem: Someone would have to move the ammunition from the barracks out to the bullet-swept parade ground. Standing on the porch, Jones commanded civilian Adam Rieke to "come to me." Adam's brother George urged his sibling to refuse because he would likely be hit as soon as he stood. Adam agreed and remained in place. Jones called to Victor, who refused to reply. His temper rising, the Regular Army sergeant turned his attention to George and issued the same command. The resentful German yelled back to the sergeant, "It is not for you to give us citizens instructions!" The frustrated Jones waved his sword in a threatening manner, to no avail. Out of viable options, Jones demonstrated his bravery by moving the shells himself by crouching and rolling them across the parade ground. The sergeant's effort may have embarrassed the German brothers into action; after all, if he could do it, maybe the risk was not so unreasonable after all. The Riekes crawled out to join Jones, rolling shells to O'Shea, who continued to work his piece with four soldiers.[32]

Andrew Rufredge of Company B, fighting to support Whipple's effort at the northeast angle, was wounded in a manner similar to Spornitz when a bullet cut his lower jaw off almost back to his ears. Henry Rieke, who was ill (and may have had a heart condition), was with the defenders on the second floor of the barracks. He was looking out a window when he saw Rufredge's jaw rip away and the soldier fall with a gaping wound and bloody face. Henry apparently believed the man was one of his brothers and was so shocked by the event that

---

32 Curtiss-Wedge, *History of Renville County,* I, 627, 641; *Minnesota in the Civil and Indian Wars,* II, 184; Wall, *Recollections of the Sioux Massacre,* 92.

he collapsed into his sister's arms. Whatever the cause, Henry died in the fort three days later.[33]

After the initial charges, the fight for Ridgely ebbed and flowed for five hours, with most of it waged at longer ranges. Some of the Renville Rangers defending the south side of the fort got into a shouting match with the Dakotas. The Indians urged the defenders to give up and come over to their side or be killed. "We will fix you, you devils!" shouted back one of the rangers. "You will eat your children before winter."[34]

The Dakotas managed to hold the old stable in the northeast corner of the fort until dusk. The position caused untold problems for the defenders for much of the day, and the simple solution to the problem should have been realized much sooner. Nightfall was approaching when Whipple received an order from Lieutenant Sheehan: blast the building apart with his artillery. His first two shells struck the building and ignited the hay. Within minutes the entire stable was engulfed in flames. When a few of the Indians manning the position attempted to flee, Ranger George Dagenais, fighting at the bakery, leveled his rifle and wounded one. When it looked as though the injured Dakota would crawl to safety, Dagenais dropped his gun, turned to fellow ranger Joseph La Tour, and said, "Come Joe." The two men made a brave and athletic run from the bakery to the stable, seized the struggling warrior, and pitched him into the flames while screaming out their own war whoops. A few seconds later they were running back for safety, dodging through a hail of bullets fired from the ravines. When they reached the bakery, breathless but exuberant, Dagenais announced, "I kill him one, I kill him one."[35]

Dakotas managed to raid the government stables in the south near the bluffs and steal some of the horses and mules housed there, but most of their damage they would inflict that day was over. Private Wall believed the tide turned about 4:00 p.m. after the Indians "had failed to force a break at any point." After that, he insisted, "they fought in disorder" until sundown. Lightning Blanket essentially agreed with Wall's assessment, saying later that

---

33 Curtiss-Wedge, *History of Renville County*, I, 642; Wall, *Recollections of the Sioux Massacre*, 151.

34 "Story of Nancy McClure," 452, *MHSC*, Vol. 6. The Dakotas were especially angry that mixed-bloods fought for white men. When the warriors returned to Little Crow's village that night they told captured mixed-blood families that they were worse than the whites and would all be killed soon. "Most of them had whiskey," recalled Nancy Faribault, "and it was a dreadful time."

35 Bryant and Murch, *Great Massacre*, 200-01; Wall, *Recollections of the Sioux Massacre*, 95.

there were about two hours of sun left when Medicine Bottle's warriors called it quits, moved around to the west side of the fort, and made for Little Crow's village. On the way they retrieved the two warriors killed during the opening of the battle in a little draw west of the fort where Little Crow's men were fighting. Their bodies were buried on either side of the road about 200 yards apart; dirt from the road was used to cover them. Lightning Blanket had no idea how many warriors had been killed in the other sectors, "but don't think there were any. We always thought no whites were killed, or not many, as it was hard to see them."[36]

In fact, there may have been more white casualties than Dakota. The defenders had suffered two killed outright (Greer and Baker) and many wounded. In addition to Good, Rufredge, and Spornitz, at least five more men had been hit. Buckshot struck Company C's Dennis Porter in the chest and leg, but he refused to put down his musket and continued fighting throughout the day without seeking any medical help. Also in Company C, Philo Henry was shot through the arm. In Company B, John L. Magill was wounded in the leg and James M. Munday was hit in the shoulder. In the Renville Rangers, Joseph Fortier took a slight wound in the face.[37]

Dr. Alfred Muller (36), a Swiss native who received his medical training at the University of Berne, spent that day and all night taxed to the limit of human endurance in the makeshift barracks hospital trying to deal with the traumatic wounds. In addition to the immediate wounded Muller also had to tend to the injured survivors who had made it back to Ridgely after Marsh's disastrous fight two days earlier—men like Blodgett, shot through the abdomen, and Sutherland, shot through the right lung—as well as scores of refugees with various wounds and the traumatized women who gave birth during the ordeal. Eliza Muller assisted her doctor husband, as did several other women including Valencia Reynolds. It is to their credit that not one wounded man who reached the care of Doctor Muller lost his life.[38] Many able-bodied women assisted in

---

36 *Minnesota in the Civil and Indian Wars*, II, 184; Wall, *Recollections of the Sioux Massacre*, 93; Anderson and Woolworth, *Through Dakota Eyes*, 155-56.

37 Orlando McFall narrative, Microfilm Reel 2, Dakota Conflict, Minnesota Historical Society; Joseph Fortier Depredation Claim #272.

38 Wall, *Recollections of the Sioux Massacre*, 167-68. Connelly, *Minnesota Massacre*, 65-66, tells a fantastic story about Eliza Muller helping Sergeant Jones operate his cannon, and dying at her post!

the hospital or helped make cartridges, saving lives with one hand and providing the means to kill with the other.

During the battle the Dakotas set fire to a few outbuildings and the artillery contributed to the conflagrations. In addition to the leveling of the old stable on the northeast corner, haystacks and some ice and root houses near the bluff were set on fire. Sheehan ordered a few buildings torched so the Indians could not use them for cover if they returned to continue fighting. The light from the burning buildings struck fear in the hearts of many of the refugees streaming toward the fort in the darkness, who reasonably believed the fort had fallen. The long and exhausting day, coupled with the darkness and flames also put the pickets on edge. "Several alarms were given during the night," remembered John Whipple, "and some 13 or 14 dogs were killed by the sentinels as they were prowling round to get into camp to eat the cattle killed by the Indians during the fight." Some of the pickets simply abandoned their posts. With lanterns in hand, sutler Ben Randall and an officer visited some of the picket posts and to their surprise found "no one was sleeping on them; they were deserted. We followed to where they had taken shelter in the barracks among the refugees, and they were ordered from under the bedsteads, to resume their guns and duties."[39]

A drenching rain began falling about midnight, which only added to the gloom and discomfort of many of the Fort Ridgely occupants. Some, however, looked upon the downpour as a gift because Indians out in the open would have a hard time keeping their powder and fire arrows dry. Old Jack Frazer used the rain as cover to seek help. He left that night for St. Peter, but his progress was slow and it took him until Friday to cover the 45 miles, arriving just about the time that Colonel Henry H. Sibley arrived there. Frazer impressed upon the former Minnesota governor how serious the situation appeared to be, and that there might be thousands of Dakotas up in arms. "The post is closely invested," Sibley wrote his wife two days later, "but Jack Frazer escaped from it on Wednesday night and says the garrison are in good health and can defend themselves until relieved, if the enemy do not succeed in firing the roofs of the buildings."[40]

---

39 Malmros, *Perspectives on the Sioux War*, 24-25; Whipple, *Central Republican*, September 10, 1862; Morris, *Old Rail Fence Corners*, 232.

40 Folwell, *History of Minnesota*, II, 148; Carley, "Sibley's Letters to His Wife," 101.

Back at the fort, meanwhile, Randall the sutler crept out into the darkness to check on the condition of his house. When he heard what he thought were Indians talking he hurried back. Soon thereafter a wailing noise rose from west of the fort. No one could recognize what it was, and Sheehan ordered Sgt. McGrew to fire a shot from his 12-pounder howitzer in that direction in case it was an Indian ruse to distract the garrison's attention. The sound continued, however, and Sheehan sent a detachment of soldiers out to investigate its source. To their surprise, they discovered a lost and exhausted woman crazed with grief and fear, and carried her into the fort.[41]

41 Wall, *Recollections of the Sioux Massacre*, 98. The unnamed woman found that night may have been Mrs. Yess, who fled from the Sacred Heart attack on Tuesday.

C hapter 13

"Is there any water in heaven?"

Lake Shetek

The settlement ~ The Sissetons visit Aaron Myers ~ Alomina Hurd ~ Maria Koch ~ Charles Hatch gives warning ~ Congregation at Wright's ~ Reasons for the settlers' discord ~ Escape to Slaughter Slough ~ The captives ~ The survivors head for New Ulm ~ Tousley's expedition ~ Rescue

L ake Shetek in Murray County was a beautiful place to settle. With plenty of water, good timber, and arable land, it rivaled the Spirit Lake area in Iowa as a mini-paradise. (Map P) By the end of August 1862 it also rivaled Spirit Lake as a mini-hell.

About a dozen or more families, perhaps 40 people in all, established a small settlement around Lake Shetek, Smith Lake, Fremont Lake, and Bloody Lake about 70 miles west of New Ulm.[1] The families who arrived between 1855 to 1861 included the names: Myer, Hurd, Koch, Ireland, Eastlick, Duley, Smith, Wright, Everett, LaBushe, and Parmlee. There were also a number of single men, including John Voight, William Jones, and Edgar Bently. Two others, said to be escaping the draft, also moved to the area. One named "Rhodes" lived part time in a tipi and part time with the settlers; the other was an older trapper named John Macabee, who erected a little shanty on an island in Lake Shetek.

---

1 "Koch Cabin Lake Shetek," in http://www.rrcnet.org/~historic/kcabin.html. Bloody Lake was not named because of the 1862 massacre. It was named years before the incident, because certain tree roots and plants on the water's edge gave the lake a rusty color (per Wayne and Connie Anderson, who live (2005) on the site of the Koch cabin).

Most of the families settled along the east side of Lake Shetek, which ran generally north-south for about five miles. Aaron Myers (37), his wife, and four children settled along the upper Cottonwood River about ten miles north of Shetek in present Amiret Township in Lyon County before moving to Fremont Lake just north of Lake Shetek. The Dakota Land Company established a town called Saratoga a few miles from Myers's first homestead. John Renniker, a company employee, erected a house there. In the spring of 1857 Renniker used Myers's ox team to fetch supplies from New Ulm that included a cask of whiskey to sell to the Indians. Mixed-blood John Campbell (the brother of Antoine Campbell, whose family was caught at Redwood Agency on August 18, 1862) saw Renniker purchase this whiskey. Campbell and several Dakota warriors followed Renniker during the 1862 uprising and murdered him at Walnut Grove in southwest Redwood County. With Inkpaduta's band also on the loose, the small young Saratoga community disintegrated. Trapper Charles Hammer disappeared, as did widower Jedidiah H. Ingalls and his children. After the 1857 incident, Ingalls, who lived upriver from Myers, moved near Yellow Medicine Agency where he thought it would be safer. He and his family were killed or captured on August 19, 1862, one day before the storm hit Lake Shetek. Another early Lyon County settler also had bad luck. James W. Lynd established a trading post on the Redwood in 1855 before moving to the Lower Agency to run Myrick's store. He was the first victim of the Dakota uprising.[2]

The Lake Shetek area may have been a little Eden, but nature unleashed periodic plagues of grasshoppers and blackbirds to prey on the region. Brown County covered much of southwest Minnesota until 1857, when Murray County was organized. The blackbirds were so bad that Brown County residents signed petitions to eradicate them. Strychnine was passed out to kill the birds in 1858 and 1859, but they always returned, though in somewhat lesser numbers. Blackbirds were also a problem in Murray County and indirectly led to the deaths of two residents. In an effort to escape the pesky creatures, settler Phineas B. Hurd and companion William Jones left on June 2, 1862, to examine new land in Dakota Territory. Hurd hired John Voight to care for his farm during his absence. Neither Hurd nor Jones reached their destination. Part of the way was through unfriendly Sisseton territory.

Exactly what happened to her husband Alomina Hurd could not say. He was expected back in one month, but it had been more than ten weeks since she

2   Bryant and Murch, *Indian Massacre in Minnesota*, 153; Rose, *Lyon County*, 34-37.

had last seen him. During this time Voight had a run-in with the Dakotas—Myers had to intervene to save him—and as a result the Indians harbored a grudge against Voight. These Indians were not to be crossed—and neither was their land. White Lodge lived about 40 miles northwest of Lake Shetek on the shores of Lake Shaokatan, and Lean Grizzly Bear lived beyond him in Dakota Territory. They were Sissetons. Unlike many of the rest of the tribe, these Sissetons refused to live on the reservation. Both chiefs detested white men. When word of the uprising reached them Monday night, they sent a messenger to Little Crow indicating that they would support him. Little Crow invited them on Wednesday to join the attack against Fort Ridgely. By this time, however, the Sissetons were already approaching Lake Shetek looking for blood, driving Phineas Hurd's wagon and riding one of his horses.[3]

The Sissetons moved down out of the north moving past Aaron Myers's place on the north shore of Lake Fremont. Some of them—White Owl, Old Pawn, a man Meyers rendered as Tizzie Tonkah, or Bad Ox, and Chaska, who was considered an "outlaw"—had been there just the day before.[4] Aaron had been up most of the night with his sick wife Mary. About six in the morning on Wednesday, August 20, their daughter Olive (8) announced, "Pa, there is a whole lot of Indians riding through our corn field, and two of them are taking down our fence." Aaron had befriended many of the Dakotas, treated them when sick or injured, and knew much of their language. Their nickname for him was "Doctor" or Siha Sisrinna (Small Feet). Perhaps disbelieving his daughter's announcement, Aaron went outside and walked to within easy speaking distance of Chaska and Tizzie Tonkah, the men taking down his fence.

When he asked them why they were destroying his property, one of them answered saucily, "Just for fun."

"I will knock some of your fun out of you," Aaron threatened.

Both warriors laughed before one replied, "You go to the house and get some breakfast and you will feel better after you get your stomach filled." Without another word the pair mounted their horses and rode off after the

---

3   Neill, *History of the Minnesota Valley*, 699; Robinson, *History of the Dakota*, 301, 305; Oehler, *Great Sioux Uprising*, 105; Currie, "Information on victims of the Lake Shetek Massacre," Microfilm Reel 1, Dakota Conflict, Minnesota Historical Society.

4   Several "Chaskas" played a role in the uprising because the Dakotas used birth order names. The firstborn male was Caske, second was Hepan, and the third was Hepi (all with variations). The firstborn female Dakota was Winuna or Winona, hence the reason for so many Winonas. Derounian-Stodola, *The War in Words*, 294n48.

others. The perplexed Aaron returned to his house and told Mary that the Indians had probably just received their annuities "and were feeling funny."[5]

After passing by the Aaron Myers home the Sissetons paid a visit to the Hurd cabin. New York native Alomina Hurd had married Phineas in 1857 and moved to Nicollet County in 1859, intending to live near St. Peter, but they joined others heading west and settled at Lake Shetek. She and her two young boys William (3) and Edward (1) had waited in vain for Phineas to return from his trip. Alomina was milking the cows early that Wednesday when about 20 Sisseton warriors appeared. Her heart sank when she realized one of them was riding her husband's horse. Alomina knew some of these Indians, who indicated they wanted to go inside to smoke. The baby began to cry once they were in the house, so Mr. Voight picked him up and went outside. Without any warning that something was wrong, one of the warriors shot him through the body leaving baby Edward to fall to the ground. As if the shot was a signal, many more Indians appeared and ransacked the place, destroying 200 pounds of butter and 23 cheeses in the process.

Alomina was ordered to take her children and leave immediately. The Indians refused to let her pack any extra food or clothing. They escorted her about three miles from the house, pointed in the direction of New Ulm, and told her to go. The rest of the whites were going to be killed, they told her, but she was free if she did not raise an alarm. As they walked, the barefoot and thinly clad William asked his mother why they couldn't go back home. He didn't know Voight had been shot and at only three years old, could not understand why his mother insisted they keep walking. He cried for a time, but after a while held her hand and shuffled along while Alomina carried Edward. Ahead of them was a long hard trek.[6]

The Sissetons passed along the east side of Bloody Lake before turning toward the Koch house on the south shore. They were approaching the Koch place when Charles D. Hatch was approaching Alomina Hurd's house. Hatch (24), who had traveled from Wisconsin to Lake Shetek with the idea of filing his own claim for land, was staying with his brother-in-law, William Everett and his sister Almira. His goal that morning was to borrow Hurd's team of oxen to help

5   Currie, "Information on victims of the Lake Shetek Massacre," Microfilm Reel 1, Dakota Conflict, Minnesota Historical Society; Aaron Myers Reminiscence, Microfilm Reel 2, Dakota Conflict, Minnesota Historical Society.

6   *Davenport* (Iowa) *Gazette*, April 28, 1863, cited in Bryant and Murch, *Great Massacre*, 367-70.

Everett build a saw mill. He had tied his horse not too far from the Koch place and used a shortcut across a slough to reach Hurd's home on foot. Hatch froze when he spotted Hurd's watchdog lying dead near the house, still attached to his chain. The house had been plundered and John Voight was lying dead in the yard. "I started back to Mr. Cook's [Koch's] where my horse was tied, as fast as I could run," remembered Hatch, "but when I got near the house I saw the Indians ahead of me." Hatch "knelt down and asked God, the great ruler, and disposer of all human events, to protect me in this my hour of danger." Once his brief supplication to heaven ended, Hatch ran like hell to the Ireland home.[7]

Germans Andreas Koch (pronounced Cook) and his wife Maria (28) built their home near the outlet from Bloody Lake to Lake Shetek in 1859 after living at Walnut Grove for two years. Childless, Maria used much of her time sprucing up the cabin and planting flowers and shrubs. She was inside sweeping the floor Wednesday morning when Andreas went out to get a pail of water.[8] A short time later Maria heard shooting and ran outside to see what was happening. Indians were in the yard, but they let her pass by when she saw Andreas lying dead near the barn. For some reason the warriors did not interfere with her and she hurried into the woods, across a natural dam on the lakeshore, and on to Ireland's house. The house was locked and no one was around, but down the road she spotted several people hurrying south. Maria ran to catch up with them.[9]

Back at the Myers house, meanwhile, Mary Myers began to feel a little better by 10:00 a.m. and was hungry for some toast. Since they had no bread in the house, Aaron sent their son Arthur (10) down to fetch some from the Hurd's at Bloody Lake. A short time later the boy was back screaming that Mr. Voight was dead, the house had been ransacked, and that feathers from the beds were scattered everywhere. Aaron figured the Dakotas had taken revenge against Voight and left to tell the Kochs. He arrived only to find Andreas

7 Silvernale, *Commemoration of the Sioux Uprising*, 12; Charles D. Hatch narrative, Microfilm Reel 2, Dakota Conflict, Minnesota Historical Society.

8 Silvernale, *Commemoration of the Sioux Uprising*, 11; Currie, "Information on victims of the Lake Shetek Massacre," Microfilm Reel 1, Dakota Conflict, Minnesota Historical Society. Another settler, Lavina Eastlick, claimed Maria Koch was in the cornfield shooting at birds, but Maria said she was in the house. Some of the lilac bushes Maria planted are said to still be in bloom at the old homesite.

9 Currie, "Information on victims of the Lake Shetek Massacre," Microfilm Reel 1, Dakota Conflict, Minnesota Historical Society.

facedown in the yard with two pails of water on either side of his outstretched arms. He had been shot through the heart. When he discovered that the house had been torn up and heard war whoops nearby, Aaron ran for home and ordered Arthur to get the oxen while he prepared the wagon. Mary grabbed what she could while readying Olive, Fred (5), and Addie (1). The Myers headed north and east hoping to get to New Ulm. None of them knew they were in the midst of an uprising and that the town was already under siege.[10]

Aaron Myers had arrived at the Koch house after Charley Hatch and Maria Koch had escaped. Hatch was the farthest ahead and reached the Ireland house first. Thomas and Sophia Waters Ireland moved to the area in November 1861. They lived in a cabin about midway down the east shore of Lake Shetek with their four daughters Rosa (9), Ellen (7), Sarah Jane (5), and Julianne (3). They tried to gather some possessions, but Hatch insisted there wasn't enough time. When he was sure the Ireland family was leaving, Lake Shetek's "Paul Revere" ran to the Eastlick cabin off the main road and away from the lakeshore. Lavina Day, born in May 1833 in Broome County, New York, married John Eastlick in Ohio in 1850. They moved to Indiana and Illinois before finally settling at Lake Shetek in October 1861. They had five sons: Merton (11), Frank (9), Giles (8), Frederick (5), and John "Johnny" Eastlick III (1).[11] A Mr. Rhodes was temporarily boarding with the family.

The Eastlick household was sitting down to breakfast when young Merton entered to announce, "Charley Hatch is coming as fast as he can run." Indians are killing the settlers, sputtered the exhausted Hatch a few moments later. "It is so," he affirmed, perhaps after sensing doubt. "They have already shot Voight." After explaining what he knew, Hatch asked for a horse to continue his ride. Rhodes the boarder, who owned two horses, willingly gave up one. A similar scene was reenacted at William Duley's house. When Duley heard the news and the plan for the residents to assemble at Smith's place, he suggested instead they go to Wright's since it was built on higher ground and was a well-constructed two-story structure. They agreed and Duley, his wife Laura, and their children Willie (11), Emma (8), Jefferson (6), Belle (4), and Frances (18 months) fled

---

10 Aaron Myers Reminiscence, Microfilm Reel 2, Dakota Conflict, Minnesota Historical Society.

11 Currie, "Information on victims of the Lake Shetek Massacre," Microfilm Reel 1, Dakota Conflict, Minnesota Historical Society. Background, names, and ages of the Eastlick family were supplied by Judith Penhiter, a descendent of Lavina through Johnny.

south as fast as they could run. Henry W. Smith's house was next, located on the west shore of Smith Lake and east of Lake Shetek. Henry and his wife Sophia were childless and therefore had a somewhat easier time gathering a few belongings. They all continued to Wright's house on the south shore of Smith Lake, where John Wright lived with his wife Julia and their children Eldora (5), John (3), and an infant, George. John, however was away in Mankato on business.[12]

No one was at Smith's by the time the Eastlicks arrived. Concluding everyone had left for Wright's place, they headed there as well. Charley Hatch rode on to Everett's, where he told his brother-in-law and sister the terrible news. They, too, gathered their children Lillie (6), Willie (5), and Charles (2) and headed north to Wright's. By the time the Irelands left their home the Indians were right behind them. Ireland decided to use himself as bait and took off on a tangent hoping the Indians would chase him. The Dakota warriors obliged, leaving his family to proceed alone. When exhaustion overtook the Duley family, William concealed everyone in the brush and made for Wright's home on his own.

The panicked settlers were approaching Wright's when they came across about ten Dakotas who had been camped nearby since Monday. "They motioned us to hurry along," recalled Lavina Eastlick, "pretending to be much frightened." An Indian woman stopped Lavina and asked what was happening. When she replied, continued Lavina, the Indian woman "pretended great sympathy for us and even pretended to weep." Some of the settlers and Dakotas appeared excited and frightened, while others acted as if it was all a big scare over nothing. Inside the house a confused Lavina found Julia Wright "very cool and collected." The Indians are our friends, she calmly explained, and "would fight for us."

Old Pawn, the same Indian Aaron Myers had noticed trampling through his cornfield, was also there with eight members of his band, supposedly on their way down the Des Moines River hunting buffalo. Old Pawn, Duley, and Everett went back to gather the stragglers and hidden members of their families. Along the way they met Maria Koch and brought her back with them. She was soaked from running through the marshes and Mrs. Wright gave her

---

12 Eastlick, "Lake Shetek Indian Massacre," Microfilm Reel 1, Dakota Conflict, Minnesota Historical Society; Silvernale, *Commemoration of the Sioux Uprising*, 12; Jefferson Duley correspondence, July 22, 1925.

some dry clothes. By this time 34 settlers had gathered at the Wright home. The question on everyone's mind was what they should do next.[13]

Their first inclination was to reinforce the house and defend it, but "as we looked over our implements of war we found only three squirrel rifles, some shot guns and a keg of powder and a few sacks of shot," explained Charley Hatch. The men distributed the guns and widened cracks between the logs to make loopholes to fire from while the women lifted axes and knives and went upstairs to use the windows and serve as lookouts. A number of Dakotas, including Old Pawn, still professed friendship and support. Most of the settlers had interacted with Old Pawn, who frequently camped in the area. The warriors coming south from Smith's were altogether different. Led by White Lodge and Lean Grizzly Bear, they were intent on committing murder. Some have speculated this group included Inkpaduta.[14]

Most of the whites argued that Old Pawn and his band should not be allowed inside, and that a defensive stand should be made in the stable. "They said they would fight for the white people," Lavina Eastlick recalled, "but they had no ammunition." As incredible as it seems given the circumstances, Old Pawn and his men were given two guns and ammunition. When Tizzie Tonkah claimed he would fight for the whites as long as there was an Indian left, Tom Ireland handed him a powder horn. Old Pawn, explained Ireland, "had been a great friend of the whites heretofore and we trusted him." Lavina remained unconvinced and told her husband she "had no confidence in them."[15]

The division of opinion among the settlers may have had its origin in incidents that occurred years earlier. In 1859, two men widely considered outlaws named Charles Wamban and Bill Clark frequented the area. Wamban befriended Aaron Myers and asked for work. Myers hired him to dig a cellar under his house and as the work progressed headed for New Ulm with

---

13 Eastlick, "Lake Shetek Indian Massacre," Microfilm Reel 1, Dakota Conflict, Minnesota Historical Society; Jefferson Duley correspondence, July 22, 1925.

14 Charles D. Hatch narrative, Microfilm Reel 2, Dakota Conflict, Minnesota Historical Society; Eastlick, "Lake Shetek Indian Massacre," Microfilm Reel 1, Dakota Conflict, Minnesota Historical Society; Beck, *Inkpaduta*, 115-16. According to Beck (p. xix) there is no primary evidence showing that Inkpaduta was present, and he is crusading for a reassessment of his character. After all, Beck writes, "up to the Spirit Lake Massacre, Inkpaduta . . . had never killed a white."

15 Currie, "Information on victims of the Lake Shetek Massacre," Microfilm Reel 1, Dakota Conflict, Minnesota Historical Society; Eastlick, "Lake Shetek Indian Massacre," Microfilm Reel 1, Dakota Conflict, Minnesota Historical Society.

neighbor William Jones for supplies. Things went smoothly until an inebriated Clark arrived and the two men began fighting over some stolen property. When Clark threatened to shoot Wamban Mrs. Myers begged them to take their quarrel elsewhere. Later, Wamban and another neighbor disarmed Clark, who left only to return with another weapon and threats of death. When he was disarmed a second time, Clark—who was said to be a mixed-blood—vowed to return with his Dakota friends and kill all the whites at the lake.

Several settlers decided this little reign of terror should end then and now, and followed Clark to Koch's. Charley Wamban and John Wright spotted him through a window sitting near the stove. "Wright told Charley to give it to him," explained Myers, "and he did, and Clark fell dead to the floor." They buried him, wrote up a paper explaining what had happened, and all the settlers involved sign it. Wright, Smith, and Wamban and Judge Joseph B. Amidon of Sioux Falls rode to New Ulm to present the document they hoped would clear everyone involved. On the way they met Myers and Jones, explained what had happened, and asked them to sign. "Neither of us would confess to a murder we had nothing to do with," said Myers. They made some "sarcastic remarks" and chastised the pair for not joining them. Phineas Hurd also refused to sign. Soon thereafter Wamban "left for parts unknown." Because of this murderous incident, explained Myers, the others "had it in for Jones and Hurd and myself."

When John Wright began selling liquor to the Indians the following year, the surrounding settlers passed a resolution prohibiting it. Wright ignored their request, bought a barrel in New Ulm, and hauled it back to the lake. When word reached the locals he was selling the alcohol, a group of settlers confronted Wright. He denied it, but the men searched his wagon and found the whiskey, broke the barrel open, and spilled it out. Wright acted like it was no big deal, telling them "it was a good joke on the whiskey," but he may well have harbored a grudge against those involved.[16]

As the settlers converged at Wright's house that August Wednesday, hard feelings lingered between some of the families and an accord about how to proceed only exacerbated their differences. Some gave Old Pawn's men weapons; others refused to allow them enter the house. Old Pawn suggested they all march out and confront the approaching war party and fire their guns in

16 Aaron Myers Reminiscence, Microfilm Reel 2, Dakota Conflict, Minnesota Historical Society; Currie, "Information on victims of the Lake Shetek Massacre," Microfilm Reel 1, Dakota Conflict, Minnesota Historical Society. As late as 1894, when Maria Koch (then remarried) was asked about the Clark killing, her reply was, "I don't want to talk about it."

a volley which, recalled Lavina Eastlick, "would frighten them away." The men agreed. Lavina begged her husband John not to fire his gun until he was sure Old Pawn and his own men had discharged their weapons. Once the settlers and Indians spotted the approaching Sissetons, the whites fired—but the Indians did not. When Lavina later learned about this she was convinced they had planned to shoot down the whites when their guns were empty, "but were too cowardly to do it when the time came to act." Whether or not that was the case, the musket volley did not deter the approaching Sissetons. Old Pawn volunteered to bargain with them.

Charley Hatch returned to the house and told some of the other settlers there "were 300 of the Indians and if we stayed there they would burn the house over our heads, but if we would leave everything and go away, they would not harm us." As usual the whites argued about what course of action to take. They finally put the matter up for a vote and by majority decision decided to leave. Hatch and Mr. Rhodes secured at the Everett house "the only team of horses that was at the lake," hitched them to a wagaon, and Mrs. Everett and the youngest children climbed aboard. Julia Wright, Lavina Eastlick and her sons Merton and Frank walked with the men. After about one mile the Indians appeared behind them. They were being followed, and their pursuers were rapidly gaining ground. "All was terror among us," Lavina admitted.[17]

The settlers tried to outdistance the Indians, but the horses were so overburdened they could barely move faster than a walk. Outpacing the Sissetons was hopeless. Thinking the Indians may be content with the horses, those in the wagon jumped out and a few of the men dropped back to provide cover. William Duley suggested making a run for a prairie slough another mile farther east that became marshy in rainy weather. Rhodes and Henry Smith, however, took off down the road, ignoring shouts to come back. Jefferson Duley remembered his father "hollering and telling them if they were going to run to leave their guns, but they did not stop." Rhodes was single, but Smith forever earned their approbation by abandoning his wife. The Indians shot at the fleeing pair but no one was hit. When the Indians reached the abandoned wagon several settlers returned fire, with one claiming he hit the warrior who first grabbed the horses. The Sissetons pursued the fleeing whites and struck

17 Charles D. Hatch narrative, Microfilm Reel 2, Dakota Conflict, Minnesota Historical Society; Eastlick, "Lake Shetek Indian Massacre," Microfilm Reel 1, Dakota Conflict, Minnesota Historical Society; Jefferson Duley correspondence, July 22, 1925.

several before they disappeared into the slough's high grass and reeds. Lavina was shot in the heel, Emma Duley in the arm, Willie Duley in the shoulder, and Julianne Ireland in the leg.

Instead of plunging into the slough, the Indians remained on the far side of a grassless stretch of ground and shot into the tall grass. One Indian Tom Ireland identified as Lean Grizzly Bear taunted someone to shoot him. When he got within range, he "opened his shirt and patted his breast for me to shoot at him," remembered Ireland. "As I shot he dropped from his pony, I aimed low and caught him as he dropped." William Duley also saw Lean Grizzly Bear's brave gesticulating and pulled the trigger about the same time. Both men claimed to have killed him. Atop the ridge, meanwhile, White Lodge, Old Pawn, and dozens of other Indians dismounted, crouched behind the wild plum trees, and looked for movement in the grass. Any rustle of the reeds brought a series of well-directed shots. The settlers could do little other than lie low.[18]

John Eastlick had a good gun, but it was wet and difficult to fire. When his wife Lavina was shot in the side John called to her. She confirmed the wound but begged him not to move and give away his own position. Charley Hatch groaned loudly when a bullet smacked into his arm. When his sister Almira Everett began crawling in his direction as the flying lead zipped through the grass in search of another target. Charley told her to stay put. He had two double-barrel shotguns lying across his wounded arm, and could use his remaining good hand to fire them. Almira may have given away her position because a short time later she was hit in the neck. The casualties began to mount rapidly. Sarah Ireland screamed when a bullet struck her in the abdomen. Eight-year-old Giles Eastlick was shot through the chest and killed, and his mother Lavina suffered a painful wound between the scalp and skull. Sophia Smith was shot in the hip. When Indian lead drew closer and closer to John Eastlick, he called to Lavina that he was going to move. The next sound she heard was the sickening soft thud of a ball smashing into human flesh. "John are you hurt?" she shouted. There was no answer. Wounded and bleeding, Lavina tried to crawl toward him but Maria Koch urged her to stay put. "Your husband is dead already," she insisted, "and you cannot possibly do him any good; so stay with your children, I beg of you."

18 Currie, "Information on victims of the Lake Shetek Massacre," Microfilm Reel 1, Dakota Conflict, Minnesota Historical Society; Eastlick, "Lake Shetek Indian Massacre," Microfilm Reel 1, Dakota Conflict, Minnesota Historical Society; Jefferson Duley correspondence, July 22, 1925.

The Indian fire fell off after about one hour of shooting. During the lull that followed Old Pawn yelled for the women to come out, insisting no one would hurt them. When William Everett called his bluff Old Pawn, who knew his voice, told Everett to come out and that he too would be spared. Everett claimed he was wounded and could not walk. "You lie," Old Pawn spat back, "you can walk well enough, if you want to." Indians fired into the grass in the direction his voice came from and a bullet shattered his elbow. Everett whispered to his wife to tell Old Pawn he was dead. Almira stood and in a dolorous voice sobbed that they had killed her husband. Old Pawn encouraged the women and children to come out, "for he wanted her and Mrs. Wright for his squaws."

Perhaps it was a good idea, suggested Everett. Obedience may well save them, and the men could get away after they left. Almira asked Lavina to go with her, but she could barely move. She next asked Julia Wright, who could speak some Dakota. Julia agreed and the women walked slowly out to meet with the Indians. Duley proposed shooting Old Pawn, but Sophia Smith and Lavina pleaded with him not to do so. "The Indians will kill us all sooner or later and I'm bound to make one less of them while I have the chance," Duley replied. The women implored him a second time, with Lavina adding that if he did not shoot he might escape and at least tell others what had happened. That made sense to Duley and he kept still and his finger off the trigger. Tom Ireland, however, rose to plead with the Indians to leave the women and children alone. Two warriors who had worked there way to within ten yards fired at him, their buckshot hitting Tom in his left arm and left lung. "Oh God, I'm killed!" he gasped as he fell to the ground.[19]

Almira and Julia returned to the slough after their meeting and repeated what they had already heard: come out and the women and children would be spared. The women figured they had no choice other than to comply or perish. Lavina crawled to her husband and found him lying dead on his side. After whispering her last farewell to her companion of 12 years she hobbled out of the slough with the help of her boy Frank. Merton carried Johnny. Sophia Ireland also said goodbye to her husband, who was still alive but appeared to be dying. Almira and Julia and their children walked and crawled to the base of the

---

19 Charles D. Hatch narrative, Microfilm Reel 2, Dakota Conflict, Minnesota Historical Society; Eastlick, "Lake Shetek Indian Massacre," Microfilm Reel 1, Dakota Conflict, Minnesota Historical Society.

ridge. One side of Almira's body was covered in blood, but her neck wound had finally stopped bleeding.

A thunderstorm broke, drenching the prairie with a heavy summer rain as the women and children moved away from the bloody slough. Once they were clear the Dakotas rushed in to claim their prizes without any intent of keeping their end of the bargain. When Lavina looked back, she saw her five-year-old son Fred emerge from the grass. An Indian woman clutching a twisted tree branch swung it at the boy's head. Fred screamed as blood streamed down his face. A frantic Lavina screamed and pleaded with those around her, to no avail. According to Jefferson Duley, the Indian woman was one of Lean Grizzley Bear's wives. She "set up an awful howling," recalled the younger Duley, "and grabbed little Fred Eastlick and raised him high above her head, and brought his head down on a rock, and then took her knife and ripped him open, and cut his heart out."

Another Indian shot Fred's nine-year-old brother Frank in the mouth and stomach. Warriors held his mother back and forced her to the bluff top with Merton and Johnny. Almira, meanwhile, ran back toward the slough but someone shot her through the back. White Lodge grabbed Mariah Koch and led her away. Two warriors claimed the two oldest Ireland girls, Rosa (9) and Ellen (7), as their own but they ended up with Chief Redwood. Old Pawn laid claim to Julia Wright and her children, and put the children on a horse. When Julia told him all the men were dead, he sent her into the slough to get their weapons. Charley Hatch gave up one of his shotguns.

When the badly wounded Sophia Smith and Sophia Ireland struggled up the bluff, two warriors chuckled at their desperate condition and shot them dead. Eleven-year-old Willie Duley was walking in front of Lavina Eastlick when a young Indian sauntered up and shot him down. All of Old Pawn's promises of safety proved false. Lavina challenged his honesty by asking whether he intended to kill her as well. Old Pawn shook his head and answered no, but a short time later he squeezed a trigger and shot her in the back. The ball tore out above Lavina's hip and pierced her right arm. She fell to the ground and Old Pawn moved on, believing she was dead. Several minutes later her son Merton crawled to her side, where she asked him to take infant Johnny and care for him as long as he lived.

Lavina rolled out of the muddy path and into the grass to avoid being trampled. When a young warrior noticed her move, he pounded her head with the butt of his rifle. She feigned death and her assailant moved on. In her semi-conscious state she heard Merton calling for her, but she dared not move or answer. The rain continued. Lavina, now freezing cold, thought it was about four in the afternoon.[20]

The Dakotas left the marsh—which whites forever after called "Slaughter Slough"—and headed for the Ireland house. Maria Koch was walking with Belle Duley, when Lean Grizzley Bear's wife, who was still not satisfied after murdering little Fred Eastlick, grabbed a board from the end gate of the wagon and struck Belle over the head, knocking her down. Mrs. Duley was held back and forced to watch as the woman beat her little girl nearly senseless before tying her to a bush. Once secure, she threw knives at Belle, piercing her numerous times until she died. Belle's brother Jefferson tried to run away but a warrior chased him down and knocked him unconscious. When he came to he saw his mother being taken toward the Wright cabin and ran to her.

Near the slough, meanwhile, the badly wounded Lavina Eastlick tried to move, but "could hear the bones grate together." The blow of the gun butt had cracked her skull. Her thick hair, three feet long, saved her from the full force of the blow. She crawled to where she heard a voice that sounded like Willie Duley's crying, "Mother, Mother." Finding she could do nothing for him she crawled on toward another voice until she discovered 6-year-old Lillie Everett leaning over her dying little brother Charles.

When Lillie saw her she asked, "Mrs. Eastlick, the Indians haven't killed us yet?"

"No," Lavina answered, "but there are very few of us left."

Lillie asked if Lavina could take care of Charley, but she explained that she could not. She had nothing to help him with, and she was trying to find her own infant Johnny. Lillie begged Lavina for a drink of water, but Lavina had none to give her. The little girl raised her eyes and with a hopeless look asked, "Is there any water in heaven?"

"When you get to heaven," Lavina said, "you will never more suffer from thirst or pain." Upon hearing this, Lillie laid herself down on her brother and seemed to consign herself to death.

Lavina crawled away and found the dead Mrs. Ireland with 3-year-old daughter Julianne lying on her breast. Farther on she found two of her sons. Giles was dead but Fred was still alive—despite Jefferson Duley's later claim

20 Bryant and Murch, *Great Massacre*, 349-50; Jefferson Duley correspondence, July 22, 1925; Charles D. Hatch narrative, Microfilm Reel 2, Dakota Conflict, Minnesota Historical Society; Eastlick, "Lake Shetek Indian Massacre," Microfilm Reel 1, Dakota Conflict, Minnesota Historical Society.

that the Indian woman had "cut his heart out." Fred's clothes had been ripped off and he had "a dreadful rattling in his throat." Lavina crawled on and found Mrs. Everett, shot through the lungs and making "a gurgling sound that made my very flesh creep. I did not, dared not touch her." Overcome with an unnamed terror, Lavina forced herself to her feet and stumbled away from the slough and across the prairie as fast as her crippled body would carry her. Young Lillie remained near her brother throughout the night.

The Indians held a great victory dance in their camp near the Ireland house, boasting of the murders and demonstrating how their victims had suffered and died. Old Pawn was selected to replace Lean Grizzly Bear as the new chief. The captives, meanwhile, were separated. White Lodge ordered Maria Koch to remain in his tipi so no one would kill her. The next morning a pair of Indians rode to the slough and searched the pockets of the dead. They found Lillie Everett shivering from cold and fear, put her on a horse and carried her to their camp. Both of the horses, she later noted, once belonged to her Uncle Charley Hatch. Her brother was still alive and Julianne Ireland was as well. "I suppose these children starved to death," she said.

When Lillie arrived, Maria Koch and Laura Duley tried to comfort her by wrapping the traumatized girl in a shawl and placing her close to the fire. A few Dakotas disliked the attention being showered upon her and shot at them in a fit of anger. One ball penetrated Laura Duley's skirt and another tore through Maria's shawl just below her shoulder. Miraculously, neither ball hit flesh. The Indians broke camp on Friday, August 22 and left with likely a dozen captives: Maria Koch, Laura Duley, Julia Wright, George Wright, Eldora Wright, John Wright, Emma Duley, Frances Duley, Jefferson Duley, Ellen Ireland, Rosa Ireland, and Lillie Everett.[21]

There were still people alive in Slaughter Slough. Merton Eastlick found Tom Ireland and told him he was going to leave, but "Uncle Tommy" replied

---

21 Jefferson Duley correspondence, July 22, 1925; Eastlick, "Lake Shetek Indian Massacre," Microfilm Reel 1, Dakota Conflict, Minnesota Historical Society; Currie, "Information on victims of the Lake Shetek Massacre," Microfilm Reel 1, Dakota Conflict, Minnesota Historical Society. The list of killed and captured varies with nearly every source consulted. For instance, Gray, "Santee and Lake Shetek," 47, incorrectly claims that Julia Wright had another daughter whose brains were "dashed out" after being captured. This child was Frances Duley. According to Jefferson Duley, she was killed six weeks after being captured. Separated from her mother the Indians "would torture her every night and the screams could be heard by my mother, until this child got so weak that they killed her." Rose, *History of Lyon County*, 40, lists Emma Duley and Mariah Everett among the killed, and an Abillian Everett among the captured. Carley, *Dakota War of 1862*, 24, claims two women and six children were captured.

that he would starve on the prairie and that it would be better to stay with him "and both die together." Merton would have none of it. "Mother told me to carry Johnny as long as I live and I'm going to do it," he answered.

Perhaps shamed by the boy's spirit while he was ready to give up, Tom agreed to accompany him as far as the road. Frank Eastlick tried to go with them but shot in the mouth, thigh, and abdomen, he could not keep up. Merton had no choice but to leave him behind. According to some sources he was found by other Dakotas, who took him to Smith's house and nursed him there for two days. Thinking he would not live, they abandoned him. Frank hung on for three weeks, eating cheese the Smiths had left behind. Mixed-blood Joe LaBushe finally found the boy and took him away. Where he took him has never been determined.

Exactly what happened to the body of 2-year-old Charles Everett remains a mystery. His corpse was not found by a burial party, and he was not captured. Twelve bodies were located and buried on October 16, 1862. They include: John Voight, Andreas Koch, Sophia Ireland, Julianne Ireland, Sarah Jane Ireland, Almira Everett, John Eastlick, Frederick Eastlick, Giles Eastlick, Sophia Smith, William J. Duley Jr., and Belle Duley.[22]

When Charley Hatch was sure the Dakotas had gone he made his way to Bill Everett, "who was badly wounded in the arm and leg and nearly helpless." Everett "was so weak from loss of blood," Hatch continued, "that I could hardly coax him to try and get away." Nevertheless, they hobbled their way toward New Ulm. Untouched and unnoticed in the slough was Edgar Bently, who joined the two wounded men on the road. He walked faster and pulled away. Hatch and Everett struggled through the night. William Duley also made it out of the slough and headed east. Perhaps the last one out was Lavina Eastlick. All of them were heading toward Dutch Charlie's.

Charles Zierke's place or Dutch Charlie's, was a rest stop for travelers in the northwest corner of Cottonwood County about 16 miles east of Lake Shetek on the New Ulm Road.[23] Zierke and his family abandoned the place on August 20

---

22 Currie, "Information on victims of the Lake Shetek Massacre," Microfilm Reel 1, Dakota Conflict, Minnesota Historical Society; William J. Duley, "Notes on Sioux Massacre," Microfilm Reel 1, Dakota Conflict, Minnesota Historical Society. Judy Penhiter, an Eastlick descendent, tells a family story that Frank survived, returned to the whites, and was called "Hambone Eastlick" because of his disfigured mouth.

23 Charles D. Hatch narrative, Microfilm Reel 2, Dakota Conflict, Minnesota Historical Society. Cottonwood County was established in 1857 and surveyed the following year. Only

when they left for New Ulm. Charlie left his family for a short time to look for food, and when he was gone Dakotas captured his wife and children and headed west. Unable to find them, Charlie struck out for New Ulm.[24]

Leaving his cabin about noon, Aaron Myers and his family took a roundabout route to avoid the main roads. They reached Dutch Charlie's about 10:00 p.m. Wednesday, several hours after Charlie left. The fire in the stove was still hot. Once inside, Myers went upstairs and tore up the floorboards to seal the four first floor windows. He was readying his three rifles and two shotguns—about the same number of weapons the settlers had at Slaughter Slough—when he heard someone outside. A moment later someone knocked on the door.

"Who is there?" Myers called out.

"Bently."

Myers knew the name but didn't recognize the voice. Holding his shotgun he unbolted the door while his son Arthur stood to the side pointing his own shotgun. When Myers swung the door open Edgar Bently threw his arms up and shouted, "Myers, for God's sake don't shoot!" Myers pulled Bently inside and slammed the door shut. The first thing he noticed was a flesh wound on his arm. Bently told Myers and his son about the massacre at the slough and that he thought everyone was dead except Hatch and Everett, who were some distance behind him. Everett, he added, was hit bad and probably would not survive. Myers got Bently some supper, put him to bed, and stood guard, peering out all night into rainy darkness.

The next morning Myers went out to a covered hayrack to find some dry hay for the wagon when he saw someone dodge around a bale. Hatch and Everett had spent a long and cold night outside by the hay after seeing lights in the house but deciding it was too risky to knock on the door. Myers got them inside, dressed their wounds, and fed them. Once everyone was ready they climbed into the wagon and started for Leavenworth. After they passed Joseph L. Brown's abandoned house Myers set out on his own to see if they could cross the Cottonwood River at that point. (Map J) Instead of a crossing he found the

one white man, Charles Zierke, was found, living on the SW quarter of section 14, Highwater Township, on present Highwater Creek. Today "Dutch Charlie County Park" is in Ann Township.

24 Currie, "Information on victims of the Lake Shetek Massacre," Microfilm Reel 1, Dakota Conflict, Minnesota Historical Society. Bryant and Murch, *Great Massacre*, 142, offer a slightly different story.

bodies of Brown, his son, daughter, and another unidentified man. Brown's wife Oratia (36) was "horribly mutilated." Myers told the others they would have to cross elsewhere. He didn't mention finding the bodies.

They reached Leavenworth at sundown. On the north side of the road were two houses belonging to brothers Bernard and Peter Kelly, with the Brink house on the south side. Myers pulled the wagon behind Brink's, unloaded it, and carried some belongings inside to spend the night. He was milking a cow when his son Arthur told him someone was coming down the road. While father and son hid to watch, about 16 Indians in two wagons stopped nearby to cut some corn for their horses. When the warriors headed for Peter Kelly's house Myers and Arthur hurried back to alert the others and move everyone to a grove about 80 yards behind Brink's house, where they stayed for the night.

Once it was dark, Myers crept over to Kelly's and watched and listened as the Indians talked and carried out pork and flour. "I learned that the country between us and town was alive with Indians, getting supplies for the warriors," he recalled. After midnight the Indians shot and cooked a cow and caroused for hours. Charley Hatch remembered hearing cannon fire from the direction of Fort Ridgely. It was not until then, he admitted, "did we know that it was a general war with the Indians." Some of the Dakotas passed close to the grove where the men were hiding, which Hatch acknowledged was "a very anxious time" because Alomina Hurd's baby (Edward) "had cried most of the night." Apparently unable to stand the stress, Bently grabbed a quilt and slipped away into the darkness.

On Friday morning, August 22, the group decided to keep off the main roads and head southeast toward the Little Cottonwood. When they stopped near the river for breakfast they saw Bently with the stolen quilt coming down a hill. "My first impulse was to shoot him," Myers said, but his wife advised him, "Do not do anything you will be sorry for." When Myers confronted Bently and demanded to know where he had been all night, the man admitted he was afraid the baby crying last night would alert the Indians. "I was so provoked that I could hardly contain myself," Myers recalled, but contain himself he did. They finished eating and moved on.[25]

25 Currie, "Information on victims of the Lake Shetek Massacre," Microfilm Reel 1, Dakota Conflict, Minnesota Historical Society; Aaron Myers Reminiscence, Microfilm Reel 2, Dakota Conflict, Minnesota Historical Society; Charles D. Hatch narrative, Microfilm Reel 2, Dakota Conflict, Minnesota Historical Society.

Before noon they saw more Indians and Myers recognized Dutch Charlie's wagon team carrying what appeared to be his captured family. Unable to help the prisoners, they avoided the Dakotas and kept moving. A short time later a large rescue/burial expedition from New Ulm frightened these same Indians, who abandoned their captives. Instead of the 17-man rescue party that left New Ulm on Tuesday, Capt. George M. Tousley of Le Sueur—who marched about 100 men to the relief of New Ulm—gathered about 140 men to march to the Leavenworth area. His strong column included three doctors: Asa W. Daniels, Otis Ayers, and William W. Mayo.

The expedition was organized because news arrived that 13 people were trapped along the Little Cottonwood. The Whiton-Hough-Covell-Van Gilder refugees had been in hiding there since Tuesday. They waited all day Wednesday, but not knowing whether it was safe to come in, they stayed put. That night, George Covell and Sidney Waite set out for help. Hiding, looking for food, and dodging Indians made for slow traveling, and it took them until 10:00 p.m. on Thursday to creep into New Ulm, where they were nearly killed when nervous pickets fired at them. Their report convinced Capt. Tousley to form a rescue party.

Tousley's expedition reached the refugees about 2:00 p.m. Friday. Cpl. W. H. Hazzard (21) of Captain Saunders's Le Sueur Tigers recalled how they "found a company of 13 in the high grass that had been hiding from the Red Skins. We made their hearts happy by rescuing them and conveying them safely to New Ulm." A grateful Mary Covell added, "They brought us food, of which our famished party eagerly partook." Unfortunately, the wounded and the exhausted had no choice other than to accompany Tousley and his men up the Cottonwood River in search of more refugees and bodies that needed to be buried. The Bluem family corpses were interred and the Indians holding Dutch Charlir Zierke's family were chased away.

By the time the expedition reached Leavenworth late Friday afternoon, 16 bodies had been found and buried. Along the way mounted Indian scouts paralleled the column and cannonading from the north was clearly audible. One doctor told his colleague that it sounded as if Indians were attacking Fort Ridgely in force. Together, the pair of doctors sought out Captain Tousley, explained their conclusion, recalled the Indian scouts watching the march, and predicted that the Dakotas would come down during the night and cut them off from New Ulm. Since they had already rescued the refugees, the doctors urged the captain to return to New Ulm rather than camp unprotected on the prairie. Tousley ordered a halt and consulted his command. "A number of the men timid or cautious were in favor of returning to town," explained William Hayden, "but the majority voted to stay all night and camp on the prairie."

They marched for another hour while the sound of cannon fire drifted down to them. The men were tired by the time the sun dipped to the horizon. Another halt was called and another vote taken. This time the men decided to go back. When the guide lost his way in the dark another man directed them. Along the gloomy trek Hayden recalled seeing "Signals made by flashing powder or burning bunches of dry grass" on both sides of them, a sure sign they were being followed. "We reached our return destination after midnight," said Dr. Daniels, "thoroughly worn out and disgusted from this long and useless march, which might have resulted not only in the destruction of the command, but perhaps in the capture of New Ulm." The day's excursion proved too much for old Ruth Van Gilder (Howard), who had been badly wounded in the arm. "She died shortly after reaching New Ulm," reported W. H. Hazzard. According to Mary Covell, "Mrs. Howard who had suffered inexpressible torture from her wound died at New Ulm on Saturday morning."[26]

*   *   *

The Tousley expedition was marching west along the Cottonwood River as the Myers-Hatch-Everett party moved east along the Little Cottonwood. By Friday night the oxen were failing and one of them slumped down and refused to move. The party struggled into a little ash grove about 12 miles southwest of New Ulm but could go no farther. Aaron Myers baked a batch of soda biscuits

---

26 Aaron Myers Reminiscence, Microfilm Reel 2, Dakota Conflict, Minnesota Historical Society; Bryant and Murch, *Great Massacre*, 134-35; Hazzard, "Autobiographical sketch," Microfilm Reel 2, Dakota Conflict, Minnesota Historical Society; Hayden, "Account of the relief expedition," Microfilm Reel 2, Dakota Conflict, Minnesota Historical Society; Daniels, "Reminiscences of the Little Crow Uprising," 327-28 MHSC, Vol. 15. According to Mary Covell, they had "scarcely buried" Ruth Van Gilder (Howard) when the Indians attacked the town. In February 1863, Mary helped George file a depredation claim for $833 in damages to their home and crops. John Jackson, Luther Whiton, and Alva Hough testified. According to Jackson, Covell "was not what you would call well off." Hough downsized the acreage Covell claimed he had under cultivation, claiming most of his grain "did not seem to have been injured," his fences weren't damaged, and that he had heard from thrashers that much of his wheat had been saved. Covell did save about three tons of hay and gave half of it to Hough. By the time the commissioners examined the claim, Mary Covell and her son were living in a rented house in St. Peter. Her "husband," she said, had gone to Michigan looking for employment. According to Alva Hough, George Covell permanently left Minnesota to get married in Michigan. "The one he lived with before the outbreak," she said, "is not his wife." The Covell claim was denied. George W. Covell Depredation Claim #127.

(Top) Acton. Site of the beginning of the Minnesota Uprising, August 17, 1862. (Middle) Annuity Center at the Lower Sioux Agency (Redwood). (Bottom) Site of Louis Robert's trading post at the Redwood Agency.

(Top) Memorial for the settlers of Milford. About 43 people were killed in the area on August 18, 1862. (Middle) Franz Massopust Sr's. Milford home is today owned by the Juni family. (Bottom) The monument to the Recruiting Party reads: "While Crossing this ravine a recruiting party of the Civil War was ambushed by the Sioux Indians on August 18th, 1862, at the noon hour. The following were killed or mortally wounded: John Schneider, Ernest Dietrich, Julius Fenske, Adolph Steimle."

The eastern road down from Lower Sioux Agency to the crossing of the Minnesota River.

Redwood Ferry on the Minnesota River below the Lower Sioux Agency.

Fort Ridgely. The Commissary building seen from the ruins of the Officers' quarters.

Fort Ridgely. View looking north to origin point of Medicine Bottle's attacks.

Above: Middle Creek. Monument to the members of the Busse and Boelter families killed in the area. Right: Beaver Creek. Memorial (right) to Clarissa Henderson, her two children, Jehiel Wedge, and Eugene White, killed August 18, 1862. Below: Middle Creek. The Schwandt Memorial. Johann, Christian, Christina, and Frederick Schwandt, and John Frass, John Walz, and Karolina Walz were killed here August 18. Mary Schwandt was captured.

(Top) Middle Creek. Area of the John Boelter home site. (Middle) Foundation of the Joseph R. Brown house, downriver from the Upper Sioux Agency. (Bottom) Upper Sioux (Yellow Medicine) Agency. Site of John and Sarah Wakefield's cabin.

(Top) Upper Sioux Agency. School-workshop-quarters on left. (Middle) Lake Shetek. Andreas and Maria Koch's cabin. (Bottom) Lake Shetek. Remnants of the cellar of Lavina Eastlick's cabin.

(Top) Slaughter Slough, where Sioux attacked the settlers fleeing Lake Shetek, August 20, 1862. (Right) Monument to the settlers killed at Lake Shetek and Slaughter Slough, August 20, 1862. (Bottom) Site of the Andreas Lundborg cabin, West Lake Settlement.

LUNDBORG CABIN

On August 20, 1862, Andrew Jackson, a circuit-rider minister, was conducting services for members of the New Sweden Church (Lebanon Lutheran) at the Lundborg family cabin at this site. Young Peter Broberg interrupted to tell his parents that Indians had frightened the children back at home in West Lake, a settlement on the Kandiyohi-Swift county border. The men left to protect their families. Thirteen settlers, including several members of the Broberg and Lundborg families, were killed in the ensuing confrontation at West Lake. Afterwards, Pastor Jackson led a relief and burial party in the area.

(Top) West Lake. Remnants of the cellar of Daniel P. Broberg's cabin. (Left) Marker for Sven Backlund and Andreas Lorentson, killed on August 21, 1862. (Bottom) Guri Endreson's cabin. Site of the massacre on August 21, 1862.

Langeland homesite in Jackson County. Mrs. Anna Langeland and her children, Anna, Agaata, Nicolai, and Knud, were killed here on August 24, 1862.

Robert H. Chaska and his family at their house near the Upper Agency.

Little Crow, the leader of the Sioux Uprising of 1862. After the uprising, Little Crow was killed while picking berries with his son near Hutchinson. His corpse was scalped and mutilated. A janitor at the Minnesota capitol building donated the scalp to the Minnesota Historical Society in 1868. Little Crow's head was taken by an officer who found his body, and the skull was donated to the historical society in 1896. The society also had other bones from Little Crow's body, so they returned them to his family in 1971 for a proper burial.

Big Eagle, born in 1827 in what is today Eagan, Minnesota, was the leader of a band of Mdewakanton Dakota Sioux. His warriors joined in the 1862 uprising and he led them against For Ridgely, at the Second Battle of New Ulm, Birch Coulee, and Wood Lake. He surrendered and was convicted and served three years in prison. He adopted Christianity late in life and is recorded to have said: "My white neighbors and friends know my character as a citizen and a man. I am at peace with every one, whites and Indians. I am getting to be an old man, but I am still able to work. I am poor, but I manage to get along." He died in 1906 in Granite Falls, Minnesota.

(Top) Col. Henry H. Sibley was in charge of suppressing the outbreak. A former Minnesota governor, Sibley's decisive victory at Wood Lake on September 23, 1862, crushed the uprising. (Bottom) Lt. Thomas P. Gere, Co. B, 5th Minnesota Infantry, helped defend Fort Ridgely and later won the Medal of Honor at the Battle of Nashville in late 1864.

A native of Ireland, Lt. Timothy J. Sheehan, Co. C, 5th Minnesota Infantry, played a key role in the defense of Fort Ridgely. Thereafter, he participated in the siege of Vicksburg (Mississippi), the Battle of Nashville (Tennessee), and in costal operations along the Gulf of Mexico.

(Right) Dr. Philander P. Humphrey and his son John.

(Left) John Otherday

New York native Charles E. Flandrau arrived in St. Paul, Minnesota, in 1853 and began practicing law. President Franklin Pierce appointed him to serve an an agent for the Sioux. Although the town of New Ulm survived repeated attacks, Flandrau's abilities as a military commander remain controversial. He died in St. Paul in 1903.

Helen Carrothers

Stephen R. and Mary L. Riggs

Mary Schwandt

before dawn, and on Saturday morning left alone to seek help. He told those remaining, including his son Arthur, that if he did not return in 24 hours to start for Mankato. Myers made a beeline across the prairie and reached a house near the Cottonwood River where he found an entire family (father, mother, son, and daughter) slaughtered in the yard. To his horror, the little girl, about six years old, "was nailed up to the side of the house, naked, arms and limbs extended, and large nails driven through hands and feet." Myers left at a run, swam the river, and reached the road that ran down the bluff and through a slough he called "the dugway"—the same place the Leavenworth Rescue party had been ambushed on Tuesday. Indians spotted him there and gave chase, but he reached the picket line surrounding New Ulm about the same time the first wave of Indians engulfed the town. Aaron Myers managed to jump out of the proverbial frying pan, but he may also have hopped into the fire.[27]

*   *   *

After the Sisseton's allowed her to leave, Alomina Hurd had walked away from her house carrying her infant Edward and holding Willie's hand. About ten in the morning a violent thunderstorm rolled in (part of the same weather system that would later drench the Shetek settlers in Slaughter Slough) that lasted so long and blew so hard that Alomina lost her way. She walked on, "not knowing whether I was right or wrong" until she found some high ground in the drenched countryside and tried to sleep for the night. Thursday morning they continued on until Alomina heard gunfire and discovered they were back near Lake Shetek. She adjusted her course but the day was overcast and no road or other distinct landmark was visible until nearly nightfall when she found "to my horror" that she and her two small sons were only four miles from home. Exhausted and discouraged, she contemplated whether it would be better to simply lay down and die. Using the road as a guide she continued on until it was too dark to see before stopping to sleep.

Friday morning dawned foggy and damp. William was sick and vomiting, so Alomina carried both children. Unable to haul both very far, she opted to carry one about one-quarter mile, set him down, go back for the other, bring

27 Currie, "Information on victims of the Lake Shetek Massacre," Microfilm Reel 1, Dakota Conflict, Minnesota Historical Society; Aaron Myers Reminiscence, Microfilm Reel 2, Dakota Conflict, Minnesota Historical Society.

him up, and then repeat the process. She traversed the remaining 12 miles to Dutch Charlie's in this exhausting manner, where she arrived about sunset. The house was empty. "Every article of food and clothing removed! My heart seemed to die within me, and I sunk down in despair."

She reached Dutch Charlie's a day and a half after Myers, Hatch, and Everett left. Alomina scrounged around until she found some carrots and onions in the garden, but Willie could not eat them and continued vomiting. The next morning (Saturday) Willie ate bits and pieces of a spoiled ham and felt better. Alomina took what was left of the ham and the few vegetables she could gather and continued walking. Her next destination was Joseph L. Brown's, about 23 miles east.[28]

*   *   *

Unbeknownst to Alomina, she had just missed running into other hungry people who also used Dutch Charlie's as a safe haven, two before she arrived and another immediately after she left. That Wednesday at Slaughter Slough, 11-year-old Merton Eastlick told Tom Ireland that he had promised his mother he would carry and watch over his infant brother Johnny as long as he lived. "Uncle Tommy" tried to keep up, but after walking about one-half mile down the road he was too weak to continue and hid in the grass. Merton kept going with Johnny. The two brothers spent the night at Buffalo Lake where Merton slept crouched over his brother to shield him from the rain. When wolves crept too close Merton shouted at them to keep them at bay. They reached Dutch Charlie's the next evening, where Merton and his infant brother ate cheese and vegetables and spent a day resting before moving on. They left just before Alomina Hurd and her two boys arrived. After he sank down to hide in the grass, the wounded and exhausted Tom Ireland could barely move for 36 hours. Somehow he felt better on Friday and began walking to Dutch Charlie's, where he arrived the following day—just after Alomina Hurd left.[29]

*   *   *

28 Bryant and Murch, *Great Massacre*, 371-73.

29 Eastlick, "Lake Shetek Indian Massacre," Microfilm Reel 1, Dakota Conflict, Minnesota Historical Society. Typical of the conflicting narratives, Alomina recalled Charlie's house was empty and made no mention of Merton and Johnny, while Lavina said her children met Alomina there and Merton found carrots in the garden for her.

Lavina Eastlick stumbled out of Slaughter Slough Wednesday evening and wandered until daylight Thursday, when she finally realized she "was lost upon the trackless prairie." Afraid the Indians would find her, she hid during the day listening to fitful bursts of gunfire and children crying, all of which convinced her she was still close to the lake. That evening Lavina spotted a grove of trees on the horizon and concluded it marked Buffalo Lake, about six miles east and on the road to Dutch Charlie's. She set out for the grove at nightfall. Thirsty, she squeezed the moisture from the bottom of her skirt and "thought it the sweetest water I ever drank." A short time later she encountered more water than she needed or wanted when a slough appeared before her. She continued on, trying to push her way through head-high grass and water at least two feet deep. She slogged on through the night until just before dawn, when she finally extricated herself from the slough and saw the timber near what she believed was Buffalo Lake.

With the Friday sun Lavina discovered to her "grief and despair" that she was back at Lake Shetek. She had walked in a giant circle, much as Alomina Hurd had done. The two women were probably no more than half a dozen miles apart. Lavina was sick and weak from hunger and knew she would have to find food or die. When she recognized the house in the distance as Tom Ireland's she dragged herself into his cornfield and grabbed the first ear she could find, tore open the husk, ate two rows of green kernels—and promptly vomited. After lying in the field until mid-afternoon, she crawled to the house and found the remains of a butchered bullock and some dead pigs, plus clothes and blankets. Lavina hid in some bushes until dark, when she returned to gnaw some meat from the carcasses. She dipped some meat in the brine at the bottom of a pork barrel, took three ears of corn, and began walking east once more. The night was clear and she used the North Star as a guide.

After sleeping for a while Lavina decided to travel during daylight only. She reached Buffalo Lake that Saturday but found her way blocked by a stream. She tried crossing on a wooden pole, but fell into the water when the wood snapped. Wounded and exhausted, it took all the energy she had to crawl up on the bank. She took off her clothes and put them, with her waterlogged food, out in the sun to dry before falling asleep once more. She had dressed and was eating when a flock of ducks burst into the sky from near the lake. She froze: something had disturbed them. A horse was approaching. Certain the Indians had found her, Lavina resigned herself to her fate until she saw that the horse was pulling a sulky (a small two-wheeled cart) with a man holding the reins. It was the mail carrier! Lavina stumbled out of the bushes and flagged him down.

August Garzene, who was on his way from Sioux Falls to New Ulm and so unaware of the uprising, was as surprised to see Lavina as she was to see him. "You look too white to be a squaw," he said in Dakota. "I am Mrs. Eastlick," she replied. "You have seen me several times at Mrs. Everett's house, but I am badly wounded." After Lavina explained, Garzene helped her into the sulky. Overcome with "the warmth of human sympathy," Lavina—who had not yet cried—admitted that the "frozen current of my tears" finally burst forth. With Garzene leading the horse they made good time and reached Dutch Charlie's about four that afternoon.[30]

Now on the alert for marauding Indians, Garzene hid the sulky and crept up to the house. Inside he found an old man who claimed he had come from Lake Shetek. Skeptical, Garzene left to get Lavina. They were approaching the door when Tom Ireland stepped outside. "I hardly knew him," recalled a shocked Lavina, "for he looked more like a corpse than a human being. His face was pale, his eyes deeply shrunk and his voice reduced to a whisper." Ireland probably had the same reaction seeing Lavina, but they embraced and "both wept like children." While Garzene cared for his horse, Lavina and "Uncle Tommy" exchanged stories. When he told her that Merton and Johnny left the slough and may have arrived in time to leave with the Zierkes, Lavina "filled with hope and joy." At least two of her children were still alive! After finding a few turnips in the garden and a final wedge of cheese in the house, the trio left Dutch Charlie's and made about eight miles before pulling well off the road to sleep for the night.

When they spied people in the road up ahead about 11:00 a.m. on Sunday morning, Garzene pulled off the road and bumped his way along a parallel ravine until they got close enough to discover a woman and two children. The woman—Alomina Hurd with her children—saw them coming, thought they were Indians, "and felt that, after all my toil and suffering, I must die, with my children, by the hand of the savage." Lavina beckoned for them to stop. Alomina appeared to be in shock. "She was unable to speak for some time," Lavina said, but when she finally snapped to awareness, she shook hands with everyone and told Lavina that her sons Merton and Johnny were but a short distance in front of her. A few minutes they found Merton still carrying his brother Johnny. Garzene put the sleeping baby in Lavina's lap. Too exhausted

---

30 Eastlick, "Lake Shetek Indian Massacre," Microfilm Reel 1, Dakota Conflict, Minnesota Historical Society.

to climb out of the sulky, Lavina reached down and held Merton's "wasted hand," describing him as "the poorest person I ever saw able to stand alone." He looked entirely changed from when she had last seen him. So did little Johnny, whose face was covered with scabs where he had scratched mosquitoes bites raw. Lavina was rightfully proud of Merton, an 11-year-old who had faithfully carried his 15-month-old brother about 50 miles. A few more miles and they reached J. L. Brown's house. It was noon, Sunday, August 24.[31]

*   *   *

By that time on Sunday, William Duley (another Slaughter Slough survivor) had passed all the Lake Shetek refugees except Aaron Myers, who was already in New Ulm. Duley hooked up that Sunday with Elijah Whiton at Henry Thomas's house on the north side of the Cottonwood about six miles from New Ulm. (Map K) Elijah Whiton, his wife Laura, and their two children had a slightly different experience than most of the others residing along the Cottonwood. They were unmolested and unaware of the murderous chaos swirling all around them for three full days. Warning of an uprising reached them on Monday the 18th, but Elijah dismissed it out of hand. He and his family went about their business without seeing or hearing anything until Thursday when, about four in the afternoon, the Whitons saw a dozen Indians chasing one of their neighbors. The warnings were true. The Dakotas had just attacked the Heydricks cabin, where they killed his wife and two children. Now they were after him. Heydricks jumped off a bridge spanning a ravine and hid beneath a log.

Elijah told his family to get ready to leave, grabbed his shotgun, and marshaled them a short distance to the Cottonwood River to hide along its bank. There, Elijah told his family he was leaving them to check on his brother Luther (Map J), and they should wait until he returned. "We never saw him again," said Laura Whiton. Once her husband left Laura took the children, forded the river, and hid in the timber on the opposite bank. They could hear Indians hitching up their wagon and loading it with their trunks, bedding, and

31 Eastlick, "Lake Shetek Indian Massacre," Microfilm Reel 1, Dakota Conflict, Minnesota Historical Society; Bryant and Murch, *Great Massacre*, 373-74. Hurd's narrative seems to place the arrival at Brown's on Monday, but Eastlick and Ireland said they arrived on Sunday. Hurd did not mention meeting Merton and Johnny at Dutch Charlie's, but she told Lavina that they were ahead of her, indicating that she must have met them somewhere during the journey.

other items stolen from the house. When Elijah did not return by 8:00 p.m. Laura decided to walk to New Ulm. About midnight she and the kids came upon the bodies of their neighbors, the Bluems, "laying dead by the road-side." They walked all night and all the next day and arrived in New Ulm Friday evening.

What Laura never knew was that her husband Elijah made it to his brother's house, but Luther had left with the others two days earlier. Elijah returned home to find his house plundered and his family no longer hiding near the river. Elijah spent Friday and Saturday searching for them in vain. Hungry and tired, he concluded that his family had been either killed or captured, and decided to walk to New Ulm. On Saturday night he nearly stumbled into an Indian camp and beat a hasty retreat to avoid discovery. The next morning Elijah met another white man heading for New Ulm. It was William Duley, who had been on the road three days since escaping from Slaughter Slough.[32]

Elijah and William traveled together to Henry Thomas's house on the north side of the Cottonwood in southwest Milford Township. They found some food inside and were eating when a pair of Dakotas walked in the door. Acting as friendly as possible, Elijah moved toward them when one of the warriors announced that this was his house. Elijah invited them to come in, to which one of the warriors responded by shooting him through the chest. Duley was sitting by the back door in the kitchen and ducked outside. The warriors left out the front to circle around the house. Duley took the opportunity to sneak back inside, grab Elijah's gun, and run into the brush to escape. The warriors yelled and shot their guns indiscriminately, but never found him. Duley crept away. His wound suffered at Slaughter Slough and exhaustion made it difficult to travel. After a while he threw away the gun and made it to New Ulm Sunday evening.[33]

While Duley was escaping from the Thomas house, about half a dozen miles to the southwest near the Little Cottonwood the Hatch-Everett party was

---

[32] Bryant and Murch, *Great Massacre*, 137-38. Researcher Marion Satterlee made the following enigmatic comment:, "There is something peculiar about this man's (Duley) adventures." He wasn't wounded, explained Satterlee, who seems to imply that Duley may have been in complicity with the Indians. Duley, however, claimed he was wounded at the slough and "have two balls in my left arm yet that I expect to carry to my grave." Tolzmann, ed., *Outbreak and Massacre*, 51-52; William J. Duley, "Notes on Sioux Massacre," Microfilm Reel 1, Dakota Conflict, Minnesota Historical Society.

[33] Bryant and Murch, *Great Massacre*, 138.

pulling out for a desperate ride to Mankato. Aaron Myers had left them Saturday morning and reached New Ulm just in time to get caught in town by the attacking Dakotas. The healthiest person left in the party was Edgar Bently, but he seemed incapable of taking charge. The wounded Charley Hatch stepped up instead. They waited until Sunday, but Myers did not return. "I was sure that something serious had happened," Hatch explained, "for he would not desert his sick wife and little children." With the others either too discouraged or too exhausted to help, Hatch hitched up the oxen, got everyone into the wagon, and drove all day in the direction of Mankato. That night they stopped at a deserted farm, where Hatch milked a cow and shared the warm liquid with everyone. Everett "seemed nearly dead" by this time, and Mary Myers, with whatever ailment she had come down with last week, "had daily grown worse until now she took no notice or care of her babe." Hatch, whose shattered hand was now "mortifying," went into the house, started a fire going, and baked some bread. No one slept well that night.

On Monday morning, August 25, Hatch found a fresh yoke of oxen, swapped them for his broken down animals, and got moving again. By four in the afternoon they reached Blue Earth County, where a body of mounted men approached them. Hatch ordered everyone to leave the team and hide in a nearby slough. Mrs. Myers fainted and had to be dragged there, and Everett could barely walk. They watched from the tall grass as men examined the wagon. Someone called out Hatch's name. Even with that they still worried it was a trick. When he determined the men were soldiers Hatch rose and hailed them. "I went out and behold they were Captain Dane's cavalry," he said. "We found friends and protection at last." The next day they traveled the last dozen miles to Mankato. "All was done for us that could be," Hatch said, "but Mrs. Myers died in a few hours after we arrived." Aaron Myers arrived in time to be at her side, but she never regained consciousness and died at 3:00 a.m. the next morning.[34]

The last of the Lake Shetek refugees were still at J. L. Brown's house. Mail carrier August Garzene made sure the Eastlicks, Hurds, and Tom Ireland were secure and left for New Ulm for help. The refugees, afraid to stay in the house on the open road, moved a quarter-mile away and hid in the brush along the

---

34 Charles D. Hatch narrative, Microfilm Reel 2, Dakota Conflict, Minnesota Historical Society; Aaron Myers Reminiscence, Microfilm Reel 2, Dakota Conflict, Minnesota Historical Society. Jerome Dane was captain of Company E, 9th Minnesota Infantry.

Cottonwood River. When darkness fell they returned. Alomina and Merton found potatoes, onions, turnips, beets, and tomatoes in the garden and enjoyed their first hearty meal in five days. Garzene returned on Wednesday night, August 27, to report finding bodies all along the road and that New Ulm appeared to be burning. Indians were all around the place, he explained, and two of them chased him away. There was nothing left to do, he continued, except go back to Sioux Falls and try to get soldiers there to come and rescue them. Lavina confessed Garzene had done all he could for them. If he got through, he explained, they should expect soldiers there in about one week. "He shook hands and bid us farewell," said Lavina, "saying that he never expected to see us again." She "wept like a child" after he left.

The Lake Shetek survivors spent the next several days scrounging for food and staying in the house or sleeping by the river. The weather was hot and muggy and mosquitoes hovered about in giant swarms. Tom Ireland was feeling better and decided he could no longer just sit there doing nothing. He proposed trying to reach New Ulm for help. "I will go and have you all rescued, or die in the attempt," he announced. On Monday morning, September 1, Alomina cooked two chickens for him and Ireland set out, telling them that with a little luck he would be in town that night and that help would arrive by Tuesday night. Ireland reached the town and reported to Lt. John R. Roberts, Company E, 9th Minnesota Infantry. Roberts and a squad of men (Ireland put the number at 30, Eastlick reported 14) left late Monday. The soldiers were guided by John Wright, who was from Lake Shetek but in New Ulm on business, and E. G. Koch, a single man who lived at Shetek but was working the harvest elsewhere when the Indians struck. The rescue party reached Brown's place before midnight on Tuesday. When the women heard noises and the dogs began to bark they were sure the Indians had found them. Lavina was getting dressed when Alomina exclaimed, "My God, Cook (Koch), is that you?" John Wright stepped through the doorway and the four clasped hands while Lavina and Alomina "wept aloud for joy."

Roberts allowed his men to rest a short time, but had everyone up and moving before dawn. One of the soldiers, Pvt. Joseph Gilfillin, who had just enlisted on August 19, may have had a problem with his horse's surcingle, a strap encircling the animal's girth to hold packs in place. In any event, Lavina saw him go into the corn crib. A few miles away, a soldier reported to Lieutenant Roberts that Gilfillin was missing and three men went back to look for him. Five miles down the road the main party passed the bodies of Joseph L. Brown and his family, which had been lying dead for two weeks. Roberts had ridden out up the Cottonwood River along on the north bank, but decided to return by the south bank. The three soldiers returned without finding Gilfillin and the entire column continued safely to New Ulm, a trip Alomina and Lavina and their children had begun two weeks earlier.

As it turned out, Gilfillan followed in their wake but somewhere along the way lost their trail. His body was found on September 3 six miles from New Ulm. The Dakotas had shot him through the chest, cut off his head, and smashed it.

The uprising was far from over.[35]

---

35 Eastlick, "Lake Shetek Indian Massacre," Microfilm Reel 1, Dakota Conflict, Minnesota Historical Society; Currie, "Information on victims of the Lake Shetek Massacre," Microfilm Reel 1, Dakota Conflict, Minnesota Historical Society; *Minnesota in the Civil and Indian Wars*, I, 446.

"Mother Endreson supplied all our wants and again bathed our wounds [and] spent a sleepless night watching over us, ever on the lookout for the savage foe."

Kandiyohi County

First Settlers ~ Church service ~ Dakotas attack the Broberg cabins ~ Survivors flee to Norway Lake ~ Island Cloud attacks Eagle Lake settlement ~ Foot and Erickson ~ Lorentson and Backlund killed ~ Guri Endreson ~ Johannes Iverson ~ Isle of Refuge ~ Flight to St. Cloud ~ Big Stone Lake ~ George Whitcomb goes to St. Paul ~ Gun ownership on the frontier

Monongalia and Kandiyohi counties hosted some of the most remote frontier settlements in northwestern Minnesota in 1862. No longer in existence, Monongalia County comprised what is today Swift County and the northern half of Kandiyohi County. Some of the first white settlers reached this area in 1856, platting the townsites of Columbia, Irving, St. John's, Whitefield, and Kandiyohi. In 1859, several Scandinavian families settled farther northwest, particularly around Norway Lake and West Lake. (Map A) The mostly rolling prairie with plenty of lakes and scattered woods proved to be some of the best wheat-producing land in the entire state, and the harvest of 1862 promised to be plentiful. The settlers never had any serious problems with the Indians, either Dakotas to the south or the Chippewas to the north. Indian troubles, like the Civil War raging elsewhere, were someone else's concern. The idyllic situation changed in August 1862.[1]

---

1   Hubbard and Holcombe, *Minnesota in Three Centuries*, III, 353; "Historical Sites in Kandiyohi County," Kandiyohi County Historical Society; Strand, *Swedish-Americans of Minnesota*, 355-56.

On Tuesday night, August 19, a man named Hart arrived at Green Lake and Nest Lake to inform the settlers of the murders at Acton two days earlier. (Map B) As was often the case, some believed the story and some did not. Wednesday morning, William Kouts, Thomas M. Clark, and Silas Foot rode to Acton to learn the truth. Three miles from their destination they talked to several other settlers who confirmed the story. Satisfied, the trio turned around to ride home and raise the alarm. They were too late: the Dakotas had already paid a morning visit to the settlement at West Lake 30 miles to the northwest.[2]

Reverend Andrew Jackson, a Swedish Lutheran minister, organized the Swedish and Norwegian settlers in one church group and formed the Norway Lake parish in 1861. He began the first of two scheduled Wednesday morning services at Andreas L. Lundborg's house in northwest Arctander Township in West Lake Settlement. (Map A) Andreas (50) and Lena Lundborg (52) had six children: Johannes Anderson (30), Anders Petter (25), Gustaf (23), Lars (21), Samuel (9), and Johanna (14). Johannes married Christina Larsdotter and was living nearby, as were his brothers Anders and Gustaf.

The Broberg brothers resided in the same general neighborhood less than two miles to the west (between today's Monson Lake and West Sunburg Lake). Anders Peter Broberg (43), his wife Christina (36), and children Anna Stina (Ernestina) (16), Johannes (13), Andreas (10), and Christina (7) lived fewer than 50 yards east of the cabin housing Daniel Peter Broberg (38), his wife Anna Stina (30), and their sons Andreas Peter (7), Alfred (4), and John (10 months). Between the Lundborgs and Brobergs lived Sven Johnson (43), his wife Christina (42), and their children Anders Petter (10) and Johanna (8). Farther east lived Michael Anderson, Lars Johnson, and Ole Knudson. No one in the area had heard an uprising was in progress.

Many of the Lundborgs, Brobergs, and Sven Johnson family members attended Reverend Jackson's service. Some of the children stayed at the Broberg cabins under the care of Christina Broberg's half-brother John Nelson. Nearly two dozen Dakotas arrived at the Broberg cabins while the service was in session. They left the reservation the day before. Only a few were mounted and most wore white men's clothing. None of them were painted and their demeanor was friendly.[3]

2 Bryant and Murch, *Great Massacre*, 389-90.

3 Lawson and Tew, Biographical Review of Kandiyohi County, cited in "Arctander Township Pioneers," www.rootsweb.ancestry.com/~mnkandiy/Arctander.htm; Hubbard

Within a short time the Dakotas assumed a belligerent posture. Young Andreas Peter Broberg slipped out of his cabin and ran through the woods to Lundborg's, where he breathlessly explained to the parishioners that the Indians were abusing the children. The families hurried out and some of the Lundborgs grabbed their guns, but the good pastor Jackson warned that guns would unnecessarily provoke the Dakotas. Andreas Lundborg, who had more faith in his gun than in Jackson's familiarity with the Indians, took his weapon with him. Andreas and four of his sons, Anders, Gustaf, Lars, and Samuel, and Anders Peter Broberg, ran along the more direct path through the woods with Andreas Lundborg lagging behind them. The others traveled toward the Broberg cabins in two wagons along the main road: Daniel Broberg and wife, Anna Stina, and sons Andreas Peter and baby John in one wagaon, and Christina Broberg with daughters Anna Stina and Christina in the other. Sven Johnson and his family traveled part way with them, but diverged off the road toward his house first.

By the time Anders Broberg and the Lundborg boys reached the cabin the Dakotas there appeared quite friendly. Anders was relaxing at his kitchen table when a warrior signaled his fellow Dakotas and the shooting began. Anders was killed so quickly he did not have time to stand up. Uncle John Nelson was also shot dead. Alfred Broberg was killed by the cook shanty and warriors using tomahawks killed Johannes and Andreas at the edge of the woods. Anders and Gustaf Lundborg were outside when the murdering began. Both were shot and killed as they tried to run for safety. Young Samuel also tried to escape but was wounded in the head, fell down, and pretended to be dead. His brother Lars Lundborg was also wounded but kept his feet and ran toward the fence east of Anders Broberg's cabin.

Lars reached the fence about the same time his slower-moving father arrived on the other side. The lumbering Andreas Lundborg could hear the firing as he trotted along the trail and arrived just in time to see his son climbing the fence—but not in time to save him. Another bullet struck Lars and he fell. Warriors ran up to him, slit his throat, and stripped off his clothes as his father watched in frozen horror, unable to do more than let out a sharp cry. The warriors fired and chased after him when he ran. The gun he carried, however,

and Holcombe, *Minnesota in Three Centuries*, III, 353. Sven Johnson (or Johanson) is sometimes called Sven Johnson Aman, Aman being a town in Sweden.

may have convinced the Dakotas to pursue with more care than they otherwise would have demonstrated.[4]

The warriors were gaining on Lundborg when they noticed three other wagons rolling on the prairie. They left Lundborg and headed for the larger more enticing wheeled prizes. Because Johnson's wagon was the farthest away the Dakotas aimed for the Broberg wagons. It was about 1:00 p.m., recalled teenager Anna Stina, when "I saw two Indians coming. One of them continued to come after us, and the other went after my Uncle Daniel." The women and children tried to get out of the wagons. One Dakota grabbed Mrs. Christina Broberg, who screamed and struggled while he shook hands with her and tried to take her away with him. Her daughters, Anna Stina and Christina, ran off. The warrior tried to catch the children, but the mother slipped out of his grip and started running. The warrior solved his dilemma by shooting Mrs. Christina Broberg in the back and running after the children. He easily caught up to little 7-year-old Christina, clubbed her to the ground with his gun, and then beat her to death. He might have continued after 16-year-old Anna Stina, but by this time the wounded Christina Broberg had staggered to her feet and the warrior went back after her. Anna was running for all she was worth but could not resist turning to look behind her. The images of the warrior bludgeoning her mother to death would remain with her forever.

As the Johnson wagon out in front pulled farther away, the occupants of the second Broberg wagon were also caught and brutalized. The second warrior killed Daniel Broberg, his wife Anna Stina, and their baby John. The first white child born in the area was slaughtered on the prairie. "The baby was cut up, pieces were cut from face and nose and legs, in sight of the mother," remembered the younger Anna Stina. Thirteen members of the Lundborg and Broberg families were dead within just a handful of minutes.

The Dakotas were unable to capture all their potential prey. Cousins Anna Stina Broberg and Andreas Peter Broberg got away. Anna Stina caught up with the running Andreas Lundborg, who had just seen his own son shot and killed at the fence line. Near his house they met Andreas' oldest son Johannes Anderson Lundborg, who had not gone to the Broberg cabins with the rest of the family. Johannes took the shocked survivors to Lundborg's house, secured

---

4 Johnson, *A Church is Planted*, in http://genforum.genealogy.com/sweden/messages/31043.html; Strand, *Swedish-Americans of Minnesota*, 357; Bryant and Murch, *Great Massacre*, 401-02; Lundblad, "Impact of Minnesota's Dakota Conflict," 213; Broberg Peterson, "Story of the Massacre," in http://www.whodeane.com/the%20story%20of%20the%20massacre.pdf.

the other Lundborg family members, and hid deep in the brush. Several Indians searched for them and even fired shots in their direction, but no one was found or hit. Andreas Lundborg carried his gun throughout the horrifying events but never fired it because both it and the ammunition were wet.

Instead of following Anna Stina, Andreas Peter Broberg made for Sven Johnson's house. He joined them as they rushed out of their wagon and ran into the cellar. When the Dakotas finished with the Brobergs they went straight to Johnson's house and broke in through the windows. Before they left they smashed furniture and dishes and took what they wanted, sliding as they did so a large chest over the cellar trap door. The Johnsons and Andreas Peter remained hidden until dark and had a tough time overturning the heavy chest to climb out.

While most of the survivors headed east Johannes Anderson Lundborg returned that evening to his house to see if he could find anyone alive. It was nearly dark when he arrived. Johannes thought he saw and heard someone call out to him, but ran away because he was worried it was an Indian trick. In fact, it was his 9-year-old brother Samuel calling out for help. After successfully feigning death the wounded boy slipped away from the Broberg's and, failing to get Johannes to help him, made his way into his house and spent the night in the cellar. The next morning Samuel met the Johnsons as they made their way to Norway Lake. On Wednesday afternoon the other survivors gathered at Ole Knudson's about three miles away.[5]

When the church service at Lundborg's was interrupted that morning Reverend Jackson packed up his books and headed east to Norway Lake, where he was scheduled to hold the next service at Thomas Osmundsen's house. On the west side of an arm of Norway Lake opposite Osmundsen's place lived Even Railson. He broke ground there in 1858 and brought his family to their new home in 1860. Ole Knudson and Even Olson joined his "expedition" and homesteaded nearby. Railson was mowing when a servant girl shouted "Indians!" Ole Knudson, who lived two miles to the west, had just arrived with news of the Lundborg and Broberg killings. The women were trying to get the laundry in; Railson admonished them to "Let the clothes be. Take the children down to the boat."

5 Johnson, *A Church is Planted*, in http://genforum.genealogy.com/sweden/messages/ 31043.html; Bryant and Murch, *Great Massacre*, 401-02; Broberg Peterson, "Story of the Massacre," in http://www.whodeane.com/the%20story%20of%20the%20massacre.pdf.

While the women gathered the children Railson ran to the home of Cristopher H. Engen and told him about the uprising. They agreed the women and children should use the boat and row across to a small island in the lake that would come to be called the "Isle of Refuge." Armed with rifles, Railson and Engen scouted the shore to make sure it was safe before crossing to the island.

After warning the settlers, Ole Knudson returned home, collected his wife and two children, and returned to Norway Lake. By this time the boat and Railsen were gone. Knudson used a hollowed-out basswood log to float his family to the safety of the island, where they joined a growing group of people with the same idea. Later that evening Railsen, Knudson, and Johannes Lundborg returned to the Knudson house to help anyone else who needed a safe haven. Although it was dark and stormy, the trio found and ferried five more people out to the island in Norway Lake.

That same afternoon a Swede (sometimes said to be Johannes Anderson Lundborg, but more likely Ole Knudson) arrived at Thomas Osmundsen's to warn about the massacre. It was the second time that day Reverend Jackson's service had been interrupted. The news may have given him second thoughts about his early admonition to be kind to the Indians, because this time Jackson rode off to spread the alarm to the Nest Lake and Green Lake settlers.[6]

*   *   *

While Dakotas killed and pillaged the West Lake settlers on the west side of what was then Monongalia County, Island Cloud and his warriors were doing the same in the eastern part of Kandiyohi County. Settlers holding an inquest regarding the Acton killings that Monday had driven Island Cloud and others out of Meeker County. When the angry Indians learned a widespread uprising was in progress they joined with enthusiasm. A dozen warriors arrived from the reservation to swell Island Cloud's group to about 25 men. Jonas Peterson spotted the group on Tuesday in the Elizabeth Lake settlement, and a meeting with other settlers convinced them all it was time to leave. Those who fled on

6   Lawson and Tew, *Biographical Review of Kandiyohi County*, cited in "Norway-L Archives," http://newsarch.rootsweb.com/th/read/norway/2004-09/1094935847; Ulvestad, *Nordma-endene i Amerika*, 100-01. Although Johannes is usually said to have delivered the warning, Anna Stina also says he was with her and his father hiding around their house most of the day before looking for survivors at the Brobergs'. Other Swedes who lived in the area and might have delivered the warning were Michael Anderson, Lars Johnson, or Ole Knudson.

Wednesday included: Peterson with his wife and four children; Jonas Olafson with his wife and three children; Charles F. Linquist, a Methodist Episcopal minister, his wife and five children, and Andrew M. Ecklund and his family. It was Ecklund's horses the Dakotas had stolen three days earlier at Acton that signaled the beginning of the uprising. Their flight was none too soon; Island Cloud's warriors began burning and robbing just a short time after they pulled out. The refugees lost household goods, crops, and livestock, but escaped with their lives.[7]

Island Cloud's men split up somewhere between Elizabeth Lake and Foot Lake, with some moving northeast toward Diamond Lake and the others scouring the Foot Lake and Eagle Lake area. (Map B) On Wednesday along the south side of Foot Lake (where the town of Willmar now stands) they killed Berger Thorson, an aging bachelor who had lived there since 1857.[8]

The Dakotas worked their way around to the east and north side of Foot Lake and on to Swan Lake. Silas's brother Solomon R. Foot lived on the isthmus between the two bodies of water with his wife Adeline Stocking Foot and their two youngest children, ages six years and 18 months. Their three older children were staying with their Uncle Silas eight miles northeast at Nest Lake. Silas Foot, Thomas Clark, and William Kouts returned to that settlement from Acton about four in the afternoon with word that the reports of an uprising were true. Reverend Jackson arrived later from Norway Lake with a similar story. The settlers around Nest Lake and Green Lake were now alerted and taking action to protect themselves and their property. The people at Foot Lake and Eagle Lake, however, were still in the dark.

Swen Swanson with his wife and three children lived on the east side of Foot Lake only a couple of miles from bachelor Berger Thorson. The sound of the gunfire that killed Thorson, together with the presence of Indians, alerted Swanson that something was amiss. His brother-in-law Andrew Nelson lived nearby and Swanson thought it best to consult with him. Nelson, another area bachelor, was helping Foot bring in his hay when Swanson arrived and reported what he saw and heard. The two men returned to help gather Swanson's family. Nelson dumped the hay out of the wagon and replaced the hayrack with the wagon body. While Swanson loaded their belongings Nelson rounded up their

7   Jonas Peterson Depredation Claim #261; Jonas Olafson Depredation Claim #617; Charles F. Linquist Depredation Claim #254.

8   Hubbard and Holcombe, *Minnesota in Three Centuries*, III, 354.

40 head of cattle. Swanson pulled out and made for Solomon Foot's cabin without Nelson, who remained behind to secure the last of the livestock. He was still rounding them up when the Indians arrived. Nelson ducked into a cornfield and tried to head north. Confused in the twilight, he splashed through a marsh and lost his way.

Swanson broke the news when he reached the Foot house on the narrow strip of land between Foot and Swan lakes about suppertime. Skeptical "on account of the frequency of such rumors in past years which proved to be unfounded," Solomon, with his wife Adeline, agreed to ride with Swanson to Oscar Erickson's one mile away on the east side of Swan Lake. Oscar (40) lived with his pregnant wife Gjetru (Gertrude) (22) and their son Erik (2). Carl Peter Jonson and his wife Anna Cathrina lived in a cabin about one-quarter mile to the north with their daughter and son-in-law, Christina and Carl J. Carlson. They moved to America from Sweden five years earlier and lived together as one family. Carl Peter was watching the cattle and his cabin, where Carl Carlson checked on his father-in-law after supper, while Anna and her daughter stayed with their neighbors.

Fifteen Dakota warriors arrived at Erickson's cabin about dark on Wednesday and told the settlers they were out hunting. Adeline didn't believe their story because they did not have any dogs with them. The Dakotas did their best to ingratiate themselves by making friendly remarks and blaming the Acton murders on "bad Indians." Their request to come into the house was refused and they huddled under some nearby trees when it began to rain. Two hours after dark Carl Carlson returned from his house and was asked by the Dakotas to visit with them. The wary Swede declined and hurried into Erickson's house. Some of the occupants were convinced the Indians were friendly, while others were just as certain they meant mischief. Solomon and Adeline stayed awake all night to keep watch. The Dakotas were still there when the sun rose Thursday morning.[9]

After losing his way the night before, that morning Andrew Nelson discovered he was on the bank of a creek connecting Eagle Lake with Swan Lake and only a short distance from Erickson's home. When he spotted Indians

9   Bryant and Murch, *Great Massacre*, 390, 394; Strand, *Swedish-Americans of Minnesota*, 363; Smith, *Sketch of Meeker County*, 59-60; "Silas Foot," http://footfamily.com/new_page_ 2.html; Ann Cathrina Jonson Depredation Claim #791. Most references to this incident mention only four familes: Foot, Erickson, Swanson, and Carlson. The Jonson depredation claim verifies that their family was also present.

surrounding the cabin he decided to high tail it seven miles east to the Diamond Lake settlement.

Meanwhile, inside the cabin Nelson wisely bypassed the concerned families discussing what to do. Solomon Foot decided to go outside and figure out what the Indians wanted. It was still drizzling when he approached the Dakotas, who told him they were cold and needed an ax and some kindling to build a fire. The request sounded reasonable and Solomon complied. A short time later they were at the door asking for potatoes; they were hungry and did not want to go out in the field and dig up their own. Although Solomon had helped them with an ax and kindling, this request struck him as odd and he warned the others to stay by the house. Carl Carlson, however, grabbed a hoe and walked toward the potato field. Solomon eventually followed. One of the warriors blasted a load of buckshot into him. The force of the blast knocked Solomon down on one knee, but he recovered his balance and ran into the house. Carl was holding a hoe in one hand and two freshly dug potatoes in the other when the warriors killed him.

The Dakotas opened fire on the Erickson cabin. Adeline bandaged Solomon's wounds and he took position at a window and fired back. He later claimed to have killed or wounded several of the warriors. Swen Swanson was apparently too terrified to load or fire a gun, but Oscar Erickson was bound and determined to defend his home. Like Solomon he found a window and opened fire, but a bullet tore into his abdomen. The siege continued fitfully for about two hours when Solomon was hit again, this time through the breast below the shoulder. The bullet bypassed his lung and exited near a kidney. Adeline took up her husband's musket and fired from the windows. With the Erickson place firmly surrounded, some warriors paid a visit to the Jonson-Carlson cabin, where they shot Carl Peter Jonson and slit his throat. Others burned down Foot's cabin.

As the hours passed the pain from Erickson's stomach wound increased to an unbearable level. "He yelled, raved around the room, seized an axe and tried to kill himself, plunged his head in a pail of water and writhed in extreme agonies," recalled Solomon. Unable to see much from her window, Adeline went upstairs to get a better view. She was firing from a window when a Dakota bullet clipped her breast and part of her arm. Adeline loaded her musket and kept shooting. Fire arrows or sparks from the shooting ignited a small fire, which the quick-thinking and cool Adeline doused with water from the tea kettle. In a state of some despair, Swen Swanson argued that their only chance for survival was to open the door and beg for mercy, to which both Solomon and Adeline swore they would shoot him if he tried. The stalemate continued until about two in the afternoon that Thursday, when the Dakotas tired of the game and broke off the siege.

Erickson had collapsed from his painful stomach wound and the women carried him upstairs to bed. Solomon was made as comfortable as possible in a bed downstairs. Both men appeared to be dying. The blood from Erickson's wound dripped through the floorboards and spattered Foot lying in the room below. It was about dusk when the Swansons, Anna Jonson, and Christina Carlson saw their chance to escape and they left. Adeline Foot, Gertrude Erickson, three children, and two wounded men remained.[10]

*   *   *

On Wednesday, while some Dakotas were killing settlers at West Lake and others were investing the Eagle Lake settlement, those around Nest Lake and Green Lake were going about their daily business waiting for proof that the rumors of war were true. Jephta Adams and his son were cutting hay that day when the sound of gunfire reached their ears. Adams supposed the Indians were hunting game. They may have been, but they were also hunting humans. It was later that afternoon when Silas Foot, Clark, and Kouts arrived from Acton and confirmed the uprising, as did Reverend Jackson a short time later.

Thursday morning about 10:00 a.m. the refugees headed for Forest City. The party included Jephta Adams, William Kouts (a single man), Silas Foot and family together with three of his brother Solomon's children, Job W. Burdick and his family, and Joseph Thomas, who sharecropped the farm of Elijah T. Woodcock for three-quarters of the production. They had only traveled a few miles when a wagon approached from the south. Jephta believed it was Solomon Foot and his family because three of his children were riding with Jephta's group. It was not Foot, but it was other settlers fleeing from the same area. (Map B)

Sven Helgeson Backlund (75), a shoemaker by trade, and his wife Steina (72) were riding with Magnus Anderson, whose cabins were near one another just west of Eagle Lake. They had fled that morning, taking with them only a few quilts to cover themselves. Before he left Backlund hid three sacks of flour

10 Bryant and Murch, *Great Massacre*, 394-95; Strand, *Swedish-Americans of Minnesota*, 363; Smith, *Sketch of Meeker County*, 60; "Silas Foot," http://footfamily.com/new_page_2.html.

in the brush and told Anderson that "he should soon be back again." To Jephta they reported hearing gunfire near Foot's cabin "and supposed they were all killed."

Right behind the Bucklands and Anderson were the families of Andreas Lorentson (Sanland), Andreas Peterson, N. A. Viren, and others. Jephta Adams's daughter Eunice Brown was living for a time at William H. Clark's cabin east of Green Lake. Her husband Charles had been killed by the Indians in June. All Eunice owned was some clothing and a few household items worth $94. When the Dakota warriors arrived they let her leave, but refused to allow her to take even her most meager possessions. She climbed into a wagon with Jesse M. Ayers and escaped an hour and a half before Dakotas burned down her house.

The growing caravan headed to Diamond Lake but by the time it arrived most of the settlers had left. The wandering and occasionally lost Andrew Nelson had already been there as early as 7:00 a.m., when he burst in upon J. H. Gates and family during breakfast. They took him at his word and, together with other local families, fled with little ado. Many of them headed toward Forest City, but some, like Nehemiah Garrison (53) and his wife, took what property they could and headed north to Paynesville. Most of the Nest Lake, Green Lake, and Diamond Lake settlers, together with some of the Eagle Lake residents, appeared to be getting away.[11]

Not everyone made it in time to join the larger caravan. Mons Oleson, his wife Anna, and five children lived two miles north of Nest Lake. They made their claim under the Homestead Act just one month earlier and were living in a rail shanty while Mons built their log cabin. A neighbor arrived to warn them that "Indians were killing everybody." Mons ordered his family into his wagon and threw aboard a few items. Mons's later claim for lost property illustrates the precarious state of existence under which some settlers lived. All told, it was worth only $47, a sum that included his unfinished cabin ($30) and 14 chickens ($1.20). By the time the Olesons reached Green Lake the sun was setting and everyone was gone. They stayed overnight and continued to Forest City in the morning, but did not see anyone else along the way. From there they headed to Kingston and on to Minneapolis. The following spring Mons lamented, "there

---

11 Bryant and Murch, *Great Massacre*, 389-91; Elijah T. Woodcock Depredation Claim #1382; Steina Backlund Depredation Claim #789; Eunice Brown Depredation Claim #1206; Nehemiah Garrison Depredation Claim #1258.

is not now a solitary white settler in that County." The Oleson family never went back.[12]

The wagon train leaving Green Lake and West Lake faced more peril. More wagons joined together the farther east it rolled. The caravan swung south of Green Lake and around the north shore of Diamond Lake. George Heywood, who had lived on the southeast shore of Green Lake since 1857, joined the wagon train with his sister and his son, as did his neighbor Daniel Delaney. When N. A. Viren had trouble with his ox team and stopped to cut a failing animal loose he asked the others to slow down and wait for him, but they refused. Many wagons bogged down in a slough east of Diamond Lake. Viren caught up with them and sounded the shallows of the lake. Finding it firm, he drove his team into the water and around the muddy slough, taking a position in front of the stalled wagons that had earlier refused to wait for him. When their occupants called to him for assistance, Viren replied that what "was sauce for the goose was sauce for the gander," smiled and waved, and drove on. He reached Forest City one day ahead of everyone else.[13]

The delay would prove costly, as would a stop for lunch at Wheeler's Grove southeast of Diamond Lake. Some halted to rest their teams and others to graze their cattle. Silas Foot, Adams, Kouts, and others had been driving their livestock in the rear and picking up strays along the way. The pace was leisurely, and more wagons joined up. The lengthy wagon train was strung out and ripe for attack. Seven Dakotas made their appearance only two miles from Wheeler Lake on the Kandiyohi-Meeker County border. They comprised one of the two groups that had split off from Island Cloud the day before. Their presence convinced nearly everyone to abandon the cattle, but Sven Backlund and Andreas Lorentson (56) refused and paid for their decision with their lives when the Dakotas ran them down. Silas Foot and William Kouts tried to offer assistance, but decided otherwise when the Indians opened fire in their direction.

The settlers made for higher ground and returned fire, but did so without much coordination, "each man acting on his own notion," explained Jephta Adams. They had about 15 guns of all types, but according to Adams only five were "fit for use." The wagons were rolling toward a hill when a couple of the Indians rode ahead and cut them off. Lashing their horses and oxen the

---

12 Mons Oleson Depredation Claim #1284.

13 George Heywood Depredation Claim #2240; Smith, *Sketch of Meeker County*, 62-63.

refugees turned in a different direction but a few more Indians blocked that route as well. With Dakotas obstructing the way north and south, the wagons pulled to a halt and the whites and Indians spent the next 20 minutes exchanging fire. Bullets zipped around the wagons but no one was hit. Adams recalled that William Kouts took aim and "had the good fortune to hit one of the red-skins, who was carried off the field, apparently dead." Rebuffed, the Dakotas pulled back, slaughtered 15 cattle, and mutilated the bodies of Backlund and Lorentson. The former's head was found in the road with his straw hat still firmly in place. Lorentson, a prolific user of snuff tobacco, was discovered with a pair of knives sticking out of his abdomen. The Dakotas had cut off his two stained "snuff" fingers and jammed them in his snuffbox before tucking it back into his pocket. Unsure whether the Dakotas would return, the settlers formed the wagons in a circle and dug a hole for shelter in the center for the women and children. The Indians never returned. They remained in the wagon corral all night before pushing on toward Forest City early on a foggy Friday morning.[14]

Even after four days of murderous uprising and widespread warnings spread in every direction, there were still some who hadn't gotten the word. Island Cloud's warriors fanned out from Erickson's cabin on Thursday and engulfed other scattered homesteads in the area. Three miles west of Erickson's was a cabin belonging to Olof Olson Haugen, who was at Green Lake picking up mail. (Map B) Dakotas killed his wife Bergeret Haugen and their son Frederick. By the time Olof reached the northeast side of West Twin Lake, about seven miles from home, he would have realized the whites had left the area. All we know today is that he was found and killed. A few days later a search party led by Reverend Jackson found his corpse floating in the lake. Reports indicate he had stuffed grass into his wounds to try and stop the bleeding.[15]

The Dakotas left Olof Haugen's place and moved two miles northwest to the Lars Endreson (Rosseland) cabin. More isolated than most, Endreson's place was tucked into a secluded wooded area on the isthmus between Solomon Lake and West Solomon Lake. Lars (59) and Gurid (Guri) (51) moved to Monongalia (Kandiyohi) County in 1857. Two of their children stayed behind

14 Bryant and Murch, *Great Massacre*, 391-93; Strand, *Swedish-Americans of Minnesota*, 365; "Silas Foot," http://footfamily.com/new_page_2.html; Steina Backlund Depredation Claim #789.

15 "Historical Sites in Kandiyohi County," Kandiyohi County Historical Society; Ulvestad, *Nordmaendene i Amerika*, 100; Dahlin, *Dakota Uprising Victims*, 71.

in Norway, but Endre (20), Gurid (16), Olav (14), Brita (9), and Anna (3) accompanied them to America. Another daughter, Gertrude, emigrated with them but married Oscar Erickson. Unbeknownst to her family, she had endured her own encounter with the Dakotas earlier that same day.

Late Thursday afternoon Lars and Endre were tending stock, Olav and his two sisters were preparing the supper table, and Guri and the baby were in the root house cellar. Four Dakotas approached carrying shotguns. Lars walked with them to the house, the Indians shaking hands with everyone. The family knew them; one they called "John" could even speak some English, even though it was not the Endresons' primary language. When John indicated they wanted some milk to drink Lars complied. He was putting the pan away when one of the Dakotas shot him. Staggered by the blast, Lars remained on his feet until the others opened fire and killed him and wounded Olav. Guri and little Anna heard the shooting from in the root cellar and remained hidden, although Guri could not resist peering through the cracks between the boards. To her horror, she watched as the Indians dragged her daughters Gurid and Brita away, the younger girl "screaming for me to save her."

Guri and Anna hid in the cellar until dark before creeping back to the house. On the way Guri stumbled across Lars and Olav and believed them both dead. With Anna in hand she decided the safest place was out on the prairie. They walked all night and the next day without finding a road or trail to help them get their bearings. Gurid and Brita, meanwhile, escaped from their captors after the Dakotas took them about half a mile from the house and camped for the evening. One version of their escape has some of the horses wandering away and the Indians searching for them, giving the two girls a chance to slip away into the tall grass. They made their way east toward Eagle Lake, where the Dakotas almost caught them again, firing into the brush but missing them. Their mother offered a different version, claming the girls escaped the day after their capture when the Indians allowed them to return to the house for food, and they used the opportunity to run away. In any case, Gurid and Brita walked east about 20 miles until Mark Piper and Otis Ferguson found them on Saturday and saw them safely to Forest City.[16]

---

16 Bryant and Murch, *Great Massacre*, 399-400; Laut, "Heroine of Kandiyohi," http://home.online.no?~torolav/guri.html; "Rosseland Family Register," http://home. online.no/~torolav/gen.html; Strand, *Swedish-Americans of Minnesota*, 364; Blegen, "Immigrant Women and the American Frontier," 26-29. The Lars Endreson (Rosseland) cabin has been preserved and stands today at the end of twisting mile-long dirt road.

*   *   *

Guri and her young daughter Anna were walking the prairie on Friday while Adeline Foot was caring for her wounded husband Solomon and Oscar Erickson. She ventured outside about 9:00 a.m. and fetched some water. When men appeared riding horses and driving ox teams, the exhausted Adeline believed they were whites coming to rescue them. Closer observation conveyed the awful truth: the men were naked warriors decorated with war paint. The Dakotas shot at the house once more and set fire to the haystack. The besieged returned fired slowly, their ammunition nearly gone. Luckily for them, the Dakotas left two hours later.

Adeline Foot and Gertrude Erickson could see cabins burning in the distance. The odds favored the Indians returning to finish the job, so they resolved to flee. Everyone assumed both men had been mortally wounded, and both husbands gave their assent to take the children and go. The women set out bread and water for their men and left. They went first to Green Lake, where several houses had been burned. Silas Foot's cabin was still standing and they found something to eat inside. They reached Forest City about 4:00 a.m. Sunday, August 24. Oscar Erickson and Solomon Foot were not ready to give up and die just yet. Both men had stopped bleeding and consumed the bread left for them. With only a little assistance they might yet get out of their dire predicament. In fact, help from an unlikely source was already on the way.[17]

Before dawn that Saturday morning Guri and Anna Endreson discovered they had been walking in circles and were still close to home. Little Anna was very hungry and Guri tried unsuccessfully to nurse her. "Thinking I could but die," Guri recalled, "I went into the house." Nearly everything had been destroyed or stolen. If she could only find one of their animals, she thought, but it soon became apparent that the livestock had been driven off—17 cows, eight sheep, eight pigs, and plenty of chickens. She found her 20-year-old son Endre's body about 60 yards from the cabin. When Guri discovered a pair of oxen she hitched them to a light sled and searched the house one last time. To her surprise and delight, she found 14-year-old son Olav hiding behind the stove. He had been shot in the shoulder "and was nearly crazy with fear and pain." Guri helped him to the sled with Anna. She placed a pillow under her dead husband's head, bid him farewell, and began walking the oxen and sled

17 "Silas Foot," http://footfamily.com/new_page_2.html.

toward the Erickson house praying that her daughter Gertrude was alive and well.

Guri reached the house about dusk but was too afraid to go inside. The next morning the dawn revealed a wagon parked near the front door. She wanted to use it to hasten her escape, but was still unsure whether Indians were lurking around the property. To her surprise, she peeked inside a window and saw two injured white men inside. One of them was her son-in-law Oscar Erickson, and the other neighbor Solomon Foot. By this time maggots had infested Solomon's wounds. "She washed our bodies, bandaged our wounds and gave us every possible comfort," he said. Guri drew Solomon's wagon "as near the door as possible, put into it bedding, blankets and other things we might need," the wounded Foot recalled. "She assisted us into it, propped us up in a half reclining position, placed my gun by my side, hitched the young unbroken oxen to it and started."

Somehow Guri managed to carry Oscar outside on her back and get him into the wagon beside Solomon. She also put the two children in, along with food and water, and led the oxen off. They traveled northeast to Green Lake and found Silas Foot's house abandoned and others burned before heading to Diamond Lake, where all the cabins were deserted. Farther east they found the bodies of two men killed on the prairie (Backlund and Lorentson), together with a dozen or more dead cattle. When they stopped for the night, Solomon explained, "Mother Endreson supplied all our wants and again bathed our wounds [and] spent a sleepless night watching over us, ever on the lookout for the savage foe."

Guri guided the wagon with children and wounded men safely to Forest City and eventually to Clearwater on the Mississippi River, where she found her daughters Gurid and Brita alive. Her teenage son Olav, however, whom she had found hiding behind the stove in their home, "lived a little more than a year and then was taken sick and died." Guri tried to make sense of her ordeal and, like so many of the settlers, accepted a supernatural explanation for the tragic events. "To be an eyewitness to these things," she later wrote to her family in Norway, "and to see many others wounded and killed was almost too much for a poor woman, but, God be thanked, I kept my life and my sanity . . . but what shall I say? God permitted it to happen thus, and I had to accept my heavy fate and thank Him for having spared my life and those of some of my dear children."[18]

*   *   *

The warring Dakotas were not yet finished with the white settlers in Kandiyohi-Monongalia County.

Johannes Iverson (40) and his wife Kari Johnsdatter Iverson (40) arrived in America from Norway in 1852 and settled in Monongalia County on the southeast side of Crook Lake six years later. (Map B) By August 1862 they had six children: Alvina Betsy Marie (Mary) (16), John Andrew (11), Bennet Martin (Bennie) (10), Sophia Margaretha (2), Lina Caroline, and Lewis Peter (infant). Johannes was cutting hay during the afternoon of a perfect summer day with no idea that the Erickson home was even then under siege just seven miles southeast at Eagle Lake; that the Endreson cabin five miles to the south at Solomon Lake was about to be attacked; and that 13 people had been killed the day before at the West Lake settlement just nine miles northwest.

Johannes looked up from his haying work to see a dozen Dakotas approaching from the south. They may have been from Island Cloud's band or some of the warriors who had terrorized West Lake the day before. Johannes knew some of them and had no reason to be concerned. The 40-year-old set aside his scythe when a few warriors rode up to him and shook his hand. Daughter Mary was in the field a quarter-mile distant watching them carry on a brief conversation when one of the men raised his rifle and shot her father dead. Mary turned and fled toward the cabin but was caught easily. The Indians manhandled her onto a pony which, frightened by the commotion, broke and ran. When she was out of sight a few seconds later Mary hopped off and hid, but the warriors were more concerned about getting the animal back than finding the worrisome girl. Depending upon the version of the story, Mary made her way back to the cabin and informed her family about what had happened, or struck out north on her own. In any event she became separated from the rest of the Iversons and was found by settlers who took her to Paynesville.

With her husband dead, and having no way of knowing that the killing was part of a much larger uprising, Kari decided to take Sophia and Lewis in the

18 Bryant and Murch, *Great Massacre*, 400-01; "Silas Foot," http://footfamily.com/new_ page _2.html.

wagon to Norway Lake to report what had happened and seek help. John, Bennie, Lina (and possibly Mary) stayed home. Afraid the Indians would return that evening, the children hid out on the prairie all night. When morning arrived and their mother had not returned, the Iverson siblings tried to get to Norway Lake, walking around the west side of Crook Lake. They became disoriented and ended up at Sven Gunderson Borgen's house about two miles northwest at Swenson Lake. (Map A) Still in shock and unsure what to do next, the three Iverson children decided to hide in the cellar.[19]

Kari Iverson found the settlers around Norway Lake in chaos when she arrived there late in the day. It didn't take long to discover that the murder of her husband was but one incident in a general murderous uprising. A handful of men had returned to the mainland from the "Isle of Refuge" to look for stragglers while others buried the Lundborg and Broberg dead. Kari demanded that someone return to her cabin and "get Johannes dug down, because the wolf might come and eat him up. You will need a spade and you will find it in the bark shanty." She gave them directions and told them where they could find the body. "You will need to take the scythe home and hang it up in the big tree in front of the house, and you must put the grind stone well into the brush behind the house," she directed. Several men agreed to go and were in the process of leaving when she called out additional instructions, including orders to bring back a whetstone Johannes carried in his pocket, as well as other things. By this time the men were tired of listening to her orders and simply walked away. When they reached the woods near the Iverson cabin, Dakota warriors spotted them approaching and shot in their general direction. Not in a hurry to end up like Johannes, they promptly turned around and headed back to Norway Lake.

Friday morning Gunder Swenson (17), the son of Sven Gunderson Borgen (52), wanted to return to their house, about two miles south of Norway Lake, to salvage any useful items. Gunder's sister Birgette (Betsy) (21) married Thomas Osmundsen (27) in Wisconsin before the families moved to Norway Lake three years early. Osmundsen, who employed Gunder on his farm, accompanied him to the house. There, they discovered the three Iverson children hiding in the cellar and took them to their mother. Kari Iverson's burial instructions and

---

19 "Johannes Iverson," http://mankell.org/iverson.html; "The Eversons in Kandiyohi County," http://ftp.rootsweb.ancestry.com/pub/usgenweb/mn/kandiyohi/bios/everson. txt; Strand, *Swedish-Americans of Minnesota*, 360; Dahlin, *Dakota Uprising History*, 351.

other orders may have been ignored, but three more of her children were now safe with her.[20]

By Saturday, August 23, the surviving settlers in the area had gathered at the island. The provisions available to them, however, were not going to be enough to sustain them for very long. Tom Osmundsen and his father-in-law, Sven Borgen, agreed to return to Osmundsen's nearby house to secure more. When they arrived, three Dakotas emerged from behind the cabin and fired at them. The men dove out of their wagon and hid in the cornfield, shouting across to the island for help. Some on the island returned the shouts while others climbed into dugouts and a small boat and began paddling back to the mainland. The Dakotas heard the shouting, realized its significance, and fled the area. The fact that Indians were still prowling the lakeshore convinced the settlers to abandon their island and seek refuge elsewhere. "[We] left the county in a body, and went to Paynesville," explained Osmundsen.[21]

Heading northeast, the refugees passed through the abandoned Lake Prairie settlement; Lars Oleson, Anfin Thorson, and the others abandoned their farms the previous day. Most or all of the whites within five miles of Paynesville had fled, including brothers Ambrose and Thomas Mayhew and Joseph Martin. Oleson heard that "some 12 persons, Swedes and Norwegians, were killed by Indians about 9 miles west of my place the day before I fled from home." He didn't wait around to confirm the news, and neither did his neighbors. "The whole country in my section was entirely depopulated," he said.

Some men from Paynesville organized a relief force and set out to locate refugees and bury bodies. Part of this relief company included Peter Heintz and Peter Le Gro, who lived about five miles west of Paynesville. Curious to learn if the rumors were true, they traveled nearly 30 miles to the West Lake settlement in time to see the 13 bodies buried. Said Le Gro, "[We] became convinced of the fact of the outbreak." The pair hurried back to get their families out and fled to St. Cloud. Once there Margaret Heintz and seven children found a place to

20 Strand, *Swedish-Americans of Minnesota*, 360; Dahlin, *Dakota Uprising History*, 385n1361; "Life of Gunder Swenson," *Willmar Weekly Tribune*, October 3, 1934. Earlier in the year, Robinson Jones hired Gunder Swenson to build the fence surrounding his property at Acton—the same fence the Dakotas crossed to steal the eggs that led to the murders.

21 Thomas Osmundsen Depredation Claim #2156. Some sources state that the two men went to Borgen's cabin when confronted by the Indians, but Osmundsen is clear that it was at his house.

stay while Peter (45), angered at the outbreak and loss of his property, joined Company D of the 1st Regiment of Mounted Rangers.

*   *   *

Andreas Lundborg and his wife Lena became separated during the chaos following the first attacks at West Lake and "entertained no hope of ever more meeting in this world." From the Paynesville men, however, Andreas learned that his wife had traveled three miles northeast to Glesne Lake and joined with Lewis Everson, his wife and five children, Even Olson (who lived with the Eversons), and Erick Kopperud. They had already reached Paynesville, they assured him, and were even then safe in town. The two reunited and rejoiced, even though they had just buried three sons. Most of the survivors were simply thankful for their lives.[22]

The murderous odyssey that had descended upon the West Lake and Norway Lake settlers was not yet at an end. Some wanted to return to their farms, but most believed that even Paynesville was too overcrowded and still not safe. Those of like mind decided to continue northeast another 25 miles to St. Cloud where, once across the Mississippi River, they would be completely safe. A cadre of St. Cloud residents, however, warned them not to go because St. Cloud was also crowded and there was not enough food there. If they would return to their farms, however, the people of St. Cloud would help furnish them with arms, ammunition, and supplies. When their pleas failed, they switched tactics and warned that the refugees would not be allowed to cross the Mississippi. In truth, the St. Cloud residents simply did not want to be on the edge of what was obviously still a very dangerous frontier and thus next in line to suffer the Dakotas' wrath; they wanted settlements farther west to act as a buffer. Intent on fleeing east, the settlers accepted the challenge and left, with more settlers joining them as they moved.

When the fleeing settlers reached the broad river, locals tried to prevent them from crossing. There was no bridge at the time and the ferry and other boats were tied up on the eastern shore. The ferryman simply refused the use of his boat. The river was running low that late August, so a frustrated Tom

---

22 Lars Oleson Depredation Claim #2155; Thomas Mayhew Depredation Claim #2143; Peter Heintz Depredation Claim #2241; Lewis Everson Depredation Claim #1235; Strand, *Swedish-Americans of Minnesota*, 361.

Osmundsen simply drove his cattle into the water and swam them across. Others followed. Once across, some of the Swedes cut the ferry boat loose for others to use. Police tried to interfere, but the settlers openly declared they would rather fight the police than fight the Dakotas. The lawmen backed off and let them pass. The allusion to Moses crossing the Red Sea was probably not lost on people so familiar with the Bible.[23]

*   *   *

On August 21, while the Dakotas were attacking the Ericksons, Endresons, and Iversons, war came to Big Stone Lake about 90 miles west of the Eagle Lake settlement and 160 miles upriver from New Ulm. For the first time in the uprising some of Inkpaduta's band joined in the killings, led not by the chief but by Striped Arrow (Wan-hde-ga).[24]

Big Stone Lake's four trading houses, run by Louis Robert, William Forbes, Nathan Myrick, and Daily, Pratt & Company, served the upper Sissetons and Wahpetons. Operations weren't as extensive as downriver and most of the employees were of French or mixed-blood ancestry. Agent Thomas Galbraith was in the process of erecting government buildings and had contracted with George Lott to build a blacksmith shop, root house, dwellings, and cut 50 tons of hay. Lott hired New Ulm brothers Anton and Henry Manderfeld and their cousin, Hilliar Manderfeld to help him with the work. John Schmerch (16) was employed at the Lower Agency to do their cooking. It took six days to reach Big Stone Lake, where they set up camp near Myrick's store.[25]

One of Myrick's clerks, John McCole, traveled to Yellow Medicine in late July to attend the anticipated annuity distribution. Once there he joined the Renville Rangers and was absent from Big Stone Lake. One of Lott's frequent visitors was Hypolite Campbell, whose wife was a cousin of Standing Buffalo and another of Myrick's clerks. Five years earlier Hypolite killed a man at

23 Strand, *Swedish-Americans of Minnesota*, 362.

24 Tolzmann, ed., *Outbreak and Massacre*, 50. According to Inkpaduta's biographer and defender, Paul Beck (*Inkpaduta*, 115-16), the chief had no involvement in the early days of the uprising.

25 *Commissioner of Indian Affairs, 1863*, 272; Bryant and Murch, *Great Massacre*, 149, 379; McConkey, *Dakota War Whoop*, 97, 316n106. According to McConkey, John's last name was Julien, while Anderson, *Little Crow*, 169, claims his last name was Euni; his Manderfeld cousin claimed John's last name was Schmerch.

Redwood Agency; the only way he stayed out of jail was by moving frequently. As a result, he could not personally show up to collect his annuity payment, but he retrieved his wife so she could collect her portion. A few days later Hypolite returned from the Lower Agency and informed Lott about the Bread Raid at Yellow Medicine on August 4. A band of Yanktons and Sissetons called "Cut-heads" were treacherous, he continued, and they planned to make trouble.

The Cut-heads were moving back upriver and Lott wanted to leave, but Hypolite convinced him that he could smooth things over. If Lott gave the Indians provisions and ammunition no one would be molested. When the Dakotas arrived Hypolite handed them flour, pork, and sugar. The surly crowd of warriors moved through Lott's camp taking clothing, knives, and virtually whatever else they wanted. "With the plunder thus obtained, they left us without doing any more harm," explained Anton Manderfeld. Everyone associated with Lott's building operation figured they had dodged a bullet. Hypolite Campbell, meanwhile, returned to the Lower Agency, where he was caught up in the initial outbreak on August 18.

Lott moved camp a mile-and-a-half from Robert's store and a mile from the lake. "Here we worked, not anticipating any danger," Anton Manderfeld remembered. All seemed well until August 21, when a Dakota arrived at their tent at daybreak and warned them to leave because "the Indians were killing all the whites, and that there was not a white man left on the whole reservation, from Big Stone Lake to New Ulm."[26]

More than 50 Dakota warriors hit the traders' stores. Many of the victims were single men with no relatives to report their loss or make inquiries as to their whereabouts. Riley Ryder was in charge of the Daily, Pratt & Company store. The Dakotas shot him down along with employees Frank Peshette, a Mr. Patnode, and a Mr. Laundre. Alexis Dubuque was killed at either Forbes's or Myrick's. The Dakotas took mixed-blood Baptiste Gubeau prisoner and tied his hands behind him with rawhide straps, but he managed to escape while they plundered the stores. With his hands still tied Gubeau ran into Big Stone Lake. Once the water loosened his rawhide bindings he swam across the foot of the lake and headed across the prairie 110 miles to St. Cloud. Even there he was not safe. By this time the uprising had triggered a wave of hysteria; locals grabbed Gubeau and accused him of being a spy. They were about to hang him when an old acquaintance vouched for him.

26 Bryant and Murch, *Great Massacre*, 380-81.

The Dakotas were approaching Lott's camp when Anton Manderfeld emerged from his tent. It had been raining all night and he noticed the Indians had wrapped their guns in blankets. Without any warning they uncovered their weapons and fired. Anton jumped into a small ravine when one of the bullets struck a tree next to where he stood. The shooting woke Anton's brother Henry, who rushed out of his tent only to be shot dead. George Lott was killed a few moments later. Anton and his cousin Hilliar ran to the lake and hid in the reeds growing along the shore. They could hear the Indians searching for them. While Anton was crouched low in the marsh Hilliar decided to stand and make a run for it. It was the wrong decision. The warriors chased after him. A few minutes later Anton heard the shots that killed him.

When night fell Anton escaped across the Minnesota River and made his way down to Lac Qui Parle, where he found Joe La Framboise Jr. and another mixed-blood, John Launche. The men had been helping Spirit Walker care for Mrs. Huggins and Julia La Framboise. After providing Anton with food and moccasins to cover his bleeding feet, they warned him that he must head northeast toward the Big Woods because if the Dakotas caught them harboring a white man they would be killed. Anton walked for a couple more days and found an abandoned cabin. A letter found inside informed him he was at Green Lake. Unsure which way to go he decided to head back south toward the Minnesota River so he could at least get his bearings. Ten long days after leaving La Framboise he stumbled into a camp of white soldiers near Fort Ridgely, joined a wagon train, and made it to St. Peter.[27]

John Schmerch, the teenage cook for Lott's operation, experienced a similar terrifying ordeal. John fled into the woods when the attack on the camp began and remained there until he thought it was safe to come out. Eu-kosh-nu, a friendly Dakota, spotted the boy back at the camp and tried to protect him by escorting John across the lake and then sending him off on his own. When he discovered Dakotas trailing him, however, Eu-kosh-nu caught up with the boy and hid him in his own tipi. Later that same day John and Eu-kosh-nu's son walked to the lake where another Indian named Hut-te-ste-mi spotted the young white man, shot him with a pistol, and then ran away. When the Indian boy told his father that John had been wounded, an angry Eu-kosh-nu set out to kill the attacker. John talked him out of it and Eu-kosh-nu settled for smashing

27 McConkey, *Dakota War Whoop*, 97-8; Tolzmann, ed., *Outbreak and Massacre*, 49; Newson, *Pen Pictures of St. Paul*, 583; Bryant and Murch, *Great Massacre*, 150-52, 381-88.

Hut-te-ste-mi's pistol with his hatchet. Now, however, Eu-kosh-nu's own life, as well as his son's, was in danger. This time he hid John in his cousin's tipi, where they removed the pistol ball from his side and cared for him.[28]

*   *   *

By Thursday, August 21, the outbreak had spread as far as Lake Shetek in the south, Monongalia County in the north, and Big Stone Lake in the west. The first murders occurred at Acton in Meeker County. There were no additional wholesale killings there for several days, but most of the settlers fled east anyway, just as those living in the counties farther west had done.

George C. Whitcomb, whom Island Cloud visited on Saturday the 16th, was in Forest City the following day when the news of the uprising arrived. He returned to his house on Lake Minnie Belle to tell his family he was going to St. Paul to seek help. Whitcomb drove his horse and buggy as fast as he dared southeast to Carver on the Minnesota River, commandeered a steamer to St. Paul, and arrived there two days later—just hours after Private Sturgis arrived with news from Fort Ridgely. Confirmations of killings from both northwest and southwest indicated the widespread nature of the uprising. After a quick meeting with Governor Ramsey, Adjutant General Oscar Malmros authorized Whitcomb to take 75 "Rifle Muskets" and 75 "Accoutrements" for the settlers to use in defense of Meeker County.

Now an acting captain, Whitcomb moved upriver to Shakopee, impressed horses and wagons, and drove to Hutchinson. When the concerned citizens there implored him to share his arms, he left 31 muskets and 1,000 cartridges and continued on. When he reached Forest City he raised a company of 60 men, but since he had given away 31 weapons, he only had 44 left to arm his men. "This scarcity of arms was complained of in all regions of the State, and the extent to which it prevailed was truly remarkable and astonishing," Adjutant General Malmros lamented, "as it was alarming to the settlers upon commencement of hostilities." How could so many citizens "located even in

---

28 McConkey, *Dakota War Whoop*, 316-317. Schmerch stayed with the Indians until September of 1863, and was probably the last of the captives to be freed.

the very frontier settlements . . . [be] destitute of any species of fire arms." He concluded that one obvious reason was "the security felt by the people."[29]

According to Col. Lucius F. Hubbard of the 5th Minnesota, "The majority of the settlers were unaccustomed to fire-arms and had none." The majority of those attacked were Germans, Swedes, and Norwegians, many or most of whom grew up under different gun-ownership traditions. Their protein came from crops and domesticated animals, not from hunting wild game. The majority of families attacked at Lake Shetek, however, arrived with an "English" heritage and tradition. These eight families (34 people) possessed three squirrel rifles and two shotguns—fewer than one gun per family. Another "English" group at Beaver Creek consisted of six families (27 people) and possessed but two muzzle-loading rifles and three shotguns that belonged to the Dakotas. Put another way, only one family out of three owned a firearm. The fact that the Minnesota settlers were not well-armed, explained Malmros, tended to "intensify the alarm and terror" even when the attacking Indians were substantially inferior in numbers. According to the Dakotas, the settlers were "as easy to kill as sheep." Armed or otherwise, there is no evidence that the majority of Dakotas harbored any special hatred for the "bad talkers" or "Dutchmen." They killed Germans, Swedes, Norwegians, Welsh, English, and Americans without discrimination.

When the tide turned and the whites got the upper hand, they too would exercise a similar non-discrimination policy toward all bands of Sioux.[30]

29 Elizabeth Whitcomb interview, Microfilm Reel 3, Dakota Conflict, Minnesota Historical Society; Malmros, *Perspectives on the Sioux War*, 50-51, 114. The lack of weapons may seem surprising given the cherished American myth of armed pioneers defending themselves on the cutting edge of the frontier. The ubiquitous firearms of frontier lore, or lack thereof, is still debated in the public forum in the 21st Century. Michael Bellesiles, in his 2001 book *Arming America*, argued that guns were scarce in early America, Americans were never well-armed, and most were uninterested in owning guns. Gun ownership was just an "invented tradition," concocted by historians and the media, and it was not until the Civil War that Americans began to get guns in significant numbers. It was a powerful declaration, but other researchers found as much evidence to prove the opposite. Clayton Cramer, in his 2006 book *Armed America*, claimed Bellesiles was deceptive and showed that Americans on the frontier did have plenty of guns, that there were laws requiring gun ownership, and gun violence may have been higher in Colonial days than today. It was a case of "dueling quotations," where historians' political leanings influenced their interpretations. Bellesiles, *Arming America*, 5, 14-15, 109, 295, 306, 428; Cramer, *Armed America*, x, xiv, 16, 29, 78.

30 Malmros, *Perspectives on the Sioux War*, 51; Hubbard and Holcombe, *Minnesota in Three Centuries*, III, 390.

C hapter 15

"If the Indians get over the barricade . . .
prepare to defend the women and children."

Second Battle of Fort Ridgely

Berating the civilians ~ Digging a well ~ Ramsey asks for help ~ Similar tactics used on both sides
~ The attack goes awry ~ Assault from the southwest ~ The artillery saves the day ~ White and
Indian casualties

A fter all they had endured, perhaps what the exhausted defenders of Fort Ridgely most needed was a good night's rest. When darkness brought an end to the fight on Wednesday, scattered shots, noises in the night, and the rescue of a half-crazed woman made for long sleepless hours. The morning of the 21st revealed a low gray rain-laden sky. Indians were moving down the Minnesota Valley and the soldiers assumed they were on their way to attack New Ulm. The men spent the day improving the barricades, providing more protection for O'Shea's gun at the southwest corner, and put Sergeant Bishop in charge of another field piece, in reserve, on the parade ground. The last two guns were loaded in case a last stand was necessary, but there were not enough crews to man them. All this activity notwithstanding, Pvt. Oscar Wall believed "the day passed uneventfully."[1]

The day wasn't so uneventful for others. Ezmon Earle slept fitfully and in the morning Lieutenant Sheehan ordered his company to assemble on the parade ground. Once Joe De Camp arranged them in single rank, Sheehan

---

1 Curtiss-Wedge, *History of Renville County*, I, 627-28; Wall, *Recollections of the Sioux Massacre*, 98-99.

"proceeded to make us a speech in which he called us all the mean names such as cowards and sneaks, etc. that he could think of," remembered Ezmon. "I was surprised for I was not aware of sneaking, but I afterward learned that many of them had deserted their posts and gone upstairs with the women and children." The lieutenant concluded his "harangue" by telling De Camp "to pick out 10 of his men, if he had so many in his company of scrubs, and detail them to go on picket duty to relieve his men."

De Camp began his task at the right end of the line by asking the first man if he could go on duty for two hours. He answered "no" and gave his excuse. De Camp asked the second man. The answer was the same, but the excuse that he had "no cartridge box" was different. The third man offered yet another excuse. When De Camp reached Ezmon, the fourth in line, the 17-year-old "was ashamed of the company" and no longer blamed Sheehan for the language he had used. "I think I would have volunteered to go if I had known I would get hurt," he admitted. When De Camp asked him, Ezmon answered loudly, "Yes, sir!"

Ezmon performed picket duty on a knoll one-quarter mile northwest of the fort with other pickets placed at 100-yard intervals. By day's end Ezmon decided he no longer wanted to be in the citizens' company. He asked Company C Sgt. Frank A. Blackmer if he could transfer to his squad, but the sergeant had no authorization to allow him to do so, and he could not get extra rations to feed him. Another soldier spoke out in favor of the transfer, urging Blackmer to "Take him in sergeant if you can for he is the only citizen I have seen that is worth a d—n." Another offered to "divide rations with him." In this manner, Ezmon was "adopted" by the squad.

Sutler Randall, who was in charge of the water supply, guided a wagon guarded by two lines of soldiers down to the springs to load the barrels. There, recalled Private McFall, they discovered that the Indians "had destroyed the tank at the spring which flowed from the bank of the river and poisoned the water." The wagon and soldiers traveled to a secondary spring in the northern ravine, where "things were found in the same condition." When Randall reported the distressing news to Sheehan, the lieutenant sought a dozen willing men to dig a well on the parade ground. Private McFall had the same opinion of the civilians as did Sheehan. "There was about 30 citizens in the fort that had done good effective work and fought bravely," explained the private, "all the rest were a curse and a hindrance and still some of them are drawing a pension from the State for bravery." Sheehan found his volunteers, however, who excavated a hole big enough for six men to work in while the remaining six hauled the dirt out with ropes and buckets. "The well was completed about 2:30 a.m. on the morning of the 22nd so they [the Dakotas] were failed in their purpose," gloated McFall.[2]

The besieged were digging the well and preparing for the next attack when the telegraph lines running between Minnesota and Washington D.C. finally began to buzz. Governor Ramsey made a proclamation to the people of Minnesota on August 21: "The Sioux Indians upon our western frontier have risen in large bodies, attacked the settlements, and are murdering men, women, and children. The rising appears concerted and extends from Fort Ripley to the southern boundary of the state." Ramsey called upon the militia to take horses, arms, and subsistence and report to Colonel Sibley, who was then moving up the Minnesota River, and appealed for the people to stay and fight rather than flee.

That same day, Ramsey telegraphed much the same message to Secretary of War Edwin Stanton. He followed up the message with another offering more details supplied by Agent Galbraith and Lieutenant Gere. He had organized an expedition under Colonel Sibley using four companies of the 6th Minnesota, just then being formed, reported the governor, who went on to implore Stanton for additional help. Minnesota's Secretary of State James H. Baker wired Assistant Secretary of War C. P. Wolcott: "A most frightful insurrection of Indians has broken out along our whole frontier. Men, women, and children are indiscriminately murdered; evidently the result of a deep-laid plan. . . . It is useless. Cannot you authorize me to raise 1,000 mounted men for the special service?"

"Send the Third Regiment Minnesota Volunteers against the Indians on the frontier of Minnesota," Gen. Henry W. Halleck ordered the following day. The entire Minnesota regiment had surrendered in July to Confederate forces near Murfreesboro, Tennessee, but instead of heading for a prison camp was promptly paroled and sent to St. Louis, where the Minnesotans became available for service. By the terms of their exchange they could not fight Confederates, but nothing said they could not be used against the Indians. Still, it would take weeks before they would be in the Minnesota Valley ready to fight.

---

2 Ezmon Earle reminiscences, Microfilm Reel 1, Dakota Conflict, Minnesota Historical Society; Orlando McFall narrative, Microfilm Reel 2, Dakota Conflict, Minnesota Historical Society. Historians Curtiss-Wedge and Folwell both incorrectly said that no well was dug within the fort until 1896.

Until then Ramsey and Sibley would have to make do with militia and several companies of Regulars.[3]

Once the fort's well was dug and flowing in the pre-dawn of Friday the 22nd, the men enjoyed a few hours of rest until muster at daybreak. Joe Coursolle left to visit his wife Jane and the baby in the barracks. His infant had been getting sicker by the hour and no one seemed to know what to do. When he arrived, Jane led him to a corner of the room and pulled back a blanket. "Our baby Joe had closed his eyes forever," lamented Coursolle.

Despite his overwhelming sadness there was no time to mourn. Joe obtained a small covered box from the carpenter, dug a small grave in the post cemetery, and put the box in the hole. Next, he wrapped his son in the blanket, carried him to the grave, and placed him inside. Only Joe, Jane, and Chaplain Joshua Sweet attended the service. They were finishing when distant shots rang out and the trio ran to the fort.

The Dakotas were back.[4]

*   *   *

This time the Dakotas arrived at Fort Ridgely with twice the number of warriors they fielded in the first fight. Andrew Good Thunder (47), a Mdewakanton who converted to Christianity in 1861, counted 800 warriors as they filed past him on the way to the fort. Lightning Blanket agreed with that figure. There were no women and children, but a number of older boys came along to cook, keep camp, and tend the horses. Little Crow rode to the battle in style in a buggy driven by David Faribault, while Antoine J. Campbell accompanied him in case it was necessary to communicate with the whites. Before the first battle the Indians had stopped to eat and prepare themselves at Three Mile Creek. This time there would be no stop to eat anything because each warrior carried his own food in his "legging sash" and ate when they could during the fighting. Private McFall later claimed "the Indians done their fighting under different tactics from what they did on the 20th," but Lightning Blanket said the plan of attack was the same as in the first battle—"three big shots from the north, followed by a rush of the men on the east, south and west

3   *Official Records*, 13, 590-91; *Minnesota in the Civil and Indian Wars*, I, 157-58, and II, 194-95.

4   Joseph Coursolle story, Microfilm Reel 1, Dakota Conflict, Minnesota Historical Society.

all at the same time." Little Crow gave strict orders to follow the plan and make sure the attack was coordinated.[5]

Employing the same basic plan that had not worked the first time demonstrated a lack of tactical imagination, but in fairness to the Dakotas, their options to do otherwise were rather limited. A favorite tactic used by the western tribes was to draw out their potential victims on a ruse to separate them from the main body or defenses, and then attack with overwhelming numbers. There was little chance the fort's defenders would fall for anything like that, so if the Dakotas wanted Ridgely they would have to go in and take it, and the only way to do that was to attack in the same basic manner. Using the same plan twice may not have worked even with double the number of attackers, but its chance of success was even lower when the attack signal was fouled up once again. This time it was because Eliphalet W. Richardson inadvertently gave up his life, and in turn may have saved the fort.

Richardson, a resident of Glencoe in McLeod County, felt an overwhelming need to go to Fort Ridgely to learn firsthand what was happening. He borrowed a fast horse from Hiram Pettyjohn and left early on August 22 for the 40-mile ride. He left Glencoe about the same time the Dakotas left Little Crow's village to surround the fort, much as they had on Wednesday. The extra 400 warriors were mostly from the Sisseton and Wahpeton tribes who had finally reached the Lower Agency, plus the Winnebago chief Little Priest (Hoonkhoonokaw) with a dozen of his warriors who had been at the ambush at Redwood Ferry and at the first fight at New Ulm. Although Little Crow was present, Big Eagle claimed "he did not take a very active part in the fight." According to Big Eagle, the main leaders that day were The Thief (Wamanonsa) and Mankato (Blue Earth), both of whom had gone to Washington in 1858 to sign the prevailing peace treaty.[6]

Some of the Dakotas, as well as several historians of the uprising, believed that capturing the fort was of overriding importance to the Indian cause. "We went down determined to take the fort, for we knew it was of the greatest importance to us to have it," explained Big Eagle. "If we could take it we would soon have the whole Minnesota Valley." In fact, the loss of Ridgely would have not made any difference in the long run because the Dakotas were too few, too

5   Anderson, *Little Crow*,145; Orlando McFall narrative, Microfilm Reel 2, Dakota Conflict, Minnesota Historical Society; Anderson and Woolworth, *Through Dakota Eyes*, 68, 148, 156.

6   Anderson and Woolworth, *Through Dakota Eyes*, 148-49, Dahlin, *Dakota Uprising Victims*, 83.

divided, and faced too many whites who were even then gathering an overwhelming force of soldiers and civilians to oppose them. Few if any of the Indians fully understood this at the time, however, so the Dakotas circled the fort about noon on Friday with the intention of capturing it.

As they had two days before, Medicine Bottle's men assumed a position on the north and northeast sides of the fort. Big Eagle's men took position on the south side. (Map I) Shortly before the predetermined three-shot signal that was to have announced the attack, Eliphalet Richardson rode into the Fort Creek ravine from the northeast. It was about 1:00 p.m. Several Indians saw him and one, said to be Wahehna, shot him off his horse. The warrior ran toward the wounded rider, who struggled to get away. Two more shots rang out and Richardson was dead.[7]

This was the same gunfire Coursolle and his wife heard in the cemetery during the burial of their son. Lightning Blanket later claimed only some of the warriors heard the shots and burst from their hiding places to attack; others were not even in position to do so. "By the time the others had commenced, the big guns were fired at them," he continued, and they "ran back under the hill, by this time all were shooting, most all of us being hid." Although Lightning Blanket believed there were "many more soldiers than were there [in] the first attack," he was mistaken. The fort had not been reinforced. Once again the Indian attack was uncoordinated, and once again the defenders were able to fight on one front at a time.[8]

The soldiers were in nearly the same positions they held on Wednesday, only this time they had a better feel for the terrain and the distances to the trees and ravines. Lieutenant Sheehan set up squads with sergeants in command and defined specific areas for each group to defend. Ezmon Earle had hoped to remain in Sergeant Blackmer's squad, which took up a position outside the fort's eastern side, but he was ordered to return to De Camp's citizen company deployed behind the log huts in the north. The northern ravine allowed the Dakotas to approach unseen to within 50 yards of the fort, so "we had to look sharp," said Ezmon. When the Indians revealed themselves and began firing into the fort, De Camp held his Sharps rifle high and walked slowly along his

---

7   Dahlin, *Dakota Uprising Victims*, 83; Heard, *History of the Sioux War*, 281. At the trials David Faribault testified that Wahehna told him he had shot Richardson as he tried to ride in to the fort. Wahehna denied it, saying the witnesses "lied on him," but he was hanged nevertheless.

8   Anderson and Woolworth, *Through Dakota Eyes*, 156-57.

line until he reached the center. There, he called out, "Boys, I am ordered to shoot the first man who leaves his post without orders, and I'll do it by God!"

A short time later Lieutenant Sheehan arrived and told De Camp to send four men to the other side of the parade ground. De Camp selected the four closest to him, including Ezmon, and the lieutenant ordered them to double-quick across the bullet-swept field. The men were not moving fast enough to satisfy Sheehan, who turned and yelled, "G-d d—m it, can't you run faster than that?" Ezmon, who was quite a sprinter, followed orders and sped past Sheehan. When he caught up, the officer ordered the teenager to take up a position on the south side east of the headquarters building "without even a spear of grass to hide behind. I could simply hug the ground and trust luck." Ezmon had only been there a short time before Sergeant Blackmer called him to return to his squad on the east side of Ridgely, where his defensive position was also out in the open and their "only protection was in shooting so well that the Indians would not dare expose themselves long enough to take good aim."

The ground in front of Blackmer's squad consisted of rolling little hills and gullies filled with tall grass, which the Dakotas infiltrated wherever the ground gave them an advantage to do so. Many of them camouflaged their heads with "turbans of grass and wild flowers." One warrior worked his way in fairly close, recalled Ezmon, and "seemed to have a particular desire to pink me." After several bullets zipped near him, Ezmon rose up on one knee to pick off the pesky warrior. Another Dakota saw his chance and fired, his bullet smashing Ezmon's third finger of his right hand and damaging the gunstock. Because of the adrenaline of battle Ezmon didn't even realize he had been hit. When he stood to get a better shot, another soldier pulled him to the ground and told him he had been hit. "I was bleeding considerably and the bone was broken," recalled Ezmon, "yet it hadn't begun to pain me."

Blackmer sent the boy to Dr. Muller to have the wound dressed and he resumed his place on the line, but by then "the feeling returned and the pain was terrific." When the pain and involuntary nerve spasms jerked his hand so much that Ezmon could no longer hold his gun, Blackmer sent him to a nearby building to keep watch. Once in the building Ezmon took cover behind a door, but his hand was hurting so much he could barely endure the pain. He stepped out intent on seeking help when a volley of bullets tore into the door and made it look "like the top of a pepper box." This time the surgeon dressed the wound with white powder that Ezmon assumed was morphine because it relieved the pain considerably. Now Sergeant Blackmer shifted Ezmon to a different location with orders to watch for any suspicious movements in that direction.

Shortly after the sergeant saw Ezmon off, recalled Private McFall, a Dakota "shot [Blackmer] through the face, his double teeth all knocked out and his tonque cut ¾ off."[9]

Some of the initial Indian attacks worked their way close to the buildings, fueling the courage of some of the Dakota warriors. "One big brave came straight at me," remembered Joe Coursolle, who burned inside with the thought that perhaps this was one of the Indians who had captured his girls. Joe took careful aim and shouted, "Take that!" as he fired. However, Joe conceded, "I am not sure I hit him."

The Dakotas approaching from the northeast were once again met with a steady fire delivered by Lt. Thomas Gere's Company B men and John Whipple's artillery battery. Sergeant James McGrew also replayed his role by running his gun out from the northwest corner, turning it to face east, and enfilading the ragged Dakota line of attack. "The first wave of charging Sioux couldn't face our fire," Coursolle boasted. "They broke and ran pell-mell back to the forest." Another attack was launched, and it also failed. After that, explained Private McFall, "most of the fighting was done from long range and from treetops. The Indians were very loath to show themselves. The lesson taught them on the 20th," he concluded, "had its effect." Unable to penetrate the fort, the Indians reverted to their former tactic of shooting fire arrows into the roofs, but the rain-soaked structures refused to burn. After a few hours when ammunition began to run low, the Ridgely defenders slowed their rate of fire.

After the first attack on the fort two days earlier, Margaret Hern and Elizabeth M. Dunn spent hours gathering a wash basin full of spent bullets and balls. The next day (Thursday) Julia Sweet joined them in the magazine where, in their stocking feet, the trio of ladies worked to make cartridges. They also melted some of the spent bullets and used molds to make new ones. About 2,000 extra rounds of ammunition were found at the fort, but the caliber was too large for the available weaponry so the women carefully shaved the balls to fit the barrels. Private McFall avowed "there never was a nobler band of heroines lived than those women were." Blacksmith John Resoft cut nail rods into short pieces to use as bullets and the screaming whistle they produced

---

9   Wall, *Recollections of the Sioux Massacre*, 100; Ezmon Earle reminiscences, Microfilm Reel 1, Dakota Conflict, Minnesota Historical Society; Orlando McFall narrative, Microfilm Reel 2, Dakota Conflict, Minnesota Historical Society.

when fired unnerved the Dakotas as much as their war whoops spooked the whites.[10]

According to at least one account, when the ammunition began running low and more canister shot was needed for the artillery, someone came up with the idea of using the $71,000 in gold buried under the floor in the commissary. "The Indians wanted their payment," explained one witness, so why not put "the gold in the cannons and give it to them that way." The proposition was rejected.[11]

The best hope to keep the fort in white hands was to keep the Indians at long range. "It was a battle on the part of the garrison to prevent a charge by the savages, which, had it been made, could hardly have failed . . . to result in the destruction of the garrison and the consequent horrible massacre of its 300 refugees," admitted Lieutenant Gere. He was almost certainly correct. A united mass attack would have put the Indians inside the fort and resulted in a hand-to-hand fight, where the Dakota numbers and individual fighting skills would have carried the day.

Although he was nominally an Episcopalian, Andrew Good Thunder fought with the Dakotas, though he and his wife Snana would later help some of the white captives. Some of the Indians managed to take possession of the sutler's store and the government stable—a dangerous foothold much too close for comfort. From those locations Dakota bullets peppered the officers' quarters and headquarters building at the southwest corner. George Quinn (Wakandayamani or The Spirit that Rattles as It Walks) recalled seeing Good Thunder, fighting near the stables, shoot at some whites who were shooting at him from the windows of a building on the fort's west side. Good Thunder, boasted Big Eagle, "acted very bravely in the fight," by running close to the fort, getting into the stables, and bringing out a good horse.[12]

When the Dakotas got possession of the buildings they seemed to realize for the first time that the southwest ravine offered the best and closest point from which to assault the fort. Fire slackened a bit in the north and east as

10 Joseph Coursolle story, Microfilm Reel 1, Dakota Conflict, Minnesota Historical Society; *Minnesota in the Civil and Indian Wars*, II, 186; Orlando McFall narrative, Microfilm Reel 2, Dakota Conflict, Minnesota Historical Society; Morris, *Old Rail Fence Corners*, 151.

11 Curtiss-Wedge, *History of Renville County*, I, 644.

12 Wall, Recollections of the Sioux Massacre, 105; Anderson and Woolworth, *Through Dakota Eyes*, 148, 157.

Dakotas changed positions. They had to make a wide detour in the northwest to stay out of range of McGrew's gun, but their shift on the open prairie was clearly visible to the defenders. Who ordered or suggested the move is unknown. Little Crow was nominally in charge, but reports say he was urging the attack in the northeast ravine when a shell from Whipple's gun exploded near his head, knocked him down, and possibly fractured his skull. If so, then Little Crow was *hors de combat* and one or more of the other chiefs made the decision.[13]

When McGrew reported the move to Sergeant Jones, they decided to bring out the 24-pounder howitzer for some added firepower. They deployed the piece south of the commissary building and threw a few shells into the area to the west where the Dakotas appeared to be concentrating, though with little effect.[14] The volume of fire against Dennis O'Shea's battery coming from the stables and sutler's store became "so hot and accurate as to splinter almost every linear foot of timber along the top of his barricades," reported one witness. The men stood by their gun, cutting their fuses as short as possible in an effort to return an effective fire. Indian bullets tore through one building, killing civilian refugee Joseph Vanosse. Jones and O'Shea swung their guns toward the sutler's store and stables and opened fire, setting both buildings ablaze. Fighting from within the embattled stables, Mixed-blood George Quinn watched as Good Thunder stole a horse and rode away. He decided he wanted one as well. "As I was leading it out a shell burst in the stable near me and the horse sprang over me and got away, knocking me down." Quinn was so angry he took out his frustration by shooting a mule. Margaret Hern saw the

---

13 *Minnesota in the Civil and Indian Wars*, II, 185; Hubbard and Holcombe, *Minnesota in Three Centuries*, III, 337.

14 Soldiers and some historians claim the rounds killed and wounded many Indians. As the story goes, women and children gathered in large numbers cooking and keeping camp a mile or so southwest of McGrew's 24-pound gun, whose shells dropped in their midst. The slaughter shocked the warriors, who believed that white soldiers did not make war on women and children. In reality, the short bombardment produced no visible effects. There were no civilians available to witness where the shells fell, and the Dakotas never made such graphic claims. The range of a 24-pounder howitzer was about ¾ of a mile (Thomas, Cannons, 31). The Dakotas would not have brought their women and children up so close to the fort during the battle, and they said they did not—only some of the older boys helped run the camp, which was far out of range. There was no one cooking, as the warriors carried their own food. Some histories that repeat the story are: *Minnesota in the Civil and Indian Wars*, II, 185; Curtiss-Wedge, *History of Renville County*, I, 630; Hubbard and Holcombe, *Minnesota in Three Centuries*, III, 337-38; Wall, *Recollections of the Sioux Massacre*, 102.

explosion of the shell that knocked Quinn down. The Indians swarmed into "a large mule barn," she said. Sergeant Jones' cannon fired, "blowing up the barn and setting the hay on fire. The air was full of legs, arms, and bodies, which fell back into the flames. We were not allowed to look out," Margaret added, "but I stood at the window all the time and saw this."[15]

A number of Renville Rangers were posted in the south around the batteries. It was about 4:00 p.m. when some of them recalled hearing a loud voice shouting instructions to the warriors. Some believed it was Little Crow, but since he had probably been knocked out of the fight, the man they heard was likely Mankato. One of the Rangers hurried over to Sergeant Jones and told him that he believed he understood what was being planned: the warriors, he explained, were concentrating down in the ravine that pointed like a spear toward the southwest corner of the fort, its head only 150 yards from O'Shea's battery. In response, Jones ordered McGrew to wheel the 24-pounder south while Sergeant Bishop rolled his reserve piece out to the southeast corner and faced it southwest. The pieces were double-shotted with canister, an anti-personnel round filled with small iron balls that exploded like a giant shotgun shell.

The Ranger was right. Within a few minutes of his warning Dakotas charged out of the ravine like a giant arrow aiming for the southwest corner of Fort Ridgely. It was a truly frightening sight. "You have no arms!" Jones shouted to the civilians on the gun crew. "If the Indians get over the barricade, run for the one door of the barracks that has been left open, and prepare to defend the women and children." Satisfied that they understood, Jones addressed the men in the service: "We are soldiers. It is our duty to stick by the gun; that is what we are here for. Fire the gun until the Indians reach it, and then spike it with a file."

The barricade Jones referred to was built of cordwood "some six or seven lengths wide, some hundred feet long, and about four feet high," recalled the Rieke brothers. "The Indians gained this barricade." O'Shea and his gunners worked their piece only 60 steps behind the overrun barricade. The rangers fell back shooting as the Dakotas poured over the structure. Once the rangers were clear, one of O'Shea's artillerists yanked the lanyard and the gun fired into the screaming Dakotas; McGrew's and Bishop's pieces followed suit.

15 *Minnesota in the Civil and Indian Wars*, II, 185; Curtiss-Wedge, *History of Renville County*, I, 629, 642; Anderson and Woolworth, *Through Dakota Eyes*, 157; Morris, *Old Rail Fence Corners*, 151-52.

Artillery may have saved the day at Ridgely and the gunners didn't have to spike their guns. The blasts of canister and solid volume of musketry killed and wounded many of the Indians cresting the wall. The rest turned and fled. Jones rolled his gun forward while Bishop and McGrew adjusted the range on their respective pieces to fire into the fleeing Dakotas all the way back to the ravine. Once the barricade was clear the Rangers ran back to the stacked wood and opened fire into the backs of the fleeing Indians, shouting defiantly as they did so, "Come on! We are ready for you!" Feeling bold about their chances, Jones and O'Shea rolled their piece out far enough so they could depress the barrel and rake the length of the ravine. The last discharge ripped the grass roots and killed and maimed perhaps as many as a dozen Dakotas. "The shells tore great holes in the ranks of the warriors and the crashing boom of the twenty-four pounder rumbled and echoed up and down the river bluffs," recalled Joe Coursolle. "The Indians skedaddled and the fighting was over." According to McFall, "in 20 minutes from the firing of this gun there wasn't an Indian to be seen."[16]

The private's claim was not quite accurate. From her perch at an upper window in the barracks, Margaret Hern watched in horror as "Indians with grass and flowers bound on their heads creep[ed] like snakes up to the fort," using the cover of the smoke from the muskets, cannons, and burning buildings to mask their approach. The warriors kept the fort under fire, but decided against launching any more assaults. Ezmon Earle believed the Indians had been badly hurt. During a lull in the firing, one of the Renville Rangers reported hearing a Dakota call out, "Come away or they'll kill us all." According to Lightning Blanket, the sun was getting low and "after we saw the men on the south and west driven back by the big guns," they decided to break off the fight. Rebuffed on two separate days of fighting, the Indians left the area by going around the northwest side of the fort.

Lieutenant Gere thought that the attacks against the fort had lasted about five hours each. By 6:00 p.m. the Indians "drew off and gave us a little rest," reported Private McFall, but by 7:30 p.m. they were back, this time shooting more fire arrows into the roofs. The weather that day was warm and sunny, and by this time some of the roofs had dried enough to catch fire. Dozens of arrows

16 Orlando McFall narrative, Microfilm Reel 2, Dakota Conflict, Minnesota Historical Society; Wall, *Recollections of the Sioux Massacre*, 102-03; Curtiss-Wedge, *History of Renville County*, I, 630, 643; Joseph Coursolle story, Microfilm Reel 1, Dakota Conflict, Minnesota Historical Society. For some reason, McFall indicates this incident happened during the first battle.

plunked into the roofs. McFall witnessed an ingenious method for setting the buildings on fire. The Dakotas tied a string onto the arrow shaft about four inches from the head with "a piece of punk," also about four inches long, secured to the string. The flammable "punk" was fired before the arrow was shot, and when the arrow stuck, the string was just long enough to allow the burning material to rest on the roof. Fortunately, only one arrow successfully landed and caught the roof on fire. About 15 men went up into the attic of the barracks with axes and hammers and found "one place that had ignited and burned a hole about as large as a bushel." When the Indians saw this, explained McFall, they began "one of those blood-freezing (hair stand on end) infernal yells that I imagine I can hear now as I write." The men doused the flames and spent a long and anxious time searching for the tips of arrowheads that had penetrated the wood. When one was spotted, a man would pound it from inside with a hammer or club to dislodge the missile so it would slide off the roof and onto the ground. Once the fighting ended, the defenders cut and placed sod and dirt from the well about two inches deep onto the roofs. Fire arrows would no longer be an issue.[17]

The Dakotas had shot their bolt. They would not attack Fort Ridgely again, although neither they nor the fort's defenders knew it at the time. The defenders spent another night making repairs, making bullets, trying to catch a few winks of sleep, and trying to clean up for the next round of fighting they assumed would begin the next morning. Trying to keep the fort clean when the latrines were not on the grounds and some 500 people were crammed into the small space for the past week was a hopeless task. "You can imagine the sanitary condition of all those people cooped up in that little fort," said Margaret Hern. "No words I know could describe it."

The hours of darkness ticked past slowly. "No mind can justly conceive of, or pen faithfully describe the mental and physical strain endured from this hour on by the garrison—a strain that burned as by a living fire, its burden into every soul," was how Private Wall dramatically described the passage of time. Many in the fort wondered why no one had arrived to help them. Several pleas for assistance had been dispatched, the first five long days earlier, but thus far there had been no response. "The world without was dead to the beleaguered Fort,"

17 Morris, *Old Rail Fence Corners*, 152; Ezmon Earle reminiscences, Microfilm Reel 1, Dakota Conflict, Minnesota Historical Society; Anderson and Woolworth, *Through Dakota Eyes*, 157; Gere, "Uncle Sam's Army," Brown County Historical Society; Orlando McFall narrative, Microfilm Reel 2, Dakota Conflict, Minnesota Historical Society.

complained Wall, who must have known as well as anyone that the defenders were nearly out of ammunition. Perhaps the soldiers could sneak out at night and fight their way to safety, he thought, but they could not abandon, nor take with them, some 300 refugees. "If these must perish," he concluded, "then the soldiers must perish with them." Sunrise that Saturday was at 5:30 a.m. "Have you ever been in great danger where all was darkness where that danger was?" Margaret Hern later asked rhetorically. "If so, you will know what an everlasting blessing that daylight was."[18]

Despite the ferocity of the attack, Fort Ridgely's defenders suffered fewer casualties on the second day of battle than they had on the first. The only person killed was civilian Joseph Vanosse. Four soldiers of Company C were wounded: Pvts. Peter E. Harris, A. J. Luther, Isaac Shortledge, and Sgt. Frank Blackmer. Ezmon Earle, also a civilian, was wounded, as were Renville Rangers Joseph Robinette, Cyprian Le Clair, and Joseph Fortier, the latter for a second time. The total casualties for both fights amounted to three killed, 15 wounded, and one (Henry Rieke) died of other causes.[19]

Dakota casualties are impossible to quantity with any precision. Lieutenant Gere estimated their killed and wounded at 100, while four Dakotas many years later recalled that only two warriors had been hit. Both estimates are implausible. "The cannons disturbed us greatly, but did not hurt many," reported Big Eagle. "We did not have many Indians killed." Contrary to what many of the white defenders claimed, Big Eagle dismissed the idea of removing the fallen. "We seldom carried off our dead," he explained. "We usually buried them in a secluded place on the battle-field when we could. We always tried to carry away the wounded."

These low estimates of Indian losses are directly challenged by white eyewitnesses who shot them down, watched as the artillery pieces tore them apart at the barricade and on the way back to the ravine, and who counted bodies after the fighting stopped. Orlando McFall recalled that "the boys went down on the bottom about 70 rods [350 yards] from the fort next day and found 16 dead braves covered up with brush and two more covered up under about

---

18 Morris, *Old Rail Fence Corners*, 148, 152; Wall, *Recollections of the Sioux Massacre*, 104.

19 *Minnesota in the Civil and Indian Wars*, II, 193a-193b. Most of the casualty compilations differ. This is the best estimate from several sources, including depredation claims. It is noteworthy that in the two "battles" at Fort Ridgely, the whites lost less than in many other encounters such as at Milford, Beaver Creek, Lake Shetek, Middle Creek, Sacred Heart, or West Lake.

four inches of earth."[20] After the post was relieved on August 27, Oscar Wall and John McCole walked into the river valley more than one-quarter of a mile southwest of the fort and found a small abandoned dug-out "in which were seven dead warriors, partially concealed by earth that had been dug from the overhanging embankment to cover them." Two more bodies were found in the underbrush near the dug-out. Wall believed that Indian losses in dead were ten times higher than they reported. He was incensed that a "chronicler" (Isaac Heard) of the event only "convert[ed] tragedy into farce-comedy when he sums up the results of the defenders of the frontier by stating seriously that the total number of Indians killed by troops and settlers during the massacre, from August 18th, exclusive of the Battle of Wood Lake, was just twenty-one."[21]

Regardless of the number of casualties they suffered, the Dakotas pulled back on Friday evening. They reached Three Mile Creek about dark and stopped there to cook some beef. Little Crow addressed his people, telling them they should not expect any additional warriors, and so would have to fight with what they had. Lightning Blanket claimed a discussion followed, with some warriors demanding a renewal of the attack against the fort in the morning before an advance against New Ulm. Others wanted to move straight to New Ulm, no doubt realizing they would not have to face artillery there. Once they took the town, argued these warriors, they could return and take the fort. Some were afraid soldiers would reach New Ulm first and make it hard or impossible for them to capture it. Little Crow argued it would be best to go to New Ulm immediately, before the sun rose and revealed their location. As usual, the discussion rippled with dissension. Little Crow, recalled Lightning Blanket, "was angry and said he would take the ones who wanted to go and capture New Ulm. He left the camp that night and started for New Ulm with part of the men," about 400 of them. The rest of the warriors remained in camp that night and returned to their villages near Redwood Agency the next morning.[22]

20 Folwell, *History of Minnesota*, II, 132; Anderson and Woolworth, *Through Dakota Eyes*, 149; Orlando McFall narrative, Microfilm Reel 2, Dakota Conflict, Minnesota Historical Society.

21 Wall, *Recollections of the Sioux Massacre*, 153-55; Tolzmann, ed., *Outbreak and Massacre*, 107-08. Heard, *History of the Sioux War*, 248, claimed that just two Indians died in the battles at Fort Ridgely as did researcher Marion Satterlee, in Tolzmann, *Outbreak and Massacre*, 107, who placed Indian losses at just two warriors killed at Fort Ridgely. Michno, *Encyclopedia of Indian Wars*, 353, in a study of Western Indian wars from 1850 to 1890, found that generally speaking, Indian casualties exceeded white casualties 69% to 31%.

22 Anderson and Woolworth, *Through Dakota Eyes*, 157.

The large concentration of Dakotas was coming apart. New Ulm, however, was about to experience a second attack with four times the number of Indians that had tested the town's defenses on Tuesday.

C hapter 16

"Then began one of the wildest scenes of frontier warfare."

Second Battle of New Ulm

Arrival of additional defenders ~ Flandrau takes over ~ Defense dispositions ~ Huey crosses the river ~ Flandrau leaves the barricades ~ Dakotas attack ~ Both sides burn the town ~ Death of Captain Dodd ~ Flandrau drives the Dakotas out of the lower town ~ Burning the windmill ~ Aaron Myers's experiences ~ Sunday attack ~ Rescue

A handful of civilian defenders and a timely thunderstorm saved New Ulm on August 19. Pickets took up positions that evening around the town and endured a long, damp, and cold miserable night. Frederick Fritsche didn't get any supper and was soaked to the bone, but he maintained his post until dawn. Fritsche and other pickets stationed on the west side near State Street began to make out something moving in the distance when the eastern sky changed from black to gray. (Map M) When someone on his right uttered the single word "Indians," several men ran back into town. Fritsche and a few others remained in place, and when the objects "came near enough to be seen plainly, they proved to be a herd of cattle." Fritsche didn't know the names of the men who ran, but concluded they were not some of the "brave men from Cottonwood" who stood with him.[1]

Advance squads of men under Henry A. Swift, William G. Hayden, Sheriff L. M. Boardman, and Aaron M. Bean had arrived to help defend the town on Tuesday, but the main force didn't appear until about ten that night. Charles E. Flandrau, who a contemporary described as "original, unique, picturesque,

---

1   Tolzmann, ed., *Brown County*, 13-14.

versatile, adventurous," and "illuminated by the light of an heroic spirit," brought in about 100 men. Flandrau selected William B. Dodd and Wolf H. Meyer to serve as his lieutenants. They left St. Peter about 1:00 p.m. and were joined by another 100 men from Le Sueur County led by Sheriff George M. Tousley. This combined force reached the Redstone Ferry about two miles downriver from New Ulm about 8:00 p.m. (Map N) It took another two hours to cross the river and move along the bottomland before they reached the town. New Ulm's commander during the Tuesday fight, Jacob Nix, recalled the joy in town when "the longed-for help from St. Peter" arrived. "Cheers and a hearty welcome greeted the brave men," he wrote. Nix was jealous of the praise heaped upon Flandrau for saving New Ulm (and also claimed that Flandrau didn't arrive until midnight).[2]

Nix, whose own brave efforts have been somewhat overlooked, had a point. According to one author, Flandrau was dubbed as the "'Savior of New Ulm' and the worker of a military miracle" who directed the fight "against overwhelming odds with off-the-cuff, intuitive brilliance." Flandrau's action in "galvanizing a panic-stricken community, under heavy siege, into an effective defense force is one of the great stories of the American frontier."[3] Much of this is simply hyperbole. The community wasn't panic-stricken when he arrived, nor was it under siege. And, Nix had already organized a defensive force that, under his steady hand drove back the first Dakota attack.

On Wednesday morning, Flandrau was chosen to command all the forces in town. He was not the first choice, however. Sheriff Roos designated William Dodd as commander, but his selection was opposed by a number of St. Peter men who claimed Dodd was "too careless with the lives of men." They called a meeting and, joined by the townsfolk, selected Flandrau. They did not trust Dodd, but the main reason for Flandrau's election was not because of his military expertise but because he had assisted many New Ulmers when they built their town. Flandrau gave them legal advice, facilitated their claims, and kept naturalization papers and a seal so he could take a declaration of anyone wanting to become a citizen to legally file for land. He also qualified many Germans for preemption, took many of them by steamboat down to Winona to enter their claims, paid for with the gold they entrusted him with, secured a post office, and often joined them in drinking some of the beer they so enjoyed

---

2   Folwell, *History of Minnesota*, II, 136; Nix, *Sioux Uprising*, 107.

3   Fridley, "Attorney at War," 116-17.

brewing. Flandrau was voted commander because of his "good ol' boy" connections.[4]

The units placed under Flandrau's command included: his own St. Peter Frontier Guards; Charles Roos's company of Brown County Militia; Louis Buggert's company of Brown County Militia; John Bellm's company of Minnesota Militia; and A. M. Bean's Nicollet County Guards. More men arrived in town during the next two days and were incorporated into the defensive arrangement, including: the St. Peter Guards under William Huey; the Mankato Company under Captain William Bierbauer; the South Bend Company under J. D. Zimmerman; and two companies of Le Sueur Tigers under Captains William Dellaughter and E. C. Saunders. The Lafayette Company under Fidel Diepolder was already organized and in New Ulm.

A company of 60 men under Capt. Theodore E. Potter arrived from Garden City, about 25 miles southeast of New Ulm. When some of the new arrivals voiced skepticism about the dire stories making the rounds, a visit paid to August Kiesling's blacksmith shop to view the bodies of the 11 men killed in the Leavenworth rescue party confirmed the uprising. The display of mutilated bodies, recalled one witness, was a "ghastly spectacle," the "remains spread out upon the floor, heads all scalped and some severed from the body, the arms and legs of some also chopped off . . . was enough to impress each one with the reality of the Indian outbreak, and many of the boys who had thought that fighting Indians would be a nice pastime began to look serious and wish themselves back home." It was, admitted Captain Potter, "a scene such as none of us had ever witnessed before." It made most of his men "anxious to return to the protection of their own homes at once."[5]

Estimates of the numbers of defenders in town ranged from as low as 325 to as many as 500. Regardless of the number, almost all of them were poorly armed. According to William Hayden, most of the firearms were short-ranged double-barrel shotguns, with only three or four rifles and one Sharps rifle available in all of New Ulm. These farmers and townsfolk were armed with only clubs, axes, or pitchforks. Few had any military training and even less discipline, and they had left families in jeopardy elsewhere but were entrusted to protect

4   Roos, "The Battles of New Ulm," Brown County Historical Society; Fridley, "Attorney at War," 120-21.

5   Hughes, *Welsh in Minnesota*, 77-79, 82; Buell, "Defense of New Ulm," 789-90, MHSC, Vol. 10, pt. 2; Potter, "Recollections," 439, 444.

from 1,200 to 1,500 women, children, and old men. They spent their days strengthening the defenses, appropriating key houses, and gathering supplies.

On Wednesday, the day after the first attack, Jacob Nix figured someone should go to Fort Ridgely and ask Sergeant Jones for artillery and ammunition. Young Xavier Zollner, who lived in West Newton Township, volunteered to make the journey. He reached the fort but was trapped and remained there during the first battle. He returned on Thursday with the news that if they wanted a cannon, they'd have to get it themselves. With enough on his plate to worry about, Flandrau did not follow up on the request.[6]

According to all indications, the Dakotas were nearby and closing on the town. Flandrau recalled that Friday as one of the most trying days of his life. He could not abandon the refugees to their fate, but Tousley's 140 men would not be available if the town was attacked, and the column itself might be jumped on the prairie and defeated in detail. Flandrau had one more worry weighing on his mind. Rumors reached New Ulm that the Winnebagoes were going to unite with the Dakotas and attack Mankato and South Bend. Some Winnebagoes had already participated in the fighting, and the proximity of their reservation to both towns made many defenders from those locales anxious about their families. As a result, about 75 men from the South Bend Company promptly marched home; the dozen who remained were incorporated into the Mankato Company.[7]

The Garden City Company also called it quits. When Flandrau refused to let them go, several simply deserted during the night. The next morning (Wednesday) Captain Potter argued with those who remained to stay put, but after what they had seen the Garden City men were convinced the Winnebagoes were knocking at their cabin doors. Flandrau ordered them to stay. When the men signed a petition and insisted on leaving Flandrau finally agreed, conceding that if they were that discontented "they would be of little use in an emergency." Potter was left with just 15 men.

The desire to abandon New Ulm for home also spread into the ranks of E. C. Saunders's Le Sueur Tigers. Brothers W. H. and Thomas Hazzard arrived in

---

6   It was on the following day, Friday, that the new commander of New Ulm sent the 140-man expedition under George Tousley (as described in Chapter 13) to secure the Whiton-Hough-Covell-Van Gilder refugees. Tousley's column returned to New Ulm about midnight.

7   Hughes, *Welsh in Minnesota*, 82; Tolzmann, ed., *Brown County*, 14; Buell, "Defense of New Ulm," 790-93, MHSC, Vol. 10, pt. 2. Hayden, "Account of the relief expedition," Microfilm Reel 2, Dakota Conflict, Minnesota Historical Society.

Minnesota from Delaware in 1859. They had farms on Rush River in Sibley County about six miles west of Le Sueur, but when they heard about the uprising they left their families forted up with a few neighbors and rode to St. Peter to enlist. By Friday they were more worried about their own families and less concerned about the families in New Ulm. As W. H. later wrote, "Then comes the thought to brother and myself . . . we had better go back to them, but we are reminded we cannot get out of town without a permit by the commander of the post." Early Saturday they approached Colonel Flandrau, who told them he wished they would stay, but he couldn't hold them against their will. He asked them to remain until noon, and if nothing developed by then he would permit them to go. It was a fair offer and they agreed, returning to their company.[8]

*   *   *

The Dakotas were coming. At least one white man had seen them in numbers moving down the left bank of the Minnesota River early Saturday morning, but he was in no position to do anything about it. Louis Robert, a storeowner and trader whose policies over the years had contributed to the dire state of affairs, was at Fort Ridgely during the first fight on Wednesday. He left for New Ulm on Friday but was only two miles from the fort when he was surrounded by warriors heading back for their second attack against the town. Robert hid in a grassy slough until that night. He tried to continue his journey but was nearly discovered and beat it back to his hiding place, where he spent most of the night standing in water holding his gun above his head. The next morning he was shocked to see but a short distance away what he considered to be 1,000 warriors passing down the road toward New Ulm. Thankful to be alive, he returned with haste to Fort Ridgely.[9]

Little Crow was indeed coming, but he could not gather the 1,000 warriors Robert claimed to have seen. The chief left his village with about 400 men, a sizeable force augmented along the way by additional warriors. By the time Little Crow reached New Ulm his column had swelled to about 650 men. Fires burning on both sides of the Minnesota River on that crisp and clear Saturday

---

8   Potter, "Recollections," 444-45; Hazzard, "Autobiographical Sketch," Microfilm Reel 2, Dakota Conflict, Minnesota Historical Society.

9   Bryant and Murch, *Great Massacre*, 202-03.

morning announced their arrival. The town's defenders surmised the fort had fallen and that the Indians were burning everything during their approach. Pickets were out to guard against a surprise attack. As Dr. Asa Daniels recalled, "The first surprise and alarm of the morning came when at guard mount, west of town, Lieutenant Edwards was instantly killed by an Indian so concealed in the grass that danger was unsuspected."[10]

A watchman on one of the roofs spotted the Indians about 8:00 a.m. Women and children sought shelter in cellars or the strongest buildings. Drs. William Mayo and Henry McMahon set up hospital in the Dakotah House, Drs. Asa Daniels and Otis Ayers set up in a house across the street, and New Ulm's own Dr. Carl Weschke prepared his own quarters. When warriors were also discovered on the opposite shore near town, Flandrau asked for volunteers to investigate. Lt. William Huey, of Traverse des Sioux, volunteered his 23-man company. To Frederick Fritsche's surprise, "the Lafayette company was ordered to join [Huey] to march to the Nicollet side of the river, and at the same time protect the ferry near the Globe Mill." (Map M) Most of the Lafayette men were on picket duty, however, so only about ten joined Huey. Others fleshed out the column and Huey left with about 75 men. An hour had passed since the first Dakotas had been spotted.

The 10 men from Lafayette "followed in disgust," admitted Fritsche, "especially as our families and loved ones were all in New Ulm, and an attack was feared." Other defenders also protested the move, claiming the demonstration was only a feint to draw them across and cut them off, while the main attack would come from another direction. Another faction believed the best course was to fight the enemy outside town, because doing nothing might be construed as cowardice.[11]

No one recorded what Flandrau said to Huey before he left, but the evidence seems clear he ordered his subordinate to cross to the far side of the river. In his initial report dated August 27, Flandrau wrote, "I thought it best to send a detachment to ascertain the design of the enemy, and if possible, give him a check." This statement implies approval, and can be read as a directive to

10 Buell, "Defense of New Ulm," 796, MHSC, Vol. 10, pt. 2; Tolzmann, ed., *Brown County*, 14; Daniels, "Reminiscences of the Little Crow Uprising," 328, MHSC, Vol. 15. Lieutenant A. W. Edwards belonged to Dellaughter's Company of Le Sueur Tigers.

11 Hughes, *Welsh in Minnesota*, 83-84; Daniels, "Reminiscences of the Little Crow Uprising," 329, MHSC, Vol. 15; Tolzmann, ed., *Brown County*, 15; *Minnesota in the Civil and Indian Wars*, II, 203-04.

cross the river. Marching as far as the low ground on the town side of the ferry would not have enabled Huey to see even as much as the observers on the rooftops could already make out: Indians were in the area. Therefore, having Huey stand idle at the ferry would not have achieved the objectives outlined by Flandrau. Huey would have to cross the river to both see what the enemy was up to and in what strength ("ascertain the design of the enemy"), and to engage or otherwise blunt the advance ("give him a check"). Fritsche, too, recorded that their orders were to march to the Nicollet side of the river. Flandrau's book published in 1900, nearly four decades after Huey left with about 20% of the town's defenders and suffered several dead, sang a different tune. "It was simply a mistake of judgment," he wrote, referring to Huey's move, "to put the river between himself and the main force." Jacob Nix disagreed and put the responsibility on Flandrau's shoulders: "one of the biggest mistakes was to order a company to cross the Minnesota River in order to fight the Indians."[12]

And so Huey marched out of New Ulm and down to the ferry, where he dropped off 20 men to guard the crossing and ferried over the balance. "We kept on going north about a distance of two miles from New Ulm," recalled Fritsche, to the neighborhood of August Rutenberg's and Adolph Schilling's farms.[13] (Map N) The men watched as seven Dakotas on horseback rode to Henry Wellner's place. Some of Huey's men fired at the riders, who were more than one-half mile distant. The Dakotas ignored them, set fire to Wellner's, and rode off.

Once Huey was well away from the river the Dakotas chased away the guards posted at the ferry, crossed to the New Ulm side, and cut the rope. Huey's men heard firing and asked him to return, but Huey thought it was just the pickets discharging their guns to clear them, emphasizing that there was no danger. When the rate and volume of fire increased, Huey finally admitted the town was under attack and issued orders to hurry back. When they reached the bluff they discovered Henry Miller's (Mueller) house on fire. When they

12 Flandrau, *History of Minnesota*, 153; Nix, *Sioux Uprising*, 115.

13 Joseph Godfrey claimed the Dakotas attacked and killed Schilling at his house south of the river in Milford. Fritsche, however, places his farm north of the river in Lafayette. Either one of these men is mistaken, Schilling had two farms, or perhaps there were two Adolph Schillings. Two depredation claims were filed with different registration numbers under the name Adolph Schilling. BLM records show two land claims filed under Adolph Schilling's name in 1861: one in section 15 in Lafayette Township, Nicollet County; and one in section 17 in Milford Township, Brown County. The latter, however, is not where Godfrey placed the cabin (near Henle's and Messmer's), but two miles to the south.

reached the ferry they discovered Dakotas in possession of the opposite bank as well as Globe Mill. The Indians opened a lively fire on them.

The Lafayette men who were familiar with the terrain advised Huey to have the men take up a position in a heavy timber where the trees were three and four feet in diameter. Both sides fired at each other from opposite sides of the river. John Summers (St. Peter Frontier Guards), who was wearing a white shirt, was severely wounded with a bullet through the lower body, and a few more men were slightly wounded. After determining he could do nothing from his position on the far side of the river, Huey ordered his men to retreat to the east. Fritsch and others demanded to know what they were going to do; many of them were St. Peter men who wanted nothing more than to return to their homes to protect their families.

"This was a hard blow for us Lafayette men," Fritsche grumbled, "but as we were only about ten men we had to follow. It was almost unbearable" to be only six or eight blocks away and unable to reach and defend their own families. Fritsche and Herman H. Beussman considered deserting, but since they had little ammunition and were exhausted they followed Huey "because we had to." By early that afternoon the men were back on top of the bluff. A long, low, and continuous rumble from town reached their ears: gunfire. To their horror, they could see New Ulm to the southeast engulfed in flames and smoke. The Eagle and Globe Mills were burning, and most of the houses in the southern part of town—which was where Fritsche's father lived—were on fire. Fritsche's heart sank, confident in the fact that his family was dead. "Well, we thought that is the last of them," he later lamented. "We will never see them again, not even the ashes." Still marking time on the wrong side of the river, Huey decided to march his command toward St. Peter, a decision that removed 50 potential defenders from the New Ulm battle.[14]

Charles Flandrau and his chief of staff, Salmon Buell, estimated that New Ulm had about 250 defenders with firearms after Huey and his men left. A small part of the Dakota force was on the Nicollet County shore, but most of the warriors had approached from the north and west side, taking advantage of the terrain by staying behind the long bluff that roughly paralleled the Minnesota River between it and the Cottonwood River. There, the warriors crossed the bluff or came down the depression that ran along the base of the bluff between

---

14 Tolzmann, ed., *Brown County*, 15-16.

two of the terraces and dispersed, hidden in the lowland or slough. And there they waited.[15]

Salmon Buell believed Little Crow had planned to wait until an ambushing force was set up at the ferry and then attack from the bluffs behind the town. Thinking an escape route was open across the river at the ferry, the townspeople and defenders would perhaps fight with less tenacity, try to break out if the pressure became too great, become trapped near the river between the two Indian forces, and slaughtered. If that was the plan, however, Huey's reconnaissance exposed it. As Chief of Staff Buell later wrote, "it may have been a blessing; for white men, surrounded by attacking Indians, fight hard, with no thought of surrender."[16]

If indeed that was Little Crow's plan something went wrong. According to Flandrau, the Dakotas "burned some stacks as a signal of their arrival, which was responded to by a similar fire in the edge of the timber, about two miles and a half from the town on the west." When they saw the signal, the Indians comprising the main force behind the town emerged from the low ground below the highest bluff and advanced toward New Ulm. "Crossing this slough, nearly in the center between the upper and lower ends of the town, was a causeway road," wrote Buell. "The Indians came in crowds" over this road, the same one where the Leavenworth Rescue Party was jumped, and when they crested the next terrace they divided, "part turning to their right and a part to their left, the latter soon being joined by another crowd that came down over the prairie bluff and above the end of the slough." Still there was no attack, as the flanking Indians circled around to surround the town. It was now 9:30 a.m.

Flandrau, who estimated that the encirclement consisted of 600 warriors, left an excellent description of their tactical movement on New Ulm: "Their advance upon the sloping prairie in the bright sunlight was a very fine spectacle, and to such inexperienced soldiers as we all were, intensely exciting. When within about one mile and a half of us the mass began to expand like a fan, and increase in the velocity of its approach, and continued this movement until within about double rifle-shot, when it had covered our entire front."

About this time, remembered Theodore Potter, a man appeared "almost in front and a little to the right of the Indians . . . entering the city on the run from a

---

15 Buell, "Defense of New Ulm," 793-94, MHSC, Vol. 10, pt. 2; *Minnesota in the Civil and Indian Wars*, II, 204.

16 Buell, "Defense of New Ulm," 797, MHSC, Vol. 10, pt. 2.

narrow skirt of timber on the west side of the bluff." The man was the beleaguered and exhausted Aaron Myers from Lake Shetek, who had left his son and others to seek help in New Ulm. According to Myers, he followed "the pickets into the town and in less than ten minutes the town was surrounded." He had made yet another miraculous escape—but was now in a town waiting to be attacked.[17]

When the Dakotas first came in view, Flandrau moved his men outside of town, "about half a mile at some points, and at a greater distance toward the point at which I conceived the attack would be made." I was "determined to give them battle in the open field," explained the town's new commander, "where I conceived would be our greatest advantage." Flandrau wanted to fight some distance from town to keep the women and children as safe as possible, but his undisciplined men were not open field fighters. Removing them from the defensive barricades and the security increased the likelihood they would be defeated and make it more likely the women and children would be killed or captured. The Dakotas were outstanding warriors, but they weren't open field fighters either. Unlike their cousins the Nakotas and Lakotas, who had fully taken up the Plains horse culture, the Dakotas were still in a state of transition, both a prairie and woodland people. They used horses to transport warriors to a fight whenever they could, but when it came to crunch time they preferred to battle on foot. Even so, dismounted Dakota warriors were more mobile than dismounted farmers and townsfolk, and they carried firearms as well as close-in shock weapons such as tomahawks, clubs, and knives. If Flandrau dispersed his men, they would not be able to deliver an effective and concerted fire and would be subject to swift Dakota concentrations against portions of their line. If Flandrau packed his men together for solid firepower, they would be easier to shoot down and more easily flanked.

It is imperative that a commander know his own capabilities as well as those of his enemy. In 1857, after Flandrau directed the chase for Inkpaduta across the prairie, he made some cogent observations about the relevant tactics employed. According to one historian, Flandrau learned his lessons and "was no novice at dealing with Indians and panic-stricken settlers." One of Flandrau's recommendations was that rifle-equipped cavalry be used against

17 Buell, "Defense of New Ulm," 794-95, MHSC, Vol. 10, pt. 2; *Minnesota in the Civil and Indian Wars*, II, 204; Flandrau, *History of Minnesota*, 150-51; Potter, "Recollections," 447-48; Aaron Myers Reminiscence, Microfilm Reel 2, Dakota Conflict, Minnesota Historical Society. Potter incorrectly wrote that William Duley and Henry Smith arrived at that time.

Indians on the prairie, "where running and not fighting is the contest." Using infantry to fight Indians, he concluded, was a waste of time. Unfortunately, however, he seemed unable to transfer his theories into practice. Flandrau did not have any cavalry at New Ulm, but that does not excuse his decision to move untrained militia out of a defensive line and into the open where the town's structures were widely scattered, and where Indians could engage them on their own terms.[18]

Flandrau moved his men forward to form a loose line, by companies with intervals between them, running generally up State Street from Center Street to about Sixth North St., where it curved right to about German Street and Ninth North St. (Map M) This formation did not have a chance of holding its ground, and the Dakotas spread quickly beyond both flanks and curled back toward its rear. Flandrau later explained that there were only about 20 to 30 rifles in the entire command, "and a man with a shotgun, knowing his antagonist carries a rifle, has very little confidence in his fighting ability." Flandrau had to have known this at the time, which further calls into question why he did not leave his men behind their protective fortifications and force the Indians to approach within range of their shotguns.

Captain Dodd moved beyond the new line, pushing his skirmishers close enough to the Indians to initiate their fire. When a horse was hit and it ran toward the Dakotas, its white rider had to leap off, barely escaping with his life. Flandrau, meanwhile, had taken up a position behind the center of the line, where he "awaited the first discharge with very great anxiety, as it seemed to me that to yield was certain destruction, as the enemy would rush into the town and drive all before them."

The nervous defenders did not have long to wait. The Dakotas made their move a little after 10: 00 a.m., driving the skirmishers back as mounted warriors moved to outflank the line. "A sudden panic seized our men in the trenches and those on horseback, and together they made a wild rush for the center of the city," reported Captain Potter, whose horse was shot and killed early in the fighting. "Down came the Indians in the bright sunlight," confirmed Flandrau, "galloping, running, yelling, and gesticulating in the most fiendish manner." The attack created a lasting impact on Salmon Buell, who remembered they "rushed with a yell never forgotten by one who heard it." Flandrau expounded

18 Flandrau, *History of Minnesota*, 150-51; *Minnesota in the Civil and Indian Wars*, II, 204; Secoy, *Changing Military Patterns*, 68-69; Fridley, "Attorney at War," 124-25.

on Buell's memory. "The yell unsettled the men a little," he admitted, "and just after the rifles began to crack they fell back along the whole line. If we had had good rifles they never would have got near enough to do much harm. . . . My men, appreciating the inferiority of their armament, after seeing several of their comrades fall, and having fired a few ineffectual volleys, fell back on the town." According to one of the men, however, not everyone panicked at the first sign of the attack and they initially fell back because they were ordered to do so. "The men had just gotten into position when mounted Dakotas rode around their flanks as if to cut them off from the town," recalled Rudolph Leonhart. "There wasn't a second to lose. The command to fall back rang out along the line and slowly it gave ground," he continued. "When the Indians saw this, they accelerated their fast march into a run, and our men were forced to follow suit." Within a short time everyone was moving at "breathtaking speed, and we were lucky to finally reach our fortifications." "The defenders fell back in panic," agreed Asa Daniels, "and the whole line retreated to the barricades." Whether the men panicked immediately or were ordered to retreat, no one disagrees they were running from the untenable position Flandrau had ordered them to assume. Most of them formed up behind the barricades, though a few sought shelter in the cellars with the women, much as had happened at Fort Ridgely.[19]

In 1862, New Ulm's town center consisted of a tighter cluster of buildings around Center Street, Broadway, and Minnesota, but the structures fanning out from this town center were fewer in number with more space in between them. Most of the dwellings were made of wood, but several were constructed of brick, whose strong walls offered outstanding defensive advantages. The dilemma was whether to occupy some of these outlying brick buildings for defense, which would expand the perimeter and disperse the men but allow some room to maneuver and keep the women and children farther from the front, or give up the buildings to the Dakotas and concentrate in a smaller tighter bastion around the town center, which would concentrate their fire but leave little room for maneuver and place the noncombatants closer to the firing.

The fleeing defenders had little time to decide on their course of action because most of the men were more concerned with their immediate safety than with tactical options. According to Flandrau, his men "committed the error of

19 Flandrau, *History of Minnesota*, 151; *Minnesota in the Civil and Indian Wars*, II, 204; Potter, "Recollections," 449-50; Buell, "Defense of New Ulm," 795, 797, MHSC, Vol. 10, pt. 2; Hughes, *Welsh in Minnesota*, 84; Leonhart, *Memories of New Ulm*, 60.

passing the outer houses without taking possession of them, a mistake which the Indians immediately took advantage of by themselves occupying them." These and other recollections confirm Flandrau had little or no control over the men and that he did not have a backup plan when he moved his defenders out of the town and onto the prairie.

Jacob Nix had another take. The Indians were not reacting to the whites, but simply changed their method of attack "with the cunning characteristic of their race." By occupying deserted buildings, he continued, "they could fire more effectively on the defenders." They decided to take the structures "best suited for their siege and to burn those which they did not wish to occupy."

Salmon Buell agreed that the Indians changed their tactical course, but it was "an irreparable error" for them to occupy the buildings abandoned by the retreating defenders. The Dakotas had the momentum, he explained, and could have chased the routed defenders into the center of town and perhaps overwhelmed it. When the Indians stopped to take up positions in the buildings, they lost that initiative.[20] Flandrau seemed to agree with Buell when he argued that if the Indians "had boldly charged into the town and set it on fire, they would have won the fight." If so then his men, albeit unwittingly, made the right decision to bypass the outer buildings during their retreat (which Flandrau earlier described as an "error"). The Dakotas may have looked upon the abrupt retreat as a ruse to draw them into an ambush in town. Instead of pushing forward, they held back and occupied buildings that offered them good firing positions into the town center area. This decision provided enough time for the defenders to collect themselves and man the barricades.[21]

Not everyone made it to the barricades. Some of the defenders were caught in the open and killed. Others were cut off and forced to take shelter in the nearest buildings, a series of impromptu outposts that offered isolated pockets of resistance shooting into the flanks and rear of the attacking Indians. Capt. E. C. Saunders and about 15 men, some from his Le Sueur Tigers, took up residence in an unfinished brick building on the northwest side of town while others took up a position on their right. When Saunders took a bullet through the body that knocked him out of the fight, he handed his valuable rifle to one

---

20 Daniels, "Reminiscences of the Little Crow Uprising," 329, MHSC, Vol. 15; *Minnesota in the Civil and Indian Wars*, II, 204; Buell, "Defense of New Ulm," 797, MHSC, Vol. 10, pt. 2.

21 Nix, *Sioux Uprising*, 111; *Minnesota in the Civil and Indian Wars*, II, 204; Hughes, *Welsh in Minnesota*, 85.

of his men. What they did not know was that the defenders to their right had fled and that they were in danger of being cut off from the town. When militiaman Henry Swift realized what was happening, he informed an officer who gathered about 40 men to move forward in an effort to save them. The move drove back the Dakotas long enough to get a messenger through to warn Saunders's men, who used the opportunity to pull out and carry their wounded commander to the hospital. Many of the men assumed a new position in another structure closer to town.

Daniel G. Shillock spotted about 15 Dakotas storming into a house near the town center, from which they could pose a serious menace to the defenders. Shillock gathered a dozen men and rushed the house, driving out the warriors and capturing it. The cost of the small victory was a wound in the leg for Shillock.[22]

In the northwest quarter, meanwhile, one of the last men to retreat became separated from his company. Otto Barth, the editor of the New Ulm *Pioneer*, described as a small man with "unkempt beard and disheveled red hair," had held back deliberately to take aimed shots at his pursuers when he looked around and realized he had been cut off by mounted Dakotas. The scribe-turned-soldier took refuge in the schoolhouse basement on Minnesota between Fourth North and Fifth North streets. From that more secure location Barth leveled his rifle and fired at any Dakota who dared approach. When they decided it was too dangerous to go in after the cornered man the Indians set the building on fire.

A squad under Lt. John F. Meagher (Bierbauer's Company) took over an unfinished building on the terrace west of town and opened a sharp fire on the Dakotas. When they realized they were too isolated Meagher ran his men back to the barricades. Most of Bierbauer's Mankato men took position on the southeast side of New Ulm. Some of the Le Sueur Tigers and Mankato Company moved quickly to occupy Roebbecke's Mill in the first block on south State Street. The 70-foot tall mill was built by Frederick Roebbecke in 1859 for grinding corn and grain. Flandrau called it an "old Don Quixote windmill," because of its "immense tower and sail-arms" that were nearly as long as the building was high. The occupants, whose numbers varied from 10 to 30 strong during the course of the day, included Lt. George W. Stewart, Evan T. Jones, E. P. Freeman, J. B. Trogdon, Thomas and W. H. Hazzard, and Rev. C. A. Stines.

During the run to the mill, W. H. Hazzard remembered that "the balls flying around our heads caused me to lose my hat." The new position satisfied Hazzard, who proclaimed the mill "a very safe place as it proved, located on a hill, [it] gave us a beautiful view of the country and [a] strong defense of the town." Indeed, the mill proved relatively secure from attack as its defenders piled wheat and flour sacks against the walls and knocked out loopholes for lines of fire.[23]

The Forster Building, which served as the post office in 1862, was another strong point. On the west side of Broadway, it was just across the street from the main barricade and as a two-story brick building was an especially critical structure. The defenders knocked loopholes in the walls to shoot out while blocking the windows with feather beds. The cellar was filled with women and children. The upper floor was just high enough to allow the defenders a field of fire to the top of the terrace to the west.

The Dakotas, meanwhile, tightened the cordon around New Ulm's town center, dodging ever closer from building to building. And then they began to set fires. Little Crow—if that chief was even in charge—had as little command control and tactical sense as Colonel Flandrau. According to Big Eagle, "There was no one in chief command of the Indians at New Ulm. A few sub-chiefs, like myself, and the head soldiers led them, and the leaders agreed among themselves what was to be done."[24] As long as dwellings remained intact the Dakotas had shelter and a means to run structure to structure, infiltrating closer to the town center to concentrate at select points with more or less impunity. For reasons that remain unclear, the Indians decided to burn their cover. The move infuriated Jacob Nix, who complained that "the red beasts now hurled the flaming torch into the homes of peaceful citizens who had never harmed them." Rudolph Leonhart, on the other hand, understood the Dakotas were making a big mistake. They burned "all isolated houses on the west end" during the morning. "In their rage, the Indians didn't seem to realize that they hurt themselves more than us, as with every house that collapsed into ashes they destroyed a position from which they could have been able to launch an attack on us."

---

23 Leonhart, *Memories of New Ulm*, 60-61; Flandrau, *History of Minnesota*, 152; Hughes, *Welsh in Minnesota*, 85; Hazzard, "Autobiographical sketch," Microfilm Reel 2, Dakota Conflict, Minnesota Historical Society.

24 Dahlin, *Dakota Uprising*, 109; Anderson and Woolworth, *Through Dakota Eyes*, 147.

The Dakotas moved in close enough to take possession of Turner Hall, only about 400 feet from the windmill. A gunfight erupted between the occupants of the two buildings that went on most of the day. Chaos reigned everywhere; Flandrau had little control over the situation. The fighting, he later reported, "became general, sharp and rapid, and it got to be a regular Indian skirmish, in which every man did his own work after his own fashion." It was the same story for Little Crow, but he found it unnecessary to state the obvious.[25]

Although the Dakotas made a mistake burning their cover, the tactical error was no comfort to those who lost their houses. Adam Joos, his wife and two children had been in New Ulm three years. An engineer at the Chicago (Eagle) Mill owned by Frederick Rehfeld and Frederick Beinhorn, Joos and his family lived in Henry Lohman's house near the sawmill. After the first fight on Tuesday, they moved to another house on north German Street where Joos thought his family would be safer. The house and the Chicago Mill were burned down; Joos lost $837 of household goods and lumber.[26]

Brickmaker and woodchopper Lorenz Muther had lived in New Ulm with his wife and three children for four years. His home was plundered and he lost the charcoal he was making for the government up near Fort Ridgely, plus all the lumber he had cut and stored near the Cincinnati (Globe) Mill, a sawmill along the river south of the Chicago Mill that was also burned down. He estimated his losses at $318.[27]

In some instances, fleeing into town didn't save the home or the goods taken from the home. Ernst Fritsche, his wife Christiane, daughter Minna (1), and his father-in-law John Schumacher (67) lived six miles south of New Ulm on the Little Cottonwood River. They got the warning early enough, and Tuesday morning loaded up most of their goods, including provisions and bedding. They reached New Ulm before the first fight Tuesday and helped the refugees by passing out their extra supplies. John Victor had known Fritsche for five years. "The provisions were eaten by the citizens," he recalled. "I helped to do it—claimant [Fritsche] gave them out." Being good Samaritans didn't help them. Much of their farm was plundered and they lost flooring, siding, and

25 Nix, *Sioux Uprising*, 111-12; Leonhart, *Memories of New Ulm*, 62; Flandrau, *History of Minnesota*, 152-53; *Minnesota in the Civil and Indian Wars*, II, 204.

26 Adam Joos Depredation Claim #77.

27 Lorenz Muther Depredation Claim #74.

fencing that they had taken to the Cincinnati Mill, for damages totaling about $545. They took refuge in the Forster Building.[28]

Within a short time the Dakotas had possession of the houses on the upper and lower ends of town. "[S]everal brave but ineffectual attempts were made to dislodge them," recalled William Hayden, "and as these efforts ended in the loss of several men, without apparent gain, Col Flandrau wisely decided to form his men behind the barricades. Each side," he added, "fought under cover as much as possible."[29]

Rudolph Leonhart was posted in the south end of town but without a firearm, and spent the morning "supervising the pouring of bullets." When the lead bars were used up, he and others found several pounds of buckshot they melted down and poured into bullet molds. During the first hour and a half, from the first ill-considered move outside the barricades until both sides hit upon a new tactic, is when Flandrau took his heaviest casualties: about ten killed and 50 wounded.[30]

Jacob Nix boasted that when he was in command during the first battle for New Ulm, only a handful of buildings went up in smoke, and this far in the second fight there was more shooting than burning. That changed about the time the wind picked up out of the southeast and swept toward the town center. The Dakotas noticed the change and shifted men to that side and began to systematically put buildings to the torch, hoping the wind, flames, and smoke would carry into town and drive the defenders out into the open. The Indians, William Hayden explained, "unable to resist the passion for burning buildings, had set on fire many of the houses." There were numerous buildings in town, and the warriors occupied many of them, particularly on the terrace to the west. These positions allowed them to see and shoot down the numbered cross streets into the center of town where the defenders had congregated, not unlike pins at the ends of bowling lanes. With gunfire sweeping its way down the lanes from the west, it was dangerous to try and cross a street in a north-south direction. After some time the defenders realized those Indian-held buildings had to be eliminated. "It soon became evident that our chances of making a successful defense would be increased by having a clear field outside of the

28 Ernst Fritsche Depredation Claim #2017.

29 Hayden, "Account of the relief expedition," Microfilm Reel 2, Dakota Conflict, Minnesota Historical Society.

30 Leonhart, *Memories of New Ulm*, 65; Flandrau, *History of Minnesota*, 153.

barricades," explained Hayden, "and the order was given to burn everything that could afford a hiding place outside of this line."[31]

Several defenders applied to Flandrau for permission to set certain structures alight. "He was loath to destroy the property of this stricken people," Hayden admitted, "but as a military necessity ordered it." All the buildings outside the central core center held by the defenders were targeted for destruction. Volunteers ran out of the barricades and torched anything flammable including haystacks, woodpiles, and structures. As they worked their way out of the town center, Indians worked their way in the ring of defenses. "Then began one of the wildest scenes of frontier warfare; burning buildings, with hideously painted naked savages running in and out of the firelight, often recklessly exposing themselves in their mad dance, yelling like fiends with that peculiar war whoop that makes the cold chills run over one," recalled Hayden. "The almost continuous discharge of guns, the shrill hiss of bullets, added to the apparent hopelessness of the situation made the bravest pale."[32]

By now, buildings were being burned by three different groups: Dakotas torched from the outer ring inward to drive the whites deeper into town and eventually trap and /or burn them out; whites forced from these outer buildings burned their way into town, destroying buildings behind them so the Dakotas could not use them for cover, and; whites in town worked their way beyond the barricades toward the Indians, burning buildings to open a wider field of fire to keep the enemy as far away as possible. The surreal scene offered a canvas of abstract and impressionist splashes of light and dark interrupted with a terrifying Picasso Guernica-like maelstrom of detached shapes flashing by in a cacophony of color and sound. "The fight became a driving by the Indians," Salmon Buell explained, "and a burning by the whites as driven back out of the buildings by superior force," which created a greater conflagration of flames and confusion.

Some of the structures that did not escape the flames included the houses along the south outskirts of town. For five years Theodore Wehrs (35) and his wife ran a painting and glazing business and owned a substantial house and two lots on German Street and Tenth South Street. The frame home, inlaid with

---

31 *Minnesota in the Civil and Indian Wars*, II, 204; Hayden, "Account of the relief expedition," Microfilm Reel 2, Dakota Conflict, Minnesota Historical Society.

32 Hayden, "Account of the relief expedition," Microfilm Reel 2, Dakota Conflict, Minnesota Historical Society; Buell, "Defense of New Ulm," 798, MHSC, Vol. 10, pt. 2.

brick, included a cellar, a central section and two wings, one and one-half stories, a pair of chimneys, and a porch the width of the house. The Wehrs abandoned it Saturday morning when they fled to the town center, where Theodore watched from an upper window as the Dakotas began burning the south end of town. A successful property loss claim requires the identity of the guilty party, and about that Wehrs had no doubt. "There were no whites in that part of the town when my house was on fire," he testified. "I saw the place on Monday the 25th, and there was nothing but ashes there." He lost everything, which was estimated at $2,804. "I am poor now."[33]

Ernst and Frederick Fritsche's father, John Karl Fritsche, had a house in the lower end of town near Front Street. While Ernst gave much of his possessions away, Frederick stored his bedding and clothing in his father's house. John Hauenstein, Frederick's brother-in-law, was posted in that part of town when the Dakotas moved in. He saw them take Frederick's wagon and set fire to the house. Frederick lost his property there, and the Dakotas broke into his house across the river in Lafayette, plundered it, and damaged his crops. He claimed $433 in losses.[34]

About noon, Leonhart watched the conflagration and rolling small arms battle from the southern part of town. "Through the smoke of the burning houses I saw the almost naked Indians moving in a zigzag fashion to dodge the aim of our troops," he wrote. "It didn't require a vivid imagination to see them as devils wandering through the flames of hell." A horseman in a red blanket charged down the slope swinging his rifle. Leonhart craved a rifle at the moment to "stuff his screaming mouth with lead." A man firing from the window next to him, however, vicariously fulfilled his wish and the two men watched as the mounted Dakota "sinks backwards from the pony, somersaults twice in falling and strikes the earth with a dull thud." His companions rushed to recover his body, continued Leonhart, while several whites "hasten forward, capture the weapons and decorations of the fallen warrior and return triumphantly to camp." William Hayden described Leonhart's compelling allusion to something straight out of Dante's Inferno as a "mad scene [that] continued through the afternoon."[35]

33 Theodore Wehrs Depredation Claim #1079.

34 Frederick Fritsche Depredation Claim #142.

35 Leonhart, Memories of New Ulm, 65-66.

As in all combats, the madness affected the perception of time and space. An episode resulting in the death of Capt. William Todd is a prime example. According to Jacob Nix, Todd was killed "at nearly 12 noon," while Salmon Buell put it "a little after noon." Flandrau, however, reported it as sometime after the Indians had taken possession of the lower town and the fighting was general on all sides (which could place it as late as the middle afternoon). Doctor Daniels pushed the captain's death well down the clock to "about five p.m." The event in question developed when 40 or 50 men dressed in civilian clothing were spotted marching in single file out of the south up the road from Mankato flying an American flag. Another source claims the column was first seen from the roof of Crone's store, near the edge of the bluff on the Mankato road, and that the men appeared uncertain as to whether they should advance. The embattled expectations of New Ulm's defenders shaped their perceptions. The mysterious men had to be Colonel Henry Sibley's anticipated reinforcements or, more likely, Lieutenant Huey and his company trying to get back into town. Huey, thought some, had marched downriver to Redstone Ferry, crossed over, and was coming up from the south. Someone informed Captain Dodd of the approaching footmen, but he may not have witnessed it himself. According to Doctor Daniels, Dodd had volunteered to fight the Confederates but was rejected "on account of impaired sight."

Whether Dodd's poor vision had any bearing on the matter is unknown, but the captain was convinced the approaching men were reinforcements who needed help. When he suggested to Lieutenant Meagher that they utilize a detachment to escort the men into town, the cautious reply warned that the escort would be in range of Indians firing from houses just a few blocks down the street. One writer argued that Dodd was brave and able but "he was fond of liquor and this the people of New Ulm foolishly distributed in unlimited quantities to all the defenders free of cost."[36]

Alcohol or otherwise, when Dodd gave "a short, impassioned speech" for volunteers that was seconded by Doctor Mayo, about 20 men agreed to follow him and escort the approaching column into New Ulm. Only Dodd and Sgt. James Shoemaker (Mankato Company) were mounted, with Dodd "on his fine black horse." Lieutenant Meagher, Thomas Y. Davis, and a few other

---

36 Nix, *Sioux Uprising*, 112; Buell, "Defense of New Ulm," 799, MHSC, Vol. 10, pt. 2; Daniels, "Reminiscences of the Little Crow Uprising," 330, 332, MHSC, Vol. 15; Flandrau, *History of Minnesota*, 152; Hughes, *Welsh in Minnesota*, 86.

Welshmen took position in Kiesling's blacksmith shop just across from the southern barricades and watched the escort head down Minnesota Street. Dodd and Shoemaker were riding well ahead of the others on foot when, about three blocks down, Dakotas opened fire on them from inside buildings. The entire column may have been trapped or heavily cut up if the Indians had let the men move another block or two. Five bullets slammed into Dodd and several more into his horse. Shoemaker's horse was also hit, but he rather miraculously emerged unscathed. The men turned back on a staggered run. Other bullets found their marks, hitting Jacob Haeberle and John Krueger, both of Milford (Roos's Company). Both made it back to the barricades, but Haeberle died a few hours later and Krueger lingered several months before succumbing. Dodd's horse carried him as far as the blacksmith shop before collapsing and throwing him to the street. Men rushed him into Kiesling's and placed him on a cot.

While some ministered Dodd on the lower level, defenders upstairs opened fire on the Dakotas. The mortally injured captain mustered a final order for everyone to leave him and go upstairs to fight. His only request was that if the building had to be abandoned, they move him so the Indians would not get his body. When the Indian pressure threatened to overwhelm Kiesling's blacksmith shop, Dodd was carried into the barricaded area and examined by Doctor Daniels. Three of his five wounds were mortal injuries. "There was little that could be done," lamented Daniels, "as he was in a dying condition, surviving only about one hour. He appreciated his condition, and met it courageously, giving me messages to his wife and to Bishop Whipple, with the utmost coolness and consideration."

The "reinforcements" were neither Sibley's nor Huey's men, but Indians using a ruse to draw the defenders outside their walls. Daniels believed their civilian clothing was obtained nearly two years earlier when 150 suits were distributed to Indians who eschewed blankets in an attempt to become farmers. Regardless of where they got the civilian garb, the ploy partially worked and killed and wounded several men. Daniels argued that the ruse was believable because Lieutenant Huey had crossed the river and the defenders anticipated his return.[37]

---

37 Nix, *Sioux Uprising*, 112; Potter, "Recollections," 451; "Defense of New Ulm," 798-99, MHSC, Vol. 10, pt. 2; Daniels, "Reminiscences of the Little Crow Uprising," 330-32, MHSC, Vol. 15.

The Dakotas, meanwhile, concentrated in the lower end of town with the wind at their backs and slowly moved forward, concealed somewhat by the smoke blowing in front of them. The advantage was slowly turning in their favor, admitted Flandrau, "the difficulty that stared us in the face was their gradual but certain approach up the main street, behind the burning buildings, which promised our destruction." He still tried to get his men to sally out and burn the structures in advance of the Dakotas, but "the risk of being picked off from the bluff was unequal to the advantage gained, and the duty was performed with some reluctance by the men."[38]

About 2:00 p.m., sentries atop the Crone building discovered a strong concentration of Dakotas behind a grove of trees in South German Park on the side of the terrace about three blocks from the barricades. Except for near the town center, most of New Ulm's dwellings were widely separated with as much as an acre or two surrounding each one. Some were fenced, while others were bordered with trees, tall grass, thickets, haystacks, barns, and sheds. Natural springs bubbled up on the side of the terrace facing the river and in those boggy areas the grass and weeds grew especially thick. The wet summer of 1862 triggered an even more luxuriant growth of vegetation than usual. All of this conspired to the advantage of the Indian attackers, who used the natural cover and manmade structures to infiltrate closer to the barricades. Now, some 75 or more Dakotas had slipped into the South German Park grove and looked to be preparing for a concentrated attack.

Asa White, a member of the Mankato Company and an old frontiersman, sought out Flandrau to fill him in on the bad news. The colonel had also seen the Indians concentrating on a side street near the park and later wrote that he "anticipated a rush upon the town from that position, the result of which I feared more than anything else, as the boys had proved unequal to it in the morning."

"Judge," White continued, "if this goes on, the Indians will bag us in about two hours."

"It looks that way;" Flandrau agreed. "What remedy have you to suggest?"

White advised the town's commander to collect everyone they could and make for a large timbered area of cottonwoods. The spot White suggested,

---

38 If faced with destruction, as Flandrau reported after the fact, the tremendous advantage gained by clearing the field of fire would easily outweigh the risk of a few men being picked off by Indians.

however, was more than two miles away. There were more than 1,000 non-combatants sheltered within New Ulm, and moving them safely that far was preposterous. Flandrau flatly refused. "White, they would slaughter us like sheep should we undertake such a movement," he replied. The only way out of their dire predicament, concluded Flandrau, was to assume the initiative. "Our strongest hold is in this town," he explained, "and if you will get together fifty volunteers, I will drive the Indians out of the lower town and the greatest danger will be passed."[39]

One of the volunteers who agreed to make the effort was Theodore Potter, who was identifying the danger point in "a thick piece of oak brush running along the north [east] side of the Mankato road" when a load of buckshot struck him in the face. The blast knocked him unconscious. Many thought he was dead, and so took his Sharps rifle, Colt revolver, and ammunition. When he regained consciousness, his comrades helped him to the hospital where Doctor McMahon removed a pair of buckshot from his left cheek, gave him "a little stimulus," and released him. Potter joined the volunteers just before they stepped out.[40]

Flandrau and nearly 60 men moved south down Minnesota Street. They expected to find the Dakotas "in a sunken road about three blocks from where we started," Flandrau reported, but by the time they moved out the Dakotas, from 75 to 100 strong, had edged closer, getting "in a deep swale about a block and a half from our barricades." The lay of the buildings and terrain, explained Salmon Buell, dictated Flandrau's moves. A pair of houses were still standing on the block in question (probably between First and Second South Streets and Minnesota and German Streets). There, Flandrau's line of defenders formed a right angle. On one side was a large frame house fronting the main street with a back lot that eventually dropped off 15 feet to the lower terrace. Fronting on a cross street was a smaller house whose lot ran along the top of the bluff and ended near the rear of the other lot. The Dakotas were below the bluff east of both houses working their way toward the center of town. The defenders holding the large house could not hit them, and those in the smaller house had only a marginal chance of doing so. Some of the Dakotas moved up the bluff and gathered behind piles of logs between the two rear lots.

39 *Minnesota in the Civil and Indian Wars*, II, 205; Hughes, *Welsh in Minnesota*, 87-88; Flandrau, *History of Minnesota*, 154.

40 Potter, "Recollections," 451.

Still uncertain as to the best tactic, Flandrau decided to burn the large house. If nothing else, its destruction would clear a large portion of one more block. Men gathered straw and bedding, doused them with kerosene and set the place aflame, pulling back on the north side. The billowing clouds of smoke blew over them, obliterating them from view. A few of the men close to the burning house could see the Indians and the smaller house. To their surprise, a defender ran out of the house on the east side to get a better shot, only to be killed by Dakotas sheltered under the bluff. Flandrau finally saw his chance. If he could draw Dakota attention to the front of the lot, he might be able to attack them in the rear. Take three men and run down the cross street and rescue the wounded man, Flandrau instructed an officer. The four obeyed, running out of the smoke to appear in front. While two of them fired their guns, the other two pulled the wounded man back to safety.

Surprised by the rush of a few men out of the smoke, the Indians under the bluff opened fire and the warriors behind the logs between the rear lots evidently believed an attack was underway and left their position to rush to the fight. The Dakotas probably considered the handful of men in front of them ripe for the killing, and therefore must have been shocked to find 50 white men, reported Flandrau, "cheering and yelling in a manner that would have done credit to the wildest Comanches" burst upon them from the bluff on their left and rear. "Colonel Flandrau," confirmed Salmon Buell, "followed this feint by rushing with his whole party out of the smoke to the rear of the lot, taking the Indians there, as it were, in their rear and flank." Some of the Dakotas opened a scattered though effective fire, which the whites returned without even slowing down. One Indian bullet struck the breech of a gun Flandrau was carrying across the front of his body during the charge, driving the weapon into his abdomen so that it "almost disabled him." An unnamed young man running next to Potter "was shot in the mouth, his tongue cut off, and he died the next day."

When the wave of white militiamen surged within 50 feet, panic swept through the Dakotas who broke and ran. The men "advanced with a cheer, routing the rascals like sheep," boasted Flandrau, whose company gave the fleeing Indians a volley at short range "that was very effectual and settled the fortunes of the day in our favor, for they did not dare to try it over." The men chased the Dakotas for one-half mile beyond the edge of the burning houses, where they halted and took up a position behind large piles of sawn logs. The Dakotas also stopped running and the two sides opened an incessant but ineffectual fire. Tellingly, the Dakotas did not make another advance against the town center from that quarter.[41]

Jacob Nix's version of Flandrau's attack is difficult to reconcile with Flandrau's and Buell's description. According to Nix, the Indians captured Kiesling's blacksmith shop on the corner of Center and Minnesota about 4:30 p.m. That success, he continued, gave them a foothold almost across from the barricades that allowed them to shoot down the length of Minnesota Street. It was at that critical moment, remembered Nix, that he and Flandrau gathered nearly 70 men, and with both of them at the head of the company, plunged over the barricades and attacked "that strategically important blockhouse." According to Nix, the Indians had four times their number, but after a short "terrible and bloody struggle" were driven away with heavy losses and "the town was saved." Nix recorded heavy white losses of five men killed and 15 to 18 wounded in the clash. "[O]ur men knew that this spot, drenched with blood," he concluded with embellished flair, "would proclaim to future generations how their small courageous number had here beaten an enemy that outnumbered them four to one. They knew that by this decisive victory over the bestial Indian hordes they had spared nearly 1,000 women and children from a terrible fate."[42]

Flandrau's spoiling attack cost the white defenders about four killed and several wounded. An "elderly gentleman" whose name Flandrau could not remember was among the dead. After they returned to the barricades, one of the men handed Flandrau a fine rifle with the words, "Some Indian lost a good gun in that run." Asa White, who was with Flandrau when the rifle was presented, recognized the weapon. "Newell Houghton is dead," White announced. "He never let that gun out of his hands while he could hold it." White was referring to Newell E. Houghton, a member of the Mankato Company. The men walked back to where the man had found the gun and, after a brief search, discovered Houghton's scalped body and brought it back to town. White's pronouncement was chillingly accurate. Flandrau especially regretted Houghton's death. He described the Mankato Company rifleman as

---

41 *Minnesota in the Civil and Indian Wars*, II, 205; Flandrau, *History of Minnesota*, 154-55; Potter, "Recollections," 452; Buell, "Defense of New Ulm," 799-800, 808, MHSC, Vol. 10, pt. 2.

42 Nix, *Sioux Uprising*, 112-13. In light of other events and time frames, Nix's estimate of a 4:30 p.m. attack is too late to reconcile with other events; the entire recollection is riddled with obvious embellishment.

cool and reliable under fire and "the best shot and deer hunter in all the Northwest."[43]

Dakota losses are much more difficult to calculate. Big Eagle later said that only a few of his band were with him, and "We lost none of them. We had but few, if any, of the Indians killed; at least I did not hear of but a few." One of the dead was 37-year-old George Le Blanc (Provencalle), a mixed-blood son of fur trader Louis Provencalle and a Mdewakanton woman found within the defensive line where Flandrau made his attack.[44]

While holding his advanced position, Flandrau "sent a party back with instructions to burn every building, fence, stack or other object that would afford cover between us and the barricades." Except for the few barricaded blocks in the center of New Ulm, nearly every structure was either burning or targeted for the flames. Until the buildings on the terrace to the west could be destroyed, however, Indian marksmen used them to lay down an effective fire upon the defenders. As a result, a number of defenders and non-combatants were killed and wounded during the day trying to cross the numbered streets running generally east to west. As Sheriff Roos described it, the long engagement was generally one of a "continual cross firing."[45]

Hiram Buck, who had fled from the upper Cottonwood to find "safety" in town, was wounded three separate times while moving among the buildings. Christian Frank, who also fled from the Cottonwood, was shot in the head and badly wounded. "His mind has been greatly impaired ever since,"explained Christian's son Frederick. Stephen and Wilhelmine Gluth lived on a farm two and a half miles west of New Ulm. Their son August (13) was captured while herding stock above Redwood Agency on Monday, and their son John (22) was shot and killed below the agency the same day. News of the uprising forced the rest of the family to seek refuge in one of the houses along the outer edge of town. When the Dakotas broke through Flandrau's outer defense line that Saturday, the Gluths fled to the town center. During the move behind the barricades, an arrow struck little Henry Gluth (5) in the back of the neck.

43 *Minnesota in the Civil and Indian Wars*, II, 205. The editor of this volume notes that the man's name was John Summers of Nicollet County. However, Frederick Fritsche claimed that Summers was badly wounded while fighting at the ferry with Huey's men.

44 *Minnesota in the Civil and Indian Wars*, II, 205; Flandrau, *History of Minnesota*, 155-56; Anderson and Woolworth, *Through Dakota Eyes*, 147, 165n1.

45 Buell, "Defense of New Ulm," 802, MHSC, Vol. 10, pt. 2; Roos, "The Battles of New Ulm," Brown County Historical Society.

Thankfully, the missile left a long scar but no other permanent damage. "Most of the killed and wounded were shot in crossing streets," including Jacob Castor, who was killed trying to reach his bakery on Broadway. It may have been Indian fire, but some claim the bullet was fired by someone in town who mistook Castor for an Indian. Eventually most of the white defenders figured out that in order to more safely cross a street, a volunteer had to rush out first to draw a volley of fire, which in turn allowed others to run across with a better chance of avoiding injury.[46]

Creszentia Schneider was certainly aware of the scores of New Ulm wounded. The widow had lived with her 15-year-old daughter in her son's house near the town center for the past eighteen months. The house survived, but was used throughout the siege as a hospital for the wounded. Creszentia allowed her sheets, tablecloths, towels, and bedding to be used as bandages; even her clothing was ripped up to dress wounds or soak up the blood. She was happy to help in the war effort, but when she returned to the house about two weeks later it was a bloody mess and everything had been stolen.[47]

Aaron Myers, who spent the day unassigned to any unit and without a weapon, wandered the streets helping wherever he could. He had "escaped" into the town just ahead of the Dakota attack, and stopped inside the barricades at what he described as "a common," where all the wagons, horses, and oxen were parked. The animals stampeded when the Dakotas attacked, prompting Myers to claim that "the people were in more danger from these than from the Indians." Oxen and horses ran down the streets, sometimes pulling careening wagons along with them. "Dogs partook of the pandemonium, biting everything they came within reach of," he continued. Men were detailed to shoot them.

Myers, a keen observer of human nature, recalled this day as the best chance in his life to study "the different temperaments of the human race." When Mr. Fuller noticed that the moccasins he had worn all the way from Lake Shetek were falling apart, he invited Myers into his general store to try on a new pair. And so it was that during a battle for their lives, Fuller tried to sell Myers a pair of new shoes. Myers, meanwhile, studied the women who packed the

---

46 Hiram Buck Depradation Claim #1153; Christian Frank Depredation Claim #2019; West, "A Lad's Version of Chief Little Crow," Microfilm Reel 1, Dakota Conflict, Minnesota Historical Society; Nix, *Sioux Uprising*, 116; Hughes, *Welsh in Minnesota*, 87.

47 Creszentia Schneider Depredation Claim #1001.

store—some crying, some laughing, some swearing, some sitting stupefied, some praying, and some, incredibly, shoplifting, hoisting their skirts and stuffing whole bolts of calico underneath. Outside, other women ran the streets calling for family members. Some, claimed Myers, had to be locked up to prevent them from running among the Indians.

After growing weary of the pandemonium inside the town, Myers asked Colonel Flandrau for a job. After explaining that a man had been killed and another was wounded carrying ammunition to the defenders in Roebbecke's windmill, the commander inquired whether Myers wanted to give it a try. Myers agreed, but only if he had some covering fire to give him a fighting chance. When the men were in place, Myers took a peck basket filled with ammunition and started running left and right, dodging his way up the hill toward the mill. Shots buzzed past him, with one cutting through his long hair and another through his sleeve. He delivered his precious cargo, but once back safely inside the barricades he did not volunteer to run the gauntlet a second time.[48]

Thomas Y. Davis (Mankato Company) also carried ammunition to various outlying houses and twice made the dangerous run to the windmill, which served as a strong point all day. According to W. H. Hazzard, one of the mill's defenders, Indians rushed up "in short range many times showing their bravery but [were] repulsed each time." After Flandrau's and Nix's victory to the south on Minnesota and German Streets and the destruction of most of the outlying dwellings around the town center, the final Dakota strongpoint was concentrated at Turner Hall where, recalled Nix, "they rained their bullets uninterruptedly towards the windmill." With a steady supply of ammunition, however, the mill's defenders stymied the Dakota advances from that quarter.

Hazzard believed it was about 4:00 p.m. when they received a command "to make a charge on the Indians who were massing their forces in the southwest part of the town hoping they might take the wind mill, capture the forces in the mill, and the town would be theirs." According to him the attack was made and "the Indians were routed, driven back, and immediately began their retreat to the western hills, and we breathed easier." Not so, according to Nix. A squad of men gathered to drive the Dakotas from Turner Hall, but "since no immediate danger to the city existed at this point," he explained, why risk the losses sure to ensue? Nix claimed the attack was canceled, but the men

---

48 Aaron Myers Reminiscence, Microfilm Reel 2, Dakota Conflict, Minnesota Historical Society.

who participated disagreed. At least one of them, W. H. Hazzard's brother Thomas, was wounded in the hip during the assault. A number of Captain Saunders's Le Sueur Tigers held the mill that day; Sgt. William Maloney and Pvts. Matthew Ahearn and Washington Kulp were killed. It is possible they lost their lives in this charge.

It was after 9:00 p.m. when an order arrived to abandon the windmill and burn it. The directive triggered both sadness and resistance, complained W. H. Hazzard, because it was still a strong point that could be held easily. Instead of complying immediately, the mill's defenders asked Lieutenant Stewart to "increase our numbers to 25 and we would hold the mill and defend it at all hazards." The request was denied and another order arrived to burn the mill and get out. A reluctant Hazzard climbed to the upper level, "and with match and straw tick did the work that destroyed the beautiful mill." The steadfast and hungry defenders fell back to the brick post office, their unpleasant task somewhat assuaged when they "found an elegant supper waiting for us."

Turner Hall also went up in flames. Nix was certain "murderous Indian firebugs" were the culprits, but it may have been destroyed by the windmill defenders when they pulled back after their attack. Nix was also incensed that the windmill, "which had contributed so much to the defense of the town," was burned, but he did not know who performed the deed. "I cannot definitely maintain that it was the Indians who sacrificed this bulwark of the defenders to the god of fire," he lamented. Nix, hardliner that he was, had a difficult time admitting the whites destroyed as many (and perhaps more) buildings in his town than "the red brutes."[49]

Rudolph Leonhart recalled the time as about ten that night when his squad near the post office got word to be on the lookout for a company of men about to abandon the windmill and head toward their position. They were warned not to fire on them which, as Leonhart remarked, "was no problem for me, as I still only had a club as a weapon." Another hour or so passed before they heard a signal cry and about 30 men "stormed down the hill and reached us safe and sound." The newcomers claimed they had set the mill on fire, but Leonhart did not see any flames. It took another hour or so, he claimed, before he spotted "a red shimmer of flames," a spectacular display he described as "one of the most

49 Hughes, *Welsh in Minnesota*, 87; Hazzard, "Autobiographical sketch," Microfilm Reel 2, Dakota Conflict, Minnesota Historical Society; Nix, *Sioux Uprising*, 113-14. According to William Hayden, the windmill wasn't set on fire until about midnight.

awesome events of my life." The siding caught first "and the framework stripped of every cover now rose into the air like a gigantic chandelier."

If burning houses during daylight hours were worthy of colorful verbiage, the nighttime fireworks exceeded anything any of them had ever witnessed. The "demon of fire" still reigned, announced Nix. "High towards the firmament whirled bursts of fire spreading afar their light, turning night into day. A spectacle so terrible and frightful, it is impossible to express in words, yet it is impressed indelibly as a horrible memory on the minds of surviving eyewitnesses." Rudolph Leonhart's evaluation was more practical. "When the houses vanished our rifles were then able to rule the prairie for a considerable distance," he wrote, "and the savages saw themselves compelled to fall back out of range." The burning windmill, reported William Hayden, was the last major fire and it "kept the town well lighted until near morning." There was nothing left within a several-block radius. The destruction was as widespread as it was personally devastating. According to Flandrau, about 190 houses "were burned by the enemy and ourselves during the encounter, leaving nothing of the town but the small portion embraced within the barricades."[50]

Even after all the destruction there was still at least one pocket of isolated resistance outside the barricades. Much earlier in the fight when the front line was collapsing, Henry Swift had helped rescue some of Captain Saunders's Le Sueur Tigers who were nearly cut off inside a building. As it turned out, some of the men either remained in place or moved to another building, where they were joined by men from other companies and held out until nightfall. Rudolph Leonhart and a number of defenders knew about 15 men were missing and spent the night believing they had been killed, though they voiced optimism while consoling worried family members.

News of the fate of these men did not arrive until late on Sunday. According to an unnamed participant, 15 men were housed in an unfinished brick building. Because of the few floorboards spanning the cellar beams, they had to step gingerly to prevent falling. They had plenty of ammunition, however, and were prepared to fight to the finish. "The first attackers paid with their lives," the anonymous narrator told Leonhart, and although it was a serious situation, they could not help but chuckle as they watched each other

---

50 Leonhart, *Memories of New Ulm*, 62, 68-69; Nix, *Sioux Uprising*, 114-15; Hayden, "Account of the relief expedition," Microfilm Reel 2, Dakota Conflict, Minnesota Historical Society; *Minnesota in the Civil and Indian Wars*, I, 733.

hop like rabbits from board to board to find a good window to fire from. Their sharp fire kept the Dakotas at bay most of the day, but when dusk fell they knew it was time to get out. Leaving, however, was not as easy as it seemed. Because of the widespread fires and heavy smoke behind them, they didn't know whether the town had been overrun. Moving toward the barricades was risky, so they headed instead for the Minnesota River.

William Gebser (Bellm's Company) remembered a farmer who kept a canoe nearby. The craft was old and leaky, but it was also large enough to carry them all across in just two trips. On the second crossing someone shifted his position and the canoe filled with water and sank, but the men all made it safely ashore. Soaked and disgusted, the men set out for St. Peter. Along the way they ran into Capt. E. St. Julien Cox's Frontier Avengers, who were marching to reinforce the defenders holding New Ulm. Most of the 15 men continued to St. Peter, but Gebser and the unnamed narrator joined Captain Cox for the journey to New Ulm.[51]

* * *

New Ulm was not the sole focus of the Dakotas that Saturday and Sunday. Parties of warriors spread throughout Brown County looting and destroying as they had in other settlements up and down the Minnesota River.

Christoph Schumann (54) and his wife lived fewer than two miles southwest of New Ulm near the Cottonwood River. (Map K) When the Dakotas arrived, the warriors threw down Schumann's fences and destroyed his crops for a property loss of $151.

One-half mile south of Schumann on the north bank of the Cottonwood, Wilhelm Alwin, his wife Wilhelmine, and their six children ran a prosperous farm. The Dakotas destroyed their crops and stole or killed their stock worth about $360. Henry Dietz (40), his wife, and their five children had lived in Cottonwood Township about three miles southeast of New Ulm for almost eight years. (Map N) They fled on August 18 and didn't return for three weeks. Dietz claimed $928 in crop losses. Nearly a dozen miles south of New Ulm, in Linden Township, Hans Johnson (46), his wife, and their four children remained at their farm oblivious to the uprising. They did not flee until August

51 Leonhart, *Memories of New Ulm*, 69-71.

24, but when they returned weeks later, their corn and hay were destroyed and their cow was dead. Johnson filed a modest claim for just $55 in losses.[52]

*   *   *

After the hell of Saturday, the nighttime hours in New Ulm passed in comparative quiet. Most of the smaller fires burned themselves out while the flickering light from the dying windmill cast its eerie shadows across the devastated landscape. "Few if any slept that night," recalled an exhausted William Hayden, "all keeping close watch, expecting an attack, but the absence of any cover whereby the Indians could approach, and a vigilant guard at every exposed point prevented any determined attempt." Somehow, despite the "vigilant guard," a dead Indian "was found inside the lines in the morning."

The last few days had worn hard on Charles Flandrau. Saturday evening after the Dakotas pulled back, some of the citizens climbed into their wagons and prepared to leave for Mankato. Flandrau and a few others argued with them that it was "simply suicide" to leave so soon, and if they were not killed outright they would probably bring on a fight and he would have to send out men to rescue them. Unable to convince them with reason Flandrau threatened to use force to hold them in town—and they reluctantly acquiesced. One man who did not heed the warning slipped away during the night, and his body was found the next morning "scalped, decapitated, and otherwise horribly mutilated."

Flandrau met with Salmon Buell a few times during the night, "heavily burdened with the responsibility upon him." The fate of more than 1,000 people hung in the balance and there were only about 190 men left fit for fighting. "If those Indians get these women and children and defenseless men," Flandrau said, "anyone in responsibility here who escapes, cannot live in this community." After relieving some of his stress by talking with Buell, Flandrau got back to work. He allowed every third man to sleep at intervals while he supervised the contracting of the inner barricades a bit and digging "a system of rifle pits on the front outside the barricades, about four rods [22 yards] apart, which completed our defense."[53]

52 Christoph Schumann Depredation #1013; Wilhelm Alwin Depredation Claim #1163; Henry Dietz Depredation Claim #423; Hans Johnson Depredation Claim #678.

53 Hayden, "Account of the relief expedition," Microfilm Reel 2, Dakota Conflict, Minnesota Historical Society; Buell, "Defense of New Ulm," 803-04, MHSC, Vol. 10, pt. 2.

As they had on other instances, Nix and Flandrau clashed on the efficacy of digging and manning rifle pits. Flandrau had ordered the digging of trenches before the battle on Saturday. According to Sheriff Roos, they were dug "so far away that it required too large a force of men to defend them." Nix seemed to agree, adding that the trenches were too scattered and unlikely to be of any use. Without his "energetic opposition," argued Nix, the pits would have been manned during the battle. If so, Nix continued, "the city would have lost at least 50 more of its bravest citizens in this struggle" because the Indians paid no attention to these pits and jumped across them with ease. The whites would have been cut off and killed or captured. Nix cited but misread Marquis de Vauban (often described as the greatest military engineer of all time) when he wrote that "trenches have always and only been used by the beleaguering parties." To the contrary, the ongoing Civil War was beginning to demonstrate just how vital breastworks and trenches were for the defense. Union Maj. Gen. John Pope, who would soon be sent to Minnesota to fight the Dakotas, discovered that firsthand on the plains of Manassas in Virginia just days after the second New Ulm battle when his men attacked Stonewall Jackson's line repeatedly without success along an unfinished railroad cut.[54]

The value of trenches at New Ulm was a moot argument, however, because it did not appear that the Dakotas were up to another face-to-face battle. There was "no attack at daylight," wrote a surprised Salmon Buell. When it was light enough to see, the defenders moved out to examine the land beyond the barricades. Some went to the schoolhouse where Otto Barth and his shotgun had taken refuge when the fight began on Saturday. They found the old man in the wreckage, burned badly but still alive. There was little the doctors in New Ulm could do for him. Barth was loaded into a wagon when the town was abandoned Monday and died in Mankato the next day.[55]

*   *   *

54 *Minnesota in the Civil and Indian Wars*, II, 206; Roos, "The Battles of New Ulm," Brown County Historical Society; Nix, *Sioux Uprising*, 116-17; Melegari, *Great Military Sieges*, 156; Hennessy, *Return to Bull Run*, 340-56. Second Manassas was but one example. Others fought later include Vicksburg, much of the Atlanta Campaign, and the fighting from the Wilderness to the James River and throughout the nine-month Petersburg Campaign.

55 Buell, "Defense of New Ulm," 805, MHSC, Vol. 10, pt. 2; Leonhart, *Memories of New Ulm*, 62.

Sometime Saturday night, Aaron Myers had run into John Wright, who was in Mankato on business and so missed the Dakota attack at Lake Shetek. Along with a Mr. Tuttle, Myers and Wright were sent to the north side of New Ulm to burn a couple of buildings. Halfway there the Dakotas saw them and tried to cut them off. The three men ran for a ravine leading to the Minnesota River. Wright could not swim so Myers tried towing him. Midway across Wright panicked when he could no longer touch bottom. During the struggle he dragged Myers beneath the water. Myers finally kicked him off and grabbed his hair in an effort to keep Wright from drowning. Tuttle swam back to help and together they pulled the unconscious man to the opposite shore. The Dakotas fired at them as they dragged Wright behind a high bank. "[We] rolled Wright about until we brought him to consciousness," remembered Myers, who was then left with his head pointing downhill while Myers and Tuttle looked for a way off the exposed bank. Once they found it, they returned for Wright and began walking for St. Peter.

After about five miles they came across "a German who was almost a raving maniac," and managed to convince the distraught man to accompany them. Near Swan Lake they came across Dakotas burning cabins and took a detour. (Map N) When Wright could walk no farther, Myers continued alone and a couple miles down the road found the advance party from E. St. Julien Cox's Company marching to New Ulm. Several men secured a wagon, went back after Myers's companions, and together they all made it to St. Peter.[56]

*   *   *

If Salmon Buell was pleased that dawn arrived without an attack, he was disappointed a short time later when the Dakotas were once again discovered moving toward the embattled town. According to William Hayden, "the firing was resumed, but with less spirit." Buell agreed, adding that when the firing began, it "was made by less than half the number of Indians." Leonhart recalled but little fighting that Sunday, the Indians "inactive and careful to stay out of range of our bullets." The Dakota seemed more interested in sneaking as close as they could to steal loose cattle and horses that had wandered away from the town center.

---

56 Aaron Myers Reminiscence, Microfilm Reel 2, Dakota Conflict, Minnesota Historical Society.

Theodore Potter, on the other hand, described a large attack. Fifty Indians appeared in the west and put on a bold front trying to draw the defenders out after them. While attention was drawn to that quarter, the main Indian force advanced from the south and east, leading Potter to believe they had "received heavy reinforcements in the night." They halted 100 yards from the barricades when the defenders let loose a devastating volley that drove them back. They also fired a make-believe howitzer. During the night the defenders fastened a stovepipe on a wheeled cart to resemble, at least from a distance, an artillery piece, with two anvils stacked one on the other and their holes filled with gunpowder. When they wheeled the "gun" out and touched off the powder in the anvils, the loud boom and smoke fooled the Indians into believing the defenders now had a cannon. Both Potter and Jacob Nix believed it was this "cannon" that scared the Indians off.[57]

According to Flandrau and Buell, the brief fighting that morning was at the upper end of town toward the river. The Indians took possession there of some unburned houses and men left the barricades to destroy them, which is what Myers, Wright, and Tuttle were trying to do when they were cut off and forced to escape across the river. Others successfully set the houses afire, even as some Dakotas moved in from behind the structures and began shooting around the corners. One of these warriors trying to fire around a burning house was wounded and fell within plain sight of the defenders. He tried to roll away but could not, and as the flames consumed the dwelling he thrashed and struggled in vain. A few men wanted to go out and pull him away from the flames, but were ordered to remain behind the barricade. The warrior burned to death.

Flandrau ordered one last building to be burned, a hotel occupied by whites but that appeared to be in danger of being captured. Everyone was ordered out. While others prepared to set it afire, an officer ran upstairs to make sure no one else was inside. To his surprise, he discovered a forgotten two-year-old, sound asleep. Dakotas attacked the family earlier in the week and had cut the child's head. The officer wrapped the youngster in a blanket and was carrying it

---

57 Hayden, "Account of the relief expedition," Microfilm Reel 2, Dakota Conflict, Minnesota Historical Society; Buell, "Defense of New Ulm," 805, MHSC, Vol. 10, pt. 2; Leonhart, *Memories of New Ulm*, 71-72; Potter, "Recollections," 452-53; Nix, *Sioux Uprising*, 119. "Several of the red scoundrels, who were among the more than 300 prisoners later interned in Mankato," recalled Nix, said "they had a deep respect for the anvil-stove-pipe cannon because they thought it was for real. They thought that it had been sent to New Ulm from Fort Snelling or from Fort Ridgely to aid in more effective defense." *Ibid.*

downstairs when a woman ran up shrieking that her baby had been left behind. The short delay saved the child and, as it turned out, the hotel as well; just before the building was fired the Indians pulled back and the order to burn it was canceled.[58]

One defender was killed that morning and two more were wounded. It was about 9:00 a.m., wrote William Hayden, when the Indians "were seen moving in squads from the river bottom and disappearing over the bluff. Uncertain as to its meaning this movement was watched with some anxiety." Rudolph Leonhart pondered similar questions: "What could this mean? Were they hatching some new tricks?" They did not have to wait long for an answer. Lookouts posted on roofs spotted men armed with muskets marching up the road from the lower ferry. Were they reinforcements, or was this another ruse like the one that cost Captain Dodd his life?

Flandrau sent an officer to find out, and he returned with welcome news: the men were from St. Julien Cox's company and Lieutenant Huey's command, which was presumed lost the day before. "The men who had borne up under the severe strain of the past thirty-six hours," admitted Salmon Buell, "broke down with joy at the thought that their trials were at last ended." Leonhart and others rushed out and the men "embraced one another even though they were strangers. Tears of joy rolled down many a bearded cheek and the expressions of joy were endless."[59]

Carried beyond normal endurance on little more than adrenalin, some of the defenders almost immediately fell asleep from exhaustion, recalled Leonhart, who with many others now had to consider "a greater number of stomachs to feed than ever before." Recovery teams went out that afternoon and brought back three or four of the dead. According to Doctor Daniels, one of them, Jerry Quane (St. Peter Guards), was found with the skin of a crow, which he called "the totem of Little Crow," pinned to his breast. Daniels claimed this emblem "was to boastfully inform us from whom the brave defender had met his death."[60]

---

58 Buell, "Defense of New Ulm," 806-07, MHSC, Vol. 10, pt. 2.

59 Buell, "Defense of New Ulm," 807, MHSC, Vol. 10, pt. 2; Leonhart, *Memories of New Ulm*, 74. As usual, time frames are disputed. Hayden and Leonhart place Cox's arrival shortly after 9:00 a.m., while Flandrau, Daniels, and Nix place his arrival about noon.

60 Leonhart, *Memories of New Ulm*, 75; Daniels, "Reminiscences of the Little Crow Uprising," 333, MHSC, Vol. 15.

When a meeting of officers was called to discuss options, a majority of those present agreed there was little choice but to evacuate New Ulm. Flandrau and Potter estimated there were now about 2,000 people in town; some 25 had been killed and about 80 wounded, and all were packed into fewer than 30 buildings. Even if they had been evenly distributed, this would have amounted to 66 people per structure. Sanitary conditions were beyond appalling, and likely worse than at Fort Ridgely. "The confined state of the town was rapidly producing disease among the women and children, who were huddled in cellars and close rooms like sheep in a cattle car," reported Flandrau. The ammunition supply was also short and there was little food. With their mills burned, surrounding farms and crops destroyed, and only 40 sacks of flour left in the entire town, feeding everyone was simply impossible. As Leonhart put it, the "poor refugees would have starved to death" if the town had not been evacuated.[61]

Not everyone agreed with this decision, including Jacob Nix. "A valid reason never existed for giving up the town, for leaving behind valuable property," that fell into the hands of marauders. According to the conspiracy-minded Nix, if Flandrau wanted to leave he could have done so on any of the three days before Saturday's fight. Flandrau, he continued, must have been influenced "by people who perhaps had thought to profit once New Ulm was given up," perhaps believing these unnamed individuals had designs on stealing whatever was left behind. What was left to steal was open to speculation. With nearly 200 buildings burned and only 30 remaining, 86% of the town was already destroyed and what was left had been used, trashed, or carried away during the evacuation. Although Nix argued that Flandrau could and should have abandoned the town earlier, he also wrote that it was much too dangerous to do so because there were many places for the Indians to set up ambushes, particularly at the crossing of the Cottonwood River, where "A slaughter would have taken place as probably never before recorded in the history of the U.S."[62]

Nix was not alone in his opinion. Dr. Asa Daniels was also against leaving and complained that none of the physicians were consulted about the decision. Reinforcements had just arrived, he complained, and "our position was stronger than ever." He went on to contradict Flandrau's dire assessment by

61 Potter, "Recollections," 453; *Minnesota in the Civil and Indian Wars*, II, 206.

62 Nix, *Sioux Uprising*, 120-21.

claiming "the sanitary condition did not necessitate great urgency in moving." Colonel Sibley, he added, was also on his way to assist them. In the end, it was probably the stress of dealing with the severely injured that most weighed on the doctors' minds. The physicians did the best they could, but could not duplicate the success Dr. Muller achieved at Fort Ridgely. Doctor Daniels had a number of serious cases: John Summers was shot through the spinal column and died; Rufus Huggins (16), the brother of Amos Huggins who was killed at Lac Qui Parle, was shot through the knee joint, refused amputation, and died; a New Ulm man who was shot in the mouth recovered, as did a Sibley County man whose fractured arm was amputated; Captain Saunders was down with his serious abdominal wound but recovered, as did A. M. Bean, whose bullet-shattered jaw would give him problems the rest of his life; a St. Paul man shot in the head lingered for two years before dying insane.[63]

Regardless of the physicians' thoughts on sanitary conditions or moving the wounded, on Monday morning the barricades came down and about 1,500 people prepared to leave. Most of those whose property was already destroyed wanted to go, while others wished to remain to save whatever was still salvageable. Zepherin Demeules, his wife, and their 18-month-old baby had lived in town for the past year and a half. He rented a house above Louis Robert's store but kept his wagon and some property at William Gallus's wagon shop. He lost his wagon and accoutrements when the wagon shop burned, but wanted to try and save the rest of his possessions. Unfortunately, the marauders feared by Jacob Nix arrived. Robert's store and the rest of Demeules' goods, worth $208, were stolen after the town was largely abandoned.[64]

Once the barricades were taken apart, 153 wagons—which formed much of the defensive breastworks—were recovered, repaired, and loaded to capacity. Flandrau limited the amount of property that could be taken away because of the need to carry so many people. Some wagon owners complained about having to leave behind their possessions, and only reluctantly made space in their wagons for the old, young, sick, or infirm who had little or no property. In the end, however, Solomon Buell explained, the wagon owners "admitted the justness, and certainly the mercy, of this order. Many have left or lost all," lamented Buell, "even their nearest and dearest ones . . . lie buried, without

63 Daniels, "Reminiscences of the Little Crow Uprising," 333-34, MHSC, Vol. 15; Flandrau, *History of Minnesota*, 157. See the Appendix for a list of casualties.

64 Zepherin Demeules Depredation Claim #175.

coffin, book, or bell, where they died, with naught to mark the spot." Those who remain, he asked rhetorically, "are going where? God knows—anywhere away from the Indians!"[65]

The caravan, described by Flandrau as a "heart-rending procession," headed downriver to Mankato. The colonel's description was sad but true. The citizens of a once prosperous town and the surrounding countryside were abandoning their homes with few if any possessions in the hope of reaching a town where their only hope was to receive food and shelter from strangers. There was a very real possibility of being slaughtered along the way as they rolled through hostile country to reach Mankato. At Crisp's Farm, about halfway to their destination, Flandrau pushed the wagons on but stopped with most of his men to form a blocking force in case any Dakotas were following them. The caravan reached Mankato late on Monday, August 25.[66]

Still on blockade duty the next morning, Flandrau suggested that a strong body of armed men return to New Ulm, but the majority of those who would have to participate in the expedition wanted nothing to do with the idea. They had not seen their families for more than a week and wanted to go home. "I did not blame them," said Flandrau. Captain Cox and his company agreed to return to the devastated town, but Flandrau did not think such a small force would be of any use. Instead, the colonel and his men marched for Mankato and arrived there later that day. Flandrau released his companies from duty. The displaced settlers found shelter in Mankato or dispersed to St. Peter and other points north and east or, as Buell put it, "anywhere away from the Indians!"[67]

---

65 Buell, "Defense of New Ulm," 809, MHSC, Vol. 10, pt. 2.

66 This is where Mrs. Harrington, as described in Chapter 8, p. 146, made her way into friendly lines after eight days in the wilderness.

67 Flandrau, *History of Minnesota*, 157-58.

C hapter 17

"What cares laughing Minnehaha for the corpses in the vale."

Nicollet County

Henry Diepolder's claim ~ Jacob Mauerle ~ Courtland killings ~ Lafayette township losses and settler disputes ~ Depredation claims procedures ~ Norwegian Grove and Scandian Grove ~ Nelson and Jonsson ~ Minnehaha

L ittle Crow may have convinced as many as 650 warriors to fight at New Ulm on Saturday, August 23, but a significant number declined to attack the well-defended town. These warriors opted for the less dangerous and potentially more rewarding choice of roaming through Brown and Nicollet counties attacking individual homesteads. The bands that came down the north bank of the Minnesota River burning and looting early Saturday chased the last of the settlers in far western Nicollet County from their homes. West Newton was about mid-way between New Ulm and Fort Ridgley, and some of the people there, like Henry Diepolder and his family, moved to the fort. The Dakotas burned 14 structures in West Newton, but only looted Diepolder's house. Diepolder—a farmer, cabinet-maker, and mill carpenter—filed a claim for $391 in losses.[1]

Henry Diepolder's case illustrates the checks and balances built into the claims filing system. His claim for losses included his money, crops, an ox, a milk cow, hogs, household items, bedding, clothing, carpenter tools, mathematical instruments, and two clarinets. Johann Linbal, who worked in the

1 Henry Diepolder Depredation Claim #2013.

neighborhood for three months before the outbreak, testified for Diepolder and basically substantiated the entire claim. Johan Voltin, who lived nearby, said he was back there about ten days after the outbreak and saw that most of Diepolder's crops were a total loss, his cow had been shot, and two calves had fallen into his cellar through broken floorboards—but he never heard that the claimant had any mathematical or musical instruments. Voltin filed his own claim for $160 in damages. Another neighbor, Alexander Harkin, who filed a clam for $650 in damages, vouched for few of Diepolder's claimed losses. But the crops, he added, could have been damaged by the bad weather; the ox was worth less than claimed; he had never heard that Diepolder lost any cows or hogs; he didn't believe he had any clarinets; "his house was not damaged," and the claimant "hid and saved all his money." Whether Harkin believed Diepolder was padding his claim or they were on unfriendly terms—or was simply a jealous neighbor—is not known. What it clearly demonstrates, however, is that some citizens were not going to simply give a free pass to someone else who might be abusing the depredation claims system.[2]

Wurtemberg, Germany native Vincent Brunner (26) had a farm in West Newton. He learned about the trouble on August 18 when a Dakota he knew told him and then asked Brunner for a wagon and horses to take word to New Ulm. The men were just leaving when the shooting began. When Brunner announced he wanted to go back and warn his neighbors, the Dakota replied that he was free to go, but that he would take Brunner's team and, if he didn't like it, he would kill him. Brunner rode with the Dakota to New Ulm, where the Indian disappeared. When he learned firsthand about the uprising from members of the recruiting party who had just been ambushed, Brunner re-crossed at the ferry in New Ulm and drove back to West Newton along the prairie road. To his dismay few people believed him, even though they must have heard the gunfire in Milford just across the river.

Brunner warned Jacob Mauerle (43), a relative from Wurtemburg who lived with his family on the east side of West Newton. Mauerle, Brunner, and several other families packed up and headed east. In Lafayette and Swan Lake they joined other families and soon about 45 teams and wagons were rolling for St. Peter. Many became convinced they had overreacted and decided to go back at least as far as Swan Lake to determine what was happening. Mauerle, however, knew many of the Dakotas and was certain they would not hurt him. He sent his

---

2 Berghold, *Indians' Revenge*, 125; Bakeman, ed., *Index to Claimants*, 18, 45.

wife and three children on to St. Paul, but against the advice of others returned to West Newton, where he owned a saloon near the Palmer Ferry. The Dakotas killed him, cut off his head, and left his body on the roadside. Some accounts have his dog sitting beside his master's body for ten days.[3]

The Dakotas pushed Lieutenant Huey and his men aside (see Chapter 16) when they reached the ferry in New Ulm on Saturday morning. Some remained to invest the town while others fanned out first into Courtland and Lafayette Townships, and then to Nicollet, Granby, and New Sweden farther east. Many men in Courtland and Lafayette had already sent their families to St. Peter or Mankato and helped defend New Ulm. Those in the eastern townships generally stayed away from New Ulm and sought refuge in St. Peter. When the panic swept through the area on Monday and Tuesday, a tide of refugees fled east. When nothing more of consequence happened by Wednesday and Thursday, they began trickling back to their homes.

Courtland was hit hard. (Map N) First organized in 1856 as Hilo, the town's name was changed to Courtland in 1865. Max Haack had a farm in Courtland Township one mile east of New Ulm and 200 yards from the Minnesota River. On Monday, August 18, he took his wife Elizabeth and their three children all the way to St. Peter. The next day Haack joined the St. Peter Frontier Guards with Colonel Flandrau and marched all the way back. He was with Flandrau in the attack that drove the Dakotas out of the lower town on Saturday, but was shot in the stomach and died that night.[4]

Most of the people had the opportunity to get away, but some returned a little too soon. Frederick G. Gerboth (52) and his wife Augusta (46) arrived from Germany in 1850, and by 1862, they and their five children worked a farm in Courtland. They reached St. Peter safely, but on August 28 Gerboth joined George Jacobs, Rudolph Kiesling, and a Mr. Hochhausen and returned to see what they could salvage from their farms. Despite warnings from the others Gerboth dropped out of the party to check his farm alone. The remaining three

---

3   Berghold, *Indians' Revenge*, 123-25. Duncan Kennedy, who left Fort Ridgely on Monday, August 25, wrote: "I stumbled over the dead body of Mauerle, who was killed the Saturday before." His gravestone, however, lists August 22 as his date of death. Bryant and Murch, *Great Massacre*, 379; Dahlin, *Dakota Uprising Victims*, 82. Mauerle's story is similar to the mysterious Redwood ferryman: killed in the road near a ferry, decapitated, and with a dog sitting by the body. Add the similar names—Jacob Mauley and Jacob Mayley—and the identity of the Redwood ferryman becomes even more confusing. Perhaps it is merely a composite of several variations.

4   Neill, *History of the Minnesota Valley*, 681; Max Haack Depredation Claim #1334.

went to Kiesling's place on the north bank of the river opposite New Ulm. The next morning, Dakotas killed Gerboth in his cornfield.[5]

August Nierens (34) emigrated from Germany in 1852, married Julia Fenske the next year, and in 1859 was licensed to preach in the Iowa Conference of the Evangelical United Brethren Church. On August 18, Nierens took his family to Fort Ridgely and helped defend the post. When the siege was over he returned to his farm, but was killed by a small war party of Dakotas on September 2.

Nierens's neighbors included Christian and Christiana Richter and their seven children. Christian was leaving his farm to enlist in the Union Army when news of the uprising changed his mind. The family spent the next two weeks moving among different homes in eastern Nicollet County and sometimes hid in the fields and woods. By September 2, they were back home. Christian and his sons William and Henry were down by the Minnesota River looking for stray oxen when a Dakota war party, likely the same one that killed Nierens, found them. Christian and William were killed and Henry was badly wounded.[6]

For the past three years William Sonnenberg, his wife Caroline, and their three children lived in Courtland near the Minnesota River six miles east of New Ulm. They fled with the first news of the outbreak but returned when they thought the trouble died down. Wilhelm Mannweiler, who lived about one mile from Sonnenberg, was visiting with him on September 2 but left just before the Indians arrived. Mannweiler moved down toward the river, near where the Richters were searching for their cattle, and the same Dakota war party killed him, too. "I saw seven Indians on 2 September," remembered William's wife Caroline. "I saw one shoot in the direction of my husband and my husband was killed. Same day they killed four men and one boy. This was on our farm."[7]

Michael Ganske lived about one and a half miles from New Ulm and a mile beyond Max Haack. He sent his wife Augusta and their children August (5) and Ida (3) to St. Peter. Ganske joined Flandrau's St. Peter Frontier Guards and participated in the second New Ulm battle, but while he was there the Dakotas raided his farm and inflicted $184 in damages. He returned to the farm in early

5   Nix, *Sioux Uprising*, 123. According to census records and family genealogies, Gerboth was either 49 or 52 years old and arrived in America in either 1849 or 1850.

6   Dahlin, *Dakota Uprising Victims*, 86-87.

7   William Sonnenberg Depredation Claim #342. Dahlin, *Dakota Uprising Victims*, 133, suggests Sonnenberg was killed August 18 or 19.

September but was frightened away when Gerboth, Nierens, Richter, and Sonnenberg were killed within four miles of his farm.[8]

Farther downriver from Ganske, and fewer than three miles from New Ulm and near Redstone Ferry lived August Buder and his wife. A mason and shoemaker by trade, Buder rode to St. Peter to enlist, but hurried back home when he heard of the uprising. Buder and his wife sought refuge in New Ulm and were there during the siege. He had already hauled logs into town to be cut at the Globe Mill, but they were burned along with the mill during the attack. His house did not go up in flames, but Buder lost a calf, crops, clothing, linens, and his shoemaker tools, all told about $357.[9]

Fewer settlers were killed north and west of Courtland in Lafayette Township, but they still suffered significant property losses. (Map N) As noted, Frederick Fritsche's house in Section 8 was plundered. Two miles upriver from Fritsche, in the northeastern corner of West Newton Township, Henry Beussmann filed a claim for $1,200. Fidel Diepolder, the lieutenant of the Lafayette Company, lived about one mile east of Fritsche in Section 9. He suffered damages of $310. Adolph Schilling, about two miles north of the ferry in Section 15, claimed losses of $190. Henry Wellner's house in Section 14 was fire damaged to the tune of $350. Jacob Spaeth lived less than three miles northeast of New Ulm in Section 10, where Indians destroyed $165 of his property.[10]

Joseph Fimeyer lived about two and a half miles northeast of New Ulm in Section 10 and about one mile from Jacob Spaeth. He, his wife Sophia, and their children Joseph, Sophia, Emmy, and Paul fled to St. Peter. Joseph returned to his farm two weeks later and claimed his carpenter and farming tools had been thrown outside and rusted, and the Indians took or destroyed wheat, rye, barley, potatoes, and oats in the amount of $784. Jurgen Durbahn (29) lived with his wife and three children in Section 5, Lafayette Township. They fled and only suffered $49 in burned fences, destroyed vegetables, and stolen poultry.[11]

Friederick Boock lived about three miles north of New Ulm and about half a mile from Durbahn. He, his wife Maria, and daughters Maria (4), Emma (2),

---

8   Michael Ganske Depredation Claim #2022.

9   August Buder Depredation Claim #139.

10 Bakeman, ed., *Index to Claimants*, 3, 11, 39, 42, 46.

11 Joseph Fimeyer Depredation Claim #2015; Jurgen Durbahn Depredation Claim #431.

and Louisa (2 months) fled to St. Peter. During the flight his children took sick, "in consequence of the exposure and sufferings caused by the Indian raid." Boock returned to his home three weeks later to find his doors and windows smashed, his silverware, clock, and watch stolen, mirrors broken, and wheat, oats, rye, corn, and rutabagas ruined. His milk cow had been clubbed or kicked in the side and her ribs broken, so Boock "had to kill her to put her out of her misery." He filed for $293 in losses, but there was no compensation for human life. A few months after the uprising, Emma and Louisa died. The heartbroken and frustrated parents knew the reason why.[12]

Most of the damage claims were straightforward, with witnesses backing the testimony. In some cases, however, as in Henry Diepolder's disagreement with Alexander Harkin, citizens disputed their neighbors' claims. Since 1858, Gottfried Kuehnel, his wife Maria, and children Eugene, Julia, Louisa, and Anna, lived on a farm in Section 15 about two miles northeast of New Ulm. On August 19, Kuehnel sent his family to St. Peter. He stayed home, traveling back and forth to New Ulm a few times over the next two days. On Saturday morning he saw "Indians within a few yards of his house coming towards the back door and immediately" ran out the front, got on his horse, and made it to town just before the Indians closed off the ferry. He returned to his badly damaged home one week later, all his property "either taken away or broken up." His stove was smashed, feather beds torn up, good clothing ripped up or stolen, fences destroyed, and stock gone. He had a wagon and sleigh burned with his hay and lost wheat, oats, barley, and beans. His cross plow was damaged and the harrow burned. Kuehnel filed a depredation claim for $1,698.

Rudolph Kiesling, who farmed one mile south, testified that he had known Kuehnel since he moved in, was familiar with his property, and vouched for the losses. William H. Sigler, on the other hand, challenged Kuehnel's claim. Sigler lived two miles from Kuehnel and scoffed at many of his claims because of his appearance. Kuehnel, he reported, "always went very commonly dressed in coarse cotton clothes" and Sigler never saw him wear anything better. "He is a poor farmer," he continued, "never raises good crops, [and] was considered in the town to be in poor circumstances." From the appearance of the farm, Sigler said, "I do not believe he had the crops on his farm for which he has charged." Sigler claimed Kuehnel only had a "rough log house" with bark still on the logs, no fences, no fine clothing, and few crops. "He ranked with the poorer class of

12 Friederick Boock Depredation Claim #2004.

farmers and was a poor man." Sigler's pointed observations suggested a personal grudge, especially when he described Kuehnel as "one of that class of Germans who is obliged and does get along with the least possible expense and is not a man to lay out means which he never had in an extravagant expenditure of dress on himself or family or furniture for house or table." As Sigler put it, there "is no human probability" that Kuehnel had the articles he claimed to have lost. In fact, Sigler concluded, in the whole neighborhood there was little property destroyed by Indians because there was little to destroy. He estimated that $200 "would amply compensate" Kuehnel for his losses.

Charles Frank countered Sigler's testimony. Frank lived one mile from Kuehnel on Section 16, was often at Kuehnel's house, and testified that he was in a very comfortable situation with clothes, furniture, and crops, and that his burned hay alone was worth $400. Frank didn't believe Sigler was acquainted with the neighborhood, stating "He never has been to claimant's [Kuehnel's] place at all I do not think." According to Frank, Sigler's occupation was teaching school a few months a year and hunting the rest, and he didn't believe Sigler went near Kuehnel's to hunt. "The neighborhood," said Frank, "do not like Sigler very well and I do not like him."[13]

Frank had a good reason not to like Sigler, because the latter had recently made similar statements about him. Frank had lived with his wife and two children for the past two years in the school section, Number 16, about half a mile from Fidel Diepolder and one mile from Kuehnel. He fled to New Ulm on Tuesday and took some of his property, but it was burned during the fight on Saturday. Frank evacuated the town with everyone else on August 25, and returned to his farm three days later to find his fences down, the cattle and hogs killed or gone, and two acres of potatoes, two acres of corn, half an acre of turnips, and half an acre of garden vegetables destroyed. Inside, his goose-feather mattress was ripped up and butternut beadstead broken apart. He lost flour, a wagon, and a dozen milk pans.

Fidel Diepolder testified that he had been at Frank's many times and knew he had lost the property. Johann Simmet, who filed his own claim asking for $875 in damages, lived about one mile from Frank, had been to his house, and testified that he had indeed lost the items. When it was Sigler's turn to support or deny the claim, he offered that Frank "did not own the land he lived on. He was very poor and had very little." Sigler argued the yield on his potato and corn

13 Gottfried Kuehnel Depredation Claim #2043.

acreage was low because Sigler's father-in-law, William Ellensdorfer, grew crops in the same fields and he did not have a good season. Sigler admitted that Frank might have lost some items, but declared that he had "more in his house immediately after [the] outbreak than he had before."

Frank rebutted Sigler's testimony by categorically saying that Sigler was "never in my house before the outbreak. He hardly knew me. It is not true that I have more property now than before the outbreak." Robert Zollner's testimony, which followed, supported Frank's claim for losses. "[I] don't think he is as well off now as before the outbreak," Zollner said. In the end, Frank only received partial payment for his claimed losses.[14]

Usually the testimony by neighbors supported a claim, but there was no guarantee they would always be friendly witnesses. The three commissioners who were appointed to take the evidence were no fools either, and if a claim was suspect it was likely to be denied. After the uprising, Minnesota Congressman Cyrus Aldrich introduced a bill to divert $1,500,000 from current and future Sioux annuities for the immediate relief of the affected settlers. The proposal was part of a process that had been in use for decades. The adjudication of depredation claims went back all the way to 1796, when Congress passed a law to provide compensation to both Indians and whites for depredations committed upon each other. The Trade and Intercourse Act was enacted in part to provide whites and Indians an avenue to settle disputes without resorting to violence.

There were four requirements for a legitimate depredation claim: the tribe had to be "in amity with the United States" (no claims would be paid if the tribe was at war); the accused white or Indian had to "cross the . . . boundary line" of Indian Territory or a reservation to commit the alleged offense (you could not commit a depredation on your own land); the victim or his representative had to provide "necessary documents and proofs" of his losses, and; the victim forfeited any right to file a claim if he tried to "obtain private satisfaction or revenge."

There were also administrative procedures. If the claim was approved, the government agent requested satisfaction from the accused party, the great majority of which were Indian tribes as a whole, since claimants rarely knew an

---

14 Bakeman, ed., *Index to Claimants*, 41; Charles Frank Depredation Claim #481. William Sigler, who comes across as being opposed to everyone else's claims, filed one of his own asking for $700 in damages. It would be interesting to learn how his neighbors testified, but this file cannot be located.

individual Indian's name. After one year, if the tribe had not provided restitution, the agent forwarded the claim to the president of the United States (or his representative) which, if approved, could pay the claimant by deducting the money from the annual stipend due to the tribe. Once again, the innocent suffered.

The Trade and Intercourse Act was amended in 1834 to shift responsibility of adjudicating the claims to the Commissioner of Indian Affairs, an office created in 1832. The amendments also said that the government would accept liability for any Indian tribes too impoverished to pay claims against them; the stipulations required that claims be filed within three years of the date of the depredation; they allowed agents to take testimony from eyewitnesses; and they indemnified whites who were legally in Indian country, such as a licensed trader or an emigrant using a road on which passage was allowed by treaty. The latter clause was clearly added to protect white Americans as they trekked ever westward.[15]

The process was banded in red tape and could take years to conclude, but what Congressman Aldrich proposed was an extraordinary measure to expedite compensation for current victims of the Dakota uprising. The Senate committee on Indian affairs was not about to simply pass out $1,500,000 without a more precise accounting. However, on February 16, 1863, it approved an initial appropriation of $200,000, providing each legitimate claimant $200. The additional money could be appropriated in a future session of Congress. The money, if appropriated, would be taken from the Sioux. Some would be from Sioux annuities—the $71,000 in gold at Fort Ridgely, for example, offered a sizeable down payment. Better yet, they could declare "all lands, rights of occupancy, annuities, and claims, heretofore accorded to said Indians . . . to be forfeited to the United States." In other words, the Dakotas no longer owned any land in Minnesota.[16]

Chairman Albert S. White, Cyrus Aldrich, and Eli R. Chase were appointed to serve as commissioners and obtain a record of applicants who suffered losses. They spent April to December of 1863 engaged in the prodigious job of hearing and recording the testimony of 2,940 claimants, which piled up "nearly 20,000 manuscript pages of legal cap." Given human nature, the three commissioners had grown sick and tired of listening to bickering and

15 Skogen, *Indian Depredation Claims*, 31-33.

16 Folwell, *History of Minnesota*, II, 246-47; Skogen, *Indian Depredation Claims*, 90-91.

contradictory evidence from the likes of Kuehnel, Frank, Sigler, Diepolder, Harkin, and hundreds of others. If there were too many inconsistencies or if the claimant did not have a convincing case, no payment was forthcoming.[17]

*   *   *

The Dakotas who bypassed New Ulm on August 23 to raid deeper into Nicollet County did not go all the way east to where the Minnesota River flows north from Mankato to St. Paul. The fringes of penetration touched Nicollet Township on the south side of the county. Robert W. McNutt (26), a farmer and "cutter of shingles," lived with his wife, Martha (21) and son Elmer (2) just north of the Minnesota River across from Crisp's Farm (present Judson) about 14 miles downstream from New Ulm. When McNutt enlisted in Company E, 9th Minnesota Infantry, at Fort Snelling on August 19, he was promised a furlough so he could go home and harvest his crops. He was on his way home when the word of the uprising arrived and leaves were canceled. Henry Toothaker, who lived next to McNutt and had enlisted the same day in Company D, was sent to find his neighbor and direct him immediately to Mankato, where the company was marching. McNutt complied and sent his family to St. Peter. He and his family were gone when the Indians reached his farm and destroyed $126 worth of property. Henry Toothaker's farm, within sight of McNutt's, was untouched.[18]

McNutt's claim was paid, but those filed by settlers living farther east were generally denied. John Schneider and John Lambert are but two examples. The men lived within half a mile of each other in Oshawa Township and only two miles from St. Peter. It wasn't until August 23 that Schneider moved his wife and four children into town. A couple of days later he returned to the farm, saw two mounted Indians, and rode back to St. Peter. For the next three weeks Schneider "returned to his farm every day" to drive out the cattle, tend his crops and fences, and stack wheat. John Lambert had a similar experience, though he claimed he saw a single Indian "skulking in the hazel bushes" near Michael Magner's house, one-half mile from Schneider's. None of the three

17 White, "Sioux Claims Commission," Microfilm Reel 3, Dakota Conflict, Minnesota Historical Society.

18 Robert McNutt Depredation Claim #827; *Minnesota in the Civil and Indian Wars*, I, 417. McNutt was in Dane's company, which was the first Regular Army unit to reach New Ulm after the evacuation. It participated in the rescue of Lavina Eastlick and Alomina Hurd.

commissioners were impressed with these stories, and didn't believe that property values went down just because an Indian happened to be seen in the neighborhood. Besides, Schneider worked his farm nearly every day. Both claims were denied.[19]

The commissioners may have rejected dubious claims like those submitted by Schneider and Lambert, but they paid others where the responsibility for the damage rested with soldiers and not Indians. One instance occurred north of Nicollet County in Sibley County. Michael Cummings (35), his wife, and their five children had lived about 20 miles east of Fort Ridgely on the road leading to Henderson. For the past eight years, Cummings ran a farm, hotel, and saloon in Section 6, just south of present-day Winthrop. Located midway between the two destinations, it was a convenient rest stop for travelers. It was also a handy stop for the army. Cummings complained that his property "was all lost or stolen during the time of the outbreak by the U. States troops in the fall of 1862." A steady stream of soldiers passed through and took his wood and water. In September, 700 troops "entirely stripped my farm of everything, and burnt up every rail they could find." Cummings was allowed $227 in damages, including restitution for items such as two beaver traps, a demijohn of sarsaparilla, and two bottles of "Dr. Sanford's Liver Remedy."[20]

Leander A. Dow also received compensation for actions undertaken by Uncle Sam's Army. Leander, his wife Maria, and their two children lived on the Fort Ridgely to Henderson Road about eight miles east of Cummings. After scores of refugees from Birch Coulee and Beaver Creek streamed by his house on Tuesday, Dow decided to leave. Together with his neighbor John Chapin, they took what belongings they could in a wagon and drove to Henderson. Dow continued on to Fort Snelling, left his family there with some relatives, and returned to see what else he could salvage from his farm. South of Belle Plaine on Sunday morning, August 24, soldiers of Company D, 6th Minnesota commandeered Dow's wagon and team, unloaded his possessions, filled the wagon with tents and camp equipage, and made him drive with them all the way to Fort Ridgely.

Dow was in service until September 1, when Colonel Sibley gave him a pass to return home. By then it was too late to salvage anything. His fences were

19 John Schneider Depredation Claim #466.

20 Michael Cummings Depredation Claim #193; Reddemann, *Henderson to Fort Ridgely Trail*, 27.

down, his hay stolen, and hogs were destroying his crops. The doors and windows of his house were broken and nearly everything inside was stolen or destroyed to the tune of $228. Dakotas did not raid that part of Sibley County, so the damages were caused by soldiers, refugees, or neighbors who had not fled. The commissioners paid Dow's claim.[21]

The Dakotas didn't penetrate into central Sibley County during the first week of the uprising, but they did visit other townships in Nicollet County. Today, Brighton Township lies east of Lafayette and north of Courtland, but until 1877 Brighton (north of Swan Lake) was in the western part of an oversized Granby Township. Christopher and John Apfelbaum (Applebaum) farmed on Section 4. (Map N) When they fled is unknown. Their bodies were found the following winter about one mile apart from each other, seven miles west of St. Peter.

The marauding Dakotas found other prey near Apfelbaum's place. Fleeing from farther west, the Johann Schwarz (Schwartz, Schwatz, Schmotz) family made it as far as Apfelbaums when the Dakotas caught them. They shot Johann, his wife Anna Maria, and their daughter Katherine, all three mortally wounded. One of the men hanged for this trio of murders was Tenazepa, or Dowansa (The Singer). He admitted being in the New Ulm fight, and Joseph Godfrey testified that he had told him he helped kill three men and two women in the Swan Lake area. Nels Nelson Sr., who lived near the Apfelbaums, found the three wounded Schwarzs in the road next to their overturned wagon and strewn possessions. Nelson managed to get them into his wagon but they all expired on the way to St. Peter.

Late in August, Governor Ramsey dispatched Lieutenant Governor Ignatius Donnelly to accompany Colonel Sibley and report how the expedition was progressing. Donnelly wrote to Ramsey from Belle Plaine and St. Peter. On the next leg of the journey to Fort Ridgely, Donnelly rode along the road through Brighton and Lafayette. His party stopped near Apfelbaum's house to examine wreckage. "In the yard of the house stood the wagons of these unfortunate people," Donnelly wrote to Ramsey from Fort Ridgely, "their trunks broken open, and the ground strewn with their effects. The trunks were old fashioned, and of German make, and bore upon the side, in large letters 'Johann Schwatz.' It was indeed melancholy to look into them and see their little

---

21 Leander A. Dow Depredation Claim #224.

trinkets, their prayer-books, their clothing; and even the toys of children; and reflect upon the sudden and brutal death which had overtaken them."[22]

The Dakotas were not finished. The farthest they struck into Nicollet County on August 23 was to the northeast in Lake Prairie and New Sweden townships. The Norwegian families of Torstein Ostensen Boen, Johan Tollefson, and Lars Svenson Rodning were the first to arrive in 1854. They built a little community at the western edge of Lake Prairie Township. The next year, Andrew Thorson and some other Swedes joined them. The growing settlement scattered around Sand Lake was called Norseland or Scandian Grove. (Map O) It was a beautiful place, wrote Thorson, and during the first winter "we lived among Indians who were numerous in our woods." Also in 1854, Charles Johnson and Andrew Webster arrived, but settled just across the township line in Granby (New Sweden). In 1856, Ole Ostensen Boen, Torstein's brother, and Gunder Nereson and Swenke Torgerson settled six miles northwest in Granby around Rice Lake near the Sibley County border (in a community later known as Norwegian Grove). During the next few years more settlers arrived, but they were not all Scandinavians. For instance, Irishman John Cronen settled in Lake Prairie in 1856. In July 1858, four families arrived that would play a central part in the drama: Carl Nelson, Pehr Carlson, Andrew Paulson, and Erik Jonsson (Johnson), all of whom settled in Section 8, Granby. Within a year more families came to the surrounding sections, including those of Lars J. Larson, Lars Solomonson, Peter M. Fritjoff, Pehr Benson, Johannes Ecklund, Swen Benson, and S. A. Herbert.[23]

The Swedish evangelical Lutherans began holding services in 1857 and organized the following year with Rev. P. A. Cederstam as pastor. "I believe that the Lord has sent me here," wrote Cedarstam, "therefore no advantages will lure me away from here nor will any dangers or difficulties drive me away." Cederstam officiated the first marriage ceremony in January 1859 at Andrew Webster's house, when Martin Peterson and Judith Webster were wed. The first post office was opened in Norseland in 1860, and in 1862 a new church went up

---

22 Neill, *History of the Minnesota Valley*, 696-97; Tolzmann, ed, *Outbreak and Massacre*, 45; Bryant and Murch, *Great Massacre*, 145; Dahlin, *Dakota Uprising*, 132, 260, 358n595.

23 Neill, *History of the Minnesota Valley*, 669-70, 690-91; Gene Estensen, "War Comes to Norwegian Grove," in *Celebrating Our Norwegian-Minnesotan Heritage*, 185-86; Nelson, "History of the early pioneers," Microfilm Reel 3, Dakota Conflict, Minnesota Historical Society. Until 1864, New Sweden Township was part of Granby Township, which today lies to the south.

in Scandian Grove at a cost of $1,500, complete with organ and bell. Things were looking up in the small but thriving community.[24]

Although the settlers knew little of what was happening on the reservations, they maintained a guarded optimism about their new lives on the Minnesota frontier. Carl Nelson's son C. C. Nelson recalled living "among the Indians four years. They made their living by hunting, fishing, and trapping muskrats. They visited us frequently and occasionally stayed all night and we accommodated them the best we could, although we didn't find them very pleasant or agreeable, however, we tried not to cross them for fear they would attack us at any time."[25]

The Swedes and Norwegians of Nicollet County didn't cross the Dakotas, but others did and they would all pay the price. At the start of the Civil War three of the locals, Herbert, Fritjoff, and John Johnson, joined the Union Army and the remaining settlers helped their families. When Andrew Paulson died, Joren Johnson married Mrs. Paulson to care for her family. They stuck together and took care of each other. Word of the uprising filtered into Scandian Grove and Norwegian Grove late on August 18. Some people left for St. Peter, but the murders and looting seemed so distant and so unlikely to reach them that most stayed behind. When word arrived that New Ulm had been attacked on the 19th, preparations were made to flee if the need arose. Pehr Carlson, Johannes Ecklund, and Joren Johnson rode to New Ulm to help fight, and the others looked after their families, too.

On Wednesday, August 20, settlers in northern Granby (New Sweden) and Norwegian Grove thought they could see fires burning far in the distance toward Fort Ridgely and New Ulm. A few of them had rifles, but according to 14-year-old Ingar Jonsson, they did not have any ammunition and it was 16 miles to St. Peter, the closest place to purchase any. They decided they should go at least a little farther east, so they hitched their oxen and drove the half dozen miles to Scandian Grove Church and spent the night there. The next day Andrew Thorson told them that scouts had not been able to find any Indians and it was safe to go home. They returned, but toward evening on the 22nd more fires were seen and the families packed once again and rode back to

24 Neill, *History of the Minnesota Valley*, 669, 690; Lundblad, "Impact of Minnesota's Dakota Conflict," 216.

25 Nelson, "History of the early pioneers," Microfilm Reel 3, Dakota Conflict, Minnesota Historical Society.

Scandian Grove Church—all except the Erik Jonsson family. "One of the neighbors was sent to tell us," explained Ingar Jonsson, "but got scared and forgot to tell us."[26]

With a bright sunrise on Saturday, the peripatetic families gathered at the church to discuss the situation. It was generally agreed they had been jumping at shadows and safe to return home. This time, several settlers with horses offered to ride beyond the settlement, look for Indians, and notify the others what they found. The horsemen, Andrew Thorson, Andrew Webster, John Nelson, Martin Peterson, Lars Larson, Erik Jonsson, and two others rode off as the families prepared their belongings. They had barely covered three miles when, at noon on Saturday, they spied mounted men in their front at the edge of timber near a large slough.The unidentified riders appeared to be beckoning them forward. Once the settlers advanced the riders (Dakotas) opened fire, but the range was too far and no one was hit. The settlers wheeled their mounts and galloped away scattering in several directions; the smaller Indian ponies were unable to catch them. "Our men didn't have time to notify us," C. C. Nelson explained, "as they had to save their own lives." Only Erik Jonsson and Lars Larson, he continued, rode straight home to rescue their families.

Larson had promised to take care of Pehr Carlson's family while he was fighting at New Ulm. Larson, who lived about one mile northeast of Carlson, was a widower living with his daughter Hannah (12). He harnessed his horse team, placed Hannah and some of their clothing and bedding in the wagon, and drove to Carlson's so Pehr's wife could throw in her belongings while he joined the others on the scout.[27]

The scouts' return set off a chain reaction. Lars Larson found everyone ready to go at Carlson's place, but within minutes "he saw six mounted Indians rapidly approaching" and whipped the horses and wagon along the road toward Norwegian Grove. No prodding was needed at Erik Jonsson's house one-half mile east of Carlson's. "Mother and we children were ready in the wagon to drive away," Ingar Jonsson recalled. "When we saw the men coming so fast we knew there was danger."

26 Nelson, "History of the early pioneers," Microfilm Reel 3, Dakota Conflict, Minnesota Historical Society; Holmquist, "Reminiscence," Microfilm Reel 2, Dakota Conflict, Minnesota Historical Society.

27 Nelson, "History of the early pioneers," Microfilm Reel 3, Dakota Conflict, Minnesota Historical Society; Lars Larson Depredation Claim #615. According to Nelson, Larson was a member of the scouting party, but Larson does not mention this in his claim.

The family consisted of Erik (40), his wife Maria (35), sons John (16), Pehr (12), Olof and Nels, August (10 months), and daughter Ingar (14). Erik gave the horse he had been riding to John, jumped into the wagon, and sped off. He tried to go east to Scandian Grove, but Indians were approaching in that direction so he veered northeast toward Norwegian Grove. They were only a few hundred yards from their house when the Dakotas drew within killing distance. Unable to escape on the road, Jonsson had no choice but to veer into the pasture. There, he ran the horses into the tall grass, the family leaped out of the wagon, and everyone scattered. Eager for good horses, some of the warriors went after Jonsson's animals while others pursued his son John. Riding unencumbered, the teenager quickly outdistanced his pursuers and caught up with Larson's wagon.

Carl Nelson's and Pehr Benson's families were a short distance behind the Jonssons. The Dakotas could have turned on them just as easily, but they had other prey in mind. According to C. C. Nelson, "the Indians overtook us but passed us without doing any harm. They were anxious to catch Erik Johnson's team of horses that was a short distance ahead of us." Pehr Benson and his wife and daughter stopped, jumped out of their rig, and hid. Carl Nelson told his sons, C. C. and John, to run and hide with the Bensons while he stayed behind and tried to unhitch the oxen. Mrs. Nelson had run out of the house before the others and, explained her son C. C., "we could not find her." The Nelson boys and the Bensons scurried through the grass and into a cornfield just beyond where the Jonssons entered. Carl Nelson, meanwhile, unhitched his oxen (for whatever good that would do him) and began hiking across the prairie.[28]

Lars Solomonson's place was less than half a mile northeast of Larson's home. Solomonson had lived there the past two years with his wife Hedda Sophia, sons John (15), Charlie, Alfred, and Ludwick, and grandson George Andersson. His oldest son Andrew was fighting in the Union army. Solomonson had the same warning as everyone else, but with all the false alarms that week he ignored the latest news and left to cut hay while his son John drove in the oxen. The Dakotas cut off John and chased him through the corn. One of them even shouted "Stop!" in plain English, but John wisely ignored the order and kept running. Several Indians fired at him, with one round passing through

28 Lars Larson Depredation Claim #615; Nelson, "History of the early pioneers," Microfilm Reel 3, Dakota Conflict, Minnesota Historical Society; Holmquist, "Reminiscence," Microfilm Reel 2, Dakota Conflict, Minnesota Historical Society.

his right hand near the wrist. They turned back when they saw Jonsson ride his wagon off the road and into the pasture.[29]

Ingar Jonsson thought it was about two in the afternoon when the Dakotas returned to the Jonsson farm and searched the grass and cornfield. Erik Jonsson with sons Nels and Olof had crawled quite a distance away and found a good place to hide. The rest were not so lucky. The Indians found Maria holding her infant August with her son Pehr and daughter Ingar next to her. Without a word, a warrior raised his gun and blasted Maria in the chest; somehow the shot missed hitting August. The woman collapsed. Her daughter Ingar went into shock. "I was in a trance," she admitted, "and could hear and feel but could not move and see." The last words she heard her mother utter were, "Lord Jesus receive my soul."

Warriors kicked Pehr Jonsson and ordered him to stand. They did the same to Ingar, but she lay transfixed. "They asked brother if I was dead," she recalled, but she could not hear his answer. Two Dakotas dragged her across the pasture by her wrists, cutting her right thigh. They dropped her and felt her pulse, but Ingar remained unresponsive. They threw a feather mattress over her and watched for awhile, but still she did not move. Either believing her dead or in some mystical state, they abandoned her. Warriors tried to get Pehr to follow them, but when he resisted they shot and killed him.[30]

Lars Solomonson was hiding with his family in his cornfield when his wounded son John raced past along the west side with Indians shooting at him. Anything Lars could do to help his boy would give away their position. He also watched from the corn as Dakotas chased down the Jonssons and shot his dog. There were many Dakotas and they were getting closer. Lars decided to move his family. He tried carrying the two little ones, but when that proved too difficult he set one down, hauled the other some distance, put him down, and returned for the first. They were getting nowhere fast.

Ahead of everyone in their horse-drawn wagon, Lars Larson, daughter Hannah, and the Pehr Carlson family were making good time. From his position in the corn Solomonson saw them ride past. Soon, another refugee wagon approached, accompanied by John Stockholm on horseback. This time

29 Lars Solomonson Depredation Claim #915.

30 Nelson, "History of the early pioneers," Microfilm Reel 3, Dakota Conflict, Minnesota Historical Society; Holmquist, "Reminiscence," Microfilm Reel 2, Dakota Conflict, Minnesota Historical Society.

Solomonson stepped out and flagged down the passers-by, asking Stockholm to take one of his small children so he and the rest could make better time; he agreed. Solomonson and the balance of his family moved more quickly now and perhaps feeling more hopeful about their chance of survival when Dakotas appeared out of a cornfield, leveled their weapons, and fired.

Lars Larson seemed to be making good time in his wagon, but while he stuck to the road the Dakotas were cutting across the prairie. There was a big curve ahead on the east side of Norwegian Grove, and when the mounted Dakotas cut the angle it appeared they would intercept the wagon, but ran instead into a stout rail fence hidden in the tall grass. Their horses refused to jump the fence and it was too strong to easily break down. By the time the warriors dismounted and climbed the fence Larson dashed past. The Dakotas fired and at least one bullet whizzed by the mounted John Jonsson and slammed into the back end of the wagon box. A minute later John Stockholm rode by and the Dakotas fired again, inflicting a flesh wound in the neck of Stockholm's horse that did not stop the animal. The frustrated Indians returned to their own horses. The hidden fence may have belonged to Ole Ostensen. Mrs. Ostensen heard the clatter, picked up one of her children and stepped outside to see what was happening. At the edge of the field, "She came face to face with the Indians who did not molest her." Why they left them unharmed is unknown. They may have realized Larson and the others were now out of reach, and were intent on getting back to the other cabins and families they had already bypassed.[31]

After watching the Indians catch the Jonssons, Pehr Benson, his family, and the two Nelson boys crawled into a cornfield to hide. They waited there for Carl Nelson (who was unhitching his oxen), but Carl never arrived. When they heard three shots from where the Dakotas had trapped the Jonssons, the Benson's decided they had to get away. Crawling and walking close to the ground, they snaked their way through the grass and corn for more than two miles until they reached Norwegian Grove. Carl Nelson, meanwhile, unhitched his animals but lost track of his two boys and the Bensons. He set out on his own toward Norwegian Grove. About a mile to the northeast Nelson found himself near John Solomonson when the Indians fired at the boy, but when he

31 Lars Solomonson Depredation Claim #915; Lars Larson Depredation Claim #615; Nelson, "History of the early pioneers," Microfilm Reel 3, Dakota Conflict, Minnesota Historical Society; Gene Estensen, "War Comes to Norwegian Grove," in *Celebrating Our Norwegian-Minnesotan Heritage*, 188.

didn't stop running, Nelson figured he wasn't hit. Young Solomonson evaded the Dakotas, but lost his other family members, who were hiding in the grass nearby.

Lars Solomonson found a spot to hide his family and crept within 200 yards of his house. Six Indians riding his neighbors' horses plundered the home between 3:00 and 4:00 p.m. Because the warriors remained inside for some time, Solomonson concluded they were eating the dinner his wife had prepared. Once outside, the Dakotas broke open a trunk and stole the contents and set fire to his wheat. Thereafter they rode south to Larson's cabin, a one-and-a-half level split-log structure with sod roof and two side additions, "which was presently set on fire and burnt up." Solomonson continued to hide there until after 5:00 p.m. before returning to get his family. Once it was dark they set out for St. Peter.

John Solomonson and Carl Nelson continued walking northeast on nearly identical courses. John wrapped a handkerchief around his wounded hand to stem the bleeding and about one mile beyond Norwegian Grove came across a fleeing family named Oleson, who welcomed him aboard their wagon. Both Nelson and Solomonson made it to Henderson, more than 15 miles away, late that evening.[32]

Erik Jonsson and his two boys, meanwhile, remained in hiding. They didn't know what had happened to the rest of their family, but they heard the same gun shots the Nelsons and Bensons heard. Like Lars Solomonson, about 4:00 p.m. they saw the same Indians half a mile to the north burn down Larson's house.

At dusk, Erik's teenaged daughter Ingar Jonsson awoke from her trance to a surreal sight. "It looked to me like the corn in the field was walking—fires all around, houses, stables, and grain." The undulating flames and shifting shadows painted a dreamlike picture similar to what the people of New Ulm were seeing that same Saturday night. She heard her infant brother August crying and found him lying next to their dead mother. She picked him up and wandered aimlessly in the field. She found some bread that had fallen from their wagon, but it was so hard and dry that she had to chew and soften it before August could swallow the food. The bread calmed the baby down and he fell

32 Lars Solomonson Depredation Claim #915; Lars Larson Depredation Claim #615; Nelson, "History of the early pioneers," Microfilm Reel 3, Dakota Conflict, Minnesota Historical Society.

asleep. Ingar carried him to an unburned part of the field and crawled with him beneath a haystack to await daylight.

Ingar was just waking up that night after sunset and about to find her baby brother when her father Erik Jonsson and two other brothers, Olof and Nels, emerged from hiding. Jonsson found his wife Maria, but no one else. He continued searching until he came upon a series of haystacks. A dog was sitting next to one, and he wondered whether he was resting by his owner. Jonsson dug through the hay and, to his surprise, discovered Mrs. Johannes Ecklund and her daughter Mary. Were others hiding inside other stacks, perhaps his own family members? He ran from one to the other, tearing through each until his efforts uncovered Ingar and little August. Both happiness and grief overwhelmed him. Jonsson gathered his charges and marched them across the prairie all the way to Scandian Grove Church.

Once the Bensons and the Nelson boys made it to Norwegian Grove, they set out for St. Peter. Keeping off the roads, they traveled across the prairie and inside the timber whenever possible. When they spotted people ahead of them they dove into the grass but it was too late: whoever it was had already seen them and was waving with a handkerchief. They emerged to discover Lars Solomonson and his family. The enlarged party decided to head to Scandian Grove Church. On the way they shared a pan of warm milk from the cellar of an abandoned house in Norseland. A company of soldiers heading to Norseland from St. Peter found them wandering in the darkness. The men informed the refugees the road beyond was clear of Indians and the tired party continued walking, reaching St. Peter about 2:00 a.m. Sunday morning. The exhausted Jonssons and Ecklunds also stumbled into luck that night when their paths crossed with the same soldiers at Scandian Grove Church.[33]

Refugees were filling the church, but there was no pastor to comfort them. Unlike Rev. Andrew Jackson, who stuck with his flock up at West Lake and Norway Lake, Rev. P. A. Cederstam and his family fled to St. Peter on Saturday. Mrs. Cederstam was pregnant and distraught that her husband might be drafted into the Union army. Reverend Cederstam wrote letters from St. Peter to Reverend T. N. Hasselquist in Illinois sharing his concerns: they were stuck in a crowded Presbyterian church, very hungry, and troubled about the sad plight of

---

33 Nelson, "History of the early pioneers," Microfilm Reel 3, Dakota Conflict, Minnesota Historical Society; Holmquist, "Reminiscence," Microfilm Reel 2, Dakota Conflict, Minnesota Historical Society.

the refugees. By Monday, August 25, Cederstam said his parishioners would probably not return to their homes and his congregation was likely "a thing of the past." On the 28th he wrote about possibly sending his family back to Illinois; on September 2, he contemplated leaving; and on the 5th, they had all fled to the safety of St. Paul before going to Illinois. Somewhat unconvincingly, Cederstam said his parishioners were "sad to see him go," but he might come back for a visit. In October, the Conference of the Augustana Synod censured Cederstam, saying that he left only because he was frightened, and many in his congregation were angry with him. Scandian Grove Church was assigned to Reverend Jackson.[34]

*   *   *

The Dakota war party that hit northeast Nicollet County wasn't that large, but the warriors inflicted extensive damage. Six houses had property damage but were not burned: Carl Nelson's, Pehr Carlson's, Swen Benson's, John Johnson's, Lars Solomonson's, and Gunder Nereson's. Others, including Pehr Benson, Peter Fritjoff, Joren Johnson, Lars Larson, and Erik Jonsson lost their homes and their crops. Johannes Ecklund lost his house and Lars Solomonson lost his grain. The families helped each other construct temporary shelters while rebuilding their farms.[35]

On Sunday morning, August 24, the soldiers from St. Peter accompanied Erik Jonsson back to Norwegian Grove to help him retrieve his wife's body and search for his son Pehr. They found Maria's remains, but could not find his son. Maria was buried in the cemetery at Scandian Grove Church. One of the soldiers named Franklin Griswold wrote to his parents about Erik Jonsson's painful plight: "to see the weeping man in failing to find anything of his children—was heart-rending." Griswold was not quite correct; by then Jonsson had found all of his children except Pehr. It was not until one week later that the 12-year-old's corpse was found; he was interred with his mother. Although it was reported that little August died of exposure two days later—and that

34 Lundblad, "Impact of Minnesota's Dakota Conflict," 217-18.

35 Bakeman, ed., *Index to Claimants*, 31; Nelson, "History of the early pioneers," Microfilm Reel 3, Dakota Conflict, Minnesota Historical Society. According to C. C. Nelson, all the families reoccupied their farms except for Pehr Benson, who moved back to Illinois. "They thought they had all the experiences with the Indians they cared for here in the wilderness," explained Nelson.

version is inscribed on the present New Sweden historical marker—August lived until February 1863, when he succumbed to measles. Ingar Jonsson had nightmares for the rest of her life.[36]

Carl Nelson reached Henderson late on Saturday and informed everyone there of what had taken place. By this time overwhelming forces were gathering to confront the uprising. Colonel Sibley's men were moving slowly up the Minnesota River when William J. Cullen and 200 men of his newly formed "Frontier Guards" entered Henderson. The citizen soldiers had assembled at Shakopee on Friday and marched to Henderson the following day. A few hundred other mounted volunteers were busy assembling at various points along the river under the command of Col. Samuel McPhail. By that Sunday, nine companies of the 6th Minnesota Volunteers under Col. William Crooks had assembled at St. Peter. The Dakotas had no chance of beating back the powerful armed commands gathering near Nicollet County's eastern border.[37]

Carl Nelson took advantage of the plentiful manpower and convinced a company of Cullen's men to travel with him to Norwegian Grove. John Fadden, who had escaped from Yellow Medicine Agency with John Otherday and had been in Henderson for the past few days, joined Nelson. Although the men conducted a thorough search, all they saw was a desolate scene of burned houses and haystacks; neither the living nor the dead were found. Some of the searchers passed near the slough where Mrs. Nelson was hiding after being separated from her family the previous day. She heard them calling but believed it was an Indian ruse and remained hidden. The soldiers marched back to Henderson while the disconsolate Carl Nelson walked to St. Peter. In a stone house on Third Street, the distressed Nelson found something to be thankful for when he discovered his two sons. With a new found optimism he vowed to return the next day and find his wife. On Monday Carl collected a party of settlers to accompany him. One mile north of Scandian Grove Church they watched a lone figure stumbling across the prairie. It was Mrs. Nelson. She had been in the slough from Saturday evening to Monday morning. As her son C. C.

36 Dahlin, *Dakota Uprising Victims*, 85; Holmquist, "Reminiscence," Microfilm Reel 2, Dakota Conflict, Minnesota Historical Society. In 1920, the 73-year-old Ingar Jonsson Holmquist finally wrote about what she experienced during the uprising. For eight months she was so nervous she could not sleep at night, thinking every noise was an Indian outside her home. For the rest of her life, she explained, she "dreamed of Indians and often woke up with a scream."

37 Nelson, "History of the early pioneers," Microfilm Reel 3, Dakota Conflict, Minnesota Historical Society; Malmros, *Perspectives on the Sioux War*, 15.

Nelson later recalled, his mother "was so exhausted that she could hardly move. We were all saved from the Indians."[38]

The Nelsons were indeed saved, but an erroneous version of what happened to them eventually found its way into print and folklore. One of the men accompanying Carl Nelson and the soldiers to Norwegian Grove that August Sunday was Richard H. Chittenden. Although usually described as a captain in the 1st Wisconsin Cavalry (which he was for a time), Chittenden had resigned on July 14, 1862, and his regiment was serving in Missouri and Arkansas. Nevertheless, Chittenden the civilian was smitten by Nelson and his tale of woe. A short time later he wrote to the New Haven *Palladium* about Nelson's ordeal. Chittenden's account, however, sounds less like Nelson's story than it does Jonsson's tragic experience. The erstwhile captain's report described burned houses, an overturned wagon with possessions strewn about, the murder of the wife in the cornfield, the disappearance of the boys, and a woman and child under a haystack—all documented elements from Jonsson's experience. Chittenden depicted Nelson as a heart-broken man, turning from his house without a tear in his eye and closing the gate. "I must confess," Chittenden concluded, "accustomed as I am to scenes of horror, the tears would come."

Chittenden was not finished. After the uprising, he was said to have visited Minnehaha Falls near St. Paul, and was inspired to put the things he had seen into verse. It does not literally follow Nelson's (Jonsson's) story, but he used it as a framework, using Nelson's name but changing the children's names to "Hans" and "Otto," adding a "Lela" who "lies unburied on the plain," a "Jennie," whose fate was "worse than death," and even a "faithful Fido." The first and last stanzas read:

> Minnehaha laughing water,
> Cease thy laughing now for aye,
> Savage hands are red with slaughter
> Of the innocent to-day.
> Nelson, as the troops were leaving,
> Turned and closed his garden gate.
> But the laughing Minnehaha
> Heeded not the woeful tale,

38 Bryant and Murch, *Great Massacre*, 146; Nelson, "History of the early pioneers," Microfilm Reel 3, Dakota Conflict, Minnesota Historical Society.

> What cares laughing Minnehaha
> For the corpses in the vale.

The words were set to music by Frank Wood, said to be Minnesota's first songwriter and composer, and was the first song to be published by a Minnesotan. "Minnehaha" was dedicated "To the memory of the victims of the Indian Massacre of 1862." The song, which wasn't quite true, about the experiences of a man who didn't fully experience them, was nevertheless correct enough—given a dash of poetic license and the temper of the times.[39]

---

39 Bryant and Murch, *Great Massacre*, 146-47; Dunn, "A Century of Song," 124-25. Because of Chittenden's errors, a number of histories have misidentified Nelson and Jonsson. Bryant and Murch, *Great Massacre*, 147, claims Nelson found his dead wife's body in St. Peter, when in fact she survived.

C hapter 18

"I understand my time has come."

Breckenridge and Jackson County

Attacks on Breckenridge and Old Crossing ~ Inkpaduta's raid on Springfield ~ Earliest settlers of
Jackson County ~ Lewison, Hjornevik, Furnes, and Langeland the first victims ~ Forde's house
attacked ~ Ole Forde escapes ~ Anders Slaabakken wounded ~ Sacrifice of Anna Furnes ~ Mrs.
Forde and Mrs. Ekse lead the children to safety ~ Settlers of Belmont and Des Moines Township
flee ~ Results of the first week of the uprising

The Sunday raid into Nicollet County on August 23 was about as far east as the Dakotas penetrated during the first critical week of the uprising. They reached their northern and southern limits in Minnesota the following day.

Fort Abercrombie was established in August 1857 on the west bank of the Red River of the North in Dakota Territory by Lt. John J. Abercrombie. Construction got underway the following year, making it the first permanent military settlement in what is today North Dakota, which is why the post became known as "The Gateway to the Dakotas." It was built to protect the valley settlers from the Sioux. At the time of the uprising it was garrisoned by Capt. John D. Vander Horck and 84 men of Company D, 5th Minnesota. The post consisted of just three buildings: the company quarters, the commissary, and the officers' quarters. Scattered huts occupied by mixed-bloods, traders, and the interpreter lined the river bank. Just like at Fort Ridgely, no fortifications or even a fence protected the post. Vander Horck detached 30 men under Lt. Francis A. Cariveau to man a post at Georgetown, about 52 miles downriver at the junction of the Buffalo River and the Red. Fifteen miles upstream from the fort was the little town of Breckenridge, founded in 1857 at the junction of the Bois de Sioux and Otter Tail rivers, which combined to form the Red River. By 1859 the new community boasted a saw mill, brickyard, a few dwellings, and a good-sized hotel. An ox-cart and stage trail from St. Cloud generally followed the Otter Tail to Breckenridge before breaking north along the Red to Fort Abercrombie.

The soldiers and settlers in this area were among the last to learn about the murderous outbreak. On August 13, a message reached Vander Horck with orders to guard a wagon train carrying treaty supplies from St. Cloud on the way north to Red Lake for a peace council with the Chippewas. The train started its journey first. The peace commissioners, following behind, reached St. Cloud on the 20th, where they got word of the uprising and sent a messenger ahead to Abercrombie to stop the train at the fort. The message didn't reach Vander Horck until the 23rd, after the train had already left the post and was beyond Whiskey Creek about two miles north. Couriers recalled the train and ordered Lieutenant Cariveau to return with his men from Georgetown.[1]

Some 100 settlers streamed into Fort Abercrombie in search of protection. Not everyone fled into the post. Martin and Maria Farrabarr and their two children had resided in Breckenridge for two months. Martin worked as a carpenter for E. L. Spencer; Maria kept house for him. Almost everyone pulled out of town on the 24th. Maria and the two children rode to the fort in a wagon with Spencer and his family, but Martin stayed behind. A Mr. Russell, Martin, and two other men who were engaged in building the hotel decided to fortify the structure and await developments. Dakotas, likely from the upper Sisseton and Wahpeton bands, descended on the town later that day. They plundered and burned, destroying almost every building except the saw mill, which they allegedly left alone because of the "evil spirits" who made terrifying noises as the logs were cut. The Dakotas murdered the four men, but whether before or after they had bound their ankles with chains and dragged them through the hotel and along the streets is unknown.[2]

One week after the beginning of the uprising, the Dakotas were raiding more than 130 miles northwest of the epicenter at Redwood Agency. After

1 Frazer, *Forts of the West*, 109; "History of Breckenridge," www.breckenridgemn.net/tourism/history.html; *Minnesota in the Civil and Indian Wars*, II, 187.

2 "History of Breckenridge," www.breckenridgemn.net/tourism/history.html; *Minnesota in the Civil and Indian Wars*, II, 187; Bryant and Murch, *Great Massacre*, 234; Maria Farrabarr Depredation Claim #1366. Farrabarr's name is also spelled Farrabach, Farribach, Farrabau, and Fehrenbach.

finishing with Breckenridge, these Dakotas (or another party) moved up the Otter Tail River and about 16 miles southeast of town came across a stage stop, stable, post office, and a small inn called "Old Crossing" run by Mrs. Scott (65) and her son Joe. A 6-year-old grandson named Jimmy Scott was also present when the Dakotas appeared about breakfast time on Sunday, August 24. The warriors killed Joe outright and wounded his mother with a shot to the breast. As she lay helpless and bleeding, the warriors destroyed her property and plundered the house. The Indians were kicking the wounded Mrs. Scott and in the process of tearing off her dress when a farmer named Mr. Bennett arrived in a loaded market wagon. The rolling prize was too tempting to resist, so the Indians ran outside, mortally wounded Bennett as he tried to run away, and commandeered the wagon.

Back inside the cabin, Mrs. Scott told her grandson Jimmy Scott to do whatever they told him and maybe they'd let him live. The warriors swarmed back inside, snatched the boy, loaded the wagon with their stolen loot, and rode off. The injured woman remained motionless until she was sure the wagon was gone, retrieved 50 silver dollars the Indians had missed, and crawled outside. She hid the money in a haystack and made her way along the Otter Tail River toward Breckenridge for help. A few miles from town she passed a Burbank & Company stage with its top cut off, horses stolen, and the driver, Charles Snell, dead. Mrs. Scott reached the destroyed little community about sunset and took refuge in the saw mill.[3]

Once Lieutenant Cariveau and his 30 men returned to Fort Abercrombie, Captain Vander Horck dispatched Lt. John Groetch with 10 men to reconnoiter as far upriver as Breckenridge. They arrived late on August 26 to find the dead inside the hotel—three men, a woman, and a child terribly mutilated. The soldiers built rough coffins out of scrap wood and carried the corpses back to the fort. According to John Winslade, a carpenter at Abercrombie, only three dead men were hauled back to the fort for burial. Winslade examined Farrabarr's body closely and reported that "he was shot through the breast, and skull broken apparently with a tomahawk." When he visited Breckenridge the following month, Winslade described Mrs. Farrabarr's

---

3 Bryant and Murch, *Indian Massacre in Minnesota*, 238-39; McConkey, *Dakota War Whoop*, 123-26; History of Breckenridge," www.breckenridgemn.net/tourism/history.html; Lounsberry, *History of North Dakota*, 201. Snell was also reported to have been killed about September 6.

house as "burnt and entirely destroyed." She filed a depredation claim for only $142 in losses.[4]

On the 27th, Lt. Groetch and his squad returned to Breckenridge to scout the area. One of the soldiers spotted someone moving in the saw mill and thought it was an Indian. Further investigation discovered the wounded Mrs. Scott in her torn clothes encrusted with blood. Grateful for the help, she told them about the destroyed Burbank & Company stage and where to find its dead driver. The scouts found Snell three miles east of town and buried him there. They found Bennett's body closer to Old Crossing. The wagon driver had been seriously wounded outside Mrs. Scott's place, but made it a long way before finally succumbing to his wounds. They decided to bring his body back with them, and so placed it in a wagon with Mrs. Scott and conveyed their macabre human cargo back to the fort. The post surgeon dressed Scott's wounds, the women of the fort gave her a different dress, and a search party that buried Joe Scott retrieved her 50 silver dollars.[5]

* * *

While some Dakotas raided the upper Red River Valley, other warriors ranged as far south as Jackson County along the Iowa border, roughly 80 miles below the Redwood Agency. These raiders were mostly Sissetons from White Lodge's band. Many of these same Indians had participated in the attack on Lake Shetek four days earlier. It was not the first time Indian raiders had visited the region.

In late March 1857, Inkpaduta and his band of 50 or more (including Wahpekutes, Yanktons, and Sissetons) killed 32 people before leaving the Spirit Lake-Lake Okoboji area. On March 27 they arrived at Springfield, where they stole 12 horses, dry goods, food, powder, lead, clothing, and quilts, and killed brothers George and William Wood, Willie Thomas (8), Josiah Stewart, his wife, and two small children, and wounded three others. Inkpaduta left the area

---

4   *Minnesota in the Civil and Indian Wars*, II, 187; Maria Farrabarr Depredation Claim #1366. Reports said either three men, four men, or three men, a woman, and a child were killed at the hotel.

5   *Minnesota in the Civil and Indian Wars*, II, 187-88; Jimmy Scott joined George Ingalls and John Schmerch when they were taken by Little Crow's followers into North Dakota. These three were among the last captives recovered. See Michno, *A Fate Worse Than Death*, 226-30.

for Dakota Territory; the remaining residents of Springfield abandoned the town.[6]

The nearly vacant region was carved into Jackson County in May 1857. The former families never returned, and only a few single men remained in the area through that summer. Several schemes to rebuild Springfield failed, but eventually enough new settlers moved in to establish another town, which was renamed Jackson. Most of the settlers before 1860 were American-born and moved from Minnesota or Iowa. After 1860 an influx of Norwegians settled along the Des Moines River, generally upriver of Jackson, in Des Moines, Belmont, and Christiania townships. (Map Q)

A large number of these immigrants were comprised of the Slaabakken families, who contributed a total of seven brothers and one sister. The second eldest brother, Anders Olson Slaabakken, visited the area in 1858 and reported back to his community in Rock County, Wisconsin. In 1860, a dozen or more families including Mestad (Midstad), Forde (Fyre, Fohre), Furnes (Furness, Furrenaes), Ramlo, Askjelson, Bradvold, and Lien, formed a wagon train and headed west, settling along the Des Moines River north of Jackson. More Norwegians arrived the following year from Wisconsin and Winneshiek County, Iowa, including Kirkevoldsmoen, Monson, Torgeson (Torgerson, Torgenson), Ostenson (Estenson), Kgostolson, Ekse (Axe), Halverson, Hjornevik (Jornevik), Olson, and Langeland, plus more Slaabakkens.[7]

Jackson County in 1862 counted about 250 rather isolated people who did not have access to a post office, telegraph, or stage line. The nearest settlements were 20 miles distant at Spirit Lake or Estherville, Iowa, and most supplies had to be hauled all the way from Mankato, Minnesota, about 60 miles northeast. The Norwegians, who had little contact with the American-born settlers downriver and spoke little or no English, kept largely to themselves. When the Civil War began, Jackson County gained a reputation for patriotism by enlisting a high percentage of its residents into the Union Army, which in turn left the region with a severe shortage of men should they be needed at home. The Norwegians knew nothing of Indian warfare and possessed few firearms. As Jackson County historian Arthur Rose put it, most of them had "probably never fired a gun in their lives." In this respect they were little different from many of

6 Beck, *Inkpaduta*, 58-59, 74, 81, 83; Bakeman, ed., Legends, *Letter, and Lies*, 34-38.

7 Rose, *Jackson County*, 83, 90, 93-94, 97-98.

the other settlers on Minnesota's frontier; whether Swede, German, English, or Norwegian the Dakotas found the Minnesotans "as easy to kill as sheep."[8]

As elsewhere, there had been few signs of open hostility. An Indian killed one of Ole Larson's cows up in Christiania Township, but the event trigged little if any response. Not until about Thursday, when a German fleeing from New Ulm arrived with news of the murderous uprising did they have an idea there was widespread trouble. Unfortunately, the language barrier prevented a full understanding of what was happening. The Jackson County residents decided to send a man to New Ulm and paid him $28 to make the trip, but he never returned. The response of the Norwegians was typical: some wanted to flee, some prepare a defense, and others simply ignored the alarm. At dusk many gathered at some of the stronger cabins, and when daylight arrived returned home to work their fields. On Saturday, August 23, they decided to build a stockade with construction set to begin the following Monday. White Lodge and his Sisseton warriors arrived on Sunday.

After terrorizing Lake Shetek, White Lodge and his warriors headed southeast toward Jackson following the general course of the Des Moines River. Old Lars Olson, one of the settlers who lived farthest north on Section 30 in Christiania Township, was returning home from Belmont Township that morning when he spotted about 50 men moving in the woods. Believing they were soldiers on their way to defend the area, Lars continued home to his wife. Apparently none of White Lodge's warriors saw Larson. They had spent the night in a copse of trees north of the Furnes cabin and began their raid shortly after Larson passed by.[9]

Lars Larson Furnes and his family, who lived in the northeast corner of Section 17 in Belmont Township on the bluff just above the Des Moines River, were among the first to suffer the wrath of these Dakota warriors. Many of the families had forted up at Ole Olson Forde's place in Section 22, less than two miles to the southeast. Lars's wife Anna Knutsdatter Langeland Furnes (30) and their 22-month-old baby Johannes were at Forde's that morning. Lars and Anna arrived from Norway in 1859, settled first and were married in Iowa, and then moved to Jackson County. The locals nicknamed Furnes "Strele," after his place of origin in Norway (Strelegroven or Strilelandet), and Furnes had named the cabin he was building Strelegroven. The family stayed overnight at Forde's,

8   Rose, *Jackson County*, 98, 100, 101.

9   Rose, *Jackson County*, 101-02; Rene, ed., "Indian War in 1862," *Vossingen*, 34.

but Lars returned early Sunday to work at his cabin while Anna and the baby stayed behind. Anna's sister, Ragnhild, her husband Jacob Nelson Ekse, and their two children sometimes stayed with the Furneses and sometimes with the Langelands, but were not at either cabin that morning when the Indians arrived. The Dakotas killed Lars, stole clothing, bedding, kitchen items, and tools, ruined his corn and wheat, killed one calf, one sheep, and two hogs, all for a loss of $285. Once finished, they moved on to the next cabin.[10]

Lars G. Hjornevik moved from Iowa to Section 9, less than half a mile from the Des Moines River, in Belmont Township. He stayed at the Forde house while staking his claim and building a cabin. With plenty of farm work to do, Hjornevik may not have slept at Forde's Saturday night. Said to have a violent temper and not one to take orders from anyone, when Hjornevik was advised to take measures to protect himself he supposedly flew into a rage, arguing that he was ready for the Indians anytime and anyplace. The Norwegian immigrant kept rocks in his pockets and was ready to hurl them at an enemy at a moment's notice. Arriving at a gunfight armed with stones, however, was not a good idea. The warriors simply shot Hjornevik dead, took what they wanted, and moved on.[11]

After hitting two farms without finding any women or children, the Dakotas may have wondered if the locals had been warned in advance of their arrival. If so, what they found at the next cabin convinced them otherwise. Knut Nilsson Langeland (37), who usually went by the name of Nelson, and Anna Knutsdatter Bjorgo Langeland (38) settled in the southeastern corner of Section 16 in Belmont, via Winneshiek County, Iowa, in 1861. They had six children: Anna Knutsdatter (9), Marta Julianna (8), Agaata (5), Julia (4), Nicolai Johan (2), and Knud (1). The Langelands either did not go to Forde's house for the night or returned to their home early that Sunday morning. When the Indians arrived, Langeland was by the river rounding up stray cows that had broken through his split rail fence. He was working below the wooded bluffs a quarter mile away, and so did not immediately hear the attack. Some of his children were playing in the cornfield chasing away blackbirds. The Dakotas began by attacking the kids

10 Lewis Lewison Depredation Claim #2690; Ivy Hjornevik correspondence, October 16, 2009; Gourley, *Astri My Astri*, 233; Monson, "Eyewitness Tells," *Windom Reporter*, October 3, 1930. The Lewison claim appears to be an Anglicized rendition of Lars Larson.

11 Rose, *Jackson County*, 102; Ivy Hjornevik correspondence, October 16, 2009. Rose believes Lars Furnes and Lars Hjornevik were killed at Forde's, but this does not appear to be the case.

they could catch. When Mrs. Langeland ran outside to find out what was happening, they turned on her. Two of the children in the cornfield saw their mother being attacked, ran out to help her, and were murdered. The killed included Mrs. Langeland, Anna, Agaata, Nicolai, and Knud. Four-year-old Julia was wounded but somehow slipped away, while 8-year-old Marta remained hidden for a while in the corn before walking to Forde's. By the time Langeland heard shooting and hurried home most of his family had been slaughtered and the Indians were gone. His wife and two of his children had been shot, and two other children beaten to death against a wall of the cabin. Overcome with shock and grief, Langeland tried to grasp what had just transpired. After figuring out which family members had been murdered, he assumed his remaining two daughters had also been killed or captured, and so grabbed a few belongings and fled. To his joy he found his wounded daughter Julia, picked her up under one arm, and carried her all the way to Spirit Lake, Iowa. The father and daughter never returned to that scene of horror.[12]

The Dakotas made an appearance at the Forde house about ten that morning. Ole Olson Forde (40) built his cabin in the northwest quarter of Section 22, Belmont, about half a mile east of Langeland. Forde had two children with his first wife: Ole F. (11) and Ole O. (9). When she died, he married Kari Olsdatter Horveid and they had one daughter, Martha (5), before moving to America. After settling in Iowa, they had Anne (4) and Guro (2), moved to Minnesota, and had one more child, Nils (1). Other families gathered at Forde's house. Johannes Ekse had lived near the Fordes in Iowa. Johannes was married to Brytteva Jonsdatter Mestad, who was once married to Johannes' brother, Nils Knutson Ekse, and had five children with him before he died: Britha (11), Knute (9), Nils (who died), John (4), and a second Nils (1). The Ekses were still at the Forde home, as were Mrs. Furnes and her son Johannes (1), and possibly Mrs. Hjornevik, when the Dakotas made their appearance.

Knut Haldorson Mestad (40) and his wife Brita Andersdatter Rote Mestad had also slept overnight but had just left for home. They lived about a mile southwest of Forde on the west side of the Des Moines River. By this time White Lodge's men had separated into several raiding parties. One of them caught and killed the Mestads along the trail between the two houses. Ole Forde

12 For more information, see Rose, *Jackson County*, 102, 105; "Knut Nilsson Langeland," www.look.no/anita/slekt/webcards/ps71/ps71_132.htm; Rene, ed., "Indian War in 1862," Vossingen, 37.

had also left his house that morning and may have walked with the Mestads for a time. The Dakotas caught him in his pigpen below the bluff between his house and the river and shot him five times.

No one inside the Forde house knew of these initial murders occurring all about them, but luckily someone looked outside and spotted Dakotas approaching. The door was slammed and locked without waiting to find out if the Indians were there simply to beg for breakfast or for something more nefarious. The Dakotas took up positions along a stout fence surrounding the house, which had an east and a west door, several windows, a raftered loft reached by a narrow staircase, and a cellar with access through a trap door in the floor of the living room. Some of the Indians raided a wagon that had been loaded in advance with household items and parked outside for a quick getaway.

Mrs. Forde, Mrs. Ekse, and Mrs. Furnes took all the children into the cellar with them. Only Johannes Ekse and Ole F. Forde remained on the ground level to keep an eye on the Indians. Unlike most of the settlers' houses, this one had four or five firearms that had been distributed by the government for homeguard use. Ole wanted to get the muskets and start shooting, but Ekse declined. They were outnumbered, he explained, and "It would merely be barbaric."[13]

While Ekse pondered the barbarity of opening fire on the Dakotas, Ole watched the Indians discover a bottle of whiskey in the wagon and surmised the situation would get much more serious very soon. The women and children had settled in the cellar and were trying to stay as quiet as possible. Keeping little Johannes from crying, however, proved impossible, so Anna tried carrying him upstairs and he finally quieted down. When she returned to the dark cellar he began screaming again. Ole remembered her trying this a couple times, to no avail. Her presence with the baby in the cellar jeopardized everyone. "I understand my time has come; I must go up again," Anna told the other women. "Your children are smaller [bigger] than mine and they keep quiet; if I stay here the Indians will find us." With that, she carried Johannes upstairs, pulled a straw mattress over the trap door, and waited. Historian Arthur Rose

13 "Ole Olson Fyre," www.look.no/anita/slekt/webcards/ps70/ps70_444.html; Gourley, *Astri My Astri*, 233-34 ; Rose, *Jackson County*, 102; Rene, ed., "Indian War in 1862," Vossingen, 34-35.

described her action as "heroism seldom equaled in the annals of Indian warfare."[14]

Emboldened by the whiskey, several Indians threw their weight against the east door and broke it open. Mr. Ekse was shot running for the stairs to the loft and some of the Indians turned toward Mrs. Furnes. Ole escaped out the west door and dodged the surprised warriors lining the fence by diving through a hole used to fetch water. Once out the other side, Ole took off down the path leading to the spring by the riverbank. He always believed the Indians hesitated while trying to figure out how he got past the stout fence so quickly. The few moments were just enough to give him a head start. The warriors gave chase and shot at him. One bullet smashed into his right elbow. He turned to see a warrior reloading and kept running, diving over the bluff and tumbling through the brush until he found a thick spot and hid there. The warrior who ran past was so close he would have tripped on Ole's legs had he not drawn them in at the last second. Ole crawled off in another direction and crossed the Des Moines River in search of help.

West of the Des Moines River lived Lars Askjelson Lid (Lee), his wife Ingeborg, a sister of Ole Olson Forde (Ole's father), and their six children. They and the Fordes lived together at the Hjornevik farm in Norway before moving to America. Once across the river Ole ran to their house but found it vacant. The Askjelsons had escaped. He ran south to the Mestad place, unaware they had both been killed. When he found another empty cabin, Ole remembered it was Sunday and a revival meeting was being held at Tarald Halstenson Ramlo's house just west of the river and about two miles south of Mestad's farm. Perhaps everyone was there, he thought. He had to warn them.[15]

While Ole ran for his life, warriors inside the Forde house tomahawked and clubbed Mrs. Furnes to death. Strangely enough, they left little Johannes alive by his mother's corpse. Those hiding in the cellar listened in terror as the Indians ransacked the cabin—and then everything fell silent. The next sound they heard was little Johannes crying once again. The women pushed open the trap door with the straw mattress covering it and emerged to find Ekse and Mrs. Furnes dead and the baby lying in a pool of his mother's blood. By this time

14 Rene, ed., "Indian War in 1862," Vossingen, 35-36; Rose, *Jackson County*, 103. Rose believed the heroine was Mrs. Hjornevik.

15 Rene, ed., "Indian War in 1862," Vossingen, 36; Ivy Hjornevik correspondence, October 18, 2009.

hogs were inside rooting about the cabin. The women snatched the baby off the floor and climbed back into the cellar to think about what to do next.[16]

The next home to endure the wrath of the warring Dakotas belonged to Englebret Olson Slaabakken (47), the oldest of the Slaabakken brothers. He and his wife Ingeborg Olsdatter Hulbkmoen Slaabakken had two sons, Ole E. Olson Slaabakken (20), who was married to Kjerstie A. Kirkevoldsmoen, and Anders Olson Slaabakken (13). Englebret lived about half a mile south of Forde, also on Section 22. One of his younger brothers, Mikkel Olson Slaabakken (31), his wife Petronelle, and their three children lived a mile southwest near the river in Section 28. They had stayed at Englebret's house Saturday night. About 10: 00 a.m., Mikkel and his nephew Anders were walking to Forde's house when they heard firing and assumed someone was shooting at blackbirds. Unbeknownst to the approaching pair, the Dakotas saw them coming and set an ambush for them. (This might account for why the Indians abandoned Forde's cabin without searching it thoroughly and locating the trap door leading to the cellar.)

Mikkel and Anders walked right into the trap. The first volley of fire tore into Mikkel, who yelled to Anders, "I am wounded and cannot run any farther!" The next ball killed him. A bullet from the first round of fire ripped through Anders's hat and another plowed a furrow through his hair and creased his scalp. The terrified teenager dropped like a rock with his face to the ground. A warrior plunged a knife into his left side and "twisted it around before he pulled it out." Anders fainted from the excruciating pain. Thinking he was dead, the Dakotas left him.

White Lodge's men moved a little farther to Englebret Slaabakken's place, but by then it was vacant because all of them had left for the revival meeting at Ramlo's. The Indians ransacked the house, taking what they wanted and destroying the rest. Englebret's younger brother Simon Olson Slaabakken (25), also lost his possessions. Simon had just been discharged from the 4th Iowa Cavalry and had only been at his brother's house for ten days—just in time to

---

16 Rose, *Jackson County*, 103; Gourley, "You are a Hjornevik," *Fillmore County Journal*, 2. Author and genealogist Deb Gourley indicates that little Johannes was her great-great-grandfather. There is an ongoing controversy as to whether the baby was the son of Lars and Anna Hjornevik, or Lars and Anna Furnes, but the latter appears to be correct. Johannes was later taken to Winneshiek County, Iowa, where his uncle, Hendrick Hendrickson, became his guardian. Hendrickson filed a depredation claim for the baby's father, Lars Larson Furnes, which was anglicized as the Lewis Lewison Depredation Claim #2690.

lose his clothing, blankets, chest, and watch worth about $70. Other warriors moved southwest to Mikkel Slaabakken's house east of the river, nearly opposite from Mestad's cabin. That premises was also abandoned. They stole possessions and destroyed crops totaling $111.[17]

By this time the Dakotas must have been wondering where all the settlers had gone. Were the whites holding a strong defensive position somewhere or perhaps rallying for a counterattack? Whatever the reason, White Lodge ended the raid and turned back upriver. Retracing their steps, the Dakotas headed back to the Forde cabin.

The women and children hiding in the Forde cellar had a short window of opportunity to make their move. They had emerged once to take baby Johannes back down with them—apparently he was all cried out— before deciding to get out in case the Indians returned. Out of the cellar, they peered from the windows to make sure no one was around and dashed for a cornfield. On the way they ran into 8-year-old Marta Langeland, who had been hiding near her house while the Dakotas were killing her family. Marta remembered being told that if there was trouble, she should make her way to the Forde house. There were now about 13 refugees hiding in the cornfield when the Dakotas returned. Once inside they spotted the open trap door and realized that settlers had been hiding just a few feet below them the entire time they had been there. The enraged warriors rushed outside and launched a short but unsuccessful search for the escapees before taking out their frustration on the bodies of Mr. Ekse and Mrs. Furnes. After stealing a few more items they continued upriver. Mrs. Forde, Mrs. Ekse, and the children remained hidden until dark before setting out for Englebret Slaabakken's cabin.[18]

---

17 Rose, *Jackson County*, 103-04; Simon Olson Slaabakken Depredation Claim #1231; Petronelle Olson Slaabakken Depredation Claim #1227.

18 Arthur Rose, in his history of Jackson County, speculates the Dakotas came down from the north and launched their first attack against the Forde house before moving south to Englebret Slaabakken's and then north to kill and rob Langeland. This scenario cannot be reconciled with existing eyewitness accounts and does not fit the pattern established by the other raiding parties during the previous week. The raiders worked out from their home bases and did not bypass targets only to attack them on the way back home, a course that would have jeopardized the element of surprise. Lars Olson reported seeing the Indians moving along the river from the northwest while on his way home. They hit Furnes, Hjornevik, and Langeland before they reached Forde's; survivor Marta Langeland's arrival at Forde's house establishes this sequence. Rose also claimed that Englebret Slaabakken's cabin was the farthest homestead attacked before the Dakotas moved upriver, but Mikkel's cabin was also ransacked. Rose, Jackson County, 103-105.

When the wounded 13-year-old Anders Slaabakken regained consciousness, he stumbled to his father's house only to find it empty and all its provisions stolen or ruined. After making his way into the stable Anders crawled into a stack of hay and hid for the night. Mrs. Forde, Mrs. Ekse, and the children arrived after dark. They spent the night in Englebret Slaabakken's blacksmith shop, as unaware of Anders as he was of them. Monday morning the two women led the small party of refugees south toward Jackson. Anders searched the stable and found two eggs to eat. When the cows returned at nightfall he tried to milk them, but the smell of blood on his clothes frightened the animals and they refused to allow Anders near them. He remained in the stable.[19]

Ole Forde, meanwhile, his wounded elbow throbbing in pain and bleeding, determined to reach Tarald Ramlo's house and warn the congregation about the murderous Dakotas. His destination was nearly two miles south of the Mestad farm, which he had managed to reach. Moving slowly to avoid the open areas, he reached Ramlo's just as the congregation was about to sing—he heard them announce the number of the hymn in the songbook. The respectful young man was doing his best to maintain some level of decorum by slipping quietly in the back when a woman noticed his disheveled and bloody appearance and alerted the others. The congregation lapsed into a moment of stunned silence before Ole tried to tell them what happened. One woman grabbed his arm to see what was wrong, smearing herself with his blood as Ole cried out in pain. Now they knew what had happened and had proof of its truth. Simon Olson Slaabakken (25), the youngest of the eight brothers, recalled that Ole entered "dripping with sweat and blood, and told that the Indians had arrived. . . . One can imagine the fright that arose. Everyone ran to their respective homes as fast as they could," gathered their families and possessions, and hurried south to Jackson.[20]

M. A. Monson, whose family lived just north of town about three miles from Ramlo's, scooped up his loved ones and ran south along the river trying to stay hidden in the thick timber. They swam across and tried to warn the families on the east side, but "we were so exicted we could hardly make ourselves understood." Ole E. Olson Slaabakken and Sigur Kgostolson ran ahead of everyone, visiting homes and spreading the warning. On the west side of the river, the only adult male with a group of four women and many children was

19 Rose, *Jackson County*, 104-05; Rene, ed., "Indian War in 1862," Vossingen, 37.

20 Rene, ed., "Indian War in 1862," Vossingen, 36; Ulvestad, *Nordmaendene i Amerika*.

Holsten Olson. He was married to Ingeborg Olsdatter Slaabakken (27) and had two young children. On their journey south they saw a man some distance north of them. With visions of marauding Indians dancing in his head, Holsten abandoned the party and took off across the prairie in a different direction. He eventually reached Mankato.

The remaining women and children reached Jackson. Simon Olson Slaabakken ran from Ramlo's to Holsten Olson's house, three-fourths of a mile north, because he knew he would find guns and ammunition there. He gathered a few muskets and had moved south about one mile before realizing that he had forgotten the percussion caps. Fighting his fear, Simon retraced his steps, retrieved the caps, and continued on. Mrs. Anders Kirkevoldsmoen and her children were hiding in a ravine unsure where to go or what to do when Simon joined them. Together, they hurried on to Jackson.

By 4:00 p.m., most of the settlers had congregated at Joseph Thomas's house. Thomas, who was well armed, advised them to stay there. With some help, he explained, they could turn his place into a fort and make a stand until soldiers stationed at Estherville arrived to help them. Mrs. Thomas fed the people as best she could, but they made the decision to flee to Iowa. Thomas could not hold the house by himself. He reluctantly joined them. The caravan left before dark. There was little in the way of obvious teamwork, recorded Ole Forde, who observed that "each seemed only to be trying to save themselves and their families." Weak from the loss of blood and exhaustion and stress of the day, Ole dropped behind. Some time passed before someone asked his whereabouts. A few turned back, found him, and made sure he took a place in a wagon. One member of the party was purportedly a deserter who knew how to bind wounds. He wrapped Ole's arm—but not before Ole's mother agreed to pay the man ten dollars.[21]

The Dakotas were not quite finished in Jackson County. Ole Estenson Lunas and Ole Torgeson (Torgenson, Torgerson) made their homes upriver on the border line of Belmont and Christiana townships. The families either received a warning or saw the Dakotas approaching. The neighbors lived just east of the Des Moines River and they congregated at one of the houses— which is unclear—and prepared a defense. Lunas (28) and his wife Anne Pedersdatter (31) had two children, Esten and Ingeborg. Torgeson (42) and his

---

21 Rose, *Jackson County*, 107-08; Monson, "Eyewitness Tells," *Windom Reporter*, October 3, 1930; Rene, ed., "Indian War in 1862," Vossingen, 36.

wife Kari had three children, Sarah, Martin, and Theander. The nine people barred the doors and windows as well as they could. Unlike most of the Norwegians in Belmont, they had guns and ammunition and were willing to use them.

The Dakotas surrounded the cabin. One of them told the whites to come out and promised they would not be harmed. No one fell for the ruse. Lunas and Torgeson opened fire and the fighting got underway. Bullets peppered the cabin, with many piercing the walls and ricocheting inside. When a bullet damaged a good cooking utensil, one of the women became so enraged that she tried to run outside and drive the Indians away by herself, but was restrained by the others. The fighting continued until after dark. It was pitch black inside the cabin, and the two men fired at the Dakota gun flashes. Eventually the Indians tired of the contest and withdrew. Reports differ as to casualties, but there is no evidence that anyone on either side was wounded or killed. White Lodge pulled out of Jackson County and headed for Dakota Territory.[22]

The whites were also pulling out. Following behind everyone were the refugees in charge of Kari Forde and Brytteva Ekse. They left Englebret Slaabakken's Monday morning, but as they trekked south all they found were abandoned cabins; even the little town of Jackson was deserted. They decided to head for Spirit Lake, but were not sure of the way. Little food was found along the way, and thirst set in. They were thirsty, but too afraid to go near the river because they were sure Indians would be moving along it. One of the Ekse children (who would all take their mother's maiden name of Mestad) recalled that Mrs. Ekse tore off a sleeve of her dress and dragged it through the dew on the grass and squeezed it into a little pan to provide water for the children. Before too long the party figured out they were lost. Panic followed despair when they spotted people approaching from the south and thought they were Indians. In fact, they were white men. One of them was Knut Langeland returning with a rescue party after taking his daughter Julia to Spirit Lake. The refugees were saved, and more incredibly, Knut found his lost daughter Marta among them.

Another rescue party from Estherville was also headed for Jackson. The two groups met in the vicinity late Monday or early Tuesday and searched for

22 Gourley, *Astri My Astri*, 234-35; Rose, *Jackson County*, 105; Hubbard and Holcombe, *Minnesota in Three Centuries*, 382-83, claim one body was found and the defenders believed they had wounded several more, but an interview with the defenders revealed that they had no knowledge of Indian casualties.

survivors. On Wednesday morning, they found Anders Olson Slaabakken still hiding in the stable. He was taken to Estherville, where he slowly recovered from his wounds. The rescue parties, remembered one eyewitness, "proceeded together to the scene of the massacre. Here the sight that met their eyes beggars description. Lying here and there just as they had been murdered were the mutilated bodies of nine victims." The rescuers spent much of their time burying bodies, eventually locating at least 13. They also located "one helpless child" who had been left behind, "too young to fully realize its condition." Perhaps the unnamed child was Johannes Furnes.[23]

Jackson County was deserted. Although the Indians inflicted substantial property damage, probably half of all losses sustained resulted from other reasons. Wild animals and untended domestic ones roamed free, eating and trampling crops. Wind, rain, sun, and prairie fires did their work. If anything was left, white scavengers from other settlements came in and cleaned it out. John Olson Slaabakken (36), for example, fled to Estherville. By the time he returned eight days later, hogs (and not the Dakotas) had ruined his crops. He went back to Estherville and filed a claim for $271 in damages. The farm owned by Lars Halverson, who lived a mile south of town, was untouched by the Dakotas. He filed a claim for $310 in losses because he and his family had to flee and animals and the weather ruined his wheat, corn, potatoes, and garden.

Aftershocks lingered. Two months later in late October, many families, including the Englebrets, the Slaabakkens (both John's and Simon's families), Mikkel Slaabakken's widow and her children, and their brother-in-law Holsten Olson and his family attempted to return to their farms. They made camp for the night of October 21 just south of the deserted town of Jackson. Justifiably leery of Indians, they avoided the woods and camped out in the open. Soon after the men left to get water from the river, a fast-burning prairie fire swept in from the west and engulfed the camp before the women could get the wagons moving. Mikkel's widow, Petronelle, and her daughter Olava (2) did not move fast enough and were caught in the blaze and badly burned, the little girl especially so. Flames burned the flesh off Holsten Olson's hands and face and he bore disfiguring scars for the rest of his life. When the settlers finally broke free and took a head count, it was discovered that Englebret's wife, Ingeborg, and a baby were missing. Once the flames roared past they hurried back but

---

23 Rose, *Jackson County*, 105; Gourley, *Astri My Astri*, 23; Rene, ed., "Indian War in 1862," Vossingen, 37-38; Bennett, "Belmont Indian Massacre," *Jackson Republic*, April 16, 1885.

were too late. Ingeborg was dead; the child on her breast lived only another few hours. The families gathered together what they could and continued to their cabins, which had been stripped bare. Somehow they managed to survive the harsh winter that followed.[24]

Most of the other Norwegian families moved south into northeastern Iowa, putting a 200-mile buffer zone between them and the Dakotas. Only a handful of settlers remained in Jackson County. In fact, only a handful of settlers remained in all of western and southwestern Minnesota. "The Indian war is still progressing," Governor Ramsey telegraphed Secretary of War Stanton on Monday, August 25. "The panic among the people has depopulated whole counties." The next day Ramsey sent a wire to President Lincoln. "The Indian outbreak has come upon us suddenly," he explained. "Half the population of the State are fugitives. . . . No one not here can conceive the panic in the State." Lincoln's secretary, John Nicolay, together with William Dole, the Commissioner of Indian Affairs, sent the president a similar wire on the 27th: "We are in the midst of a most terrible and exciting Indian war. Thus far the massacre of innocent white settlers has been fearful. A wild panic prevails in nearly one-half of the State."[25]

The whites fled north, east, and south, some of them not stopping until they had put the Mississippi River between them and the Indians. The Dakotas, however, had stopped chasing after them. The uprising had covered a swath of territory stretching about 120 miles east to west and 200 miles north to south. After a week of murderous rage their energy abruptly dissipated. The collapse came quickly. Like the force of a great explosion, the shock wave travels only so far before it spends itself. The Dakotas did not have the political, social, and cultural organization, the physical means, the economic base, the unity, the manpower, or the will to achieve their goals. They had no plan other than a general desire to sweep away the whites and take back their land. After the twin failures at Fort Ridgely and New Ulm, the warriors moved back upriver, packed

24 Rose, *Jackson County*, 111-12; Monson, "Eyewitness Tells," *Windom Reporter*, October 3, 1930; Petronelle Oleson Slaabakken Depredation Claim #1227; John Olson Slaabakken Depredation Claim #1230; Lars Halverson Depredation Claim #1234. The story of Mrs. Englebret Slaabakken and a baby dying in the fire comes from Rose. Monson also tells of it, although he was not an eyewitness. I could find no other independent verification. Their deaths are not mentioned in the Slaabakken claims. Holsten Olson says only that a baby of Petronelle's was badly burned.

25 *Official Records*, vol. 13, 596, 597, 599.

up their villages, and headed west and north. Thousands of square miles of territory where the two peoples had once intermingled were now a no-man's land.

The majority of the Dakotas had opposed the uprising, but their views were not strong enough to prevail. Once the war began, the Dakotas could not field enough warriors to achieve their main objectives. They had many chiefs, but no real leaders. The fact that they chose war in the first place was only because they had no statesman with the force of character and will to take charge of a volatile situation and prevent a kamikaze-like assault that could only result in self-immolation. Little Crow has often been described as a great leader, but in the summer of 1862 he failed in the most important task: knowing when to choose war or peace.

The whites were also poorly led, by politicians who were not statesmen and by officers who were not very good soldiers. Charles Flandrau, asserted one historian, "emerged as the ablest battlefield commander on either side"—an arguable conclusion at best.[26] If Flandrau was indeed a "capable battlefield commander," it was not because he was so good but because the others were so poor. The attacks against Fort Ridgely and New Ulm were the largest and most intense battles waged by any tribe against any fort or town during the entire western Indian Wars. After the first week there would be other battles at Fort Abercrombie, Forest City, Hutchinson, Acton, and Wood Lake, but the Dakotas fought them with fewer warriors and with much less enthusiasm. The fighting at Birch Coulee on September 2 was a bloody and close-run affair, but the Dakotas were unable or unwilling to make the final charge that would likely have won the battle. Perhaps they had learned of the futility of charges at Ridgely and New Ulm.

The Dakotas' war of rage could only thrive as long as the warriors were facing and overwhelming unprepared bystanders, and in that they succeeded very well. The exact number of deaths will never be known. Marion P. Satterlee, a newsman and student of the war who interviewed survivors, counted 447 white deaths, both civilian and military. Governor Ramsey estimated the dead at 500. Some put the number as high 800 and more. Only King Philip's War in colonial Massachusetts, Connecticut, and Rhode Island—which lasted from June 1675 to August 1676 and killed nearly 1,000 colonists—surpassed the

---

26 Fridley, "Attorney at War," 125.

Dakota uprising in the number of white deaths.[27] The earlier war spanned more than 14 months; the uprising in Minnesota killed about 400 people in just a single week.

How well did the whites fight? "If there were many instances of courageous or commendable conduct on the part of the white settlers to be noted," wrote historians Hubbard and Holcombe, "the attempt might be made to give them. But, save in a very few instances, the whites were killed without resistance." They credit William Duley at Lake Shetek for killing Lean Bear, and Lunas and Torgeson in Jackson County for making a stand in their cabin. Otherwise, they concluded, "The other white men that were killed made no fight."[28]

In fairness, the majority of Minnesota's frontier settlers did not own firearms and were unaccustomed to them. When the uprising began, the state did not have enough muskets on hand to arm its own people. On September 6, Adjutant General Oscar Malmros asked Wisconsin's Governor Edward Salomon for help. "The Indian war assumes daily greater proportions. Our people are massacred because we have not a sufficient number of muskets to arm our troops," explained Malmros. "Can you send us some—say 1,000— muskets by express? The emergency is great." Salomon forwarded the wire to Secretary of War Stanton. "I have no arms to send him," the governor explained. "What shall I reply?"[29]

As much as Americans like to believe they descended from ancestors who all carried "Old Betsy" by their sides and could grin down a grizzly bear and shoot the eye out of a squirrel at 100 paces, the truth is that many settlers lived unarmed. Those on the cutting edge of Minnesota's frontier at least, did their cutting not with sabers but with scythes and plows. Many were Germans and Scandinavians, but even those with English and American ancestry were poorly armed. Women and children had a right to rely on their husbands and fathers for protection, explained Hubbard and Holcombe, but for the pity and shame of it, "their natural defenders could not defend themselves."[30]

Considering the settlers' circumstances, living largely unarmed was not as odd or unreasonable as it might first appear. These settlers had lived from

27 Leach, *Northern Colonial Frontier*, 59.

28 Hubbard and Holcombe, *Minnesota in Three Centuries*, 389-90.

29 *Official Records*, vol. 13, 617.

30 Hubbard and Holcombe, *Minnesota in Three Centuries*, 390.

months to several years in proximity of the Dakotas. They talked with them, traded with them, and often fed them. No reasonable person would have expected that one morning, no different than hundreds of other mornings, the Indians would draw their weapons and murder them without warning. This lack of foreseeability made it even less likely that the settlers would have their weapons ready, whether firearm, ax, scythe, or hickory stick, and go after the Dakotas in a pre-emptive strike. They remained neighborly, conciliatory, and docile until it was too late. Whether one likes to admit it or not, this was a traditional frontier characteristic. Contrary to many movies and novels, frontier people did not "shoot first and ask questions later." A stranger was a friend until he proved otherwise, and only when threatened with imminent physical harm and death did a man have "no duty to retreat"—the right to defend himself with deadly force. But the settlers would not be caught off guard again. As Frederick Fritsche succinctly explained, the settlers returned to their farms, and when the Indians eventually reappeared, "they were driven away instantly, as everybody was armed and no mercy was allowed."[31] Fool me twice, shame on me.

As usual, Indian losses are much harder to determine and will never be known with certainty. One chronicler, Isaac Heard, concluded that prior to the Battle of Wood Lake on September 23, 1862, only 21 Dakotas had been killed during the uprising. Researcher Marion Satterlee placed the number of deaths at 30. These low counts upset Oscar Wall, who had participated in the battles at Fort Ridgely. Heard, Wall sarcastically asserted, "serio-comically" assured his readers that the counts were right because he asked the Indians how many dead they had and because he searched for their bodies. These methodologies were faulty, Wall concluded, and so Heard's numbers could not be taken seriously. Wall believed Indian losses exceeded Heard's estimation tenfold.[32]

Mercy is a grace in short supply during war. Much has been written about the carnage committed by the Dakotas. In the first decades following the outbreak, white historians emphasized these atrocities, often painting the Indians as a monolithic force with one mindset: to kill and capture whites. That was obviously incorrect. Many of the Dakotas had been opposed to war, a minority actually took up arms, and a small percentage of those committed atrocities. The pendulum of late has swung to the other extreme, with some

---

31 Tolzmann, ed., *Brown County*, 17.

32 Wall, *Recollections of the Sioux Massacre*, 153-54.

authors downplaying Dakota violence while trivializing the white settlers' sufferings.

Author Roy Meyer, in his Santee Sioux history, likens the settlers' experiences to a type of Falstaffian farce that crumbles upon close examination. According to Meyer, instances of torture and mutilation were rare, and that the hundreds of people who were captured, wounded, or escaped from the rampaging Dakotas were exaggerating or hallucinating. Meyer misuses the testimony of Dr. Jared W. Daniels, who did not see any mutilated bodies while accompanying a burial party, by erroneously concluding that bodies weren't mutilated. That fact that Daniels did not see any mutilated bodies doesn't mean there weren't any—it only means that he didn't see any in his narrow view of the uprising. Jared's brother, Dr. Asa Daniels, had a different experience. Meyer calls these atrocities "isolated instances" that "were multiplied in the imagination of refugees."

Another author, Ellen Farrell, in an article that appeared in *Journal of the Indian Wars*, takes a similar line. The Dakotas, she insists, did not engage in "indiscriminate rampage" even though they were provoked, which is true, but when she contends that much of the supposed Indian barbarism was the result of self-serving white imagination, she belittles the white settlers' experience.[33]

It is easy for authors writing 150 years after the fact to be cavalier about an ordeal they did not live through. The participants suffered the direct and indirect consequences and knew what it was like. Colonel Sibley's voice is representative. "Don't think there is exaggeration in the horrible pictures given by individuals," he wrote to Governor Ramsey. "They fall short of the dreadful reality."[34]

It is not politically correct today to portray white settlers as victims, but during the opening week of the Dakota uprising they certainly were victims. The hundreds who were killed and wounded and the thousands more driven from their homes, many of them peaceful Scandinavian and German emigrants, did not deserve their fates. At the same time, the Dakotas did not deserve the years of poor treatment they had received that pushed them over the edge into violence. Innocent people on both sides were victims. The Western Indian Wars were essentially guerrilla wars, and the losers were not the warriors and

33 Meyer, *History of the Santee Sioux*, 120; Farrell, "Dakota Conflict in White Imagination," 30-34.

34 Malmros, *Perspectives on the Sioux War*, 15.

soldiers. It is in the Indian villages and the frontier settlements where the tragedy of the Indian Wars is found.

The Dakotas simply wanted the whites to go away, and had often considered using force to drive them off. They wanted their land back. Five years earlier Wabasha had told President Buchanan that his "chief desire" was to have his own land. The land, the soil, mother earth, had always been the focal point of contention. To reiterate, it was land ownership, by treaty or conquest, which was the *sine qua non* of Dakota and American existence. At the end of one brief week in August 1862 the Dakotas had realized their objective: the settlers were gone and they could once again tread on soil free of white men's boots and plows. One week was all it took. One week was a thin dividing line between peace and prosperity and catastrophic war.

None but the wisest, however, could have realized that the Dakotas had already reached their zenith. Their offensive was virtually over. Never again could the Dakotas amass the willing manpower gathered for the battles at Fort Ridgely and New Ulm. The Dakotas' bubble burst even before the white soldiers arrived.

Their dawn, their restored old order, was a red sky at morning, poised, delicate, ephemeral, and boding ill winds of approaching dispersion and destruction.

Postscript

The decisive first week of the Dakota Uprising was over, but the fighting and killing continued. Col. Henry Sibley gathered 1,500 men and moved up the Minnesota River. An advance force of 160 men under Capt. Hiram P. Grant was encamped at Birch Coulee when about 200 warriors under Mankato, Big Eagle, and Gray Bird attacked them there on September 2. The two-day battle nearly destroyed Grant's command before reinforcements arrived to drive the Indians away. The whites lost 24 killed and 67 wounded; Dakota losses were only two killed and four wounded.[1]

On September 3, Little Crow and 110 warriors battled Capt. Richard Strout and 55 men of the 5th Minnesota near Hutchinson, killing six and wounding 23. More Dakotas attacked Fort Abercrombie on the Red River on September 3 and 6, killing and wounding four soldiers.

One of the largest battles occurred near Wood Lake just below the Upper Agency on September 23. Sibley's forces, now more than 1,600 men, defeated Little Crow and his 740 warriors. Sibley lost seven killed and 34 wounded, but the Dakotas suffered about 25 killed and 40 wounded. Chief Mankato was among the former, killed by a cannonball.

The cumulative losses suffered by Little Crow's force demoralized and scattered most of the remaining warriors. Many of the farmer Indians gathered

---

1 Justina Krieger, rescued just the day before, spent many long hours during the intense fighting at Birch Coulee prostrate in the back of a wagon. As noted earlier in Chapter 9, somehow she escaped further injury or death even though the wagon was hit by some 200 bullets.

most of the captives taken during the preceding weeks. On September 26 at Camp Release (near present Montevideo), the friendly Dakotas turned over 269 white and mixed-bloods to Colonel Sibley. Those released included many people whose stories appeared in this book, including: Minnie Busse, Helen Carrothers, Margaret Cardinal, Martha Clausen, Justina Frass, August Gluth, Wilhelmina Inefeldt, Maria Koch, Mary Schwandt, George Spencer, Sarah Wakefield, and Urania White.

Some of those who escaped made their way back to safety. Maria Hartman survived 17 days in the wilderness after escaping from the Milford massacre. The record, however, belongs to Justina Boelter, who survived the Middle Creek massacre. She with her children Emilia and Ottilie hid in the woods until September 24, when Emilia died of starvation. Justina and Ottilie ate grapes and raw potatoes and wandered the woods until late October—nine weeks after the massacre—when Sibley's soldiers found them near the Upper Agency.

During the weeks after the Camp Release surrender about 1,700 Dakotas, the innocent and the guilty, gave themselves up. A military commission was organized to punish those responsible for the "murder, rape, and other outrages." A series of "trials" were held. Some lasted mere minutes, and no formal defense was offered to the captives. By the time the proceedings ended in early November 1862, 16 Indians had been sentenced to prison and 307 others to death. A few of the latter were reduced to imprisonment. A final list of 303 condemned was sent to President Abraham Lincoln, who had ordered that no executions take place without his presidential approval. Lincoln reduced the list of condemned from more than 300 to just 39, all of whom had been convicted of rape or murder. One final Dakota received a last-minute reprieve. On December 26, 1862, 38 Dakotas were led to a massive gallows constructed in Mankato. Some admitted their guilt and faced death stoically, while others protested their innocence to the end. One, Rdainyanka, claimed he had been deceived. "You told me that if we followed the advice of General Sibley, and give ourselves up to the whites," he argued, "all would be well; no innocent man would be injured. I have not killed, wounded, or injured a white man . . . and yet today I am set apart for execution." He asked that his children be told that their father died because "he followed the advice of his chief, and without having the blood of a white man to answer for to the Great Spirit."[2]

---

2 Carley, *Dakota War of 1862*, 72-73.

Another innocent man was also hanged. Chaska had saved Sarah Wakefield and protected her until her release. Sarah insisted he was innocent, but her defense was looked upon with a jaundiced eye by many whites who could not understand how a white woman could be so "friendly" with a Dakota man. Chaska was supposed to be released, but on the last day his name was confused with a guilty warrior named Chaskadon, and so he was hanged by mistake.

When the drum rolled three times that morning, the executioner cut the rope. When the platform dropped all 38 Indians simultaneously, a prolonged cheer erupted from the 1,400 soldiers and hundreds of civilians surrounding the square. They had just witnessed the largest mass execution in American history. Ironically, the hangman was William Duley, who believed his wife and children had all been killed or captured at Lake Shetek. In fact, they had been ransomed and were safe at the Yankton Agency in Dakota Territory.

More revenge was about to be exacted. In the spring of 1863, about 1,300 Dakotas and 1,900 Winnebagos, who had only marginally participated in the uprising, were removed from the state and set up on reservations along the Missouri River in Dakota Territory. Of the Dakotas imprisoned at Fort Snelling, 160 died during the first winter. Of the prisoners originally taken to Mankato, 38 had been executed, while 49 were acquitted, and 27 died in confinement. The remaining 278 were transferred to Camp McClellan near Davenport, Iowa, where they remained for three years. Another 120 died before they were freed. By any count, more Dakotas died in confinement than perished in battle. Those still alive in 1866 were finally allowed to join their families. Unfortunately, the majority of those responsible for the uprising and killings escaped, while many Dakotas who had resisted fighting and saved white captives paid the price by losing their homelands and their lives. Once again the innocent suffered the most.[3]

On July 3, 1863, the spurned Little Crow and his son Wowinape were picking berries in the woods about six miles north of Hutchinson; Nathan Lamson and his son Chauncey were hunting in the same area. A gun battle broke out that wounded Nathan in the shoulder and killed Little Crow. Wowinape escaped to Devil's Lake, where soldiers found him later in the month. After hearing Lamson's story, soldiers and civilians found the dead chief. Someone scalped him and his corpse was carried back for display as part

3 Carley, *Dakota War of 1862*, 75, 78-80; Keenan, *Sioux Uprising*, 80-82; Monjeau-Marz, *Dakota Internment*, 100, 109.

of the Fourth of July celebration. His head and forearms were later cut off and his body was thrown into a pit by the slaughterhouse. Such was the ignoble end of the Dakota who is usually held most responsible for the uprising and its tragic consequences.[4]

The experiment to maintain Indian reservations within the borders of Minnesota had failed. Pushing the tribes farther away had only postponed the next confrontation. The initial shockwaves from the Dakota Uprising dissipated with the hangings, but the consequences continued. Had the vengeful whites been content with executing some prisoners, imprisoning others, and banishing the rest, the uprising might have been confined to Minnesota and ended in 1862. Instead, over the next three years Army columns moved into Dakota Territory. In theory, these soldiers were hunting renegade Dakotas, but in practice they were fighting their Nakota and Lakota cousins. Once more, the innocent were being punished.

The relatively contained fighting in Minnesota thus spread some 1,000 miles across the northern plains and involved tribes that had nothing to do with the 1862 uprising. Before it was over the Dakota Uprising grew into the greatest of the Sioux Wars, eclipsing the misnamed "Great Sioux War" of 1876-77. The 1862-65 fighting in Minnesota and the Dakotas witnessed higher casualties for both sides in both killed and wounded, involved more soldiers in the field, and cost millions of dollars more than did the "Great Sioux War" of 1876-77. The earlier conflict also had more important far-reaching consequences. It essentially terminated hostile Indian actions east of the Missouri River. After the 1863-64 battles, the Sioux never again sought out large-scale open-field battles with the soldiers.

*   *   *

As news of the initial conflagration circulated, isolated white communities felt they, too, were in mortal danger. If something like that could happen in Minnesota, it could happen anywhere. Fear spread. The paroxysm of rage that began along the Minnesota River on an August morning in 1862 spread across the western plains, igniting a killing spree that would continue fitfully until the final meeting at Wounded Knee Creek in South Dakota in 1890.

---

4 Folwell, *History of Minnesota*, II, 283-86; Anderson, *Little Crow*, 178-79; Anderson and Woolworth, *Through Dakota Eyes*, 280-81.

Appendix

Numbers of Killed and Wounded at Select Locations

ACTON, Sunday, August 17: 5 killed

Howard Baker, Robinson Jones, Ann Baker Jones, Viranus Webster, Clara D. Wilson

REDWOOD AGENCY, Monday, August 18: 21 killed

Joseph Belland, Joseph Brosseau, Lathrop Dickinson, George W. Divoll, John Gluth, Francois La Bathe, John Lamb, James W. Lynd, Patrick McClellan, Andrew Myrick, Joseph Robinette, William Taylor, George Thomas, August H. Wagner, Antoine Young, "Old Fritz," unnamed four men and one woman

BIRCH COULEE, Monday, August 18: 16 killed

Thomas Brook, Charles Clausen, Frederick Clausen, Balthasar Eisenreich, John Hayden, Patrick Hayden, Anna Maria Juni, Henry Kaertner, Hubert Milier, Peter Pereau, Eusebius Piquar, St. Germain, Mrs. Carl Witt, Gottfried Zimmerman, John Zimmerman, John Zimmerman Jr.

BEAVER CREEK, Monday, August 18: 14 killed

Andrew Bahlke, John Carrothers, William Carrothers, Radnor Earle, Dorothea Frohrip, Frederica Frohrip, John Frohrip, Maria Bahlke Frohrip, Mary Frohrip, Clarissa Henderson, two Henderson children, Jehiel Wedge, Eugene White

FORT RIDGELY ROAD, Monday, August 18: 11 killed

David O'Conner, Gertrude Humphrey, Jay P. Humphrey, Philander P. Humphrey, Susan A. Humphrey, Patrick Kelly, Edward Magner, Ole Sampson, two Sampson daughters, Thomas Smith

SMITH CREEK, Monday, August 18: 19 killed

Ernest Hauff, Mrs. Hauff, two Hauff daughters, William Inefeldt, Caroline Meyer, three Meyer children, John Sieg, Caroline Sieg, three Sieg children, Mrs. Louis Thiele, one Thiele child, John Zitloff, Michael Zitloff, Mary Zitloff

MIDDLE CREEK, Monday, August 18: 39 killed

Gottlieb Boelter, Mrs. Gottlieb Boelter, John Boelter, Justine Boelter, three Boelter children, Gottfried Busse, Wilhelmina Busse, Augusta Busse, Bertha Busse, Caroline Busse, John Frass, John Kochendorfer, Catherine Kochendorfer, Sarah Kochendorfer, John Lettou, Lettou child, Gottlieb Mannweiler, Annie Reyff, Benjamin Reyff, Eusebius Reyff Jr., Margreth Reyff, John Roessler, Mrs. John Roessler, Frederick Roessler, two Roessler sons, Louise Schmidt, William Schmidt, two Schmidt children, Johann Schwandt, Christian Schwandt, Christina Schwandt, Frederick Schwandt, Louis Seder, John Walz, Karolina Walz

REDWOOD FERRY, Monday, August 18: 24 killed

Charles R. Bell, Joseph S. Besse, Edwin F. Cole, Russell H. Findley, Charles E. French, John Gardner, Jacob A. Gehring, John Holmes, Christian Joerger, Durs Kanzig, James H. Kerr, Wenzel Kusda, John Marsh, Henry McAllister, Wenzel Norton, Moses P. Parks, John W. Parks, John Parsley, Harrison Phillips, Nathaniel Pitcher, Peter Quinn, Henry A. Shepherd, Nathan Stewart, Charles W. Smith

MILFORD, Monday, August 18: 43 killed

Ernst Dietrich, Benedict Drexler, Julius Fenske, John M. Fink, Monika Fink, Max Fink, Christian Haag, Florian Hartman, Anton Henle, Maria Henle, Martin Henle, Carl Maerkle, Franz Massopust Sr., Franz Massopust, Mary Ann Massopust, Julia Massopust, Anton Messmer, Joseph Messmer, Maria Messmer, Johann Pelzel, Brigitta Pelzel, John Rohner, Regina Rohner, Adolph Schilling, Louise Schilling, John Schneider, Adolph Steimle, Caroline Stocker, Max Zeller, Lucretia Zeller, Monica Zeller, Cecelia Zeller, Conrad Zeller, Martin Zeller, John B. Zettel, Barbara Zettel, Elizabeth Zettel, Johanna Zettel, Stephen Zettel, Anton Zettel, two teamsters, one unnamed man

NEW ULM TO REDWOOD ROAD, Monday, August 18: 6 killed

Mary Anderson, Le Grand Davies, George Gleason, Antoine La Blaugh, Francois Patoile, Philander Prescott

COTTONWOOD RIVER, Monday, August 18: 24 killed

Martin Bluem, Elizabeth Bluem, Margaret Bluem, Lizie Bluem, Adam Bluem, Charles Bluem, Joseph L. Brown, Jonathan Brown, Oratia Brown, Joseph Emmerich, Seth Henshaw, Henry Heyers, Dorothea Heyers, Carl Heyers, Joachim Heyers, John Heyers, Philetus Jackson, Sebastian May, Barbara May, Henry May, Bertha May, George Roeser, Barbara Roeser, unnamed man

NEW ULM, LEAVENWORTH RESCUERS, Tuesday, August 19: 11 killed

William B. Carroll, George Lamb, DeWitt Lemon, Almond D. Loomis, Uriah Loomis, Nels Olson, Ole Olson, Tore Olson, Thomas Riant, Jan Thomson, William H. Tuttle

SACRED HEART CREEK, Tuesday, August 19: 24 killed

Uris Andermack, August Frass, Emil Grundmann, Mrs. Grundmann, one Grundmann daughter, one Grundmann son, August Heining, Rosina Heining, two Heining sons, Frederick Kreiger, one Krieger daughter, Paul Kitzman, Mrs. Kitzman, Wilhelmina Kitzman, Pauline Kitzman, Gustav Kitzman, William Lammers, Mr. Tille, Mrs. Tille, two Tille sons, Mr. Wagner, Gottlieb Zabel

NEW ULM, FIRST BATTLE, Tuesday, August 19: 2 killed

Emilie Pauli, August Riemann

YELLOW MEDICINE AGENCY, HAWK CREEK, Tuesday, August 19: 6 killed

Louis Constans, Stewart B. Garvie, Jedidiah H. Ingalls. Mrs. Jedidiah Ingalls, Charles Lauer, James W. Lindsay

FORT RIDGELY, FIRST BATTLE, Wednesday, August 20: 3 killed

Robert Baker, Mark M. Greer, Henry Reike

LAKE SHETEK, Wednesday, August 20: 13 killed

Belle Duley, William Duley Jr., John Eastlick, Giles Eastlick, Frederick Eastlick, Almira Everett, Charles Everett, Julianne Ireland, Sarah Jane Ireland, Sophia Ireland, Andreas Koch, Sophia Smith, John Voight

WEST LAKE, NORWAY LAKE, Wednesday, August 20: 13 killed

Alfred Broberg, Anders Broberg, Andreas Broberg, Christina Broberg, Christina Broberg (child), Daniel Broberg, Anna Stina Broberg, John Broberg, Johannes Broberg, Anders Lundborg, Gustaf Lundborg, Lars Lundborg, John Nelson

FOOT LAKE, EAGLE LAKE, Thursday, August 21: 7 killed

Lars Endreson, Andre Endreson, Olof Olson Haugen, Bergeret Haugen, Frederick Haugen, Johannes Iverson, Carl Peter Jonson

BIG STONE LAKE, Thursday, August 21: 8 killed

Alexis Dubuque, Mr. Laundre, George Lott, Henry Manderfeld, Hilliar Manderfeld, Mr. Patnode, Frank Peshette, Riley Ryder

FORT RIDGELY, SECOND BATTLE, Friday, August 22: 2 killed

Eliphalet Richardson, Joseph Vanosse

NEW ULM, SECOND BATTLE, Saturday, August 23: 25 killed

Matthew Ahearn, Otto Barth, Louis Buggert, Jacob Castor, William B. Dodd, A. W. Edwards, William England, Max Haack, Jacob Haeberle, Newell E. Houghton, Rufus Huggins, Julius Kirchstein, John Krueger Sr., Washington Kulp, Ferdinand Krause, William Lusky, William Maloney, Matthias Meyer, John C. Michaels, William Nicholson, Jerry Quane, August Roepke, Leopold Senske, Luke Smith, John Summers

GRANBY TOWNSHIP, Saturday, August 23: 7 killed

Christopher Apfelbaum, John Apfelbaum, Maria Jonsson, Pehr Jonsson, Johann Schwartz, Anna Maria Schwartz, Katherine Schwartz

JACKSON COUNTY, Sunday, August 24: 13 killed

Johannes Ekse, Ole Olson Forde, Lars Larson Furnes, Anna K. Furnes, Lars G. Hjornevik, Anna K. Langeland, Anna K. Langeland (child), Agaata Langeland, Nicolai Langeland, Knud Langeland, Knut H. Mestad, Brita A. Mestad, Mikkel O. Slaabakken

Breckenridge, Old Crossing, Sunday, August 24: 7 killed

Mr. Bennett, Martin Farrabarr, Mr. Russell, Joe Scott, Charles Snell, and two white adult males.

*   *   *

ESCAPED WITH JOHN OTHERDAY: 62 people

Mr. Ashley, J. D. Boardman, Oscar Canfil, Mary Charles, Edward Cramsie, Mary J. Dailey, Carter H. Drew, Henry Eschle, Mrs. Henry Eschele, five Eschele children, John Fadden, Mrs. John Fadden, three Fadden children, Mrs. Thomas Galbraith, three Galbraith children, Ebenezer Goodell, Mrs. Ebenezer Goodell, Goodell children, Nelson Givens, Mrs. Nelson Givens, Mrs. Givens's mother, three Givens children, John German, Mrs. John German, Ellen Hanrahan, Z. Hawkins, Mary Hayes, Mr. Hill, Matthew E. Hurd, Mrs. Links, Links children, Nehemiah Miller, Jane K. Murch, Mr. Parker, Frederick Patoile, Mrs. Frederick Patoile, one Patoile child, Josephine Patoile, Parker Pierce, E. Rider, Mr. Rotwell, Mrs. Rotwell, Rotwell children, Lizzie Sawyer, Noah Sinks, Mrs. Noah Sinks, two Sinks children, John L. Wakefield, Elizabeth Zeiher

ESCAPED WITH STEPHEN RIGGS: 36-40 people

H. D. Cunningham, Mrs. H. D. Cunningham, one sister of Cunningham, one child of Cunningham, Adrian Ebell, Andrew Hunter, Elizabeth Hunter, D. Wilson Moore, Mrs. D. W. Moore, Richard Orr, Jonas Pettijohn, Fannie Pettijohn, Albert Pettijohn, William Pettijohn, Laura Pettijohn, Alice Pettijohn, Stephen Riggs, Mary Ann Riggs, Martha Riggs, Isabella Riggs, Anna Riggs, Thomas Riggs, Henry Riggs, Robert Riggs, Mary Cornelia Riggs, Thomas Williamson, Margaret Williamson, Jane Williamson, ten or more unnamed refugees and employees of Yellow Medicine Agency

B ibliography

Newspapers

Central Republican (Faribault, Minnesota)
Davenport (Iowa) *Gazette*
Jackson (Minnesota) *Republic*
Mankato (Minnesota) *Free Press*
Mankato (Minnesota) *Weekly Review*
Minnesota Statesman (St. Peter)
New Ulm (Minnesota) *Journal*
New York Times
St. Paul (Minnesota) *Pioneer Press*
Willmar (Minnesota) *Weekly Tribune*
Windom (Minnesota) *Reporter*

Government Publications

Report of the Commissioner of Indian Affairs 1861. Washington: GPO, 1862.
Report of the Commissioner of Indian Affairs 1862. Washington: GPO, 1863.
Report of the Commissioner of Indian Affairs 1863. Washington: GPO, 1864.
U.S. War Department. *The War of the Rebellion: A Compilation of the Official Records of the Union and Confederate Armies.* 128 vols. Washington: GPO, 1880-1901.

Repositories

Brown County Historical Society (New Ulm, MN)

Gere, Thomas P. "Journal from January 1st, 1862 to May 15th, 1865. Life in 'Uncle Sam's' Army."

Roos, Charles. "Sioux Uprising: The Battles of New Ulm, An Account Written by Sheriff Roos." Manuscript Collection, Brown County Historical Society.

"The Ill-Fated Leavenworth Expedition and Marker." Unpublished Manuscript.

Minnesota Historical Society

Rose and Borden Family Papers. Catalog No. P1957

Coursolle, Joseph. "Story as told by grandson Clem Felix." M582, Dakota Conflict of 1862. Microfilm Reel 1.

Currie, Neil. "Information on victims of the Lake Shetek Massacre obtained by correspondence and personal testimony." M582, Dakota Conflict of 1862. Minnesota Historical Society, Microfilm Reel 1.

Duley, William J. "Notes on Sioux Massacre." M582, Dakota Conflict of 1862. Microfilm Reel 1.

Earle, Ezmon W. "Reminiscences." M582, Dakota Conflict of 1862. Microfilm Reel 1.

Eastlick, Lavina Day. "The Lake Shetek Indian Massacre in 1862." M582, Dakota Conflict of 1862. Microfilm Reel 1.

Friend, Andrew. Thomas J. Hughes, collector. "Collected statements on the Sioux Outbreak of 1862 in Butternut Valley Township." M582, Dakota Conflict of 1862. Microfilm Reel 2.

Hatch, Charles D. "Narrative of Charles D. Hatch's experiences in the Indian war in Minnesota in 1862." M582, Dakota Conflict of 1862. Microfilm Reel 2.

Hayden, William G. "An account of the relief expedition sent from St. Peter to New Ulm, August 22, 1862." M582, Dakota Conflict of 1862. Microfilm Reel 2.

Holl Hahn, Margareta. "Notes of Interview. Irene Persons, interviewer." M582, Dakota Conflict of 1862. Microfilm Reel 2.

Holmquist, Ingar Johnson. "Reminiscence." M582, Dakota Conflict of 1862. Minnesota Historical Society, Microfilm Reel 2.

McClure Huggan, Nancy. Letter to William R. Marshall. M582, Dakota Conflict of 1862. Microfilm Reel 2.

McFall, Orlando. Narrative of the Sioux Massacre. M582, Dakota Conflict of 1862. Microfilm Reel 2.

Meagher, John F. Letter, December 26, 1887. M582, Dakota Conflict of 1862. Microfilm Reel 1.

Myers, Aaron. "Reminiscence and biographical data." M582, Dakota Conflict of 1862. Minnesota Historical Society, Microfilm Reel 2.

Nairn, John. "Recollections." M582, Dakota Conflict of 1862. Minnesota Historical Society, Microfilm Reel 3.

Nelson, C.C. "History of the early pioneers of this neighborhood." M582, Dakota Conflict of 1862. Minnesota Historical Society, Microfilm Reel 3.

Robertson, Thomas A. Reminiscence. M582, Dakota Conflict of 1862. Microfilm Reel 3.

Satterlee, Marion P. "The Massacre at Sacred Heart." M582, Dakota Conflict of 1862. Microfilm Reel 2.

West, Harry B. "A Lad's Version of Chief Little Crow." M582, Dakota Conflict of 1862. Microfilm Reel 1.

Whitcomb, Elizabeth. Interview by Irene Persons. M582, Dakota Conflict of 1862. Microfilm Reel 3.

White, Albert Smith. "Sioux Claims Commission data." M582, Dakota Conflict of 1862. Microfilm Reel 3.

National Archives and Records Administration, Washington, D.C.

Record Group 75, Entry 702. Depredation Claims:

Alwin, Wilhelm. #1163.
Back, Henry L. #1159.
Backlund, Steina. #789.
Bell, Elizabeth. #1201.
Buck, Hiram A. #1153.
Bennett, James L. #171.
Berthiaume, Rocque. #748.
Bibeau, Edward. #160.
Boock, Friederick. #2004.
Brown, Eunice #1206.
Buder, August. #139.
Buhrer, Johann. #338.
Carpenter, David. #315.
Covell, George W. #127.
Cramsie, Edward. #232.
Crawford, Charles. #152.
Cummings, Michael. #193
Dailey, Mary Jane. #501.
Demeules, Zepherin. #175.
Dickinson, James F. #757.
Diepolder, Henry. #2013.
Dietz, Henry. #423.
Dow, Leander A. #224.

Drew, Carter H. #618.
Durbahn, Jurgen. #431.
Everson, Lewis. #1235.
Fadden, James. #601.
Farrabarr, Maria. #1366.
Feie, Ole Anderson. #1019.
Fimeyer, Joseph. #2015.
Fortier, Joseph. #272.
Frank, Charles. #481.
Frank, Christian. #2019.
Fritsche, Ernst. #2017.
Fritsche, Frederick. #142.
Ganske, Michael. #2022.
Garrison, Nehemiah. #1258.
Glock, Katherine. #258.
Gorman, James. #343.
Guerin, Narcisse. #278.
Haack, Max. #1334.
Halverson, Lars. #1234.
Hanrahan, Ellen. #245.
Harrington, Benjamin. #215.
Hayes, Mary. #274.
Heintz, Peter. #2241.
Heywood, George. #2240.
Hough, Alva B. #2029.
Hurd, Matthew E. #255.
Ives, Russel #2034.
Johnson, Hans. #678.
Jonson, Anna Cathrina. #791.
Joos, Adam. #77.
Kratke, John P. #259.
Kuehnel, Gottfried. #2043.
La Framboise, Joseph Jr. #1108.
Larson, Lars John. #615.
Le Clair, Cyprian. #161.
Lewison, Lewis. #2690.
Linquist, Charles F. #254.
McConnell, Joseph #200.
McNutt, Robert. #827.
Mayhew, Thomas. #2143.
Mireau, Moses. #159.
Morin, Theodore. #163.
Muther, Lorenz. #74.
Olafson, Jonas. #617.
Oleson, Lars. #2155.
Oleson, Mons. #1284.
Osmundsen, Thomas. #2156.

Patoile, Josephine. #836.
Patoile, Peter. #1097.
Peterson, Jonas. #261.
Resca, Henry. #166.
Riemann, August. #325.
Riggs, Martha T. #219.
Robinette, Vanesse. #1136.
Robinson, Thomas. #1217.
Scheible, Christian. #56.
Schneider, Creszentia. #1001.
Schneider, John. #466.
Schumann, Christoph. #1013.
Seder, Louis. #1085.
Slaabakken, John Olson. #1230.
Slaabakken, Petronelle Olson. #1227.
Slaabakken, Simon Olson. #1231.
Solomonson, Lars. #915.
Sonnenberg, William. #342.
Thinnes, Nicholus. #1210.
Wehrs, Theodore. #1079.
Williams, Martha M. #165.
Woehler, Charles E. #237.
Woodcock, Elijah T. #1382.
Zander, Hubert. #202.
Zeiher, Elizabeth. #238.

Internet

"Arctander Township Pioneers." Http://www.rootsweb.ancestry.com/ ~mnkandiy/Arctander.html

"A Church is Planted." www.genforum.genealogy.com/ sweden/ messages/ 31043.html

"Dakota Conflict Trials." www.law.umkc.edu/faculty/projects/ftrials/ dakota/ trialrecl

"The Eversons in Kandiyohi County." ftp.rootsweb.ancestry. com/pub/usgenweb/mn/kandiyohi/bios/everson.txt

"History of Breckenridge." www.breckenridgemn.net/ tourism/history. html

"The Ingalls Inquirer." www.home.comcast.net/~ingalls pages/Inquirer/ 9-1.html

"Johannes Iverson." Www.mankell.org/iverson.html

"Knut Nilsson Langeland." Www.look.no/anita/slekt/webcards/ps71/ ps71_132.html

Laut, Agnes C. "The Story of Guri Endreson The Heroine of Kandiyohi." www.home.online.no?~torolav/guri.html;

"Nordmaendene i Amerika." Translation by Olaf Kringhaug. www.freepages.genealogy.rootsweb.com/~maggiebakke/minnesota.html

"Norway-L Archives." www.newsarch.rootsweb.com/th/read/norway/2004-09/1094935847

"Ole Olson Fyre." www.look.no/anita/slekt/webcards/ps70/ps70_444.html

"Rosseland Family Register." www.home.online.no/~torolav/gen.html

"Silas Foot." www.footfamily.com/new_page_2.html

"The Story of the Massacre." www.whodeane.com/the%20story%20of%20the%20massacre.pdf

Books and Periodicals

Anderson, Gary C. *Little Crow Spokesman for the Sioux*. St. Paul, MN: Minnesota Historical Society Press, 1986.

Anderson, Gary Clayton. "Myrick's Insult: A Fresh Look at Myth and Reality." *Minnesota History* (Spring 1983):198-206.

Anderson, Gary Clayton, and Alan R. Woolworth, eds. *Through Dakota Eyes: Narrative Accounts of the Minnesota Indian War of 1862*. St. Paul: Minnesota Historical Society Press, 1988.

Bakeman. Mary Hawker, ed. *Index to Claimants for Depredations following the Dakota War of 1862*. Roseville, MN: Park Genealogical Books, 2001.

———. *Legends, Letter, and Lies: Readings about Inkpaduta and the Spirit Lake Massacre*. Roseville, MN: Park Genealogical Books, 2001.

Baker, Frank, et. al. *American Anthropoligist New Series*. Vol. 3. New York: G.P. Putnam's Sons, 1901.

Barton, Winifred W. John P. Williamson. *A Brother to the Sioux*. Redwood Falls, MN: Sunny Crest Publishing Co., 1980. Reprint, New York: Fleming H. Revell Company, 1919.

Beck, Paul N. *Inkpaduta Dakota Leader*. Norman, OK: University of Oklahoma Press, 2008.

Belanger, Dian Olson. "The True Story Behind the Fort Ridgely Medal." *Minnesota History*, 47 no. 6 (Summer 1981): 233-239.

Bellesiles, Michael A. *Arming America: The Origins of a National Gun Culture*. New York: Vintage Books, 2001.

Bennett, H. L. "The Belmont Indian Massacre." *Jackson Republic*, April 16, 1885.

Berghold, Rev. Alexander. *The Indians' Revenge or Days of Horror*. Don Heinrich Tolzmann, ed. Roseville, MN: Edinborough Press, 2007. Originally published, San Francisco: P.J. Thomas, 1891.

Bergland, Betty Ann. "Guri Endreson and Gendered Representation of the Landtaking in the Wake of the Lakota Rebellion: Norwegian Immigrants and Indigenous People in 19th Century Midwest, U.S.A." Paper presented at the Seventh International Interdisciplinary Women's Congress, Tromso, Norway, June 1999.

Blegen, Theodore C. "Immigrant Women and the American Frontier." *Studies and Records*, V. Norwegian-American Historical Association (1930): 14-29.

―――. *Minnesota: A History of the State*. Minneapolis, MN: University of Minnesota Press, 1963.

Broberg Peterson, Anna Stina. "The Story of the Massacre." *Pennington County History*, Vol. 2. 1991: 171.

Brown, John A. *History of Cottonwood and Watonwan Counties Minnesota*. Vol. 1. Indianapolis, IN: B. F. Bowen & Company, Inc., 1916.

Buell, Salmon A. "Judge Flandrau in the Defense of New Ulm During the Sioux Outbreak of 1862." *Collections of the Minnesota Historical Society*, Vol. 10, pt. 2. St. Paul, MN: Minnesota Historical Society, 1905.

Carley, Kenneth. *The Dakota War of 1862: Minnesota's Other Civil War*. St. Paul, MN: Minnesota Historical Society, 1976.

―――. "The Sioux Campaign of 1862 Sibley's Letters to His Wife." *Minnesota History*, 38 (September 1962): 99-114.

Connolly, Alonzo P. *A Thrilling Narrative of the Minnesota Massacre and the Sioux War of 1862-63*. Chicago, IL: A.P. Connolly, n.d.

Connors, Joseph. "The Elusive Hero of Redwood Ferry." *Minnesota History* (Summer 1955): 233-38.

Cramer, Clayton E. *Armed America: The Remarkable Story of How and Why Guns Became as American as Apple Pie*. Nashville, TN: Nelson Current, 2006.

Curtiss-Wedge, Franklyn. *The History of Redwood County*, Volume I. Chicago, IL: H.C. Cooper Jr., & Company, 1916.

―――. *The History of Renville County*, Vols. 1 & 2. Chicago, IL: H.C. Cooper Jr., & Company, 1916.

Dahlin, Curtis A. *Dakota Uprising Victims Gravestones & Stories*. Edina, MN: Beaver Pond Press, Inc., 2007.

Daniels, Dr. Asa W. "Reminiscences of the Little Crow Uprising." *Collections of the Minnesota Historical Society*, Vol. 15. St. Paul, MN: Minnesota Historical Society, 1915.

De Camp Sweet, Jannette E. "Mrs. J. E. De Camp Sweet's Narrative of her captivity in the Sioux Outbreak of 1862." *Collections of the Minnesota Historical Society*, Vol. 6. St. Paul, MN: Minnesota Historical Society, 1894.

Derounian-Stodola, Kathryn Zabelle. The *War in Words Reading the Dakota Conflict through Captivity Literature*. Lincoln, NE: University of Nebraska Press, 2009.

Dietz, Charlton. "Henry Behnke New Ulm's Paul Revere." *Minnesota History* (Fall 1976): 111-115.

Dunn, James Taylor. "A Century of Song Popular Music in Minnesota." *Minnesota History*, 44. (Winter 1974): 123-126.

Dunn, Mrs. J. W. "The Sioux Massacre of '62." *Jackson Republic*, July 20, 1888.

Estensen, Gene. "War Comes to Norwegian Grove." *Celebrating Our Norwegian-Minnesotan Heritage: The Norwegian Statehood Pioneer Project*, 185-92. LaPorte, MN: The Norwegian Statehood Pioneer Project, 2009.

Farrell, Ellen. "The Most Terrible Stories: The 1862 Dakota Conflict in White Imagination." *Journal of the Indian Wars*, Vol. 1, no. 3: 21-37.

Flandrau, Judge Charles E. *The History of Minnesota and Tales of the Frontier*. St. Paul, MN: E. W. Porter, 1900.

Folwell, William Watts. *A History of Minnesota*, Vol. II. St. Paul, MN: Minnesota Historical Society, 1924. Revised edition, 1961.

Frazer, Robert W. *Forts of the West*. Norman, OK: University of Oklahoma Press, 1965.

Fridley, Russell W. "Charles E. Flandrau Attorney at War." *Minnesota History* (September 1962): 116-125.

Fritsche, L. A. *Memories of the Battle of New Ulm: Personal Accounts of the Sioux Uprising. L.A. Fritsche's History of Brown County, Minnesota* (1916). Don Heinrich Tolzmann, ed. Westminster, MD: Heritage Books, Inc., 2007.

Gilman, Rhoda R. *Henry Hastings Sibley: Divided Heart*. St. Paul, MN: Minnesota Historical Society Press, 2004.

Gourley, Deb Nelson. *Astri, My Astri: Norwegian Heritage Stories*. Waukon, IA: Astri my Astri Publishing, 2004.

———. "You are a Hjornevik, but who are you?" *Fillmore County Journal*. (November 2001).

Heard, Isaac V. D. *History of the Sioux War and Massacres of 1862 and 1863*. New York: Harper & Brothers, Publishers, 1863.

Henig, Gerald S. "A Neglected Cause of the Sioux Uprising." *Minnesota History*, 45, no. 3 (Fall 1976): 107-110.

Hennessy, John J. *Return to Bull Run The Campaign and Battle of Second Manassas*. New York: Simon & Schuster, 1993.

Holcombe, Return I. *Sketches Historical and Descriptive of the Monuments and Tablets Erected by the Minnesota Valley Historical Society in Renville and Redwood Counties, Minnesota*. Morton, MN: Minnesota Valley Historical Society, 1902.

Hubbard, Lucius F. and Return I. Holcombe. *Minnesota as a State, 1858-1870*. Vol. 3 of *Minnesota in Three Centuries, 1655-1908*. Mankato, MN: The Publishing Society of Minnesota, 1908.

Hughes, Reverends Thomas E. and David Edwards, Hugh G. Roberts, and Thomas Hughes, eds. *History of the Welsh in Minnesota, Foreston and Lime Springs, IA. Gathered by the Old Settlers*, n.p., 1895.

Humphrey, John Ames. "Boyhood Remembrances of Life Among the Dakotas and the Massacre in 1862." *Collections of the Minnesota Historical Society*. Vol.15. St. Paul, MN: Minnesota Historical Society, 1915?

Johnson, Rev. Emeroy. *A Church is Planted: The Story of The Lutheran Minnesota Conference, 1851-1876.* Minneapolis, MN: Lutheran Minnesota Conference, 1948.

Kappler, Charles J., ed. *Indian Treaties 1778-1883.* Mattituck, NY: Amereon House, 1972.

Keenan, Jerry. *The Great Sioux Uprising Rebellion on the Plains August-September 1862.* Cambridge, MA: Da Capo Press, 2003.

Koblas, John. *Let Them Eat Grass: The 1862 Sioux Uprising in Minnesota,* Vols. 1-3. St. Cloud, MN: North Star Press of St. Cloud, Inc., 2006.

Kvasnicka, Robert M. and Herman J. Viola, eds. *The Commissioners of Indian Affairs, 1824-1977.* Lincoln, NE: University of Nebraska Press, 1979.

Lamson, Frank B. *History of Meeker County.* Dassel, MN. Area Historical Society, nd.

Lawson, Victor E. and Martin E. Tew. *Illustrated History and Descriptive and Biographical Review of Kandiyohi County Minnesota.* St. Paul, MN: Pioneer Press Manufacturing Department, 1905.

Leonhart, Rudolf. Memories of New Ulm: *My Experiences During the Indian Uprising in Minnesota.* Don Heinrich Tolzmann ed. and trans. Roseville, MN: Edinborough Press, 2005.

Lounsberry, Col. Clement A. *Early History of North Dakota.* Washington, D.C.: Liberty Press, 1919.

Lundblad, Larry. "The Impact of Minnesota's Dakota Conflict of 1862 on the Swedish Settlers." *The Swedish-American Historical Quarterly.* LI, no. 3 (July 2000): 211-221.

McClure Huggan, Nancy. "The Story of Nancy McClure." *Collections of the Minnesota Historical Society,* Vol. 6. St. Paul, MN: Minnesota Historical Society, 1894.

McConkey, Harriet E. Bishop. *Dakota War Whoop: Or, Indian Massacres and War in Minnesota, of 1862-'3.* St. Paul, MN: Wm. J. Moses Press, 1864. Reprint. Chicago, IL: R. R. Donnelley & Sons Company, 1965.

Malmros, Oscar. *Perspective on the Sioux War: Oscar Malmros.* Mary Hawker Bakeman, ed. Roseville, MN: Park Genealogical Books, 2007.

Map, "Historical Sites in Kandiyohi County." Kandiyohi County Historical Society, 2002.

Mason, Augustus Lynch, A. M. *The Romance and Tragedy of Pioneer Life.* Cincinnati, OH: Jones Brothers and Company, 1883.

Melegari, Vezio. *The Great Military Sieges.* New York: Thomas Y. Crowell Co., 1972.

Meyer, Roy W. *History of the Santee Sioux.* Lincoln, NE: University of Nebraska Press, 1993.

Michno, Gregory and Susan Michno. *A Fate Worse Than Death: Indian Captivities in the West, 1830-1885.* Caldwell, ID: Caxton Press, 2007.

Minnesota Board of Commissioners. *Minnesota in the Civil and Indian Wars, 1861-1865,* Vols. 1-2. St. Paul, MN: Pioneer Press, 1891.

Monjou-Marz, Corinne L. *The Dakota Indian Internment at Fort Snelling, 1862-1864.* St. Paul, MN: Prairie Smoke Press, 2006.

Monson, M. A. "Eyewitness Tells of Indian Uprising." *Windom Reporter*, October 3, 1930.

Morris, Lucy Leavenworth Wilder, ed. *Old Rail Fence Corners The A.B.C's. of Minnesota History.* Austin, MN: The Old Settlers by the Book Committee, 1914.

Neill, Rev. Edward D. *History of the Upper Mississippi Valley: Explorers and Pioneers of Minnesota.* Minneapolis, MN: Minnesota Historical Society, 1881.

Neill, Rev. Edward D. and Charles S. Bryant. *History of the Minnesota Valley, Including the Explorers and Pioneers of Minnesota, and History of the Sioux Massacre.* Minneapolis, MN: North Star Publishing, 1882.

Newcombe, Barbara T. "'A Portion of the American People: The Sioux Sign a Treaty in Washington in 1858." *Minnesota History*, 45, no. 3 (Fall 1976): 83-96.

Newson, T. M. *Pen Pictures of St. Paul, Minnesota, and Biographical Sketches of Old Settlers.* St. Paul, MN: By the Author, 1886.

"New Ulm 2009 Visitors Guide." New Ulm, Minnesota Chamber of Commerce.

Nix, Jacob. *The Sioux Uprising in Minnesota, 1862: Jacob Nix's Eyewitness History.* Don Heinrich Tolzmann, ed. Indianapolis, IN: Max Kade German-American Center and Indian German Heritage Society, Inc., 1994.

Oehler, C. M. *The Great Sioux Uprising.* New York: Oxford University Press, 1959.

Ostler, Jeffrey. *The Plains Sioux and U.S. Colonialism from Lewis and Clark to Wounded Knee.* New York: Cambridge University Press, 2004.

Paulson, Robert J. Franz Massopust, *German-Bohemian Pathfinder and Founder of New Ulm: A Tragic Family Saga.* Roseville, MN: Park Genealogical Books, 2004.

Pettijohn, Jonas. *Autobiography, Family History and Various Reminiscences of the Life of Jonas Pettijohn.* Clay Center, KS: Dispatch Printing House, 1890.

Potter, Theodore E. "Captain Potter's Recollections of Minnesota Experiences." *Minnesota History Bulletin*, Vol. 1, no. 8 (November 1916): 419-521.

Prescott, Philander. "Autobiography and Reminiscences of Philander Prescott." *Collections of the Minnesota Historical Society*, Vol. 6. St. Paul, MN: Minnesota Historical Society, 1894.

Reddemann, Ahle. *The Henderson to Fort Ridgely Trail.* Henderson, MN: Sibley County Historical Society, 2003.

Rene, Knut A., ed. "From the Indian War in 1862." *Vossingen Organ for Vosselagst*, no. 3-4 (December 1925): 33-38.

Renville, Gabriel. "A Sioux Narrative of the Outbreak in 1862, and of Sibley's Expedition in 1863." *Collections of the Minnesota Historical Society*, Vol. 10, Pt. 2. St. Paul, MN: Minnesota Historical Society, 1903.

Riggs, Stephen R., D.D., LL.D. Mary and I. *Forty Years with the Sioux.* Williamstown, MA: Corner House Publishers, 1971. Reprint, Boston, MA: Congregational Sunday-School and Publishing Society, 1880.

Robbins, Roy M. *Our Landed Heritage: The Public Domain 1776-1936.* New York: Peter Smith, 1950.

Robinson, Doane. *A History of the Dakota or Sioux Indians*. Minneapolis, MN: Ross & Haines, Inc., 1974.

Rose, Arthur P. *An Illustrated History of Jackson County Minnesota*. Jackson, MN: Northern History Publishing Company, 1910.

———. *An Illustrated History of Lyon County Minnesota*. Marshall, MN: Northern History Publishing Company, 1912.

Russo, Priscilla Ann. "The Time to Speak is Over: The Onset of the Sioux Uprising." *Minnesota History*, 45, no. 3 (Fall 1976): 97-106.

Satterlee, Marion P. "Narratives of the Sioux War." Vol. 15, *Collections of the Minnesota Historical Society*. St. Paul, MN: Minnesota Historical Society, 1915.

Schultz, Duane. *Over the Earth I Come: The Great Sioux Uprising of 1862*. New York: St. Martin'sPress, 1992.

Schwandt, Mary. *The Captivity of Mary Schwandt*. Fairfield, WA: Ye Galleon Press, 1999 (Originally in Collections of the Minnesota Historical Society, Vol. 6, 1894.)

Secoy, Frank Raymond. *Changing Military Patterns of the Great Plains*. Lincoln, NE: University of Nebraska Press, 1992.

Smith, A. C. A *Random Historical Sketch of Meeker County, Minnesota. From its First Settlement to July 4, 1876*. Litchfield, MN: Belfoy & Joubert, Publishers, 1877.

Stevens, John H. *Personal Recollections of Minnesota and Its People, and Early History of Minneapolis*. Minneapolis, MN: 1890.

Strand, A. E. *A History of The Swedish-Americans of Minnesota*. Vol. 1. Chicago, IL: The Lewis Publishing Company, 1910.

Thomas, Dean S. *Cannons: An Introduction to Civil War Artillery*. Gettysburg, PA: Thomas Publications, 1985.

Tolzmann, Don Heinrich, ed. *German Pioneer Accounts of the Great Sioux Uprising of 1862*. Milford, OH: Little Miami Publishing Co., 2002.

———. *Outbreak and Massacre by the Dakota Indians in Minnesota in 1862, Marion P. Satterlee's Minute Account of the Outbreak, with Exact Locations, Names of All Victims, Prisoners at Camp Release, Refugees at Fort Ridgely, etc.* Westminster, MD: Heritage Books, Inc., 2001.

Ulvestad, Martin. *Nordmaendene i Amerika: Early Norwegian Settlements in Minnesota*. Minneapolis, MN: History Book Company's Forlag, 1907.

Wakefield, Sarah F. *Six Weeks in the Sioux Teepees: A Narrative of Indian Captivity*. Edited, Annotated, and with an Introduction by June Namias. Norman, OK: University of Oklahoma Press, 2002.

Wall, Oscar Garrett. *Recollections of the Sioux Massacre: An Authentic History*. Lake City, MN: Home Printery, 1909.

Waters, Thomas F. *The Streams and Rivers of Minnesota*. Minneapolis, MN: University of Minnesota Press, 1977.

Whipple, Henry Benjamin. *Lights and Shadows of a Long Episcopate, Being Reminiscences and Recollections of the Right Reverend Henry Benjamin Whipple, D.D., L.L.D., Bishop of Minnesota*. New York: Macmillan, 1912.

Wilson, Raymond. Forty Years to Judgment The Santee Sioux Claims Case."
Minnesota History (Fall 1981): 281-91.

Woolworth, Alan R. and Mary H. Bakeman, eds. *Camera and Sketchbook Witnesses to the Sioux Uprising of 1862.* Roseville, MN: Park Geneological Books, 2004.

Index

Big Eagle (Wamditanka), Chief, 23, 395; travels to Washington, D.C., 8; Treaty of 1858, 8; causes of the uprising, 10, 24, 26-27, 35, 38; Acton massacre, 46, 49, 52-53; Redwood Agency massacre, 56, 58n, 61, 63; Beaver Creek massacre, 75; Redwood Ferry massacre, 114n; New Ulm, First Battle of, 193; Fort Ridgely, First Battle of, 220-221, 229; Fort Ridgely, Second Battle of, 297-298, 301, 306; New Ulm, Second Battle of, 323, 334

Big Stone Lake, causes of the uprising, 28, 43, 60, 165, 287-288, 290

Big Stone Lake massacre, 402

Big Thunder, chief, 4

Big Woods, 14-15, 48, 140, 289

Billings, Henry G., 28, 65

Birch Coulee massacre, 75-76, 86, 88, 92, 97, 155, 189, 359

Birch Coulee, second battle of, 164, 390, 395, 399

Bishop, Harriet E., 11

Bishop, Sgt. John F., 110n, 111-112, 114-116, 222, 225-225n, 293, 303-304

Bjorkman family and home, 97

Bjorkmann, Peter, 99, 107

Blackfeet Lakota Indians, 2

Blackmer, Sgt. Frank A., 294, 298-299, 306

Blackwell, John, 50-51

Blair family and home (Lydia, Minnie, Stuart), 174

Blair, Charles, 173-175

"Blanket Indians," 1, 16-17, 25, 27

Blodgett, Pvt. William, 117-118, 118n, 234

Bloody Lake, 237, 240-241

Blows on Iron (Mazabomdu) Indian warrior, 128-129, 139

Blue Earth County, 81, 89n, 263

Blue Earth, Chief, 297

Blue Face, Indian warrior, 167

Blue Sky Woman, 68-69

Bluem family and home (Adam, Charles, Elizabeth, John, Lizzie, Margaret, Martin), 255

Bluem, Martin, 143, 197, 401

Boardman, J. D., 170-171, 178, 403

Boardman, L. M., 202, 202n, 204-206, 206n, 309

Boelter family and home (Emilia, Gottlieb, John, Justina, Justine K., Michael, Ottilie), 97, 100-104, 104n, 105-106, 133, 154, 174, 396, 400

Boelter, Gottlieb, 102, 400

Boelter, John, 100, 104n, 400

Boelter, Justina, 102-103, 106, 396, 400

Boelter, Justine K., 102, 105

Boelter, Michael, 100, 102-106, 133, 154

Boen, Ole O. and Torstein O., 361

Boesch, Anna and Werner, 226

Bogaga, Indian warrior, 177

Bois de Sioux River, 374

Boock family and home (Emma, Friederick, Louisa, Maria, and child Maria), 353

Borgen, Sven Gunderson, 284-285

Borgersrode, Col. Rudolph von, 222

Bourat, William, 60

Bowen, Evan, 202

Bradvold family and home, 377

Brandt, J., 14

Bread Raid, 1, 32-33, 38, 40, 43, 114, 140, 208, 288

Breaking Up (Ka-om-de-i-ye-ye-dan), Indian warrior, 48, 51

Breckenridge Township, 373-376, 403

Brennan, Pvt. John, 116

Brighton Township, 360

Brink family and home, 254

Brisbois family and home (Antoine, Elizabeth, Louis P., Louis (child), Margaret), 90-91

Broberg (Anders Peter) family and home (Anders Peter, Anna Stina (Ernestina),

author

Award-winning author Gregory F. Michno is a Michigan native and the author of three dozen articles and ten books dealing with World War II and the American West, including *USS Pampanito: Killer-Angel*, *Lakota Noon*, *Battle at Sand Creek*, *The Encyclopedia of Indian Wars*, *The Deadliest Indian War in the West*, and *Circle the Wagons*. Greg helped edit and appeared in the DVD history "The Great Indian Wars: 1540-1890." He lives in Longmont, Colorado, with his wife Susan.